D0819743

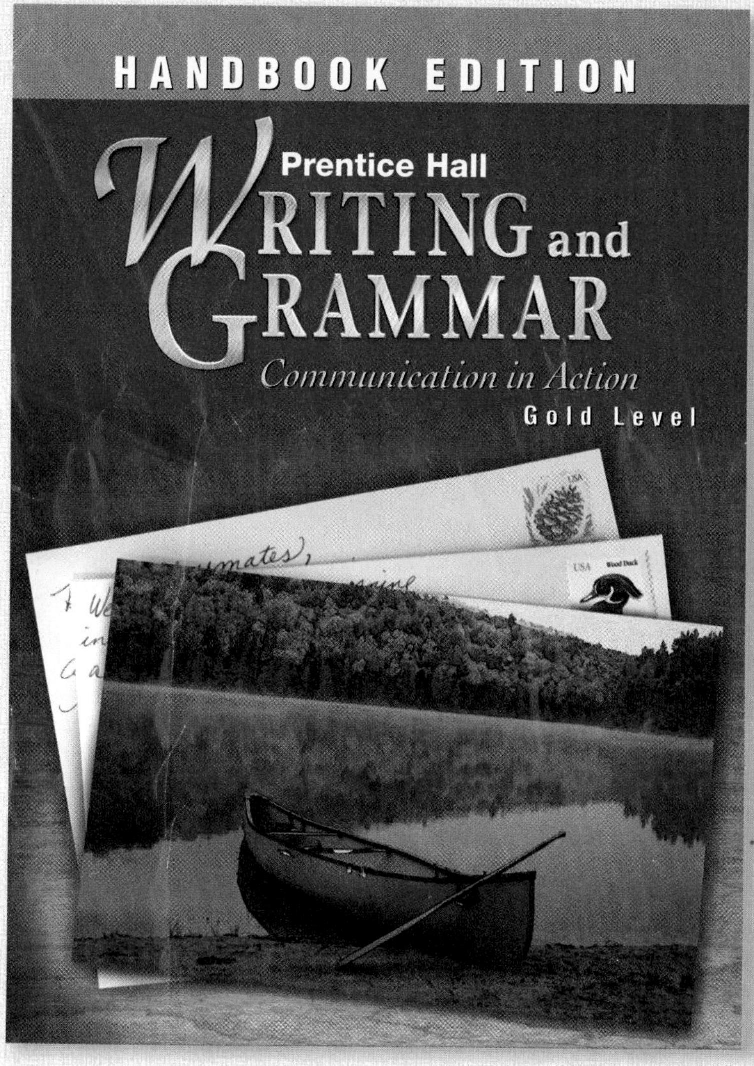

HANDBOOK EDITION

Prentice Hall

WRITING and GRAMMAR

Communication in Action

Gold Level

Gold Level
Handbook Edition

Upper Saddle River, New Jersey
Glenview, Illinois
Needham, Massachusetts

ISBN 0-13-037299-4

6 7 8 9 10   08 07 06 05 04

Handbook Edition

Copper
Bronze
Silver
Gold
Platinum
Ruby
Diamond

Program Authors

The program authors guided the direction and philosophy of *Prentice Hall Writing and Grammar: Communication in Action.* Working with the development team, they contributed to the pedagogical integrity of the program and to its relevance to today's teachers and students.

Joyce Armstrong Carroll

In her forty-year career, Joyce Armstrong Carroll, Ed.D., has taught on every grade level from primary to graduate school. In the past twenty years, she has trained teachers in the teaching of writing. A nationally known consultant, she has served as president of TCTE and on NCTE's Commission on Composition. More than fifty of her articles have appeared in journals such as *Curriculum Review, English Journal, Media & Methods, Southwest Philosophical Studies, Ohio English Journal, English in Texas,* and the *Florida English Journal.* With Edward E. Wilson, Dr. Carroll co-authored *Acts of Teaching: How to Teach Writing* and co-edited *Poetry After Lunch: Poems to Read Aloud.* Beyond her direct involvement with the writing pedagogy presented in this series, Dr. Carroll guided the development of the Hands-on Grammar feature. She co-directs the New Jersey Writing Project in Texas.

Edward E. Wilson

A former editor of *English in Texas*, Edward E. Wilson has served as a high-school English teacher and a writing consultant in school districts nationwide. Wilson has served on the Texas Teacher Professional Practices Commission and on NCTE's Commission on Composition. With Dr. Carroll, he co-wrote *Acts of Teaching: How to Teach Writing* and co-edited the award-winning *Poetry After Lunch: Poems to Read Aloud.* In addition to his direct involvement with the writing pedagogy presented in this series, Wilson provided inspiration for the Spotlight on Humanities feature. Wilson's poetry appears in Paul Janeczko's anthology *The Music of What Happens.* Wilson co-directs the New Jersey Writing Project in Texas.

Gary Forlini

Gary Forlini, a nationally known education consultant, developed the grammar, usage, and mechanics instruction and exercises in this series. After teaching in the Pelham, New York, schools for many years, he established Research in Media, an educational research agency that provides information for product developers, school staff developers, media companies, and arts organizations, as well as private-sector corporations and foundations. Mr. Forlini was co-author of the *S.A.T. Home Study* program and has written numerous industry reports on elementary, secondary, and post-secondary education markets.

National Advisory Panel

The teachers and administrators serving on the National Advisory Panel provided ongoing input into the development of *Prentice Hall Writing and Grammar: Communication in Action.* Their valuable insights ensure that the perspectives of teachers and students throughout the country are represented within the instruction in this series.

Dr. Pauline Bigby-Jenkins
Coordinator for Secondary English Language Arts
Ann Arbor Public Schools
Ann Arbor, Michigan

Lee Bromberger
English Department Chairperson
Mukwonago High School
Mukwonago, Wisconsin

Mary Chapman
Teacher of English
Free State High School
Lawrence, Kansas

Jim Deatherage
Language Arts Department Chairperson
Richland High School
Richland, Washington

Luis Dovalina
Teacher of English
La Joya High School
La Joya, Texas

JoAnn Giardino
Teacher of English
Centennial High School
Columbus, Ohio

Susan Goldberg
Teacher of English
Westlake Middle School
Thornwood, New York

Jean Hicks
Director, Louisville Writing Project
University of Louisville
Louisville, Kentucky

Karen Hurley
Teacher of Language Arts
Perry Meridian Middle School
Indianapolis, Indiana

Karen Lopez
Teacher of English
Hart High School
Newhall, California

Marianne Minshall
Teacher of Reading and Language Arts
Westmore Middle School
Columbus, Ohio

Nancy Monroe
English Department Chairperson
Bolton High School
Alexandria, Louisiana

Ken Spurlock
Assistant Principal
Boone County High School
Florence, Kentucky

Cynthia Katz Tyroff
Staff Development Specialist and Teacher of English
Northside Independent School District
San Antonio, Texas

Holly Ward
Teacher of Language Arts
Campbell Middle School
Daytona Beach, Florida

Grammar Review Team

The following teachers reviewed the grammar instruction in this series to ensure accuracy, clarity, and pedagogy.

Kathy Hamilton
Paul Hertzog
Daren Hoisington
Beverly Ladd
Karen Lopez
Dianna Louise Lund
Sean O'Brien

CONTENTS IN BRIEF

Chapters 1–15

Part 1: Writing 1

Chapters 16–29

Part 2: Grammar, Usage, and Mechanics 215

Chapters 30–34

Part 3: Academic and Workplace Skills . . 543

Resources

Chapter 1 The Writer in You 2

Chapter 2 A Walk Through the Writing Process 6

Chapter 3 Paragraphs and Compositions

Structure and Style 20

Chapter 4
Narration
Autobiographical Writing 32

Student Work IN PROGRESS

Featured Work:
"Cedar Avenue Recycling: The Rise and Fall of a Family Business"
by Sara Holman
Towson High School
Towson, Maryland

INTEGRATED SKILLS

Chapter 5

Narration

Student Work IN PROGRESS

Featured Work:
"A Stranger's Lesson"
by David Friggle
Columbia High School
Maplewood, New Jersey

INTEGRATED SKILLS

Chapter 6

Description

Student Work IN PROGRESS

Featured Work:
"My 'Sister'"
by Allison Lutes
Butler Traditional High School
Louisville, Kentucky

INTEGRATED SKILLS

Chapter 7

Persuasion

Student Work IN PROGRESS

Featured Work:
"Who Wrote *West With the Night*?"
by Janaki Spickard-Keeler
Clark High School
San Antonio, Texas

INTEGRATED SKILLS

Chapter 8

Persuasion

Student Work IN PROGRESS

Featured Work:
"Pets Complete the Family Picture"
by Caitlin Mahoney
Darien High School
Darien, Connecticut

INTEGRATED SKILLS

Chapter 9

Exposition: *Comparison-and-Contrast Essay* 112

Student Work IN PROGRESS

Featured Work:
"Working Out Possibilities"
by Elizabeth Dunbar, Maggie McCray, Cassie McKinstry, and Emily Szeszycki, with additional reporting by Liz Humston
Staff of *the little hawk*
City High School
Iowa City, Iowa

INTEGRATED SKILLS

Chapter 10 Exposition

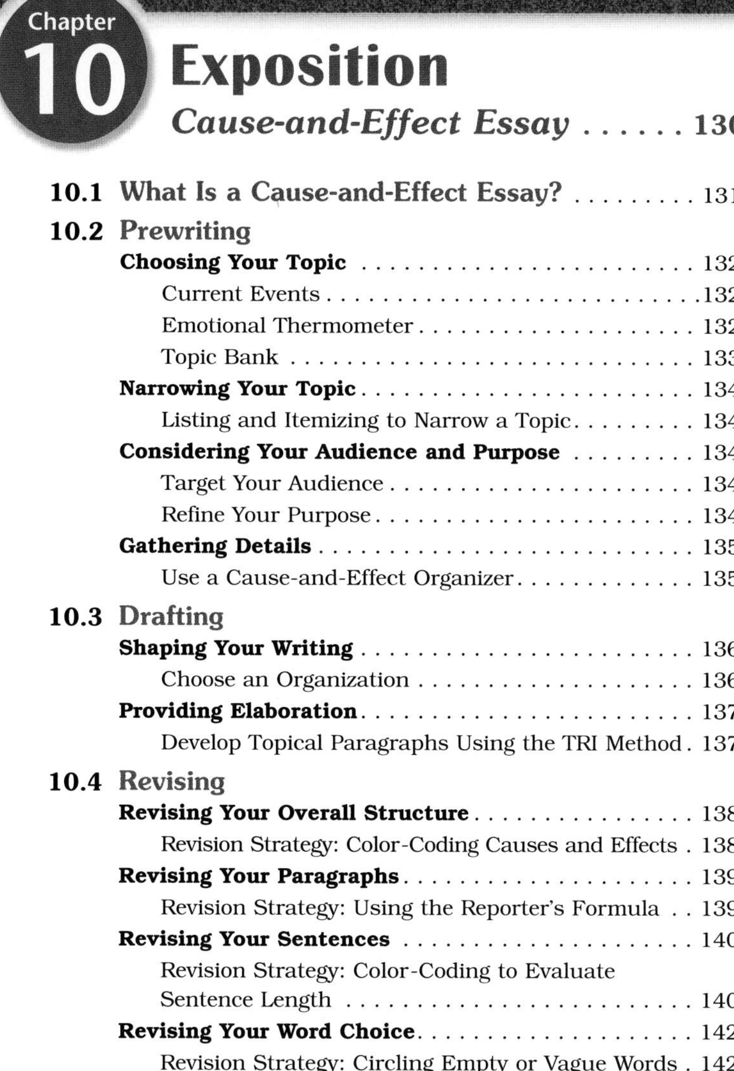

Student Work IN PROGRESS

Featured Work:
"The Music of the Soul" by
Sonia Reimann
Athens High School
Athens, Texas

INTEGRATED SKILLS

Chapter 11 Exposition

Problem-and-Solution Essay . . 148

Student Work IN PROGRESS

Featured Work:
"Safety and Progress"
by Michael C. Mahoney
St. Stephen's School
Hickory, North Carolina

INTEGRATED SKILLS

Chapter 12

Research

Student Work IN PROGRESS

Featured Work:
"Tracking the Success of Bubble Gum"
by Angelika Klien
Sunnyslope High School
Phoenix, Arizona

INTEGRATED SKILLS

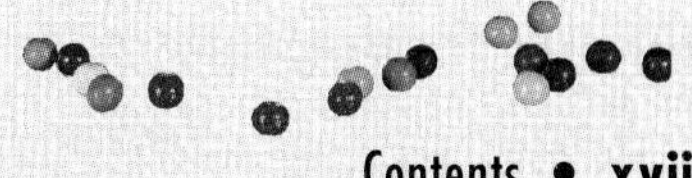

Chapter 13

Response to Literature

Student Work IN PROGRESS

Featured Work:
"The Poetic Power of 'The Raven'"
by Andrea Montgomery
Omaha Northwest High School
Omaha, Nebraska

INTEGRATED SKILLS

Chapter 14

Writing for Assessment 196

Student Work IN PROGRESS

Featured Work:
"The Lesson of 'The Scarlet Ibis'"
by Megan Holbrook
Buena High School
Ventura, California

INTEGRATED SKILLS

Chapter 15 **Workplace Writing** 206

Chapter 30 Speaking, Listening, Viewing, and Representing . . . 544

Chapter 31 Vocabulary and Spelling 564

Chapter 32

Reading Skills

Chapter 33

Study, Reference, and Test-Taking Skills

Workplace Skills and Competencies

Resources

Writing

Benjamin Comfort (detail), Percy Ives, Detroit Historical Museum

Chapter 1 The Writer in You

▲ Critical Viewing What kind of writing might the students in the photograph be doing? **[Speculate]**

One of the biggest mistakes that some people make when they think about writing is to consider writing to be a chore. The truth is that writing isn't a chore: It's an opportunity. It is an opportunity to express your ideas, to open up your imagination, to persuade others to agree with your point of view.

Writing in Everyday Life

Writing is already an important part of your everyday life. If you have access to computers, you most likely exchange e-mail messages with friends. You probably also write notes and cards to friends and family members to say thank you or to celebrate a special occasion. In addition, you may keep a journal in which you jot down private thoughts and feelings. As a student, you also do a substantial amount of writing—papers, stories, essay tests. The various types of writing you do every day give you an opportunity to capture and share your feelings and to demonstrate what you know.

Why Write?

Developing your writing skills will not only help you to express yourself more effectively, it will also help you achieve success in life. Being a strong writer will help you do well in school and it will serve you well in a wide range of occupations—from law and medicine to nursing and auto mechanics.

Writers in ACTION

Writing is not limited to the nation's classrooms and newsrooms, as this quotation from Larry Cataldo, an auto mechanic, proves:

"People would be surprised by how important writing is to my job. Without a clearly written work order, I wouldn't know what to look for when I inspect a car. And if I didn't write careful notes about what the problem was, what the repair was, and what procedure I had used, customers wouldn't have a clear understanding of what work had been done and why."

What Are the Qualities of Good Writing?

Ideas Sometimes the hardest part of writing is coming up with ideas. However, there are ideas for writing all around you—you just may not recognize them. Most of the things that interest you—sports, music, clothes—are a source of an unlimited number of writing ideas. Starting with an idea that interests you makes it more likely that you will produce a good piece of writing. It is important, however, to consider whether potential readers will also find the idea interesting. Even the best pieces of writing won't succeed if the audience is uninterested.

Organization Once you have the ideas for a piece of writing, you must decide how to arrange them. Good writing has a clear and consistent organization that suits the topic. For example, if you are telling a story, you will probably want to arrange your details chronologically, or in the order in which they occurred.

Voice Voice refers to all of the distinctive qualities of your writing—from the type of language you use and the way you put together sentences and paragraphs to the ideas you like to write about and the attitude you convey to readers.

Word Choice Not surprisingly, word choice is a key element of good writing. By choosing words that convey your meaning as precisely as possible and capture your attitude toward your subject, you will help to ensure that readers understand your points and will increase the likelihood that you can sway them to accept your viewpoint.

Sentence Fluency In a piece of good writing, sentences seem to flow seamlessly from one to another. Transitions make it clear how one sentence connects to the next. A variety of lengths, structures, and openers helps to create a rhythm that engages readers.

Conventions Finally, it is essential for a piece of writing to follow the conventions of English grammar, usage, and mechanics. Errors in these areas will distract readers.

Learn More

To learn about strategies to help you develop writing that has these qualities, see Chapter 2, "A Walk Through the Writing Process," p. 6.

1

Developing Your Writing Life

There isn't just one correct way to approach the writing you do. Instead, writers experiment with different routines and approaches to writing until they find one that works for them. Following are some suggestions to help you develop your own writing routine:

▼ Critical Viewing
What type of writing do you imagine that this girl is doing? Why?
[Speculate]

Keep Track of Your Ideas

A great idea is only great if you remember it. Keep track of your thoughts and observations.

Notebook Take a tip from many professional writers and keep a small notebook with you at all times. In it, record thoughts, ideas, snippets of overheard conversation (great for helping you write realistic dialogue), and anything else that grabs your interest throughout the day. If coming up with a topic ever presents a problem, your notebook may contain the solution.

Writer's Journal Like a notebook, a writer's journal can be a great source of writing ideas. The writing in a writer's journal is writing you do for yourself alone, so this is a place where you can experiment with different writing styles or just let your ideas flow without stopping to edit yourself. A writer's journal is also a place where you can keep drawings, clippings, or other mementos that might inspire future writing projects.

Learning Log Often, writing about something can help you understand it. This is one of the benefits of keeping a learning log. A learning log is a place to record information you have learned—anything from methods for solving equations to a new technique for stopping on in-line skates. Writing something in a learning log that you want to remember might inspire you to conduct further research on the same topic, to turn it into a larger writing project.

Learning Log

October 26

What I Learned	Where I Learned It	Connections I Make
Not every number is something you count with. Some numbers are like a vanishing point that a series of numbers gets closer and closer to but never reaches.	Math class	This idea reminds me of what happened to the crew of the *Space Cat* on last week's episode—they got closer and closer to the center of the black hole but never reached it.
When putting a new string on a guitar, always start winding the string at the bottom of the peg and wind up.	Kevin next door	My strings used to buzz a lot before I tried this—I wonder if it will help.

Keep Track of Your Writing and Reading

Writing Portfolio Keeping a writing portfolio can also help you develop as a writer. Looking over your old work can remind you which writing strategies have worked well for you and which have not. A portfolio is a place where you save your written work and also monitor your progress as a writer. In a portfolio you can collect finished pieces as well as the notes and drafts you developed during the writing process. If you work on a computer, you might keep a portfolio disk instead of—or as well as—a paper portfolio.

Reader's Journal You can learn from other writers by keeping a journal in which you jot down quotations that you particularly like. Review these before you write; they may inspire you. Also, by familiarizing yourself with writing that has impressed you, you will develop an ear for effective style.

▼ Critical Viewing Compare and contrast the setting in which this girl is writing with a more formal setting—such as a classroom. **[Compare]**

Try Different Approaches

Just as you have your own tastes, likes, and dislikes, you will find that you will develop a unique approach to writing. Following are suggestions to help you find your own approach:

Getting Started There are many different ways of getting started on a piece of writing. You may find that simply sitting quietly and gathering your thoughts is your first step. In contrast, you may discover that sitting in front of a blank computer screen is the best way to begin.

Finding Ideas If you keep a learning log or journal (see page 4), you may turn to its pages to find inspiration for your writing. You might also look to the media as a valuable source for writing topics.

Writing a Draft Once you have assembled ideas and research, you might like to write a draft—on-line or by hand—in one continuous burst of writing. Another good method is to work out a few ideas, leave your writing for a while, and then come back to it.

Improving Your Work You might like to improve your sentences and paragraphs as you write, erasing or crossing out and rewriting before you have finished a draft. Alternatively, you may work best by improving a finished draft. Collaborate with a peer reviewer to revise and edit your work.

Experiment

Don't be afraid to try new strategies from time to time. As you develop as a writer, pay attention to the techniques that work best for you so that you can develop the most effective writing process.

Chapter 2

A Walk Through the Writing Process

▲ **Critical Viewing** Identify two ways in which libraries support effective writing. **[Support]**

Writing is a process that begins with the exploration of ideas and ends with the presentation of a final draft. The steps of the writing process can help you make your finished product the best it can be.

Types of Writing

Often, the types of writing are grouped into **modes** according to form and purpose. The chart at right shows the writing modes you will encounter in this book.

Writing can also be classified as *reflexive* or *extensive*. **Reflexive writing** refers to writing for which you choose the subject and the form. Often, reflexive writing is written for the writer alone and is not shared with an outside audience. **Extensive writing,** on the other hand, is writing for which you are given a subject or a range of subjects. Writing extensively results in sharing your writing with an audience—often your teacher.

The Modes of Writing

- Narration
- Description
- Persuasion
- Exposition
- Research Writing
- Response to Literature
- Writing for Assessment
- Workplace Writing

The Process of Writing

These are the stages of the writing process:

- **Prewriting** is the stage in which you explore possible topics, choose a topic, and then gather details you can include in your writing.
- **Drafting** involves putting ideas down on paper in a rough format.
- **Revising** is the stage in which you rework your rough draft to improve both its form and its content.
- **Editing and proofreading** are the stages in which you polish your writing, fixing errors in grammar, spelling, and mechanics.
- **Publishing and presenting** are the sharing of your writing.

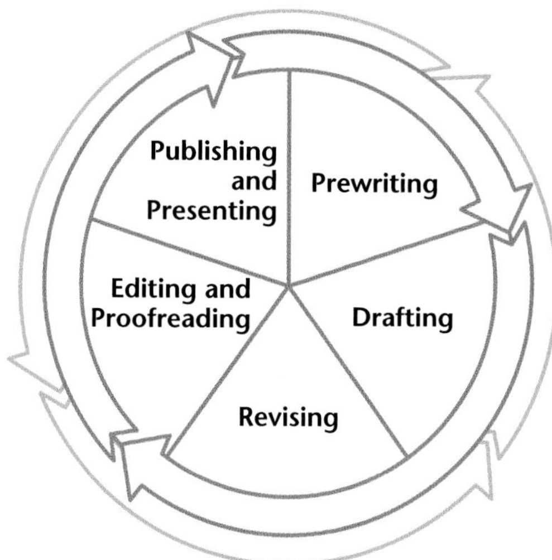

Although it may appear to be the case, these stages do not form a linear sequence. As a writer, you may find yourself skipping stages or returning to earlier stages. For example, you may begin drafting and find that you need to go back to do more research for more material with which to work. In another case, you may plunge right into drafting a story without taking time to jot down your ideas.

A Guided Tour

Use this chapter as a guided tour of the stages of the writing process. Learn about the steps of the process, and experiment with the sample strategies that are presented. In the chapters that follow, you will learn about many other strategies that you can use for each stage of the process.

What Is Prewriting?

Even experienced writers can feel challenged when faced with a blank sheet of paper. Prewriting acts as a preparation for writing by helping to flex and stretch your creative muscles, just as athletes' warm-up activities help prepare them for a meet or competition. Prewriting serves as a mental warm-up. It consists of activities and strategies to help you get started.

Choosing Your Topic

Obviously, you can't create a piece of writing if you don't have a topic. If a topic hasn't been assigned to you and if one doesn't immediately spring to mind, there are a variety of strategies you can use to generate possible topics. Following is one such strategy:

Learn More

For additional prewriting strategies suited to specific writing tasks, see Chapters 4–15.

SAMPLE STRATEGY

When you can't see the words you are entering, you won't be tempted to edit your thoughts as you enter them.

Writing With Invisible Ink Turn off your computer monitor, and begin writing about the events of a typical day. Let one idea flow freely into the next. When you have written freely for approximately ten minutes, turn the monitor back on. Review what you have written, and see whether any of the ideas might make a good topic. If you are unable to work on a computer, you can write using a pen with no ink on a piece of paper placed over carbon paper with a clean sheet of paper underneath.

Write with monitor turned off.

Turn on monitor to reveal what you have written.

Narrowing Your Topic

Even the most interesting topic won't lead to an effective piece of writing if the topic is too broad. For example, if you chose "sports" as your topic, you might not be able to cover it thoroughly unless you wrote a whole series of books. However, if you narrowed this topic to focus on the impact of rule changes in basketball, you would have a topic just right for a short paper. Following is one strategy you can use to narrow a topic:

SAMPLE STRATEGY

Using a Planning Web or Cluster Diagram Draw a diagram, beginning with a central circle with extending lines. Write your central thought, topic, or story title in the center circle. Draw additional circles around the central circle and use lines to connect them to the central circle. In each of these circles, jot down thoughts that the central subject or topic inspires. Each of the circles may generate new circles of its own or may serve as a natural stopping point—it's up to you. In this example, the writer narrowed the broad topic "Soccer" to "Loss Against Burton High."

SAMPLE PLANNING WEB

Considering Your Audience and Purpose

Before you begin writing your first draft, it is important to identify your audience; these are the people or person who will read your work. Next, consider your purpose; this is the goal you wish to accomplish through your writing. Both your audience and purpose will affect your use of language and choice of details.

Considering Your Audience Identify who will read your work. Think about what your audience does and does not know about your topic, and consider the type of language that would suit them. For instance, if you are writing a children's story, your language and descriptions should be simple and clear. On the other hand, if you are writing a personal essay for a college application, you should use much more sophisticated language and include details about yourself that might appeal to a college admissions board.

To help you identify the needs of your audience and keep these needs in mind as you write, develop an audience profile on a note card. Use the one below as a model. Refer back to your audience profile as you develop and draft your paper.

Audience Profile			
Age:	Children	Teenagers (circled)	Adults
Appropriate Language:	Very Informal	Informal (circled)	Formal
Audience Knowledge of Topic:	______		
What Will Interest the Audience Most:	______		

Considering Your Purpose Next, identify what you want to accomplish through your writing. For example, you may want to influence readers to accept your point of view, or you may simply want to entertain and amuse your audience. Keep your purpose in mind as you develop your paper, and use language and details that will help you achieve this purpose.

Gathering Details

Just as a scientist planning to conduct a laboratory experiment first gathers the specific information and ingredients he or she needs, you must gather the details and materials that you need before you write your first draft. Collecting information at this stage ultimately makes writing easier. Methods you can use to gather details include talking to other people, conducting research, and analyzing a topic.

SAMPLE STRATEGY

Using the Reporter's Formula When news reporters gather information for a story, they use a simple yet effective strategy often referred to as the five *W's and H.* They ask the questions **Who? What? When? Where? Why?** and **How?** You can also use this technique as you gather information for many of the types of writing you do. Use the five *W's and H* to guide you as you conduct research in the library, on the Internet, or by interviewing experts. Carefully record all the information you gather.

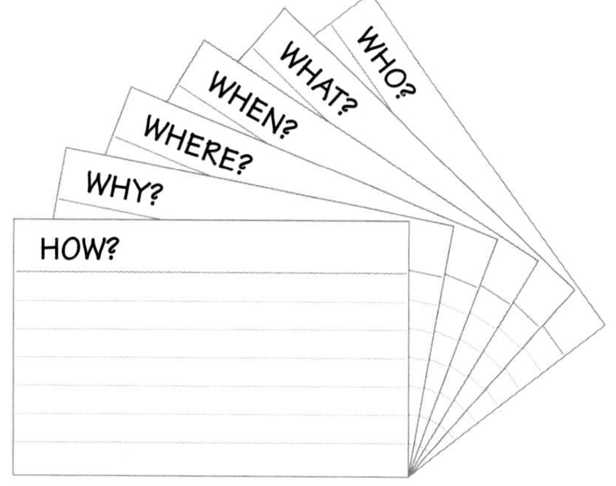

SAMPLE STRATEGY

Completing a Hexagonal When writing about literature, you can use a technique called hexagonal writing. Hexagonals, like the one shown at right, help you focus on different aspects of a piece of literature and make it easier for you to arrive at a thoughtful, thorough analysis. Complete each side of the hexagonal using the instructions shown here. Then, gather more details from the selection to support your analysis.

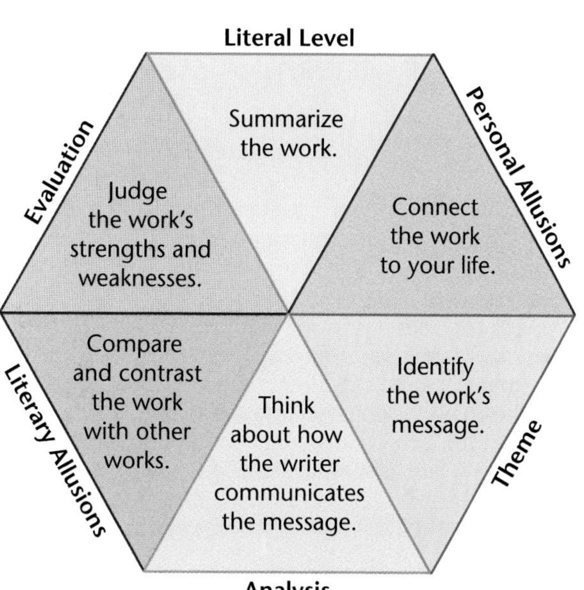

SAMPLE STRATEGY

Making a Timeline A timeline is an excellent tool to help you gather and arrange details in chronological order. Before you begin writing, you may want to construct a timeline like the one below. As you prewrite, challenge yourself to insert as many events and details as you can. While you may not ultimately include all of these ideas in your draft, knowing the sequence of events will enrich your draft. Use your timeline to guide you as you write.

MAKING A TIMELINE

Topic: Starting High School

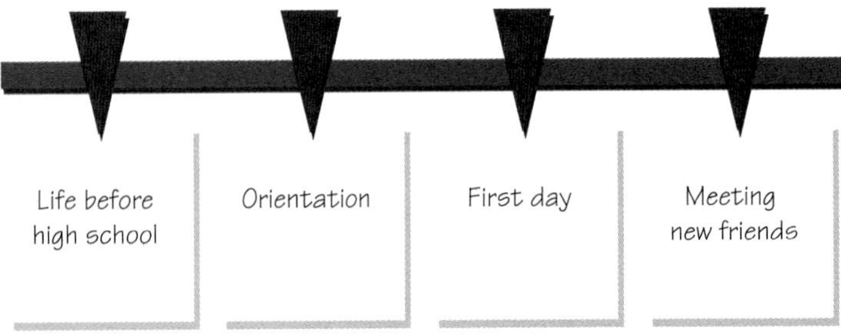

APPLYING THE PREWRITING STRATEGIES

1. Try out the Invisible Ink strategy to generate possible writing topics. Record any potential topics in your notebook for later use.
2. Use a Planning Web or Cluster Diagram to help you narrow one of the topics you generated using the Invisible Ink strategy. Choose one of the narrowed topics in your web as the focus of a piece of writing.
3. Prepare two different audience profiles for a personal essay on courage. Make one profile for a group of your ninth-grade classmates. Make the other for a college admissions board.
4. Use the Reporter's Formula questions to gather details about an event for a news story for your school paper.
5. Complete a Hexagonal for a short story or novel you have recently read.
6. Prepare a timeline showing what you did over a typical weekend.

2.2 What Is Drafting?

Shaping Your Writing

Focus on the Form Each form of writing has its own set of objectives: *narration* tells a story, *persuasion* convinces, and *exposition* explains. Whatever your final product, keep the particular objectives of the form in mind as you write.

Attract Your Readers' Attention With a Strong Lead Write your opening paragraph so that it entices your audience to keep reading. To compose a strong "lead," begin with an intriguing quotation, a surprising or provocative statement, or an evocative description.

WRITING MODELS

"Off there to the right—somewhere—is a large island," said Whitney. "It's rather a mystery—"

—Richard Connell, "The Most Dangerous Game"

The writer arouses interest by suggesting a mysterious situation.

I had called upon my friend, Mr. Sherlock Holmes, one day in the autumn of last year and found him in deep conversation with a very stout, florid-faced, elderly gentleman with fiery red hair. With an apology for my intrusion, I was about to withdraw when Holmes pulled me abruptly into the room and closed the door behind me.

—Sir Arthur Conan Doyle, "The Red-headed League"

The writer uses detailed description and creates suspense with an unexpected event.

I was six when my mother taught me the art of invisible strength. It was a strategy for winning arguments, respect from others, and eventually, though neither of us knew it at the time, chess games.

—Amy Tan, from "Rules of the Game"

This piece begins with an intriguing statement and shows its possible applications.

Ticktock, ticktock: time to type the labels. Ticktock, ticktock: time to schedule next week's lunch appointments. Ticktock, ticktock: time to fax out the budget proposals. Ticktock, ticktock: time to go home.

—Marcia A. Reed-Woodard, "From 'Ho-hum' to More Fun"

A clever lead shows readers an exaggerated scenario. The essay to follow will provide solutions for the problem presented.

Do you want to take a trip abroad but don't think you can spring for the airfare and hotel costs? Discount travel consolidators may be your solution.

—George Alexander, from "Thinking of Venturing Abroad?"

A question invites readers to connect to the writer's ideas.

Providing Elaboration

As you develop each of the paragraphs in the body of your paper, focus on elaborating, or developing, your key points by providing a thorough set of facts, examples, and details. One strategy that you can use to ensure that you elaborate on the key point of each paragraph is called the SEE method.

SAMPLE STRATEGY

Using the SEE Method The SEE method of *Statement, Extension,* and *Elaboration* is a systematic approach to developing paragraphs. Think of the SEE method as a way to shed more light on your subject. Start with a statement of the main idea. Then, write an extension by restating or explaining the first sentence. Elaborate further by providing even more detail about the main idea. Look at this example:

STATEMENT: To learn to play the piano, she practiced every day.

EXTENSION: From scales to simple melodies, she began to see improvement in weeks.

ELABORATION: After several months, she was playing sonatinas with grace.

APPLYING THE DRAFTING STRATEGIES

1. Write an exciting or interest-grabbing lead for a review of a school play.
2. Complete the following statements, and use the SEE method to elaborate your ideas.
   a. My favorite sport is __?__.
   b. To save some money, try __?__.

Learn More

The types of paragraphs that you include in a piece of writing vary, depending on the form and purpose of the writing. You will learn about the types of paragraphs most appropriate to each form in Chapters 3–15.

2.3 What Is Revising?

Using a Systematic Approach

Once you've finished writing, revise your work carefully. In this book, you will learn a systematic revision process called **ratiocination** (rash´ ē äs ə nā´shen). The word *ratiocination* refers to logical thinking. As a revision approach, the word refers to applying logic to the way you look at your work by color-coding items for analysis. Begin by looking at your overall structure, and then look at your paragraphs, sentences, and words. At each stage, use a process of color-coding and marking clues in your work to help you revise.

Writers in ACTION

Edgar Allan Poe's detective stories featured C. Auguste Dupin, an amateur detective who was a master of ratiocination skills. In "The Murders in the Rue Morgue," Dupin made an analytical study of a crime scene to solve the crime.

Revising Your Overall Structure

Start by examining the soundness of your structure, or overall organization. Your ideas should flow logically from beginning to end. You may strengthen the structure by reordering paragraphs or by adding information to fill in gaps.

SAMPLE STRATEGY

REVISION STRATEGY
Highlight to Frame Your Writing

To view the structure of your writing, highlight the statement of the main point of your paper and the key sentence in your conclusion. Then, in a second color highlight the main idea of each paragraph. Evaluate whether the progression of your writing is sound, or logical, and rearrange or add information as needed. With the details stripped from the example at right, you can analyze the structure of the essay.

EVALUATING STRUCTURE

On the whole, the advantages of having a part-time job outweigh the disadvantages.

Working may take time away from study and extracurricular activities. . . .

While working at a job, a student learns what it means to have responsibilities, which is excellent preparation for the future. . . .

Another advantage is the salary, which the student can use for various worthwhile purposes, such as class trips or a college fund. . . .

Despite the time commitment and scheduling issues, a part-time job is a valuable experience for a student.

Revising Your Paragraphs

Next, examine each paragraph in your writing. Consider the way each sentence contributes to the point of the paragraph. As you evaluate your draft, rewrite or eliminate any sentences that are not effective. Try the strategy below:

SAMPLE STRATEGY

REVISION STRATEGY
Color-Coding to Check Connections

Go through each paragraph, and circle the places in which you introduce a specific example, a cause, an effect, a comparison, or a contrast. Use different symbols to identify each of these relationships. Then, evaluate whether each idea follows logically from the one before it. Add transitional words or phrases to make connections more clear. This chart suggests symbols for color-coding and provides effective transitions for each relationship.

IDENTIFYING RELATIONSHIPS

Relationship	Symbol	Transitionals
Comparison	●	both, all, similarly, moreover, and, too
Contrast	■	although, but, however, yet, nevertheless, instead
Example	▼	for instance, for example
Cause and Effect	➡	because, as a result, consequently, since, so

Revising Your Sentences

When you study the sentences in your draft, check to see that they flow smoothly from one to the next. Look to see that you have avoided the pattern of beginning most of your sentences in the same way.

Learn More

To learn specific strategies for varying your sentences, see Chapter 22, "Effective Sentences."

SAMPLE STRATEGY

REVISION STRATEGY
Listing Sentence Starters to Vary Sentence Beginnings

Make a list of the first word in each sentence of your draft. Review your list, and eliminate repetition by rearranging the word order or adding introductory material to begin each sentence in a different way.

Revising Your Word Choice

The final step in the process of revising your work is to analyze your choice of words. Make sure that each word conveys the exact meaning you intended. Also, look for the repetition of words, and make revisions to reduce the number of the most commonly repeated words.

SAMPLE STRATEGY

REVISION STRATEGY
Circling Repeated Words

Go through your writing, and circle any nouns, verbs, adjectives, or adverbs that you have used more than once. Then, evaluate each of these repeated words to decide whether you should replace it with a synonym.

EVALUATING REPEATED WORDS

The concert was excellent. The band played many ~~excellent~~ ^popular songs and the crowd was enthusiastic. The special effects added to the excitement of the ~~concert.~~ ^event

Peer Review

After you've finished revising your draft, work with one or more classmates to get a fresh perspective on your writing.

Focus Your Peer Reviewer To get the most specific feedback possible, focus on one element or provide questions that lead to suggestions for improvement. Look at the sample questions at right.

Evaluate the Peer Responses Weigh the responses of your peer reviewer, and determine which suggestions you want to incorporate in your draft. Ask your peer reviewer for clarification of any points that seem unclear.

FOCUSING PEER REVIEW

- Which parts were most confusing to you?
- Where did I leave out details?
- Where was I repetitive?

APPLYING THE REVISION STRATEGIES

Choose a piece of writing that you did last year or one you've written recently. Go through the piece, using each of the revision strategies described on the preceding pages. Then, write an explanation of how the strategies helped you make additional improvements to your work.

What Are Editing and Proofreading?

Don't let errors in grammar, usage, mechanics, and spelling ruin the impact of your writing. Carefully proofread your work to identify and correct these types of errors.

Focusing on Proofreading

In each of the chapters that follows, you will find a specific proofreading focus—an area on which to place extra attention. Address the suggested element; however, you should always take care to find and eliminate *all* types of errors. Here are the broad categories you should address:

- Spelling
- Grammar
- Usage
- Mechanics
- Accuracy
- Legibility

Using Proofreading Symbols As you proofread your paper, use the symbols below to mark corrections. If you are working on a computer, enter the changes, and print out a clean final copy. If you are not working on a computer, mark the corrections as neatly as possible before turning in your paper.

PROOFREADING SYMBOLS

∧	insert letters or words here	B̸	make this letter lowercase
#	insert space here	b (triple underline)	capitalize this letter
∽	switch the order of two letters or words	⁀	link inserted material
¶	begin a new paragraph		

APPLYING THE EDITING AND PROOFREADING STRATEGIES

Write a one-paragraph composition on a topic that interests you. For the purposes of a proofreading exercise, intentionally include a variety of different types of errors in your work. Then, exchange papers with a classmate. Using the proofreading symbols above, identify and mark the necessary corrections.

Technology Tip

Don't make the mistake of thinking that a spell-check feature on a computer will catch all of your spelling errors. Doing a spell check is a great first step, but you still need to carefully proofread your work.

2.5 What Are Publishing and Presenting?

Moving Forward

This walk through the writing process gives you a preview of the strategies and techniques that you can incorporate into your writing process. Chapters 4–15 will provide more specific instruction focused on the modes of writing, offering you effective strategies for improving your writing.

Building Your Portfolio Save your finished writing products in a folder, file, box, or other safe and organized container. Your portfolio will serve as a record of your development and growth as a writer. To see this change, you may want to compare recent work with writing that you completed some time ago. Your portfolio can also act as a resource for future writing: In a section of your portfolio, keep partly completed pieces of writing, writing ideas, clippings, and photos that inspire you.

Reflecting on Your Writing Every time you complete a piece of writing, you are presented with a learning experience, a chance to learn something about yourself, something about your topic, and something about your writing process. Questions at the end of each writing chapter will help you think about what you have learned and how you have learned it. To help you learn from your experiences, add your reflections to your portfolio.

Assessing Your Writing In each chapter, you'll find a rubric, or set of criteria, on which your work can be evaluated. Refer to the rubric throughout the writing process to be certain you are addressing the key issues.

APPLYING THE PUBLISHING AND PRESENTING STRATEGIES

1. Choose a prewriting strategy you used in this introduction to the writing process. Put your prewriting ideas in your portfolio to be worked into a fully developed piece of writing at a later time.
2. Start your reflection by answering these questions:
   - Which of the strategies or activities did you find most useful or usable? Explain.
   - What are your strengths as a writer?

Chapter 3

Paragraphs and Compositions

Structure and Style

▲ Critical Viewing In what way do the items on this table fit together to create a whole? **[Connect]**

What Are Paragraphs and Compositions?

A **paragraph** consists of a group of sentences that share a common topic and work together as a unit of expression. A new paragraph is indicated by visual clues, such as an indentation or an extra space between lines of text. When you write, your organization and meaning will determine how you insert these breaks.

In a **composition,** paragraphs are organized around a main idea. Each paragraph supports, develops, or explains the main idea of the whole work. Essays, speeches, autobiographical narratives, and research reports are just a few of the types of compositions.

3.1 *Writing Effective Paragraphs*

Main Idea and Topic Sentence

Most paragraphs develop one main idea. This main idea is usually stated in the paragraph's **topic sentence.** The remaining sentences of the paragraph support, explain, develop, or illustrate the topic sentence.

When the main idea of a paragraph is not directly stated, all the sentences in the paragraph work together to support the **implied main idea.** In a paragraph that has an implied main idea, the reader infers the point of the paragraph based on the details that are provided.

WRITING MODELS

from Silent Spring

Rachel Carson

There was once a town in the heart of America where all life seemed to live in harmony with its surroundings. The town lay in the midst of a checkerboard of prosperous farms, with fields of grain and hillsides of orchards where, in spring, white clouds of bloom drifted above the green fields. In autumn, oak and maple and birch set up a blaze of color that flamed and flickered across a backdrop of pines. Then foxes barked in the hills and deer silently crossed the fields, half hidden in the mists of the fall mornings.

In this passage, the stated topic sentence is shown in blue italics.

from Arthur Ashe Remembered

John McPhee

His mother was tall, with long soft hair and a face that was gentle and thin. She read a lot. She read a lot to him. His father said of her, "She was just like Arthur Junior. She never argued. She was quiet, easygoing, kindhearted."

In this passage, all the sentences work together to suggest the unstated main idea that Arthur Ashe's mother was a beautiful person—personally and physically.

Exercise 1 **Identifying a Stated Topic Sentence** Identify the stated topic sentence in this paragraph from Amy Tan's "Rules of the Game."

I was six when my mother taught me the art of invisible strength. It was a strategy for winning arguments, respect from others, and eventually, though neither of us knew it at the time, chess games.

Exercise 2 **Identifying an Implied Main Idea** Identify the implied main idea in the following paragraph from "Children in the Woods" by Barry Lopez.

I have never forgotten the texture of this incident. Whenever I recall it I am moved not so much by any sense of my young self but by a sense of responsibility toward children, knowing how acutely I was affected in that moment by that woman's words. The effect, for all I know, has lasted a lifetime.

Writing a Topic Sentence

Each topic sentence presents a main point within your whole piece of writing. You may often develop topic sentences in the planning stages of your writing, before you actually write your paragraphs. As you revise your work, you may want to rework some of these sentences.

To write a topic sentence, review the details you will include in your writing. Look for groups of details that have something in common. For each group, make a statement that expresses the idea or quality that these details have in common. Use this statement as the topic sentence of a paragraph that includes the grouped details.

Exercise 3 **Writing a Topic Sentence** Write a topic sentence for a paragraph about each of the following topics.

1. Why you do or don't participate in an after-school club or activity
2. Which aspect of your best friend's personality you find most appealing
3. The reasons you do or do not enjoy a particular sports activity
4. The contents of your backpack
5. How you get to and from school each day

Writing Supporting Sentences

Your topic sentence, whether stated or implied, will direct the remaining sentences in the paragraph. These other sentences should give enough information to support, explain, or develop the topic sentence completely.

You can support or develop the main idea by using one or more of the following strategies:

Use Facts Facts are statements that can be verified. They support your key idea by providing concrete evidence or proof.

TOPIC SENTENCE: Antarctica has the most hostile environment on Earth for humans.

SUPPORTING FACTS: Not a tree or bush grows there. No human beings are native to the land. The only permanent inhabitants of Antarctica—such as seals, penguins, and a few other birds—must feed in the sea.

Use Statistics A statistic is a fact, usually stated using numbers.

TOPIC SENTENCE: The children's zoo is very busy on Saturdays.

SUPPORTING STATISTIC: Surveys reveal that the zoo receives 70 percent of its visitors on weekends.

Use Examples, Illustrations, or Instances An example, illustration, or instance is a specific thing, person, or event that demonstrates a point.

TOPIC SENTENCE: Seals are very popular zoo attractions.

ILLUSTRATION: Last weekend, spectators lined up twenty minutes in advance to view the seals' afternoon feeding.

Use Details Details are the specifics of your writing. They make your point or main idea clear by showing how all the pieces fit together.

TOPIC SENTENCE: Families like to watch the seals being fed.

DETAILS: Adults and children gasp with awe, clap excitedly, and cheer happily as the seals bark, catch the fish, and perform tricks.

▼ Critical Viewing What details would you use to support the statement that these seals are healthy? **[Support]**

Exercise 4 **Writing Supporting Sentences** Write two supporting sentences for each of the following topic sentences.

1. Exercise and a balanced diet contribute to good health.
2. Competitive athletes work hard to achieve their goals.
3. Space exploration may result in new lifestyle options.

3.1

Placing Your Topic Sentence

The topic sentence presenting your main idea can be located at any point in the paragraph. You may place it at the beginning, in the middle, or at the end of the paragraph; or you may leave it unstated. When the topic sentence comes at the beginning of a paragraph, it gives a preview of and direction to the sentences that come after it. Placed at the end of the paragraph, the topic sentence may draw a conclusion or function as a summary. When you leave the topic sentence unstated, the reader can synthesize the information you have presented.

Topic, Restatement, Illustration With the TRI pattern (Topic, Restatement, Illustration) you "build" a paragraph with the following elements:

TOPIC SENTENCE:	You state your key idea.
RESTATEMENT:	You interpret your key idea—put it into other words.
ILLUSTRATION:	You support your key idea with an illustration or an example.

T Dragons were often associated with royalty.
R Mythic figures, dragons suggest power and majesty.
I When Uther, father of King Arthur of the Round Table, became king, he had a golden dragon made to carry with him, and he took the name Pendragon.

Once you have identified the basic elements of your paragraph, experiment with variations of the TRI pattern, such as TIR, TRI, or ITR, until you are satisfied with the effect.

Exercise 5 **Placing a Topic Sentence** Identify the topic sentence that expresses the main idea of the following group of sentences. Then, use two variations of the TRI pattern to organize the sentences. Use transitions and, if necessary, additional sentences. Choose the arrangement you think is most effective.

1. The winds of a hurricane swirl at 75 miles per hour or more.
2. The force of a hurricane is frightening and devastating.
3. Strong winds tear down trees and buildings.
4. Flood waters make roads impassable and damage property.
5. Hurricanes cause great destruction.

3.2 Paragraphs in Essays and Other Compositions

Unity and Coherence

Maintain Unity

Unity in a paragraph or composition means that all the parts are related to a single key idea. In a unified composition, the main idea of each paragraph is clearly connected to the main idea or **thesis statement** of the composition. In a paragraph that has unity, all the sentences either develop, support, or explain the stated or implied topic sentence.

In the following paragraph, one sentence is marked for deletion because it interferes with the unity of the paragraph.

▲Critical Viewing What statement communicates your overall impression of this cat? **[Describe]**

WRITING MODEL

Some of the domestic cat's features resemble those of all felines. For instance, a cat's whiskers help it gauge spaces through which it may fit, and its night vision is powerful, as with most other felines. ~~Artists have portrayed the domestic cat in many different ways through the ages.~~ Its playfulness as a kitten and hunting habits mimic those of feline counterparts in the wild.

Exercise 6 **Revising for Unity** On a separate sheet of paper, copy the following paragraphs. Mark for deletion any sentences that interfere with the unity of the paragraphs.

Reactions to poison ivy vary. Some people seem to be immune to it, although the immunity may not continue throughout a lifetime. Usually, those who are allergic to poison ivy develop an itchy skin rash when they come into physical contact with the vine. The smoke from burning poison ivy vines can also carry the poison. For many people, the severity of the rash diminishes with each exposure.

Runners and hikers may contract poison ivy on their legs as they brush past the weed. The leaves of this plant are quite distinctive. Children often get rashes on their hands and faces while playing outdoors.

Construct Coherence

Coherence means that ideas are organized in a logical order and in a way that allows readers to see the connections and understand the flow of ideas.

When you write your draft, arrange the order of the sentences of each paragraph so that one leads logically to the next. Choose an organization for your paragraphs, and use it consistently throughout the composition. Indicate the connections between ideas by using transitional words and phrases.

TRANSITIONAL WORDS AND PHRASES To Show Comparison, Contrast, and Development		
again	however	like
along with	in contrast	namely
also	in fact	next
although	instead of	similarly
as a result	for example	than
as in	for instance	therefore
both	furthermore	together
consequently	in addition	too
finally	in conclusion	
To Show Time		
after	first	next
at last	last	now
before	later	soon
finally	meanwhile	then
To Show Location		
above	beneath	inside
ahead	beyond	near
behind	in back of	next to
below	in front of	outside
To Show Importance		
another	furthermore	next
even greater	moreover	one
finally	most important	second
first	most significantly	third

Exercise 7 **Revising for Coherence** On a separate sheet of paper, revise the following paragraph to construct coherence. If necessary, reorder sentences and add transitions.

Many people find the microwave a useful tool to solve the problems presented by the lengthy meal preparation times demanded by traditional cooking. America is a country always on the move. Many American citizens no longer have or want to take the time to cook a full meal. Microwave cooking can provide a quick, tasty, nutritious meal.

The Parts of a Composition

To compose means "to put together." In a written composition, sentences and paragraphs are put together and organized to develop a single focus. No matter what type of organization is used, most compositions have three main sections or parts: an *introduction*, a *body*, and a *conclusion*.

Introduction

The **introduction** of a composition does what its name suggests: It introduces the focus of the composition, usually in a sentence called the **thesis statement.** In addition, the introduction usually captures readers' interest with a strong **lead.** An attention-getting lead may be an interesting quotation, a surprising statement, or a unique observation.

Body Paragraphs

The **body** paragraphs of a composition develop the thesis statement. They provide supporting facts, details, and examples. The paragraphs in the body are organized in a logical order, such as time order, order of importance, or spatial order.

Conclusion

The **conclusion** brings a composition to a close. Usually in the conclusion, the thesis statement is restated and the support is summarized. An effective conclusion also ends with a striking image or thought that will stick in readers' minds.

For more information about organizing paragraphs, see page 24.

Exercise 8 **Planning a Composition** On a separate sheet of paper, outline the parts of a persuasive composition on an issue of importance to you. Write a thesis statement and a possible lead. Then, plan the topic sentences for each of several body paragraphs. (Although you may not have specific facts and statistics at hand, you can plan the points you will try to support.) Finally, restate your thesis statement in a way that you could use in a conclusion.

Types of Paragraphs

Topical Paragraphs

A **topical paragraph** is a group of sentences that contains one main sentence or idea and several sentences that support or develop that key idea. Most paragraphs are topical paragraphs, but many compositions also include functional paragraphs.

Functional Paragraphs

Functional paragraphs serve a specific purpose. Although they may not have a topic sentence, they are unified and coherent because the sentences (if there is more than one sentence) all follow a logical order and are clearly connected. Functional paragraphs can be used for the following purposes:

To Create Emphasis A very short paragraph of one or two sentences lends weight to what is being said because it breaks the reader's rhythm.

WRITING MODEL

from **An Entomological Study of Apartment 4A**

Patricia Volk

The phone rings. It rings all day. Louis Sorkin is the 911 of insect emergencies. If you open your safe and bugs fly in your face or you need to know whether New Mexican centipedes produce cyanide, Sorkin's your man.

He studies two flies I found on the bathroom windowsill. There's no masking his disgust.

The short, direct second paragraph following the longer, more conversational paragraph emphasizes Louis Sorkin's reaction.

To Indicate Dialogue One of the conventions of written dialogue is that a new paragraph begins each time the speaker changes.

To Make a Transition A short paragraph can help readers move between the main ideas in two topical paragraphs.

Paragraph Blocks

Sometimes, a key idea requires an amount of support or development that is too extensive for a single paragraph. Therefore, you may occasionally use several paragraphs to develop a single idea. These paragraphs function as a "block." Each paragraph within the block contributes support to the key idea or topic sentence. By dividing the development of the ideas into chunks, you make your ideas clear and accessible.

Topic sentence: Recycling is one of the most beneficial ways to reduce waste.

Paragraph 1	It's economical.	**B L O C K**
Paragraph 2	It's more economical than reducing consumption.	
Paragraph 3	It creates new jobs.	

Exercise 9 **Identifying Functional Paragraphs** Skim a book review or some other piece of persuasive writing to find examples of functional paragraphs that create emphasis, indicate dialogue, and make transitions. Explain to a partner how these paragraphs work within the longer piece of writing.

Exercise 10 **Analyzing Types of Paragraphs** Photocopy a newspaper or magazine article. Analyze each type of paragraph and identify its type. Draw a box around topical paragraphs. Underline any stated topic sentences. Write implied topic sentences in the margin of the article, next to the paragraph. Put a red star next to functional paragraphs that create emphasis, a blue star next to dialogue, and a green star next to paragraphs that create transitions. Then, mark paragraph blocks with a brace: { }. Discuss with a partner why each paragraph type is or is not an effective choice.

Writing Style

Developing Style

You can express your personal style in any number of ways: through clothing, hairstyle, movie preferences, choices in friends, and so on. Just as your style may be apparent in the people and things you identify with, so your style is reflected in your writing. Your writing style may be affected by a number of elements.

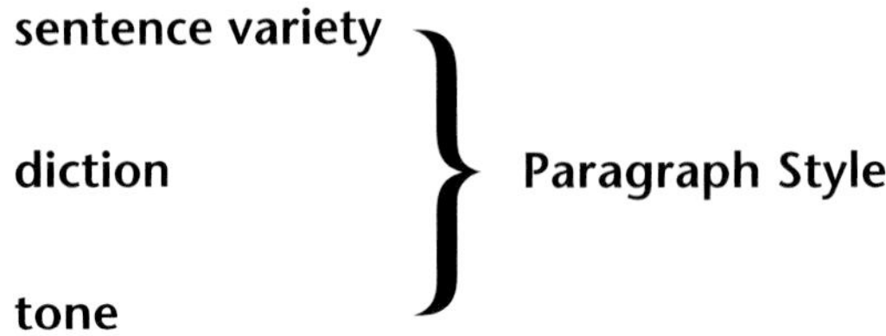

Sentence Variety The variety of outfits in your closet may reflect different aspects of your style and the various ways you perceive yourself. You may choose to project one image on one occasion and an entirely different image on another. You have options in your writing style as well. When you write, you choose from a variety of sentence types, lengths, and structures. Vary your sentences to express your style.

Diction The overall effect, or style, of a paragraph is affected by the words you choose. You can achieve an eccentric or offbeat style by using words with unusual or unexpected associations, or you can use words with formal or scholarly connotations if you want to assume a more authoritative stance. The sounds of words can also contribute to the style of a paragraph.

Tone Tone is your attitude toward your subject. You may feel any number of ways about your subject—passionately opinionated, amused, saddened, or objective. If you are writing a letter of reference, your paragraphs will have a businesslike, formal tone. If you are e-mailing your sister or brother about a comical family event, your paragraphs will probably have a lighthearted, informal tone.

Exercise 11 **Identifying Paragraph Style** Read the two Writing Models on page 21. Study the sentence lengths and structures, the word choice, and the tone of each paragraph. Discuss with a partner how the styles of the two paragraphs are similar and different. Then, write a paragraph of your own, modeled on the style of the paragraphs you read.

Formal and Informal English

Standard English can be either formal or informal. Informal English is used when you want to achieve a conversational tone in your writing and for casual writing. Formal English is used to address subjects in a serious way.

Use the Conventions of Formal English

Formal English is appropriate for research projects, essays, speeches, business letters, and most of your school assignments. When writing in formal English, you should observe the following conventions:

- Do not use slang.
- Avoid contractions.
- Use standard English and grammar.

▼ **Critical Viewing** Do you think this girl is using formal or informal English? Explain. **[Deduce]**

Use Informal English

Informal English is conversational in tone. It is appropriate for friendly letters, humorous writing, casual notes, some narratives, and much dialogue. When using informal English, you can:

- Use contractions.
- Use slang and popular expressions.

FORMAL ENGLISH: Please contact me at your earliest convenience if I can be of any further assistance.

INFORMAL ENGLISH: Feel free to give me a call whenever you've got a moment.

Exercise 12 **Using Formal and Informal English** On a separate sheet of paper, rewrite the following sentences. Use formal English for those written in informal English. Use informal English for those written in formal English.

1. This awesome song really rules.
2. The facts to which the reporter referred were of unquestionable veracity.
3. It was such a bummer when the storm ended the concert early.
4. The enthusiastic English teacher gratefully acknowledged her students' efforts and thanked them effusively.
5. Park yourself over there and grab yourself some grub.

Chapter 4

Narration

Autobiographical Writing

▲ Critical Viewing What good memories of your family can provide the source for an interesting narration? **[Evaluate]**

Autobiography in Everyday Life

At first glance, the word *autobiography* may seem a suitable writing form only for famous people with great accomplishments. However, when you take a closer look at this form, you'll realize that you don't have to be famous to have an interesting life story. The humorous anecdotes relatives tell about your antics as a child, an account of your participation in a championship game, the story about the way you met your best friend—these, too, are "life stories," or autobiographical narratives. In fact, each individual life unfolds like a story. Whenever you retell a part of your life story, you are sharing an autobiographical narrative.

What Is Autobiographical Writing?

When you write an **autobiography,** you are telling a story from your own life. Effective autobiographical writing includes

- a series of events involving the writer as a main character.
- a conflict or event that changed the writer's viewpoint.
- details about people and places.
- an insight based on the events narrated.
- a logical organization.

To preview the criteria on which your autobiographical writing will be judged, see the Rubric for Self-Assessment on page 46.

Writers in ACTION

Isabel Allende is a Chilean writer who began her writing career as a journalist. She frequently draws on her own experience when writing:

"Memory always betrays me. That's why I write—to preserve memory."

Types of Autobiographical Writing

Each type of autobiographical writing has a name that reflects its unique purpose:

- **Autobiographical sketches** often include information about the writer's life and his or her personal qualities.
- **Memoirs** focus on the writer's relationship with a particular person, place, or animal.
- **Reflective essays, personal essays, or autobiographical incidents** share a personal experience and include the writer's reflections on the significance of the experience.
- **Anecdotes** are brief, usually humorous accounts of a single event.

In this chapter, you will follow the work of Sara Holman, a student at Towson High School, in Towson, Maryland. Sara recounts her activities as a nine-year-old entrepreneur. As you will see, she used prewriting, drafting, and revising techniques to develop her autobiographical piece.

Prewriting

Choosing Your Topic

Your life is full of stories, so you may have trouble choosing only one! On the other hand, you might think you have no experiences interesting enough to write about. Either way, the following strategies will help you select or discover a topic.

Strategies for Generating Topics

1. **Song List** Make a list of your favorite songs. For each, record the memories each song inspires. Review your list, and choose one of the ideas to develop as your topic.
2. **Blueprinting** Draw a blueprint of someplace you remember. It can be a home, park, camp, or any place you value. Label each room or area. Then, jot down words and phrases you associate with these areas. Choose one of your ideas as the topic of your narrative.

For more help finding a topic, explore the activities and suggestions in the Choosing a Topic section of the Narration lesson.

Student Work IN PROGRESS

Name: *Sara Holman*
Towson High School
Towson, MD

Using a Blueprint to Choose a Topic

Sara used a blueprint to find ideas for an autobiographical sketch. She decided to write about a recycling project she ran as a child.

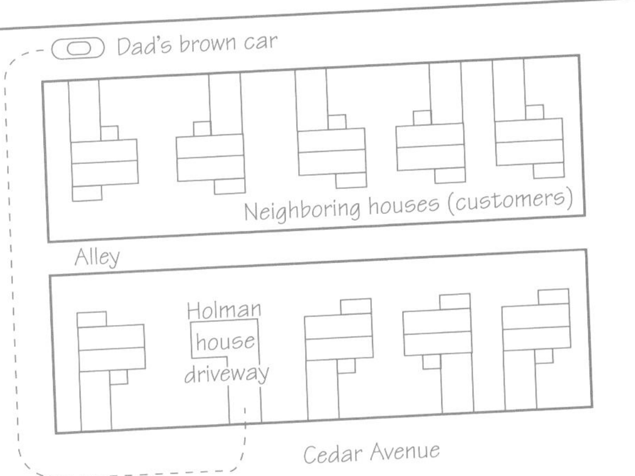

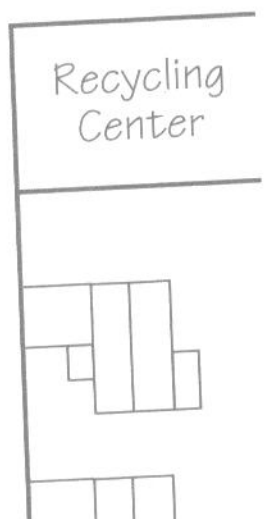

TOPIC BANK

If you are having trouble choosing a topic, consider these possibilities:

1. **Account of a Competition** Recall some particularly exciting competition that you witnessed or in which you participated. Write an autobiographical narrative that focuses on your reactions to the outcome of the competition.
2. **Anecdote About a Humorous Experience** Tell the story of a humorous mix-up or misunderstanding that you have experienced. In addition to details showing what happened, include your thoughts and feelings about the event.

Responding to Fine Art

3. *Travelling Carnival* may remind you of summer adventures or weekends of fun. In an autobiographical essay, describe an event this painting brings to mind. Like the artist, capture the excitement and atmosphere of your experience.

Travelling Carnival, John Sloan, National Museum of American Art

Responding to Literature

4. In Robert Frost's poem, "The Road Not Taken," the speaker reflects on an important decision. Read the poem, and use a quotation from it to inspire an essay about a time that you chose to follow an unusual or unexpected path. You can find this poem in *Prentice Hall Literature: Timeless Voices, Timeless Themes,* Gold.

Cooperative Writing Opportunity

5. **Group Autobiography** Work with a group to tell the narrative of a shared experience, such as a field trip or other school event. Some members can create a timeline of the events, others can interview one another for eyewitness accounts, and some can create pictures and captions to highlight the important moments of the experience.

4.2

Narrowing Your Topic

An autobiographical narrative is like putting a moment of your life under a magnifying glass. By enlarging a single moment or event, you make visible the unique qualities of the event that might otherwise go unseen. Narrow your topic so that you can describe and analyze it effectively. One way to narrow your topic is to use "invisible writing."

Use Invisible Writing to Narrow a Topic

If you can't see what you are writing as you write, you are more likely to write freely and continuously, concentrating on your ideas. Use the following steps to complete an invisible-writing exercise.

1. To prepare to write, slip a piece of carbon paper between two sheets of lined paper. Use a pen with the cap on or an empty ballpoint pen. Alternatively, start a new writing file on a word processor and turn the monitor off.
2. Write freely and continuously about your general topic for five minutes. Allow your thoughts to wander within the limits of the general topic, and note whatever ideas come to mind.
3. When you are finished, reveal what you have written. Review your notes, and circle key ideas that interest you.
4. Narrow your topic by choosing one moment, event, or detail that was most memorable or significant. Use this as the focus of your autobiographical writing.

▼ Critical Viewing
If you were writing for an audience of your peers, what level of language might you use to address them? **[Connect]**

Considering Your Audience and Purpose

Identify Your Audience Your audience is the person or people who will read your work. Their expectations and knowledge should influence your writing. For example, if you are sharing a story with your grandparents, you may need to define some terms they may not know, but you won't necessarily need to describe your family in full detail.

Refine Your Purpose Your purpose is your reason for writing. Look at these specific purposes and suggestions. Then, consider your goal for writing, and include language and ideas to achieve it.

- **To entertain** Include descriptions of situations or events that were especially funny.
- **To reflect** Focus on an event that is completed, and include information about how you have changed as a result of your experiences.

Gathering Details

Once you have chosen an incident on which to focus, gather details to bring the experience to life. Consider reviewing photographs or journals to gather details for your writing. You may even want to talk to relatives or friends to learn more about the events or experiences you'll narrate. To help focus your work, examine your topic by making a timeline of key events.

Make a Timeline

Create a detailed record of events by making a timeline. Write down the first event or incident related to the subject of your narrative. Record each event in the relative order each occurred.

To help find the appropriate words to describe your setting, use the Setting Profile and the Sensory Word Bins in the Narration lesson.

Name: Sara Holman
Towson High School
Towson, MD

Using a Timeline to Gather Details

Sara used a timeline to help her recall all the incidents and the sequence in which they occurred. She placed the events on the line in the order in which they happened, leaving spaces between events in case she wanted to insert details she remembered later.

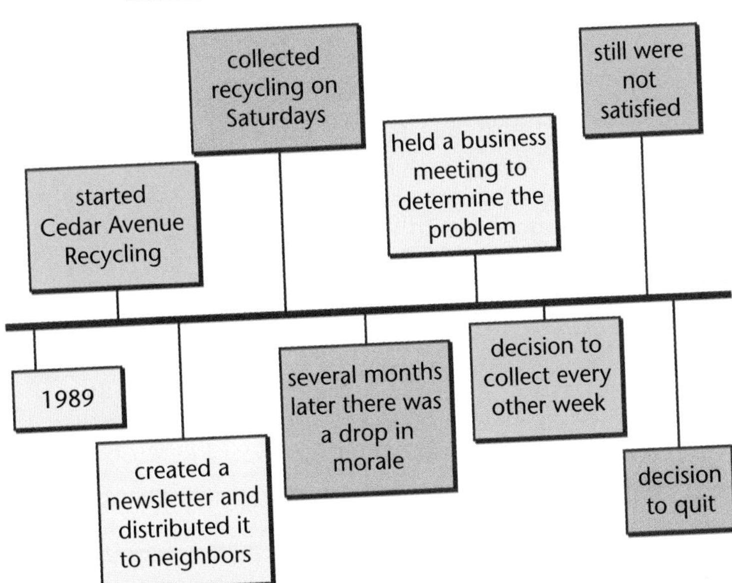

Drafting

Once you've done all your prewriting work, use the drafting stage to give shape to the details. Arrange the details you have gathered into a logical order that leads up to the turning point of your narrative—the moment of decision or insight.

Shaping Your Writing

Identify Your Main Point

Identify the turning point around which your details will be organized. To help you identify your turning point, think about why your topic experience is memorable or significant to you. It may be that you learned something from the experience or that the experience changed the way you look at life. Ask yourself the questions that follow. Then, use your answers to help you recognize the moment that moves your narrative forward.

- **What have I learned?**
- **What do I want my audience to understand?**

Once you have identified the main point of your narrative, begin organizing details to communicate it.

Use the Audio-Annotated Literary Models that show different ways to organize a narrative. You can find them in the Narration lesson.

Organize to Convey Your Main Point

You will probably want to organize the events of your narrative in chronological, or time, order. While you may want to include many episodes of your experience, remember that not every event is of equal importance. As you review the details you have gathered, look for the following narrative elements to include in your draft:

Conflict Identify the problem that set the events in motion. Introduce the conflict at the beginning of your narrative. Provide details and comments that show the event as the root of the narrative.

Rising Action Several events will probably occur between the introduction of your narrative and the climax, or most significant moment. These events should build on one another to create tension in the narrative. Organize them in chronological order to give your readers a context for understanding the conflict or insight that is at the heart of your narrative.

Climax The turning point in your narrative, the climax, is the moment in which you make a decision or a realization that changes your outlook or your situation.

Conclusion After the climax of the narrative, include a reflection that provides insight about your experience.

For more instruction on the elements of storytelling, see Chapter 5.

Providing Elaboration

As you draft your narrative, elaborate to help readers understand the significance of your experience. Provide details of what you thought and felt to allow readers to see the experience from your perspective.

Use Thought Shots to Elaborate

Cut from colored paper several "thought shot" balloons like the one shown on this page. After you complete each episode in your draft, slide a balloon down your draft as you look for places to add details about your reactions or thoughts. When you find a place, write the details on the balloon and tape or clip it in the margin where you want to make an addition. To strengthen your writing, include the ideas in your next draft.

Challenge

Whenever possible, provide sensory details that appeal to the five senses. This will enrich your writing and help your readers experience the events you are narrating.

Student Work IN PROGRESS

Name: Sara Holman
Towson High School
Towson, MD

Elaborating With Thought Shots

Sara intensifies the conflict by providing more information about what her narrator was thinking.

However, as time passed, company morale began to drop drastically. I called an executive meeting. We gathered on the driveway and sat in a circle. Will spoke first: "I hate this junk. We have to work really hard, and we only get paid ten cents a bag! That's nothing! I need time to work on my new invention—a hovering skateboard—and this is getting me nowhere."

Next, Jane shared her opinion: "I hate it, too. Every single Saturday, I have to do all this work. I just wanna play. I never even have time to play house with you, Sara."

When I heard these comments, I realized I felt the same way. When was I going to finish my friendship bracelet?

I gave an executive order. We stopped going every Saturday, and, instead . . .

4.4 Revising

Revision is your chance to polish your writing. As you revise, take a fresh look at your narrative. Add details that convey your ideas more effectively. Begin revising by evaluating the overall structure of your narrative.

Revising Your Overall Structure

Focus on Unity

When you check the unity of your writing, you analyze the way all the details fit together to present one idea. Here are two ways to create unity in your narrative:

Cut Unnecessary Events The significance of the experience you are relating may be lost if you include every event that occurred. Review your draft, and eliminate any events that do not contribute to developing the main point.

Establish Relationships As a participant in the action of your narrative, you know how one event was related to another. Your readers may need some clarification. Look for places where you have moved from one event to another or one time period to another. Add explanations and transitions to clarify relationships between events.

REVISION STRATEGY
Color-Coding to Improve Unity

Draw a box around the climax or turning point in your narrative. Then, use yellow to underline causes of the event, red to underline effects of the event, and green to highlight details that build the background, context, or tension. Then, evaluate any remaining details to see whether they should be eliminated or clarified. Use these tips to guide your revision:

Evaluate	Revise
• Does any unmarked text add to the narrative?	• Find ways to incorporate additional details to clarify the relationship of the event to the turning point.
• Do all the marked passages flow smoothly in a logical order?	• Consider reordering some passages to improve the writing.

Challenge

Take a tip from filmmakers who show only scenes or actions that add to their stories. For example, you may never see a film's main character actually working at a job unless the filmmaker can tie it to the story in a meaningful way.

Revising Your Paragraphs

Build Interest by Adding Information

Your narrative focuses on a single event or incident. To enrich each paragraph of your draft, add details that build the significance of the experience you narrate. You can do this in a number of ways:

- Add adjectives to make a word picture more vivid.
- Add dialogue to bring a scene to life.
- Add personal insights to show what you were thinking.

REVISION STRATEGY
Exploding a Moment

Read your draft, and identify the most significant moments in the narrative. Consider paragraphs that describe conflict or episodes that build tension. For each, use a small piece of paper to expand your presentation of the moment. Jot down details to show *what, where, when, how,* or *why* something happened. Then, incorporate your ideas into the revised draft.

Student Work IN PROGRESS

Name: Sara Holman
Towson High School
Towson, MD

Exploding a Moment

Sara added details to her narrative by identifying critical moments. She found an uncomfortable moment between her brother and herself. The details she added make the struggle more obvious.

"Let's go, Will! We still have five more houses!" My younger brother and junior partner responded to my urging. [by sticking out his tongue] He and I were not getting along too well. [because we were doing hard work]

Several months earlier, Will and I had started Cedar Avenue Recycling.

4.4

Revising Your Sentences

Vary Sentence Length

To improve your writing, consider revising not only what you say, but how you say it. One way to improve your writing style is to eliminate a string of short, choppy sentences by combining some of them.

REVISION STRATEGY
Combining Sentences to Vary Sentence Length

Bracket any short sentences in your draft that only provide more information about a noun or pronoun in a nearby sentence. Combine these sentences with the ones they support.

SHORT SENTENCES: It was a great day. I'll never forget it.
COMBINED: It was a great day that I will never forget.

Grammar in Your Writing

Relative Pronouns

A **relative pronoun** begins a subordinate clause and connects it to another idea in the sentence. The relative pronouns are *who, whom, whose, which,* and *that.*

You can combine two sentences by inserting *who, which,* or *that* in place of the subject of one sentence. Then, insert the new subordinate clause into the other sentence to modify its subject. Look at these examples.

Two Sentences: Janice sometimes teases me. She is older than I am.
Combined: Janice, **who** is older than I am, sometimes teases me.

You can instead use *whom, which,* or *that* in place of the object of one sentence. Then, insert the resulting clause into the other sentence.

Two Sentences: Paul is young. Janice teases him often.
Combined: Paul, **whom** Janice often teases, is young.

Find It in Your Reading Review a short story that you have read recently. Find two sentences that contain relative pronouns. Identify whether the clause introduced by the relative pronoun gives more information about a noun.

Find It in Your Writing Look through your draft to find places where you have used relative pronouns. Challenge yourself to combine sentences by including at least three relative pronouns in your final draft.

For more information on using relative pronouns, see Chapter 16.

Revising Your Word Choice

Make Verbs Work for You

Strong verbs work to build vivid pictures in the minds of your readers. Use precise action verbs to communicate exactly what is happening in your narrative. Choose the most vivid action verb for your meaning. Look at these examples.

VAGUE: Urgency *moved* through us.
VIVID: Urgency *flashed* through us.

VAGUE: She *turned* the pages, looking for the coupon.
VIVID: She *flipped* the pages, looking for the coupon.

REVISION STRATEGY
Circling Action Verbs

To circle the action verbs in your draft, ignore *being* verbs such as *am, is, are, was, were, be, being,* and *been.* Evaluate each circled verb to decide whether a more vivid verb might be better suited to your needs.

Learn More

For more about the difference between action and linking verbs, see Chapter 17.

Student Work IN PROGRESS

Name: Sara Holman
Towson High School
Towson, MD

Evaluating Action Verbs

In the paragraph that described how Sara and her siblings conducted their recycling business, Sara replaced vague verbs with action verbs to better convey the feeling she wanted.

Our business was fairly simple. Every Saturday morning, we ~~went with~~ pulled our wagon from house to house and ~~gathered~~ collected recycling for a mere ten cents a bag. Then, we ~~put~~ hauled the bags into our big brown van, and Dad ~~brought~~ drove them to a nearby recycling center.

At first, ~~putting~~ loading these bags of pickle jars, milk jugs, and soup cans into our red wagon was fun.

Peer Review

Having a peer review your work will help you identify problems in your writing that you may be too close to catch. After you have done a thorough revision of your draft, ask a peer to read it with a critical eye. To focus the review, ask your reader to identify vague words or clichés that don't communicate an idea in an interesting way.

Writing Lab CD-ROM

For more tips on peer reviews, see the checklist of peer revision strategies. You can find it in the Narration lesson.

REVISION STRATEGY
Color-Coding Word Choice and Clichés

Make a photocopy of your draft, and give it to a peer reviewer. Ask your reader to mark imprecise words with a check and to box any clichés or overused expressions. When your peer reviewer has finished marking your writing, meet to discuss the problems the reviewer found. Consider these tips:

- Work together to share ideas about how a cliché might be replaced with a fresher expression.
- Brainstorm to list words that might be more precise than the ones you have chosen.

Consider your reviewer's suggestions, but use your own judgment as you revise your draft.

Student Work IN PROGRESS

Name: Sara Holman
Towson High School
Towson, MD

Using Peer Revision to Evaluate Word Choice

After a peer reviewer checked vague words and boxed clichés and overused expressions, Sara used the evaluation to revise her draft.

At first, loading these bags of pickle jars, milk jugs, and soup cans into our ~~cart~~ red wagon was fun. However, ~~we were soon down in the dumps again.~~ as time passed, company morale began to drop drastically. Anxious to determine the cause of this problem, I ~~gathered the troops.~~ called an executive meeting. We gathered on the driveway and sat in a circle.

4.5 Editing and Proofreading

Once you have completed revising the content of your narrative, check your draft for spelling, grammar, punctuation, and capitalization. Strive to make your final draft error-free.

Focusing on Punctuation

As you proofread, pay special attention to whether you have punctuated your sentences correctly. Look at these specific punctuation problem areas:

- **End punctuation** Check the end of each sentence to see that you have chosen the correct mark.
- **Dialogue** Review the conventions for punctuating dialogue, and confirm that you have used them correctly in your writing.
- **Commas** While a comma can create a necessary pause, it is also frequently misused. Review your draft to see whether you have inserted commas only where necessary.

Learn More

Check the rules for punctuating dialogue. You can find them in Chapter 29.

Grammar in Your Writing

Using an Exclamation Mark to Show Emotion

An **exclamation mark** can be used to signal a strong emotion or force. It can also indicate that words are spoken loudly or with intensity. Whether the emotion is enthusiasm, anger, or surprise, an exclamation mark puts power behind the words. Weigh your interpretations of these two sentences:

I found it under the sink. I found it under the sink!

Use exclamation marks sparingly. Too many of these marks in your writing will diminish their effectiveness.

Find It in Your Reading Find an example of a sentence in an essay you have read that is punctuated with an exclamation mark. Discuss with a partner what emotion is expressed and why it is being expressed with intensity.

Find It in Your Writing Look through your narrative to see whether there is a sentence or two that could be more effectively punctuated with an exclamation mark than with a period.

For more on end punctuation, see Chapter 29.

Publishing and Presenting

Consider sharing your autobiographical writing with a large or small audience. The following suggestions offer two ideas for presenting your work to others.

Building Your Portfolio

1. **Submit It to Your School Newspaper or Magazine** Talk to the editor or a faculty advisor to find out what the requirements are for submitting work. Review and revise your narrative as necessary to meet these requirements. Then, submit your work.
2. **Send an Audiotape** Record a reading of your narrative on audiotape and add music to enhance the ideas. Then, send the tape to a friend or relative who lives far from you.

Reflecting on Your Writing

Reflect on your writing process by answering the following questions in your notebook or writing journal:

- How is writing about yourself different from other kinds of writing you've done?
- In what ways did writing about an event or experience change your view of it?

To see model essays scored with this rubric, go to **www.phschool.com**

Rubric for Self-Assessment

Use the following criteria to evaluate your autobiographical writing:

	Score 4	Score 3	Score 2	Score 1
Audience and Purpose	Contains details that engage the audience; provides a clear insight about an experience	Contains details appropriate for an audience; addresses a clear reason for writing	Contains few details that appeal to an audience; gives a reason for writing	Is not written for a specific audience or purpose
Organization	Organizes events to relate an interesting narrative	Presents clear sequence of events	Presents a confusing sequence of events	Presents no logical order of events
Elaboration	Contains rich details that shape vivid characters; clearly elaborates an insight	Contains details that develop character and describe setting; elaborates an insight	Contains characters and setting; provides a context for the experience	Contains few or no details to develop characters or setting; does not set experience in context
Use of Language	Uses an excellent variety of sentence beginnings; contains no errors in grammar, punctuation, or spelling	Uses a good variety of sentence beginnings; contains few errors in grammar, punctuation, and spelling	Introduces some variety in sentence beginnings; contains some errors in grammar, punctuation, and spelling	Uses monotonous pattern of sentence beginnings; has many errors in grammar, punctuation, and spelling

Connected Assignment Firsthand Biography

In an autobiography, the writer tells his or her own life story. In contrast, the writer of a biography tells the story of someone else's life. A **firsthand biography** combines the writer's personal observations from an interaction or knowledge of the subject with objective information gathered through research to create an engaging narrative. Because the writer knows the subject, a firsthand biography takes on a more intimate tone than a formal biography does.

The following writing process steps will help you write a firsthand biography of someone you know.

Prewriting Choose your subject by thinking about the people in your life. Consider the people who have been special to you, and decide whose life or personality would be interesting to address.

Once you've chosen your biography subject, focus on a moment that especially captures his or her spirit or that particularly impresses you. Complete a timeline like the one shown here to gather details about a specific period in your subject's life. Use the timeline to spark ideas and observations about your subject's behavior, appearance, and attitude.

▲ **Critical Viewing** How would your own interactions with a person change the way you describe them to others? **[Analyze]**

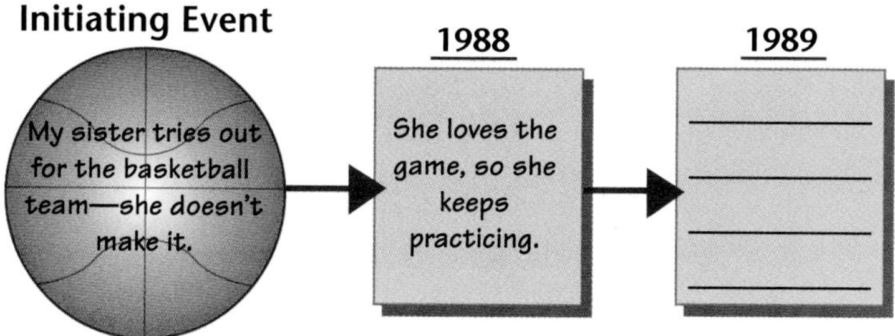

Drafting Refer to your notes as you draft your biography. Try to balance objective facts with personally observed data as you include details that bring your subject to life. Keep your relationship with the subject clear by writing in the first person and using possessive phrases such as *my friend.*

Revising and Editing As you review your biography, look for places where you could elaborate your own interpretations and impressions. Check that you've maintained first-person narration throughout. Replace overused verbs with more precise and engaging language.

Publishing and Presenting After you have completed your firsthand biography, put the essay and selected photographs together in a booklet to share with classmates or your subject.

Chapter 5

Narration

Short Story

▲ Critical Viewing What kind of story might be inspired by this sculpture? **[Hypothesize]**

Stories in Everyday Life

Narratives are stories—something you hear and tell every day. Some are true: They're a way to share the events of your latest experiences, and they're a way to reveal the events in the world. These stories are **nonfiction.** But not all stories have to be true. When the stories are made up, they are called *fiction*, and they can take on a life all their own. You see, hear, and imagine fictional stories when you watch television sit-coms, read novels, or daydream about becoming a movie star. One kind of imaginative narration is the **short story**—a written piece of fiction that follows specific rules and has its own unique characteristics.

What Is a Short Story?

A **short story** is a brief fictional narrative that combines elements to create a world that attracts the reader's attention and interest. An effective short story

- uses details to create a setting of time and place in the reader's mind.
- presents a main character who takes part in the action.
- introduces and develops a conflict, or a problem, to be resolved.
- relates a series of events that make up the story's action, or plot.
- suggests a theme or generalization about life.

To see the criteria on which the final draft of your short story may be evaluated, preview the Rubric for Self-Assessment on page 62.

Writers in ACTION

Isaac Bashevis Singer wrote short stories and novels that seem magical but reveal people's truest feelings. As this quotation suggests, Singer looked at the everyday life around him for story ideas.

"Life itself is a story."

Types of Short Stories

Short stories, as well as other forms of fiction, may be categorized according to the types of setting or conflict they present. Here are a few examples of the types of short stories you might read or write:

- **Mysteries** present a story with important missing information, which is revealed as the plot unfolds.
- **Westerns** usually focus on a specific combination of character, setting, and time: cowboys in the western parts of the United States in the second half of the nineteenth century.
- **Thrillers** create a high level of tension by introducing danger in the conflict they present.

PREVIEW Student Work IN PROGRESS

In this chapter, you will find the work of David Friggle, a student at Columbia High School in Maplewood, New Jersey. David tells of a young person who learns something about life through the death of an uncle he barely remembers. As you will see, David used prewriting, drafting, and revising techniques to develop his short story "A Stranger's Lesson."

Prewriting

Choosing Your Topic

You can build a story from a single strong element. Start with a compelling conflict, an interesting character, or an unusual setting. The following strategies can help you choose an element to expand into a short story:

Strategies for Generating Topics

1. **Sentence Starters** Let your imagination wander by completing a sentence-starter exercise. Draw from your opinions, memories, or creativity to develop interesting situations or settings. Use one sentence starter to freewrite for five minutes. Then, review your writing. Circle intriguing settings, characters, conflicts, or themes, and choose one to build into a story. Consider these beginnings:

   What if I were to . . .
   One person I will never forget is . . .
   All of a sudden . . .

2. **List and Itemize Interests** To help find a conflict to build your story around, list your favorite pastimes. Jot down activities, hobbies, and sports you enjoy. Next to each entry, note a conflict the activity might create or a generalization about life that the conflict could illustrate. Review your notes to find a seed for a short story.

For more help finding a topic, explore the activities and suggestions in the Choosing a Topic section of the Narration lesson.

Student Work IN PROGRESS

Name: David Friggle
Columbia High School
Maplewood, NJ

Listing and Itemizing to Find a Topic

David listed the events that have happened in the last month. From this list, he brainstormed for potential conflict and theme ideas that each topic suggested. He decided to write about a funeral that sparked an interesting writing idea.

School play — competition among friends; winning isn't everything

Family activities — discussions about school; bonding with my parents

Family funeral — learning through sadness; loss brings self-knowledge

TOPIC BANK

Here are some other possibilities for generating story ideas:

1. **Short Story About a Challenge** Whether a character faces a struggle with nature, like getting home in a storm, or an internal conflict, like trying to overcome a bad habit, challenges provide rich opportunities for writing fiction. Write a short story showing how a character faces challenge—and whether he or she overcomes the conflict.
2. **Short Story in an Unusual Setting** Imagine life far into the future or many years in the past. Switch gears, and imagine a world where people fly or pets rule the family home. To make the setting even more significant, write a story in which your narrator is a visitor, not a resident.

Responding to Fine Art

3. Because conflict is the essence of competition, sports are the perfect arena for short stories. *Basketball Superstars*, at right, might remind you of a competition in your own life. Write a short story about the tension and the celebration or defeat that comes out of a sports competition.

Basketball Superstars, LeRoy Neiman

Responding to Literature

4. Read "I Have a Dream" by Martin Luther King, Jr. Use King's celebrated ideas to spark a story about a person fighting for personal justice. You can find the speech in *Prentice Hall Literature: Timeless Voices, Timeless Themes*, Gold.

Cooperative Writing Opportunity

5. **Short Story With Multiple Authors** With a group, plan and write a story. Draft the story together, and then assign each writer a revision focus. One student can add details about setting, another can strengthen the conflict, a third can improve characterization. When you are done, evaluate the experience of co-authoring.

5.2

Narrowing Your Topic

Once you have chosen the general subject of your short story, select incidents that will be at the heart of the writing. Summarizing the plot in one or two sentences is one strategy to narrow your topic.

Summarize the Plot

Briefly describe the incidents that make up the plot of your story. If you need more than a few sentences to do this, you may be involving your characters in too much activity or presenting them in too many settings. To narrow the focus of your story, cross out the less important incidents, characters, or settings until you can summarize your plot in one or two sentences.

Considering Your Audience and Purpose

Consider Your Audience

When you write, think about who is going to read your story. For example, if you write a story for your friends, you can use different language than you might choose if you were writing for an audience of younger children. Identify the audience for which you are writing, and tailor your language accordingly.

For help in defining your audience and shaping your story to interest them, use the Audience Profile activity in the Narration lesson.

Refine Your Purpose

As you prepare to create fiction, take a moment to identify the purpose of your story. You may want to tell a funny story to make readers laugh, you may want to make a statement about the world as you see it, or you may want to lift your readers' spirits. This chart offers suggestions about how to achieve those purposes.

If your purpose is to . . .	include . . .
• make readers laugh	• an exaggerated situation
• make a statement about the world	• situations that are based in reality
• lift your readers' spirits	• characters overcoming obstacles

Consider your own specific reasons for writing, and then plan the details you'll need to include in your story.

Gathering Details

To bring the characters and conflict of your story to life, provide enough detail to let your readers imagine the world you create. While you don't have to include every bit of information you imagine, a wide knowledge of the elements of your story will help you choose the most effective points to include.

Know the Elements of Storytelling

Most stories have the common elements of character, setting, conflict, and action. Collect information to help you make the most of these key features of your story.

- **Characters** Jot down a few adjectives for each character in your story to help you make each one a specific individual. Plan their clothing, speech habits, attitudes, and relationships to the other characters in the story.
- **Setting** Note interesting and relevant details about your setting. For example, the time of year or climate may be important to your story.
- **Conflict** Isolate the conflict of your story. Decide who the conflict affects, how long it lasts, and how each character reacts to the problem.
- **Action** Identify the specific events that your plot will include. It may help to make a timeline so you can plan what happens first, next, and last. As you plan the action, decide how the conflict intensifies and how it is resolved.

Student Work IN PROGRESS

Name: David Friggle
Columbia High School
Maplewood, NJ

Gathering Details About Characters

To develop characters, David started with character types and listed traits that made the characters distinct.

Character	Description	Actions
Aunt	gregarious	talks loudly talks fast
people at funeral	uncomfortable	wore painted smiles asked the same, obvious questions

Drafting

Shaping Your Writing

Choose a Narrator

A narrator provides the voice of the storyteller and guides the reader through the events of the story. Because the narrator's presentation of information will influence the way the story is received by an audience, decide who you want your narrator to be. First-person and third-person narrators are common choices in short stories.

First Person When you use first-person narration, the narrator is a character in the story. This personal type of storytelling lets you share the narrator's thoughts with readers. Although you use the first-person pronoun *I*, writing in the first person does not mean writing as yourself. You can adopt the voice of a completely fictional person.

FIRST-PERSON NARRATION: I get good grades, but I want to be a soccer player. My brother doesn't care about my dreams of being a great athlete.

Third Person Third-person narration allows you to include information about the thoughts of each character. This narrative style can provide a more objective approach because the narrator is not necessarily a participant in the story's events. When you use a third-person narrator, you can describe the thoughts and feelings of one character or of all the characters.

Third-Person Narration

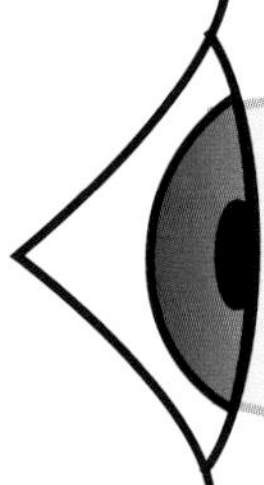

Juliet Harris is a quiet, mousy girl, who is a good student but clumsy. She really wants to be a star on the soccer team, but she is afraid to say anything. Her brother would be jealous and make fun of her.

Writers in ACTION

Toni Cade Bambara was an African American writer whose stories often focused on the emerging identity of black women. Her collections of short stories describe relationships, friendships, and struggles. This quotation explains her inspiration for writing:

"I write because I really think I've got hold of something that, if I share, might save somebody else some time, might lift someone's spirits, or might enable someone to see more clearly."

Providing Elaboration

Plan the flow of your story, and then fill in details to create a complete picture for your reader. Remember that you are constructing a specific effect. Choosing what to tell and what not to tell is an important ingredient of good storytelling.

Show, Don't Tell

If you find yourself writing sentences that simply tell readers what you want them to think, challenge yourself to be a better storyteller. To do this, provide the instances that will make the writing speak for itself. Use characters' actions, details of setting, and dialogue to show readers what you want them to see.

Follow up "telling" sentences with "showing" ones. Look at this example:

TELLING:	My four-year-old brother Jake loves me.
SHOWING WITH INSTANCES:	For instance, when I come home from school, my four-year-old brother, Jake, runs out of the house, hugs me, and gives me a kiss.

Grammar and Style Tip

While you want to make the world of your story vivid, be especially careful not to bog down your writing with too many adjectives and adverbs. Keep the action of your story moving, and add description with the nouns and verbs you use.

Student Work IN PROGRESS

Name: David Friggle
Columbia High School
Maplewood, NJ

Using Elaboration to Show Instead of Tell

By adding examples of the confusion the narrator felt, David shows his audience more about the character and the conflict.

The initial shock of being told about a death quickly subsided, to be replaced with confusion.

PROVIDE INSTANCES

Who was Great-Uncle Paul? Was he nice? Had I ever met him? Why don't I remember him? *Should* I remember him? Thoughts of my great-uncle Paul stayed in my mind until I was asleep.

Revising

Review your draft to find ways to improve your writing. Focus on the plot, the dialogue, and the language you have chosen. Use the strategies that follow to revise your story.

Revising Your Overall Structure

Track the Conflict

The higher you climb to the top of a slide, the greater the anticipation of the ride becomes. Use a chutes-and-ladders diagram to think of your story's conflict in the same way.

REVISION STRATEGY

Using Chutes and Ladders

Write the events that build the conflict of your story on a diagram like the one shown here. Put the climax of the story—the highest point of interest or suspense of your story—at the top of the slide. Review your diagram, and consider adding more events to your draft to make the conflict stronger.

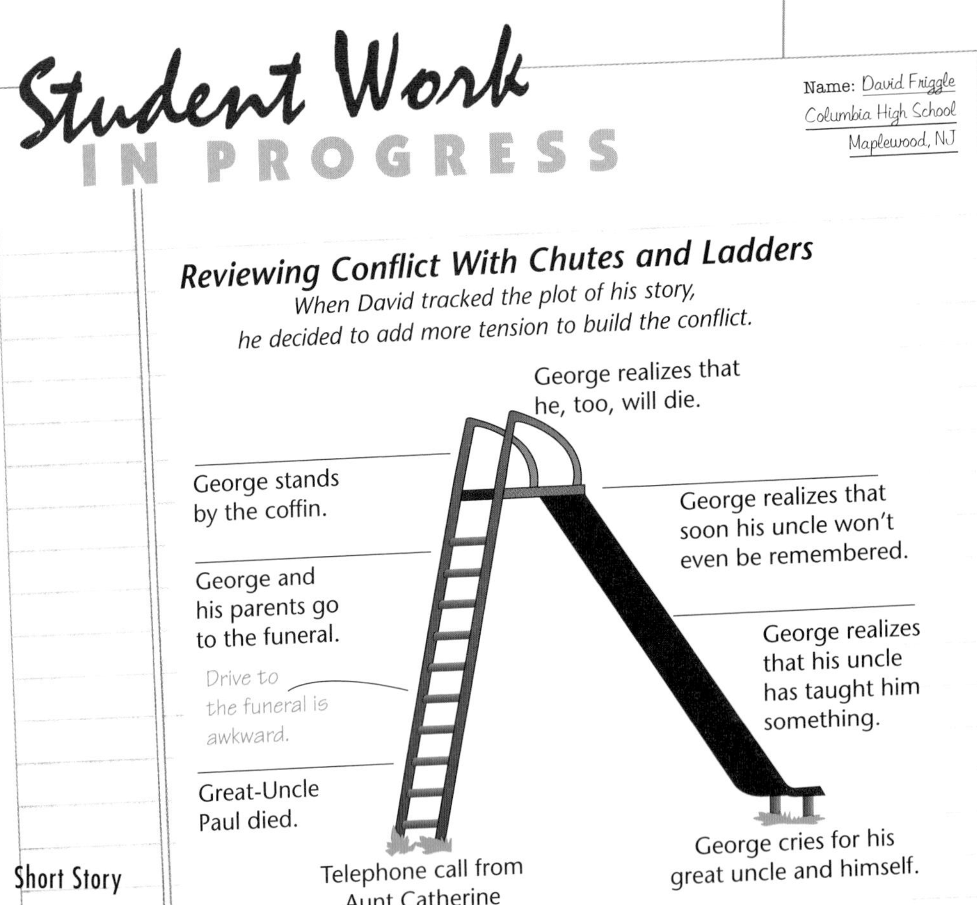

Revising Your Paragraphs

Make Dialogue Sound Realistic

Dialogue gives credibility to your characters and your story. To hone your skill at writing authentic dialogue, listen to the speech habits of friends and family. Broaden your study by noticing the variety of speech patterns you hear in school, in stores, and at restaurants. Then, apply the conversational habits you've overheard to your story's dialogue to make your characters sound more real.

▲ **Critical Viewing** What emotions might the dialogue between these children convey? **[Hypothesize]**

REVISION STRATEGY
Reading With a Partner

Ask a partner to read your dialogue aloud with you. Jot down dialogue that sounds stiff or unnatural. Later, you can make the words your characters say sound more realistic.

REVISING FORCED DIALOGUE

Forced Dialogue

"Mother, please write a note for school," Sam asked, looking down at the ground.

"I'd be happy to write that for you," she said.

"Thank you so much," Sam said, handing her a sheet of paper. His eagerness raised her suspicion.

"By the way, what is this for?"

- ☑ Change formal language to informal words when appropriate.
- ☑ Have characters interrupt each other or speak in half-uttered sentences.
- ☑ Insert interjections that show character.

Realistic Dialogue

"Mom, could you write me a note for school?" Sam asked.

"Sure, I'd be . . ." but Sam was jumping ahead of her.

"Thanks!" he said, handing her a sheet of paper. His eagerness raised her suspicion.

"What is this for, anyway?"

Revising Your Sentences

Use the Active Voice

To create dynamic sentences in which your characters are acting instead of being acted upon, choose the active voice. Its opposite, the passive voice, can make your characters and actions dull and slow. Using the active voice helps you create characters that act on their emotions and shape their own lives.

ACTIVE VOICE: Daniel *caught* the ball

PASSIVE VOICE: The ball *was caught* by Daniel.

REVISION STRATEGY
Highlighting Verbs

Read each sentence in your draft, focusing on the action performed in each case. As you analyze your writing, identify whether each sentence is written in the active or passive voice. Using a highlighter, mark all the passive verbs in your essay. Evaluate each use of the passive voice, weighing whether changing the sentence to active voice could make the writing more interesting or direct. Challenge yourself to change some of your passive-voice verbs to active-voice ones.

Student Work IN PROGRESS

Name: David Friggle
Columbia High School
Maplewood, NJ

Highlighting Verbs to Identify the Active Voice

In his first draft, David used the passive voice often. To make the writing more lively, he changed passive to active. In these examples, he recast the sentences.

Our house is old, and you can half hear when ~~a joke is told~~ someone talks downstairs. You may not hear the joke, but you know someone told one. But there was no laughter from my mom, nor was there any idle chatter. ~~In muffled voices, seriousness, gloom, and worry were mentioned.~~ The muffled voices spoke of seriousness, gloom, and worry. Someone had died, I was sure of it.

Grammar in Your Writing

Active vs. Passive Voice

Two different voices of verbs are used to show how an action is performed. In sentences written in the **active voice,** the subject performs the action. In sentences written in the **passive voice,** the action of the sentence is performed on the subject.

Active voice: The musician **turns** the page.

(*Musician,* the subject of the sentence, performs the action of the sentence, *turns.*)

Passive voice: The page **is turned** by the musician.

(*Page,* the subject of the sentence, has the action of the sentence, *turn,* performed upon it.)

Use the active voice

- to emphasize the actor:

The conductor **inspires** his orchestra.

The violists **harmonize** with the violins.

- to create vibrant writing:

The audience **applauds** his efforts.

The symphony hall **brims** with excitement.

Use the passive voice

- to emphasize the action:

The budget **was slashed** by the board in the latest meeting.

Each day, newspapers **are delivered** to these homes.

- to draw attention away from the performer of the action or to indicate action even when the performer is unknown:

The funds **will be lost** for years.

The decision **has been called** disastrous.

Find It in Your Reading Review a short story that you have read. Identify three uses of the active voice. For each, demonstrate how the subject of the sentence performs the action. Notice that the writer avoids the passive voice.

Find It in Your Writing Review your short story, and identify all of the places where you have used the passive voice. Unless you have a specific reason for using it, change the passive voice to the active voice.

For more on active and passive voices, see Chapter 23.

Revising Your Word Choice

Analyze Nouns

You can often get more mileage out of a specific noun than you can from several adjectives. By reviewing the nouns you have chosen and finding more precise ones, you can make your writing more efficient, so that it communicates exactly what you want to say.

VAGUE NOUN: Yellow and blue *papers* covered the desk.

PRECISE NOUNS: *Bills* and *advertisements* covered the desk.

REVISION STRATEGY
Circling Vague Nouns

When you choose specific nouns, you make your writing concrete and clear. This will help readers picture exactly what you had in mind. Review your draft to find vague nouns that do not suggest clear images. Where you can, replace these words with precise nouns. Look at these examples:

GENERAL NOUNS	Potential Revisions	SPECIFIC NOUNS
vehicle		dump truck, station wagon, sports car
instrument		guitar, cello, tambourine
book		novel, biography, comic book

Peer Review

Pointing

In a small group, read your story two times. The first time, ask people just to listen. The second time, ask each person to point out a specific passage he or she especially liked.

This strategy will help you identify the successful parts of your draft. For example, you may learn that you have conveyed a setting effectively or that a you developed the conflict in your narrative successfully. You may wish to extend the discussion by asking reviewers for suggestions about improving the sections that need attention.

Speaking and Listening Tip

To get the most of your peer review, resist the urge to interrupt your partner or to finish the sentence. When you are truly listening, be patient enough to hear what your reviewer has to say.

5.5 Editing and Proofreading

To make your writing error-free, check spelling, punctuation, and grammar before you write your final draft. The primary purpose of using correct mechanics, including punctuation, in your writing is to make your short story easy to follow.

Focusing on Punctuation

Punctuation, especially the end marks of sentences, helps to convey emotion to the reader. Check your draft to see that you have chosen the right end marks.

Periods identify the ends of most sentences.
Question marks identify the ends of questions.
Exclamation points indicate the ends of sentences that show strong emotion.

Grammar in Your Writing

Punctuating Dialogue Correctly

The conventions of punctuating dialogue help readers to follow a conversation even when it involves several people. Enclose each speaker's words in quotation marks. Follow these rules when punctuating dialogue:

• **Dialogue that ends the sentence:** Introduce the quotation mark with a comma, and put the ending punctuation inside the quotation marks.

Mary said, "I have to go now."

• **Dialogue that begins the sentence:** Use a comma inside the quotation marks unless a question mark or exclamation point is needed to make sense of the speaker's words.

"I'll be late for this appointment if I don't leave now," said Mary.
"So go already!" her brother shouted.

• **Dialogue that is interrupted by tag words:** Use commas to set off the two parts of the quotation.

"Steven," she said, glaring at him, "we can't leave until you're ready!"

Find It in Your Reading Review a short story that you have read. Find examples of the three conventions of dialogue shown here.

Find It in Your Writing As you proofread your short story, double-check the punctuation of any dialogue you have used.

For more on punctuating dialogue, see Chapter 29.

Publishing and Presenting

Building Your Portfolio

When you have finalized your draft, share your short story with others. Here are some suggestions:

1. **Illustrate Your Story** An illustrated presentation of your short story can give your writing a polished and professional look. Create several illustrations that help express the mood of your story, choose the correct placement, and bind the work together.
2. **Create an Author's Forum** Invite classmates to share their short stories with the rest of the class. Following a reading, you may want to encourage a discussion of the story and the techniques the writer used.

Reflecting on Your Writing

After you have finished writing your short story, jot down your ideas about the process. Use these questions to get started:

- How did writing a short story enhance your understanding of techniques used by the writers of short stories you read?
- Which element of the short story did you find easiest to elaborate? Which was the most difficult? Explain.

Internet Tip

To see model short stories scored with this rubric, go to **www.phschool.com**

Rubric for Self-Assessment

Use these criteria to evaluate your short story.

	Score 4	Score 3	Score 2	Score 1
Audience and Purpose	Presents details targeted at a unique audience; successfully narrates the events of a story	Presents details suited to an audience; narrates the events of a story	Presents few details suited to an audience; some ideas conflict with narration of story	Supports no purpose; is not written for a specific audience
Organization	Presents events that create a clear narrative; writes from a consistent point of view	Presents sequence of events; told from a specific point of view	Presents a confusing sequence of events; contains inconsistent points of view	Presents no logical order; uses an inconsistent point of view
Elaboration	Contains details that provide insight into character; contains dialogue that reveals characters and furthers the plot	Contains details and dialogue that develop characters	Contains characters and setting; contains some dialogue	Contains few or no details to develop characters or setting; no dialogue provided
Use of Language	Uses fresh word choice and tone to reveal story's setting and character; contains no errors in grammar, punctuation, or spelling	Uses interesting and fresh word choices; contains few errors in grammar, punctuation, and spelling	Uses clichés and trite expressions; contains some errors in grammar, punctuation, and spelling	Uses uninspired word choices; has many errors in grammar, punctuation, and spelling

5.7 Student Work IN PROGRESS

FINAL DRAFT

◀ Critical Viewing How does this photograph combine with the story's title to set a mood? [Respond]

A Stranger's Lesson

David Friggle
Columbia High School
Maplewood, New Jersey

That Friday night started out normally. I was watching television when a jarring ring broke into the studio audience's laughter. Normally, I can wait out a phone call until the answering machine or one of my parents picks it up. This time, however, my resistance gave out first, and I picked it up, slightly annoyed.

The opening paragraph provides the story's contemporary setting.

"Hello?" *This had better be good*, I thought to myself, as I muted the television.

"Hi, John?" The woman on the phone mistook me for my father, which led me to believe she was either a co-worker of his or a distant relative who'd not seen me for quite some time.

David chose to use a first-person narrator to bring the reader closer to the character's thoughts and emotions.

"No, this is George. Who's speaking?"

"Georgie? That's you? I can't believe it! You sound just like your father! You've grown so much since the last time I saw you!"

Dialogue establishes two of his characters: the narrator and his aunt.

"Really? Thanks. Yeah, it's George. Who's this?"

She suddenly took on a more serious tone.

"This is your Aunt Catherine, dear. May I talk to your mother?"

"Sure, just hold on a sec. MOM!"

"YES?"

"Aunt Catherine on the phone!"

There was a pause, then some footsteps, then a click on the line. Suddenly, my mother's voice came on, "Thanks, George, you can hang up now."

Our house is old, and you can half hear when someone talks downstairs. You may not hear the joke, but you know someone told one. But there was no laughter from my mom, nor was there any idle chatter. The muffled voices spoke of seriousness, gloom, and worry. Someone had died, I was sure of it.

By showing the character's reaction before revealing the conflict, the writer adds tension to the plot.

The click of the phone hanging up led to a hushed conversation between my mom and dad in the living room. Then, as if on cue, I was called down to talk.

I asked what was wrong. My mom searched for words, her mouth moving as if to start saying every phrase she pondered, before finally telling me that my great-uncle Paul had died.

The conflict of the story is announced: There has been a death in the family.

The initial shock of being told about a death quickly subsided, to be replaced with confusion. Who was Great-Uncle Paul? Was he nice? Had I ever met him? Why don't I remember him? *Should* I remember him? Thoughts of my great-uncle Paul stayed in my mind until I was asleep. The funeral was Saturday. At least the mystery would be solved soon.

The car ride to the funeral home was awkward. My parents' obvious grief and my persistent curiosity were offset by the saccharine voice of "Cousin Brucie," the oldies station's morning disc jockey. For an hour and a half, Cousin Brucie was the only one in the car who was talking. Herman's Hermits and Derek and the Dominos didn't seem to excite the same exuberance in my family as it did in Brucie.

To develop the conflict, the writer contrasts the enthusiasm of the radio disc jockey with the mood of the characters in the car.

The funeral service was no better. The generally uncomfortable mood during the car trip was evident tenfold at the funeral. Pop music was replaced by forced smiles, but jittery hands, nervous tapping of feet, and conversation without mention of my great-uncle Paul challenged the validity of any of the smiles. At least Cousin Brucie was genuinely excited about his silly asides.

Details like "forced smiles" and "jittery hands" convey the mood of the situation.

Sitting in the corner, I felt like a complete stranger. Everyone seemed to know who I was, however. Cousins of uncles and sisters-in-law of aunts all came over to me in an effort to "cheer me up." Half of them told me that if I thought high school was good, I'd love college, and the other half made some sort of weird joke when I told them I fenced in my spare time. I did my part by putting on a happy face and answering everything politely, but the whole time I wondered who was being comforted.

After a while, it was time for everyone to pay their respects. Although I had no idea what to do when I got there, I went up because I didn't know what else to do. There were several pictures of Great-Uncle Paul, in various stages of his life. He looked like my mother's side of the family, but besides that, there was nothing I recognized about him.

The narrator faces the climax of the story when he approaches the coffin.

Standing in front of a coffin next to mourning people makes one think, and think I did. I thought about the impact he left on so many people. I thought about how I should have known him, how I should have remembered him, and how I no longer had a chance for any of that.

The narrator shares his thoughts to show how his attitude and feelings have shifted, leading to the resolution in the last paragraph.

Suddenly, I stopped thinking about him as Great-Uncle Paul and started thinking of him as Paul Horenburg. Paul Horenburg, who told jokes to friends at work, who laughed, who fell in love, who cried on occasion, who got angry, and just a few days earlier, died. I realized that although Paul Horenburg had died, the world didn't. In days, weeks, months, or possibly years, the mourning would stop, and everyone would go back to their normal lives. Memories of Paul Horenburg would crop up occasionally, as co-workers remembered funny stories he had told, or as friends looked back on evenings they had spent with him, or when his family remembered the helpful advice he had given them in times of trouble. Then, I finally realized that he had taught me something, too.

The events of the story illustrate a generalization about life and death. The narrator—and the reader—take a second look at the importance of living fully, despite life's fragility.

And on that Saturday, I cried for a man I didn't know.

◀ **Critical Viewing**
How does this photograph convey hope and despair, the two emotions developed in the story? **[Support]**

Chapter 6 Description

▲ **Critical Viewing** This is a photograph of the Seattle skyline at sunset. How would you describe the scene? **[Describe]**

Description in Everyday Life

Every time you share a meaningful experience, tell someone the details of a beautiful sight, or explain why you enjoyed a book or movie, you use description. Similarly, whether you sit down to write a poem about clouds, a song about love, a historical essay about the Civil War, or a scientific report about cell structure, you use description. Without even realizing it, you probably use description—both in speaking and in writing—many times a day.

What Is Description?

Our senses enable us to experience the world around us. We can see a beautiful sunset or hear the roar of a wave crashing against the shoreline. We can smell the spicy aroma of oven-fresh pizza, and we can taste the refreshing tang of lemonade. **Description** is writing through which we can share these sensations with others. Effective description includes

- sensory details that convey sights, sounds, smells, tastes, and physical sensation.
- vivid language that brings a subject into focus.
- figurative language that compares its subject with other objects.
- a logical organization.

To see the criteria against which your descriptive writing may be evaluated, preview the Rubric for Self-Assessment on page 81.

Writers in ACTION

Science-fiction writers use description to create pictures of imaginary creatures and far-off planets. In her science-fiction literature Anne McCaffrey develops her descriptions by placing herself in her imaginary settings:

"You, the author, have to be where your story is taking place. You have to be there, in it. And if you are there, in it, for the duration of the story, that comes across."

Types of Descriptive Writing

Many forms of writing include description. Other forms are purely descriptive. These forms include the following:

- A **description of a person, place, or thing** may focus on the physical appearance or the significance of the subject.
- A **description of an idea** uses concrete images to show an abstract, complicated, or otherwise intangible concept.
- An **observation** objectively describes an event that the writer has witnessed.
- A **remembrance** of a person, place, or thing uses vivid details to capture a memorable part of the writer's past.
- A **vignette,** also known as a "picture painted with words," captures a specific moment in the life of the writer.

In this chapter, you'll see the work of Allison Lutes, a student at Butler Traditional High School in Louisville, Kentucky. Allison used prewriting, drafting, and revising strategies to write "My 'Sister,'" a description of a treasured friend.

Prewriting

Choosing Your Topic

When choosing a topic for a description, consider people, places, things, and experiences that strike you as memorable, important, or special. Your enthusiasm for your topic will shine through in your writing. Use one of the following strategies to choose a topic:

For more help finding a topic, explore the activities and suggestions in the Choosing a Topic section of the Description lesson.

Strategies for Generating Topics

1. **Observation** For a few days, carry a note pad with you. Be alert to the sights, sounds, smells, tastes, and textures you encounter. Wherever you go, jot down notes about the interesting people, places, and things that you see. Then, review your notes, and select a topic for your description.
2. **Trigger Words and Objects** A single word or object can trigger a flood of ideas. For example, words like *friendship* or *fire* may remind you of people or places or evoke an emotion in you. Objects, like a leaf or a blue ribbon, may be equally suggestive. Working with a group, take turns calling out trigger words or holding up trigger objects. As each person takes a turn, jot down whatever comes to mind. When the activity is finished, review your notes and choose a topic.

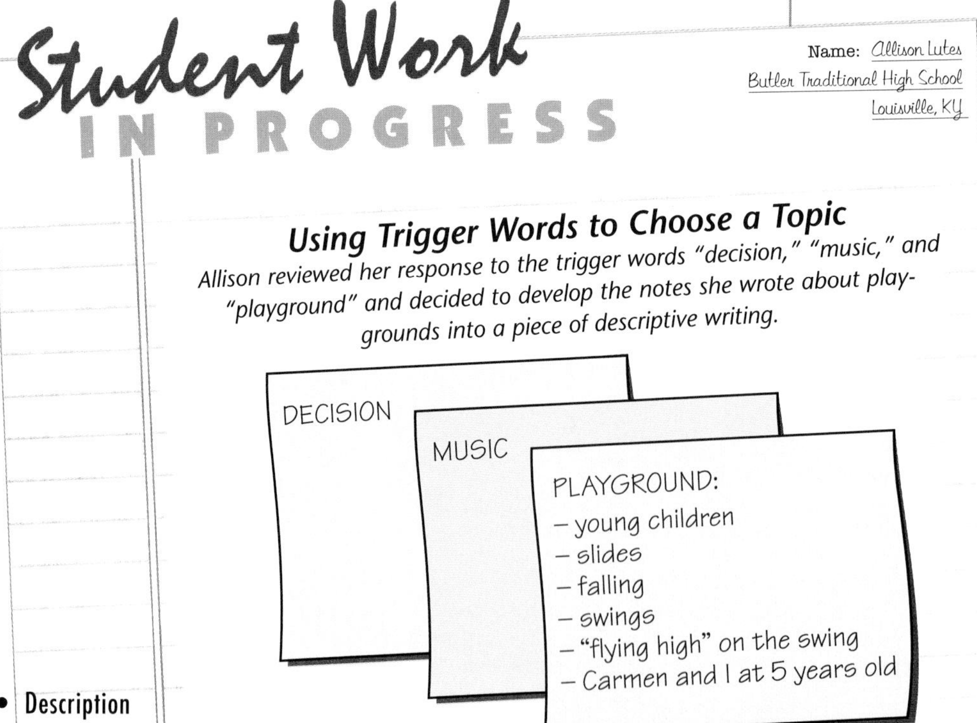

TOPIC BANK

1. **Description of Freedom** A dictionary can define freedom, but the concept may be harder to convey. Using concrete images and examples, describe what the concept of freedom means to you.
2. **Description of a Sports Event** Radio announcers have the special skills needed to capture the action at a sports event in words. Write a description of a championship game so readers can envision all the action.

Responding to Fine Art

3. Vincent van Gogh painted this picture of his bedroom at Arles, France. Write a description of the room as he portrayed it, or use your reaction to this painting as a springboard for an idea of your own. For example, you might describe a room you'd like to call your own.

Bedroom of Van Gogh at Arles Vincent van Gogh
Musee d'Orsay, Paris, France

Responding to Literature

4. In his short story "The Secret Life of Walter Mitty," James Thurber uses descriptive language to convey the excitement the title character conjures up in his daydreams. Read this story to see how a comic writer makes use of descriptive language. Use Thurber's writing as a model and describe another daydream Mitty might have had. You can find this story in *Prentice Hall Literature: Timeless Voices, Timeless Themes,* Gold.

Cooperative Writing Opportunity

5. **Travel Brochure** Work with a group to write a travel brochure about a place that is real or imagined. One student can write a profile of the area's geographic features; another can write about its key places; others can draw maps or create or gather pictures. When you have completed all of these tasks, work together to assemble the pieces into a finished brochure.

Narrowing Your Topic

Once you have chosen a topic, ask yourself whether you can cover it thoroughly in a brief description. A topic such as "the desert" is too broad. To make the job more manageable, you might whittle "the desert" down to "cactus." Here is a technique you might use to narrow your topic:

Use an Index-Card Camera

1. Find or create a picture of your topic or, if possible, look at the actual person, place, or thing.
2. Study the picture or actual subject as it is, noting as many sensory details as possible.
3. Cut a small hole in the center of an index card.
4. Use your "index-card camera" to zoom in on a smaller aspect of your subject. Let the camera help you to focus on details that you may have overlooked.
5. Choose one of the specific details you saw with your "camera" to use as the specific topic of your description.

▼ Critical Viewing What other topics related to this desert scene might the writer have focused on using the index-card camera? **[Make a Judgment]**

Considering Your Audience and Purpose

Identifying Your Audience Before you write, consider your audience. The knowledge level and interests of your readers may direct the vocabulary you use or the depth and complexity of your description.

Refining Your Purpose While your writing will be descriptive, you probably have another purpose in mind. For example, you may write to inform your readers about a place they've never been. Once you clarify your purpose, use details and language that will help you achieve it.

Use the Interactive Audience Profile to record information about your audience's age, interest, and familiarity with your subject. You can find it in the toolkit.

Gathering Details

To create a vivid picture of your subject, use precise, concrete details. Using the strategy of cubing will help you gather as many details as you can.

Cubing to Gather Details

Cubing is a technique that helps you gather details by exploring your subject from a variety of angles. Draw a cube, or build one using a piece of paper. Then, use each of the six sides of the cube to jot down notes from these specific "angles":

Describe your topic. Note relevant sights, sounds, smells, textures, and tastes.

Associate it. Jot down words or experiences that your subject suggests to you.

Apply it. Note the ways in which your subject can be used.

Analyze it. Break your subject into parts. Then, consider how these parts work together.

Compare or contrast it. Identify examples of other items or ideas that are similar to your subject.

Argue for or against it. Take a position.

Internet Tip

Depending on your topic, you may find it helpful to conduct research to gather details. If you're describing a well-known person, place, thing, or event, use the Internet to learn more about your subject.

Student Work IN PROGRESS

Name: Allison Lutes
Butler Traditional High School
Louisville, KY

Cubing to Gather Details

Allison used the cubing strategy to help her gather details about her friend Carmen. Here are her notes on three cubing "angles."

Apply
I learned to use my imagination—playing store... finding fun...

Associate
She was like a sister to me.

Analyze
Her appearance—natural, never fussy, comfortable with herself
Her smile and laugh—shy, honest, funny

Drafting

Shaping Your Writing

Once you have all the details you need, choose an organizational plan to present them. Here are two organizational patterns you might use.

Choose an Organization That Suits Your Topic

Spatial Organization For a physical description of a person, place, or thing, use spatial order. Describe your topic from top to bottom, left to right, front to back, or outward from the most prominent feature. To keep your order clear, use such transitional words and phrases as *to the left* and *above*.

Order of Importance To describe an idea, grab your readers' interest with your second most important point. Then, address your less important points, and build to your strongest. To use this type of order, place a number next to each of the details you'll use, so you can plan the order in which you will present them. Follow this list as you draft.

Name: Allison Lutes
Butler Traditional High School
Louisville, KY

Creating a General Impression Through Organization

To show all the ways that Carmen is like a sister to her, Allison chose an order-of-importance organization.

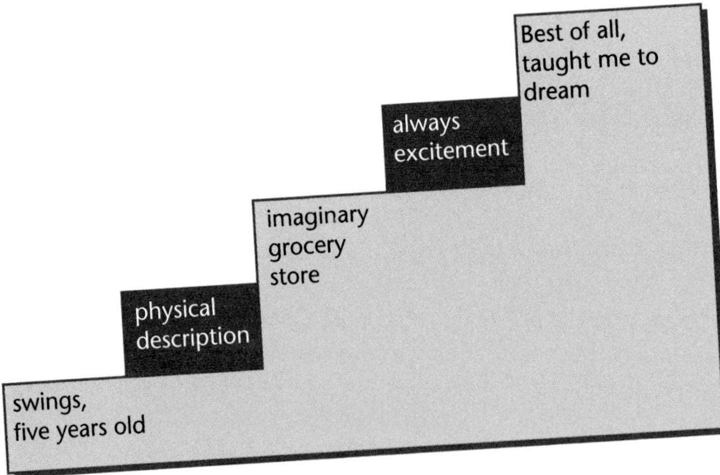

Providing Elaboration

As you draft your description, focus on providing vivid sensory details—details appealing to any of the five senses. These will create a strong picture of your subject in the minds of your readers.

Add Figurative Language

In addition to sensory details that describe your topic exactly as it appears, use figurative language to capture your readers' interest. Figurative language is not meant to be taken literally; instead, it builds comparisons and helps suggest new ways of looking at an object. Two types of figurative language you might use are similes and metaphors.

Simile A *simile* compares one thing to another using the word *like* or *as*. The example below stresses the force of a storm's wind by comparing it to a power saw.

EXAMPLE: During the storm, the wind tore through branches *like* a power saw.

Metaphor A *metaphor* compares two unlike things by setting them up as equals. It describes one object as if it were another. This example calls hefty tree trunks matchsticks to convey the power of the storm.

EXAMPLE: Tree trunks *were* matchsticks as they snapped in the hurricane-force winds.

Collaborative Writing Tip

Work with a partner to build your experience with figurative language. Discuss both types of comparisons, and suggest specific ones that your partner might use to elaborate his or her draft with sharp and creative details.

▼ Critical Viewing
What other similes or metaphors might you use to describe this storm? **[Describe]**

6.4 Revising

Once you have completed a first draft, review your description by polishing its overall structure, analyzing its paragraphs, studying its sentences, and evaluating the word choice.

Revising Your Overall Structure

Analyze the General Impression

Remember that the purpose of descriptive writing is to paint a picture of your subject with words. To achieve this goal, your paper should convey a single impression of your subject. All of your paragraphs should contribute to that impression; your first or last paragraph should include a statement that sums up the impression.

REVISION STRATEGY

Color-Coding to Highlight Your Main Impression

Use different-colored highlighters to mark words that reveal the main impression of each paragraph. Then, evaluate your draft using these questions as a guide:

Evaluate	Revise
• Does each paragraph contribute to a general impression? What is that impression?	• Eliminate paragraphs that are irrelevant or distracting, or revise them so they *do* contribute.
• Have you included a generalization that expresses the overall impression you want to create?	• Look carefully at your last sentence, and consider revising it or adding another sentence.

◄ Critical Viewing What is the main impression you get from looking at this train station? **[Analyze]**

Revising Your Sentences

Eliminate Run-ons

As you add more descriptive details to your draft, be on the lookout for run-on sentences. A run-on sentence is two or more complete sentences written as if they were a single sentence. To revise a run-on sentence, consider one of these three strategies:

REVISING RUN-ON SENTENCES

EXAMPLE SENTENCE: The apple is sweet the skin is smooth.	
Strategy	**Example**
Add a comma and a conjunction.	The apple is sweet, and the skin is smooth.
Add a semicolon	The apple is sweet; the skin is smooth.
Split the run-on into two or more sentences.	The apple is sweet. The skin is smooth.

REVISION STRATEGY
Color-Coding to Identify Run-ons

Using alternate colors for every other sentence, bracket the beginning and end of every sentence in your draft. Review each sentence to analyze its construction. Revise any run-on sentences you find.

Student Work IN PROGRESS

Name: Allison Lutes
Butler Traditional High School
Louisville, KY

Bracketing to Identify Run-on Sentences

[It was her Pop, and he screamed when he found out about all the food we had taken.] [He wanted us to give it back, but we explained to him that it didn't work that way.] [If he wanted the food back, he would have to pay.] [After all, we were running a business.] [Her Pop finally gave in; he would give us fifty cents if we returned all of the food.] [We agreed, because we had had our fun.]

6.4

Grammar in Your Writing

Semicolons

Semicolons can create compound sentences by connecting two simple sentences. Semicolons can indicate a strong connection between ideas or they can indicate a direct contrast.

To show a strong connection:

The fans jumped to their feet in anticipation of a win; the game was on the line.

To show a direct contrast:

The fans jumped to their feet in hopes of a win; the pitcher dug in his heels.

When the relationship between clauses is not clear, add a transition or a conjunctive adverb to clarify the sentence. Place the phrase immediately after the semicolon.

Transitional Words and Phrases

as a result	for example	on the other hand
at this time	for instance	second
first	in fact	that is

Example: They cheered for the home team; **in fact,** they clapped until their hands were sore.

Conjunctive Adverbs

also	furthermore	instead
besides	however	otherwise
consequently	indeed	therefore

Example: Fans had high hopes of victory; however, the championship was lost.

Find It in Your Reading Read "See Ya' at the Subway" on pages 102–105, and identify any sentences that include semicolons. For each, indicate whether a transition or a conjunctive adverb makes the connection clear.

Find It in Your Writing Review your draft, looking for places where you can use semicolons to join two simple sentences. Consider whether you need transitions or conjunctive adverbs to make the relationship between clauses clear.

For more on semicolons, see Chapter 29.

Grammar in Your Writing

Semicolons

Semicolons can create compound sentences by connecting two simple sentences. Semicolons can indicate a strong connection between ideas or they can indicate a direct contrast.

To show a strong connection:

The fans jumped to their feet in anticipation of a win; the game was on the line.

To show a direct contrast:

The fans jumped to their feet in hopes of a win; the pitcher dug in his heels.

When the relationship between clauses is not clear, add a transition or a conjunctive adverb to clarify the sentence. Place the phrase immediately after the semicolon.

Transitional Words and Phrases

as a result	for example	on the other hand
at this time	for instance	second
first	in fact	that is

Example: They cheered for the home team; **in fact,** they clapped until their hands were sore.

Conjunctive Adverbs

also	furthermore	instead
besides	however	otherwise
consequently	indeed	therefore

Example: Fans had high hopes of victory; however, the championship was lost.

Find It in Your Reading Review a story from your favorite book. Identify any sentences that include semicolons. For each, indicate whether a transition or a conjunctive adverb makes the connection clear.

Find It in Your Writing Review your draft, looking for places where you can use semicolons to join two simple sentences. Consider whether you need transitions or conjunctive adverbs to make the relationship between clauses clear.

For more on semicolons, see Chapter 29.

Revising Your Word Choice

Use Precise Verbs

As you revise, put some punch into your writing style. Find tired, vague, weak verbs and throw them away. Replace them with precise, vivid verbs that express exactly the meaning that you want to convey to your readers. Here are some examples:

Throw These Out:	Replace Them With:
• go	• race, creep, streak, tumble
• say	• whisper, yell, suggest, demand
• think	• imagine, brainstorm, agonize, worry, anticipate, plan, wonder

In addition to replacing vague verbs, strengthen your use of adjectives. Use the vague-adjectives revision checker to help you do so.

REVISION STRATEGY

Circling Verbs to Enliven Writing

Read through your paper, and circle the verbs you've used. As you review the circled words, analyze each one to decide whether it seems vague. Consult a thesaurus to tap the variety of words that may suit your needs. Then, consider replacing some of the verbs you've circled with words that more precisely convey the action you intended.

Student Work IN PROGRESS

Name: Allison Lutes
Butler Traditional High School
Louisville, KY

Circling Verbs to Evaluate Word Choice

In this passage, Allison has circled dull verbs and inserted replacements to make the description stronger.

The two of us, sneaky thieves on a mission, waited until the coast was clear and then ~~went~~ sneaked down to the kitchen. We ~~took~~ loaded our arms with as much as we could carry, taking foods like oranges and peanuts and other things that wouldn't spoil quickly, and ~~went~~ ran back up to her room.

Peer Review

Once you have polished and improved your draft, enlist the help of a classmate. At this stage in the writing process, you have become so familiar with your piece of writing that you really need the assistance of a fresh pair of eyes. Take turns being those "fresh eyes" for each other, reviewing and commenting on each other's work.

Encourage Specific Peer Review

Ask Open-Ended Questions Avoid questions that can be answered with a yes or no response. Instead, probe with questions that ask what, how, or when.

YES/NO QUESTION:	Did you like my introduction?
OPEN-ENDED QUESTION:	What did you like best about my introduction? How could I improve it? When did you know for sure what I was describing?

Direct Your Peer's Attention Instead of asking a reviewer to comment on your whole draft, limit your peer's response. Ask questions that direct peers to comment on specific elements of your writing.

VAGUE QUESTION:	Did you like this draft?
DIRECT QUESTION:	Which comparison worked best? Was there any comparison that I should improve or delete?

Ask Follow-up Questions Use a peer's response as a springboard for a discussion. In this sample conversation, the writer asks follow-up questions to direct the revision.

SAMPLE PEER REVIEW DIALOGUE

Writer: What did you like best about the part that describes the arcade?

Reviewer: I could really see the bright lights.

Writer: Which words conveyed that?

Reviewer: "Dazzling" and "blinking" let me see what you were describing.

Writer: I was also trying to show the noise. Did you get that?

Reviewer: Not really. There isn't any description of the noise. Maybe you should add some there.

Editing and Proofreading

While you want your description to convey an impression, prevent distractions by correcting mistakes in your final draft. Carefully check your writing to catch and correct errors in grammar, spelling, punctuation, and capitalization.

Focusing on Agreement

As you proofread, focus your attention on subject-verb agreement. Identify the subject and verb in each sentence, and double-check that they agree.

Grammar in Your Writing

Making Verbs Agree with Indefinite Pronouns

Indefinite pronouns often refer to people, places or things, without specifying which ones. Here are some common indefinite pronouns:

Common Indefinite Pronouns

Singular		Plural	Singular or Plural
anybody	nobody	both	all
anything	no one	few	any
everybody	nothing	many	more
everyone	someone	several	most

- Singular indefinite pronouns take singular verbs; plural indefinite pronouns take plural verbs.

  Singular: Anybody in the club is allowed to attend the meeting.

  Plural: Both of us want to hear the report.

- When an indefinite pronoun can be singular or plural, study the sentence. Use the antecedent, the pronoun's reference, to make the agreement choice.

  Singular: More of the money is spent in December. (refers to singular *money*)

  Plural: More of the gifts are bought at that time. (refers to plural *gifts*)

Find It in Your Reading Read a recent newspaper article. Identify any indefinite pronouns used as subjects. For each, identify whether the verb it takes is singular or plural.

Find It in Your Writing Review your draft to correct any agreement errors involving indefinite pronouns.

For more help with subject-verb agreement, see Chapter 25.

6.6 Publishing and Presenting

Building Your Portfolio

There are numerous ways in which to share your descriptive writing. Consider these strategies:

1. **Prepare an Oral Presentation** Descriptive writing that is rich in sensory detail is well suited to reading aloud. Gather props, illustrations, or music to enhance your reading. Then, share your description with an audience.
2. **Create an Illustrated Anthology** Put several descriptions in a collection. Include at least one illustration or photograph with each piece of writing. Create a cover and a table of contents, and invite others to share your anthology.

Reflecting on Your Writing

Consider the experience of writing your descriptive paper. Use these questions to inspire a written reflection. Keep a copy of your reflection, along with a copy of your essay, in your portfolio.

- How did your view of your subject change or grow as a result of your writing about it?
- What did you find most enjoyable about this kind of writing?

Internet Tip

To see model essays scored with this rubric, go to **www.phschool.com**

Rubric for Self-Assessment

Use these criteria to evaluate your descriptive writing.

	Score 4	Score 3	Score 2	Score 1
Audience and Purpose	Contains details that work together to create a single, dominant impression of the topic	Creates through use of details a dominant impression of the topic	Contains extraneous details that detract from main impression	Contains details that are unfocused and create no dominant impression
Organization	Demonstrates clear organization well-suited to the topic	Demonstrates clear organization	Demonstrates inconsistent organization	Presents information randomly
Elaboration	Contains creative use of figurative language, creating interesting comparisons	Contains figurative language that creates comparisons	Contains figurative language, but the comparisons are not fresh	Contains no figurative language
Use of Language	Contains sensory language that appeals to the five senses; contains no errors in grammar, punctuation, or spelling	Contains some sensory language; contains few errors in grammar, punctuation, and spelling	Contains some sensory language, but it appeals to only one or two of the senses; contains some errors in grammar, punctuation, and spelling	Contains no sensory language; contains many errors in grammar, punctuation, and spelling

Chapter 7

Persuasion

Persuasive Essay

Trial by Jury, 1985, Adele Alsop, courtesy of Schmidt Bingham Gallery, NYC

▲ Critical Viewing What clues in this painting indicate that the man standing in the center is speaking persuasively? **[Analyze]**

Persuasion in Everyday Life

Whenever you argue with a friend over which movie to see or debate the merits of one musical group over another, you're using persuasive skills. **Persuasion** is writing or speaking that attempts to convince others to accept a position or take a desired action. Effective persuasion can decide a defendant's fate in a trial, lead to a change in government leadership, or even end a war.

What Is a Persuasive Essay?

A **persuasive essay** is a piece of writing that presents a position and aims to convince readers to accept that position or take action. An effective persuasive essay

- addresses an issue of concern or importance to the writer.
- addresses an issue that is arguable and has at least two sides.
- presents a position that is supported with relevant facts, examples, or personal experience.
- addresses the knowledge level, experiences, and concerns of the intended audience.

To see the criteria on which your final persuasive essay may be judged, preview the Rubric for Self-Assessment on page 97.

Writers in ACTION

Although you may not have heard of Victorian writer Edward Bulwer-Lytton, his words have become a motto for the power of persuasion. Since the nineteenth century, people have quoted his famous line:

"The pen is mightier than the sword."

Types of Persuasion

From the brief note you write to ask a friend a favor to the formal proposals that nonprofit agencies develop to secure million-dollar grants, persuasion takes many forms. Several types of persuasive writing are similar to the persuasive essay. These specialized types of persuasion have names that reflect their unique purposes:

- **Editorials** are published by the editors of a newspaper to offer their opinions about a current event.
- **Position papers** are prepared to influence policy on current issues.
- **Persuasive speeches** are presented aloud to an audience.

PREVIEW Student Work IN PROGRESS

In this chapter, you'll follow the work of Janaki Spickard-Keeler, a student at Clark High School in San Antonio, Texas. In her essay, Janaki addresses the controversy over the autobiography of pilot and adventurer Beryl Markham. As you'll see, she used prewriting, drafting, and revising techniques to develop her persuasive essay "Who Wrote *West With the Night*?"

Prewriting

Choosing Your Topic

To write an effective persuasive essay, consider issues that have more than one side and select one that touches your life. Use these strategies to select a topic you'd like to develop:

Strategies for Generating Topics

1. **Hot Topics** Whether a sports hero gets into trouble off the field or a new bill is being introduced in Congress, the day's news often sparks controversy. Watch television, scan newspapers, or listen carefully to the hot issues your friends and family are discussing right now. In a chart like the one below, identify the two sides of several controversial topics, and then decide whether you feel strongly enough to present either argument.

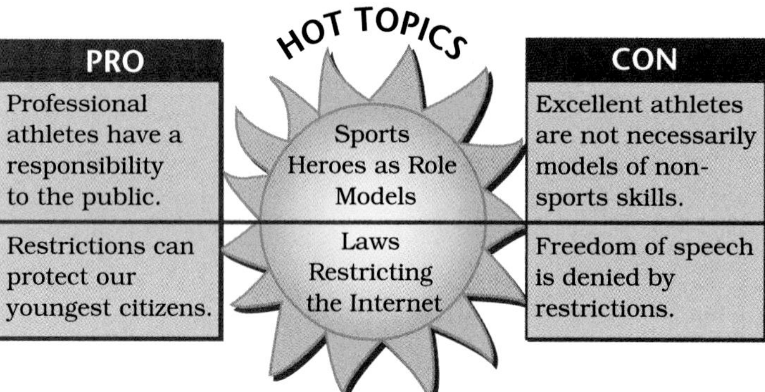

2. **Discussion Group** Meet with a group of students or residents of your community to find out what issues these people find most important. With the group, jot down a list of topics, noting those that create the most controversy or disagreement. You may decide that one of these ideas can lead to a strong persuasive writing topic.
3. **Notebook Review** Use your own classroom experiences to help you find a topic. Skim through the notebooks you keep for various subject areas. Most likely, you will come across topics you have debated in social studies or science classes, or you may be reminded of literature you have read that you would like to urge others to read. Use a highlighter to mark any topics about which you have strong opinions. Then, review the highlighted sections to choose the topic that means the most to you.

For more help finding a topic, explore the activities and topic suggestions in the Choosing a Topic Section of the Persuasion lesson.

TOPIC BANK

If you're having trouble coming up with your own topic, consider these possibilities:

1. **Editorial About Violence on Television** Television networks have come under attack for the violence that is telecast on the news and in dramas. Write an editorial in which you criticize or defend a network's programming choices.
2. **Persuasive Essay on Equal Funding for Girls' Sports** Schools and colleges budget large amounts of money for traditionally male sports. In some states, football receives more funding than field hockey. In a persuasive essay, argue for or against this financial situation.

Responding to Fine Art

3. This painting, *The Pond*, might inspire you to find the beauty of your community's natural spaces. Write a persuasive essay on an action that impacts the local environment. For example, you might evaluate the effect of mandatory recycling programs or weigh the results of the increased building of shopping malls and housing.

The Pond, 1985, Adele Alsop, courtesy of Schmidt Bingham Gallery, NYC

Responding to Literature

4. Read "The Cask of Amontillado" by Edgar Allan Poe. As a lawyer, write a persuasive essay in which you either defend or prosecute Montresor for his actions. You can find this story in *Prentice Hall Literature: Timeless Voices, Timeless Themes*, Gold.

Cooperative Writing Opportunity

5. **Persuasive Brochure on Volunteerism** With a group, split the task of researching volunteer work. Each group member can research a different aspect of the topic; for example, one might report on the benefits to the volunteer, while another could focus on the benefits to others. Together, create a pamphlet on the values of volunteering.

2

Narrowing Your Topic

Once you've chosen a topic, consider all the points you will have to make in order to convince your readers. For example, if you plan to argue that animals should be protected from harm, you'll have to identify all the hazards animals face. That might take hundreds of pages to do well. In contrast, a narrowed topic such as "Additives in Dog Food Can Harm Your Pet's Bones" focuses your writing. Limiting your topic to one specific issue or problem enables you to cover your topic thoroughly. Looping is one strategy to narrow your topic.

Use Looping to Narrow a Topic

These are the steps of looping. First, write freely on your topic for about five minutes. Read what you have written, and circle the most important idea. Write for five minutes on that idea. Continue this process until you come to a topic that is narrow enough to address in your persuasive writing.

Student Work IN PROGRESS

Name: Janaki Spickard-Keeler
Clark High School
San Antonio, TX

Looping

Here is how Janaki used looping to narrow a broad topic:

Broad topic: The controversy surrounding Beryl Markham's autobiography

I've studied the life of Beryl Markham, a pilot, adventurer, and writer. Markham may be known for her aviation feats. She may be best known because of her autobiography, *West With the Night.* Markham was a horse trainer and a breeder.

Autobiography: *West With the Night* is an exciting and gripping book that Hemingway called "wonderful." I was surprised to learn that some people have questioned whether Beryl Markham wrote it! How could they make such a claim? She describes things that no one else could have known!

Narrowed topic: Beryl Markham is the only person who could have written *West With the Night.*

Considering Your Audience and Purpose

Your purpose in writing a persuasive essay is to convince readers to accept your position or to take action. A knowledge of your audience will be a critical element in achieving your purpose.

To help identify your audience and shape your argument appropriately, use the Audience Profile activity in the Persuasion lesson.

Analyze Your Audience

The interest, concerns, and attitude your readers bring to your subject should help direct the approach you take. For example, if you were to write a persuasive essay to promote exercise, you'd want to address the characteristics of your audience. This chart shows the arguments you might use to persuade specific groups of people:

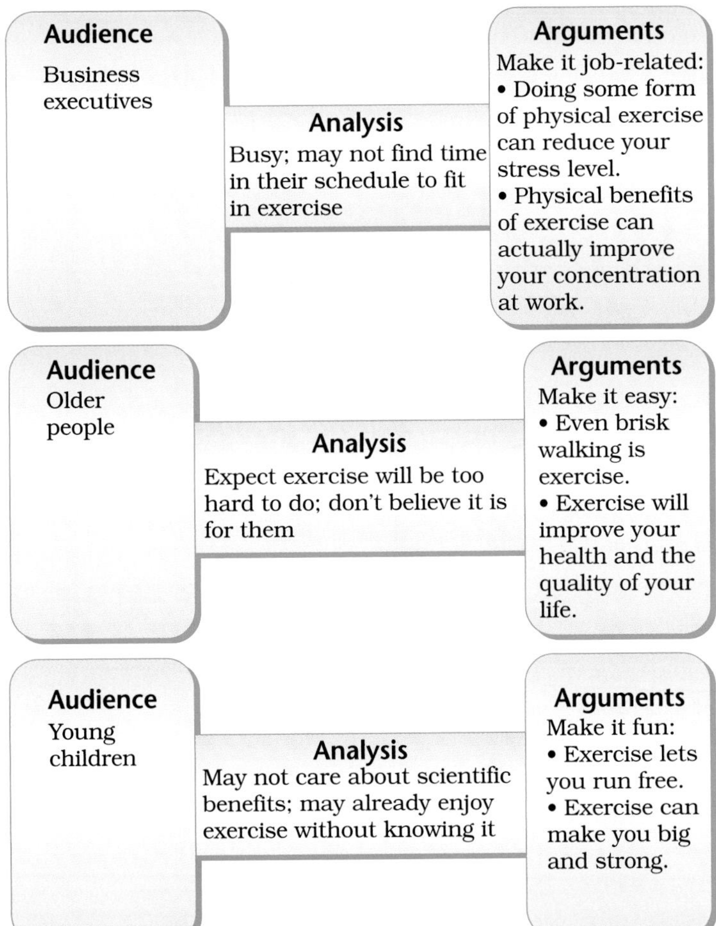

7.2

Gathering Evidence

To write a strong persuasive essay, you must back up your claim with convincing proof. In order to do this, you need to gather as much evidence as you can. Consider these strategies for collecting supporting information that will prove your point to your audience:

Conduct Research

To collect facts, statistics, and examples, use reliable resources: books by experts, accounts of people with experience, and primary sources such as letters and speeches. Keep bibliographic information such as title, author, and date of publication to include in your final draft. As you research, you may discover details that support an opposing position. Take notes on both sides of the argument using a T-chart.

Complete a T-Chart Write your position across the top of a sheet of paper. Then, fold the paper in half to create two columns. In one column, jot down facts and ideas that support your position. In the other column, note evidence that might be used to argue against your idea. Begin thinking about how you can answer these opposing arguments.

Student Work IN PROGRESS

Name: Janaki Spickard-Keeler
Clark High School
San Antonio, TX

Organizing Research With a T-Chart

Janaki consulted several sources to support her argument that Beryl Markham had been the sole author of West With the Night. *She used a T-chart to establish evidence for both sides of the issue.*

Position: Beryl Markham did write *West With the Night.*

Evidence Markham didn't write WWTW	Evidence she did write it
Claims of illiteracy	She was well read.
Father's role in her education	She had a large library.

7.3 Drafting

Shaping Your Writing

Develop a Thesis Statement

An effective persuasive essay is built around a clearly worded **thesis statement,** a statement of the position you will prove.

SAMPLE THESIS STATEMENTS

New drivers should be required to log 100 hours with a licensed driver before obtaining a driver's license.

Any drivers who can pass a road test should receive a driver's license no matter how long they have been practicing.

As you begin drafting, introduce your topic and state your thesis. Then, in the body of your essay, provide the arguments that support and prove your thesis statement. Your arguments may consist of facts, reasons, and other examples that support your position.

Writing Lab CD-ROM

To help you organize your argument, use the Note Cards activity in the Persuasion lesson.

▼ Critical Viewing
What statement about Beryl Markham could you support using details from this picture? **[Support]**

Organize to Emphasize the Strongest Support

Every point in your essay should support your thesis statement. Some details provide stronger support than others. Organize your essay so that you use your strongest support to its best advantage. Consider the following suggestions:

- Save your best reason for last to finish with power.
- Use your second-best argument to get off to a strong start.
- Organize the remaining facts and details in ascending order of importance as you build toward your most powerful reason.
- Before you deliver the strongest argument, acknowledge the opposition. Show and argue against a conflicting side of the issue.

Beryl Markham, pilot and adventurer

Providing Elaboration

As you draft, build a strong case for your position by thoroughly developing each of your supporting arguments. Use a variety of methods to elaborate on each argument. For example, as the chart below demonstrates, you can use personal experiences, comparisons, and statistics.

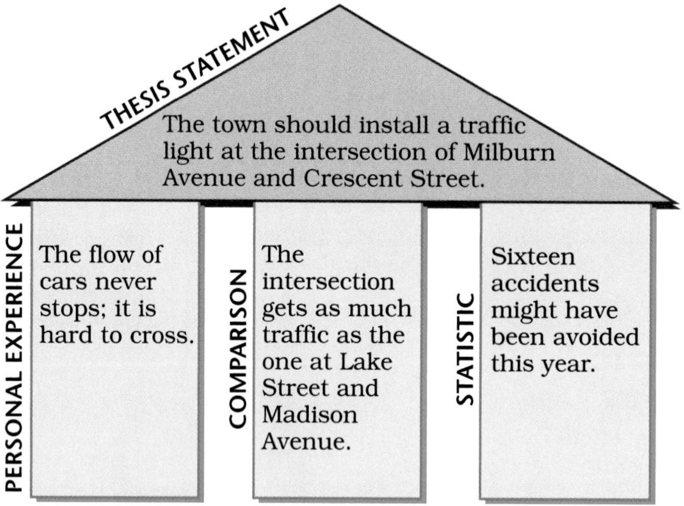

The following are some other strategies you can use to elaborate on your main point.

Describe the Situation Use sensory language to help your readers see the conditions you address. For example, to convince readers that the food in a certain restaurant is fantastic, describe the best entree you were served.

Show a Contrast Explain how your subject is different from another one. For example, to argue that toddlers need to use specialized car restraints, show how small children's safety needs are different from those of adults.

Provide an Anecdote Share a story that proves your point. For example, to support the position that a healthy diet is worth the effort, show how following a food plan changed one person's life.

7.4 Revising

Once you have written your first draft, start looking for ways to improve it. Moving from the big picture of overall structure to the small details of word choice, the work you do in revising will make your essay more persuasive.

Revising Your Overall Structure

Support Your Arguments

The convincing power of a persuasive essay topples when supporting arguments are weak. Review your paper to strengthen each reason you provide to back up your opinion.

REVISION STRATEGY
Color-Coding Main Points

Using a highlighter, identify the points that support your thesis statement. For each, underline the evidence you've provided.

Evaluate

- Does the support prove the thesis statement?

Revise

- If a point needs more evidence, return to your notes to find details. If there is no stronger evidence, eliminate the point.

Research Tip

To improve your essay, consult reference materials to get the additional facts you need. It is never too late to check *Facts on File,* recent journals, or other sources to find the statistic that will seal your case.

Student Work IN PROGRESS

Name: Janaki Spickard-Keeler
Clark High School
San Antonio, TX

Evaluating Support for Your Arguments

By highlighting the main idea and underlining her support, Janaki analyzed this paragraph to evaluate her evidence. At this point, Janaki is revising for organization, rather than grammar or style.

For anyone who has read *West With the Night,* I think the real proof lies in the actual work. No one could have written the story without having been there. You'd have to have lived it to write like that. No matter what analysts say, the soul of the story is Beryl's.

The underlined statement does not give evidence to support the claim. The main point needs more evidence to support it.

To strengthen this point of her essay, Janaki decided to add a specific example of Markham's writing. See the final draft on pages 148–149.

Revising Your Paragraphs

Address the Critics

Give your essay greater credibility by showing another side of the argument. Identify an opposing point by thinking like your critics. First, imagine what your opponent might say to challenge your ideas. Then, list a few ideas, and choose one you can answer with a strong rebuttal. Finally, to find a place to insert this opposing argument and rebuttal effectively, analyze your essay at the paragraph level.

REVISION STRATEGY

Finding a Place to Address the Opposition

Using self-sticking notes, write the opposing argument you will refute. Move this note down the margin of your essay, stopping at each paragraph to judge where the information would best fit. Once you decide on the best placement, write the idea out fully and incorporate it into your essay. Then, address the contrast between the opposition and your thesis. You may have to add a sentence or two to smooth out the connection.

Student Work IN PROGRESS

Name: Janaki Spickard-Keeler
Clark High School
San Antonio, TX

Addressing the Critics

Janaki reviewed the main point of each paragraph. She decided to introduce the opposing view into the paragraph that contains her thesis.

First paragraph: For years, no one even knew the question existed. . . .

Second paragraph: Readers were thrilled with the book; it was an instant success. . . .

People claim Raoul's notes were on the manuscript.

Third paragraph: It is my opinion that Beryl Markham—and no one else—wrote her autobiography. . . .

Grammar in Your Writing

Punctuating Adverb Clauses

You may find that in your essay you have used many adverb clauses. Adverb clauses show the relationship between ideas by telling *where, when, how, why, to what extent,* or *under what condition.*

Time relationship (when): After the book was published

Cause-and-effect relationship (why): Because so many people like the book

Opposing relationship (under what condition): Although many thought it was well-written

All adverb clauses contain a subject and a verb and begin with a subordinating conjunction.

Common Subordinating Conjunctions That Introduce Adverb Clauses

after	although	as
because	before	if
since	unless	until
when	whenever	where
wherever	whether	while

When an adverb clause introduces a sentence, use a comma to separate it from the rest of the sentence. Note, however, that it is usually not necessary to use a comma before an adverb clause at the end of a sentence.

Introductory adverb clause

After the book was published, critics came forward to question its source.

Adverb clause at the end of a sentence

Hemingway praised the writer because he thought she was talented.

Find It in Your Reading Review a selection from a book of short stories. Identify two sentences that contain introductory adverb clauses.

Find It in Your Writing Review your draft to identify three adverb clauses. Be sure that you have placed a comma after those that start sentences. If you cannot identify three adverb clauses, challenge yourself to add at least one more to your writing. You may like the improvement you've made.

For more on adverb clauses, see Chapter 21.

Revising Your Sentences

Use Transitions

Minor revisions to sentences can make a big difference. Look at each sentence to see whether rearranging or adding words will make your meaning more clear to your readers. Use transitions to clarify or reinforce the connections between ideas.

REVISION STRATEGY
Using Transition Boxes

You may want to try this strategy with one paragraph:

1. Draw a box between the end punctuation of one sentence and the first word of the next sentence.
2. Identify the relationship that connects the sentences on either side of the box.
3. Evaluate your writing as it exists. Place a check in the box if the relationship between the sentences it connects is clear.
4. If the relationship is not clear, add a transition. (Use the chart on the next page as a reference.) Place the new word or phrase at the point where the box is located. As an alternative, you might draw a line from the box to a space where the transition makes the most sense.

Challenge yourself to apply this strategy to other paragraphs in your essay.

Use the Transition Word Bin in the Persuasion lesson to help improve your sentences.

Student Work IN PROGRESS

Name: Janaki Spickard-Keeler
Clark High School
San Antonio, TX

Using Transition Boxes to Smooth Writing

In the paragraph that argued that Beryl Markham was not illiterate, Janaki saw that readers might not see the connections she wanted them to see. She added several transitions to make the writing more clear.

Beryl practically worshiped her father[, so naturally,] she would do as he wished and read the classics. She [also] had quite a library, and Denys Finch-Hatton encouraged her to educate herself. [Furthermore,] she wrote diligently with a practiced hand in her logbook. [✓] She also had to write a lengthy theory paper to pass her flying exam.

The first sentence gives a reason for the second sentence. The transition "so naturally" clarifies the relationship.

TRANSITIONS THAT INDICATE LOGICAL RELATIONSHIPS			
Point to a Reason	Identify a Single Conclusion	Show a Contrast	Signal a Sequence
since, because, if	therefore, consequently, as a result, thus, hence, accordingly, so, then, in conclusion	although, even though, however, despite, yet, but, on the other hand, in contrast, except for	first, second, then, next, finally, before, after, later, soon, daily, recently, when

Revising Your Word Choice

Use Persuasive Language

The words you choose can influence the readers' reactions to your argument. If you maintain a polite tone, you can use language that points readers in the direction you want them to go.

When you want to sharpen criticism: Use words like *unfounded, shameful,* and *implausible.*

When you want to polish a recommendation: Add words like *superior* and *wise.*

When you want to defend your ideas: Include words like *obvious, clear,* and *evident.*

REVISION STRATEGY
Reading Aloud

Read your draft aloud, as if it were a speech. Mark the ideas or sentences that you would want to stress to a crowd. Then, go back into your draft, adding the forceful words you need.

▲ Critical Viewing
In what ways might a peer conference like the one shown here help you fine-tune your persuasive essay? **[Hypothesize]**

Peer Review

Say Back

In a small group, share your revised draft. Read your persuasive essay twice, asking readers to listen the first time and respond the second time. Use these questions as a starting point for group discussion:

1. What is the most persuasive point?
2. About which point would a reader want to know more?

After you've heard from your classmates, consider using their suggestions to improve your draft.

Editing and Proofreading

Errors in persuasive writing can lessen your power to persuade readers. To make your writing error-free, check spelling, punctuation, and grammar before you create your final draft.

Focusing on Fact-Checking

Be sure you have included accurate information. Compare your draft to research notes you made, or consult reference materials to confirm details you have cited. Double-check the following kinds of details, and make corrections when necessary:

Names and dates Confirm the spelling of people's names. Make sure that the dates you cite are accurate.

Statistics Be on the lookout for numbers that may have been mistakenly transposed. For example, you may have copied 56,513 instead of 53,516 in your draft.

Quotations Check the wording of any quotations you include.

Grammar in Your Writing

Using the Conventions for Writing Titles

As you proofread, make sure you have used the conventions for writing titles. Long works are set off by underlining or italics. In addition to the titles of novels and plays, other titles that are italicized include the names of newspapers, magazines, movies, paintings, and sculptures.

Enclose short works in quotation marks. In addition to the titles of poems and short stories, other titles that are enclosed in quotation marks are essays, articles, chapters, and songs.

Titles of books: *West With the Night* by Beryl Markham
Titles of short stories: "A Day's Wait" by Ernest Hemingway
Titles of long poems: *Paradise Lost* by John Milton
Titles of short poems: "The Bells" by Edgar Allan Poe

Find It in Your Reading Find three titles in the table of contents of an anthology. Explain the conventions used for writing the titles.

Find It in Your Writing As you proofread your persuasive essay, check that you have written all titles correctly.

For more on writing titles correctly, see Chapter 29.

7.6 Publishing and Presenting

Building Your Portfolio

Sharing your essay may prove powerful—your ideas could change a law, inspire a turnaround in people's habits, or provoke readers to see an idea in a new way. Consider these ideas for publishing and presenting your work:

1. **Encourage Action** Sponsor a read-aloud of several persuasive essays. As a group, choose one of the issues on which to act. Discuss ways to begin the process of making a change for the better—and then get started!
2. **Mail Your Essay** Invite a local, state, or federal elected official to act on the issue your essay addresses. Use government directories to find the address of the most appropriate official. Save a copy of the letter and any response you receive in your portfolio.

Reflecting on Your Writing

Take a moment to jot down your ideas about the persuasive writing experience. Save a copy of your ideas in your portfolio. These questions might direct your reflection:

- What have you learned about your topic?
- Which writing strategy might you recommend to a friend?

To see model essays scored with this rubric, go to **www.phschool.com**

Rubric for Self-Assessment

Use the following criteria to evaluate your persuasive essay:

	Score 4	Score 3	Score 2	Score 1
Audience and Purpose	Demonstrates highly effective word choice; clearly states focus on persuasive task	Demonstrates good word choice; states focus on persuasive task	Shows some good word choices; minimally states focus on persuasive task	Shows lack of attention to persuasive task
Organization	Uses clear, consistent organizational strategy	Uses clear organizational strategy with occasional inconsistencies	Uses inconsistent organizational strategy; presentation is not logical	Demonstrates lack of organizational strategy
Elaboration	Provides convincing, well-elaborated reasons to support the position	Provides two or more moderately elaborated reasons to support the writer's position	Provides several reasons but few are elaborated; only one elaborated reason	Provides no specific reasons or does not elaborate
Use of Language	Incorporates many transitions to create clarity of expression; includes very few mechanical errors	Incorporates some transitions to help flow of ideas; includes few mechanical errors	Incorporates few transitions; does not connect ideas well; includes many mechanical errors	Does not connect ideas; includes many mechanical errors

Chapter 8 Persuasion

Advertisement

◀ Critical Viewing How does this artwork convey enthusiasm for reading? **[Analyze]**

Advertisements in Everyday Life

You are bombarded by advertisements every day—on television and radio, on billboards, in magazines and newspapers, on the walls of buses and trains, and on the Internet. Advertisers do their best to get you to read, hear, and be persuaded by their messages. If you've ever accepted a free food sample or allowed yourself to be spritzed with a new fragrance in a department store, you know that advertising can go beyond words and images to address even the senses of taste and smell. As a form of persuasion, advertisements must convince; however, they have a more focused purpose: to encourage consumers to buy products or services.

What Is an Advertisement?

An **advertisement** is produced by a company or an organization to persuade an audience to buy a product or service, accept an idea, or support a cause. Advertisements in print form appear in newspapers, magazines, or on billboards. Ad writers can create audio or visual commercials presented on radio, television, or the Internet. An effective advertisement may include

- a memorable slogan to grab the audience's attention.
- a call to action that encourages the readers to do something.
- details that provide practical information, such as price, location, date, or time.
- a deliberate use of layout, images, or print styles.

To see the criteria by which your final advertisement may be judged, preview the Rubric for Self-Assessment on page 110.

Writers in ACTION

Rosser Reeves, a successful advertising professional, encourages new advertising writers to find the element of a product that creates good feelings and to capitalize on that. Reeves coined the phrase, "Sell the sizzle, not the steak."

Types of Advertisements

From a flyer announcing a school musical to a campaign for the presidency of the United States, advertising takes many forms. Here are a few of the most common types of advertising:

- **Political campaigns** use print ads, posters, and television spots to educate and persuade voters about a candidate.
- **Infomercials** mix a talk-show or news format with persuasive techniques to promote a product or service.
- **Product packaging** takes advantage of the container or wrapping of a product to persuade consumers to buy it.
- **Public-service announcements** provide persuasive information to educate audiences about issues of social concern.

In this chapter, you'll follow the work of Caitlin Mahoney, a student at Darien High School in Darien, Connecticut. Caitlin used prewriting, drafting, and revising techniques to create a flyer. Her interest in animal adoption inspired her ad for the Doggy Palace Animal Shelter. Her final advertisement appears at the end of this chapter.

8.1 Model From Literature

Like most theater companies, the Michigan Opera plans a season by identifying several productions it will present in a given year. The advertisement below, sent to homes before the first curtain, announces the operas to be performed in one season.

Incorporate Design Elements As you finalize your advertisement, use color, lines, or fonts to communicate your ideas.

MICHIGAN
OPERA
THEATRE

"This world is a comedy to those who think, a tragedy to those who feel."

Think. Feel. See an Opera.

The Barber of Seville
October 2 – 10

Werther
October 29 – November 14

Der Rosenkavalier
April 15 – 30

Tosca
May 6 – 14

Peter Grimes
June 3 – 11

LITERATURE

For another example of a print ad, see the advertisement for an automobile in the Analyzing Real-World Texts section of *Prentice Hall Literature: Timeless Voices, Timeless Themes*, Gold.

The logo at the top identifies the company that sponsored the ad.

The ad's memorable slogan "Think. Feel. See an Opera." echoes the quotation printed in a large type size. It targets a specific audience and appeals to a perceived desire to live life fully.

Details such as prices, ticket-office phone numbers, and the opera's address are essential to ticket sales. These practical details are printed on the reverse side of the mailer.

8.2 Prewriting

Choosing Your Topic

To write a convincing advertisement, choose a product, service, or event that you would like to promote. Use these strategies to generate a topic you'd like to develop:

Strategies for Generating Topics

1. **Products and Services Schedule** In a chart, break your day into logical segments, such as before, during, and after school. For each block of time, make a list of the products and services that you use every day. Review your chart to find a topic for your advertisement.
2. **Classroom Interest Poll** Survey your classmates to find out what products and services they buy. Develop a questionnaire or conduct a group discussion to identify the brand names of on-line services, magazines, musical groups, clothing, or stores they enjoy. Review the results of your poll, and choose a topic for your advertisement.

For more help finding a topic, explore the activities and suggestions in the Choosing a Topic section of the Persuasion lesson.

TOPIC BANK

Consider these suggestions for more topic ideas:

1. **Advertisement for an Invented Product** Imagine a product that would make your life more manageable or interesting. Develop the concept, and then devise an advertisement that introduces your idea to consumers.

Responding to Literature

2. **Public-Service Announcement** After reading "The Birds," by Daphne du Maurier, write a public-service announcement based on the events of the story. You can find "The Birds" in *Prentice Hall Literature: Timeless Voices, Timeless Themes*, Gold.

Cooperative Writing Opportunity

3. **Ad Campaign** With a group, decide upon a product or service to promote with a series of advertisements. Develop individual ads to appeal to specific audiences. For example, one writer can create an ad for teenagers; another can design one for families; and a third can make the product appealing to businesses.

Narrowing Your Topic

The topic of your advertisement should be the product or service you've identified. However, you will need to find an angle that makes your product appealing. Use the cubing strategy to study your topic and narrow the focus of your advertisement.

Narrow a Topic With Cubing

Cubing allows you to look at your topic from six angles:

1. **Describe It** Explain the physical attributes of your topic.
2. **Associate It** Show how your topic may remind your audience of something else.
3. **Apply It** Tell how your topic can be used.
4. **Analyze It** Separate your topic into smaller parts.
5. **Compare and Contrast It** Explain how other products are similar to and different from yours.
6. **Argue for It** Traditionally, in cubing, you promote or reject an idea. However, narrow this cubing angle to collect only positive ideas for promoting your topic.

After you've studied your product or service from each angle, review your list. Circle the elements of the product or service that you will address in your advertisement.

CUBING TO NARROW AN AD'S FOCUS

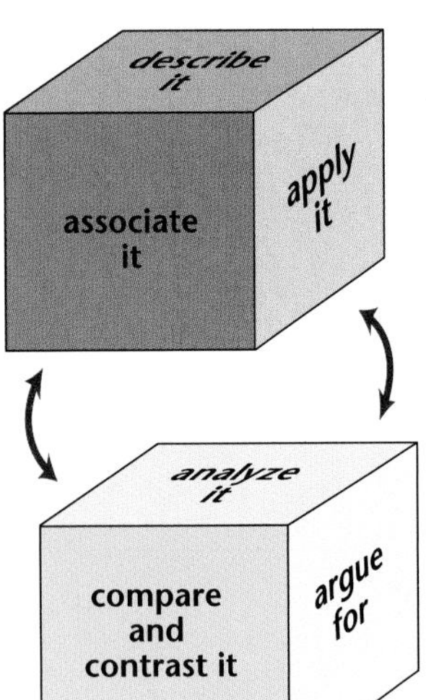

Product: Pack and Go Radio

Describe:
credit card size
AM-FM radio; available in 8 colors

Associate:
like other high-tech gadgets; something a spy might use

Apply:
take news or music with you anywhere

Analyze:
digital tuner; clock feature; built-in antenna and speakers

Compare and contrast:
provides stereo-quality sound;
smaller than any home stereo

Argue for or against:
convenient; modern

Narrowed focus: size and quality

Speaking and Listening Tip

To help identify those features of your topic that need more focus, do the cubing exercise with a group. As you address each angle, ask group members if you have provided a clear explanation.

Considering Your Audience and Purpose

Generally, advertisements serve a predictable purpose: to show a product, service, or idea in a positive light and therefore encourage readers to take actions such as buying, voting, or participating. However, specific sales techniques will appeal to some audiences and not to others. Consider the audience you want to reach with your ad, and then devise an appeal that will move that group.

Match Your Audience With Your Purpose

A knowledge of your audience will be a critical element in achieving your purpose. Identify your target audience, list what you know about the people you want to reach, and then decide on the best way to appeal to them.

To gather information about your target audience, use the Audience Profile activity in the Persuasion lesson.

Student Work IN PROGRESS

Name: Caitlin Mahoney
Darien High School
Darien, CT

Matching Your Audience With Your Purpose

Before drafting her ad, Caitlin made a list of benefits that might persuade her audience to adopt a pet. Then, she chose a specific angle.

Audience: Families
- Both old and young members
- Varied interests
- Want to spend quality time together
- Parents may want value or affordability
- Kids may prefer animals that are active and fun
- Looking for ways to bring the family together and create memories

Angle: Pets complete the family picture

Gathering Details

To write a strong advertisement, back up your pitch with details that will help convince your audience of the merits of your service, product, or cause.

Make a Link to Audience and Angle

Use a knowledge of your audience to gather details that will be persuasive. Jot down ideas that will help you prove that the product is suitable for your audience's needs, lifestyle, financial situation, and interests. Look at these suggestions:

Lifestyles If the people in your target audience lead hectic lives, show how your product or service is convenient, time-saving, or relaxing. If your readers want to add excitement to their lives, show how your product can help them do that.

Finances If you are trying to reach an audience of people who keep to a strict budget or those who want to save money, emphasize the cost and value of your product. If money is not a concern, you may choose not to address this issue.

Interests Some audiences are impressed by status—the prestige or importance that owning an item may bring them. Others are more concerned with the way a product can help their business, improve their health, or help them achieve some other goal. Gather information to address these specific interests of your target audience.

Challenge

Consult the professionals by scanning newspapers and magazines to find effective ads. Consider applying the techniques you see by using them in your own advertisement.

Student Work IN PROGRESS

Name: Caitlin Mahoney
Darien High School
Darien, CT

Linking Audience, Angle, and Details

Caitlin made a list of details to show how adopting a dog could be valuable for families. She crossed off ideas that would not appeal to her target audience.

Audience: families
Angle: Pets complete the family picture.
Details: Pets can offer families:
unconditional friendship
lively companionship
loyalty and love
~~status~~
~~popularity~~
the chance for adults to stay young
the chance for children to learn responsibility
health benefits

8.3 Drafting

Shaping Your Writing

Organize to Persuade

Although the number of words in an advertisement is drastically fewer than the count for a fully developed essay, your words must communicate your ideas and persuade your audience. Be sure your writing addresses each of these features:

- **Slogan** An effective ad is based on a catchy and memorable message. Write a short phrase or sentence that announces your main idea. Make a play on words or use rhyme to encourage your audience to learn more about your product or service.
- **Images** Pictures can often say more than words. If possible, find an appropriate photograph or illustration for your advertisement.
- **Supporting Information** Include supporting details to appeal to your target audience. Somewhere on your ad, provide information about where your readers can learn more.

Grammar and Style Tip

Use alliteration, the repetition of initial consonant sounds, to make your slogan more memorable. For example, one restaurant chain launched a successful campaign with the phrase "Food, folks, and fun."

Providing Elaboration

Include the Facts

While your slogan presents the strongest selling point of your product or service, it is also important to include details to answer the readers' basic questions. As you write your advertisement, include factual information, such as what the product is, what it does, why it is useful, and where to get it.

◀ Critical Viewing In your opinion, what is the most important information on this political advertisement? Why? **[Evaluate]**

Revising

Revising Your Overall Structure

Review the Visual Layout

After you've completed your first draft, look for ways to make your advertisement visually appealing to your audience. Try several layouts, and choose the one that seems most logical. To make your organization more obvious, identify the main ideas your ad presents.

REVISION STRATEGY

Circling Main Ideas to Improve the Layout

Review the first draft of your advertisement, and circle the ideas you want to convey most. To make these items stand out, evaluate their placement on the page. Decide whether a different font, size, or color would make the ideas more visible. Alternatively, consider adding bullets to call more attention to the key points. The illustration below offers one potential layout for your advertisement.

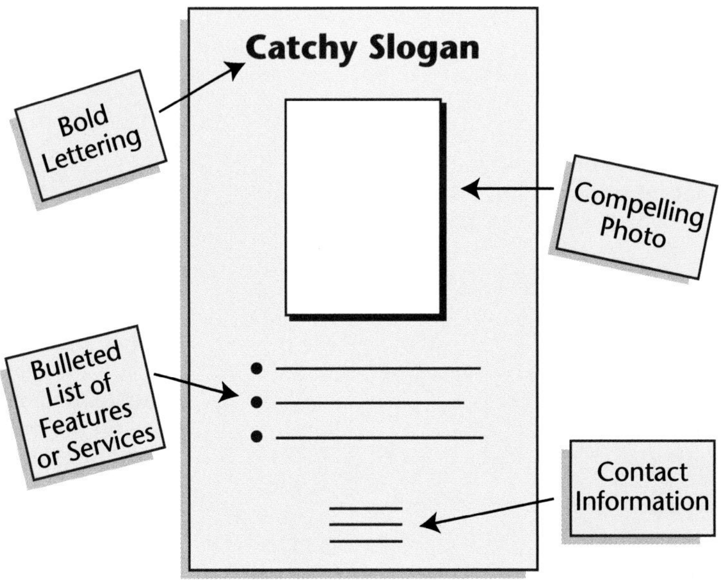

Learn More

In addition to images images and layout, advertisements rely on the power of words to sell products or services. See Chapter 6 and Chapter 7 to review the key qualities of descriptive and persuasive writing.

Revising Your Paragraphs and Sentences

Improve Sentence Power

To make their point quickly and effectively, advertisements depend on short, punchy sentences or phrases. Review your draft, and replace long, wordy sentences with leaner, more powerful ones.

REVISION STRATEGY
Shortening Your Sentences

Look at the length of the sentences in your draft in an effort to shorten each one. Revise complicated sentences by limiting many of them to a single subject, its verb, and any modifiers.

To address your audience directly, change declarative sentences to imperative ones. Look at this example:

DECLARATIVE: We advise you to compare our prices.
IMPERATIVE: Compare our prices.

Student Work IN PROGRESS

Name: Caitlin Mahoney
Darien High School
Darien, CT

Shortening Sentences

To get directly to the point and add authority to her writing, Caitlin reduced wordiness by shortening many sentences in her final draft.

- ~~You'll find~~ a dog is a lively companion and a loyal friend to adults and children.
- ~~All our customers report~~ a dog will love you unconditionally for the rest of your lives together.

Revising Your Word Choice

Choose Words With Positive Connotations

Because people respond to the connotations or emotional meanings of words, advertising professionals know the importance of a precise label. While the words *satisfying, filling,* or *hearty* may seem similar, their connotations may appeal to one audience but alienate another. To reach your audience, review the words you've used in your draft.

Research Tip

To find the exact words to convey an idea to your audience, consult a thesaurus.

REVISION STRATEGY
Color-Coding to Improve Word Choice

Use a highlighter to identify words that you'd like to make more persuasive. Besides indicating dull words, mark words that are overused. To make your ad more persuasive, replace the words you've identified with more powerful ones. Use a thesaurus to spark your revision choices.

Student Work IN PROGRESS

Name: Caitlin Mahoney
Darien High School
Darien, CT

Using Color-Coding to Improve Word Choice

Caitlin used a highlighter to identify dull words and then replaced them with punchier ones.

A dog is a ~~nice~~ lively companion and a ~~good~~ loyal friend to adults and children.

A dog will love you ~~a lot~~ unconditionally for the rest of your lives together.

Peer Review

Focus Groups

Before advertisements hit the pages of a magazine or the airwaves, they are tested to be sure they communicate the intended message. After a group previews your ad, use feedback to make final revisions to your work. Ask these questions to get specific responses:

- What do you think the product or service is?
- Would you buy the product or use the service based on this advertisement?

8.5 Editing and Proofreading

Review your writing carefully for errors. Be sure to check spelling, punctuation, and grammar before creating your final draft.

Focusing on Spelling

Unless they are intended to grab your audience's attention, errors in spelling will detract from the persuasive power of your ad. Be especially careful to spell place names and product names correctly.

Grammar in Your Writing

Using Abbreviations

An abbreviation is a shortened form of a word or a phrase. It usually consists of the first several letters of a word or the first letter of each word in a longer phrase.

Titles The most common abbreviations are the social terms *Mr.* and *Mrs.* Note these abbreviations for government leaders:

President	Pres.	Senator	Sen.	Representative	Rep.
Governor	Gov.	Treasurer	Treas.	Ambassador	Amb.

Time The abbreviations that distinguish between morning and evening can be written in three styles, as shown below. Choose one format for consistency.

A.M., a.m., am : ante meridiem, before noon

P.M., p.m., pm : post meridiem, after noon

Months of the Year Most months of the year are abbreviated to their first three letters.

January	Jan.	February	Feb.	March	Mar.
April	Apr.	May	May	June	June
July	July	August	Aug.	September	Sept.
October	Oct.	November	Nov.	December	Dec.

Find It in Your Reading As you review professional advertisements, notice the use of abbreviations to convey information.

Find It in Your Writing Circle words you have abbreviated in your ad. Double-check these to be sure you have followed standard conventions.

For more on abbreviations, see the Abbreviation Guide on pages 866–869.

Publishing and Presenting

Building Your Portfolio

Advertising is meant to convince others to buy your product or service, support your cause, or attend your event. Try these ideas for presenting your work:

1. **Bulletin Board** Make a display to share the creative talents of your class. Next to each ad, include a few words from the writer that explain the ideas behind the work.
2. **Mail Your Ad** If your advertisement is for a product or service that exists, share your work with the company. You should be able to locate an address on the product's packaging, through library resources, or on the Internet.

Reflecting on Your Writing

Reflect on the experience of writing an advertisement. Use these questions to direct a written reflection. Include your ideas in your portfolio.

- How did the purpose of your advertisement become clear as you began to create it?
- How is drafting an advertisement different from creating other types of writing?

To see a model essay scored with this rubric, go to **www.phwg.phschool.com**

Rubric for Self-Assessment

Use the following criteria to evaluate your advertisement:

	Score 4	Score 3	Score 2	Score 1
Audience and Purpose	Presents effective slogan; clearly addresses specific audience	Presents good slogan; addresses specific audience	Presents slogan; minimally addresses specific audience	Does not present slogan; shows lack of attention to specific audience
Organization	Uses layout and design elements to convey clear, consistent organizational strategy	Uses layout and design elements to convey clear organizational strategy with few inconsistencies	Uses inconsistent layout and design strategy; creates illogical presentation	Demonstrates lack of organizational strategy; creates random presentation through layout and design elements
Elaboration	Successfully combines words and images to provide convincing, unified support for a position	Combines words and images to provide unified support for a position	Includes some words or images that detract from a position	Uses words and images that do not support a position
Use of Language	Successfully communicates an idea through clever use of language; includes very few mechanical errors	Conveys an idea through adequate use of language; includes few mechanical errors	Misuses language and lessens impact of ideas; includes many mechanical errors	Demonstrates poor use of language and confuses meaning; includes many mechanical errors

8.7 Student Work IN PROGRESS

FINAL DRAFT

Caitlin Mahoney
Darien High School
Darien, Connecticut

Pets Complete the Family Picture

Why adopt a dog?

- A dog is a lively companion and a loyal friend to adults and children.
- A dog will love you unconditionally for the rest of your lives together.
- Caring for a dog and playing with a dog can keep adults young and help teach children responsibility.
- Our dogs need good homes.
- Doggy Palace Animal Shelter needs your support.

What will you find here?

- A puppy or an adult dog that will fit happily into your household
- Pets in many colors, sizes, breeds, and barks

When and where?

Monday, Sept. 23 – Friday, Sept. 27 3 P.M. – 9 P.M.
Saturday, Sept. 28 – Sunday, Sept. 29 9 A.M. – 9 P.M.

Doggy Palace Animal Shelter
11 Peters Street
Trentville

Caitlin made her headline bigger than the other text and centered it to grab the attention of readers more effectively.

◀ **Critical Viewing**
How does the photograph convey positive feelings about pets? **[Analyze]**

Caitlin uses bold subheads and icons to call out main points.

Details beneath each main point provide more information aimed at a specific audience.

At the end of the advertisement, Caitlin includes practical information such as dates and times.

Chapter 9

Exposition

Comparison-and-Contrast Essay

▲ Critical Viewing What would make these marbles a good subject for a comparison-and-contrast essay? **[Evaluate]**

Comparisons and Contrasts in Everyday Life

When you make a decision about whether to try skiing instead of snowboarding, whether to wear a pair of jeans or a pair of corduroys, or whether to have a chicken sandwich instead of a salad for lunch, you are using comparison-and-contrast skills. Although choosing the contents of a meal or selecting the day's wardrobe may not have lasting consequences, you will also apply comparison-and-contrast analysis to more important decisions: what career to pursue, where to live, whom to elect to office. In each case, you consider two or more options that are similar in some ways and different in others. In the end, you use the skills of comparison and contrast to weigh all factors and make a decision.

What Is a Comparison-and-Contrast Essay?

A **comparison-and-contrast essay** addresses two or more subjects to show their similarities and differences. It may describe or explain, reveal strengths as well as weaknesses, or persuade a reader to value one subject over another. An effective comparison-and-contrast essay

- identifies similarities and differences between two or more things, people, places, or ideas.
- provides factual details about each subject.
- identifies a purpose for comparison and contrast.
- addresses each subject equally by presenting information in one of two organizations: subject by subject or point by point.

To preview the criteria by which your final comparison-and-contrast essay may be evaluated, see the Rubric for Self-Assessment on page 126.

Writers in ACTION

Carl Sagan, an astronomer who made the galaxies accessible to millions, valued discovery. Just as uncovering hidden stars takes research, good comparison and contrast may take some study, but the acquired insight is worth the effort. As Sagan explained, a bold revelation has value:

"When you make the finding yourself—even if you're the last person on Earth to see the light—you'll never forget it."

Types of Comparison-and-Contrast Essays

The comparison-and-contrast format is suitable for a wide range of topics. Following are some common types of comparison-and-contrast essays:

- **Essays on historic figures or events** ("The Visions of Martin Luther King, Jr., and Nelson Mandela")
- **Comparison and contrast in the humanities** ("Monet's Impressionism vs. Seurat's Pointillism")
- **Reports on consumer goods** ("This Year's New Cars")

In this chapter, you will read the work of several students at City High School in Iowa City, Iowa. As you'll see, they used techniques of the writing process to write "Working Out Possibilities," a comparison-and-contrast article published in *the little hawk*, the school newspaper.

Prewriting

Choosing Your Topic

There is virtually no limit to the kinds of topics you can address in a comparison-and-contrast essay. Choose two or more subjects that invite comparison because they are related in some way or because they are aspects of the same subject. Use the following strategies to choose a topic:

For more help finding a topic, explore the activities and suggestions in the Choosing a Topic section of the Exposition lesson.

Strategies for Generating a Topic

1. **Finding Related Pairs** Explore possible topics in terms of clear opposites (*spring–autumn*), clear similarities (*marching band–symphonic band*), or close relationships (*photographs–videotape*). Start with names of people, places, objects, or ideas. Then, note a related subject that comes to mind. As you create the list, be aware of the relationships that interest you, and then choose one to develop.
2. **Listing and Itemizing** To find a topic that is relevant to your life, make a list of subjects that interest you. For example, you might list sports, music, celebrities, and current events. For each, itemize by brainstorming for a list of comparison-and-contrast pairs that the subject suggests. Review your work to choose a topic you'd like to develop.

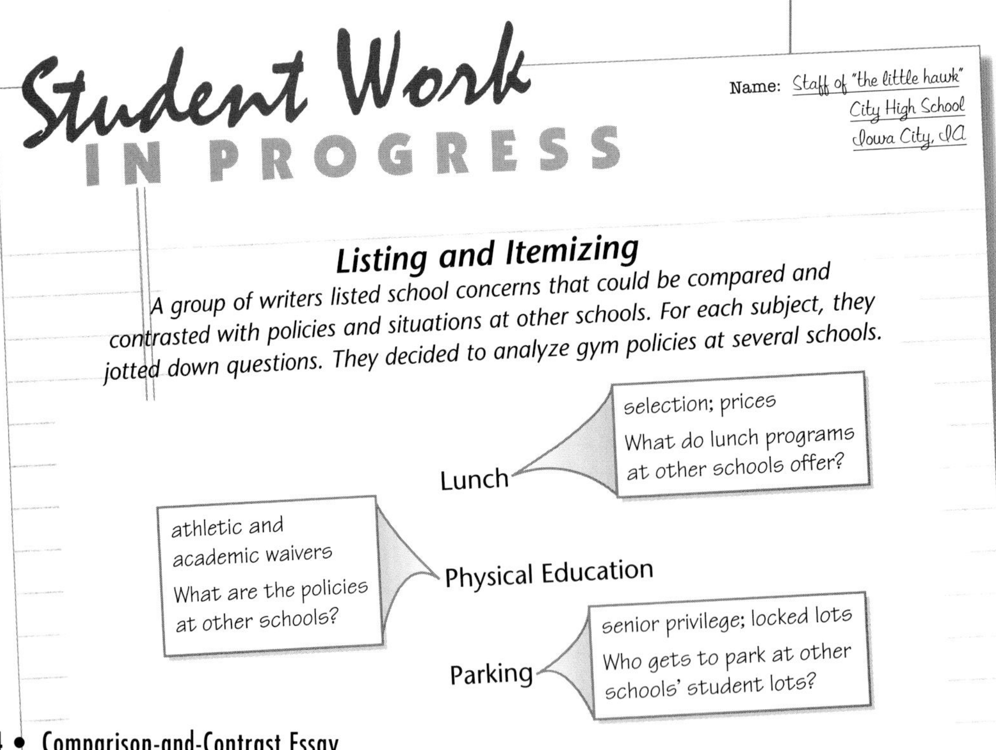

TOPIC BANK

If you are having difficulty finding a topic, consider the following ideas:

1. **Regions of the United States** The national landscape contains a remarkable variety of habitats and climates, ranging from the frigid wilderness of northern Alaska to the tropical bamboo forests of Hawaii. Choose two regions of the United States to compare and contrast.
2. **Famous Athletes** When each was still at the top of his or her game, Michael Jordan retired from basketball, Wayne Gretzky ended his professional hockey career, and Steffi Graf retired from tennis. Write an essay to compare and contrast the positive and negative aspects of a planned early retirement from professional sports.

Love in Ice, Veronica Ruiz de Velasco, Courtesy of the artist

Responding to Fine Art

3. Although dance is common in most cultures, dance styles can vary according to generation, region, and even purpose. Let "Love in Ice" inspire your own comparison and contrast of dance. In an essay, discuss the similarities of at least two dance styles.

Responding to Literature

4. In Shakespeare's *Romeo and Juliet*, the playwright tells a love story in contrasts. Using the Capulets and the Montagues as your subjects, compare and contrast the two families at the center of the feud. You can find the play in *Prentice Hall Literature: Timeless Voices, Timeless Themes*, Gold.

Cooperative Writing Opportunity

5. **Comparison of Exercise Programs** With a group, compare and contrast the exercise plans your classmates follow. One student can study the benefits of team sports; another can report on the benefits of aerobic exercise; a third can research the results of weight training. Share your findings with the class.

9.2

Narrowing Your Topic

Once you've chosen a topic, consider how much information you'll need to present in order to develop all points of comparison and contrast. Some topics are so broad that they cannot easily be managed in an essay. For example, a useful comparison and contrast of New York City and Paris might require hundreds of pages. However, by narrowing the focus to address a specific topic—such as museums, tourist attractions, or transit systems—you could present an effective comparison-and-contrast essay.

Considering Your Audience and Purpose

Identify Your Audience

Take a moment to think about the people you expect to read your comparison-and-contrast essay. Your intended audience will direct the types of information you include—from the level of vocabulary you choose to the level of detail or analysis you pursue. For example, as the chart at the bottom of this page suggests, your audience may even direct your purpose.

Specify Your Purpose

To identify a purpose for your essay, consider what kind of insight you want your readers to gain. Look at these options:

- **To persuade:** If you want your readers to accept your opinion that one subject is better or more desirable than the other, your purpose will be to persuade.
- **To explain:** If you want your readers to understand something about the subjects, your purpose will be to explain.

Consider your topic, your audience, and your purpose to arrive at a framework for the direction your writing will take.

Topic: The Internet vs. The Library	
Audience	**Purpose**
All readers	To **describe** the similarities and differences
Older adults who prefer to use a library	To **persuade** readers that the Internet is a more convenient research tool
Children and readers who aren't familiar with the Internet	To **explain** how each works, what each can do, and how they are similar and different

To help define your specific purpose in writing a comparison-and-contrast essay, use the interactive examples of writing purposes. You can find them in the Exposition lesson.

Gathering Details

To make your writing detailed and concrete, include facts, examples, descriptions, and other information that will show the similarities and differences between your subjects. You might need to tap your own personal experiences, find out about the experiences of your friends, or conduct more extensive research. To make this information collecting easier, use your preliminary findings to identify a limited number of comparisons to pursue.

Identifying Points of Comparison As you generate the details to use in your comparison-and-contrast essay, look at the ideas you've collected, and then consider the main elements you will discuss in your draft. Here are some examples:

TOPIC: Paper Bags vs. Plastic Bags at the Grocery Store

POINTS OF COMPARISON: Convenience, durability, effects on the environment

TOPIC: Action Movies vs. Romantic Comedies

POINTS OF COMPARISON: Story lines, insight into life, special effects

Once you identify the main points of comparison, use this information to guide further detail gathering.

Research Tip

If you need to consult reference material, gather details for each one of your subjects separately.

Student Work IN PROGRESS

Name: Staff of "the little hawk"
City High School
Iowa City, IA

Identifying Points of Comparison

The staff of the little hawk *found that in some schools, athletes or those who carried a heavy academic load were sometimes excused from taking gym. The writers chose three schools to compare and generated this chart to help them gather details about this situation.*

	Physical Education Requirement	Academic Waivers	Athletic Waivers
City High	Gym class once every three days	no	yes
Solon	One credit of PE each year	yes	no
CR Washington	One class of PE every other day	juniors and seniors only	yes

Drafting

Shaping Your Writing

Organize to Show Comparisons and Contrasts

Once you have identified points of comparison and contrast, you have done a large part of the organization of your ideas. Next, think about the order in which you want to present your details. Consider these options:

- **Subject-by-Subject Organization** When you use this organization, you compare your subjects as complete units. First, discuss all the features of one subject, and then discuss all the features of the other. While this format allows you to focus on one subject at a time, be careful to address the same features and to devote equal time to each subject.
- **Point-by-Point Organization** This organization allows you to move between your subjects as you discuss points of comparison. First, compare one element of both subjects, and then address another element of both subjects, until you have addressed all the features. This method allows you to sharpen your points of comparison and contrast. It also makes it easier to address each feature for both subjects.

For more instruction on organizing your essay, see the audio-annotated models of comparison-and-contrast organization. You can find them in the Exposition lesson.

Student Work IN PROGRESS

Name: Staff of "the little hawk"
City High School
Iowa City, IA

Planning a Subject-by-Subject Organization

The writers arranged their information using a subject-by-subject organization. This plan allows readers to understand each school's program as a whole.

City High
- A. Requirements
- B. Waivers—academic and athletic
- C. Program's strengths or weaknesses

Solon
- A. Requirements
- B. Waivers—academic and athletic
- C. Program's strengths or weaknesses

CR Washington
- A. Requirements
- B. Waivers—academic and athletic
- C. Program's strengths or weaknesses

Providing Elaboration

Whether your purpose in comparing and contrasting two subjects is to describe, to persuade, or to explain, provide enough detail to fully develop your points of comparison and contrast. It is not enough to say that cereal is a more nutritious meal than buttered toast. A good writer supports this conclusion with facts.

Support Generalizations With Specifics

Don't point out differences and similarities without including facts or information to back up your assertions. For example, if you were comparing and contrasting classical music and popular music, you'd need to do more than just state conclusions you've drawn. Include support that develops each point you make.

In this example, the writer supports a generalization by showing how it applies to a specific piece of music.

▲▼ Critical Viewing What points of comparison do these photographs emphasize? **[Compare and Contrast]**

GENERALIZATION: With some attention, listeners can usually identify a main musical theme and its variations in classical music.

SUPPORT: For example, Pachelbel's *Canon* takes an eight-note phrase and, through harmony and variation, develops it into a complex composition.

In the next example, the writer offers a generalization to comment on the prevalence of popular music as a soundtrack to life. To elaborate on this idea, a supporting sentence identifies several instances in which music provides such a soundtrack.

GENERALIZATION: In contrast, popular music forms a soundtrack in our lives, and in some cases, we may not even be listening.

SUPPORT: Popular music can be heard as we drive to work, shop in a store, watch a movie, or eat dinner in a restaurant.

Revising

After you complete your first draft, review your structure, analyze your paragraphs, study your sentences, and evaluate your word choices. This revision will strengthen your writing.

Revising Your Overall Structure

Frame Your Findings: Revive Your Introduction

Your comparison-and-contrast essay should include at least two subjects, their similarities and differences, and your reasons for writing about them. To make your purpose clear to readers, take advantage of the opportunities your introduction presents. This opening paragraph should introduce the main idea you want to convey about the comparison and contrast, and it should also prove to readers that the analysis is valid.

REVISION STRATEGY

Improving Your Lead

Your lead, the first several sentences of your introduction, should set the stage for your comparison by presenting your subject in an interesting light. Journalists often use quotations, statistics, or descriptions to show readers the relevance or importance of the story that will follow. Review the lead you've written. Borrowing from news writers, brainstorm for ideas that will perk up your lead. Jot down several different suggestions, and then choose the one that you like best.

Student Work IN PROGRESS

Name: Staff of "the little hawk"
City High School
Iowa City, IA

Improving Your Lead

The writers of this article wanted their readers to be interested as soon as they started reading, so they improved their lead with more vivid language.

Ever since the dawn of required physical education in the public-school systems of America, complaints about nine-minute runs have echoed throughout locker rooms across the country. CHS is no different.

^ The Iowa legislature mandates that every student attending a public high school in the state must complete at least one fifty-minute physical education class per week for every term enrolled.

Revising Your Paragraphs

Make Comparisons and Contrasts Clear

Once you confirm your overall structure, focus on individual paragraphs. Whether you use a subject-by-subject organization or a point-by-point plan, each body paragraph should be unified: All of the sentences should work together to develop a single main idea.

Point-by-Point Body Paragraphs These paragraphs offer a convenient place to show comparisons and contrasts. As you move from a discussion of one subject to the other, use transitional words that make the similarities and differences clear.

EXAMPLE: *In terms of size,* the parrot is larger than the parakeet.

Subject-by-Subject Body Paragraphs Your points of comparison will be spread into separate paragraphs when you use a subject-by-subject organization. To remind readers of the connections and contrasts you want to show, use comparative or superlative forms of modifiers. In some cases, readers may not get the full elaboration until a later paragraph, but words like *cleaner, more powerful,* or *most expensive* will guide them through your analysis.

EXAMPLE: The parrot is *more friendly, more social, and more colorful* than the parakeet.

▲ Critical Viewing
If you were to compare this parrot to a bird common in your region, what points of comparison might you emphasize? **[Analyze]**

REVISION STRATEGY
Refining or Adding Connecting Sentences

Review each body paragraph to be sure that you lead the reader to see the comparisons and contrasts that you draw. Identify the places where you address each subject: Use one color to underline every instance in which you refer to one subject, and use a second color to underline every reference to the other subject. To evaluate your writing in places where the colors meet, judge the connection between the two subjects. Add transitional words or phrases to make the shift more clear.

- **Transitions that show similarities:** *all, similarly, both, in the same way, equally*
- **Transitions that show differences:** *on the other hand, in contrast, however*
- **Comparative modifiers to compare two items:** *richer, busier, brighter, more confusing, more colorful*
- **Superlative modifiers to compare three or more items:** *richest, busiest, brightest, most confusing, most colorful*

Revising Your Sentences

To review your essay at the sentence level, review the verb tense used most in your draft. Revise any unnecessary changes in verb tense.

Make Verb Tense Work for You

The tense of a verb expresses time by showing when events happened in a sequence. Unless you want to show action in the past, present, or future, the verb tense of your writing should be consistent. For example, if you are writing about two subjects that still exist, use the present tense exclusively. On the other hand, if you discuss an event that happened in the past or compare items in different time periods, you may need to make use of the past tense. Evaluate the verbs in your draft to avoid unnecessary shifts in verb tense.

Language Lab CD-ROM

For more on the six tenses of verbs, see the Principal Parts of Verbs lesson and the Verb Tense lesson.

REVISION STRATEGY
Listing Verbs to Evaluate the Use of Tense

Skim through your draft to find all the verbs, and write them on a narrow strip of paper. As you read each sentence, confirm that the verb tenses you've chosen make sense. Review your list to identify verb shifts, and make sure that any verb shifts you see are necessary to indicate a time shift. Make revisions as necessary.

Student Work IN PROGRESS

Name: Staff of "the little hawk"
City High School
Iowa City, IA

Evaluating Verb Tense

By making a list of the verbs they used, the writers were able to see how they could change some verb tenses for more consistency in their writing.

are required

is
~~has been~~
can choose
~~have chosen~~

Students at Solon are required to take one credit of PE each year, or one-half credit of PE each semester. Since the school's calendar ~~has been~~ is based on quarters and semesters, students ~~have chosen~~ can choose whether to take one semester of PE every other day or one quarter of PE every day.

Grammar in Your Writing

Six Tenses of Verbs

The **verb tenses** express time and clarify the sequence of events. The basic forms of the six tenses show the time of an action or condition in the present, past, or future. Each verb form shows when an action happens and whether it is still happening. Use the following as a guide to the correct use of the six tenses of verbs.

Present indicates an action that happens regularly or states a general truth:

I take my dog Squeegee for a walk every morning.

Past indicates an action that has already happened:

We walked earlier than usual yesterday.

Future indicates an action that will happen:

We will walk on the beach this summer.

Present perfect indicates an action that happened at some indefinite time in the past or an action that happened in the past and is still happening now:

We have walked here almost every day for two years.

Past perfect indicates an action that was completed before another action in the past.

We had walked around the corner when Squeegee started to bark.

Future perfect indicates an action that will have been completed before another:

We will have walked two hundred miles before I need new shoes.

Find It in Your Reading Review an essay you have read. Look for examples of at least four verb tenses. Note the way in which these verb tenses indicate how an action relates in time to other actions being discussed.

Find It in Your Writing As you revise your draft, identify any shifts in verb tense. Make sure that each one is correct and necessary.

To learn more about verbs, see Chapter 17.

Revising Your Word Choice

Vary Word Use

In your essay, you move back and forth between two subjects, frequently naming your subjects and points of comparison for clarity. While you want to communicate clearly, avoid repeating the same words over and over. For variety, use synonyms, words that are similar in meaning, or pronouns, such as *it* or *they*, to break up repetition. Look at this example:

REPETITIVE WORD: At amusement parks, I enjoy the *Ferris wheel* most. I go to the *Ferris wheel* first. The *Ferris wheel* offers fantastic bird's-eye views, and the *Ferris wheel* is slow enough that I don't feel sick.

REVISED: At amusement parks, I enjoy the *Ferris wheel* most. I go to *that ride* first. *This giant hoop* offers fantastic bird's-eye views, and *it* goes slowly enough that I don't feel sick.

▲ Critical Viewing What other amusement park attraction might make a good subject for comparison and contrast with the Ferris wheel? **[Evaluate]**

REVISION STRATEGY
Identifying Repeated Words

As you review your draft, create a color-coding system to identify words that you've used frequently. Use one color to circle your first point of comparison, a second color to circle your second point of comparison, and two other colors to circle the names of your main subjects. Using the colors you assigned, underline pronouns or synonyms you've used to create variety. Evaluate each word you've identified by studying your draft one color at a time. If you have used a highlighted word frequently without using any synonyms or pronouns, challenge yourself to introduce at least two synonyms and one pronoun.

Peer Review

Once you've finished revising your essay on your own, ask a small group of classmates to provide feedback on it. Peer reviewers can give objective opinions about whether your points of comparison and contrast are clear.

Showing

Read your essay twice to the group. During your first reading, have your classmates simply listen. Ask your peers to complete two lists as you read your draft again. Reviewers can jot down one list of similarities they feel you've communicated or shown effectively and a second list of differences that you made clear. Use their lists—and any discussion the reading generates—to decide whether you have done your job effectively.

9.5 Editing and Proofreading

Errors in spelling, punctuation, and grammar can distract your readers from the content of your essay. Carefully proofread your essay so that it is error-free.

Focusing on Grammar

As you proofread your paper, look closely at the grammar of words you have chosen. Use these guidelines to help you:

- **Pronoun reference** Wherever you used a pronoun—such as *he, she, it, they,* or *them*—check the clarity of the reference.
- **Degrees of comparison** Be sure that you have used the correct form when comparing two items. For further instruction, review the box below.

Learn More

For more on pronoun and antecedent agreement, see Chapter 25.

Grammar in Your Writing

Degrees of Comparison

Most modifiers have a *positive* form, a *comparative* form for comparing two items, and a *superlative* form for comparing more than two items.

ADJECTIVES

Positive	Comparative	Superlative
tall	taller	tallest
eager	more eager	most eager
good	better	best

ADVERBS

Positive	Comparative	Superlative
early	earlier	earliest
eagerly	more eagerly	most eagerly
well	better	best

When in doubt about forming a comparison, check a dictionary. If no acceptable *-er* or *-est* forms are listed, use *more* and *most.*

Find It in Your Reading Review an essay you have read. Find two examples of modifiers that demonstrate a degree of comparison.

Find It in Your Writing Identify at least two modifiers that show a degree of comparison in your essay. If you have not used two, challenge yourself to add one. In all cases, check that you have used the correct form.

To learn more about degrees of comparison, see Chapter 26.

9.6

Publishing and Presenting

Building Your Portfolio

Sharing your comparison-and-contrast essay with others can give them a fresh insight into your subject. Consider the following suggestions for publishing and presenting:

1. **Make a Photo Montage** Using images that stress the comparisons and contrasts your essay develops, create a poster that combines your essay with the photographs or illustrations that support your ideas.
2. **Publish Your Essay On-line** Share your comparison-and-contrast essay with others who are interested in your subject by posting it on your school Web site. To reach a wider audience, consider other sites on the Web that may reach people who could benefit from your analysis.

Reflecting on Your Writing

Think about the experience of writing your essay. Use the questions that follow to help you get started. Then, jot down your ideas, and add your reflection to your writing portfolio.

- Did you start to look differently at your subjects?
- Which strategy for prewriting, drafting, revising, or editing helped you the most?

Internet Tip

To see model essays scored with this rubric, go to **www.phschool.com**

Rubric for Self-Assessment

Use the following criteria for evaluating your comparison-and-contrast essay:

	Score 4	Score 3	Score 2	Score 1
Audience and Purpose	Clearly provides a reason for a comparison-and-contrast analysis	Adequately provides a reason for a comparison-and-contrast analysis	Provides a reason for a comparison-and-contrast analysis	Does not provide a reason for a comparison-and-contrast analysis
Organization	Successfully presents information in a consistent organization best suited to the topic	Presents information using an organization suited to the topic	Chooses an organization not suited to comparison and contrast	Shows a lack of organizational strategy
Elaboration	Elaborates several ideas with facts, details, or examples; links all information to comparison and contrast	Elaborates most ideas with facts, details, or examples; links most information to comparison and contrast	Does not elaborate all ideas; does not link some details to comparison and contrast	Does not provide facts or examples to support a comparison and contrast
Use of Language	Demonstrates excellent sentence and vocabulary variety; includes very few mechanical errors	Demonstrates adequate sentence and vocabulary variety; includes few mechanical errors	Demonstrates repetitive use of sentence structure and vocabulary; includes many mechanical errors	Demonstrates poor use of language; generates confusion; includes many mechanical errors

9.7 Student Work IN PROGRESS

FINAL DRAFT

◀ Critical Viewing
How does this gym class compare with the ones you attend? **[Relate]**

Working Out Possibilities

Elizabeth Dunbar, Maggie McCray, Cassie McKinstry, and Emily Szeszycki, with additional reporting by Liz Humston

***Staff of* the little hawk**
City High School
Iowa City, Iowa

Ever since the dawn of required physical education in the public-school systems of America, complaints about nine-minute runs and stinky sweat pants have echoed throughout locker rooms across the country. CHS is no different. The Iowa legislature mandates that every student attending a public high school in the state must complete at least one fifty-minute physical

In the introductory paragraph, precise details like "nine-minute runs" and "locker rooms" invite readers to relate to the subject of high-school gym classes.

education class per week for every term enrolled. If students wish to graduate early, they are not required to make up the PE credits that they will be missing by doing so.

The final sentence of the introduction explains that each school has a different gym requirement. Next, the writers use a subject-by-subject, or school-by-school, analysis set off by subheads.

Despite these low state requirements, many Iowa high schools, including CHS, require their students to take (and pass) more gym classes than necessary in order to graduate. But even though the schools in IC and surrounding cities all require more than the minimum, their methods of acquiring the credits differ greatly.

City High

First, the writers discuss their own school, addressing three points of comparison: requirements, academic and athletic waivers, and the strengths or weaknesses of the school's program.

CHS's graduation requirement of gym class (55 minutes) once every three days, with the exception of an athletic waiver, including one trimester of Health PE, exceeds those of the state.

Even with the extra 50 minutes a week, PE instructor Diane Delozier thinks the students need more gym time. "Because gym is only once every three days, we see no consistency in a student's performance," Delozier said. "There's no chance for improvement. The student comes back after two days and is struggling to do the activities."

However, Delozier does think that CHS has advantages over other schools. The juniors and seniors get to choose what units they do, unlike those in some other schools. Also, CHS has some units that other schools don't offer, such as rappelling, CPR, social dancing, and cross-country skiing.

Academic waivers have also come up in discussion among CHS students. "I think they're a great idea," Clare Martin, '00, said. "It seems ridiculous that we need to take four years of PE and only two years of math and science."

Delozier, however, disagrees. "It's not the same thing. It's an issue of activity versus intellect," Delozier said. "Students won't get a workout with a good GPA."

Solon

Second, the writers discuss Solon High School, addressing the same three points of comparison.

Students at Solon are required to take one credit of PE each year, or one-half credit of PE each semester. Since the school's calendar is based on quarters and semesters, students can choose whether to take one semester of PE every other day or one quarter of PE every day.

Instead of rewarding athletes with PE waivers, Solon High School has a different waiver system. If students are taking so many classes that they don't have room in their schedule for PE, they can get a waiver. Students can waive one half credit each year, but they must take the other half credit.

Not only is Solon's scheduling of PE flexible, but students can also choose what kind of PE class they want to take. The two specialized classes are conditioning class, which includes training and weight lifting; and aerobics, which includes stunts and tumbling. Students also have the option of taking a normal PE class that is separated by grade and includes various units.

If senior Kurt Kruckeberg could change something about the PE system, he would want the option of athletic waivers. A lot of people have pushed for waivers, but nothing has really happened. However, Solon is expecting some new administrators, and the issue of athletic waivers might come up again. "I think [waivers] would be very helpful," Kruckeberg said. "I have a lot of friends who get frustrated because they have to take PE in addition to weight lifting and practicing outside of school."

Shorter paragraphs and direct quotations are part of the format for newspaper articles.

CR Washington

CR Washington runs on a trimester system, and PE classes meet every other day. Students at Washington are allowed one athletic PE waiver each year. Juniors and seniors are also allowed one academic waiver each year. If a student's schedule is completely full, he or she does not have to take PE for that trimester. Jim Rusick, the head of the school's athletic department, feels that the program has advantages and disadvantages.

An analysis of the third school follows the established format by presenting the same three points of comparison.

"It rewards students who are working hard," Rusick said. "But it also allows the kids who might really need the strength and physical activity to slip through the cracks."

Some students are able to avoid physical education for an entire year if they are especially involved. Senior Erika Fry is one of those students. "I haven't had PE for the last two years, and I think it's great," Fry said. "I play golf, and I have a full schedule, so I am really glad I have that option."

Although students at Washington may not be seasoned social dancers like the students at CHS, the student body seems to have a positive attitude about it.

"Of course, some people complain, some always will," Rusick said. "But I think that most students are satisfied with how much PE they have to take."

Following journalistic style, which calls for main ideas at the start of articles, this article has no formal concluding paragraph. However, the story's title and the text of the article suggest the writers' conclusion: City High might learn from the experience of the other schools.

◀ Critical Viewing Identify two points of contrast to guide an analysis of the two photographs accompanying this article. **[Analyze]**

Chapter 10 Exposition

Cause-and-Effect Essay

▲ **Critical Viewing** What are three causes that led to the development of the space shuttle program? **[Analyze]**

Cause-and-Effect Analysis in Everyday Life

From the time we were young children, we began analyzing causes and effects. What causes the sun to rise every morning? Why does it snow? Why are the days shorter in the winter than they are in the summer? As we grow older, our questions often become more complex or more focused on specific areas of interest. We might consider what enables a rocket to be propelled into space, examine the effects of increased traffic on busy city streets, or look for a reason that a popular rock band decided to break up. Examining all of these types of causes and effects helps us better understand and appreciate our world, and it can even help us shape the directions of our lives.

What Is a Cause-and-Effect Essay?

Expository writing is writing that informs or explains. A **cause-and-effect essay** is a specific type of expository writing that focuses on an action or a series of actions that cause other actions or results. A good cause-and-effect essay features

- an introduction that presents a general statement about how one event or situation causes another.
- an analysis of the features or aspects of the **cause,** the event or condition that produces a specific result.
- an explanation of the **effect,** the outcome or result.
- facts, statistics, and other types of details to support the conclusions about both the causes and the effects.
- a clear and consistent organization.

To see the criteria upon which your cause-and-effect essay may be judged, preview the Rubric for Self-Assessment on page 144.

Writers in ACTION

Writer Henry David Thoreau conducted an experiment to test cause-and-effect relationships on a large scale. He built a cabin himself and lived there in solitude for two years. In his book Walden, *he wrote:*

"I went to the woods because I wished to live deliberately, to front only the essential facts of life, and see if I could not learn what it had to teach, and not, when I came to die, discover that I had not lived."

Types of Cause-and-Effect Essays

Cause-and-effect writing is suitable for subjects in a variety of fields. Following are some specific types of cause-and-effect essays you may encounter:

- **Lab reports** give causes and effects in a science experiment.
- **History papers** explain relationships among events.
- **Health articles** discuss connections among factors influencing well-being; for example, links among diet, heredity, behavior, and lifestyle.

In this chapter, you can follow the development of an essay written by Sonia Reimann of Athens High School in Athens, Texas. Sonia used the stages of the writing process to explore the beneficial effects of laughter. You can see her final draft at the end of the chapter.

10.2 Prewriting

Choosing Your Topic

A successful cause-and-effect essay begins with a topic involving two events that are clearly linked. One of the events must be a cause of the other. However, if the causes and effects are too obvious, readers may not be interested. Here are some methods you can use to generate potential topics:

1. **Current Events** Scan newspapers or magazines for headlines that interest you. Jot them down in the center column of a three-column chart. To the left of each of the headlines, write causes; to the right, list possible effects. Then, review this chart to choose a topic to develop.

2. **Emotional Thermometer** In a sketch of a thermometer, list the different intensities of various emotions, from least to most intense. To the left of each emotion, list an event that might cause it; to the right, list an effect this emotion can produce. Review your work to choose an interesting topic for a cause-and-effect essay.

For more help choosing a topic, explore the activities and suggestions in the Choosing a Topic section of the Exposition lesson.

Student Work IN PROGRESS

Name: Sonia Reimann
Athens High School
Athens, TX

Using an Emotional Thermometer

Sonia made a thermometer to chart a series of emotions. She decided to write about the causes and effects of laughter.

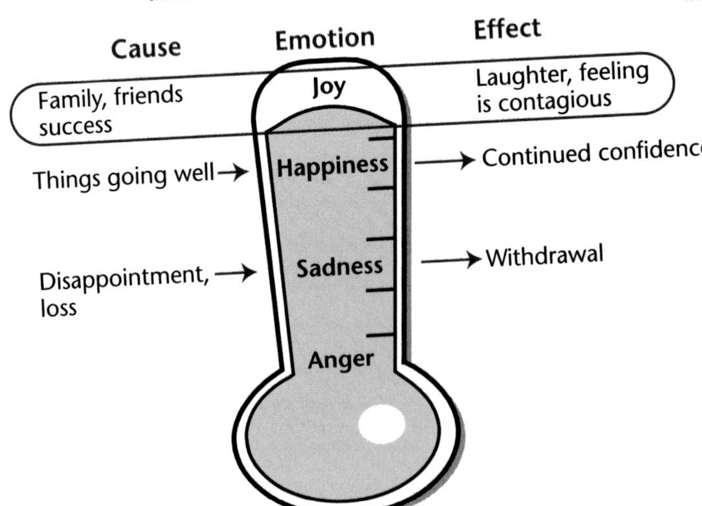

TOPIC BANK

If you have difficulty developing a topic on your own, consider one of these suggestions:

1. **Essay About Year-Round Schools** Year-round schools have effects on students, parents, and teachers. Learn more about the causes and effects of this school schedule, and write an essay to share your findings.
2. **Report on the Effects of Technology** Choose a technological development, such as the spread of cellular phones or the availability of the Internet. In an essay, examine the causes and effects of this development.

Responding to Fine Art

3. Use the painting *Two Lane Road Cut* to spark your own investigation of the construction of a road in your area. In a cause-and-effect essay, explain why the road was built and how the road has changed your community.

Two Lane Road Cut, Woody Gwyn, Courtesy of the artist

Responding to Literature

4. Read "Georgia O'Keeffe" by Joan Didion. Use the piece as the starting point for an essay about the impact of O'Keeffe's work on other artists. You can find "Georgia O'Keeffe" in *Prentice Hall Literature: Timeless Voices, Timeless Themes,* Gold.

Cooperative Writing Opportunity

5. **Survey on the Causes and Effects of Extracurricular Activities** With a group, survey students in your school to learn more about extracurricular activities. Together, devise and use a questionnaire to gather information. Then, split the task of evaluating the results. One writer can analyze the factors influencing students' choices. Another group member can study the effects of the extracurricular involvement. Present your findings to school officials or classmates.

Narrowing Your Topic

You can't produce an effective essay if your subject is too broad to analyze. For example, a topic such as the civil rights movement might captivate readers, but there are too many causes and effects of this movement to address in a short essay. A narrowed focus—like the causes and effects of the March on Washington—might be a more manageable topic for a short paper. Use listing and itemizing to narrow your topic.

Listing and Itemizing to Narrow a Topic

1. Break your subject into subtopics.
2. Itemize each subtopic by identifying causes and effects.
3. Review your list of subtopics and their associated causes and effects, and choose the one you would like to pursue in your cause-and-effect essay.

Research Tip

Before narrowing your topic, read more about the general subject you've chosen. As you complete a preliminary study, you may identify a narrow topic that suits the scope of your writing and your interests.

Considering Your Audience and Purpose

Target Your Audience

Shaping your writing to appeal to your audience is one of the keys to successful writing. To define your audience and target your writing to their needs and interests, prepare an audience profile using the questions shown below. Then, keep these answers in mind as you draft and revise.

AUDIENCE PROFILE

1. **Readers** Who will read your work?
2. **Knowledge Level** How much do your readers already know?
3. **Language** What type of language will best suit your audience?
4. **Interests** What will interest your audience most about your topic?

Refine Your Purpose

The general purpose of a cause-and-effect essay is to explain. However, you might have a more specific purpose in mind, such as to convince readers to take action or to encourage a change. Once you've clarified your purpose, consider how it will affect your choice of language and details.

Gathering Details

Once you've focused your topic and defined your audience and purpose, you may want to plunge right in to writing your first draft. However, you will probably find it easier to write if you take some time to collect facts, statistics, examples, descriptions, and other details that you can use to clearly illustrate the causes and effects you plan to describe. It's not enough simply to say that one event or situation causes another; you have to show *how*.

Use a Cause-and-Effect Organizer

You may want to use an organizer such as the one below to record causes and effects. Write your topic in the center. List causes above it and effects below it. If you know your topic well, you will find it easy to fill in the organizer. If you don't, you may want to do some research to gather the details you'll need.

Writing Lab CD-ROM

You can find a cause-and-effect organizer in the Exposition lesson.

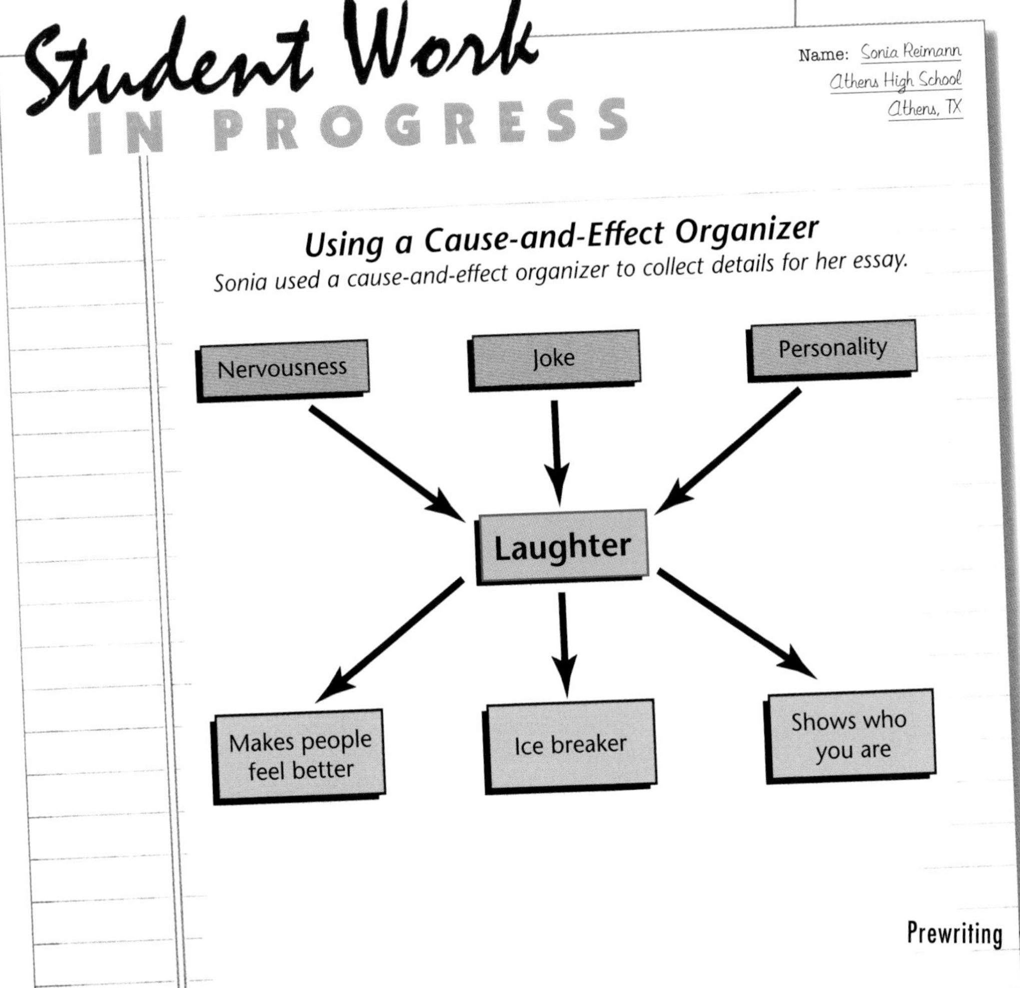

3 Drafting

Shaping Your Writing

Choose an Organization

As you prepare to write your first draft, you should have an organization in mind. Following are two of the possible methods for organizing your essay:

Chronological Order If you describe causes and effects that happen over time, arrange them in the order in which they happened. For example, this type of organization might be appropriate for analyzing the development of a new policy.

EVENT 1 (CAUSE)	Color films become the industry standard in Hollywood.
EVENT 2 (CAUSE/EFFECT)	Interest develops in colorizing old films.
EVENT 3 (CAUSE/EFFECT)	Controversy over this technique builds.
EVENT 4 (CAUSE/EFFECT)	Film critics and moviegoers boycott.
EVENT 5 (EFFECT)	New policies over colorizing emerge.

Order of Importance You can also organize your essay in a sequence based on the relative importance of each idea, event, or situation you are presenting. Begin with your least important point, and work toward your most important point. This type of organization is especially effective when you are presenting a series of effects of a single event. For example, you might use this organization to present the effects of a tornado.

ORDER OF IMPORTANCE

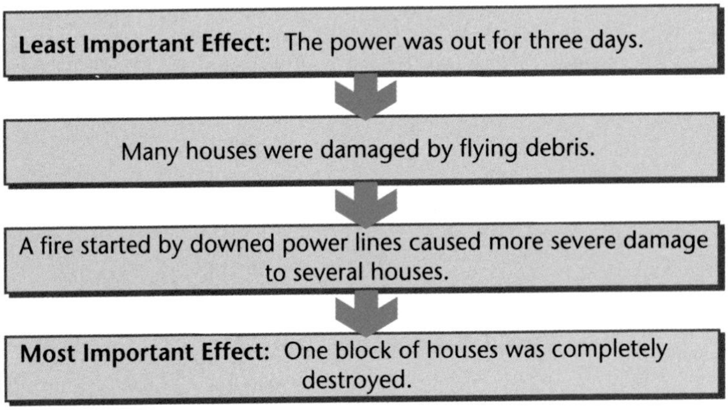

Least Important Effect: The power was out for three days.

↓

Many houses were damaged by flying debris.

↓

A fire started by downed power lines caused more severe damage to several houses.

↓

Most Important Effect: One block of houses was completely destroyed.

Providing Elaboration

As you draft your essay, illustrate each cause and effect through layers of supporting facts, details, examples, and other types of illustrations. In your opening paragraph, introduce your topic, and illustrate why it is important. Follow with a series of topical paragraphs—body paragraphs focusing on a single subpoint of your main topic.

Develop Topical Paragraphs Using the TRI Method

To develop your topical paragraphs fully, try the TRI method. To use this strategy, follow these steps:

1. Write a sentence stating your topic; label it (T).
2. Write a sentence restating your topic; label it (R).
3. Illustrate your point through details, facts, examples, or personal experience; label this section (I). The illustration part of the paragraph may include several sentences.

Once you feel comfortable with the TRI pattern, you can vary the elements to suit the information you address. Consider a TIR or ITR approach when it would work best.

Internet Tip

Search the Internet for more information about your topic. If you are looking for a phrase on an Internet search engine, put parentheses around the phrase when you type it in the search window.

Student Work IN PROGRESS

Name: Sonia Reimann
Athens High School
Athens, TX

Developing Topical Paragraphs

Sonia developed her opening paragraph using TIR, a variation of the TRI pattern. As you can see below, she began by stating the topic. She followed by illustrating how the message affected her, and then she restated the topic in the final sentence.

[T-topic] Laughter can break the tension of some very serious moments. [I-illustrate] On one specific occasion I was ending a visit to Switzerland. I was saying goodbye to my cousin Martin and his family. My aunt gave me a big hug and the sadness began to build. Next was Martin. The tears in my eyes threatened to burst out at any moment. But Martin did something that made me burst with laughter, not tears. He pulled a huge polka-dot handkerchief out and started dabbing my eyes. [R-restatement] Adding laughter changed the scene completely.

10.4 Revising

Revising Your Overall Structure

When a soccer player misses a game-tying goal, he or she usually doesn't get a second chance to score. As a writer, you do have a "second chance" to correct your work and find ways to improve it. This occurs during revision. Take advantage of the opportunity by evaluating your draft carefully.

Clarify Cause-and-Effect Relationships

First, review your entire draft, focusing specifically on the causes and effects you have presented. Check to see that the relationship between the causes and effects is clear. Highlighting these key elements of your draft will help you see the connections you've made.

Use the Revision Checker for transition words to identify places where your writing could be revised for clarity. Find this tool in the Exposition lesson.

REVISION STRATEGY
Color-Coding Causes and Effects

With two highlighters, use one color to mark phrases that present causes and another to mark those that discuss effects. Evaluate the connections between the two. You may need to add details to strengthen the connections, use transitional words or phrases to make the link clear, or eliminate the causes or effects that do not support your main point.

Student Work IN PROGRESS

Name: Sonia Reimann
Athens High School
Athens, TX

Highlighting Sentences to Evaluate Structure

Sonia used highlighting to evaluate the structure of her essay. She added transitional words and phrases to clarify the cause and effect she discussed.

We used his trademark laughter ^so that^ we could get through the pain. . . .

^Because^ I began remembering the powerful effect Martin's laughter had on me,

I started talking about all the crazy things he had said and done. . . .

Revising Your Paragraphs

Add Details to Show Cause and Effect

Once you're confident that the relationships among your causes and effects are clear, analyze each paragraph to see that you have provided a thorough set of facts, details, statistics, examples, or other types of support to illustrate each cause and effect. To identify places to add support for your ideas, use this strategy perfected by professional journalists:

▲ Critical Viewing
What is the effect of having a standard set of questions ready before conducting an interview? **[Evaluate]**

REVISION STRATEGY
Using the Reporter's Formula

Journalists use the five *W*'s to get all the facts into an effective news story. Reporters double-check to be sure they have provided information to tell *who, what, when, where,* and *why* an event happened. You can use this strategy to identify the details you want to add in order to strengthen cause-and-effect connections you've established. Review your paragraphs, and answer the questions shown below. If you cannot answer some of these questions fully, add the information that will provide the answer.

Reporter's Formula	
Who	are the people involved or affected?
What	were the specific reasons it happened? What evidence is there to support this conclusion?
When	did the events take place or the situation develop? When did it start, and when did it end?
Where	did the events take place? Where was the impact greatest?
Why	did it happen?

Revising Your Sentences

Combine Short Sentences

Good writing not only provides the information that readers need, but it also has a rhythm that keeps readers engaged. One way to create a rhythm in your writing is to vary the length of your sentences. As you revise, look for places to combine short sentences and establish greater sentence variety. This will eliminate choppiness and build an interesting rhythm. Use color-coding to analyze the length of your sentences.

REVISION STRATEGY
Color-Coding to Evaluate Sentence Length

Count the number of words in every sentence in your essay. Write the number of words in the margin beside each sentence. When you're done, scan the numbers you've recorded and highlight the sentences you'd like to revise. If you discover that you have many sentences with fewer than ten words, look for places where you can combine short sentences to create longer sentences. Consider these tips:

- Add transitional words or phrases to show clearer connections among the ideas you address.
- Combine two sentences using subordinating clauses that start with conjunctions such as *after*, *although*, *despite*, *if*, and *whenever*.
- Use coordinating conjunctions such as *and*, *but*, *or*, *nor*, *for*, *so*, and *yet*.

Grammar and Style Tip

Short sentences can be used occasionally for a dramatic effect. For instance, if you are describing a person who has experienced a tragic event, you might end the description with a short sentence, such as "He collapsed."

Student Work IN PROGRESS

Name: Sonia Reimann
Athens High School
Athens, TX

Color-Coding Short Sentences

Here is an example of how Sonia color-coded and combined her short sentences.

11 On one specific occasion when I was ending a visit to Switzerland, I was
11 saying goodbye to my cousin Martin and his family. My aunt gave me
13/3 a big hug, and the sadness began to build. Next was Martin, and the tears
12 in my eyes threatened to burst out at any moment.

Grammar in Your Writing

Using Appositive Phrases to Combine Sentences

An **appositive** is a noun or a pronoun placed near another noun or pronoun to identify, rename, or explain it. An **appositive phrase** is an appositive accompanied by other words that modify it.

An appositive phrase functions as a unit, renaming or amplifying the word that precedes it. Appositive phrases are a useful tool for combining sentences. Look at the following examples.

Individual Sentences:	My little brother is a rascal if there ever was one. He's always getting into trouble.
Combined Sentence:	My little brother, **a rascal if there ever was one**, is always getting into trouble.
Individual Sentences:	Advance planning is essential. It is the most effective means of avoiding the problem.
Combined Sentence:	Advance planning, **the most effective means of avoiding the problem**, is essential.
Individual Sentences:	I've devised a more organized schedule. My plan will make life easier for me.
Combined Sentence:	My plan, **a more organized schedule**, will make life easier for me.
Individual Sentences:	The dramatic series won many awards. It also attracts heavy viewer ratings.
Combined Sentence:	The dramatic series, **winner of many awards**, also attracts heavy viewer ratings.
Individual Sentences:	Paulson is the committee leader. Paulson spoke to a group of reporters about the progress of the job.
Combined Sentence:	Paulson, **the committee leader,** spoke to a group of reporters about the progress of the job.

Find It in Your Reading Review a story you have read. Identify one of the appositive phrases that it includes. Then, explain how this appositive phrase adds useful information to the sentence in which it appears.

Find It in Your Writing Combine at least three pairs of short sentences in your draft by using appositive phrases.

For more on appositive phrases, see Chapter 21. For more on combining sentences, see Chapter 22.

Revising Your Word Choice

Delete or Replace Empty and Vague Words

Empty and vague words—such as *really, very, somewhat, thing, good, bad, nice,* and *awful*—do not add to your analysis. Review your draft to identify such language in your writing.

REVISION STRATEGY
Circling Empty or Vague Words

Circle empty or vague words that you find in your writing. Evaluate each word you've marked. Delete those that do not add to the draft, and replace the others with more precise language.

Student Work IN PROGRESS

Name: Sonia Reimann
Athens High School
Athens, TX

Evaluating Empty or Vague Words

Sonia circled weak words, deleting some and replacing others.

Laughter is ~~like~~ a symbol that can instantly join people and solidify ~~real~~ friendships. I became a friend of a girl named Krystle not because she possessed the ~~good~~ qualities of honesty, reliability, and kindness that I normally seek in friends, but because she had an even ~~better~~ rarer quality—she could ~~really~~ make me laugh.

Peer Review

Read Aloud

When you've finished revising on your own, work with a group to make additional revisions. When you read your work aloud to a group, your peers may notice some points you have missed. After you have read your essay twice, choose one of the following points for discussion.

- Is the relationship between cause and effect clear to you?
- Do I need more examples to illustrate any causes or effects? What types of examples would be helpful?

Use feedback from your peers to make further revisions of your draft.

10.5 Editing and Proofreading

Before you create your final draft, correct errors in spelling, punctuation, and grammar.

Focusing on Sentence Clarity

To ensure that your sentences are clear, check that the subjects agree with the verbs, that modifiers are properly placed, and that your punctuation is correct.

- **Subject-Verb Agreement** Find the subject-verb combinations in each sentence, and make sure that you use the form of the verb that agrees with the subject.
- **Punctuation** Check to make sure that you have the right punctuation in the right places. Pay close attention to opening punctuation, such as parentheses or quotation marks, and make sure that each is followed by the related closing punctuation.
- **Placement of Modifiers** In most cases, adverbs and adjectives should be placed next to the words they modify. Check your essay, and make corrections where necessary.

Technology Tip

If you are using the spell-check function on a computer, enter frequently used proper names in the custom dictionary. This way, the correctly spelled name will not be identified as a misspelled word.

Grammar in Your Writing

Placement of Adverbs

Adverbs modify verbs, adjectives, or other adverbs. The placement of adverbs can change the meaning of a sentence. In the following sentences, the location of the adverbs *only* and *usually* affects the meaning.

She learned **only** yesterday that she was hired.
She learned yesterday that **only** she was hired.

She was **usually** cheerful on Monday mornings but not on Tuesdays.
She was cheerful on Monday mornings but **usually** not on Tuesdays.

Find It in Your Reading Rewrite this sentence from "Murderous Mitch" by moving the adverb *just.* Explain how the meaning is altered.

It was "a terrible, towering wall that just fell out of the clouds."

Find It in Your Writing Check all of the adverbs in your essay to make sure that they are placed in a way that makes your intended meaning clear.

6 # Publishing and Presenting

Building Your Portfolio

Once you've completed your final draft, think about the best ways to share it with others. Consider these ideas:

1. **Post It on the Web** If your school has its own Web site, consider using it to publish your complete essay. Another possibility is to search the Web for sites related to your topic. See if one of these sites would be interested in posting your essay.
2. **Create a Class Anthology** Others in your school—including students studying how to write cause-and-effect essays—might benefit from a class anthology of cause-and-effect essays. Work with classmates to assemble your essays into a booklet: design a cover, prepare a title page and table of contents, and choose illustrations.

Reflecting on Your Writing

Take some time to reflect on the experience of writing your essay by answering these questions:

- What would you say are the most effective ways to establish cause and effect?
- Which process skill will help you most in future writing?

Internet Tip

To see model essays scored with this rubric, go to **www.phschool.com**

Rubric for Self-Assessment

Use these criteria to evaluate your cause-and effect-essay.

	Score 4	Score 3	Score 2	Score 1
Audience and Purpose	Consistently targets an audience through word choice and details; clearly identifies purpose in thesis statement	Targets an audience through most word choice and details; identifies purpose in thesis statement	Misses a target audience by including a wide range of word choice and details; presents no clear purpose	Addresses no specific audience or purpose
Organization	Presents a clear, consistent organizational strategy to show cause and effect	Presents a clear organizational strategy with occasional inconsistencies; shows cause and effect	Presents an inconsistent organizational strategy; creates illogical presentation of causes and effects	Demonstrates a lack of organizational strategy; creates a confusing presentation
Elaboration	Successfully links causes with effects; fully elaborates connections among ideas	Links causes with effects; elaborates connections among most ideas	Links some causes with some effects; elaborates connections among most ideas	Develops and elaborates no links between causes and effects
Use of Language	Chooses clear transitions to convey ideas; presents very few mechanical errors	Chooses transitions to convey ideas; presents few mechanical errors	Misses some opportunities for transitions to convey ideas; presents many mechanical errors	Demonstrates poor use of language; presents many mechanical errors

10.7 Student Work IN PROGRESS

FINAL DRAFT

◀ **Critical Viewing** In what ways do friendship and laughter make your daily experiences more pleasant? **[Connect]**

The Music of the Soul

Sonia Reimann
Athens High School
Athens, Texas

One year at the State Fair of Texas, I received a free sample of chocolate. Inside the wrapper, there was a brief note: "Take time to laugh; it's the music of the soul." I hung this chocolate wrapper on a bulletin board above the bed in my room where it remains today. As I scurry through my busy life, sometimes I briefly glance up at

To capture her reader's attention, Sonia begins her essay with a vivid description of an event in her life. She also uses the paragraph to state her thesis.

the note and reflect on this message. When you stop to think about it, the powerful effects of laughter might surprise you.

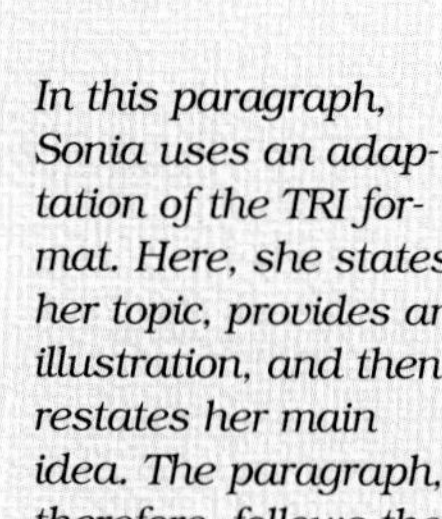

Laughter is a symbol that can instantly join people and solidify friendships. I became a friend of a girl named Krystle not because she possessed the qualities of honesty, reliability, and kindness that I normally seek in friends, but because she had an even rarer quality—she could make me laugh. One day she and I were walking in the mall, window-shopping and running out of conversation. At that point of our friendship, I wasn't sure whether we would be good friends. Suddenly, I saw her picking up a plastic ball in a toy store, dribbling the ball across the floor, and saying, "Come on. Let's play catch!" No one else may have seen the humor in this incident, but I could not control my laughter. Krystle's ability to make me laugh is what makes her special to me. We've been close friends ever since. In this case, laughter cemented a friendship.

In this paragraph, Sonia uses an adaptation of the TRI format. Here, she states her topic, provides an illustration, and then restates her main idea. The paragraph, therefore, follows the TIR format.

Laughter can break the tension of some very serious moments. My immediate family and I live in Texas, but the rest of my relatives live in Switzerland, so I hardly ever get a chance to see them. On one specific occasion when I was ending a visit to Switzerland, I was saying goodbye to my cousin Martin and his family. My aunt gave me a big hug, and the sadness began to build. Next was Martin, and the tears in my eyes threatened to burst out at any moment. But Martin did something that made me burst with laughter, not tears. He pulled a huge polka-dot handkerchief out of his pocket and began dabbing my eyes. Adding laughter changed the scene completely. Martin did things like this all the time—making the unexpected joke, pointing out the ridiculous while everyone else saw the serious, creating laughter where there was none.

In each of the body paragraphs, Sonia uses a chronological order to express the relationship of cause and effect.

Later, tragedy struck. Martin died last May, unexpectedly, at the youthful age of twenty-two. We used his trademark laughter so that we could get through the pain of this terrible loss. I remember my father telling us about his death. My sisters, my mother, and I were weeping. It was a painful moment filled with sorrow. After a short time, however, I thought about Martin's laughter. Because I began remembering the powerful effect Martin's laughter had on me, I started talking about all the crazy things he had said and done. We all began to laugh. My family joined in with more stories about Martin, and, in this way, a sorrowful scene became an on-the-spot, uplifting remembrance of Martin's unique personality.

Sonia shows how Martin's laughter and sense of fun helped his family accept the tragedy. She develops this cause-and-effect connection with details from shared experiences.

Besides changing the tone of some awkward moments, laughter can lighten the mood of a stressful and ordinary day. Some days, I come home from school feeling the pressure of homework or tests or even papers looming on the school horizon. I know many adults get caught up in the same kind of thinking; they may spend free moments thinking about money troubles or work troubles or just hoping to pull themselves out of exhaustion. This mindset doesn't correct itself easily, either. To help myself turn it around, I visit my neighbor. Her children are young and adorable. When I watch her one-year-old laughing over the repetition of climbing in and out of a toy tunnel, I realize that dwelling on my own troubles may not be the right focus. Laughing with children makes me remember what it was like being younger myself. A child's special gifts, curiosity and playfulness, often make me laugh regardless of my previous mood. Maybe this is why the laughter of a child is the most beautiful sound in the world.

In this paragraph, Sonia discusses laughter's power to reduce stress.

You may not always take the time to laugh, but when you take a moment to stop and reflect, you will probably see that humor can help you to cope with many difficult situations, such as major exams, first dates, or even the loss of a loved one. So my chocolate fortune proves truer than I may have previously thought. In the end, there is nothing like a good laugh.

Sonia wraps up her essay by restating her thesis and providing a list of familiar events that broadens her discussion of the effects of laughter.

◀ **Critical Viewing**
Does your first response to this picture support or refute Sonia's ideas? **[Connect]**

Chapter 11

Exposition

Problem-and-Solution Essay

▲ Critical Viewing How do volunteer groups that build low-cost housing provide a unique solution to a problem? **[Analyze]**

Problem-and-Solution Analysis in Everyday Life

During the course of a day, you encounter problem-and-solution analyses in many forms: On radio and television, newscasters report troubles around the world and then share the innovative ways people are working to fix them; advice columnists offer suggestions for problems ranging from grape-juice stains to bankruptcy; and bookstore shelves are full of books on managing time, improving memory, and living a healthier life. While some problems affect individuals and others affect whole communities or countries, each of these is an example of problem-and-solution thinking in action.

What Is a Problem-and-Solution Essay?

A **problem-and-solution essay** is a piece of writing that identifies and explains a problem and then offers a possible solution. An effective problem-and-solution essay includes

- a statement of a problem that is focused enough to be fully developed and supported in an essay.
- a suggested solution.
- facts, statistics, and details that illustrate the problem and how it can be solved.
- a logical organization.

To see the criteria on which your final problem-and-solution essay may be judged, preview the Rubric for Self-Assessment on page 160.

Writers in ACTION

As a public radio journalist, Gene Bryant Johnson reports on the issues that trouble our times. He analyzes problems that face the country and reports on solutions people have undertaken. Johnson says solutions to most problems are within sight:

"The ideas . . . are all around you. Everything that happens in your neighborhood and in your community has a reason and it has an effect. So pay attention."

Types of Problem-and-Solution Writing

Solutions to problems can be presented in a variety of written formats. In addition to essays, the following types of writing can address problems and offer solutions:

- **Formal letters** are sometimes used to offer solutions to public problems. Usually, they are addressed to the person or group with the power to implement a solution.
- **Advice columns** offer solutions to specific problems faced by individuals.
- **Memos and proposals** are used to formally suggest solutions to problems faced by businesses or organizations.

In this chapter, you will follow the development of an essay by Michael C. Mahoney of St. Stephen's School in Hickory, North Carolina. He suggests a solution to the problems caused by increased traffic in his community. You will see how Michael used prewriting, drafting, and revising to develop his essay "Safety and Progress."

2 # Prewriting

Choosing Your Topic

When you select a topic for a problem-and-solution essay, be sure to choose one for which you can offer a realistic solution.

Strategies for Generating Topics

1. **Newspaper Scan** Look through a newspaper for stories about community problems. List problems for which you can imagine a practical solution. Choose one as the topic of your essay.
2. **Sentence Starters** Using the sentence starters on this page, complete each sentence and jot down a few ideas to complete your thoughts. Then, review your writing to choose one of the problems as the topic for your essay.

One thing that really annoys me is __?__.

The biggest problem people my age face is __?__.

A problem I'd like to see solved in my town or city is __?__.

For more help finding a topic, explore the activities and suggestions in the Choosing a Topic section of the Exposition lesson.

Student Work IN PROGRESS

Name: Michael C. Mahoney
St. Stephen's School
Hickory, NC

Using Sentence Starters

Michael used a sentence-starters exercise to find a problem-and-solution essay topic. After completing each sentence starter and talking with family members and neighbors, Michael decided to write his essay on the topic of sidewalks as an investment in community safety.

Life would be better in my community if . . . we recycled.

The biggest problem my town faces is . . . litter.

✓ Our neighborhood would be a better place to live if ~~everyone~~ . . . adults and children were safe from traffic.

A problem I'd like to solve in my school is . . . long lines in the cafeteria.

Most students would like to see a change in . . . the after-school activities offered.

TOPIC BANK

If you have trouble coming up with a topic on your own, consider one of these suggestions:

1. **Essay on School Spirit** Take a look around your school for evidence of student interest in clubs, sports, and school pride. Use your school as the problem or the solution, and write an essay offering advice to any school suffering from a lack of school spirit.
2. **Essay on Recycling Participation** Most communities encourage residents to recycle. Some communities have laws requiring citizens to recycle because people might otherwise not take the trouble to do so. Write an essay in which you suggest a solution to the problem of a lack of participation in voluntary recycling.

Responding to Fine Art

3. While *Gust of Wind at Ejiri, in the Province of Suruga* shows one way to react to dangerous weather conditions, a more practical approach to rain, flood, or strong winds may be more successful. In an essay, advise others about preparing for dangerous weather.

Gust of Wind at Ejiri, in the Province of Suruga. From the series The Thirty-six Views of Fuji, Hokusai, Metropolitan Museum of Art

Responding to Literature

4. Cynthia Rylant's story "Checkouts" tells of a girl who moves to another town. Read the story. Then, in a problem-and-solution essay, suggest methods for overcoming the loneliness such a move presents. You can find this story in *Prentice Hall Literature: Timeless Voices, Timeless Themes*, Gold.

Cooperative Writing Opportunity

5. **Study-Habit Flyers** With a group, create flyers that provide solutions to common study-habit problems. Some group members can interview classmates to identify study problems, others can outline solutions, and others can organize and design the layout of the flyer.

Narrowing Your Topic

After you have selected a problem that needs attention, be sure that it is not too complicated to cover in your essay. Focus your topic so that you can propose realistic solutions. Completing a target diagram may help you narrow a topic.

Use a Target Diagram

Use a target diagram, like the one below, to narrow a broad topic. In the outer circle, write your general topic. Then, to narrow your topic, consider what part of your topic affects you. In the second circle, identify a single aspect of the broad topic. To complete the diagram, challenge yourself to write an even narrower topic in the center of the target.

NARROWING A TOPIC WITH A TARGET DIAGRAM

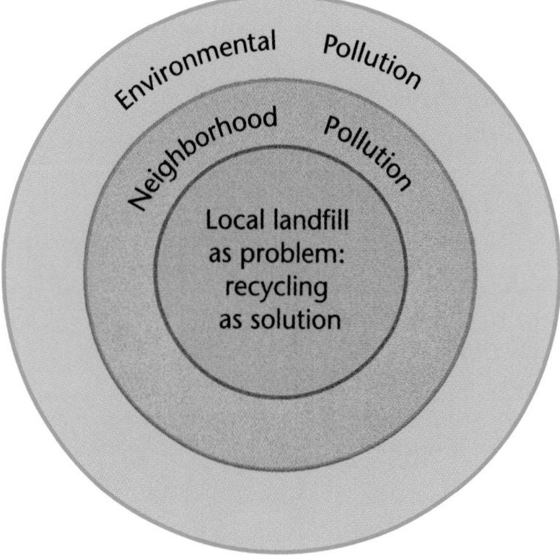

Considering Your Audience and Purpose

Identify Your Audience

When you write a problem-and-solution essay, keep a specific audience in mind: readers who have the ability to implement your suggestions. Use details and vocabulary that will appeal to that audience.

State Your Purpose

You may want to direct your readers to take action, change their behavior, or think about your topic in a new way. State your purpose in a single sentence, and use this purpose to direct your writing.

To help you identify an audience and tailor your appeals for action, use the Audience Profile activity.

Gathering Details

Once you have identified your audience, gather the details that you'll need to write your problem-and-solution essay.

Analyzing the Problem Take the time to jot down information that will clarify the problem. Define the issue, explain why it happens, note who it affects, and collect any other information that will help readers see the trouble.

Seeing the Solution Before you write, gather as much information as you can about the solution you suggest. Note the costs involved, outline the steps that must be taken, consider complications that might arise, and note the benefits of your ideas.

Record Details on a T-Chart

To collect the information you'll need, complete a T-chart like the one shown here. For each solution you propose, write a benefit that will appeal to your audience.

Student Work IN PROGRESS

Name: Michael C. Mahoney
St. Stephen's School
Hickory, NC

Gathering Details With a T-Chart

Michael used a T-chart to make sure he could show the benefits of each part of his suggested solution.

Problem: Wide Roads Are a Danger to Pedestrians, Bike Riders, and Children

SOLUTIONS	BENEFITS
Build sidewalks	Serve as buffer between families' yards and road Give pedestrians a safe place to walk
Add bike lanes	Promote safe bike traffic Enable bikers to travel in safety away from pedestrians
Install railings and dividers	Further ensure that traffic is kept at a safe distance

3 Drafting

Shaping Your Writing

Your problem-and-solution essay must clearly identify and develop two ideas: It must establish the problem and develop a workable solution. To best address this unique form of expository writing, choose an organization that allows you to show the connection between the ideas.

Choose an Appropriate Organization

Review the two approaches presented below. Then, take a look at your prewriting work to decide on the best organization plan.

Point-by-Point Plan To show that your solution addresses a many-sided problem, use a point-by-point organization that explains each part of a problem and its solution in turn. Use this organization if you can break the problem you address into several components.

Point-by-Point Organization

Problem: High-school students have no time.
Solution: They should make an effort to change.

Problem 1: School workload has increased.
Solution 1: Students should set aside time each day.

Problem 2: They have too many commitments.
Solution 2: Setting priorities will help reduce commitments.

Block Plan A block plan allows you to develop the problem fully and then address your solution. This organization is especially useful if you want to outline the steps of your solution.

Block Organization

Problem: Teenagers often want more spending money than they have.
Solution: They should get a handle on their finances.

Problem: A student's life can be expensive.
- movies and entertainment
- clothing
- food

Solution: Establish a plan for informed spending.
- make a budget
- find activities that are inexpensive

Providing Elaboration

Unless you are an expert yourself, your proposed solution will not make instant believers of your readers. You must demonstrate—with facts, statistics, examples, anecdotes, testimonials, or personal experiences—that your solution is both workable and likely to be the best one proposed. This may require some research on your part to locate data that will support your solution.

Using Examples and Anecdotes Depending on your topic, you can draw examples from case studies or personal experiences. Examples help your readers to see vivid and powerful depictions of the problem, as well as the proposed solution. Such examples can help you persuade your readers to agree with you.

Pointing to Supports Look for places where an example or anecdote would help you clarify your point or help persuade your readers. If you don't have such material available as you draft, indicate an idea in your draft. Later, go in search of these details, and add them to your essay.

Student Work IN PROGRESS

Name: Michael C. Mahoney
St. Stephen's School
Hickory, NC

Pointing to Supports

As Michael shaped his essay and selected his point-by-point action statements, he looked for details that would support his suggestions.

Give Personal Experience

Our town has always been known as a friendly place. People are out walking, children play in the yards, and bike riders wheel around the neighborhood. Many of the places I used to ride to on my bike will be off-limits for safety reasons. My friends and I will be driven to places that we used to be able to ride to on our own.

Revising Your Overall Structure

Be sure that your paragraphs make sense in the order in which you have arranged them. The main point of one paragraph should lead logically to the main point of the next.

REVISION STRATEGY
Highlighting Topic Sentences

To evaluate the order of your ideas, highlight the topic sentence of each paragraph. Review your paragraph order, assigning numbers to show a revised order if necessary.

Revising Your Paragraphs

Look at your paragraphs to be sure that the details support or explain the main idea.

REVISION STRATEGY
Color-Coding to Eliminate Generalizations

Look back at the main idea you highlighted in each paragraph. In blue, underline sentences that restate the idea. In red, underline sentences that support or develop the idea. If you have more sentences underlined in blue than in red, you are probably making generalizations without supporting them.

Student Work IN PROGRESS

Name: Michael C. Mahoney
St. Stephen's School
Hickory, NC

Supporting Generalizations

In this paragraph, Michael discovered that he was restating the problem several times without providing concrete support. He added details to support his main idea.

Building new roads without sidewalks will make our town more like a highway attraction, where people are always enclosed by their cars. New roads will cause more traffic to come to my neighborhood. ^The additional traffic will create the potential for more accidents, injuries, and deaths. Many of the places I used ride to on my bike will be off-limits for safety reasons.

Revising Your Sentences

Combine for Sentence Variety

A series of short, choppy sentences may prevent your readers from seeing the connections between your ideas. Whenever possible, vary your sentence structure by combining two or more short sentences into one longer sentence. One way to combine sentences is to create a complex sentence.

REVISION STRATEGY
Color-Coding to Identify Sentences to Combine

Reread your essay. In red, bracket each sentence that is made up of a single independent clause. If ideas in two consecutive simple sentences are related, consider combining them in a complex sentence.

Use the revision checker to analyze your sentence length. You can find it in the Toolkit.

Grammar in Your Writing

Creating Complex Sentences

A **complex sentence** includes one independent clause and one subordinate clause linked by a subordinate conjunction.

Common Subordinate Conjunctions

after	because	since	when
although	before	so that	whenever
as	even though	unless	whether
as soon as	if	until	while

When combining two independent clauses, look for a relationship between the ideas and use a subordinating conjunction to create a complex sentence.

To show a time relationship: After she read the newspaper, she told her friends about the candidate's speech.

To show cause and effect: We'll need to get an early start if the weather is bad.

To show a contrast: Although he was disappointed, he knew he had done his best.

Use a comma to separate an introductory subordinate clause from the rest of a sentence. Do not use a comma to separate a subordinate clause at the end of a sentence.

Find It in Your Reading Find an example of a complex sentence in a short story you have read. Identify the relationship between the two clauses.

Find It in Your Writing Find any complex sentences you have used. If you cannot find any complex sentences, challenge yourself to create one.

To learn more about combining sentences, see Chapter 22.

Revising Your Word Choice

Choose Words That Fit Your Audience

Your intended audience has the power to implement the solution you suggest. Evaluate your word choice to make sure that you are using the right level of language for your readers.

REVISION STRATEGY
Circling Suspect Words

Review your draft as if you were a member of the audience you intend to reach. Circle words that such readers may not understand, terms that may need to be defined, or vocabulary that seems too low for your readers. To improve your writing, consider revising the words you've circled.

Student Work IN PROGRESS

Name: Michael C. Mahoney
St. Stephen's School
Hickory, NC

Refining Word Choice

Michael circled and revised words in his draft that were inappropriate for an audience of his classmates.

Another (part) [aspect] of the problem is that many of the (older people) [senior citizens] in our town, who often walk for exercise, will not feel safe on the shoulder of a busy street with traffic flying by [at 40 mph]! A sidewalk with a divider between the street and walking area would (help) [protect] the walkers and allow them to continue their exercise.

Peer Review

Read Aloud

Read your draft to a group of classmates. Ask them to consider these questions as they listen to you read:

- What did you want to know more about?
- Where did you need the connections to be shown more clearly?

Use your reviewers' responses to begin a discussion about your work. Then, make any revisions you feel would improve your writing.

11.5 Editing and Proofreading

Once you have revised your essay for content, review your draft to correct spelling, punctuation, and grammatical errors.

Focusing on Semicolons

Check your draft to make sure that you have used semicolons correctly. They can be used for the following purposes:

- **To separate independent clauses that are related:**
  We hoped for rain; the storm followed immediately.
- **To separate items in a series when the items are lengthy or complicated:**
  I expect to hear from Steven and Joe in St. Louis; Peter and Mariah in Moscow; and Sam in Altoona, Pennsylvania.

Grammar in Your Writing

Punctuating Compound Sentences With Commas and Semicolons

Compound sentences are composed of two independent clauses. They can be punctuated in one of two ways: with a comma or with a semicolon.

• A **comma** must be followed by a coordinating conjunction such as *and, but, or, for,* or *nor*.

INCORRECT: We want improvement, we can't agree about the solution.
CORRECT: We want improvement, **but** we can't agree about the solution.

• A **semicolon** can be used alone to join independent clauses in a compound sentence. It may or may not be followed by a coordinating conjunction.

CORRECT: We want improvement; **however,** we can't agree about the solution.
CORRECT: We want improvement; we can't agree about the solution.

Find It in Your Reading Find an example of a compound sentence in a story you have read recently. Rewrite the sentence using a semicolon.

Find It in Your Writing Check to make sure that you have correctly punctuated the compound sentences in your problem-and-solution essay.

For more on punctuating compound sentences, see Chapter 29.

6 # Publishing and Presenting

Building Your Portfolio

To make the best use of your problem-and-solution essay, share it with people who can help you make a difference. Consider these ideas:

1. **Send a Letter** If your essay addresses a public problem, send it to someone who can put your suggestions into action. Send your essay to the appropriate government official, agency, or group. Save a copy of your letter in your portfolio, along with any reply you receive.
2. **Create a Solutions Handbook** If your essay addresses a problem faced by individuals—such as managing study time—make copies available for others to read. Ask readers for feedback on your ideas.

Reflecting on Your Writing

Reflect on what you've learned by answering these questions in a written response. Add your reflections to your portfolio.

- What have I learned about the problem that I addressed?
- In what ways is a problem-and-solution essay similar to and different from other types of writing?

Internet Tip

To see model essays scored with this rubric, go to **www.phschool.com**

Rubric for Self-Assessment

Use the following criteria to evaluate your problem-and-solution essay:

	Score 4	Score 3	Score 2	Score 1
Audience and Purpose	Contains language and details to successfully engage audience; clearly identifies problem and proposes solution	Contains language and details appropriate for audience and identifies problem and solution	Contains some language and details not suited for audience; contains some details not related to problem or solution	Contains language and details that are not geared for a particular audience; has an unclear purpose
Organization	Presents information clearly in an organization suited to topic consistently, logically, and effectively	Presents most information according to an appropriate organization	Presents several details that detract from main organization	Demonstrates lack of organization
Elaboration	Clearly explains problem; presents a well-elaborated, realistic solution	Has a solution that is supported with details	Presents solution; contains few details to support it	Presents unclear solution; offers no details to support it
Use of Language	Includes wide variety of sentence styles; contains no errors in grammar, punctuation, or spelling	Contains some variety of sentence styles; contains few errors in grammar, punctuation, and spelling	Contains little variety of sentence style; contains some errors in grammar, punctuation, and spelling	Contains no sentence variety; contains many errors in grammar, punctuation, and spelling

Connected Assignment Question-and-Answer Column

When your running shoes wear out unevenly, you can ask for help at the local shoe store or you can write to an expert at a specialty magazine. These experts offer printed or electronically transmitted problem-and-solution essays in a question-and-answer format. Like a traditional problem-and-solution essay, a **question-and-answer column** includes a clearly explained problem, proposes a solution, and explains how the solution would work.

To write a question-and-answer column, use the writing process tips outlined here:

▲ Critical Viewing Why do you think people put creative energy into choosing the gifts they give? **[Hypothesize]**

Prewriting Identify an area of your expertise. For example, you may know a great deal about computers or getting along with friends. Announce your area of expertise, and invite a group of classmates to write questions.

When you receive a question you'd like to answer, use a problem-and-solution organizer like the one shown here to focus your thoughts. Jot down as many solutions as you can imagine. Later, you can decide which ones to develop in your response.

Problem	Solution
Want to find a unique holiday gift without spending lots of money	• Offer services like babysitting or laundry • Put together a memory book • Bake cookies, and include the recipe with the batch

Drafting First, draft the question so that it provides a clear explanation of the problem. Next, draft your answer. Offer one or more possible solutions, explaining how each idea you suggest will solve the problem. You may need to provide direction about implementing the solution you offer. In both question and answer, use polite, formal language.

Revising and Editing Share your draft with a classmate, and discuss whether the problem is sufficiently explained. Ask your partner to tell you whether the solutions are realistic and helpful. If necessary, add details to clarify the problem or suggested solutions.

Publishing and Presenting Get together with classmates to create a question-and-answer bulletin board. Invite other students to submit questions for your response.

Chapter 12

Research

Research Paper

Icebergs, Frederic Edwin Church

▲ **Critical Viewing** What resources could you consult to learn more about the terrain featured in this painting? **[Hypothesize]**

Research in Everyday Life

Your curiosity often directs your informal research—whether you are learning more about a specific breed of puppy by talking to a veterinarian, following your favorite actor's career by watching his biography on television, or scanning books, library resources, or the Internet to understand a weather pattern or to follow up on a science experiment. When your search becomes a more formal pursuit, skills in research and organization allow you to gather information by consulting sources outside your own experiences and to share your findings with others. In the process, research helps you become an expert and provides you with information to help others understand more about the subject you have studied.

What Is a Research Paper?

A **research paper** is a formal, written presentation of your findings on a topic based on information you have gathered from several sources. Effective research writing has

- a clearly stated thesis statement.
- factual support from a variety of outside sources, including direct quotations whose sources are credited.
- a clear organizational strategy.
- a bibliography or a works-cited list that provides a complete listing of research sources.

To preview the criteria upon which your research paper may be evaluated, see the Rubric for Self-Assessment on page 178.

Writers in ACTION

A collector of African American folklore, the writer Zora Neale Hurston (1891–1960) documented the cultural heritage of the American South. By gathering stories and retelling them, Hurston combined research techniques and writing skills to share the legacy of the oral tradition. Of her work, Hurston has said her personal interest fueled her success:

"Research is formalized curiosity. It is poking and prying with a purpose."

Types of Research Papers

Like the range of subjects suited to research, research writing comes in a variety of forms. Following are some of the types of research writing you will encounter:

- **Lab reports** record the purposes, processes, and results of an experiment.
- **Annotated bibliographies** help researchers by providing a list of sources related to a topic. In addition to source information such as title, author, and publication date, the researcher provides evaluations of the material.
- **Documented essays** are short versions of research papers. Because they include only a limited number of research sources, these essays provide full documentation parenthetically within the text.
- **Documentaries** use video, photographs, personal interviews, and narration to present the results of research.

PREVIEW Student Work IN PROGRESS

In this chapter, you will follow the work of Angelika Klien, a student at Sunnyslope High School in Phoenix, Arizona. As you will see, she used writing process strategies to develop her research essay on the history and uses of bubble gum.

2 Prewriting

Choosing Your Topic

When you set out to write a research paper, choose a topic that will hold your interest for the extended amount of time you will devote to it. Beyond this commitment to a topic, be sure there are enough sources of information available. To find a subject, consider one of the following strategies:

1. **Category Brainstorming** Identify a general area of interest, and brainstorm for a list of narrower categories. For example, from the general area of science, you might identify the categories of inventions, technology, and researchers. Within each of these categories, you can narrow your list even further. Review your brainstorming list to choose a topic you'd like to research.
2. **Sentence Starters** Finish one of the following sentence starters to begin generating ideas. Write for five minutes, elaborating on the idea your completed sentence starter presented. Review what you have written to see if you have identified a suitable research topic.

   I wonder why __?__

   I'd like to learn more about __?__
3. **24-Hour List** List the activities, ideas, and items that you encounter during a 24-hour period. Generate a research question that each point on your list suggests. As you jot down ideas, be open to the research possibilities your curiosity generates. Choose one to develop into a research paper.

For more help finding a topic, explore the activities and suggestions in the Choosing a Topic section of the Research Writing lesson.

Student Work IN PROGRESS

Name: *Angelika Klien*
Sunnyslope High School
Phoenix, AZ

Creating a 24-Hour List

Angelika noted her activities over the course of a day. For each point she jotted down, she suggested a potential research question. This list provided her with the inspiration for her research paper on bubble gum. Here are some highlights:

10 A.M. Go to math class: How has geometry affected architecture?

3 P.M. Chew bubble gum on the way home: How did this product get invented?

5 P.M. Volunteer at community center: Why are community centers necessary?

7 P.M. On the telephone to friends: How have the telephone and the Internet changed business?

TOPIC BANK

If you are having trouble finding a topic for your research paper, consider these suggestions:

1. **Report on Television Accuracy** Television combines fact with fiction to create entertaining stories. For example, television dramas set in hospitals contain realistic medical jargon; courtroom dramas incorporate elements of the modern court system. Choose a television drama, and conduct research to identify the elements of the show that are based in reality. In a report, evaluate the program's accuracy.
2. **Amazing Achievement Report** Focus on a historic event that amazed the public in its time. For example, research Lindbergh's famous flight across the Atlantic or investigate the *Titanic*'s maiden voyage. In a paper, explain how the event generated excitement or interest.

Responding to Fine Art

Three Studies of a Dancer in Fourth Position, c. 1879/80 (detail), Edgar Degas, Art Institute of Chicago

3. *Three Studies of a Dancer in Fourth Position* reveals the artist's attention to research and detail. Learn more about Edgar Degas and his work. In a paper, report on his life, work, and legacy. Alternatively, research the fundamentals of ballet, including arm and leg positions.

Responding to Literature

4. Read "A Celebration of Grandfathers" by Rudolfo A. Anaya. Use his ideas about older people in today's society as inspiration for your writing. Research the work of an older person who has made a significant contribution to society. You can find Anaya's essay in *Prentice Hall Literature: Timeless Voices, Timeless Themes*, Gold.

Cooperative Writing Opportunity

5. **Technology Update** With a small group, brainstorm to identify the major technological advances of recent years. Consider inventions that affect medicine, communication, and transportation. Assign each group member one innovation to research. Combine your reports into an anthology.

Narrowing Your Topic

Conduct Preliminary Research

Before you finalize the topic you'd like to explore, conduct preliminary research to assess the amount of material available to you. Use your general idea as a starting point, and surf the Web or browse through relevant books, magazines, and indexes at the library. As you conduct this preliminary research, jot down the names, ideas, and events that appear most often. Use this information to narrow your focus.

For example, you might have started your research with the topic of the best educational programs on television. After some early research, you may have discovered that many articles address children's educational programs and that one series is analyzed frequently. Limiting your topic to a discussion of this series allows you to research your original interest while effectively narrowing the research and writing required.

To narrow your focus by dividing and subdividing your topic, use the Topic Web activity in the Research Writing lesson.

Considering Your Audience and Purpose

Analyze Your Audience

The degree of your audience's familiarity with your topic helps you determine the level of research to conduct and the level of information to include. For example, if your audience is unfamiliar with your topic, the ideas you address should be described in general terms and any special terminology should be defined or modified. When you write for an expert audience, use terminology more freely, defining only those terms you feel your readers may not know. This chart illustrates how an audience's knowledge level should direct your research goal and help refine your topic.

Matching Audience's Knowledge With Research Goals

Audience	Research Goal	Sample Topic
Novices	Discuss the topic in a general, nontechnical way	Types of fish
General Audiences	Give some background, and define all the special terms used	Specific needs and habits of one species
Experts	Report the results of your research	Effect of a new environment on a group of migrating fish

Refine Your Purpose

Your purpose shapes the details you choose to include in your essay and directs the points or arguments you choose to emphasize. Here are three common purposes for research writing, along with suggestions for meeting these goals:

- **To Persuade** Include support from acknowledged authorities. Provide details that will convince your readers to accept your position.
- **To Honor** Use vocabulary that offers a positive impression and captures the best qualities of the topic.
- **To Show Cause and Effect** Include evidence that establishes logical connections among the causes and effects you identify.

Match Your Purpose With Your Research

To get the most out of the time you spend researching, consider creating a list of the types of information you will need to achieve your purpose. As you find facts or details that address each item, check them off your list.

Student Work IN PROGRESS

Name: Angelika Klien
Sunnyslope High School
Phoenix, AZ

Using Purpose to Direct Research

Angelika's purpose is to entertain her audience with interesting facts about her topic. To guide her research, she identifies several questions that may lead to interesting results. Checks indicate the information she has found in the initial stages of her research.

Purpose: To entertain by providing a lighthearted look at bubble gum.

✓ Is there evidence for the early use of gum chewing?

✓ Who invented bubble gum?

What are the ingredients in bubble gum?

Are there unusual uses for bubble gum?

✓ Are there unusual facts about bubble gum?

12.2

Gathering Information

Consult a variety of library sources, including books, encyclopedias, magazines, and newspapers. You can also find a wide range of information on the Internet.

Locate Sources

You can find sources of specific information through a card catalog, an on-line search, or these more complex resources:

Indexes: Locate magazine or newspaper articles by consulting the *Readers' Guide to Periodical Literature.*

Databases: Access databases of information to find appropriate sources; for example, the Modern Language Association database indexes articles on topics within the humanities.

Take Notes Systematically

As you locate information, take notes efficiently. This will help when you draft your paper and create a reference list.

Source Cards For each source, create a single card to note the information you'll need. Note the title, author, publisher, and city and date of publication. Assign a number to each source; then, use this number to link note cards to source cards.

Note Cards Use note cards to record specific items of information. Place only one item on a card, and include a categorizing label to identify the contents.When copying a direct quotation, record the words accurately. In addition to any notes, indicate page numbers on which you found the information.

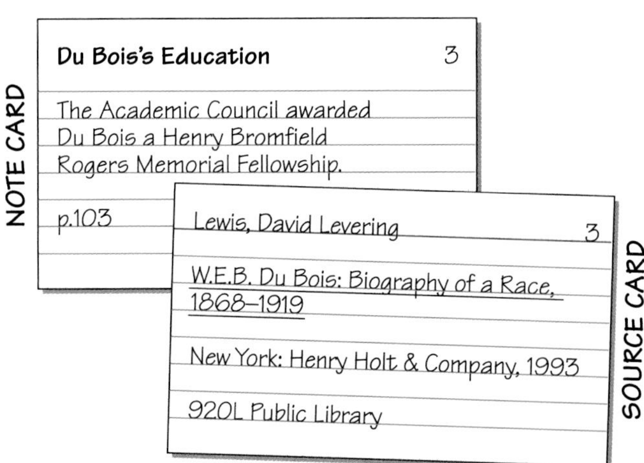

High-Tech Options Print out information you find on-line or photocopy articles that address your topic. Include bibliographical information for later use.

Learn More

For more information on specialized reference material, see Chapter 33.

12.3 Drafting

Shaping Your Writing

When you have gathered enough information for your research paper, think about organizing it. Begin with a proposal for a thesis statement.

Propose a Thesis Statement

An effective thesis statement expresses an idea that can be supported by research. To propose your thesis statement, review your research notes and look for one idea that can be supported by a majority of the information you have found in your research. Confirm that the thesis is narrow enough to address the ideas you will present. Then, use this thesis to guide your draft. If you find your ideas shifting as you write, be prepared to revise the sentence.

Sample Thesis Statement

- Spain offers a variety of pleasant activities for vacationers.
- The roots of the Northern Ireland conflict date back many centuries.
- During the first year of its life, a baby shows an amazing ability to learn.

Choose an Organization

Use your thesis statement, your audience, and your purpose as a basis for choosing an organizational strategy. Consider these options:

Types of Organization	Sample Topics
Chronological Order • Presents events in the order in which they occur • Ideal for reporting the history of a subject	Explaining the events leading up to the election of a president
Order of Importance • Presents details in order of increasing or decreasing importance • Ideal for writing persuasively or building an argument	Analyzing the elements of laboratory safety
Comparison and Contrast • Presents similarities and differences • Ideal for addressing two or more subjects	Discussing the themes of two works by the same author

Challenge

You may choose to organize your paper using *inductive reasoning*. With this strategy, you cite specific examples and build to the generalization they illustrate. In contrast, a paper organized according to *deductive reasoning* starts with a general claim and concludes with a specific statement.

Write an Outline

Roman Numeral Outline When you have decided how you want to organize your information, prepare an outline to guide your drafting. Give each of your subtopics a Roman numeral, each of your major pieces of supporting information a capital letter, and each smaller detail an Arabic number. Refer to the sample outline on this page as a model for your work.

Sentence Outline To begin developing the tone of your writing and deciding on the way you will present your ideas, you might want to create a sentence outline. Write complete sentences for each topic and subtopic you'll address. You can use this skeletal essay as the basis for your draft.

Student Work IN PROGRESS

Name: Angelika Klien
Sunnyslope High School,
Phoenix, AZ

Creating a Roman Numeral Outline

Angelika planned her essay using a chronological organization. Her outline helped her organize the key ideas she presents.

Thesis Statement: Bubble gum is big business in the United States.

I. Introduction —The prevalence of bubble gum

II. History of Gum Chewing
- A. Archaeological Evidence
- B. Invention
  1. Fleer Corporation
  2. Walter Deimer
  3. William J. White

III. Manufacture and Promotion of Commercial Gum
- A. Manufacturing—Ingredients and Process
- B. Promotion

IV. Funny Facts
- A. Other Uses
- B. Bubble Gum Alley

V. Snappy Summary and Conclusion

Providing Elaboration

Use a Variety of Outside Sources

Although the voice of your writing should integrate all the ideas you are reporting, support your ideas with the statistics, facts, examples, and quotations you have found through research. Consider these options:

Make Direct Reference to Sources You can use one of these three methods to incorporate the information you've learned through research.

- **Direct Quotation** When using a writer's exact words, enclose the entire statement in quotation marks. If you delete words from a lengthy sentence for clarity, be sure your editing does not change the intention of the quotation. Remember to show your deletions by the insertion of ellipses, or three dots.
- **Paraphrase** This technique involves restating a writer's specific ideas in your own words. You can paraphrase a sentence or a paragraph to convey the mood or intensity of the writer's description or ideas.
- **Summary** You can include the material you found through research by summarizing or reporting key ideas.

Incorporate Visuals To make your topic more understandable, consider including a visual representation, like the one shown here, when appropriate. For example:

- **Charts** can summarize information.
- **Graphs** can show comparisons and contrasts or indicate growth or decline over time.
- **Maps** can illustrate a variety of topics, including geography, war zones, and population.

Integrate References by Framing Whenever you include information gathered through research, smooth your writing by providing a context for the material you use. First, introduce the material. Then, present the quotation or visual. Finally, complete the frame by explaining how the material supports the point you are making.

Prepare to Credit Sources

When you include a direct quotation, present an idea that is not your own, or provide a fact that is available in only one source, you must include documentation. As you draft, circle all ideas and words that are not your own. At this stage, for each circled item, use parentheses to note the author's last name and the page numbers of material used. Later, you can use these notes to create formal citations.

Research Tip

Avoid the temptation to present someone else's work as your own. When using another writer's words, quote the author directly. If you summarize or rephrase, be sure the words are your own and give the author credit.

Access to Media

	USA	Japan
Newspaper circulation per 1,000	230	578
Radios per 1,000	2,076	906
Television sets per 1,000	741	611

Source: *Europa World Yearbook; World Factbook*

▲ Critical Viewing How could this chart help demonstrate a contrast between two countries' media access? **[Analyze]**

4 Revising

Finishing the first draft of your research paper is an achievement. Take the time now to polish your work, creating a final draft that reflects the amount of time and commitment you have already devoted to this writing. Review your draft several times, focusing on a different element of the writing each time.

▲ **Critical Viewing** In what situation might revising your paper send you back to do more research? **[Hypothesize]**

Revising Your Overall Structure

Refine Your Thesis Statement

In the process of drafting your paper, you may have learned something new, changed your interpretation of your subject, or developed a slightly different focus from the one you had planned. To avoid presenting a research paper that does not support your thesis statement, review your draft to be sure that all the details fit together to present a unified idea.

REVISION STRATEGY

Tracking the Thesis From Introduction to Conclusion

Review your draft, identifying the organizational skeleton you originally planned. Highlight the thesis statement in which you first present the main idea of your paper. As you read through the body of your paper, highlight the topic sentences of each topical paragraph. Finally, highlight the thesis as restated in your conclusion. Looking only at what you have marked, evaluate the clarity of your paper. Use these tips to guide your revision:

Evaluate	Revise
• Does the thesis statement presented in the introduction match the idea presented in the conclusion?	• If not, locate the point in your paper where the writing changed course. Revise your thesis or your conclusion to reflect the body of your paper. You may need to adjust the body paragraphs to correct the conflict.
• Is the sequence of main ideas logical?	• Consider reordering paragraphs or adding transitional words, phrases, or sentences that will make the sequence logical.

Learn More

For more instruction on topical paragraphs, those that develop a topic sentence, see Chapter 3.

Revising Your Paragraphs

Evaluate Your Paragraph Patterns

Because research often addresses complex subjects, you may have included a majority of long topical paragraphs in the body of your draft. This could make the writing seem dense and complicated. Consider adding functional paragraphs that increase readability and maintain reader interest.

Introduce Functional Paragraphs Short, functional paragraphs can create variety in the body of your draft by summarizing data, emphasizing points, or presenting special effects. Review your essay to decide whether a functional paragraph will improve the flow of ideas.

REVISION STRATEGY
Seeing the Pattern

Using self-sticking notes, indicate the subject of each topical paragraph in your essay. Wherever you see a series of long topical paragraphs, consider inserting a functional paragraph to break the pattern. These paragraphs give your readers a chance to interpret the material you've presented, review what you've said, or anticipate your next point.

Student Work IN PROGRESS

Name: *Angelika Klien*
Sunnyslope High School
Phoenix, AZ

Seeing the Paragraph Patterns

Angelika noticed several long paragraphs in the body of her essay and decided to add a functional paragraph to break the pattern. She jotted down several ideas and chose the best one.

Walter Diemer

. . . the true bubble gum age arose when a 23-year-old accountant at the Fleer Corporation named Walter Diemer mixed up a 300-pound batch of bubble gum. . . .
^ Insert functional paragraph for emphasis?

Flavoring

The first flavored gum featured peppermint flavoring. In 1880, William J. White found that adding sugar to the gum would allow the mixture to hold a flavor. . . .
^ Insert functional paragraph to show transition? ✓

Business

With so many companies competing in a global market, it is important to chew through the business of bubbles to see just how these companies continue to expand. . . .
^ Insert functional paragraph of dialogue?

Revising Your Sentences

Combine Sentences to Make Connections

In many cases, you can join simple sentences by using coordinating conjunctions such as *and, but, for, or, so,* and *yet* or subordinating conjunctions such as *after, because, until,* and *wherever.* To strengthen your writing, combine short sentences into longer ones that show these relationships between ideas.

SEQUENCE OF EVENTS:	*Once* he learned skills, he found a job.
CAUSE AND EFFECT:	He was offered many other positions *because* he was so qualified.
COMPARISON AND CONTRAST:	She expected him to be happy with the offer; *however,* he was not.

REVISION STRATEGY
Underlining Short Sentences

Review your draft, and underline sentences of eight words or less. If you see two or three short sentences in a row, challenge yourself to combine them into a compound one by clarifying the relationship between ideas.

Grammar in Your Writing
Semicolons

Semicolons can create compound sentences by linking clauses that otherwise stand as separate sentences. The semicolon emphasizes the close connection between ideas.

Example: The game was critical; fans streamed into the stadium.

To create a compound sentence using a semicolon, use the punctuation mark to separate main clauses. If you are introducing a transition such as *however, finally, consequently,* or *therefore,* place the word immediately after the semicolon and separate the transition from the second main clause with a comma.

Example: The game was critical; **consequently**, fans streamed into the stadium.

Find It in Your Reading Review a short story. Identify one compound sentence created with a semicolon. Explain the relationship between the two main clauses.

Find It in Your Writing Strive to use the semicolon construction correctly at least twice in your final draft.

For more on semicolons, see Chapter 29.

Revising Your Word Choice

Examine Language Variety

Except for the specific terminology associated with your topic, avoid using the same word over and over. Increase language variety with pronouns, synonyms, and specific proper nouns like names of people and places.

REVISION STRATEGY
Compiling a Synonym Bank

Identify words that are key to your topic, and review your writing to find words that you have repeated. Circle them as you go. Using a thesaurus, generate a list of possible synonyms, and substitute them as appropriate. Look at these examples:

SYNONYM BANKS

technology
innovation,
invention,
product,
brainchild

theory
belief, policy,
system, position,
idea

Woodrow Wilson
president,
government official,
leader

Grammar and Style Tip

Although you should try to avoid repetition of key words in your draft, do not substitute another word unless you are certain its meaning is appropriate.

Peer Review

Analytical Reading

In a research paper, it is especially important to document information that comes from someone else. Ask a small group of classmates to read a draft that indicates which statements or ideas you plan to cite with formal documentation. Ask each reader to evaluate your writing according to these questions:

1. Do I provide enough evidence of research?
2. Do you see enough variety of sources?
3. Which quotation is best integrated into the writing? Do any need better framing?
4. Do you see more statements of facts, ideas, or discoveries that should be referenced?

When appropriate, incorporate your reviewer's ideas into your final revision.

▼ Critical Viewing
How can a peer review group like the one shown here help you fine-tune your research paper? **[Analyze]**

5

Editing and Proofreading

By the time you've arrived at the point of editing and proofreading, you may have completed the hardest work of your research paper. With researching, organizing, drafting, and revising behind you, you can focus on the final touches.

Writing a Reference List

Whether you use a bibliography or a works-cited list, your paper should document your sources of information. A works-cited page provides information on each source you reference in your paper. In contrast, a bibliography offers a complete list of your research sources. In both cases, items are arranged alphabetically by author or, for works with no known author, by title. Identify the format your teacher requires, review your source cards, and create your reference list.

Consult Style Manuals

For consistency within the community of scholars who publish their research, conventions for documentation are set by several organizations.

Papers on literature and the arts often follow the specifications described in *MLA Handbook for Writers of Research Papers* or *The Chicago Manual of Style (CMS).* Papers on scientific or social science topics usually follow the style developed by the American Psychological Association (APA).

Before you draft your reference list, identify the format your teacher requires. Then, consult models of that style, and make sure that each entry is complete and properly punctuated.

Focusing on Mechanics

Take the time to review your research paper for misspelled words, problems with punctuation, and other errors in mechanics. Pay special attention to these conventions for including quoted material:

- When quoting a few words or part of a sentence, make sure the quoted material fits grammatically with the rest of the sentence.
- When providing a quotation of five lines or more, indent the text ten spaces. When you present a quotation this way, do not use quotation marks.

Learn More

To double-check your knowledge of mechanics issues, see the chapters on capitalization and punctuation.

Grammar in Your Writing

Conventions for Documentation

To credit sources within a research paper, include direct documentation in the form of footnotes, endnotes, or parenthetical citations. At the end of your paper, provide a reference list giving complete bibliographic information.

Bibliographic Form Present your sources in a standardized format. Include authors' names, source titles, places of publication, publishers, and the dates of publication. For on-line references, indicate the date on which you accessed the site. The following examples are in MLA format:

For a book with one author:
Wolfe, Tom. *The Right Stuff.* New York: Bantam Books, 1979.

For a book with more than one author:
Aaron, Hank, with Lonnie Wheeler. *I Had a Hammer: The Hank Aaron Story.* New York: HarperCollins, 1991.

For an article:
Quittner, Joshua. "Digital Video Daze." *Time.* 2 Nov. 1998: 112.

For an on-line source:
"Half Past Autumn: Newshour Transcript" *Online Newshour.* 19 Oct. 1999. <http://www.pbs.org/newshour/bb/entertainment/jan–june98/gordon_1/>

Footnotes and Endnotes When using footnotes or endnotes to provide citation, include full details about the source and cite the page number. Indicate a citation by placing a number at the end of a passage. Place footnote documentation at the bottom of the page on which the number appears; place endnote documentation on a page preceding the reference list.

First footnote or endnote for a book:

1. Tom Wolfe, *The Right Stuff* (New York: Bantam Books, 1979), 61.

Subsequent footnotes or endnotes citing same source:

2. Wolfe 92.

Parenthetical Citations To cite parenthetically, include the source information in parentheses immediately after the quoted material. This information, along with your reference list, directs readers to your source.

In her analysis of heroic behavior, Lewis suggests, "If you look inside yourself, you might find a hero waiting" (Lewis 90).

Find It in Your Reading and Writing As you finalize your paper, make the format of your documentation consistent with one style.

For a complete discussion of documentation styles, see *Citing Sources and Preparing Manuscript,* pp. 848–854.

6 Publishing and Presenting

Building Your Portfolio

Now that you have finished your research paper, share what you have learned with others. Here are some suggestions:

1. **Publish On-line** If your school has a Web site, post your paper on the school Web page. You might choose to group research papers with similar topics or arrange for the creation of links to Web sites you used as resources.
2. **Organize a Panel Discussion** If several of your classmates have written on a similar topic, plan a panel to compare and contrast your findings. Speakers can summarize their research before opening the discussion to questions.

Reflecting on Your Writing

Reflect on the experience of writing a research essay. Add your thoughts, along with a copy of your research paper, to your portfolio. Use these questions to direct your reflection:

- How did writing a research paper affect your appreciation, understanding, or opinion of your topic?
- What were the best and worst parts of this experience?

Internet Tip

To see model essays scored with this rubric, go to **www.phschool.com**

Rubric for Self-Assessment

Use these criteria to evaluate your research paper.

	Score 4	Score 3	Score 2	Score 1
Audience and Purpose	Focuses on a clearly stated thesis; gives complete citations	Focuses on a clearly stated thesis; gives citations	Focuses mainly on the chosen topic; gives some citations	Presents information without a focus; gives few or no citations
Organization	Presents information in logical order, emphasizing details of central importance	Presents information in logical order	Presents information logically, but organization is inconsistent	Presents information in a scattered, disorganized manner
Elaboration	Draws clear conclusions from information gathered from multiple sources	Draws conclusions from information gathered from several sources	Explains and interprets some information; cites some sources	Presents information with no interpretation or synthesis; cites few sources
Use of Language	Shows overall clarity and fluency; contains few mechanical errors; consistently uses documentation conventions	Shows good sentence variety; contains some errors in spelling, punctuation, or usage; demonstrates minor errors in documentation style	Uses awkward or overly simple sentence structures; contains many mechanical errors; demonstrates several errors in documentation style	Contains incomplete thoughts and mechanical errors that make the writing confusing; does not follow conventional documentation format

Connected Assignment Documented Essay

Like a traditional research paper, a **documented essay** presents a thesis that is supported by evidence. The difference in these two research products is in the length of the writing and in the number of sources consulted. In a documented essay, writers refer to a limited number of sources. They cite researched information and include quotations from books, interviews, or electronic sources, using full citation information parenthetically rather than providing a works-cited list. A documented essay can also be slightly less formal in tone.

Follow the writing process steps below to develop your own documented essay:

▲ **Critical Viewing** Who might you interview to learn more about students who hold after-school jobs? **[Apply]**

Prewriting As with any research paper, choose a topic that interests you, so that you'll want to devote the necessary time to it. For ideas, flip through magazines, scan on-line news services, or chat with friends. Consider a more contemporary topic than you might choose for a research paper.

Develop a thesis statement to focus your research. Identify candidates for interview or experts on the subject you are researching; their quotations will lend your essay a more personal tone. As you collect information, devise a note-card system for recording facts and sources. This will help later with your referencing. Look at these sample note cards.

Topic: Trends related to teens who go to school and work

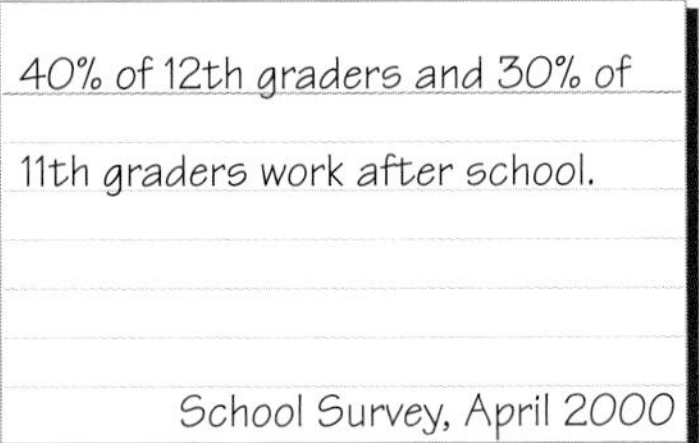

40% of 12th graders and 30% of 11th graders work after school.

School Survey, April 2000

"Working after school gives me extra spending money and it helps me budget my time better."

-Shane Rowe (11th grade)

Interview, May 1, 2000

Drafting Choose an organization that fits your ideas, and draft an outline to help plan your writing. For an essay about a current trend, you might use a pro-and-con organization to present opposing views about the topic. Refer frequently to your note cards for evidence to support your ideas.

Revising and Editing To improve the tone and readability of your essay, replace wordy explanations with livelier examples or direct quotations.

Publishing and Presenting When the final draft of your documented essay is complete, submit it to your school newspaper or class magazine.

Chapter 13 Response to Literature

Marshian Boy, Christian Pierre, Private Collection

▲ Critical Viewing What message does this painting convey about reading? **[Infer]**

Response to Literature in Everyday Life

Have you ever read a poem, play, or story that you couldn't put out of your mind? A character may have appealed to you or appalled you, the ending may have surprised or disappointed you, or you may simply have enjoyed the craft of a specific author. To extend your reading experience, you may have discussed your ideas with a friend or family member, or you may have compared responses with classmates at school.

In addition to reacting to the fiction you read, you may also find yourself analyzing the effectiveness of an advertisement, the persuasiveness of a speech, the realism of a movie script, or the clarity of another type of writing. In all cases, you are using the same set of critical response skills—the ones you'll learn and refine in this chapter.

What Is a Response-to-Literature Essay?

When you write a **response-to-literature essay,** you express the *what, how,* and *why* behind a piece of literature's effect on you as a reader. An effective response-to-literature essay

- analyzes the content of a literary work, its related ideas, or the work's effect on the reader.
- focuses on a single aspect of the work or gives an overall view of it.
- relies on evidence from the literary work to support the opinions the writer presents.
- uses a logical organization to convey ideas clearly.

To see the criteria on which your response-to-literature essay may be judged, preview the Rubric for Self-Assessment on page 195.

Writers in ACTION

As a book reviewer whose work appears in a magazine, Lawrence Chua believes a book reviewer's job is to be aware of the power of literature:

"We pay attention to the way that we're reading, how we're processing the information that's on the page, how we're understanding it, what that's doing to us, what emotions that might provoke in us, what rage, anxiety, despair, . . . love, that might provoke in us, and why the text does that."

Types of Responses to Literature

There are many ways to share your response to literature. Here are some of the most common:

- **Literary interpretations** show how literary elements combine to create a general effect in a work of literature.
- **Critical reviews** present an evaluation of a piece of writing, citing evidence in the work to support the reviewer's opinions.
- **Character studies** analyze the actions, beliefs, behaviors, or motivations of one character in a literary work.
- **Comparisons of works of literature** compare two or more works of literature. These may discuss two works by one author, compare the work of two writers, or examine one literary element in several pieces of literature.

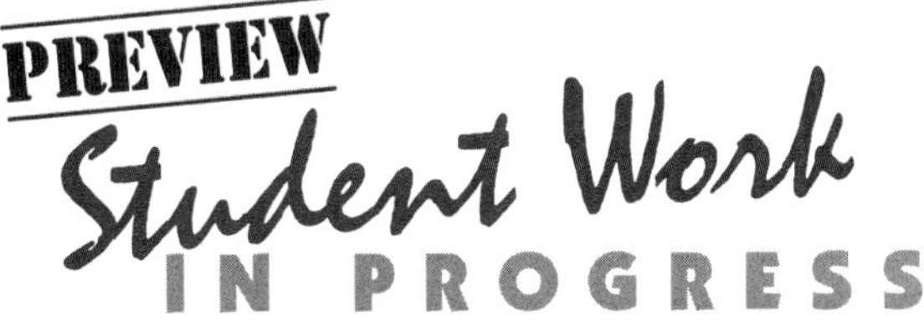

In this chapter, you will follow the work of Andrea Montgomery, a student at Omaha Northwest High School in Omaha, Nebraska. You will see how Andrea used writing process strategies to evaluate the success of the poem "The Raven," by Edgar Allan Poe.

2 # Prewriting

Choosing Your Topic

Choose a selection to which you had a strong response. Use one or more of the following strategies to select a topic on which to write:

Strategies for Generating Topics

1. **Class Book Awards** Conduct a class survey to discover which books are favorites. You can narrow the focus of your survey by asking about books with the most interesting characters, the most suspenseful plot, or the most descriptive writing. Compare your own favorites against the list of winners, and choose a topic to develop.
2. **Sentence Starters** Sometimes, starting with an open-ended sentence can stimulate memories and opinions about literature. Complete the sentences below, and develop each idea for five minutes. Review your work to choose a topic for your essay.
   - A poem that moved me was . . .
   - One piece of writing that helped me understand life better was . . .
   - The most exciting ending I remember was . . .
   - I wish something had happened differently in . . .

For more help finding a topic, explore the activities and suggestions in the Choosing a Topic section of the Response to Literature lesson.

Student Work IN PROGRESS

Name: Andrea Montgomery
Omaha Northwest High School
Omaha, NE

Using Sentence Starters to Find a Topic

When Andrea completed this sentence starter, she realized she had a poet whose work she could address in a response-to-literature essay.

A poem that had a strong effect on me was "The Raven." I read "The Tell-Tale Heart" by Poe in middle school. It was scary, but not like Stephen King. I like the way Poe writes. I think he has an interesting style. The rhymes seem to pull you into the eerie settings.

TOPIC BANK

If you are having trouble finding a topic, review the following possibilities:

1. **Response to a Biography** Biographers often choose subjects who have lived a life worth examining. Consider the biographies you have enjoyed, and write a response in which you explain what readers can learn from the subject's experiences, philosophy, or actions.
2. **Letter to an Author** Write a letter to an author explaining your reaction to a particular work. In your letter, use specific evidence to back up your opinions, but take the opportunity to ask questions that your own analysis has left you unable to answer.

Responding to Fine Art

3. *Mexican Market* conveys a strong impression of its subject. Like art, literature can show you places you've never been. Consider the stories you know that are especially successful at creating a fictional setting or conveying a real-life exotic one to readers who may never have visited it. In an essay, evaluate the setting of the work you selected.

Mexican Market (detail), Jane Scott, Schalkwijk

Responding to Literature

4. Read Toni Cade Bambara's story "Blues Ain't No Mockin Bird," which shows the conflict between the media and a person's right to privacy. Then, in an essay, explain how the author develops this conflict and identify your own position on this issue. You can find the story in *Prentice Hall Literature: Timeless Voices, Timeless Themes*, Gold.

Cooperative Writing Opportunity

5. **Comparison of Short Stories** Work with a group to identify several stories that are related by theme, by setting, or by conflict. Split the task of analyzing each story according to the link that you identify. Present your essays in a booklet. To put your responses in context, include an introduction that presents the comparisons you have found.

2

Narrowing Your Topic

To present an effective response that is clear to your readers, narrow your focus by finding a single point to address.

Use Hexagonal Writing to Narrow a Topic

By studying your topic from six basic angles, you can focus your response. Follow the directions below to complete each section of a hexagon like the one shown below. When the hexagon is finished, review your notes to focus your topic.

Plot Summarize the selection.

Personal Allusions Jot down experiences from your own life that the selection suggests to you.

Theme Identify the theme or generalization about life that the selection presents.

Analysis Provide evidence from the selection to support the theme you have identified.

Literary Allusions Jot down other works of literature that have a similar theme.

Evaluation Give your opinion of the work.

Student Work IN PROGRESS

Name: Andrea Montgomery
Omaha Northwest High School
Omaha, NE

Using Hexagonal Writing to Narrow a Topic

Completing a hexagon helped Andrea narrow her topic to the effects of repetition in creating a mood.

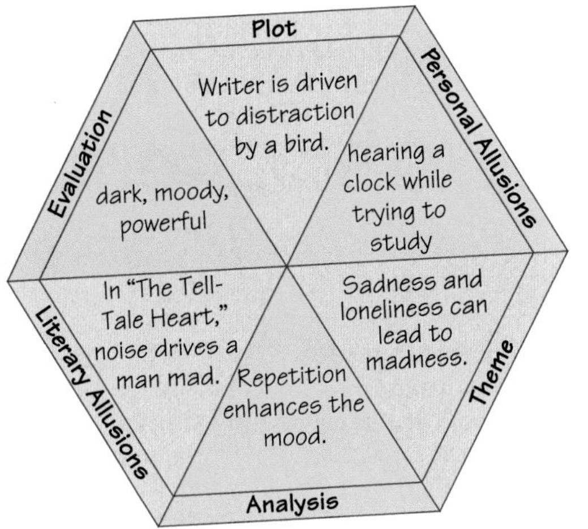

Considering Your Audience and Purpose

After narrowing the focus of your response, consider the format your writing will take. For example, if you are writing to introduce the play *Romeo and Juliet* to an audience who has not studied it, include background information and a summary. In contrast, if you want to write a critical review of the play for an audience of classmates, you need not provide extensive introductory context for the play. Instead, include your opinions and support them with direct evidence from the text. Evaluate your audience and purpose to help you identify the level of information that will make your writing successful.

To help you evaluate your audience, use the Audience Profile activity in the Response to Literature lesson.

Analyze Your Audience

Use the questions that follow to help you develop an audience profile that identifies the readers you expect to reach. Note your answers, and use them to guide the level of language and detail you include in your essay.

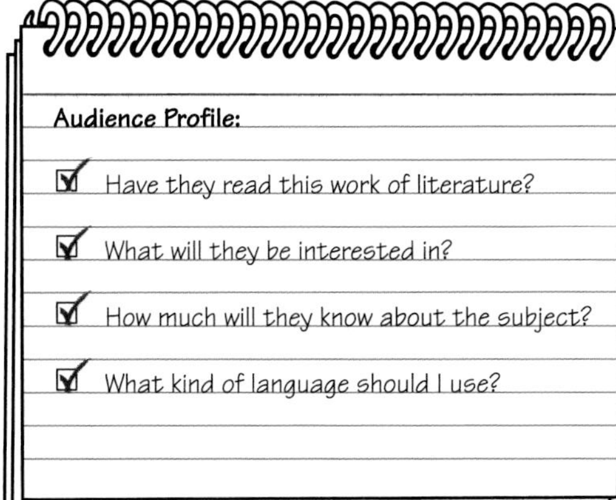

Analyze Your Purpose

Whether you are responding to the work of a well-known writer, providing an interpretation of a piece of literature that you have discovered, or writing to achieve another goal, include language and details that support your purpose. Consider these tips:

- **To praise:** Include concrete details to back up your enthusiasm for the work.
- **To analyze:** Support your interpretation with evidence from the text.
- **To show a personal response:** Make the connection between your ideas, opinions, or experience and the writing you are addressing.

2

Gathering Details

Find Details to Support Your Position

To find evidence to support your points, gather details from the literature, such as examples, excerpts, and direct quotations. Identify the main ideas you want to convey, and then return to the literature with a research goal: to find the proof.

Using Index Cards Prepare a series of index cards with each main point written across the top. Underneath, put your notes on the details you gathered to support that point.

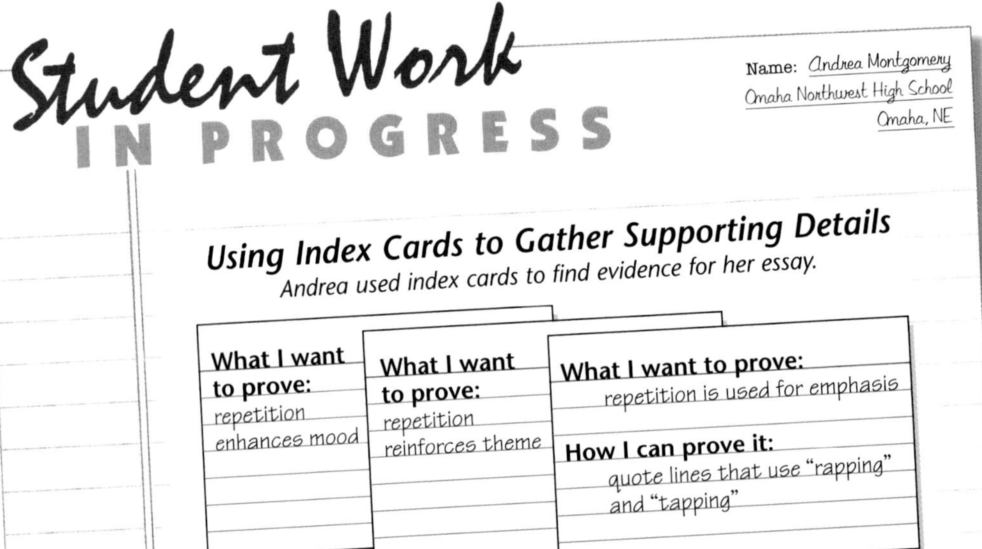

Use these tips to gather details about literary elements:

- **Character** When you analyze a character, find evidence that shows the character's actions, beliefs, and motivations. Note other details, including the ways other characters respond to the character you discuss and any change you see.
- **Setting** To provide an interpretation of the setting, find words that describe time and place and note the mood or atmosphere the setting generates.
- **Diction** Locate examples of word choice by considering the vocabulary level and formality of the language. Also, evaluate the connotation or emotional meanings of the writer's words.
- **Sound Devices** When analyzing poetry, address rhyme, rhythm, and repetition. Note examples of figurative language—such as simile or metaphor—that create meaning.

13.3 Drafting

Shaping Your Writing

Develop a Thesis Statement

Your draft should have a clear statement of the main idea, or thesis, you intend to develop. Review your prewriting notes, looking for a single idea that brings together the ideas you've generated and the support you've gathered. Write this as a single sentence. Use this sentence, your thesis statement, to direct the writing of your response to literature.

SAMPLE THESIS STATEMENTS

- Daphne du Maurier's "The Birds" presents a gripping series of events to illustrate the unpredictability of nature.
- In "One Ordinary Day, With Peanuts," by Shirley Jackson, the main character is motivated by a wish to be kind to strangers.
- Even though it was written more than two thousand years ago, Homer's epic the *Odyssey* presents a hero that today's audiences can respect.

▲ Critical Viewing What elements of this photograph would complement the frightening tone of a story such as Daphne du Maurier's "The Birds"? **[Connect]**

Organize to Support Your Ideas

Presenting your ideas in an organized way helps you guide your readers in following your thoughts and ideas.

Introduction After an inspired lead that grabs your audience's attention and links to your main ideas, your introduction should meet three more expectations:

- Identify the title and author of the work.
- State your thesis.
- Offer a brief summary of the work you are discussing.

Your response to literature should be evaluative or analytical, so avoid devoting too much attention to your summary. The length and level of this summary should be appropriate to your intended audience's needs.

Body Paragraphs Your development of a thesis is the main part of your essay. To build your thesis, offer several supporting ideas. Introduce each key idea in a new paragraph, and then use the details that you have gathered from the selection to support each idea.

Conclusion Your conclusion should restate your main ideas or make a final point. You can also present something new, such as your recommendation or opinion.

3

Providing Elaboration

In everyday conversation, you probably often say, "You know what I mean." When you find your listener doesn't understand the point you imply, you can offer more explanation. Writing is not as interactive as conversation; help your reader know what you mean by providing elaboration to develop your points.

Instead of asking readers to trust your analysis, include specific examples from the text that illustrate your ideas.

Include References to Support Your Thesis

Include citations from the literary work to support the points you are making. These can include quotations of a character's dialogue, an example of a specific literary element, or an excerpt from the work. Consider these specific suggestions:

- **Quotations** Include quotations to illustrate a character's attitude, a writer's word choice, or an essay's argument.
- **Examples** Insert an example of a specific literary element to enhance your analysis of a writer's style.
- **Paraphrases** To develop a writer's theme, discuss the conflict, analyze the character, or restate key ideas from the literature in your own words.

Collaborative Writing Tip

If you meet to discuss your ideas with a partner, you may discover the points that need the most explanation. Use your experience to guide you as you draft.

Student Work IN PROGRESS

Name: Andrea Montgomery
Omaha Northwest High School
Omaha, NE

Incorporating References From the Text

To make her essay more effective, Andrea included direct quotations from the text to make her points. In the excerpt shown here, references to the text are underlined.

Poe . . . produces rhythms and patterns that make the motion of the poem faster. To do this, Poe uses sets of three words that sound similar. For example, in the second stanza, Poe plays off the ending *-ember* with "remember/December/ember" and the ending *-orrow* with "morrow/borrow/sorrow." To extend the movement of the rhythm, Poe also intertwines the rhymes of "floor/Lenore/evermore" to pull the stanza together. Throughout the poem, Poe provides this type of triple rhyme.

Revising Your Sentences

Review Sentence Clarity

When you are adding quotations from literature to your own writing, the resulting sentences may be unclear. To be sure your points are clear, review each sentence in your draft. Make sure that each one is grammatically correct. A strategy for doing this is to circle all the subjects and verbs.

REVISION STRATEGY
Circling Subjects and Verbs

To evaluate the sentences in your draft, circle the subjects and verbs in each sentence. Be sure that the subjects and the verbs in each sentence agree. Be especially wary of sentences whose subjects and verbs are separated by modifiers, phrases, or clauses.

SEPARATED BY A PHRASE: The *celebration*, usually attended by thousands, *attracts* intense media coverage.

SEPARATED BY A CLAUSE: The *revelers*, who have been here since dawn, *remain* peaceful despite their number.

If you are not sure about subject-verb agreement in a sentence, take out all the modifiers and look again.

Grammar in Your Writing

Agreement in Inverted Sentences

In an **inverted sentence,** the verb precedes its subject. Despite this format, the subject and verb must still agree. In this example, the subject *seat* follows the verb *is*.

Example: Near the bookcase **is** the most comfortable **seat** in the library.

The words *there* and *here* at the beginning of a sentence often signal an inverted sentence. These words are not the subject of the sentence; instead, the subject appears after the verb. For example, in the first of the following sentences, the singular subject *article* takes the singular verb *is*. In the second sentence, the plural subject *articles* takes the plural verb *are*.

Example: Here **is** the best **article** on the topic.
Example: Here **are** the more useful **articles** on the topic.

Find It in Your Reading Locate at least three inverted sentences in a story you have read, and analyze the agreement between subject and verb.

Find It in Your Writing Review your draft to find inverted sentences. Confirm the correct subject-verb agreement, and revise as necessary.

For more on subject-verb agreement, see Chapter 25.

Revising Your Paragraphs

Review Topical Paragraphs

The topical, or body, paragraphs of your essay should state, develop, and support a key idea. Ultimately, they should contribute to your thesis statement. Each topical paragraph has a topic sentence that states an idea. Other sentences in the paragraph should expand, elaborate, and support the idea. To tune up your topical paragraphs, highlight all the topic sentences in your draft, and then be sure that each idea is well supported.

REVISION STRATEGY
Highlighting Topic Sentences

Use a highlighter to mark the topic sentences of each of your topical paragraphs. For each, review the sentences that support the main idea, and evaluate the effectiveness of the paragraph. When possible, add more explanation, refine word choice to clarify your ideas, or review the literature you are discussing to find an example that will strengthen your point.

Student Work IN PROGRESS

Name: Andrea Montgomery
Omaha Northwest High School
Omaha, NE

Highlighting Topic Sentences

When Andrea highlighted the topic sentence of this paragraph, she saw several opportunities for revision. In addition to adding specific language from "The Raven," she planned to add a complete reference to make her ideas more clear.

Poe also repeats words to emphasize a point. For example, to let the reader feel the nervousness created by the bird's knocking, Poe repeats ^the^ word~~s~~ ^"rapping" three times in^ ~~throughout~~ the first stanza. ^He^ adds the word "tapping" to complete the repetition of the sound.

Add reference from poem.

Revising Your Sentences

Review Sentence Clarity

When you are adding quotations from literature to your own writing, the resulting sentences may be unclear. To be sure your points are clear, review each sentence in your draft. Make sure that each one is grammatically correct. A strategy for doing this is to circle all the subjects and verbs.

REVISION STRATEGY
Circling Subjects and Verbs

To evaluate the sentences in your draft, circle the subjects and verbs in each sentence. Be sure that the subjects and the verbs in each sentence agree. Be especially wary of sentences whose subjects and verbs are separated by modifiers, phrases, or clauses.

SEPARATED BY A PHRASE: The *celebration*, usually attended by thousands, *attracts* intense media coverage.

SEPARATED BY A CLAUSE: The *revelers*, who have been here since dawn, *remain* peaceful despite their number.

Grammar and Style Tip

If you are not sure about subject-verb agreement in a sentence, take out all the modifiers and look again.

Grammar in Your Writing

Agreement in Inverted Sentences

In an **inverted sentence,** the verb precedes its subject. Despite this format, the subject and verb must still agree. In this example, the subject *seat* follows the verb *is*.

Example: Near the bookcase is the most comfortable seat in the library.

The words *there* and *here* at the beginning of a sentence often signal an inverted sentence. These words are not the subject of the sentence; instead, the subject appears after the verb. For example, in the first of the following sentences, the singular subject *article* takes the singular verb *is*. In the second sentence, the plural subject *articles* takes the plural verb *are*.

Example: Here is the best article on the topic.
Example: Here are the more useful articles on the topic.

Find It in Your Reading Review "Lederer's 'Miracle' Is His Well of Wit and Wisdom With Words" on pages 282–285. Locate at least three inverted sentences, and analyze the agreement between subject and verb.

Find It in Your Writing Review your draft to find inverted sentences. Confirm the correct subject-verb agreement, and revise as necessary.

For more on subject-verb agreement, see Chapter 25.

4

Revising Your Word Choice

Add Evaluative Modifiers

Although all the modifiers in your draft should be powerful, the words you use to convey praise or criticism should be especially precise. These evaluative adjectives and adverbs will help you describe and clarify your opinions. Consider these suggestions as you revise your writing:

MILD PRAISE: *accurate, adequate, factual, intelligent, solid*

HIGH PRAISE: *brilliant, excellent, entertaining, honest, original*

MILD DISAPPROVAL: *confusing, dull, inconsistent, predictable, unfocused*

STRONG DISAPPROVAL: *biased, pointless, ugly, misguided*

REVISION STRATEGY

Bracketing Modifiers

With a colored pen or pencil, bracket any modifiers you've used. Evaluate each one, deciding whether you might add a more precise word. Notice any words that convey positive or negative criticism. If you've chosen vague or overused words, consider replacing them with words that more precisely capture your response.

Student Work IN PROGRESS

Name: Andrea Montgomery
Omaha Northwest High School
Omaha, NE

Color-Coding Modifiers

Andrea bracketed all the modifiers in her conclusion, changing several to make her evaluation more precise.

Stanza after stanza, Poe creates [~~an interesting~~] a compelling rhythm through repetition. . . . These examples show how [~~an easy~~] a simple concept such as repetition can give a poem depth and intrigue. Poe was a master of repetition, and "The Raven" is [~~a good~~] an excellent example of the ways he could apply it to achieve [~~many~~] a variety of results.

Andrea inserted the words "compelling" and "excellent" to convey her high opinion of Poe's writing.

◀ Critical Viewing
How would you guide a peer review like this one to help you improve your writing? **[Connect]**

Peer Review

Plus and Minus Scoring

Gather a small group of classmates to help you evaluate your revised draft. Using the criteria in the chart below, ask your readers to score your work. You may want to customize the chart to target your own draft and your own concerns.

As you read the criteria in each category, ask your reviewers to give your draft a plus or minus score. Record responses, and ask your reviewers to explain their evaluations. Take notes when necessary, or begin a discussion to clarify any suggestions your reviewers may offer. Then, use your classmates' responses to revise your draft.

PLUS AND MINUS CHART

CRITERIA	Group Members			COMMENTS
	1	2	3	
Interesting introduction: First two sentences hook readers				
Identifiable thesis				
Identifiable title and author				
First idea clearly stated and elaborated				
Second idea clearly stated and elaborated				
Successful conclusion				
Overall evaluation				

5

Editing and Proofreading

An essay free of errors in spelling, grammar, and punctuation will help your readers enjoy your writing and devote more attention to considering the ideas you present. Check that your essay is free of errors.

Focusing on Spelling

Review your draft to be sure that each word is spelled correctly. One effective strategy for checking spelling is to read blocks of text from end to beginning. This helps you focus less on meaning and more on spelling. In addition, follow these suggestions:

- **Check Problem Words** As you develop a writing portfolio, build a list of words you often misspell. Keep this list handy, and check these words in your writing. Use a dictionary to confirm the spelling of any words you question.
- **Confirm Names** Your draft contains at least two proper nouns: the author and title of the work you address. Be sure that these and other names and places in your essay are spelled correctly.

Spelling Tip

The spell-check feature on your word-processing software will not catch a word that is spelled correctly but is used incorrectly; for example, it will not alert you to a discrepancy between *he* and *be*. Make sure that you check your final draft carefully.

Grammar in Your Writing

Avoiding Common Homophone Errors

A **homophone** is a word that sounds the same as another word but has a different meaning and a different spelling. Here are some common homophones to consider as you review your draft:

your/you're: *Your* is generally used as a possessive adjective; *you're* is a contraction of the words *you* and *are*.

right/write: *Right* is usually an adjective meaning "correct"; *write* is most often a verb meaning "to communicate using printed words."

Use a dictionary to clarify the spelling and meaning of homophones that present a problem to you.

Find It in Your Writing As you proofread your response to literature, check that you have not used a homophone instead of the word you intended.

To learn more about homophones, see Chapter 27.

13.6 Publishing and Presenting

Regardless of the strategy you choose, getting reactions from others will expand your insight into your response to literature. Consider these ideas for sharing your work:

Building Your Portfolio

1. **Library Display** Talk with your school librarian about establishing a Readers' Choice area where books are displayed next to students' written responses.
2. **Book Group** Bookstores and libraries often organize groups to discuss works of literature. Participate in a book group, and offer to read your essay as the starting point of a discussion on the literature you have analyzed.

Reflecting on Your Writing

Take a moment to reflect on the experience of writing your response to literature. Write your ideas, and add them to your writing portfolio. Use these questions to direct your thinking:

- What did you discover about the literature as you wrote?
- If you could start the writing process again, what might you do differently? Why?

Internet Tip

To see model essays scored with this rubric, go to **www.phschool.com**

Rubric for Self-Assessment

Use the following criteria to evaluate your response to literature.

	Score 4	Score 3	Score 2	Score 1
Audience and Purpose	Presents sufficient background on the work(s); presents reactions forcefully	Presents background on the work(s); presents reactions clearly	Presents some background on the work(s); presents reactions at points	Presents little or no background on the work(s); presents few reactions
Organization	Presents points in logical order, smoothly connecting them to the overall focus	Presents points in logical order and connects them to the overall focus	Organizes points poorly in places; connects some points to an overall focus	Presents information in a scattered, disorganized manner
Elaboration	Supports evaluations with elaborated, well-chosen examples from the text	Supports evaluations with specific reasons and examples from the text	Supports some evaluations with reasons and examples from the text	Offers little support for evaluations; provides no reference to the text
Use of Language	Shows overall clarity and fluency; uses precise, evaluative words; makes few mechanical errors	Shows good sentence variety; uses some precise evaluative terms; makes some mechanical errors	Uses awkward or overly simple sentence structures and vague evaluative terms; makes many mechanical errors	Presents incomplete thoughts; makes mechanical errors that create confusion

Chapter 14

Writing for Assessment

▲ Critical Viewing How can preparation help you succeed on in-class tests? **[Analyze]**

Assessment in School

To make sure that you are learning and mastering the information and skills you are being taught in school, teachers frequently assess your knowledge. Tests, essays, oral reports, lab reports, performances, and research papers are different forms of assessment that evaluate your progress. Besides helping you to focus your learning and evaluate your own strengths and weaknesses, assessment gives you the chance to earn higher grades and show what you know. In this chapter, you will learn how to improve your performance skills for a common type of written assessment: the essay test.

What Is Assessment?

By the time you've reached this stage of your school career, you should recognize essay tests as one of the most common forms of **writing for assessment.** In contrast to standardized tests that evaluate your critical thinking ability and writing skills, in-class exams require you to draw on the material you have studied in school. An effective essay-test response includes

- a direct response to the test question or prompt.
- a clearly worded and well-supported thesis statement or main idea.
- specific information about the topic, drawn from your reading or from class discussion.
- a clear organization.

To see criteria by which essay-test responses may be evaluated, preview the Rubric for Self-Assessment on page 205.

Writers in ACTION

The value of education has been celebrated by leaders in every generation. Education becomes an issue for campaigns, both local and national, with leaders offering their perspectives on the importance of learning. These words spoken by Booker T. Washington ring as true today as on the day he said them in 1895:

"There is no defense of security for any of us except in the highest intelligence and development of all."

Types of Assessment

The topics you address in essay tests depend on the classes you are studying. However, the format the essays take is often limited to a few familiar types of writing. In your academic classes, you can expect to encounter the following types of essays:

- **Explain a process** ("How a Script Becomes a Movie")
- **Defend a position** ("Why a Candidate Was Elected")
- **Compare and contrast** ("Tornadoes vs. Hurricanes")
- **Show cause and effect** ("Analyzing the Growing Popularity of E-mail")

Megan Holbrook, a student at Buena High School in Ventura, California, wrote an essay-test response about a short story. In this chapter, you will see her work in progress, including strategies she used to draft and revise.

14.1 Prewriting

Choosing Your Topic

On some essay tests, a single writing topic is assigned. In other cases, you may have the opportunity to choose a topic from several that are offered. Time pressure requires that you make a commitment to one prompt early in the process. Follow these guidelines for choosing a topic:

Consider What You Know Examine which questions will take the least time. To stay focused, identify the topics you have reviewed most recently. Try jotting down a list of specific details for each topic. If you find you can list several ideas quickly for one prompt but only one idea for another, choose the one you can answer more fully.

Pinpoint Your Strengths The prompt for an essay question may ask you to address specific critical thinking skills in your writing; for example, you may need to *analyze,* to *predict,* or to *explain.* Find a question that connects with your strengths, and choose a prompt for which you can provide facts to support the type of response required.

Draft a Single Sentence Choose a topic for which you can develop a focus or main idea. For example, if a test prompt asks an open-ended question that requires you to select an important event, character, or theme, decide what you might discuss. In a single sentence, identify the main idea you would develop. Then, evaluate your ability to write an essay based on the sentence you've written.

TOPIC BANK

Following are two essay-test questions. If you plan to practice writing for assessment, choose one of these or ask your teacher to provide you with one.

1. **Role Models for Your Generation** Choose two Americans, living or deceased, as role models for today's youth. In a brief essay, compare and contrast the achievements and leadership qualities of these two heroes.
2. **Body Systems** The human body contains several major organ systems, including the skeletal system, the digestive system, the respiratory system, and the circulatory system. In an essay, explain how one of these organ systems works. Identify the organs involved, and describe the function the system performs.

Narrowing Your Response

Circle Key Words to Identify Your Purpose

As you prepare to write your essay, circle key words and make any notes to help you interpret the directions. Note especially the verbs, nouns, and important phrases in the question. The chart below shows how the specific verbs you encounter direct the purpose of your writing.

Key Words	Essay Objectives
Analyze	Examine how various elements contribute to the whole.
Describe	Give main features and examples of each.
Compare and Contrast	Stress how two works or other items are alike and different.
Discuss	Support a generalization with facts and examples.
Explain	Clarify by probing reasons, causes, results, and effects.
Defend	Support your position with reasons and examples.

Student Work IN PROGRESS

Name: Megan Holbrook
Buena High School
Ventura, CA

Circling Key Words in Questions

Before she began writing, Megan circled the important verbs in the prompt she had chosen. By adding her own notes to paraphrase the question, she clarified the assignment.

Review the short stories we have studied in this unit. Consider the criteria you think are most important in a successful short story, and identify the story that best meets these standards. Explain your response.

List qualities of stories

Choose one story

Show how one story meets these standards

2 **Drafting**

Shaping Your Writing

Find a Focus

After you choose your topic, develop a focus for your essay. Consider the type of writing you are creating, and draft a statement that directly responds to the prompt. This sentence will shape an effective response. Use these suggestions:

- **Exposition** Develop a thesis statement to address the question. For problem-and-solution, cause-and-effect, or comparison-and-contrast essays, phrase your thesis statement to reflect the expectation of these types of writing.
- **Persuasion** Choose a position to argue, and identify the support you'll use to defend it.
- **Response to Literature** In a single sentence, identify your focus. For example, you may decide to evaluate a character, analyze a setting, or compare two works.

Learn More

To review the unique qualities of each type of writing, review the appropriate chapters in Part One.

Plan a Structure

Quick Outline When you sketch an outline for your essay, divide it into three parts: introduction, body, and conclusion.

The **introduction** should state your thesis. The **body** of the essay should present at least two main points that support your thesis. The **conclusion** should restate the answer to the essay question and sum up the main points in the body. Look at this example:

THESIS: The fire in the Triangle Shirtwaist Factory led to major reforms in fire safety standards.

INTRODUCTION: State thesis; summarize the fire.

BODY 1 Reforms: Women's Trade Union League and Red Cross collaborate to urge city to fix fire safety standards

BODY 2 Reforms: Labor union demonstrations lead to state legislation

CONCLUSION: Tragedy leads to inspiration for safer working conditions

Fill in the Details Before you draft, collect the evidence, facts, and examples you'll need to prove your point. Jot down as many details as you can remember or generate.

Providing Elaboration

The proof of your knowledge is in the details you use. To demonstrate your mastery of the subject, include details from class discussions or readings to support your main idea.

Support Your Thesis With Specifics

Whatever your purpose, you need to include specific details to support your answer. Generally, these details must come from your memory or personal experience. Consider developing your ideas with these types of elaboration:

- **Facts, Dates, Names** Whenever you can, provide facts to make your response concrete. Instead of writing that an agreement was signed to end the war, name the treaty, indicate the date, and tell which leaders were involved in the negotiations.
- **Specific Examples** Provide examples that prove your point. For example, to illustrate that Robert Frost's poems are often set in rural areas, name and discuss several poems.
- **Explanations** It is not enough to say that a character changes. Elaborate by explaining the ways the character changes or showing what experiences cause the change.
- **Quotations or Paraphrases** You probably can't quote long passages from memory, but adding paraphrases or memorable quotations can bring your writing to life. For example, an essay on leadership could be strengthened by a few famous lines used by United States presidents to inspire the nation.

Student Work IN PROGRESS

Name: Megan Holbrook
Buena High School
Ventura, CA

Including Details to Support a Thesis

In this passage, Megan used insert marks neatly to make her examples and details more specific.

One meaningful change was the shift in Doodle's brother ^from selfishness to love and sensitivity. At first, he was embarrassed ^by Doodle's disability. ~~and~~ His effort to teach Doodle ^to walk sprang from his own shame at having a disabled brother. However, the scene in which Doodle walks ^on his sixth birthday brings out the change in Doodle's brother. The narrator now understands ^that by teaching Doodle to walk he himself has been learning to love his brother. ~~the situation better.~~

3 Revising

While time is limited during an essay test, you should still leave yourself enough time to check your writing for accuracy and clarity.

Revising Your Overall Structure

Get the Big Picture

Your grade will be based in large part on your ability to answer the question presented. Review your response to be sure you have addressed each part of the question.

REVISION STRATEGY
Reviewing the Question Against Your Answer

When you have finished writing, check to see that you have followed the instructions in the question. For example, if the question asks you to give examples of a specific literary technique in two of the works on a list, make sure that the examples in your discussion are drawn from two different works. If you are asked to explain at least two causes of the Vietnam War, check to see that your essay has covered at least two reasons.

Revising Your Paragraphs

Confirm the Coherence

While most writers take several drafts to move from inspiration to published work, the restrictions of an in-class essay test make such drastic revisions unlikely. However, if you change your thesis as you write, your essay-test response can be confusing to your reader. To be sure you present one idea coherently, look for transitional sentences that guide the flow of ideas, and compare your introduction with your conclusion.

REVISION STRATEGY
Checking the Introduction Against the Conclusion

Compare the first paragraph of your essay with the last. The first paragraph should contain your focus or thesis in response to the essay question. The final paragraph should restate the thesis and sum up the main points.

If the main points in these paragraphs do not match, revise either paragraph to make the writing more coherent. If necessary, revise body paragraphs or add transitional sentences to bring the essay together.

To review transitions that can improve the coherence of your response, see the Transitions Word Bin. You can find it in the Toolkit.

Revising Your Sentences

Double-Check for Relevance

In an essay test written under time limitations, every sentence is important, but details that do not contribute to the main ideas you are presenting can detract from your success. Review the sentences to be sure they are relevant to your thesis.

REVISION STRATEGY
Deleting Irrelevant Ideas

For each paragraph in your essay, identify the main idea you address. Read the supporting sentences, checking for any details that veer away from the main idea. Use transitional words or phrases like *at the same time, in contrast, eventually,* or *although* to tighten the paragraph. If you cannot link the details, delete them to strengthen your writing.

▲ **Critical Viewing** Why do you think students often neglect the revising process during exams? **[Relate]**

Revising Your Word Choice

Improve Your Diction

Examine your sentences for word choice, asking yourself whether you have selected words and phrases carefully in order to express exactly what you mean.

REVISION STRATEGY
Evaluating Informal Language

An essay test is an opportunity for you to present information in a serious and thoughtful way. Review your draft to be sure the language you have chosen is appropriate to your purpose. Circle any words that are chatty and informal. To replace them, choose more refined, precise language. Look at these examples:

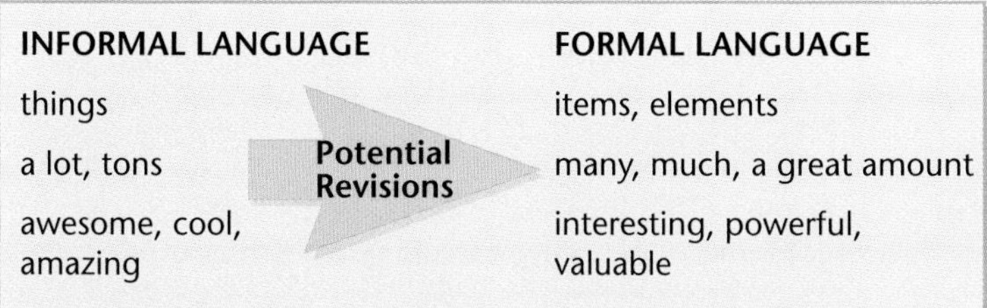

INFORMAL LANGUAGE	Potential Revisions	FORMAL LANGUAGE
things		items, elements
a lot, tons		many, much, a great amount
awesome, cool, amazing		interesting, powerful, valuable

4 # Editing and Proofreading

Focusing on Eliminating Errors

Because you must write quickly on a test, you may introduce some unintended errors in spelling, grammar, or punctuation. Review your draft, with special attention to these areas:

- **Sentence Construction** Be sure every sentence expresses a complete idea. Be especially aware of subordinate clauses punctuated as if they were sentences. In those cases, add information to complete the idea.

  FRAGMENT: Although the main theme of Pachelbel's *Canon* is not complex.

  CORRECT: Although the main theme of Pachelbel's *Canon* is not complex, the variations create depth.

- **Spelling** Review your work to catch any misspelled words. Neatly correct the errors you find.
- **Legibility** If you notice some words are written in a scrawl too difficult to read, neatly write them again.

Learn More

For more instruction on writing effective sentences, see Chapter 22.

Grammar in Your Writing

Homophones

Homophones are words that sound alike and are often confused. Check your essay for the proper usage of the following groups of homophones.

its, it's *Its* is a possessive pronoun showing ownership. *It's* is a contraction of the words *it is* or *it has.*

We need to find its proper place. Until then, it's going to create confusion.

their, there, they're *Their* is a possessive adjective showing ownership. *There* can be used to begin a sentence or to indicate place. *They're* is a contraction of the words *they are.*

They're going to post their ideas over there.

affect, effect *Affect* is almost always a verb meaning "to influence." *Effect* is usually a noun meaning "result."

The change will affect the system. We should study the effect closely.

Find It in Your Writing As you revise an essay-test response, be sure you've chosen the correct word of a homophone group to convey your ideas.

For more on homophones and other usage errors, see Chapter 27.

14.5 Publishing and Presenting

Building Your Portfolio

After your test is graded, keep a copy of your essay in your portfolio. Consider these suggestions to make further use of it:

1. **Organize a Study Group** Compare your responses with those of your classmates. This will help all of you to review the material you have learned during the year.
2. **Prepare for Future Exams** Use your essay as a study tool. Review the grade you received and the scorer's comments to help you improve your performance on the next essay test you encounter.

Reflecting on Your Writing

Whether you address the strategies outlined in this chapter or consider your own experiences during a recent essay test, take a moment to reflect on your strengths and weaknesses in test situations. Write down your ideas, and include them in your portfolio. Use these questions to get started:

- What strategy presented in this chapter might best help you complete your next essay test?
- What do you find is the most challenging element of an essay test?

Internet Tip

To see model essays scored with this rubric, go to **www.phschool.com**

Rubric for Self-Assessment

Use these criteria to evaluate your writing.

	Score 4	Score 3	Score 2	Score 1
Audience and Purpose	Uses appropriately formal diction; clearly addresses writing prompt	Uses mostly formal diction; adequately addresses prompt	Uses some informal diction; addresses writing prompt	Uses inappropriately informal diction; does not address writing prompt
Organization	Presents a clear, consistent organizational strategy	Presents a clear organizational strategy with few inconsistencies	Presents an inconsistent organizational strategy	Shows a lack of organizational strategy
Elaboration	Provides several ideas to support the thesis; elaborates each idea; links all information to thesis	Provides several ideas to support the thesis; elaborates most ideas with facts, details, or examples; links most information to thesis	Provides some ideas to support the thesis; does not elaborate some ideas; does not link some details to thesis	Provides no thesis; does not elaborate ideas
Use of Language	Uses excellent sentence and vocabulary variety; includes very few mechanical errors	Uses adequate sentence and vocabulary variety; includes few mechanical errors	Uses repetitive sentence structures and vocabulary; includes many mechanical errors	Demonstrates poor use of language; generates confusion; includes many mechanical errors

Chapter

15 Workplace Writing

▲ **Critical Viewing** Why are skills such as the ability to write and speak effectively important in business? **[Draw Conclusions]**

Workplace Writing in Everyday Life

When you send a thank-you letter to a neighbor who participated in a school fund-raiser or when you complete an application for a local youth services job bank, you're using workplace writing skills. Workplace writing helps co-workers, classmates, businesses, and even governments communicate important information and work together across geographic distances. Effective workplace writing can lead to school success and job possibilities, notify a company of customer satisfaction or dissatisfaction, invite people to important events, and even communicate urgent messages to resolve community problems.

What Is Workplace Writing?

Workplace writing takes many forms—each appropriate to a specific situation. The way you write in the workplace will change, depending on the tasks you undertake and the places in which you work. Despite these differences, workplace writing usually results in a fact-based, written product that communicates specific information to readers in a structured format that most people recognize. Effective workplace writing

- communicates its information and message clearly, directly, and briefly.
- focuses on key topics and anticipates answers to questions readers may have.
- reflects thorough attention to accuracy and neatness.

Writers in ACTION

Perhaps more than any other form of written communication, workplace writing involves specific and accepted traditions. These rules require practice to achieve success.

Popular children's writer Betsy Byers showed great insight into workplace writing when she made this comment:

"Writing is like baseball or piano playing. You have to practice if you want to be successful."

Types of Workplace Writing

From the comments your teachers write on your report card to the application you complete to work in the public library, workplace writing is part of your life. There are several forms of workplace writing—both electronic and print. Each reflects particular audiences and purposes. These are several common formats:

- **Business letters** are created to communicate information or to address issues of almost any kind.
- **Meeting minutes** are generated to provide a written record of the decisions and plans discussed at a meeting. These notes benefit those attending and other interested parties.
- **Forms and applications** are completed to provide specific factual information necessary for a particular purpose, such as shopping on-line or obtaining a part-time job.

PREVIEW

Chapter Contents

In this chapter, you'll see several examples of workplace writing—such as a letter requesting information about a recycling program, the minutes of a student government meeting, an application for a personal savings account, and the forms typically used to introduce facsimiles (faxes) and to note phone messages. As you'll see, using the stages of the writing process can make these business forms more effective.

1 Business Letter

What Is a Business Letter?

From a letter offering a job candidate a position to a letter requesting charitable donations, business letters are among the most common type of workplace writing. Whatever the subject, an effective business letter

- includes six parts: the heading, the inside address, the salutation or greeting, the body, the closing, and the signature.
- follows one of several acceptable forms: In *block format*, each part of the letter begins at the left margin; in *modified block format*, the heading, the closing, and the signature are indented to the center of the page.
- uses formal language to communicate respectfully, regardless of the letter's content.

The **heading** indicates the address and business affiliation of the writer. It also shows the date the letter was sent.

Model Business Letter

In this letter, Yolanda Dodson uses modified block format to request information.

The **inside address** indicates where the letter will be sent.

A **salutation** is punctuated by a colon. When the specific addressee is not known, use a general greeting such as "To whom it may concern:"

The **body** of the letter states the writer's purpose. In this case, the writer requests information.

The **closing** "Sincerely" is common, but "Yours truly" or "Respectfully yours" are also acceptable. To end the letter, the writer types her name and provides a **signature**.

Students for a Cleaner Planet
c/o Memorial High School
333 Veterans' Drive
Denver, Colorado 80211

January 25, 20 – –

Steven Wilson, Director
Resource Recovery Really Works
300 Oak Street
Denver, Colorado 80216

Dear Mr. Wilson:

Memorial High School would like to start a branch of your successful recycling program. We share your commitment to reclaiming as much reusable material as we can. Because your program has been successful in other neighborhoods, we're sure that it can work in our community. Our school includes grades 9–12 and has about 800 students.

Would you send us some information about your community recycling program? For example, we need to know what materials can be recycled and how we can implement the program.

At least fifty students have already expressed an interest in getting involved, so I know we'll have the people power to make the program work. Please help us get started.

Thank you in advance for your time and consideration.

Sincerely,

Yolanda Dodson

Yolanda Dodson

TOPIC BANK

To write a business letter that communicates successfully, choose a real-life topic that interests you and focus on just one or two aspects of it. That way, you can keep your letter brief. If you're having trouble coming up with your own topic, consider these possibilities:

1. **Letter to an Author** Review the books you've enjoyed recently. Choose the one you liked best, and write a letter to the author. Express your pleasure in reading the work, and ask about the writer's plans for future books.
2. **Letter to a Workplace** Consider a career or job you might be interested in pursuing. Then, write a letter to a local professional to ask for an interview that will help you to learn more about what the job demands.

Prewriting If possible, identify the name and title of the person who will receive your letter. Then, jot down the information you want to convey. To make the best use of your reader's time and to increase the chances that your letter will generate a positive response, identify your most important point and plan to present it early in the letter.

Drafting As you draft, use a formal tone and provide any background information your reader will need.

Revising Because your letter must introduce and address an issue, check that the topic and main point are clear in the first paragraph. Review your draft to make the most efficient and effective use of details, adding those that are necessary and deleting those that are not.

Editing and Proofreading Carefully check your letter's format. Make absolutely certain that you've spelled the person's name correctly and that you have the right business name and address. Correct grammar, usage, and mechanics problems.

Publishing Write, type, or print your letter on standard business paper or send it by e-mail. Use a neutral color of paper, such as white or ivory. To mail your letter, fold it neatly into thirds and put it in a properly addressed matching envelope.

2 # Meeting Minutes

What Are Meeting Minutes?

When people hold a meeting to discuss issues of interest to them all, it's important to have a written record. Meeting minutes can provide the details. Effective meeting minutes

- provide a list of those who attended and identify the date, time, and place of the meeting.
- itemize the issues discussed and objectively summarize the views taken by those present.
- list action items and the people responsible for completing them.

Model Meeting Minutes

As a member of his school's Student Council, Brian Pretkowski recorded these minutes of a meeting.

The title clearly identifies the group that is meeting, and the date helps all readers keep track of the progress of individual projects.

In addition to a list of those who attended, the writer indicates an absent member to recognize him as a participant.

Meeting minutes are typically organized into ongoing, or "old," business and new business. In each section, the writer titles the topic, briefly recounts the discussion, and lists the action items with the people responsible.

Boldfaced type and underlining help organize the minutes and make it easier for readers to find the information they need.

Portland High School Student Council
Monthly Meeting: April 4, 20 – –

Attended: Luz Delgado, Roger Cash, Justin Healy, Clare Picone, Kathleen O'Rourke, Dory Marsh, Brian Pretkowski
Absent: Simon Weathers

Business Discussed:

- Minutes of last month's meeting were read by Justin Healy, who had recorded them. The minutes were approved as written.

Old Business:

- Fund-raising for the Yearbook: We are still exploring different ways to raise money for the yearbook. Clare strongly stated her feeling that we should not ask for student donations. Kathleen disagreed, pointing out that we can write a letter explaining that people will not be pressured to donate and that no donation is too small.

Action Item: Get advice from parents and teachers about donation issue. Report at next month's meeting. (Roger, Dory)

New Business:

- Representative for School Board: The School Board has created a spot for a student representative. They've asked the Council to select that member. Luz suggested that we invite all students to write an application letter telling why they would be good a representative. Brian felt that such a process would take too long and be too subjective. He suggested instead a lottery of interested students. We could set minimum qualifications, such as being in good academic standing. A motion was made and accepted to follow Brian's idea.

Action Item: Write letter announcing and explaining the lottery. (Brian) Photocopy letter. (Dory) Distribute letter.

Next Meeting: May 7, 20 – –

TOPIC BANK

To write effective meeting minutes, arrive at the meeting prepared to take notes. Focus on accuracy and objectivity. If you'd like to practice writing meeting notes and need some help to get started, consider these possibilities:

1. **Minutes of a Club Meeting** In schools and communities, people form clubs to share common interests, such as gardening, bowling, or reading. Attend the meeting of a club you belong to or ask permission to visit the meeting of another one. Record and write up minutes of the meeting.
2. **Minutes of a Public Meeting** In communities of many different sizes, citizens gather at public meetings to discuss issues such as education, library funding, and recreation. Contact city offices to learn of such meetings. Attend a meeting and record its minutes. To prepare, read local newspapers and the minutes of the previous meeting.

Prewriting Before you write up any minutes, attend a meeting. Record the names of participants, and take accurate notes about what happens. As each issue is addressed, identify the subject. Then, briefly summarize the views expressed. List actions to be taken, and name the people identified to follow up.

Drafting Use your notes to draft your meeting minutes. As you list and discuss each topic, present ideas objectively; record what was said, and do not take sides in any disputes. Use complete sentences, and identify any questions raised.

Revising Use a numbering system or bullets to organize topics, and use boldfaced type or underlining to help readers locate topics of interest. Revise to make the notes brief and to maintain a consistently objective tone.

Editing and Proofreading Check your final copy against your original notes. Be sure you have represented all discussions accurately and have spelled names correctly. Check that the formatting you have chosen is consistent.

Publishing Distribute your meeting notes before the next meeting. This courtesy gives participants a chance to review your notes with two goals in mind: First, club members will want to be sure they remember what decisions were made; second, they may need to be reminded of the actions they agreed to take.

15.3 Forms and Applications

What Are Forms and Applications?

In the fast-paced world of computer databases and printouts, forms and applications are everywhere—at school to help students join clubs, in the workplace to help people obtain jobs, and even in the home as people order from a catalog. Forms and applications are preprinted with blank spaces for specific information. To effectively complete these documents

- write legibly so that information can be read.
- read all the labels and instructions to make sure you're supplying the correct information.

Model Form: Fax (Facsimile) Cover Sheet

When people send a fax, they usually use a cover sheet to make the communication more formal. Cover sheets tell who sent the fax, who should receive it, and how many pages the complete fax contains. Most provide a space for a brief handwritten message. Look at this example:

A company letterhead clearly identifies the sender of the fax.

The sender completes information thoroughly, providing the recipient's fax number and the total number of pages.

The remarks on a fax cover sheet should be brief and to the point. Longer or more in-depth comments should be included in a properly formatted business letter, which can be faxed along with the cover sheet.

Your Yearbook!
5 Harr Court • Columbus, Ohio 43229
phone 614.555.2637 • fax 614.555.2601
e-mail: jay@address.com

Fax

FACSIMILE COVER SHEET/TRANSMITTAL

DATE: *10/19/20--*

TO: *Luke Pelliccio – Photos by Pelliccio*

FAX NUMBER: *614-555-1200*

FAX SOURCE TRANSMISSION NUMBER: *614-555-2637*

FROM: *Elaine Rothman*

TOTAL NUMBER OF PAGES (including this cover sheet): 3

REMARKS:

Luke - When will you be able to review the photos you took for Medford High? I need to set aside time for any reshoots that may be necessary. Let me know.

Thanks, Elaine

Model Application

Opening your first bank account is an exciting moment. In the model below, notice how one teenager completed the application for such an account.

GULFPORT SAVINGS BANK
Biloxi • Gulfport • Hurley

NAME(S): Anthony Coratella
Judith Coratella

ADDRESS: 171 Central Avenue
Biloxi, MS 39531

TELEPHONE (HOME AND WORK):
Home: (228) 555-6035
Work: (Judith): (228) 555-3400 x51

TAX ID NUMBER(S):
Anthony: 999-00-9999
Judith: 888-00-8888

DATE(S) OF BIRTH:
(FOR CUSTODIAL ACCOUNT, INCLUDE MINORS)
Anthony: 7/5/89 Judith: 5/1/62

ACCOUNT NUMBER: *(for internal use)*

ACCOUNT TYPE:
☐ NOW ☐ Statement Savings
☐ Money Market ☑ Passbook Savings
☐ Checking

ACCOUNT OWNERSHIP:
☐ Individual ☐ Corporation
☑ Joint w/Survivorship ☐ Partnership/Firm
☐ Joint w/o Survivorship ☐ Custodial

SPECIAL INSTRUCTIONS:

Account # ____________ Chex System ☐

CUSTOMER TAXPAYER IDENTIFICATION BACKUP WITHHOLDING CERTIFICATION
Under penalties of perjury, I certify that the number shown on this form is my correct Taxpayer Identification Number. I also certify that I am not subject to backup withholding either because I have not been notified that I am subject to backup withholding as a failure to report all interest and dividends, or because the Internal Revenue Service has notified me that I am no longer subject to backup withholding.

Signature *Judith Coratella* Date 10/28/20--

By signing this form, I/We agree to the rules and regulations regarding this account of Gulfport Savings Bank. I/We certify receipt of a Deposit Account Agreement, Schedule of Interest and Charges, Funds Availability Agreement, Electronic Funds Transfer Agreement and Truth-in-Savings Disclosures.

DATE	SIGNATURE
10/28/20--	*Judith Coratella*
10/28/20--	*Anthony Coratella*

Date Opened: 10/28/20-- Initial Deposit: $25 ☐ Check ☑ Cash Opened by: ______

A writer includes only the specific information requested. In fact, some spaces are left blank as the directions request.

When there doesn't seem to be enough space, writers should write small but legibly or find out how to include requested information.

The writer neatly checks off the type of account desired. In this case, a bank employee can explain the different choices.

Noting one person's name inside parentheses helps readers know which information goes with each person listed on the form. Slashes might also help separate this information when it is entered on the same line.

Knowing in advance that an adult's signature will be required avoids delays. Sometimes forms can be taken home and returned with the necessary signatures.

Grammar, Usage, and Mechanics

In Celebration, 1987, Sam Gilliam, National Museum of American Art, Washington, D.C.

Chapter 16 Nouns and Pronouns

▲ Critical Viewing Nouns can name parts of things as well as things themselves. How many parts can you name on this grasshopper? **[Relate]**

This chapter presents nouns and pronouns, which are the words we use to name people, places, things, and ideas. If you were to take a walk in the country and wanted to relate what you saw, you would use nouns: *tree, flowers, bees, ants, animals, leaves, stream, grass, sky, sun.* All these words are nouns. If you saw people during your walk, you would use nouns to identify them, too: *man, woman, children, gardener, Bob Smith, Clara.*

Sometimes you need a replacement for a noun—a word like *he* or *she, him* or *her, I* or *me.* These replacements are called pronouns, and they take the place of nouns in sentences.

In this chapter, you will study both nouns and pronouns.

Diagnostic Test

Directions: Write all answers on a separate sheet of paper.

Skill Check A. Copy these sentences. Underline the common nouns, put two lines under compound nouns, and circle the proper nouns.

1. Because insects are so small, they must have creative ways to protect themselves, Sunday through Saturday, 365 days a year.
2. A saddleback caterpillar has sharp hairs that will break and release poison when they prick your skin.
3. An inchworm and a walking stick use camouflage.
4. Often insects like syrphus flies, which cannot defend themselves, mimic other insects that have better defenses.
5. One species, found in North America, looks like a type that tastes bad to birds.

Skill Check B. Copy the following sentences. Underline each pronoun, and draw an arrow to its antecedent.

6. Insects do not learn their behavior from their parents.
7. In fact, an adult usually dies before her young are born.
8. Consequently, an insect must rely on its instincts to survive.
9. The behavioral patterns are built deep in the nervous system, and they are apparent when stimulated.
10. Every insect reacts to its surroundings.

Skill Check C. Write the reflexive or intensive pronouns in these sentences, and label them.

11. If a cockroach sees a light, it will hide itself in a dark area.
12. If you're near a light at night, you may find yourself surrounded by moths.
13. People often find themselves bothered by mosquitos.
14. Animals themselves attract fleas by the warmth of their bodies.
15. Insects seem to think for themselves, but instinct rules.

Skill Check D. Write and label the demonstrative, interrogative, or relative pronoun in each sentence.

16. A female wasp that is ready to reproduce finds a place where she can build a nest.
17. She then seeks prey, which is usually a tarantula or caterpillar.
18. This is a tarantula captured by a wasp.
19. Those are the books with more facts about wasps.
20. Who borrowed one of the books?

Skill Check E. Write the indefinite pronoun from each sentence.

21. Insect behavior varies by species; most of it is ruled by instinct.
22. However, many do have some ability to learn.
23. A honeybee learns colors and specific landmarks, and it watches both as it returns to its hive.
24. Every species is different; each follows inherited patterns.
25. Behavioral patterns are characteristic of some species but not others, and they have been developed over time.

Section 16.1 Nouns

The word *noun* comes from the Latin word *nomen*, which means "name."

KEY CONCEPT A **noun** is a word that names a person, place, or thing. Nouns name things that can be seen and touched as well as those that cannot be seen and touched. ■

Notice in the chart below that among the things nouns can name are ideas, actions, conditions, and qualities.

People			
Uncle Mike	Catherine	neighbor	boys
Places			
Canada	library	garden	city
Things			

Things You Can See and Touch		Ideas and Actions		Conditions and Qualities	
cicada	trees	justice	rebellion	joy	illness
store	mayfly	peace	election	beauty	bravery

Note About Collective Nouns: Nouns that name *groups* of people or things are known as *collective nouns.*

EXAMPLES: swarm, crowd, group, committee, family, herd

Theme: Insects

In this section, you will learn about nouns. All the examples and exercises are about insects.

Cross-Curricular Connection: Science

Exercise 1 **Identifying Nouns as People, Places, or Things** Write the two nouns in each group, and label each as a *person, place,* or *thing.*

1. scientist thorax eat
2. insect flutter identification
3. smelled scent laboratory
4. color botanist bright
5. immature appearance swamp
6. clear nest grocer
7. butterfly growth near
8. forest undergo abdomen
9. shell country exhausting
10. technician belief direct

More Practice

Language Lab CD-ROM
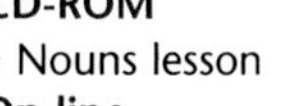
- Nouns lesson

On-line Exercise Bank
- Section 16.1

Grammar Exercise Workbook
- pp. 1–2

Compound Nouns

Nouns may not always be just one word. A name such as Uncle Mike is a noun. So, too, are other words that must stand together to name a person, place, or thing.

KEY CONCEPT A **compound noun** is a noun that is made up of more than one word. ■

As the following chart shows, *compound nouns* are written in several different ways.

TYPES OF COMPOUND NOUNS		
Separated	**Hyphenated**	**Combined**
bubble bath station wagon	daughter-in-law hand-me-down	shipwreck handstand

Historically, most compound nouns begin as separate words. Over a long period of time, more and more people start to hyphenate the words. Finally, many compound nouns come to be written as one word. If you are not sure how to spell a compound noun, check a dictionary. If the compound noun you are looking for is not entered in the dictionary, you can safely spell it as separate words.

▼ **Critical Viewing** The name of this bee is a compound noun. What do you think it might be? **[Deduce]**

Exercise 2 **Recognizing Compound Nouns** List the ten compound nouns you find in the following paragraph.

EXAMPLE: Last weekend, Jane collected insects with her grandparents.

ANSWER: weekend; grandparents

Insects are fascinating animals. Each one has something unique about it. Any notebook belonging to a bug collector is full of interesting facts. Here are a few: The *Chrysiridia madagascarensis*, a moth, is full of vibrant colors. A railroad worm, the larval form of a beetle found in South America, makes its own light. A flea has a broad jump of over 33 centimeters. Honeybees do a dance to communicate where a specific flower is located, and the queen bee of bumblebees gives birth to every bee that lives in her beehive!

16.1

Common and Proper Nouns

All nouns can be divided into two groups: *common nouns* and *proper nouns*.

KEY CONCEPTS A **common noun** names any one of a class of people, places, or things. A **proper noun** names a specific person, place, or thing. ■

As you can see in the following chart, proper nouns always begin with a capital letter.

Common Nouns	Proper Nouns
writer	Mark Twain, Emily Dickinson
order	Odonata, Neuroptera
building	White House, Monticello

Exercise 3 Distinguishing Between Common and Proper Nouns Write the one proper noun in each group, adding the necessary capitalization.

EXAMPLE: planet neptune star
ANSWER: Neptune

1.	insect	bumblebee	north america
2.	reptile	india	ocean
3.	thorax	professor	monday
4.	wings	antennae	professor jones
5.	venus	plant	fly
6.	tarantula	chicago	condition
7.	jurassic period	dinosaurs	jaw
8.	syrphus fly	food	national bug week
9.	dandelion	mothers' day	mothers
10.	june	autumn	month

More Practice

Language Lab CD-ROM
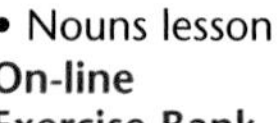
- Nouns lesson

On-line Exercise Bank
- Section 16.1

Grammar Exercise Workbook
- pp. 3–4

◀ Critical Viewing Would you use more common nouns or more proper nouns in a description of this picture? Why? **[Explain]**

Section 16.1 Section Review

GRAMMAR EXERCISES 4–10

Exercise 4 **Identifying Nouns** Write the nouns in the following sentences.

1. Many insects die when winter comes.
2. However, some manage to survive by migration or hibernation.
3. Some hibernate as adults in a warm place, such as a barn or house.
4. Other insects hibernate in eggs, in cocoons, or as larvae.
5. The monarch is a kind of butterfly that migrates.

Exercise 5 **Identifying Compound Nouns** Write the compound nouns from the following sentences.

1. The life span of insects is different for each species.
2. An adult male mayfly never lives to see his offspring; he lives only a few hours.
3. A queen termite can live up to 50 years, although her lifestyle consists of populating the hive.
4. An individual dragonfly does not live long, but this species has survived about 250 million years.
5. The American cockroach survives because of its adaptability to change.

Exercise 6 **Spelling Compound Nouns Correctly** Use a dictionary to help you write compound nouns. On your paper, write the correct spelling from each of the following sets.

1. lifetime	life time	life-time
2. lifesize	life-size	life size
3. swandive	swan-dive	swan dive
4. often times	oftentimes	often-times
5. stonefly	stone-fly	stone fly

Exercise 7 **Recognizing and Writing Proper and Common Nouns** Copy each sentence. Capitalize proper nouns, and underline common nouns.

1. During class, professor dominguez lectured about the order orthoptera.
2. Tree crickets are a species in this order.
3. Dragonflies and mayflies have noticeable wings, natasha pointed out.
4. We visited the beane museum to get a closer look at insect mouthparts.
5. Professor dominguez told us that beetles and grasshoppers have chewing mouthparts.

Exercise 8 **Find It in Your Reading** Skim magazines or newspapers to find five examples each of proper and common nouns and at least one collective noun. Bring your examples to class.

Exercise 9 **Find It in Your Writing** Look through your portfolio, and select a piece of your writing. Identify at least one example of each type of noun (*common*, *proper*, *compound*, and *collective*).

Exercise 10 **Writing Application** Write a comparison of two insects. Use at least three compound and five proper nouns. Underline the compound nouns, and circle the proper nouns.

Section 16.2

Pronouns

You would probably never say, "Michael said Michael lost Michael's watch." Once you had clearly identified Michael as the person you were talking about, repeating the noun *Michael* would sound awkward. Instead, you would probably say, "Michael said he lost his watch." The words *he* and *his* are called *pronouns.* They stand for the noun *Michael.*

KEY CONCEPT **Pronouns** are words that stand for nouns or for words that take the place of nouns. ■

Antecedents of Pronouns

Pronouns get their meaning from the words they stand for. These words are called *antecedents.*

KEY CONCEPT **Antecedents** are nouns (or words that take the place of nouns) for which pronouns stand. ■

In the following examples, the arrows point from pronouns to their antecedents. In the first sentence, the pronouns *he* and *his* stand for the noun *Michael,* their antecedent. In the second, the pronouns *they* and *their* stand for the noun *Levines,* their antecedent. In the third, the pronoun *it* stands for an entire group of words that takes the place of a noun. This group of words is the antecedent of the pronoun *it.*

EXAMPLES: *Michael* said *he* lost *his* watch at the fair.

When the Levines moved, *they* gave *their* pets to neighbors.

[Attending the Mardi Gras] can be tiring, but *it* can be a lot of fun!

Antecedents do not always appear before their pronouns, however. Sometimes, an antecedent *follows* its pronoun.

EXAMPLE: Because of *its* carnival, Rottweil, Germany, is my favorite city.

There are several kinds of pronouns. Most of them have specific antecedents, but a few do not.

Theme: Carnivals

In this section, you will learn about pronouns. The examples and exercises are about celebrations from a variety of countries and cultures.

Cross-Curricular Connection: Social Studies

▲ **Critical Viewing** If you were to use the pronouns *it, they,* and *them* in referring to this photograph, what could be the antecedents of these pronouns? **[Apply]**

GRAMMAR IN LITERATURE

from The Cask of Amontillado

Edgar Allan Poe

In the following excerpt, notice the underlined pronouns. The antecedent of each is italicized.

The thousand injuries of *Fortunato* I had borne as I best could, but when he ventured upon insult I vowed revenge. You, who so well know the nature of my soul, will not suppose, however, that I gave utterance to a threat. At length I would be avenged; this was a *point* definitely settled—but the very definitiveness with which it was resolved precluded the idea of risk.

Exercise 11 **Recognizing Antecedents** Write the antecedent of each underlined pronoun.

1. Carnivals have varied their images over time.
2. Many carnivals developed from festivals in Europe that were held every year.
3. They included markets where merchants sold their wares.
4. Eventually, these carnivals adopted rides, games, shows, and exhibits that often included sideshows.
5. Another type of carnival is made up of merrymaking; it is celebrated just before a traditional time of fasting.
6. Rottweil, Germany, has its carnival in February or March.
7. There, the people dress themselves in fabulous costumes.
8. Rio de Janeiro, Brazil, also has a grand carnival; it is famous all over the world.
9. To prepare for it, samba dancers teach their skills in classes.
10. New Orleans, Louisiana, hosts Mardi Gras during February or March; thousands of people flock to it each year.

Exercise 12 **Writing With Pronouns and Antecedents** Write a sentence or two using each of the following nouns, accompanied by a pronoun that uses the noun as an antecedent.

1. clowns
2. festival
3. dancer
4. New York City
5. fireworks

More Practice

Language Lab CD-ROM
- Pronouns lesson

On-line Exercise Bank
- Section 16.2

Grammar Exercise Workbook
- pp. 5–6

16.2

Personal Pronouns

The most common pronouns are those that you use to refer to yourself and the people and things around you. These pronouns are called *personal pronouns.*

KEY CONCEPT **Personal pronouns** refer to the person speaking (first person), the person spoken to (second person), or the person, place, or thing spoken about (third person). ■

PERSONAL PRONOUNS		
	Singular	Plural
First Person	I, me my, mine	we, us our, ours
Second Person	you your, yours	you your, yours
Third Person	he, him, his she, her, hers it, its	they, them their, theirs

Spelling Tip

When using *its* as a pronoun, be sure to omit the apostrophe. *It's* is a contraction for *it is* and is never used as a pronoun.

Exercise 13 **Identifying Personal Pronouns and Their Antecedents** Write the personal pronouns and their antecedents. HINT: The antecedent may be in a previous sentence.

EXAMPLE: Liz handed her brother his coat.
ANSWERS: *her*, Liz; *his*, brother

1. Keiko and her family went to the carnival in the city this weekend.
2. Her father went straight toward the Ferris wheel.
3. He told them that the first Ferris wheel was built by George W.G. Ferris.
4. It was 250 feet in diameter and had 36 cabs that held 60 people each.
5. Keiko was astounded when she thought of 2,160 people on one Ferris wheel.

More Practice

Language Lab CD-ROM
- Pronouns lesson

On-line Exercise Bank
- Section 16.2

Grammar Exercise Workbook
- pp. 5–6

Reflexive and Intensive Pronouns

The ending *-self* or *-selves* can be added to some personal pronouns to form *reflexive* and *intensive pronouns.*

KEY CONCEPTS A **reflexive pronoun** ends in *-self* or *-selves* and indicates that someone or something performs an action to, for, or upon itself. Reflexive pronouns point back to a noun or pronoun earlier in the sentence. An **intensive pronoun** ends in *-self* or *-selves* and simply adds emphasis to a noun or pronoun in the same sentence. ■

The following chart lists the eight reflexive and intensive pronouns used in English.

REFLEXIVE AND INTENSIVE PRONOUNS		
	Singular	Plural
First Person	myself	ourselves
Second Person	yourself	yourselves
Third Person	himself, herself, itself	themselves

A reflexive pronoun is essential to the meaning of a sentence. In the examples below, *herself* tells who was helped to some turkey and *themselves* tells for whom the milk was poured.

REFLEXIVE: Joy helped *herself* to some turkey.

They poured *themselves* some milk.

An intensive pronoun, on the other hand, simply adds emphasis. If you omit an intensive pronoun, the sentence will still contain the same basic information.

INTENSIVE: The mayor *herself* attended the carnival.

An intensive pronoun usually comes directly after its antecedent, but not always.

INTENSIVE: Frank fixed the refrigerator *himself.*

Don't use a pronoun that ends in *-self* or *-selves* in place of a personal pronoun.
Incorrect: Josh sent postcards from New Orleans to Les and myself.
Correct: Josh sent postcards from New Orleans to Les and me.

Exercise 14 **Distinguishing Between Reflexive and Intensive Pronouns** Write the reflexive or intensive pronoun in each sentence. Then, label each *reflexive* or *intensive.*

EXAMPLE: The dancer spun herself in circles.
ANSWER: herself (reflexive)

1. Mardi Gras itself has become an event.
2. It was originally intended to allow people to enjoy themselves before a time of fasting.
3. If you yourself have ever attended one, you know it is a week-long celebration.
4. Participants dress themselves in colorful costumes.
5. The mayor himself enjoys the festivities.

More Practice

Language Lab CD-ROM
- Pronouns lesson

On-line Exercise Bank
- Section 16.2

Grammar Exercise Workbook
- pp. 7–8

Demonstrative, Relative, and Interrogative Pronouns

Another group of pronouns can be used to direct attention, relate ideas, or ask questions.

Demonstrative Pronouns *Demonstrative pronouns* help specify one of many different people, places, or things.

KEY CONCEPT **Demonstrative pronouns** direct attention to specific people, places, or things. ■

The following chart lists the four demonstrative pronouns.

DEMONSTRATIVE PRONOUNS	
Singular	Plural
this, that	these, those

Demonstrative pronouns may come before or after their antecedents.

BEFORE: *This* is the person we want to hire.

AFTER: Of all the celebrations in the world, *that* is my favorite.

Relative Pronouns *Relative pronouns* relate clauses. (See Chapter 21 for more details about clauses.)

KEY CONCEPT A **relative pronoun** begins a subordinate clause and connects it to another idea in the sentence. ■

The chart below lists the five relative pronouns.

RELATIVE PRONOUNS				
that	which	who	whom	whose

The following examples show the way relative pronouns are used in sentences.

Independent Clause	Subordinate Clause
We planted a shrub	*that* attracts ladybugs.
I saw a cicada,	*which* was a surprise.
Louisa is the player	*who* pitched first.
Phil is the debater	*whom* the judges chose.
We visited Grandmother,	*whose* house is in New Orleans.

◀ **Critical Viewing** Do you think this costume is designed more to reflect the meaning of Mardi Gras or the heritage of the individual wearing the costume? What do you think that heritage is? **[Deduce]**

Interrogative Pronouns Most relative pronouns can also be used as *interrogative pronouns.*

KEY CONCEPT An **interrogative pronoun** is used to begin a question. ■

The following chart lists the five interrogative pronouns.

INTERROGATIVE PRONOUNS				
what	which	who	whom	whose

An interrogative pronoun may or may not have a specific antecedent. In the following, only *which* has an antecedent.

EXAMPLES: *What* do you mean?

Which of the vegetables do you want?

Who will go with me to the park?

Exercise 15 **Recognizing Demonstrative, Relative, and Interrogative Pronouns** Write the pronoun in each sentence. Then, label each *demonstrative, relative,* or *interrogative.*

EXAMPLE: Alice chose the place that her family visited.
ANSWER: that (relative)

1. Mardi Gras is a carnival that is held before Lent begins.
2. This is the grand finale of a long carnival season.
3. Mardi Gras, which is a French tradition, was introduced to the United States in the early 1700's.
4. Several southern states started Mardi Gras as an annual tradition, and these still celebrate it today.
5. This is a holiday in a few states.
6. Which of the states has a famous celebration?
7. New Orleans, which is famous for its Mardi Gras celebration, starts activities early.
8. Societies that organize the event are called *krewes.*
9. Who comes to celebrate?
10. Tourists, who come from around the world, join locals to participate in Mardi Gras.

More Practice

Language Lab CD-ROM
- Pronouns lesson

On-line Exercise Bank
- Section 16.2

Grammar Exercise Workbook
- pp. 9–10

Indefinite Pronouns

Indefinite pronouns resemble interrogative pronouns in that they often lack specific antecedents.

SPECIFIC ANTECEDENT: *Some* of the tourists were late.

NO SPECIFIC ANTECEDENT: *Everyone* ate *something.*

KEY CONCEPT **Indefinite pronouns** refer to people, places, or things, often without specifying which ones. ■

The following chart lists the indefinite pronouns.

INDEFINITE PRONOUNS				
Singular			Plural	Singular or Plural
another	everyone	nothing	both	all
anybody	everything	one	few	any
anyone	little	other	many	more
anything	much	somebody	others	most
each	neither	someone	several	none
either	nobody	something		some
everybody	no one			

Exercise 16 **Identifying Indefinite Pronouns** Write the indefinite pronoun or pronouns in each sentence.

EXAMPLE: Most of us know something about carnivals.
ANSWER: Most; something

1. Before 1900, no one moved Ferris wheels from place to place.
2. Eventually, somebody working for the Eli Bridge Company started making portable Ferris wheels.
3. This someone was William E. Sullivan.
4. Many were sold to carnivals that wanted to travel.
5. Now, everyone could enjoy a ride on a Ferris wheel.
6. Most of the carnivals started selling popular carnival foods.
7. One could play games at most traveling carnivals.
8. A few may even win some prizes.
9. The carnivals had exhibits for anything considered spectacular.
10. Several had sideshows that featured natural wonders.

More Practice

Language Lab CD-ROM
- Pronouns lesson

On-line Exercise Bank
- Section 16.2

Grammar Exercise Workbook
- pp. 11–12

16.2

Hands-on Grammar

Noun Classification Fold-up

Cut a square for which the sides are at least six inches. Fold it in half diagonally to form a triangle. Fold the triangle in half. Unfold the square to reveal that you have created four triangular sections. Cut along each of the folds toward the center of the square, leaving a little bit of the fold uncut so that the triangles do not fall apart. Then, label the triangles as shown below.

Turn the square over, and label the other sides of the triangles as shown.

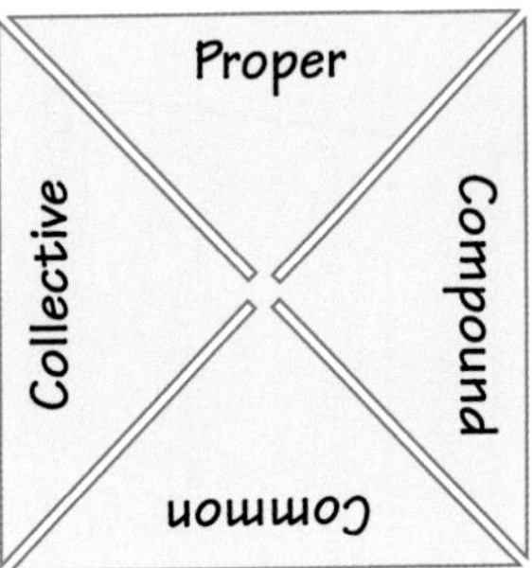

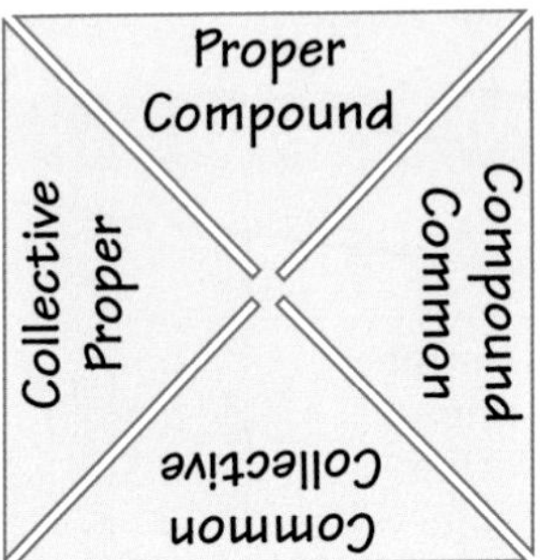

When you have finished labeling and cutting, fold one triangle over the other to show how nouns can fall into more than one category. For example, some nouns are common, but other nouns are both common and collective. Fold each triangle over the other to show combinations of noun types. On each triangle, write at least two nouns that fit the label for each section.

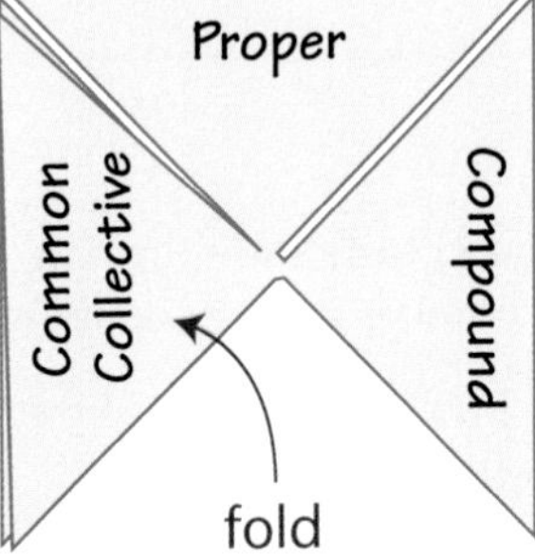

Find It in Your Reading Add nouns to each category as you find examples in your reading. You can begin by adding nouns from the excerpt from "The Cask of Amontillado" on page 223.

Find It in Your Writing Look through the writing in your portfolio to find examples that you can add to each section. If there is a particular type of noun that you cannot find, challenge yourself to add an example to a piece of writing.

Section 16.2 Section Review

GRAMMAR EXERCISES 17–23

Exercise 17 **Recognizing Pronouns and Antecedents** Write the antecedent for each underlined pronoun. If it has no antecedent, write *none*. HINT: The antecedent may appear in a previous sentence in the exercise.

1. The merry-go-round is the oldest amusement ride that is still in use.
2. It has also been called a carousel, and it always has wooden animals fastened to its platform.
3. They are painted bright colors, and anyone may ride.
4. Mules were hooked to the old merry-go-round models, and they would pull the merry-go-round themselves.
5. Later on, these were replaced by electric or gas motors.

Exercise 18 **Recognizing Relative, Demonstrative, and Interrogative Pronouns** Write and label the relative, demonstrative, and interrogative pronouns from each numbered item.

(1) What is the history of carnival? (2) This is celebrated in many Roman Catholic countries. (3) Carnival has origins that are obscure. (4) It started in Italy—that is certain. (5) There are those who believe it was linked to ancient Roman festivals.

Exercise 19 **Recognizing Indefinite Pronouns** Write the indefinite pronoun in each sentence.

1. Many throughout the world know of the carnival in Rio de Janeiro, Brazil.
2. Most of the carnival centers on the samba, Brazilian dance music.
3. The carnival tradition is one rooted in the history of Brazil—rhythms from African slaves and cultural touches from Portugal.
4. Costumes are showy, and some include large headdresses.
5. Everyone spends his or her time dancing and enjoying the music.

Exercise 20 **Classifying Pronouns** On your paper, name the type of each underlined pronoun.

Veracruz, Mexico, celebrates (1) its carnival in February. (2) It started as the Festival of Masks, (3) which was approved by Maximilian (4) himself in 1866. (5) He gave permission to (6) his people to disguise (7) themselves in fancy masks and costumes. (8) These were worn as (9) they walked through the streets on (10) their way to the dance halls.

Exercise 21 **Find It in Your Reading** Read the excerpt from "The Cask of Amontillado" on page 347. How many personal pronouns are there in the excerpt? There are two other types of pronouns in the passage; identify and label them.

Exercise 22 **Find It in Your Writing** Review a selection in your writing portfolio, and identify the pronouns you use. Personal pronouns are probably the most common, but which do you use least? Why are they used less?

Exercise 23 **Writing Application** Write a descriptive paragraph about a celebration you attended. Use a variety of pronoun types. Identify each type you use.

Chapter 17 Verbs

▲ **Critical Viewing** What verbs could you use to describe the action you see in this picture? **[Analyze]**

The verb is perhaps the most important part of speech in English. Without it, there would be no sentences. A **verb** is a word that expresses time while showing an action, a condition, or the fact that something exists.

If you say, "Artists *paint* portraits," the verb *paint* shows an action. If you say, "Treasures *are* on display," the verb *are* shows a condition. If you say, "The king *was* there," the verb *was* expresses existence.

In this chapter, you will learn about *action verbs*, *linking verbs*, and *helping verbs*.

Diagnostic Test

Directions: Write all answers on a separate sheet of paper.

Skill Check A. Identify the action verb in each sentence. Then, label each *V* (*visible action*) or *M* (*mental action*).

1. The earliest Chinese people lived in the Yellow River valley.
2. Written records go back more than 4,000 years.
3. The Chinese believed in the importance of history.
4. Archaeologists wondered about the origin of the Chinese people.
5. They investigated ancient sites.

Skill Check B. Identify the action verb in each sentence. Then, label it *transitive* or *intransitive*.

6. The Shang dynasty once ruled the territory of present-day China.
7. Agriculture sustained the early Chinese.
8. The people worked hard on small patches of land.
9. They also raised pigs, dogs, sheep, and oxen.
10. The rulers lived in fine palaces.

Skill Check C. Write the following sentences. Underline the linking verb, and draw a double-headed arrow connecting the words linked by the verb.

11. The Shang was an aristocratic society.
12. The king became the head of a military nobility.
13. The rulers of each territory were his appointees.
14. The other classes may have been less influential.
15. The commoners remained the largest group.

Skill Check D. Write the verb in each sentence. Then, label it *linking* or *action.*

16. The Zhou dynasty remained powerful for a time.
17. Peasants grew millet, wheat, barley, and rice.
18. Men and women grew tired from long hours in the fields.
19. They turned over the harvest to the ruler.
20. This system appears unfair to people today.

Skill Check E. Write the verb phrase in each sentence. Include all helping verbs, but do not include any words that interrupt the verb phrase.

(21) The Qin dynasty had contributed much to the Chinese culture. (22) However, the accomplishments of the Qin dynasty must have been achieved at an enormous cost of wealth and human life. (23) Taxation and forced labor might have been responsible for the resentment of the dynasty. (24) The indignant population will always be remembered because they rebelled. (25) This power struggle could possibly have caused the fall of the dynasty.

Section 17.1

Action Verbs

Action verbs tell what happens. *Sit* and *throw*, for example, are action verbs.

KEY CONCEPT An **action verb** is a verb that tells what action someone or something is performing. ■

EXAMPLES: The king rules.
Famine struck the people.

The person or thing that performs the action is called the *subject* of the verb. The verb *rules* tells what the subject *king* does. The verb *struck* tells what the subject *Famine* did.

KEY CONCEPT Action verbs show *mental* action as well as *visible* action. ■

VISIBLE ACTION: We *chose* two books about China.

MENTAL ACTION: They *remember* the film about China.

Exercise 1 **Recognizing Action Verbs** Identify the action verb in each sentence, and label it *V* (*visible*) or *M* (*mental*).

EXAMPLE: Sarah attended the concert. attended (V)

1. Chinese artists of the Bronze Age made beautiful carvings.
2. Kings had tombs decorated extravagantly for themselves.
3. Artists painted the walls with scenes of daily life.
4. The Chinese remembered their ancestors.
5. They hoped for harmony between human beings and nature.

GRAMMAR IN LITERATURE

from The Golden Kite, the Silver Wind

Ray Bradbury

Notice in the following sentences how the verbs said, call, will whisper, *and* will know *express the actions of the characters.*

"Then," *said* the daughter, "*call* in your stonemasons and temple builders. I *will whisper* from behind the silken screen and you *will know* the words."

Theme: China

In this section, you will learn to recognize action verbs and to distinguish between those that are transitive and those that are intransitive. The examples and exercises in this section are about China.

Cross-Curricular Connection: Social Studies

Transitive and Intransitive Verbs

An action verb can be *transitive* or *intransitive.*

KEY CONCEPTS An action verb is **transitive** if it directs action toward someone or something named in the same sentence. An action verb is **intransitive** if it does not direct action toward someone or something named in the sentence. ■

The receiver of the action of a transitive verb is called the *object* of the verb. Intransitive verbs, however, have no objects.

TRANSITIVE: Pat *carried* her books to the lecture on Asia.
INTRANSITIVE: The temperature *fell* quickly.

▼ Critical Viewing
This statue army was found when the tomb of an ancient Chinese ruler was unearthed. What might have been its purpose? In your response, use at least one transitive and one intransitive verb. **[Infer]**

Transitive or Intransitive? Most action verbs can be transitive in one sentence and intransitive in another. To determine whether a verb is transitive or intransitive, ask *Whom?* or *What?* after the verb. If you can find the answer in the sentence, the verb is transitive. If not, the verb is intransitive.

TRANSITIVE: Bill *reads* books about Asia.
INTRANSITIVE: Bill *reads* every night before going to bed.

Exercise 2 **Distinguishing Between Transitive and Intransitive Verbs** Identify the action verb in each sentence. Then, label each *transitive* or *intransitive.*

1. The Shang people began as a clan of villagers in central China.
2. Their rule occurred during two separate periods.
3. The first period came before the establishment of the capital city.
4. Archaeologists discovered most of the artifacts from the first period in graves.
5. The art of metalwork advanced greatly during this period.
6. During the second period, the rulers practiced a complex system of ancestor worship.
7. Kings of the Shang dynasty constructed elaborate tombs.
8. They worried about being remembered.
9. Artisans worked with jade, stone, and bronze.
10. They carved the jade in the shape of birds and animals.

More Practice

Language Lab CD-ROM
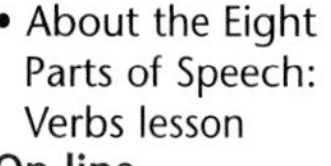
- About the Eight Parts of Speech: Verbs lesson

On-line Exercise Bank
- Section 17.1

Grammar Exercise Workbook
- pp. 13–14

Hands-on Grammar

Transitive and Intransitive Verb Explorer

Use a Verb Explorer flip book to understand the difference between transitive and intransitive verbs. To begin, cut out a piece of paper 5" long and 3" wide. Then, cut out ten 1-1/2" x 3" rectangles, and write a subject and one of the action verbs below on each one. Stack them neatly, and staple them to the left edge of the 5" x 3" paper.

play	sing	go	read	cook
sit	paints	write	watched	drive

Next, cut out thirty 4" x 1" rectangles, and print the word *TRANSITIVE* on ten of them and *INTRANSITIVE* on the other twenty. On the opposite side of each "transitive" rectangle, print the word *NOUN* in one corner. On the other side of ten "intransitive" rectangles, print the word *ADVERB* in a corner. On the remaining ten, print *PREPOSITIONAL PHRASE.* Stack them neatly by category, and staple them (part-of-speech side up) to the right edge of the 5" x 3" rectangle. (See the example below.)

Now, fill in your Verb Explorer. Complete each sentence, first with a noun, next with an adverb, and finally with a prepositional phrase. Check the back of each 4" x 1" rectangle to remind yourself which ones are transitive and which are intransitive. (If you come across a sentence that can't be completed by a noun, you will have found a verb that is always intransitive.)

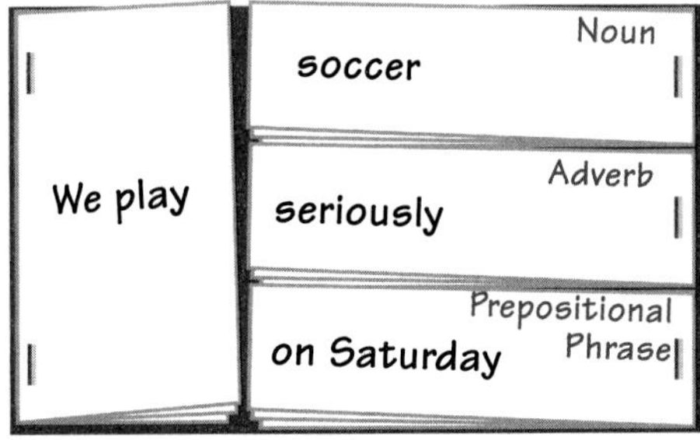

Find It in Your Reading Read the excerpt from "The Golden Kite, the Silver Wind" on page 234. Identify each verb in the second sentence as *transitive* or *intransitive.*

Find It in Your Writing Review a piece of writing from your portfolio. Identify three transitive and three intransitive verbs. Challenge yourself to revise two sentences, changing the verbs from intransitive to transitive.

Section 17.1 Section Review

GRAMMAR EXERCISES 3–8

Exercise 3 Recognizing Action Verbs Identify the action verb in each sentence.

1. Many regard Confucius as the most influential philosopher of China's Golden Age.
2. He belonged to a minor aristocratic family.
3. Confucius served as a local administrator.
4. The rulers of the time valued his advice.
5. Confucius wanted a system of morality and just government.
6. He believed strongly in the rulers of the period.
7. They ruled an ideal society by the example of personal virtue.
8. Confucius hoped for a class of virtuous and cultivated rulers.
9. These men led the people through their example.
10. People remember Confucius today because of his beliefs.

Exercise 4 Distinguishing Between Visible and Mental Action Write the action verb in each sentence. Then, label each *V* (*visible*) or *M* (*mental*).

1. Chinese civilization affected many other peoples.
2. The influence of the Tang dynasty reached from Japan to western China.
3. The Japanese of the time adopted some Chinese rituals and customs.
4. They were taught about the teachings of Zen Buddhism.
5. The Japanese, like the Chinese, believed in the importance of culture and education.

Exercise 5 Recognizing Transitive and Intransitive Verbs Write the action verb in each sentence, and label it *transitive* or *intransitive*.

1. The fall of the Shang dynasty occurred about 1000 B.C.
2. The last Shang monarch ruled unjustly.
3. The king of Chou overthrew him.
4. The people of Chou lived on the northwestern fringes of the Shang domain.
5. The Chou culture reflected the influence of the Shang civilization.
6. Chou rulers wanted as much control over the entire region as possible.
7. They delegated power to vassals.
8. The vassals ruled walled towns and the surrounding territories.
9. Lords with hereditary positions controlled many towns.
10. The structure of the social system created a ruling class.

Exercise 6 Find It in Your Reading In the excerpt from "The Golden Kite, the Silver Wind" on page 362, tell which verbs are transitive and which are intransitive.

Exercise 7 Find It in Your Writing Find five examples of action verbs in your own writing. Tell whether the verbs are transitive or intransitive.

Exercise 8 Writing Application Summarize what you learned about the Shang dynasty. (You may refer to page 363.) Include a verb that shows mental action, a verb that shows visible action, a transitive verb, and an intransitive verb.

Section 17.2

Linking Verbs

Linking verbs do not show action. Though few in number, these verbs are widely used. A linking verb helps one word in a sentence name or describe the condition of another word in the sentence.

KEY CONCEPT A **linking verb** is a verb that connects a word at or near the beginning of a sentence with a word at or near the end. ■

Forms of *Be*

KEY CONCEPT In English, the most common linking verb is some form of the verb *be*. ■

Notice how the forms of *be*—*is*, *are*, and *was*—connect words at the beginning of the following sentences with words at the end.

EXAMPLES: Sara *is* an astronaut.

He *was* glad.

The following chart lists the forms of the verb *be*.

THE FORMS OF *BE*			
am	am being	can be	have been
are	are being	could be	has been
is	is being	may be	had been
was	was being	might be	could have been
were	were being	must be	may have been
		shall be	might have been
		should be	must have been
		will be	shall have been
		would be	should have been
			will have been
			would have been

Note About Verbs Expressing Existence: The verb *be* is not always used as a linking verb. Sometimes, it simply expresses existence, generally by showing where something is located.

EXAMPLES: The missile *should be* on the launch pad.
Here *is* your ticket.

Theme: Apollo 13

In this section, you will learn to recognize linking verbs and to distinguish between linking verbs and action verbs. The examples and exercises in this section are about the mission of *Apollo 13.*

Cross-Curricular Connection: Science

Exercise 9 **Recognizing Forms of *Be* Used as Linking Verbs** Write each sentence on a separate sheet of paper, underlining the linking verb. Then, draw a double-headed arrow to show which words are linked by the verb.

1. The *Apollo 13* mission was successful.
2. It may be the most famous lunar-landing mission.
3. It would be difficult to name a more courageous crew.
4. Their names are James A. Lovell, Jr.; John L. Swigert, Jr.; and Fred Wallace Haise, Jr.
5. These men were aboard during an explosion on the module.

More Practice

Language Lab CD-ROM
- About the Eight Parts of Speech: Verbs lesson

On-line Exercise Bank
- Section 17.2

Grammar Exercise Workbook
- pp. 15–16

Other Linking Verbs

Verbs other than *be* may also be used as linking verbs.

KEY CONCEPT Other verbs may be used in the same way as *be* to link two parts of a sentence. ■

OTHER LINKING VERBS					
appear	feel	look	seem	sound	taste
become	grow	remain	smell	stay	turn

In the examples below, you can see how these verbs act as linking verbs by helping words at the end of the sentences name or describe the place or thing at the beginning.

EXAMPLES: The situation on board *remained* serious.

The astronauts *grew* anxious.

Exercise 10 **Identifying Other Linking Verbs** Write each sentence, underlining the linking verb. Then, draw a double-headed arrow to show which words are linked by the verb.

1. The astronauts felt concerned after sensing the explosion.
2. After the system malfunction, the situation turned serious.
3. The tension in the module grew thick.
4. The levels of oxygen, water, and power appeared lower.
5. Conditions became critical.
6. The moon landing seemed unlikely.
7. The lunar module remained a refuge for longer than expected.
8. The return to Earth looked impossible.
9. A minor mid-course correction became the only solution.
10. On Earth, Mission Control stayed positive.

Section 17.2

Linking Verb or Action Verb?

Most of the verbs in the chart on page 239 can be used as either linking verbs or action verbs. To determine whether a verb is being used as a linking verb or as an action verb in a sentence, you can substitute *am, are,* or *is* for the verb. If the substituted verb makes sense and connects two words, then the original verb is being used as a linking verb in that sentence. If the substituted verb makes the sentence illogical or fails to connect two words, then the original verb is an action verb.

KEY CONCEPT A verb is functioning as a linking verb if *am, are,* or *is* can logically be substituted for the verb. ■

Linking Verbs	Action Verbs
The pears *taste* sweet. The pears *are* sweet. (linking)	I *taste the red pepper.* I *am* the red pepper. (not linking)
Apollo 13 appears ready. *Apollo 13* is ready. (linking)	*Apollo 13* appears suddenly. *Apollo 13* is suddenly. (not linking)
The runner *grew* tired. The runner *is* tired. (linking)	He *grew* a beard. He *is* a beard. (not linking)

Exercise 11 Distinguishing Between Linking Verbs and Action Verbs Write the verb or verbs in each sentence. Then, label each *linking* or *action.*

EXAMPLE: Astronauts felt the heat through their suits.
ANSWER: felt (action)

1. The *Apollo 13* mission seemed routine in its early stages.
2. An electrical surge turned a successful mission into a perilous one.
3. The surge occurred as a result of wires making contact.
4. The astronauts felt vibrations from the explosion.
5. They grew concerned about sparks igniting insulation.

More Practice

Language Lab CD-ROM
- About the Eight Parts of Speech: Verbs lesson

On-line Exercise Bank
- Section 17.2

Grammar Exercise Workbook
- pp. 17–18

Section 17.2 Section Review

GRAMMAR EXERCISES 12–16

Exercise 12 Identifying Linking Verbs Write each sentence, underlining the linking verb. Then, draw a double-headed arrow connecting the words linked by the verb.

1. The *Apollo 13* astronauts were often tired during their extensive screening.
2. Computer-based aids became necessary in the astronauts' training.
3. Knowledge of basic water survival would be crucial to the *Apollo 13* astronauts.
4. After the first year of training, they seemed well prepared.
5. The *Apollo 13* crew was completely ready for their mission.
6. Suddenly, a bright flame became visible.
7. The oxygen content of the air in the craft may have been low.
8. The craft smelled smoky.
9. The control center sounded chaotic to listeners.
10. Everyone felt relieved after the astronauts' safe return.

Exercise 13 Identifying Verbs as Linking or Action Verbs Write the verb in each sentence, and label it *linking* or *action*.

1. The space program looks for qualified candidates.
2. Physical and mental health requirements remain important.
3. Can astronauts grow a beard?
4. Astronauts seem ready for isolation and fear.
5. Most stay in the program.
6. Integrity, ability, and self-confidence appear essential.
7. The selection process looks rigorous.
8. The candidates grow anxious for a decision.
9. Many of the candidates appear at press conferences.
10. Some remain afterward for autograph signing.

Exercise 14 Find It in Your Reading In this excerpt from Jim Lovell and Jeffrey Kluger's *Apollo 13*, identify the linking verb that is part of a contraction. Which words does the verb link?

> "Roger," Lousma responded, in the mandatory matter-of-factness of the Capcom, "we copy your venting."
>
> "It's a gas of some sort," Lovell said. "Can you tell us anything about it? Where is it coming from?"

Exercise 15 Find It in Your Writing Look through two or three pieces of writing in your portfolio. Find five examples of linking verbs. In each case, identify the words that are linked by the verbs.

Exercise 16 Writing Application Write a short explanation of why you would or would not want to take part in a space mission. Use at least one of the following verbs as both an action verb and as a linking verb: *look, appear, grow, stay.*

Helping Verbs

Often, a single verb is formed from as many as four words. *Helping verbs* may be added to a verb such as *sung* to make a *verb phrase,* such as *had sung* or *should have been sung.*

KEY CONCEPT **Helping verbs** are verbs that can be added to another verb to make a single verb phrase. ■

Recognizing Helping Verbs

Learning the forms of *be* in the chart on page 366 and the other verbs that can be used as helping verbs will help you recognize helping verbs in sentences.

KEY CONCEPT Any of the many forms of *be* as well as some other verbs can be used as helping verbs. ■

HELPING VERBS OTHER THAN THE FORMS OF *BE*			
do	have	shall	can
does	has	should	could
did	had	will	may
	would	might	
		must	

Verb phrases are created by the addition of helping verbs to other verbs. The following chart lists six examples, but the possibilities are almost endless.

VERB PHRASES	
Helping Verbs	**Verbs**
am	talking
did	play
can	write
will be	studying
should have	seen
might have been	considered

Helping verbs are sometimes called *auxiliary verbs* or *auxiliaries* because they add meaning to other verbs. Notice how using helping verbs can change the meaning of a sentence.

WITHOUT HELPING VERBS: They *sing* in the morning.

WITH HELPING VERBS: They *will sing* in the morning.
They *might sing* in the morning.

Theme: Apollo 13

In this section, you will learn how to use helping verbs to form verb phrases. The examples and exercises in this section tell more about the mission of *Apollo 13.*

Cross-Curricular Connection: Social Studies

GRAMMAR IN LITERATURE

from Apollo 13

Jim Lovell and Jeffrey Kluger

Notice how the helping verbs had been *and* might have *add meaning to the verbs* launched *and* metamorphosed *in the following sentences.*

. . . No one said anything out loud, no one declared anything officially, but the controllers began to recognize that the *Apollo 13*, which had been launched in triumph just over two days earlier, might have just metamorphosed from a brilliant mission of exploration to one of simple survival.

More Practice

Language Lab CD-ROM
- About the Eight Parts of Speech: Verbs lesson

On-line Exercise Bank
- Section 17.3

Grammar Exercise Workbook
- pp. 19–20

Exercise 17 **Identifying Helping Verbs** Identify the helping verb(s) in each sentence.

EXAMPLE: Al will be watching the mission on television.
ANSWER: will be

1. Did you hear about the *Apollo 13* mission?
2. Many journalists have written about this historic flight.
3. People will be talking about the events of the *Apollo 13* mission for years to come.
4. On the way to the moon, *Apollo 13* must have experienced technical difficulties.
5. An electrical surge had occurred inside a fuel cell.
6. The following explosions might have been caused by the electrical surge.
7. The astronauts had been taught to enter the lunar module in case of emergency.
8. They could survive in the lunar module for 45 hours.
9. After 95 hours in the module, all supplies should have been exhausted.
10. The astronauts' courage has been admired by people throughout the world.

▶ **Critical Viewing** Use a verb phrase to describe this sight at the blastoff of *Apollo 13*. **[Relate]**

Section 17.3

Finding Helping Verbs in Sentences

Verb phrases are often interrupted by other words.

KEY CONCEPT Other words may sometimes separate helping verbs from main verbs in sentences. ■

The following examples show the words of a verb phrase together as well as verb phrases interrupted by other words.

WORDS TOGETHER: They *will be flying* in the morning.

WORDS SEPARATED: They *will* definitely not *be going* with us.

Have you and the others *met* our friends?

Exercise 18 **Identifying Verb Phrases** Write the verb phrase in each sentence. Include all helping verbs, but do not include any words that come between the helping verb and the main verb.

EXAMPLE: Most of this planet's galaxy has not been explored.

ANSWER: has been explored

(1) Differing accounts have sometimes been written of the events of the *Apollo 13* mission. (2) However, you will be impressed by the courage of the *Apollo 13* crew. (3) Had sparks been created by contact between two electrical wires? (4) A fire in space can be caused by any number of sources. (5) A fire would certainly result in limited supplies. (6) An astronaut in trouble must always keep a clear mind. (7) Fortunately, the *Apollo 13* crew had been trained to deal with emergencies. (8) The astronauts did not panic. (9) With correct propulsion adjustments, the moon's gravity will send a spacecraft back to Earth. (10) This voyage may have been the most successful failure in the annals of spaceflight.

Exercise 19 **Writing Sentences With Verb Phrases** Write sentences containing verb phrases, using the verbs and topics given below. Include these helping verbs: *have, will, did, can,* and *would.*

1. admire—astronauts' courage
2. like—space adventure
3. eat—freeze-dried food
4. hear—broadcasts from space
5. learn—space program

Grammar and Style Tip

Even though an adverb might interrupt a verb phrase, it is not considered part of the verb phrase.

More Practice

Language Lab CD-ROM
- About the Eight Parts of Speech: Verbs lesson

On-line Exercise Bank
- Section 17.3

Grammar Exercise Workbook
- pp. 19–20

Section 17.3 Section Review

GRAMMAR EXERCISES 20–25

Exercise 20 Identifying Helping Verbs Write the helping verb(s) in each sentence.

1. The *Apollo 13* mission may have been the most exciting in history.
2. The mission should have proceeded normally.
3. However, problems would arise from an electrical surge.
4. An electrical surge can cause an explosion and a fire.
5. The crew had quickly moved to the lunar module.
6. The crew's water-retaining strategy may have saved their lives.
7. During the mission, the crew was exposed to near-freezing temperatures.
8. The ship did return to Earth five days after the initial launch.
9. According to NASA, *Apollo 13* officially must be classed as a failure.
10. The mission will be viewed differently by those who know the full story.

Exercise 21 Identifying Verb Phrases Write all verb phrases, but do not include any words that come between the helping verb and the main verb.

1. NASA was diligently studying the causes of the crisis.
2. Such an event should never happen again.
3. Since *Apollo 13*, other missions have been sent to the moon.
4. By 1972, astronauts had landed on the moon six times.
5. They were wearing protective clothing.
6. Scientific instruments have always been carried on each flight.
7. A seismograph can easily detect small movements on the moon's surface.
8. Did astronauts always recover samples from the lunar surface?
9. Drills were sometimes used for collecting soil samples.
10. The *Apollo 13* lunar module would carry two astronauts.

Exercise 22 Supplying Helping Verbs Complete each sentence with an appropriate helping verb.

1. They __?__ land near a crater.
2. The crater __?__ originally been the target of *Apollo 13*.
3. During the *Apollo 15* mission, astronauts __?__ driving a lunar rover.
4. Our knowledge of the moon __?__ increased through these missions.
5. Much space technology __?__ later applied to other fields.

Exercise 23 Find It in Your Reading In this excerpt from Jim Lovell and Jeffrey Kluger's *Apollo 13*, identify the verb phrases.

> . . . If a tank of gas is suddenly reading empty and a cloud of gas is surrounding the spacecraft, it's a good bet the two are connected, especially if the whole mess had been preceded by a suspicious ship-shaking bang.

Exercise 24 Find It in Your Writing Identify the verb phrases in a recent piece of your writing. Underline the helping verb(s) in each verb phrase.

Exercise 25 Writing Application Write a description of one thing you would take with you on a voyage to the moon. Use at least three verb phrases in your sentences. Underline the helping verbs.

Chapter 18 Adjectives and Adverbs

▲ **Critical Viewing** Ocean liners like this one are often described as "majestic" or "grand." Do you think these adjectives are fitting? Why? **[Evaluate]**

Often a noun cannot express the exact meaning you have in mind. Imagine, for example, that a relative of a missing person reports, "She sailed off in a boat yesterday." "What kind of boat?" a Coast Guard officer might ask. If the relative were to answer, "She sailed off in a *white two-masted sailing* boat," the officer would have a clearer picture of the boat. Words that describe or explain nouns are called *adjectives*.

Adverbs, another part of speech, work in much the same way except that they describe or explain verbs, adjectives, and other adverbs. For example, the officer might have asked the relative, "Did the boat sail *north* or *south*?" These words are used as *adverbs*.

This chapter will examine both adjectives and adverbs. Together, these two parts of speech are known as *modifiers*. Used carefully, they can clarify and enliven your sentences.

Diagnostic Test

Directions: Write all answers on a separate sheet of paper.

Skill Check A. List the adjectives, but not the articles, in these sentences.

1. Sir Samuel Cunard was a successful merchant.
2. The British shipowner sailed from Canada to England in 1838.
3. With several merchants, he formed a British and North American shipping company.
4. Later, this growing steamship company became known as the Cunard Line, Ltd.
5. The company dispatched the first steamship in 1840.

Skill Check B. Identify the underlined word as either a *definite* or *indefinite article*, or as a *demonstrative, interrogative, indefinite, compound,* or *proper adjective.*

6. Which ship was called the *Britannia*?
7. Its fourteen-day, eight-hour voyage from Liverpool to Boston was one of many milestones.
8. It marked the beginning of regular steamship service across the Atlantic.
9. The *Britannia* was followed across the ocean by Cunard's first iron ship, the *Persia*, in 1855.
10. In 1862, Cunard sailed his first screw-propelled ship, the *China*.

Skill Check C. List the adverbs in these sentences.

11. Public demand for transcontinental rail connections was originally inspired by two American statesmen.
12. This demand was further increased by the California Gold Rush of 1849.
13. The need for transcontinental lines was felt so urgently that construction began during the extremely costly Civil War.
14. The Union Pacific rails began in Omaha, Nebraska, and stretched westward.
15. The Central Pacific rails began in Sacramento, California, and later stretched eastward.

Skill Check D. Identify the underlined word as either an *adverb* or an *adjective*. If it is an adverb, identify the word it modifies as well as the part of speech of that word.

16. The two rails were joined at Promontory, Utah, in 1869.
17. Thus, the coast-to-coast connection for trains was finally completed.
18. It was now possible to cross the country in a matter of weeks instead of months.
19. Migration west was greatly accelerated by the transcontinental railroad.
20. Western cities very soon began to flourish due to the swifter arrival of eastern supplies.

Section 18.1

Adjectives

Whenever you are asked to describe something—your favorite animal, your best friend, or the longest trip you ever took—you are likely to give an answer that is filled with *adjectives*.

KEY CONCEPT An **adjective** is a word used to describe a noun or pronoun or to give a noun or pronoun a more specific meaning. ■

The process by which an adjective describes a word or makes it more specific is called *modification*.

The Process of Modification

To *modify* means to "change slightly." An adjective modifies meaning by answering any of four questions about a noun or pronoun.

KEY CONCEPT Adjectives answer the question *What kind? Which one? How many?* or *How much?* about the nouns and pronouns they modify. ■

The following are adjectives answering each of these questions:

What Kind?	
red boat	*silver* jewelry
sick passenger	*cool* water
Which One?	
third chance	*any* piece
this train	*those* apples
How Many?	
six cars	*several* reasons
both answers	*few* letters
How Much?	
enough space	*more* energy
no rain	*little* effort

Exercise 1 **Coming Up With Examples of Adjectives** Come up with five additional adjective-noun pairs, answering each of the questions in the chart above.

Theme: Travel

In this section, you will learn about adjectives. The examples and exercises in this section are about various types of travel.

Cross-Curricular Connection: Social Studies

More Practice

Language Lab CD-ROM

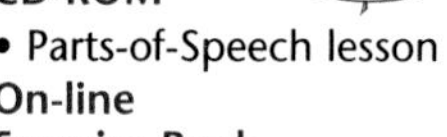

• Parts-of-Speech lesson

On-line Exercise Bank

• Section 18.1

Grammar Exercise Workbook

• pp. 21–22

GRAMMAR IN LITERATURE

from The Long and Winding Road

John Lennon and Paul McCartney

Notice how the highlighted adjectives long, winding, wild, *and* windy *describe the road and the night in the song lyrics that follow. They answer the question* What kind?

The *long* and *winding* road that leads to your door,
Will never disappear,
I've seen that road before
It always leads me here,
Leads me to your door.

The *wild* and *windy* night the rain washed away,
Has left a pool of tears crying for the day.

▲ **Critical Viewing** What three adjectives would you use to give a vivid description of the light in this photograph? **[Describe]**

An adjective usually comes before the noun it modifies. It may, however, come after the noun.

BEFORE THE NOUN: The *sick* child lay in bed.

AFTER THE NOUN: The child, *sick* with fever, lay in bed.

An adjective generally comes after a pronoun it modifies, usually directly after a linking verb such as *is, was, look,* or *seemed.* It may, however, come before the pronoun.

AFTER THE PRONOUN: She was *sick* for a week.

BEFORE THE PRONOUN: *Sick* in bed, he was very bored.

Exercise 2 **Identifying Adjectives and the Words They Modify** Identify each adjective in the following sentences. Then, indicate the word each adjective modifies and the question that it answers (see the chart on page 248).

1. Small work boats were sailed extensively for pleasure in early colonial times.
2. The first pleasure schooner was built in 1816.
3. It was built specifically as a large, luxurious yacht.
4. American yacht clubs started around the 1840's.
5. Six members of the New York Yacht Club financed America's first racing yacht.

More Practice

Language Lab CD-ROM

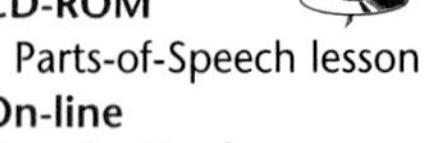

- Parts-of-Speech lesson

On-line Exercise Bank

- Section 18.1

Grammar Exercise Workbook

- pp. 21–22

Exercise 3 **Revising Adjective Placement** In the paragraph below, identify the words modified by the underlined adjectives. Then, revise the paragraph, changing the placement of at least three adjectives.

(1) The 100-foot schooner *America* was finished in 1851. (2) Its fine lines and slimmer bow changed yacht designs. (3) Its victory in an international regatta in 1851 stimulated American yachting. (4) The America's Cup trophy, named for the *America*, became the most famous prize in yacht racing. (5) Competition for the America's Cup continues today with racing fleets of one-design crafts, each manufactured to meet rigorous specifications.

Articles

Three adjectives—*the*, *a*, and *an*—are called *articles*. *The* is called the *definite article*; *a* and *an* are called *indefinite articles*.

KEY CONCEPTS The **definite article,** *the*, indicates that the noun it modifies refers to a specific person, place, or thing. The **indefinite articles,** *a* and *an*, indicate that the nouns they modify refer to any one of a class of people, places, or things. ■

Look at the examples below:

DEFINITE: *The* catcher wore *the* face mask.

IINDEFINITE: Give me *an* essay that you think I would enjoy.

Notice that *an* is used before a vowel sound; *a* is used before a consonant sound. The emphasis is on the sound, not the letter. The letter *h* is a consonant, but it may sound like a vowel. *O* and *u* are vowels, but they may sound like consonants.

Consonant Sounds	Vowel Sounds
a *b*aseball	an *a*pple
a *h*istory lesson (*h* sound)	an *h*onest man (no *h* sound)
a *o*ne-horse town (*w* sound)	an *o*nly child (*o* sound)
a *u*nion (*y* sound)	an *u*gly hat (*u* sound)

Exercise 4 **Completing Sentences With Definite and Indefinite Articles** Write the article needed to complete each sentence.

EXAMPLE: In (definite) 1800's, trains became popular modes of transportation.
ANSWER: the

1. (definite) first passenger train cars were 15 feet long and 17 feet wide.
2. They were built like (indefinite) stagecoach with railroad wheels.
3. Later, six wheels were placed on (definite) passenger cars.
4. Today, there are (indefinite) variety of passenger cars.
5. (definite) typical passenger car has (indefinite) aisle with seats on either side.

▼ **Critical Viewing** What adjectives could you use to describe a train that moves quickly? **[Analyze]**

Nouns Used as Adjectives

Articles and descriptive words—such as *quick, red,* or *new*—are not the only kinds of words that can act as adjectives. In fact, nouns themselves may sometimes be used as adjectives before other nouns.

KEY CONCEPT A noun used as an adjective answers the question *What kind?* or *Which one?* about a noun that follows it. ■

EXAMPLES: guitar — *guitar* music (*What kind* of music?)
evening — *evening* meal (*Which* meal?)

Internet Tip

Nouns used as adjectives make great search words and help to specify the information wanted. For example, just typing in *flares* will produce a variety of sites on flares. By typing in *road flares,* you will find only sites with that specific type of flare.

Exercise 5 **Identifying Nouns Used as Adjectives** Write the noun or nouns that are used as adjectives in each sentence. Make sure each one modifies another noun.

(1) For a fun vacation, some families plan road trips to state monuments and historic sites. (2) This type of family vacation requires a careful review of state maps to plan a route that covers restaurants, motels, and the sites themselves.

(3) The first step is for family members to choose a destination. (4) Next, several different highway routes should be highlighted and studied for the best stops and visitor attractions. (5) Once a route is chosen, the road miles should be calculated, the travel time should be estimated, and a detailed itinerary should be made.

More Practice

Language Lab CD-ROM
- Parts-of-Speech lesson

On-line Exercise Bank
- Section 18.1

Grammar Exercise Workbook
- pp. 23–24

Exercise 6 **Writing Sentences With Nouns Used as Adjectives** Write sentences in which you use each of the following nouns as adjectives.

1. plane	3. beach	5. ground
2. automobile	4. airport	

Proper and Compound Adjectives

In addition to the types of adjectives already mentioned, there are *proper* and *compound* adjectives.

Proper Adjectives *Proper adjectives* can be simply proper nouns. Others are formed from proper nouns.

KEY CONCEPT A **proper adjective** is a proper noun used as an adjective or an adjective formed from a proper noun. ■

When proper nouns are used as adjectives, the form of the proper noun is not changed.

However, when an adjective is formed from a proper noun, the form of the proper noun is changed, as shown below.

EXAMPLES:	Alcott	*Alcott* novel (*What kind* of novel?)
	Chicago	*Chicago* storm (*What kind* of storm?)

EXAMPLES:	Jefferson	*Jeffersonian* democracy (*What kind* of democracy?)
	Mexico	*Mexican* art (*What kind* of art?)

Proper adjectives generally begin with a capital letter.

Grammar and Style Tip

Possessive nouns can act as adjectives. *England's*, for instance, may be considered a proper adjective when it shows ownership: *England's* waterways.

Compound Adjectives Adjectives made up of more than one word are called *compound adjectives.*

KEY CONCEPT A **compound adjective** is an adjective that is made up of more than one word. ■

Compound adjectives are often written as hyphenated words. However, a number of them are open or are written as combined words. Consult a dictionary whenever you are in doubt about the spelling of a compound adjective.

EXAMPLES:	*far-off* land	*farsighted* leader
	hard-shell crabs	*hardhearted* neighbor

▼ **Critical Viewing**
Describe this picture by telling what kind of ship it is, how many masts it has, how much wind there is, and what kind of ocean it is. What adjectives did you use in your description? **[Describe]**

Exercise 7 **Identifying Proper and Compound Adjectives** Write the proper and compound adjectives in each sentence.

(1) Late in 1577, Francis Drake left England to attempt a three-year circumnavigation of the globe. (2) After crossing the Atlantic Ocean, Drake sailed down the South American coast. (3) Drake lightened the expedition by disposing of two unfit ships and one high-spirited gentleman.

(4) Drake then sailed quickly through the Straits of Magellan and ran into a Pacific storm. (5) For the next five and a half months, his crew raided Spanish settlements at will, committing very little violence but taking many treasures.

Exercise 8 **Revising to Include Proper and Compound Adjectives** Revise the following paragraph so that it consists of sentences that each contain proper or compound adjectives.

(1) This summer, we took our vacation in London. (2) Our flight there took six hours. (3) Even though we traveled all night, our first day was packed with excitement. (4) We visited Buckingham Palace and ate in a restaurant where we sampled various foods that England has to offer. (5) In the days that followed, we visited famous sites throughout London.

Pronouns Used as Adjectives

The previous section presented descriptive adjectives, articles, nouns used as adjectives, proper adjectives, and compound adjectives. This section will discuss pronouns that can be used as adjectives.

KEY CONCEPT A personal pronoun that can be used as an adjective answers the question *Which one?* about a noun that follows it. ■

Possessive Pronouns as Adjectives Seven of the personal pronouns can be considered both pronouns and adjectives. *My, your, his, her, its, our,* and *their* can be thought of as pronouns because they have antecedents. They can also be thought of as adjectives because they modify nouns by answering the question *Which one?*

EXAMPLE: *My* (adj.) *daughter* (word modified) left *her* (adj.) new *backpack* (word modified) at school.

Exercise 9 **Recognizing Personal Pronouns That Act as Adjectives** Write each possessive pronoun or adjective in the following sentences, followed by the word it modifies.

EXAMPLE: Yacht owners sail their boats long distances.
ANSWER: their boats

1. Have you asked a professional captain for his advice?
2. A professional can help you chart your course.
3. My sister enjoyed her friends' boat.
4. Their boat is large and has eight cabins.
5. Our goal is to have a small boat someday.

More Practice

Language Lab CD-ROM
- Parts-of-Speech lesson

On-line Exercise Bank
- Section 18.1

Grammar Exercise Workbook
- pp. 25–26

◀ **Critical Viewing** What pronouns acting as adjectives might you use in describing this photograph? **[Describe]**

KEY CONCEPT A demonstrative, interrogative, or indefinite pronoun becomes an adjective if it answers the question *Which one? How many?* or *How much?* about a noun that follows it. ■

Demonstrative Adjectives All four of the demonstrative pronouns—*this, that, these,* and *those*—can be used as adjectives. When demonstrative pronouns are used as adjectives, they are called *demonstrative adjectives.* Remember that *demonstrate* means "point out."

PRONOUN: She sailed these.

ADJECTIVE: She sailed these boats.

Interrogative Adjectives Only three of the interrogative pronouns—*which, what,* and *whose*—can be used as adjectives. When used as adjectives, they are called *interrogative adjectives.* Remember that *interrogate* means "ask."

PRONOUN: *Which* did she see?

ADJECTIVE: *Which* ship did she see?

Indefinite Adjectives Many of the indefinite pronouns can also be used as adjectives. When used as adjectives, they are called *indefinite adjectives.* Singular forms of indefinite adjectives can be used to modify singular nouns; plural forms modify plural nouns.

EXAMPLES: *Each* boat had *several* sails.

They bought *more* rigging.

Exercise 10 Recognizing Other Pronouns Used as Adjectives Write the pronouns used as adjectives. Label each *demonstrative, interrogative, indefinite,* or *possessive.*

EXAMPLE: This sailing vessel is safe.

ANSWER: This (demonstrative)

1. Each stateroom has a private breakfast room.
2. Some cruise ships stop in the Bahamas.
3. Those ships depart often from East Coast ports.
4. Many boats sail to Central and South America.
5. What kind of cruise would you like to take?

Spelling Tip

Its should not be confused with *it's*. *Its* is a possessive adjective: There is the dog's bowl and *its* bone. *It's* is a contraction of *it is* or *it has*: It's (*it is*) time for dinner. *It's* (*it has*) been a long day.

18.1

Hands-on Grammar

Adverb and Adjective Wheel

Cut two large equal-sized circles out of light-colored construction paper. Then, cut out two rectangles—one long and thin and one with a width that nearly matches the diameter of the circles.

Next, cut three windows out of the larger rectangle. The windows should be equally spaced apart, as shown in the diagram. Write verbs on one circle and nouns on the other circle. Write words that can function as either adjectives or adverbs on the thin rectangle, and write on the larger rectangle the words shown on the diagram.

Finally, use paper fasteners to attach the circles to the large rectangles. Do it so that the verbs and nouns show through the windows in the rectangle. Use tape and strips of construction paper to attach the narrow rectangle to the other rectangle so that you can slide the narrow rectangle up and down.

With a group of classmates, experiment with different combinations of words. Notice how the words in the center can be used to modify either verbs or nouns and that the word being modified dictates the part of speech assumed by the modifier.

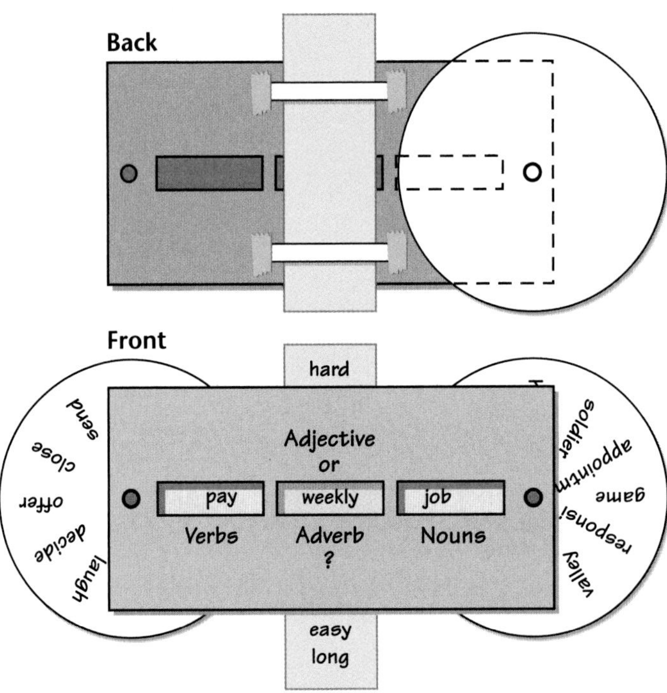

Find It in Your Reading Try this activity with words from one of your favorite literature selections.

Find It in Your Writing Try this activity with words from a piece of your own writing.

Section 18.1 **Section Review**

GRAMMAR EXERCISES 11–18

Exercise 11 Identifying Adjectives List all adjectives, including articles, in the following sentences.

1. The wagon used by American pioneers was called the Prairie Schooner.
2. It was a common farm wagon.
3. The canvas top was supported by horseshoe-shaped wooden arches.
4. It had oval-shaped openings.
5. These openings allowed air to enter.

Exercise 12 Distinguishing Between Adjectives and Nouns Identify each underlined word as an adjective or a noun used as an adjective.

1. recreational area
2. evening meal
3. fresh meat
4. wagon train
5. guitar music

Exercise 13 Identifying and Using Proper, Compound, Definite, and Indefinite Adjectives Label each adjective *proper, compound, definite,* or *indefinite.* Then, use each one in a sentence.

stump-filled	muddy	American
the	underway	some
one-year-old	down	surprising
special	an	Atlantic
Jeffersonian	Irish	farsighted

Exercise 14 Identify Pronouns Used as Adjectives Decide whether the underlined words, function as adjectives, pronouns, or both.

1. Have you heard of that Greek myth about Demeter and Persephone?
2. Demeter was Persephone's mother, and both were beautiful goddesses.
3. They lived on Mount Olympus with other gods and goddesses.
4. Demeter loved Persephone so dearly that she spent each second of every day with her.
5. Demeter, the goddess of the harvest, performed these duties with Persephone at her side.

Exercise 15 Identifying Possessive, Demonstrative, Interrogative, and Indefinite Adjectives Copy the headings below. Place the words that follow in the correct category.

Demonstrative *Interrogative* *Indefinite*

whose	few	this	another
those	any	which	some

Exercise 16 Find It in Your Reading Reread "The Long and Winding Road" on page 381. Write down and label all indefinite, demonstrative, interrogative, and possessive adjectives in the passage.

Exercise 17 Find It in Your Writing Choose a paragraph from your portfolio. Underline the demonstrative adjectives, circle indefinite adjectives, and draw a box around interrogative adjectives.

Exercise 18 Writing Application Imagine that you are traveling though the wilderness on the Oregon Trail. Write a week's worth of journal entries. In each day's entry, include at least one proper adjective, one compound adjective, and one noun used as an adjective.

Section 18.2

Adverbs

Adverbs add meaning to three parts of speech:

KEY CONCEPT An **adverb** is a word that modifies a verb, an adjective, or another adverb. ■

Adverbs Modifying Verbs

Adverbs can add meaning to verbs in many different ways:

KEY CONCEPT An adverb modifying a verb answers the questions *Where? When? In what way?* or *To what extent?* ■

Adverbs can also be placed in many different positions. As shown in the chart, they can come after or before a verb or verb phrase or even between the words in a verb phrase.

ADVERBS MODIFYING VERBS

Where?	
fell *below*	move *aside*
went *there*	climbs *down*
When?	
arrived *today*	left *early*
should have spoken *before*	begins *then*
In What Way?	
happily ran	will end *abruptly*
danced *awkwardly*	had been sung *loudly*
To What Extent?	
partly understands	wash *completely*
have *not* completed	*hardly* would have known

Exercise 19 **Coming Up With Examples of Adverbs** Come up with five additional adverb/verb pairs answering each of the questions in the chart.

Theme: The Night Sky

In this section, you will learn about adverbs. The examples and exercises in this section are about the night sky.

Cross-Curricular Connection: Science

▲ **Critical Viewing** Describe the moon by telling in what way or to what extent it shines. Which question did you answer? Which adverb(s) did you use? **[Analyze]**

GRAMMAR IN LITERATURE

from Tonight

Leonard Bernstein and Stephen Sondheim

Notice how the highlighted adverbs in the following excerpt from the song answer the questions When? *and* Where?

...Tonight, tonight,

It all began **tonight**.

I saw you and the world went **away.**

Exercise 20 **Identifying Adverbs That Modify Verbs** Make four columns with the headings shown below. Then, identify the adverb in each sentence, and place it in the correct column.

Where? When? In What Way? To What Extent?

1. Ancient peoples often saw designs in the stars, called constellations.
2. They carefully named the constellations after various religious figures, animals, and objects.
3. Constellations are sometimes imagined to be groupings of bright stars.
4. Eighty-eight constellations are recognized today.
5. The names are derived in part from Greek mythology.
6. Draco, the dragon, bravely defended the goddess Hera's apple tree.
7. Hercules subdued him quickly in a struggle to get apples.
8. Hera placed Draco overhead in the stars to remember him.
9. Draco is one of the constellations now.
10. The constellation Hercules is very near Draco.
11. Hercules originally was represented as a kneeling man with his foot on Draco.
12. The constellations fully symbolize the Greek myth.
13. In another Greek myth, Leo the Lion ferociously devoured Peloponnesian villagers.
14. Hercules' weapons scarcely touched the lion.
15. If a weapon hit Leo, it bounced off him harmlessly.
16. Confidently, Hercules wrestled Leo.
17. Hercules brilliantly won the battle.
18. He then wrapped the lion's pelt about himself for protection.
19. Leo went away to the heavens to commemorate the battle.
20. The constellation Leo is undeniably easy to see in the sky.

More Practice

Language Lab CD-ROM

- Parts-of-Speech lesson

On-line Exercise Bank

- Section 18.2

Grammar Exercise Workbook

- pp. 27–28

18.2

Adverbs Modifying Adjectives and Adverbs

Many descriptions can be made more meaningful by adding an adverb to an adjective.

KEY CONCEPT An adverb modifying an adjective answers only one question: *To what extent?* ■

When an adverb modifies an adjective, it usually comes directly before the adjective, as shown in the examples in the following chart.

ADVERBS MODIFYING ADJECTIVES	
very glad	*almost* ready
absolutely wrong	*entirely* grateful

Sometimes adverbs are used to sharpen the meaning of other adverbs.

KEY CONCEPT An adverb modifying another adverb answers just one question: *To what extent?* ■

An adverb modifying another adverb generally comes directly before the adverb it modifies. In the following examples, *very* modifies *quickly*, *almost* modifies *over*, *not* modifies *completely*, and *only* modifies *just*.

ADVERBS MODIFYING ADVERBS	
moved *very quickly*	*not completely* wrong
climbed *almost over*	*only just* recognizable

▼ Critical Viewing What pairs of adverbs and adjectives might you use in describing this photograph? **[Describe]**

Exercise 21 **Recognizing Adverbs That Modify Adjectives and Adverbs** Identify all of the adverbs. Then, indicate the word each adverb modifies.

1. A glow just barely appears on the northern horizon.
2. Lights move unexpectedly fast across the sky.
3. A glowing curtain of light forms more clearly.
4. It arches farther forward.
5. It swirls and dances somewhat closer to the Earth.
6. I watch very quietly in awe.
7. I have only just comprehended the beauty of the night sky.
8. The light starts to move more quickly away from us.
9. The glow is almost completely gone.
10. The Northern Lights will never completely disappear from my memory.

More Practice

Language Lab CD-ROM

- Parts-of-Speech lesson

On-line Exercise Bank

- Section 18.2

Grammar Exercise Workbook

- pp. 29–30

Exercise 22 **Revising to Eliminate Unnecessary Adverbs** Adverbs serve an important purpose in your writing. However, it is important to avoid using adverbs that do not significantly add to meaning. Revise this passage, eliminating unnecessary adverbs or replacing them with adverbs that add meaning.

(1) Last night's sunset was really and tremendously beautiful. (2) It was truly one of the most exciting points of our trip. (3) The sky was filled with very brilliant, flaming reds and oranges. (4) As the sky grew darker, the colors gently faded. (5) Finally, the sunset gave way to an incredibly brilliant star-filled night.

Adjective or Adverb?

Some words can be either adverbs or adjectives, depending on how they are used.

KEY CONCEPT An adverb modifies a verb, an adjective, or another adverb; an adjective modifies a noun or a pronoun. ■

Notice in the examples below that the adverb modifies a verb, while the adjective modifies a noun.

ADVERB: I awoke *early*.

ADJECTIVE: I had an *early* class.

The word *early* takes the same form whether used as an adjective or adverb. Most such words, however, have an adjective form and an adverb form.

Adjectives	Adverbs With *-ly* Endings
gentle hands	handle *gently*
bright paint	painted *brightly*

Do not, however, think that all words ending in *-ly* are adverbs. Some are adjectives formed by adding *-ly* to a noun.

Nouns	Adjectives With *-ly* Endings
a head of *curls*	*curly* hair
a close *friend*	*friendly* neighbors

Never identify a word as an adverb simply because it ends in *-ly*. Check to see whether it modifies a verb, an adjective, or an adverb.

Exercise 23 Distinguishing Between Adverbs and Adjectives Identify each underlined word as an adverb or an adjective.

1. Often when you look out your window at night, you see the kindly face of the Man in the Moon.
2. You will also see in the far reaches of the sky the stars that form the many constellations.
3. Some people think that the idea of constellations is silly.
4. However, constellations serve well as memory devices for identifying stars.
5. When you're staring at 11,000 to 11,500 stars, you'll have a hard time telling which is which.
6. However, once you recognize the stars of the constellation Orion the Hunter, for example, you will find the stars of his hunting dogs near him.
7. Ancient cultures saw pictures in the stars late at night.
8. They looked high into the heavens and saw the Lion, the Bull, the Fish, and the Scorpion.
9. The Crane is a modern constellation found deep in the southern sky.
10. Al Nair, a bright star on the Crane's foot, is spinning fast—at least 236 kilometers per second!
11. Early efforts to catalog the stars date back roughly 6,000 years.
12. Some constellations are seen low on the horizon.
13. Other constellations are much higher.
14. Some are seen most clearly in late summer.
15. Whether the constellations seem far or near depends on the rotation of the Earth.

More Practice

Language Lab CD-ROM
- Parts-of-Speech lesson

On-line Exercise Bank
- Section 18.2

Grammar Exercise Workbook
- pp. 31–32

Section 18.2 Section Review

GRAMMAR EXERCISES 24–30

Exercise 24 **Identifying Adverbs** Identify each adverb and tell which question it answers: *Where*? *When*? *In what way*? or *To what extent*?

1. The Maya were very accomplished astronomers.
2. Their primary interest was in carefully observing Zenithal Passages.
3. A special event occurred when the sun crossed directly over the Mayan latitudes.
4. The sun travels annually to its summer solstice point, latitude $23^{1}/_{3}$ degrees north.
5. Mayan cities were always located south of this point.

Exercise 25 **Identifying Adverbs That Modify Adjectives** Identify all of the adverbs that modify adjectives in the following sentences.

1. The ghost story was thoroughly scary.
2. She looked extremely pale.
3. It was unusually dark tonight because of the rain clouds.
4. I was somewhat hopeful that she would sleep tonight.
5. My assumption was partially correct.

Exercise 26 **Recognizing Adverbs That Modify Other Adverbs** Identify all the adverbs that modify other adverbs in the following sentences.

1. The sun is almost completely hidden.
2. The red color of the sunset spreads quite rapidly across the sky.
3. The sky darkens surprisingly fast.
4. The first star is just barely visible.
5. I make my wish as the star glows more clearly now.

Exercise 27 **Distinguishing Between Adjectives and Adverbs** Identify each underlined word as an adverb or an adjective.

1. Vincent van Gogh painted *Starry Night* <u>late</u> in his career.
2. It was a very <u>hard</u> time in his life, and he was not well.
3. Although Van Gogh often discussed his paintings with his brother, he apparently said <u>little</u> about *Starry Night.*
4. In the painting, cosmic gold fireworks seem to swirl <u>fast</u> against the sky.
5. In contrast to the raging night sky, the <u>little</u> village below seems peaceful.

Exercise 28 **Find It in Your Reading** Read a recent newspaper article, and make a list of the modifiers in the first paragraph. Label each modifier *adverb* or *adjective*, and explain how each one contributes information to the sentence.

Exercise 29 **Find It in Your Writing** Find five sentences in your portfolio that would be clearer if you added an adverb or replaced an adverb with a more specific one. Revise the sentences.

Exercise 30 **Writing Application** Most constellations in the night sky have a story or myth about their creation. For example, Leo the Lion stands as a symbol of Hercules' power in Greek mythology. Create your own story about a constellation. Use at least ten adverbs and ten adjectives. Label them, identify the word they modify, and tell what question they answer.

Chapter 19

Prepositions, Conjunctions, and Interjections

▲ Critical Viewing What prepositions can you use to describe the relationships of the people in this picture to each other and to the objects around them? **[Relate]**

Three parts of speech act as relaters, joiners, and attention-getters in sentences. They are *prepositions, conjunctions,* and *interjections.*

Consider the following sentence: Basketball can be played outdoors, *but* it began as an indoor exercise for the winter months.

The conjunction *but* helps to join the two ideas in a way that clarifies their relationship.

In this chapter, you will learn more about these three parts of speech—prepositions, conjunctions, and interjections—and about the ways they connect and relate words in sentences.

Diagnostic Test

Directions: Write all answers on a separate sheet of paper.

Skill Check A Write the prepositional phrase(s) in each sentence. Underline each preposition.

1. James Naismith invented basketball in December 1891.
2. Basketball is a court game played by two teams, with five players on each team.
3. Putting a ball into a basket, and thus scoring points against the opposing team, is the object of the game.
4. Naismith hung two peach baskets at opposite ends of a room.
5. During the winter, his YMCA athletes played the game with a soccer ball.
6. Players threw the soccer ball into the assigned basket.
7. People quickly heard about the new game.
8. It was soon being played throughout the eastern United States.
9. Women also played the game before 1900.
10. The rules today are based on the rules of Naismith's game.

Skill Check B Label each underlined word *preposition* or *adverb.*

11. Basketball's popularity led to improvements in equipment.
12. Peach baskets were soon thrown out, and metal hoops were used.
13. The use of a backboard behind the net began in 1895.
14. Improvement in playing skills did not lag behind.
15. The number of spectators increased throughout the country.

Skill Check C Write each conjunction, and label it *coordinating, correlative,* or *subordinating.*

16. In early games, following each point, the opposing centers would face each other at mid-court and jump for the ball.
17. The team with the ball would either pass it or dribble it until a player was about 10 feet from the basket.
18. Although the early game was slow-paced, it drew many fans.
19. Its popularity grew when rules were adopted to speed up play.
20. The ball had to be moved past mid-court within 10 seconds, and players could remain within the foul lanes for only 3 seconds.

Skill Check D Rewrite the first three sentences by adding a conjunctive adverb. Add an interjection to the last two sentences.

21. Several events in the 1930's spurred the growth of basketball; these events made the game more exciting for the players.
22. College games played in Madison Square Garden became highly successful; colleges began building their own arenas for basketball.
23. Stanford University players shot one-handed while jumping; one Stanford player could outscore an entire opposing team that shot two-handed while standing still.
24. Those basketball scores shot up!
25. Women have played basketball since 1890.

Section 19.1 Prepositions

Prepositions—such as *at, by, in, on,* and *with*—play an important role in English. They are used to relate words within a sentence.

KEY CONCEPT A **preposition** is a word that relates a noun or pronoun that appears with it to another word in the sentence. ■

The following chart lists several of the most commonly used prepositions.

FREQUENTLY USED PREPOSITIONS				
about	behind	down	off	till
above	below	during	on	to
across	beneath	except	onto	toward
after	beside	for	opposite	under
against	besides	from	out	underneath
along	between	in	outside	until
amid	beyond	inside	over	up
among	but	into	past	upon
around	by	like	since	with
at	concerning	near	through	within
before	despite	of	throughout	without

Although most prepositions are single words, some prepositions are made up of two or three words. These prepositions are called *compound prepositions.* Some compound prepositions are spelled without a space between them, such as *without, throughout, into, underneath,* and *outside.* The chart above lists some compound prepositions.

Other compound prepositions are spelled as separate words, as shown in the chart below.

COMPOUND PREPOSITIONS			
according to	because of	in place of	next to
ahead of	by means of	in regard to	on account of
apart from	in addition to	in spite of	out of
aside from	in back of	instead of	owing to
as of	in front of	in view of	prior to

Theme: Basketball

In this section, you will learn about prepositions and prepositional phrases. The examples and exercises in this section are about basketball.

Cross-Curricular Connection: Physical Education

Internet Tip

Prepositions are sometimes used to narrow a topic on the Internet. For example, using *basketball at . . .* as a search word instead of just *basketball* would narrow the topic down to places where basketball is played.

GRAMMAR IN LITERATURE

from Slam, Dunk, & Hook

Yusef Komunyakaa

Notice the highlighted prepositions in the following excerpt.

Dribble, drive *to* the inside, feint,
& glide *like* a sparrow hawk.
Lay ups. Fast breaks.
We had moves we didn't know
We had. Our bodies spun
On swivels *of* bone and faith . . .

▲ **Critical Viewing** What prepositions can you use to tell where you might stand in relation to a basketball net? **[Speculate]**

Exercise 1 **Identifying Prepositions** Write each sentence, replacing the underlined preposition with another preposition that makes sense.

EXAMPLE: The player stood <u>in</u> <u>front</u> <u>of</u> the coach.
ANSWER: The player stood <u>behind</u> the coach.

1. Does the basketball season generally come <u>before</u> the football season?
2. The standard length <u>of</u> a basketball court is 94 feet, and the width is 50 feet.
3. A basket attached to a backboard hangs <u>over</u> each end of the court.
4. Her free throw hit the backboard <u>above</u> the basket, and she failed to score.
5. Is the center considered the most important player <u>on</u> the team?
6. A player can advance the ball only <u>with</u> dribbling or <u>with</u> passing.
7. The forward dribbled the ball <u>over</u> the court and then passed it to a teammate.
8. The coach gives instructions to the players <u>during</u> the game.
9. An official may stand <u>along</u> the sideline.
10. Scorekeepers and timekeepers sit at a table <u>behind</u> the sideline.

More Practice

Language Lab CD-ROM
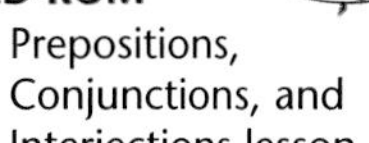
- Prepositions, Conjunctions, and Interjections lesson

On-line Exercise Bank
- Section 19.1

Grammar Exercise Workbook
- pp. 33–34

Prepositional Phrases

Prepositions are almost always followed by nouns or pronouns.

KEY CONCEPT A **prepositional phrase** is a group of words that includes a preposition and a noun or pronoun. ■

Generally, the *object of a preposition* is the noun or pronoun that follows the preposition.

PREPOSITIONAL PHRASES	
Prepositions	**Objects of the Prepositions**
near before according to	me the storm her

Most *prepositional phrases* contain two or three words. However, they may be longer, depending on the number of words modifying the object and the length of the preposition.

EXAMPLES: *near* the tall, gently swaying *trees*
on account of the *rain*

Exercise 2 **Identifying Prepositional Phrases** Write the prepositional phrase or phrases in each sentence. The number at the end of each sentence tells how many prepositional phrases the sentence has.

EXAMPLE: Spectators in the stands cheered wildly. (1)
ANSWER: in the stands

1. College basketball tournaments came into their own in 1939. (2)
2. Since that time, players have been setting records. (1)
3. Players are often named all-American for outstanding performances. (1)
4. A few players join professional teams after graduation from college. (2)
5. Some teams win medals at international games. (1)
6. The best players are noted for their leadership on the court. (2)
7. In time, women's basketball grew in popularity. (2)
8. Thousands of cheering fans fill the stands. (1)
9. The college season runs from November through March. (2)
10. The unpredictability of the game is very exciting for fans. (2)

Grammar and Style Tip

Whenever possible, avoid ending a sentence with a preposition. For example, *This is a good court to play on* can be rewritten *This is a good court for playing* or *This is a good court on which to play.*

More Practice

Language Lab CD-ROM

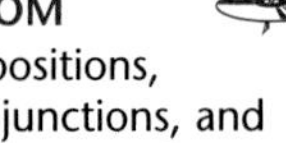

- Prepositions, Conjunctions, and Interjections lesson

On-line Exercise Bank
- Section 19.1

Grammar Exercise Workbook
- pp. 35–36

Preposition or Adverb?

Many words that act as prepositions can also act as adverbs, depending on how they are used.

KEY CONCEPT Remember that prepositions always have objects; adverbs do not. ■

If a word that can be used either as a preposition or as an adverb has an object, the word is acting as a preposition.

PREPOSITION:	The ball flew *through* the net.
ADVERB:	We were waved right *through*.
PREPOSITION:	We play *behind* the school.
ADVERB:	Leave your worries *behind* when you go on vacation.

For a word to act as a preposition, it must have an object and be part of a prepositional phrase. In the preceding examples, only the first and third sentences show prepositions with objects.

▲ Critical Viewing
Use *up* in two sentences about this picture. In the first sentence, use *up* as an adverb. In the second, use it as a preposition. **[Analyze]**

Exercise 3 Distinguishing Between Prepositions and Adverbs Label each underlined word *preposition* or *adverb.*

EXAMPLE:	His sneakers had holes underneath in three places.
ANSWER:	adverb

1. Have you ever seen a live college basketball game before?
2. A sign outside the arena said my two favorite teams were playing inside.
3. Come along; let's get to our seats before the game starts.
4. The teams came out to warm up before the game.
5. Two aggressive players fouled each other throughout.
6. At half time, one team was ahead by eight points.
7. A player threw the ball in from the sideline.
8. We walked around during half time.
9. After the game, the winners were given the championship trophy inside the locker room.
10. Despite losing in the playoffs, that team had a winning record for the season.

More Practice

Grammar Exercise Workbook
- pp. 33–36

Hands-on Grammar

Preposition Pet on a Leash

To increase your understanding of prepositions, create and play Preposition Pet on a Leash.

First, build a house. Cut a piece of 8-1/2″ x 11″ paper into two 5-1/2″ x 8-1/2″ pieces. Fold each piece in half the short way and in half again, to make three parallel creases in the paper; then, unfold. On the creases, fold one of the pieces into an open triangle shape, and tape the overlapping edges to form a roof. Fold the other piece into an open rectangular box, and tape the edges where they meet to form the bottom of the house. Cut a small door (about 1-1/2″ high) in the middle of the taped edge. Then, tape the roof to the house at the open edges at each end. (See illustration.)

Now, make your pet and its leash. Cut out a small, simple dog or cat, about 1″ to 1-1/2″ long and high. Take a piece of string about 12″ long, and tape one end around the neck of your pet, to resemble a collar. Tape the other end to the door of your house. If you like, give your pet a name—Preppy, perhaps.

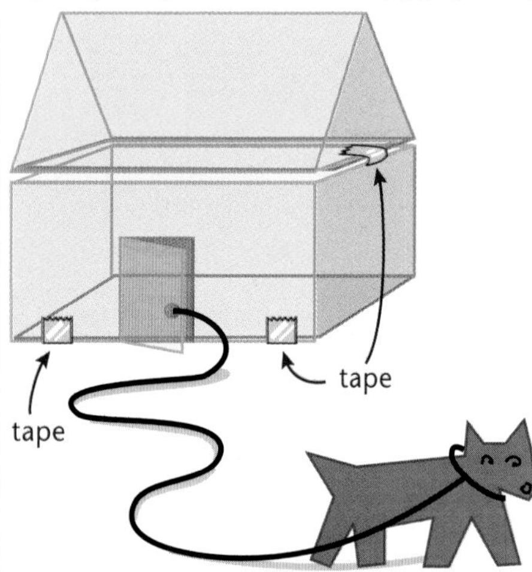

Finally, join with two or three of your "neighbors," and demonstrate where your pets can go on their leashes. Each person should take a turn moving his or her pet to different parts of the house, using prepositional phrases to explain where the pet is or is going. Then, take turns changing the prepositions to function as adverbs. Example: "Preppy goes *inside* the house." (preposition) "Preppy goes *inside* to eat." (adverb)

Find It in Your Reading Read a short newspaper or magazine article, and underline the prepositional phrases. Which prepositions are used most frequently? Circle any words that can be prepositions but are actually functioning as adverbs.

Find It in Your Writing Review a piece of your writing, and identify the prepositional phrases. See if there are places where you can add a prepositional phrase to clarify or expand on an idea.

Section 19.1 Section Review

GRAMMAR EXERCISES 4–10

Exercise 4 **Recognizing Prepositions** List the prepositions and the compound prepositions in each sentence.

1. Prior to the game, the coach gave all the members of his team a pep talk.
2. According to their coach, this season would be among the best.
3. The team entered the court through the doors next to the bleachers.
4. The first pass was thrown out of bounds by a player.
5. The game went into overtime on account of a tied score.

Exercise 5 **Identifying Prepositional Phrases** Write the prepositional phrase or phrases in each sentence. The number at the end of each sentence tells how many prepositional phrases the sentence has.

1. John Robert Wooden was one of the greatest college basketball coaches. (1)
2. He was a three-time, all-American player at Purdue University before his coaching career. (2)
3. Wooden arrived at UCLA in 1948. (2)
4. He compiled 667 victories between the years 1946 and 1975. (1)
5. For his playing and coaching, Wooden was elected to the Basketball Hall of Fame. (3)

Exercise 6 **Supplying Prepositions** Rewrite the following paragraph, supplying appropriate prepositions to fill the blanks.

Basketball star Kareem Abdul-Jabbar was coached __?__ John Wooden. This all-time great played __?__ UCLA __?__ the 1960s. Kareem Abdul-Jabbar was an All-American __?__ three years and College Player __?__ the Year twice.

Exercise 7 **Distinguishing Between Prepositions and Adverbs** Label each underlined word *preposition* or *adverb.*

1. She turned the radio <u>on</u> to hear a program <u>about</u> basketball statistics.
2. The announcer listed MVPs <u>in</u> playoff games.
3. In the playoffs, the right forward made the last three-point shot as the buzzer went <u>off</u>.
4. The announcer said that the player hit the final shot just before time ran <u>out.</u>
5. <u>Throughout</u> the program, the announcer's love of the game came <u>through</u>.

Exercise 8 **Find It in Your Reading** In the excerpt from "Slam, Dunk, & Hook" on page 403, identify the complete prepositional phrase that each highlighted preposition begins.

Exercise 9 **Find It in Your Writing** In a recent piece of your own writing, identify the prepositional phrases. Are there places where you can add prepositional phrases to give more information?

Exercise 10 **Writing Application** Choose a sport that you enjoy playing or watching. Write an explanation of how to play the game. Include at least five prepositional phrases in your sentences. Underline each prepositional phrase.

Conjunctions and Interjections

The last two parts of speech discussed in this chapter are *conjunctions* and *interjections.* Of the two, conjunctions are more important because they link ideas. Interjections add emotion to a sentence but do not link ideas.

Theme: The Environment

In this section, you will learn about three kinds of conjunctions and the use of interjections. The examples and exercises in this section are about the environment.

Cross-Curricular Connection: Science

Different Kinds of Conjunctions

Prepositions simply relate different words, but conjunctions make a direct connection between words.

KEY CONCEPT A **conjunction** is a word used to connect other words or groups of words. ■

The three main kinds of conjunctions are *coordinating conjunctions, correlative conjunctions,* and *subordinating conjunctions.*

Coordinating Conjunctions *Coordinating conjunctions* connect similar kinds of words or similar groups of words.

COORDINATING CONJUNCTIONS						
and	but	for	nor	or	so	yet

EXAMPLES: My sister *and* brother ran the program.
They wrote a short *yet* effective report.
The dog barked *but* wagged its tail.
Put the bags on the table *or* in the closet.
Bob left early, *so* I left with him.

Correlative Conjunctions *Correlative conjunctions* also connect similar words or groups of words. However, they always appear in pairs.

CORRELATIVE CONJUNCTIONS		
both . . . and	neither . . . nor	whether . . . or
either . . . or	not only . . . but also	

EXAMPLES: He watched *both* lions *and* tigers.
Neither Don *nor* she will go.
Jean recycled bottles and cans *not only* consistently *but also* carefully.

Subordinating Conjunctions *Subordinating conjunctions* connect two complete ideas by making one of the ideas subordinate to the other. To *subordinate* means to "place below another in rank or importance."

FREQUENTLY USED SUBORDINATING CONJUNCTIONS		
after	before	till
although	even though	unless
as	if	until
as if	in order that	when
as long as	since	whenever
as soon as	so that	where
as though	than	wherever
because	though	while

Notice that the subordinating conjunction always comes just before the subordinate idea.

EXAMPLES: We protect the wetlands *because* they are important to the ecosystem.
As soon as the volunteers arrived, the cleanup work began.

Subordinating Conjunction or Preposition? *After, before, since, till,* and *until* can be subordinating conjunctions or prepositions, depending on how they are used. In the first example below, *until* is a subordinating conjunction because it connects two complete ideas. In the second example, *until* is the first word in a prepositional phrase.

SUBORDINATING CONJUNCTION: *Until* you finish your wetland research, you are not ready to begin writing.

PREPOSITION: *Until* recent decades, people were not as proactive in preserving the environment.

◀ Critical Viewing Explain the probable role of the wetlands in the survival of this egret. Use a sentence with a subordinating conjunction in your response. **[Infer]**

GRAMMAR IN LITERATURE

from To the Residents of A.D. 2029

Bryan Woolley

The correlative conjunctions in the following excerpt are highlighted.

Because of man's amazing record of making his dreams come true, I refuse to be pessimistic about the future, despite the frightening aspects of the present. As long as we—*both* as a race *and* as a crowd of individuals—retain our capacity for dreaming, we also keep the possibility of doing.

▲ **Critical Viewing** Use correlative conjunctions in a sentence that compares or contrasts at least two features of this picture. **[Compare and Contrast]**

Exercise 11 **Identifying Conjunctions** Write the conjunction(s) in each sentence. Then, label each *coordinating, correlative,* or *subordinating.* Write *none* if a sentence contains no conjunction.

EXAMPLE: In science, we studied both ecology and the environment.

ANSWER: both, and (correlative)

1. The term *environment* refers to the surroundings of either an individual organism or a community of organisms.
2. The word *surroundings* refers to all living and nonliving materials around an organism.
3. These materials include both food and water.
4. An organism is influenced not only by its immediate surroundings but also by physical forces.
5. When we use the word *environment,* we often think about the adverse effects of human activities.
6. Environmental groups work to prevent or lessen damage caused by human activities.
7. We study ecology because we want to analyze the interactions of organisms with their environment.
8. Since the 1970's, people have paid more attention to the environment.
9. After a ship struck the sandbar, an oil spill occurred.
10. Although volunteers arrived quickly, some wildlife could not be saved.

Conjunctive Adverbs

Some words act as both conjunctions and adverbs at the same time.

KEY CONCEPT A **conjunctive adverb** is an adverb that acts as a conjunction to connect complete ideas. ■

Conjunctive adverbs are often used as *transitions*. Transitions serve as bridges between different ideas.

FREQUENTLY USED CONJUNCTIVE ADVERBS		
accordingly	finally	nevertheless
again	furthermore	otherwise
also	however	then
besides	indeed	therefore
consequently	moreover	thus

The following examples show how conjunctive adverbs can be used to make transitions between different ideas.

EXAMPLES: Maureen loves animals; *moreover,* she is a student of plant and animal life.
I arrived late; *furthermore,* I forgot my books.

Exercise 12 **Recognizing and Supplying Conjunctive Adverbs** Read each sentence to see whether it contains a conjunctive adverb. If it does, write the conjunctive adverb. If it does not, rewrite the sentence to include a conjunctive adverb.

EXAMPLE: Gather your information; begin writing your report.

ANSWER: Gather your information; then, begin writing your report.

1. Human activities sometimes have damaging effects on the environment; therefore, society develops ways to prevent or lessen these damages.
2. Humans produce all kinds of waste; recycling is one way to reduce waste accumulation.
3. Recycling reduces the amount of waste; also, it conserves resources and cuts costs.
4. Beverage bottles can be reused for their original purpose; indeed, they can be used fifteen to twenty times before they break.
5. Some European countries encourage the reuse of beverage bottles; U.S. law does not permit the reuse of food or drink containers.

More Practice

Language Lab CD-ROM
- Prepositions, Conjunctions, and Interjections lesson

On-line Exercise Bank
- Section 19.2

Grammar Exercise Workbook
- pp. 37–38

Interjections

Interjections are used to express emotion.

KEY CONCEPT An **interjection** is a word that expresses feeling or emotion; it functions independently of a sentence. ■

Interjections—such as *aha, bravo, goodness, great, hurray, oh, oops, well, ugh,* or *whew*—express different feelings or emotions. Several different emotions are being expressed by the interjections below. Because an interjection is unrelated to any other words in the sentence, set it off from the other words by inserting an exclamation mark or a comma.

PAIN: *Ouch!* That burns.
JOY: *Wow!* This is great!
CONTEMPT: *Oh,* go away.
HESITANCY: Do you, *uh,* believe that?

Though common in speech, interjections should be used sparingly in writing.

More Practice

Language Lab CD-ROM
- Prepositions, Conjunctions, and Interjections lesson

On-line Exercise Bank
- Section 19.2

Grammar Exercise Workbook
- pp. 39–40

Exercise 13 **Supplying Interjections** Write each sentence, adding an interjection that conveys the indicated emotion.

EXAMPLE: (weariness) We worked hard cleaning the park.
ANSWER: Whew! We worked hard cleaning the park.

1. (disappointment) Look at the garbage left on the ground.
2. (delight) The park certainly is cleaner since the town provided more garbage cans.
3. (happiness) Here comes the recycling truck at last.
4. (pain) I stumbled on that tree root.
5. (annoyance) I missed the trash can.
6. (uncertainty) Are you sure that plastic is recyclable?
7. (enthusiasm) That was a magnificent cleanup effort!
8. (disinterest) Could you bring back that petition another time?
9. (unintended mistake) I didn't mean to mix up the clear glass bottles with the green ones.
10. (discovery) Now I get it!

▼ Critical Viewing What interjections can you use in response to this picture? **[Relate]**

Section 19.2 **Section Review**

GRAMMAR EXERCISES 14–19

Exercise 14 **Identifying Conjunctions** Write the conjunction(s) in each sentence. Then, label each *coordinating, correlative,* or *subordinating.* If there is no conjunction, write *none.*

1. Organisms live together in communities comprised of both plants and animals.
2. Communities may be very small or very large.
3. Biomes are extensive communities that occupy wide geographic areas.
4. Not only arctic tundras but also tropical jungles are considered biomes.
5. Some animals are found in only one layer of a biome, but most animals range through several layers.
6. In a biome, some species of animals are active during the day, whereas some are active at night.
7. Since they are active at different times, many organisms can occupy the same area.
8. If there are many species in a community, it is said to have a rich diversity.
9. After a disaster, a community will eventually restore itself.
10. Restoration occurs very slowly in the desert and the tundras because the climactic and soil conditions are not as rich or varied.

Exercise 15 **Recognizing and Supplying Conjunctive Adverbs** Write the conjunctive adverbs in the following sentences. If a sentence has no conjunctive adverb, rewrite the sentence to include one.

1. Lichens and grasses are among the first species to invade a recovering area; they are called pioneers.
2. They are not the only pioneers; indeed, trees such as elm and aspen are, too.
3. These pioneers increase the organic content of the soil; moreover, they change the moisture conditions.
4. Some species release nitrogen into the soil; therefore, they fertilize the soil.
5. Many ecologists study ecosystems; accordingly, they determine how organisms retain and recycle minerals.

Exercise 16 **Supplying Interjections** Supply an appropriate interjection for each sentence.

1. Those hot ashes burned me!
2. The fire ruined the animals' homes.
3. I wish the campers had put out their campfires.
4. Grass is already starting to grow after the forest fire.
5. I see new animals here already!

Exercise 17 **Find It in Your Reading** Identify the subordinating conjunction in the excerpt from "To the Residents of A.D. 2029" on p. 410.

Exercise 18 **Find It in Your Writing** Look through your writing portfolio. Find three coordinating conjunctions and two subordinating conjunctions in your own writing.

Exercise 19 **Writing Application** Identify an area in your school or town that needs a cleanup. Create a poster persuading volunteers to join a cleanup project. Use at least three conjunctions and at least two interjections for emphasis.

Chapter 20

Basic Sentence Parts

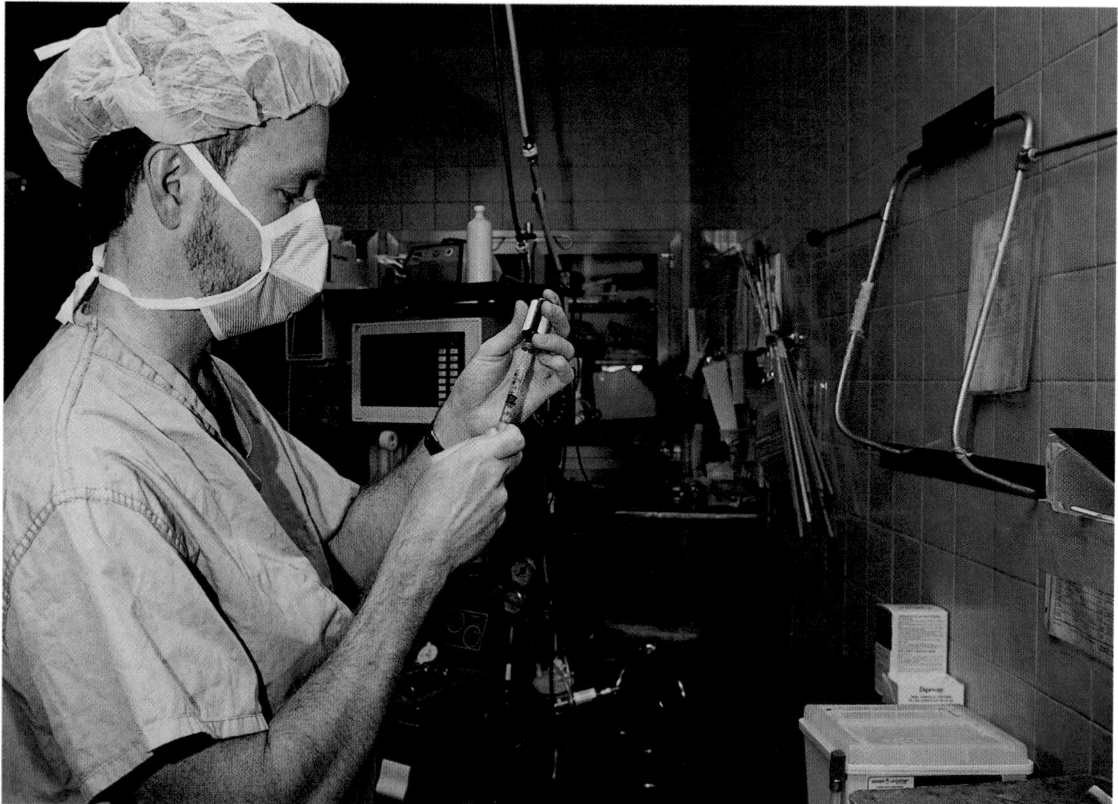

▲ **Critical Viewing** What do you think are some of the things that inspire medical researchers to choose their career? Answer in a complete sentence. **[Speculate]**

To work effectively in a career or job, one must use sentences to communicate with others. Nurses, doctors, architects, cooks—all must have good writing and speaking abilities. Effective writing and speaking depend on the ability to form sentences.

Every sentence clearly written in the English language follows certain basic patterns that can be described in grammatical terms. This chapter will explore some of the basic patterns, giving you a better understanding of the variety of expressions that you have at your command.

Diagnostic Test

Directions: Write all answers on a separate sheet of paper.

Skill Check A. Write each sentence, drawing a vertical line between the complete subject and complete predicate. Then, underline each simple subject once and underline the verb twice.

1. High-school graduates have a great variety of career choices.
2. The amount of additional schooling for these careers varies.
3. Few careers accept less than a high-school diploma.
4. Educational programs in vocational schools, junior colleges, and universities help to prepare students for their professions.
5. Graduating from an institution of higher education shows determination and accomplishment.

Skill Check B. Make two columns on your paper, one labeled *subject* and one labeled *predicate.* Write the noun or nouns that make up each simple subject under the subject column and the verb or verbs under the predicate column.

6. Researchers and librarians work in information science.
7. These professionals seek, utilize, and even organize information.
8. Computer science, mathematics, and engineering are considered important areas of information science.
9. Libraries and archives store and catalog information.
10. Librarians and archivists must learn and use various research methods.

Skill Check C. Write the subject of the following directions, questions, and inverted-order sentences.

11. How much schooling does a physical therapist need?
12. Eventually, after college training, comes private practice.
13. There is the physical therapist's office.
14. Visit the physical therapist and practice your exercises.
15. Here are the exercises to strengthen your arm.

Skill Check D. Label each underlined word *direct object, indirect object,* or *object of the preposition.*

16. Most careers require some kind of higher <u>education</u>.
17. A teacher receives his or her <u>degree</u> in education.
18. His college granted <u>him</u> a degree in social work.
19. My friend received <u>information</u> about a management degree.
20. Mathematics courses are required for civil engineering <u>students</u>.

Skill Check E. Label each underlined word(s) *predicate nominative, predicate adjective,* or *objective complement.*

21. Generally, a nurse must be a <u>college graduate</u>.
22. Nurses are extremely <u>busy</u> with multiple responsibilities.
23. In addition, nurses must be both friends and <u>caregivers</u>.
24. The hospital appoints head nurses <u>leaders</u> of their departments.
25. Nurses must be <u>flexible</u> and must provide genuine care.

Complete Subjects and Predicates

Every *sentence* has two main parts.

KEY CONCEPT A **sentence** is a group of words with two main parts: a *complete subject* and a *complete predicate*. Together, these parts express a complete thought. ■

The chart below shows the two main parts of three complete sentences. In each sentence, the *complete subject* includes a noun or pronoun that names the person, place, or thing that the sentence is about. Each *complete predicate* includes a verb that tells something about the complete subject.

Complete Subjects	Complete Predicates
Several pilots from various countries	have vanished in or near the Bermuda Triangle.
The Bermuda Triangle, the area in question,	lies between Florida, Bermuda, and Puerto Rico.
The U.S.S. *Cyclops*	disappeared there in 1918.

As you can see in the following examples, the complete subject or complete predicate can consist of several words or just one word.

EXAMPLES: He | read about many different careers.
COMPLETE SUBJECT | COMPLETE PREDICATE

The nurse in the white uniform | arrived.
COMPLETE SUBJECT | COMPLETE PREDICATE

Exercise 1 **Recognizing Complete Subjects and Predicates** Write each sentence, drawing a vertical line between the complete subject and the complete predicate.

EXAMPLE: The tired nurse | completed her rounds.

1. Nurses teach preventive care and rehabilitation.
2. Most nurses work in hospitals.
3. Other nurses provide their services in health agencies, nursing homes, offices, schools, and industries.
4. Nurses can be educators, administrators, or supervisors.
5. Most nursing was done at home in the nineteenth century.

Theme: Helping Professions

In this section, you will learn about simple and compound subjects and predicates. The examples and exercises in this section are about professionals who help others.

Cross-Curricular Connection: Social Studies

More Practice

On-line Exercise Bank
- Section 20.1

Grammar Exercise Workbook
- pp. 41–46

Simple Subjects and Predicates

Every complete subject and complete predicate contains a word or group of words that is essential to the sentence.

KEY CONCEPTS The **simple subject** is the essential noun, pronoun, or group of words acting as a noun that cannot be left out of the complete subject. The **simple predicate** is the essential verb or verb phrase that cannot be left out of the complete predicate. ■

Notice that all the other words in the complete subject add details to the simple subject. Similarly, all of the other words in the complete predicate either modify the simple predicate or help it complete the meaning of the sentence.

	SIMPLE SUBJECT	SIMPLE PREDICATE
EXAMPLES:	Two of his *friends*	*studied* law enforcement.
	COMPLETE SUBJECT	COMPLETE PREDICATE
	SIMPLE SUBJECT	SIMPLE PREDICATE
	Sick in bed, *she*	*had missed* her job interview.
	COMPLETE SUBJECT	COMPLETE PREDICATE

Note About *Simple Subjects*: The simple subject is never the object of a preposition.

EXAMPLE: Most nations of the world have their own police.

In this example, *nations* is the simple subject of the sentence; *world* is the object of the preposition *of.*

▼ Critical Viewing Using a complete sentence, name one way in which law enforcement officers protect us. **[Relate]**

Exercise 2 Recognizing Simple Subjects and Predicates Write each sentence, drawing a vertical line between the complete subject and complete predicate. Underline the simple subject once and the verb twice.

EXAMPLE: A friend of mine | visited the police barracks.

1. The police are government agents.
2. They protect citizens from unlawful acts.
3. The U.S. police establishment operates at several levels.
4. The Federal Bureau of Investigation (FBI) is the largest and most important department.
5. Two other federal departments are the Secret Service and the Customs Service.

Compound Subjects

Some sentences have two or more subjects.

KEY CONCEPT A **compound subject** is two or more subjects that have the same verb and are joined by a conjunction such as *and* or *or*. ■

In each of the following examples, the parts of the compound subject are underlined once and the verb twice.

EXAMPLES: You and she took entrance tests yesterday.
Either the actor or the tailor will talk at our career day.
Snow, ice, and flooding made the roads treacherous.

▼ **Critical Viewing** What are some of the ways in which computers have changed methods used by doctors and physical therapists? Answer using a compound subject. **[Connect]**

Exercise 3 **Recognizing Compound Subjects** Write the nouns that make up each compound subject.

EXAMPLE: Carpenters and plumbers spoke to us about their trades on our career day.
ANSWER: carpenters, plumbers

1. The physical therapist and his patient plan exercises.
2. Heat, light, water, and massage are used to treat certain physical disabilities.
3. Stiff joints and pain are generally eased with heat.
4. A hot bath or a hot compress heats deep, sore tissues.
5. The patient and the therapist work together to help the patient relearn motor functions.
6. Physical therapy and occupational therapy help patients improve their motor abilities.
7. In occupational therapy, tools and hands-on materials are used rather than exercise aids.
8. Doctors and therapists help patients reestablish basic physical skills and contact with the world outside the hospital.
9. Stroke victims and people who have been seriously injured sometimes have to relearn basic skills, such as handling a spoon or fork.
10. Physical therapists and occupational therapists should feel proud of their work with patients.

Compound Verbs

Just as a sentence can have a compound subject, it can also have a *compound verb*.

KEY CONCEPT A **compound verb** is two or more verbs that have the same subject and are joined by a conjunction such as *and* or *or*. ■

In the next examples, each subject is underlined once and the parts of the compound verb are underlined twice.

EXAMPLES: I neither want nor need your help on the test.
The little children hopped, skipped, and jumped around the playground.

Sometimes, a sentence has both a compound subject and a compound verb.

EXAMPLE: The boys and girls danced and listened to records for hours.

Exercise 4 **Recognizing Compound Verbs** Write the verbs that make up each compound verb.

1. Some students go to college and study to become computer programmers.
2. Programmers write and encode application programs.
3. Operating systems programs run the user's input and output requests and process them.
4. Operating systems programs connect to a network and interpret data requests.
5. Applications programs tailor the computer's powers and perform specific tasks.

More Practice

On-line Exercise Bank
- Section 20.1

Grammar Exercise Workbook
- pp. 47–48

Exercise 5 **Combining Sentences With Compound Subjects and Verbs** Combine each pair of sentences into one using a compound subject or a compound verb.

1. Computer programmers encode programs. They also test them.
2. Often, a programmer will discuss a line of code. The discussion will take place with his or her colleagues.
3. A computer programmer will uncover defects in design specifications. He or she will also fix them.
4. Design defects must be eliminated. System bugs must be eliminated, as well.
5. Programmers work long hours writing code for a new application. They have a great sense of satisfaction when it works well.

20.1

Hands-on Grammar

Simple Sentence Builders

Make and use Simple Sentence Builders to see how a sentence can grow with compound subjects and verbs. To begin, take two sheets of paper in different colors, and cut twelve 2" x 2" squares from each sheet. Take a third sheet of paper, and cut five T shapes, with the stems 1" wide and 2" high and the top 3" across. Next, on each of the squares of one color, write a noun that will serve as a subject. Examples: *Tony, Juan, Lisa, my brother, my sisters, our friends, I, we, they, the team, the cat, the dogs,* and so on. On the other squares, write past tense verbs—a few with complements. Examples: *ran, sang, played, danced, chased the ball, ate lunch, slept until noon,* and so on. Then, write the word *and* on the stem of each T shape. Finally, turn the T shapes over, and draw a comma on the back of each one.

Now, begin building sentences. Take one subject square, and place it next to one verb square. Then, fit an *and* T over the subject and add another subject square to its left. Next, fit an *and* T over the verb, and add another verb square to its right. Then, fit a *comma* T over the second subject, and add a third subject square. To add a third verb, you must turn over the T shape so that a comma shows; then, add another *and* T and the new verb. (See illustrations.)

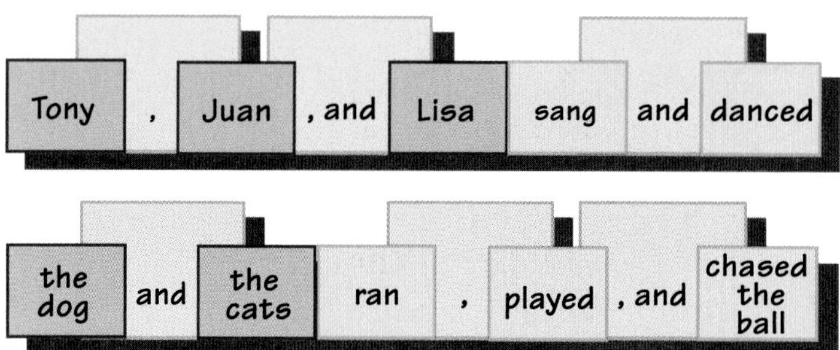

You might try variations using *but* on one of the T shapes:

Find It in Your Reading Read some directions for building, fixing, installing, or cooking something. Notice where compound subjects and verbs are used.

Find It in Your Writing Review a piece of your writing, and note where you have used simple sentences. See if you can combine any short, simple sentences by making compound subjects and verbs.

Section Review

GRAMMAR EXERCISES 6–11

Exercise 6 **Recognizing Compound Subjects** Write the noun or nouns that make up the subject in each sentence.

1. Accounting and bookkeeping help people and businesses make economic decisions.
2. The figures in a bookkeeper's ledger follow basic accounting principles.
3. Businesses and other types of organizations use financial statements for their financial planning.
4. Investors and stock traders are supplied with accounting information to make decisions about companies.
5. Large corporations and small firms need the services of accountants.
6. Investors, creditors, and the general public have uses for financial reports.
7. Stockholders and other outsiders receive information about a company's financial standing from these reports.
8. The balance sheet and other important statements provide a way of examining a company's performance.
9. Financial accounting and tax accounting are the two major areas in the accounting field.
10. Tax accountants must keep up with the frequent changes in tax laws.

Exercise 7 **Recognizing Compound Verbs** Write the verbs that make up each compound verb.

1. Orthodontists diagnose and correct teeth and jaw abnormalities.
2. An orthodontist adjusts and corrects tooth positions by using braces.
3. Braces are attached to teeth and are tightened and retightened.
4. Over a period of time, an orthodontist examines braces and makes corrections.
5. Sometimes, they recommend additional time in braces or prescribe a retainer.

Exercise 8 **Revising a Paragraph to Combine Sentences** Revise this paragraph, combining the short sentences into longer ones with compound subjects or compound verbs.

Crusty snow covered the sidewalk. There were patches of ice on the sidewalk too. Suddenly, I slipped. I fell. I twisted my ankle. The doctor examined my injury. He gave me some advice. I was to soak my ankle. I was to rest it for several days. Eventually, the pain would subside. The swelling would also subside.

Exercise 9 **Find It in Your Reading** Read a newspaper or magazine article. Find at least one sentence with a compound subject and one with a compound verb. Write the sentences, underlining the subjects once and the verbs twice.

Exercise 10 **Find It in Your Writing** Review a paper from your portfolio, and write down any sentences that contain compound subjects or verbs, underlining the compound subjects once and the compound verbs twice. See if there are places where you can combine two short sentences into one sentence with a compound subject or compound verb.

Exercise 11 **Writing Application** Write a paragraph about where you hope to be ten years from now. You may include educational, career, or personal goals. Write at least two sentences that contain compound subjects and two that contain compound verbs.

Section 20.2 Hard-to-Find Subjects

Basic methods for finding the subject and verb of a sentence were explained in Section 20.1. This section presents ways of finding subjects that are hard to find or that appear to be missing.

Theme: Plants and Animals

In this section, you will learn to locate hard-to-find subjects. The examples and exercises in this section are about plants and animals.

Cross-Curricular Connection: Science

Subjects in Orders and Directions

In most sentences that give orders or directions, the subject is understood rather than actually stated.

KEY CONCEPT In sentences that give orders or directions, the subject is understood to be *you.* ■

In the following chart, sentences are given with and without the understood *you.* In the second example, the subject is still understood to be *you* even though the sentence contains a *noun of direct address*—that is, the name of the person being addressed.

Orders or Directions	With Understood Words Added
Look at the bird perched on the branch.	[You] look at the bird perched on the branch.
Michael, come here.	Michael, [you] come here.

Exercise 12 **Finding Subjects in Orders or Directions** Write each sentence, inserting the understood subject.

EXAMPLE: During the autumn, enjoy the scenery.
ANSWER: During the autumn, [you] enjoy the scenery.

1. Ted, plan on having different garden chores to do each season.
2. In the fall, rake the leaves and put them into special large leaf bags.
3. In the winter, cover the tender plants to protect them from harsh weather conditions.
4. Fertilize your soil and plant your beds of annual flowers in the spring.
5. When summer at last arrives, remember to water the lawn and plants and keep your shrubs trimmed.

More Practice

On-line Exercise Bank
- Section 20.2

Grammar Exercise Workbook
- pp. 49–50

Subjects in Questions

In most sentences, the subject comes before the verb. However, in some sentences, including many sentences that ask questions, the subject comes after the verb. Such sentences are said to be *inverted*.

KEY CONCEPT In questions, the subject often follows the verb. ■

Questions that are in inverted order will generally begin with a verb, with a helping verb, or with one of the following words: *how, what, when, where, which, who, whose,* or *why*. The following examples show all three types of inverted questions. The subjects are underlined once and the verbs or verb phrases, twice. In the last two examples, notice that the subject comes between the parts of a verb phrase.

VERB FIRST: Are the sunflowers very tall?
HELPING VERB FIRST: Have you collected the seeds?
ADVERB FIRST: When will Anike roast them?

▲ **Critical Viewing** What is it about sunflowers like these that would make them an appealing subject for an artist? Use a sentence with an inverted subject and verb in your response. **[Relate]**

To find the subject in questions with inverted order, mentally rephrase the question as a statement. This will place the subject before the verb. Then, follow the same steps that you would follow to find any other subject and verb.

Questions	Reworded as Statements
Is dinner ready?	Dinner is ready.
Are you working here?	You are working here.
When will it snow?	It will snow when.

Note About *Questions*: Not all questions are in inverted order. Sometimes, questions beginning with an adjective or a pronoun are in the usual subject-verb order.

EXAMPLES: Whose flower garden is in bloom?
What is being planted next year?

20.2

Sentences Beginning With *Here* and *There*

Some inverted sentences begin with the word *here* or *there*.

KEY CONCEPT The subject of a sentence is never *here* or *there*. ■

In sentences that begin with the word *here* or *there*, the subject will usually be found after the verb. In each of the following three examples, *here* and *there* are adverbs. Each of them answers the question *Where?* and modifies the verb in the sentence.

EXAMPLES: There is the aromatic eucalyptus tree.
Here are photographs of the beautiful, towering coconut palms.
There goes the tree specialist to fertilize our neighbor's Japanese maple.

Like inverted questions, sentences beginning with *here* or *there* can usually be rephrased mentally in order to place the subject in the normal position before the verb. All you need to do is make a logical sentence that does not begin with *here* or *there* out of the other words given in the sentence. Then, follow the same steps that you would for finding any subject in a sentence.

Sentences Beginning With *Here* or *There*	Reworded With Subjects Before Verbs
There is your train to Arizona.	Your train to Arizona is there.
Here are the pictures of the Grand Canyon.	The pictures of the Grand Canyon are here.
There goes the senator.	The senator goes there.

In some sentences, you may find that the word *there* is used just to get the sentence started. In these situations, *there* is not an adverb modifying the verb. Instead, it just fills out the sentence. When the word *there* is used simply to fill out a sentence, it is called an *expletive*.

EXAMPLES: There were a large saguaro cactus and a barrel cactus visible from our room.
There are many types of cactus.

Internet Tip

For links to a wealth of information about plants and botanical gardens and arboretums around the country, go to the Web site of the Big Island Association of Nurserymen at **http://www.hawaiiplants.com/links.htm#Botanical Gardens and Arboretums**

Sentences With Expletive *There*	Questions for Finding Subject
There were four misspelled words in the article.	*Question: What* were? *Answer:* words
There are two reasons for her resignation.	*Question: What* are? *Answer:* reasons

Rephrasing a sentence to place the subject first is not always possible when *there* is used as an expletive. The important thing to remember is that *there* will never be the subject. To find the subject in a sentence that cannot be rephrased, drop the word *there* and ask *Who?* or *What?* before the verb.

Note About *Inverted Sentences:* Some sentences beginning with *here* or *there* are not inverted but are in normal word order.

EXAMPLE: There they are.

Other Inverted Sentences

Occasionally, sentences are inverted to draw attention to the last words in the sentence.

KEY CONCEPT In some sentences, the subject is placed after the verb in order to give it greater emphasis. ■

In the following example, notice how the order of the words creates suspense by leading up to the subject *eagle.*

EXAMPLES: High on the cliff overlooking the rugged landscape was an eagle.
Bright is her smile, but heavy is her heart.
Soon after the sound of the drums came the marchers.

These sentences can be mentally rephrased in normal subject-verb order.

Inverted Word Order for Emphasis	Reworded With Subject Before Verb
High on the cliff overlooking the rugged landscape was an eagle.	An eagle was high on the cliff overlooking the rugged landscape.

Spelling Tip

The words *there, their,* and *they're* are homophones—words that sound the same but are spelled differently and have different meanings. Remember that *there* is an adverb or an expletive, *their* is a possessive pronoun, and *they're* is a contraction of *they are.*

GRAMMAR IN LITERATURE

from I Wandered Lonely as a Cloud

William Wordsworth

Notice in these lines from the poem that the subject I *follows the verb* saw. *This inverted order maintains the rhythm of the line.*

Ten thousand *saw I* at a glance,
Tossing their heads in sprightly dance.

Exercise 13 Finding Subjects in Questions and Inverted Sentences Write the simple subject of each sentence.

EXAMPLE: In her hand was a beautiful starfish.
ANSWER: starfish

1. Where in the world is the deep blue sea?
2. Beyond the edge of the continental shelf and below the level of light penetration are the ocean waters of the deep blue sea.
3. How far is the penetration of sunlight into ocean water?
4. There is not much penetration of sunlight below a few hundred meters.
5. What is the percentage of ocean water in the deep sea?
6. In the deep sea is more than 90 percent of the ocean volume.
7. Among the Earth's least-known environments is the deep sea.
8. Sinking below the lighted surface waters are organic materials.
9. What are some characteristics of the deep sea?
10. There is a range of 20 to more than 1,000 atmospheres of pressure in the deep sea.
11. There are various effects on the organisms in the deep sea caused by the lack of light.
12. Also present in the shallower parts are fish with very large eyes.
13. Have you ever seen the fish and invertebrates with their own light-making organs?
14. There are many deep-sea fishes with large mouths.
15. Why do they have such large mouths?

More Practice

On-line Exercise Bank
• Section 20.2
Grammar Exercise Workbook
• pp. 51–52

Section 20.2

Section Review

GRAMMAR EXERCISES 14–19

Exercise 14 **Finding Subjects in Orders or Directions** Write each sentence, inserting the understood subject.

1. If you're looking for a great vacation spot, consider the Grand Canyon.
2. To get the most out of your trip, pack binoculars.
3. Drive west on Highway 40 into Arizona.
4. From Highway 40, take the exit to Highway 64.
5. Enjoy the open roads.

Exercise 15 **Finding Subjects in Questions and Inverted Sentences** Write the subject of each sentence.

1. There are vast arid lands in the world.
2. Are there other types of deserts besides the hot, dry ones?
3. Yes, there are semiarid deserts and coastal deserts.
4. Lying about 25 degrees north and south of the equator are most of the world's deserts.
5. Can plants and animals survive with such little water?
6. There are certain plants and animals well adapted for survival in dry climates.
7. Among the more interesting animals are the tarantula and the gila monster, a type of lizard.
8. There are also many varieties of cactus with the ability to store water.
9. Probably most familiar is the giant saguaro, found in the southwestern United States and Mexico.
10. Low to the ground and widely spaced is typical desert vegetation.

Exercise 16 **Revising Sentences to Invert Subjects and Verbs** Revise these sentences, following the instructions. You may have to add or omit some words.

1. Many plant adaptations are here in the desert. (begin with *Here in . . .*)
2. Spines, hairs, and thick leaves are included among the adaptations. (begin with *Included among . . .*)
3. Some seeds lie dormant for many years. (begin with *There are . . .*)
4. The seeds finally germinate. (change to a question.)
5. The new shoots come after a rare desert rainfall. (begin with *After a . . .*)

Exercise 17 **Find It in Your Reading** Read this excerpt from Emily Dickinson's "'Hope' is the thing with feathers—" and explain how the inverted subject and verb maintain the poem's rhythm.

And sweetest—in the Gale—is heard—
And sore must be the storm—
That could abash the little Bird
That kept so many warm—

Exercise 18 **Find It in Your Writing** In your writing, find two examples of inverted statements. Rewrite them so that the subject precedes the verb. If you don't find any, choose two statements and reword them so that they are inverted.

Exercise 19 **Writing Application** Write a three- or four-line description of something you are learning about in one of your other classes. In it, include the following types of sentences: a question, an inverted statement beginning with *there*, and a statement that is inverted to emphasize the subject.

Section 20.3

Complements

In addition to a verb, the complete predicate of a sentence often contains a *complement.*

KEY CONCEPT A **complement** is a word or group of words that completes the meaning of the predicate of a sentence. ■

It is, of course, possible to have a complete sentence with just a subject and verb. However, most of the sentences you read and write will contain one or more complements that are needed to complete the meaning of the sentence.

Different kinds of complements will be presented here and in the next two sections. This section discusses one of the most important complements, the *direct object.*

Theme: Sports

In this section, you will learn about direct and indirect objects and subject and objective complements. The examples and exercises in this section are about sports.

Cross-Curricular Connection: Physical Education

Direct Objects

Direct objects are generally found after action verbs.

KEY CONCEPT A **direct object** is a noun or pronoun that receives the action of a transitive action verb. ■

You can determine whether a word is a direct object by asking *Whom?* or *What?* after an action verb. In the following examples, the subjects are underlined once; the action verbs, twice; and the direct objects are boxed and labeled. Notice how each direct object answers the question *Whom?* or *What?*

EXAMPLES: The hailstorm bombarded the picnickers. (DO: picnickers)

Bombarded *whom? Answer:* picnickers

The rugby players are running the ball. (DO: ball)

Are running *what? Answer:* ball

Not all action verbs have direct objects. Transitive action verbs do; intransitive action verbs do not. Because some action verbs can be either transitive or intransitive, knowing that a verb is an action verb will not tell you whether or not it has a direct object. You will always need to ask the question *Whom?* or *What?* after the verb to see whether there is a direct object.

Learn More

For more about transitive and intransitive verbs, see Chapter 17.

EXAMPLES: Jenn won the match. (DO: match)

Won *what? Answer:* match

Jenn won yesterday.

Won *what?* There is no answer, so there is no direct object.

GRAMMAR IN LITERATURE

from I Had a Hammer: The Hank Aaron Story
Hank Aaron

Notice how the direct objects ball *and* field *complete the meaning of the sentence in this excerpt.*

My father threw out the first *ball*, and then we took the *field* against the Dodgers. Their pitcher was Al Downing, a veteran lefthander whom I respected.

Note About *Direct Objects in Questions*: When a question is inverted, the direct object is sometimes located near the beginning of the sentence, before the verb. To find the direct object in an inverted question, reword the question as a statement.

QUESTION: Which bus should I take?

REWORDED AS A STATEMENT: I should take which bus. (DO: bus)

Like subjects and verbs, direct objects can be compound.

KEY CONCEPT A **compound direct object** is two or more nouns or pronouns that receive the action of the same verb. ■

EXAMPLE: We photographed the players and the coach. (DO: players; DO: coach)

If a sentence contains a *compound direct object*, asking the question *Whom?* or *What?* after the verb will lead to two or more answers.

Exercise 20 **Recognizing Direct Objects** Write the sentences, underlining the direct object or objects in each.

EXAMPLE: Most football players own a football.

(1) Football rivals baseball as the most popular athletic event for spectators in the United States. (2) Millions of people watch football games on the high-school, college, and professional levels. (3) Half-time shows, with marching bands and alumni or fan-club gatherings, usually accompany the games. (4) Football teams usually play eight to sixteen games in a season. (5) The best of the teams enter post-season playoffs.

More Practice

On-line Exercise Bank
• Section 20.3
Grammar Exercise Workbook
• pp. 53–54

Direct Object or Object of a Preposition? Do not confuse a direct object with the object of a preposition.

KEY CONCEPT A direct object is never the noun or pronoun at the end of a prepositional phrase. ■

The first example below contains a direct object only. The second contains a direct object and a prepositional phrase. The third contains a prepositional phrase only.

EXAMPLES: They bought a dilapidated Victorian [mansion.] (DO)
Bought what? *Answer:* mansion

They restored the [downstairs] (DO) of the mansion. (PREP PHRASE)
Restored *what? Answer:* downstairs

Soon, they moved into the mansion. (PREP PHRASE)
Moved *what? Answer:* none

Exercise 21 **Distinguishing Between Direct Objects and Objects of Prepositions** Write the direct object in each sentence. If a sentence does not have one, write *none.*

EXAMPLE: Baseball players have used metal bats for a long time.
ANSWER: bats

(1) Spectators love the popular game of baseball. (2) Two teams of nine players take turns on the field and at bat. (3) The teams play nine innings, with the home team batting last. (4) The team at bat sends its nine men to the plate, one at a time, in a specified sequence. (5) Each batter attempts to hit a ball. (6) The pitcher throws the ball at varying speeds and placement within the strike zone. (7) The batter runs to as many bases as possible without being tagged out. (8) Each player on the field wears a leather glove on one hand. (9) The players use the gloves to catch any balls hit toward them. (10) With the ungloved hand, they throw the ball to a teammate.

For a list of prepositions and more on prepositional phrases, see Chapter 19.

▼ **Critical Viewing** How will the umpire call this play? Answer using a direct object. **[Speculate]**

Indirect Objects

In addition to a verb and direct object, the complete predicate of a sentence may contain an *indirect object.*

KEY CONCEPT An **indirect object** is a noun or pronoun that appears with a direct object and names the person or thing that something is given to or done for.

A sentence cannot have an indirect object unless it has a direct object. You can tell whether a word is an indirect object by finding the direct object and asking *To or for whom?* or *To or for what?* after the action verb.

EXAMPLE: I gave my brother (OI) new skis (DO).
Gave *to whom? Answer:* brother

Like subjects, verbs, and direct objects, indirect objects can be compound.

EXAMPLE: We wrote Sue (IO) and Al (IO) letters (DO) about our trip.
Wrote *to whom? Answer:* Sue and Al

Exercise 22 **Recognizing Indirect Objects** Write the indirect object in each sentence.

EXAMPLE: He brought me his old bowling shoes.
ANSWER: me

1. Many colleges offer students bowling as an elective course.
2. The instructor teaches each class basic rules.
3. My father lent John and me his bowling balls.
4. My friend gave me a wrist brace to help keep my wrist straight as I bowled.
5. Mr. Neil taught us the history of bowling.

More Practice
On-line Exercise Bank
• Section 20.3
Grammar Exercise Workbook
• pp. 53–58

Exercise 23 **Supplying Indirect Objects** Supply an indirect object that logically completes each sentence.

EXAMPLE: I lent __?__ my new racquet.
ANSWER: Philip

1. Philip told __?__ the time of the match.
2. I gave __?__ a call to remind her to come.
3. She asked __?__ a question about the tickets.
4. I said that I had given __?__, __?__, and __?__ the extra ones.
5. We all enjoyed the match and cheered loudly when the sponsor awarded __?__ the first-place trophy.

Indirect Object or Object of a Preposition? Do not confuse indirect objects with objects of prepositions.

KEY CONCEPT An indirect object never immediately follows a preposition in a sentence. ■

In the first of the following examples, *conductor* is an indirect object. In the second, however, *conductor* is the object of the preposition *to*.

INDIRECT OBJECT: I gave the conductor (IO) our tickets (DO).

OBJECT OF A PREPOSITION: I gave our tickets (DO) to the conductor (OBJ of PREP).

Exercise 24 Distinguishing Between Indirect Objects and Objects of Prepositions In the following sentences, change each indirect object into a prepositional phrase. Change each prepositional phrase, if possible, into an indirect object. If you can't change a prepositional phrase into an indirect object, write *none*.

EXAMPLE: Janet taught a gymnastic routine to you.
ANSWER: Janet taught you a gymnastic routine.

1. Gymnastics coaches teach physical tumbling and acrobatic skills to gymnasts.
2. Gymnasts sometimes offer local schools gymnastic demonstrations.
3. Dr. Dudley Allen Sargent introduced the sport of gymnastics to the United States.
4. His inventions gave more than thirty pieces of apparatus to the sport.
5. Six gymnasts make up the teams for international competitions.
6. Rhythmic routines are performed individually or in group performances for six gymnasts.
7. Judges give gymnasts relatively unbiased scores by using specific guidelines.
8. In 1774, Johann Bernhard Basedow taught physical exercises to students at his school.
9. Gymnast Olga Korbut earned the Soviet Union considerable popularity in the international games.
10. The performances of Nadia Comaneci gained widespread recognition for Romania in the 1976 games.

More Practice

On-line Exercise Bank
• Section 20.3
Grammar Exercise Workbook
• pp. 57–60

Subject Complements

The last two sections were about complements that help complete the meaning of sentences with transitive action verbs. Sentences with linking verbs contain a different kind of complement: a *subject complement.*

KEY CONCEPT A **subject complement** is a noun, pronoun, or adjective that appears with a linking verb and tells something about the subject of the sentence. ■

A subject complement will almost always be found *after* a linking verb. The two kinds of subject complements are known as *predicate nominatives* and *predicate adjectives.*

Predicate Nominative The word *nominative* comes from the same Latin word (meaning "name") that the words *noun* and *pronoun* come from.

KEY CONCEPT A **predicate nominative** is a noun or pronoun that appears with a linking verb and renames, identifies, or explains the subject of the sentence. ■

In a sentence with a predicate nominative, the linking verb acts as an equal sign between the subject and the predicate nominative. They refer to the same person or thing.

In the examples, subjects are underlined once, linking verbs twice, and predicate nominatives are boxed and labeled.

EXAMPLES: The winner of the tournament is our [team.] (PN)
Team renames *winner.*

The new captain of the team will be [Sue.] (PN)
Sue renames *captain.*

Their first choice was [you.] (PN)
You identifies *choice.*

KEY CONCEPT A **compound predicate nominative** is two or more nouns or pronouns that appear with a linking verb and rename the subject of the sentence. ■

EXAMPLE: The co-captains are [you] (PN) and [Chris.] (PN)
You and *Chris* identify *co-captains.*

Journal Tip

This section contains information on a variety of sports. In your journal, jot down some notes about those that interest you. Then, review them later to find a topic for an essay or research report—perhaps on the development of a particular sport.

Exercise 25 **Recognizing Predicate Nominatives** Write the predicate nominative(s) in each sentence.

1. A sport is physical exertion for recreation or competition.
2. From a historical standpoint, the ancient Olympic Games were the birth of organized sports.
3. About 5,000 years ago, wrestling was essentially a survival skill.
4. Rugby is a game accidentally invented by students at Rugby School in Rugby, England.
5. Professional sports in the twentieth century were a profitable business, often involving highly paid athletes.

Predicate Adjective The other kind of subject complement is called a *predicate adjective.*

KEY CONCEPT A **predicate adjective** is an adjective that appears with a linking verb and describes the subject of the sentence. ■

EXAMPLES: The swimmer was fast. (PA: fast)
Fast describes *swimmer.*

A compound predicate adjective is two or more adjectives that appear with a linking verb and describe the subject of the sentence.

EXAMPLE: The uniforms are green and white. (PA: green; PA: white)

Exercise 26 **Recognizing Predicate Adjectives** Write the predicate adjective(s) in each sentence.

EXAMPLE: Jean seemed tired after her swimming lesson.
ANSWER: tired

1. Swimming is good for strengthening muscles.
2. The popular crawl stroke appears easy.
3. The backstroke is similar to the crawl stroke.
4. Leg and arm movements are simultaneous in the breast stroke and the butterfly stroke.
5. The butterfly stroke appears graceful.

Grammar and Style Tip

Use vivid subject complements to add interest as well as information to a description of your subject.

▼ Critical Viewing
How strong and how skilled do you think this swimmer is? Use predicate adjectives in your response. **[Assess]**

Objective Complements

Indirect objects generally come before direct objects. Complements called *objective complements* generally come after direct objects and give additional information about them.

KEY CONCEPT An **objective complement** is an adjective or noun that appears with a direct object and describes or renames it. ■

To find an objective complement, say the verb and the direct objective, and then ask *What?*

EXAMPLES: She painted her room green. (DO: room; OC: green)
Painted room *what?* Answer: green

The coach appointed David captain of the team. (DO: David; OC: captain)
Appointed David *what?* captain

Exercise 27 Recognizing Objective Complements Write the objective complement in each sentence.

EXAMPLE: The race made him weak.
ANSWER: weak

1. Track and field participants call the competitions *meets*.
2. The track coach made Brian a sprinter in the track meet.
3. He also called Brian his best distance runner.
4. The sprint made Brian tired.
5. The coach classifies Sue a high jumper.
6. Sue made 6 feet the new school record in the high jump.
7. The judges considered Sue a qualifier for the finals.
8. Qualifying in the event made Sue happy.
9. The coach made the last track meet Saturday.
10. The newspaper named Joe Klepak Coach of the Year.

More Practice
On-line Exercise Bank
• Section 20.3
Grammar Exercise Workbook
• pp. 59–64

Exercise 28 Writing Sentences With Objective Complements Write sentences with objective complements, using the verbs and direct objects given below.

1. consider swimming
2. called the captain
3. is making me
4. classifies the sport
5. dubbed the mascot

Section

20.3 Section Review

GRAMMAR EXERCISES 29–40

Exercise 29 **Recognizing Direct Objects** Write the direct object in each sentence.

1. A YMCA instructor invented basketball in 1891.
2. In basketball, players put a ball through a basket to make points.
3. The winning team scores the most points.
4. Spectators first watched basketball in the nineteenth century.
5. Most states now hold championships in basketball.

Exercise 30 **Distinguishing Between Direct Objects and Objects of Prepositions** Write the direct object in each sentence. If a sentence does not have one, write *none*.

1. Volleyball is played by hitting a ball back and forth over a net.
2. Each team has six players.
3. In beach volleyball, teams consist of two players.
4. William G. Morgan invented the game in 1895 as a recreational pastime.
5. The game was originally called *mintonette*.

Exercise 31 **Supplying Indirect Objects** Supply a logical indirect object in each sentence.

1. Pam told __?__ the highlights of the basketball game.
2. At the beginning of the game, the center tipped __?__ the jump ball.
3. A foul gave __?__ a chance to score.
4. In the last 30 seconds of the game, the guard passed __?__ the ball and he made a three-pointer.
5. As a result, the home team gave __?__ another victory.

Exercise 32 **Distinguishing Between Indirect Objects and Objects of Prepositions** In the following sentences, change each indirect object into a prepositional phrase. Change each prepositional phrase, if possible, into an indirect object. If you can't, write *none*.

1. Stefan told the rules of ice hockey to Jason.
2. The players wear ice skates for the game.
3. Using a hockey stick, a hockey player passes the puck to his teammate.
4. Hockey coaches can give a timeout to their team.
5. Canada and Russia have given many active players to the game of hockey.

Exercise 33 **Revising to Combine Sentences Using Direct and Indirect Objects** Revise this paragraph, combining short sentences into longer ones with compound direct or indirect objects.

Sam told Jill the events of his soccer game. He also told Simran. Sam made three goals for his team. He had three assists, as well. He passed the ball to the right wing several times. He passed the ball to the left wing several times. One midfielder had a number of shots on goal. He also had a number of corner kicks.

Exercise 34 **Recognizing Predicate Nominatives** Write the predicate nominative in each sentence.

1. Lugeing and bobsledding are forms of tobogganing.
2. Bobsledding is a fast and dangerous winter sport.
3. The luge is a small sled used for one- and two-man and one-woman competitions.
4. Eugenio Monti was a great bobsledder between 1957 and 1968.
5. St. Moritz was the home of the first bobsled event in 1888.

Exercise 35 **Recognizing Predicate Adjectives** Write the predicate adjective(s) in each sentence.

1. Tobogganing became popular in the northern United States and Canada in the 1930's.
2. Tobogganing remains well received as a sport today.
3. The toboggan sled is runnerless.
4. The sport of tobogganing is recreational and exciting.
5. Cresta tobogganers, or tobogganers in the Cresta Valley at Saint Moritz, are adventurous.

Exercise 36 **Supplying Objective Complements** Complete each sentence with one or more objective complements as indicated.

1. Weight lifting makes participants __?__.
2. It makes muscles __?__ and __?__.
3. Powerful weight lifters leave spectators __?__.
4. Being unable to lift the desired weight leaves the lifter __?__.
5. In recent decades, people have come to consider weight lifting a __?__.

Exercise 37 **Writing Sentences With Subject Complements** Use each subject and verb to write a sentence. Add words to form the kind of complement indicated in parentheses.

1. game seemed (predicate adjective)
2. parents were (predicate nominative)
3. team remained (predicate nominative)
4. captain named (objective complement)
5. Matt felt (predicate adjective)

Exercise 38 **Find It in Your Reading** Read this excerpt from *I Had a Hammer.* Write it on your paper. Underline the subjects once; underline the verbs twice; and box and label direct objects, indirect objects, and objects of prepositions.

> " . . . Their pitcher was Al Downing, a veteran lefthander whom I respected. Downing always had an idea of what he was doing when he was on the mound, and he usually pitched me outside with sliders and screwballs."

Exercise 39 **Find It in Your Writing** Look through your portfolio for one example of each of the following: direct object, indirect object, object of a preposition, predicate nominative, predicate adjective, and objective complement. Write the sentences and label each complement.

Exercise 40 **Writing Application** Write an account of a sports event you recently participated in or witnessed; or you can make up an event. In it, include at least one of each of the following: direct object, indirect object, object of a preposition, predicate nominative, predicate adjective, and objective complement. Write down the sentences, and label each complement.

Chapter 21

Phrases and Clauses

▲ Critical Viewing
Use a phrase to add details to this sentence about the picture: An Apache warrior stands by his tepee. **[Analyze]**

Knowing when and how to use the parts of speech and the basic parts of a sentence will enable you to begin building strong sentences. This chapter will help you expand on your sentences by introducing two additional elements, the *phrase* and the *clause*. A **phrase** is a group of words, without a subject and verb, that functions in a sentence as one part of speech. A **clause** is a group of words with its own subject and verb. Some clauses can stand by themselves as complete sentences; others can only be parts of sentences.

The Native American tepee pictured above was put together carefully so that it would be strong. In the same way, you tie words together to create strong sentences. Phrases and clauses allow you to form effective sentences in which ideas are clear and concise. Whether writing about Native Americans or travel to Africa, phrases and clauses provide important details that add meaning to your sentences.

Diagnostic Test

Directions: Write all answers on a separate sheet of paper.

Skill Check A. Write the prepositional phrase(s) from each sentence. Label them *adverb* or *adjective.*

1. Arrowheads are made of stone, bone, or metal.
2. They are fastened to the end of an arrow shaft.
3. A notch at the top of the arrow shaft is cut.
4. The arrowhead is then secured in the arrow shaft with sinew.
5. Finally, the arrow shaft is fitted with feathers.

Skill Check B. Write the appositive phrases from each sentence. Then, label the underlined phrase *infinitive* or *prepositional.*

6. Flint, a rock that chips easily, is used to make arrowheads.
7. The process results in a sharp point, the arrowhead, chipped to the perfect shape.
8. A special process of making percussion fractures, chipping off smaller pieces by applied pressure, is then used to sharpen the edge.
9. The arrow, a simple yet effective weapon, enabled Native Americans of earlier times to protect themselves and to hunt for animals.
10. The arrowhead was even able to pierce the thick hide of their most common prey, the buffalo.

Skill Check C. Label the underlined word(s) in each sentence *present participle, past participle, gerund,* or *verb.*

11. For many Native American tribes, hunting buffalo was important for all aspects of life.
12. Dried brush from buffalo plains was often used as fuel for fire.
13. Hides were wrapped around wooden frames to make tepees and war shields as well as a covering for boats.
14. Some tribes followed the herd of buffalo as they were grazing.
15. Ceremonies were performed, honoring the buffalo.

Skill Check D. Copy the following sentences. Label each sentence *simple, complex, compound,* or *compound-complex.* Underline the subordinate clauses, and label them *adjective, adverb,* or *noun.*

16. Southwestern tribes hold a festival when the first corn of the year is harvested.
17. During this week of festivities, whatever debts or injuries a person has at the time are forgiven.
18. The Utes, an Indian tribe from the Utah area, celebrate the Bear Dance every spring.
19. The dance grounds are made to resemble a bear's den, and one opening faces the East.
20. A woman asks a man to dance by brushing him with her shawl, but if the man tries to avoid dancing, he is put back into line by the "Catman," who is chosen to keep order!

Section 21.1

Phrases

This section will explore the ways several different kinds of phrases can be used to add variety and meaning to sentences. There are several types of phrases, among them *prepositional, appositive, participial, gerund,* and *infinitive* phrases.

Theme: Native Americans

In this section, you will learn how phrases are used to modify nouns, pronouns, verbs, adjectives, and adverbs. The examples and exercises in this section are about Native Americans.

Cross-Curricular Connection: Social Studies

Prepositional Phrases

A *prepositional phrase,* such as *by the lake* or *out of gas,* is made up of a preposition and a noun or pronoun, called the object of the preposition. Prepositions may also have compound objects, such as *for Maria and me* and *to the kitchen, hallway, or living room.* (See Section 19.1 to review prepositions.) Prepositional phrases function either as adjectives by modifying nouns and pronouns or as adverbs by modifying verbs, adjectives, and adverbs.

Adjective Phrases

When acting as an adjective, a prepositional phrase is called an *adjective phrase.*

KEY CONCEPT An **adjective phrase** is a prepositional phrase that modifies a noun or pronoun by telling *what kind* or *which one.* ■

EXAMPLES: The tepee *of buffalo hide* was sturdy.

The decoration *on the hide* was painted carefully.

The opening *in the front* was narrow.

At other times, more than one adjective phrase may be used to modify the same noun.

EXAMPLE: The drawing *of a warrior on the tepee* was painted in red.

Exercise 1 **Identifying Adjective Phrases** Write each sentence, underlining the adjective phrase or phrases in each. Then, draw an arrow from each phrase to the word it modifies.

EXAMPLE: Native American tribes <u>in the Northwest</u> were numerous.

1. There are several different kinds of Native American tribes in North America.
2. The culture of each tribe varies.
3. The tribes of western Louisiana and eastern Texas are the Caddo.
4. Farming provided their main source of food.
5. Also important was the annual hunt for buffalo.

More Practice

On-line Exercise Bank
- Section 21.1

Grammar Exercise Workbook
- pp. 41–43

Exercise 2 **Writing Sentences With Adjective Phrases** Using the following prepositional phrases, write sentences of your own. Use each prepositional phrase as an adjective phrase.

EXAMPLE: of farming
ANSWER: Native Americans taught their ways *of farming* to colonists.

1. of the culture
2. about Native American tribes
3. for fishing
4. from buffalo
5. in the Utah area

▼ Critical Viewing These totems in Stanley Park, Vancouver, were made by Native Americans. Describe the totems with two sentences. Use an adjective phrase in one and an adverb phrase in the other. **[Describe]**

21.1

Adverb Phrases

When a prepositional phrase functions as an adverb, it is called an *adverb phrase.*

KEY CONCEPT An **adverb phrase** is a prepositional phrase that modifies a verb, an adjective, or an adverb by pointing out *where, when, in what way,* or *to what extent.* ■

MODIFYING A VERB: Abstract animal figures were carved *in totem poles.* (carved *where?*)

Southwestern art dates back *before Columbus.* (dates back *when?*)

MODIFYING AN ADJECTIVE: The forest was quiet *before dawn.* (quiet *when?*)

They are happiest *at the playground.* (happiest *where?*)

MODIFYING AN ADVERB: He arrived late *for lunch.* (late *to what extent?*)

While an adjective phrase almost always comes directly after the word it modifies, an adverb phrase may be separated from the word it modifies.

EXAMPLE: Put the package *in the closet.* (put *where?*)

Two or more adverb phrases may also be used to modify the same word.

EXAMPLE: *On Saturdays,* my cousin studies *at the Native American Art Museum.* (studies *when?* studies *where?*)

▲ **Critical Viewing** Use the prepositional phrases *in his hands* and *on his head* as adverb phrases to describe the dancer in this Native American artwork. **[Describe]**

Exercise 3 **Identifying Adverb Phrases** Write each sentence, underlining the adverb phrase or phrases in each. Then, draw an arrow from each phrase to the word it modifies.

EXAMPLE: Native American tribes divided *for different reasons.*

1. The Pawnee divided themselves into four different tribes.
2. Most of them lived in earth lodges.
3. One tribe, the Skidi Pawnee, became part of the Grand Pawnee in the early 1800's.
4. Religion was very important to this tribe.
5. In their religion, they paid homage to the morning star.

More Practice

On-line Exercise Bank
- Section 21.1

Grammar Exercise Workbook
- pp. 41–43

Exercise 4 **Writing Sentences With Adverb Phrases** Using the following prepositional phrases, write sentences of your own. Use each prepositional phrase as an adverb phrase.

1. in different sections of the United States
2. during the festival
3. after the hunt
4. with a hard stone
5. from farming and fishing

Appositives and Appositive Phrases

Appositives and *appositive phrases* are used to develop the meaning of nouns and certain pronouns.

Appositives

KEY CONCEPT An **appositive** is a noun or pronoun placed near another noun or pronoun to identify, rename, or explain it. ■

Notice in the following example that the appositive is set off by commas, which indicates that it is not essential to the meaning of the sentence and can be removed.

EXAMPLE: A tribe of the Northeast, the *Iroquois,* made pottery, baskets, beadwork, and quill work.

In the example below, the appositive is not set off by commas because it is needed to complete the meaning of the sentence.

EXAMPLE: The Native American writer *N. Scott Momaday* won a Pulitzer Prize for his novel *House Made of Dawn.*

Appositive Phrases

When an appositive has its own modifiers, it forms an *appositive phrase.*

KEY CONCEPT An **appositive phrase** is a noun or pronoun with modifiers, placed next to a noun or pronoun to add information and details. ■

The modifiers added to make an appositive phrase can be adjectives, adjective phrases, or other groups of words acting as adjectives. Notice the construction of the appositive phrases in the following chart. Also, note how they are used to add important information to the sentence.

APPOSITIVE PHRASES
Unmarried Hopi girls often wore their hair in twisted buns, *the design of squash blossoms.*
The horrible smoke, *a blend of burnt rubber and industrial fumes*, made her choke.
The dog, *a large Saint Bernard*, crushed the flowers in the garden.

Although many appositives and appositive phrases follow the subject, they can accompany almost any noun or pronoun used in a sentence. Following are some examples:

EXAMPLES: Her toy is a Kachina doll, *a doll made by Pueblo Indians.*

The man took his daughter, *a talented artist*, to see Native American paintings.

Appositives and appositive phrases also make it possible for a writer to combine sentences with similar ideas.

TWO SENTENCES: Navajo is a tribe in the West. They developed silver-working skills for making jewelry.

COMBINED: The Navajos, *a tribe in the West*, developed silver-working skills for making jewelry.

Appositives can be compound.

EXAMPLE: Symbols of wealth, *copper* and *horses*, were important to Northwestern tribes.

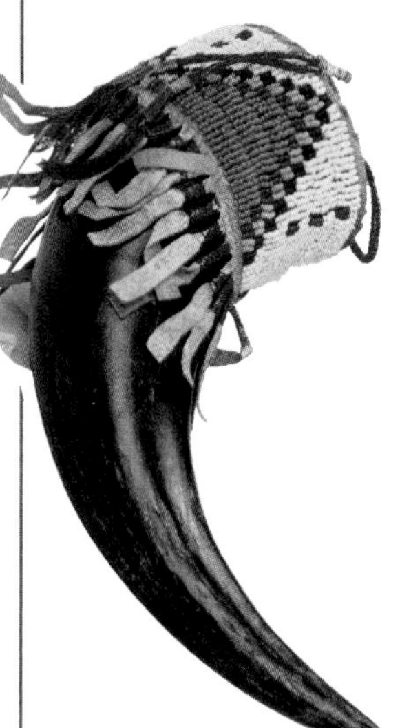

▲ Critical Viewing
This horn was used by Native Americans as a container. Use an appositive or appositive phrase in a sentence that tells what the container might have held.
[Speculate]

Exercise 5 **Identifying Appositive Phrases** Write the appositive phrase in each sentence. Then, write the word or words each appositive phrase renames.

1. Sugar cane, a plant with a strong stem, was used to make armor for Creek warriors.
2. Clubs, slings, lances, and bows and arrows—the usual weapons of war—were made of cane, rock, and other materials found in the area.
3. A war post, a cane stalk painted red and hung with feathers and arrows, signified the start of a war party.
4. Those who wanted to enlist would hit the post as hard as they could with a war club, a piece of cane painted red.
5. Then, warriors would put themselves through a purification rite, a physically strenuous ceremony.

Exercise 6 **Combining Sentences Using Appositive Phrases** Combine the two sentences by making the information in one into an appositive phrase.

EXAMPLE: A headdress was placed upon the warrior's head. The headdress was rows of feathers fastened together.

COMBINED: A headdress, rows of feathers fastened together, was placed upon the warrior's head.

1. Feathers were used not only for headdresses but also for acts of bravery. These feathers were called honor feathers.
2. Markings on the feathers identified the brave deed. The markings were cuts or adornments.
3. A small piece of colored feather appeared at the end of one feather. This feather represented a warrior riding into battle without weapons.
4. A feather with a split meant that the warrior had been wounded. The split was a tear down the center of the feather.
5. Counting *coup* was the bravest deed a warrior could perform. Counting *coup* was using a stick to touch a live enemy in battle without killing him.

More Practice

On-line Exercise Bank
- Section 21.1

Grammar Exercise Workbook
- pp. 67–70

◄ **Critical Viewing** Use "a beaded band decorated with feathers" as an appositive phrase in a sentence about the picture. **[Describe]**

21.1

Participles and Participial Phrases

Sometimes certain forms of verbs are used not as verbs but as other parts of speech. Verb forms used as other parts of speech are called *verbals.*

Verbals may be used alone or in phrases. Like verbs, they can have complements or be modified in different ways.

This section will cover the verbal known as the *participle.*

KEY CONCEPT A **participle** is a form of a verb that can act as an adjective. ■

Participles fall into two groups: *present participles* and *past participles.* You can identify these two different kinds of participles by their endings. Present participles end in *-ing* (*dancing, playing, waiting*). Past participles generally end in *-ed* (*danced, played, waited*), but they may also have irregular endings such as *-nt* or *-en* (*burnt, spoken*). (See Section 23.1 for lists of irregular verb endings.)

Like adjectives, participles answer the questions *What kind?* or *Which one?* The following chart shows how these participles are used as adjectives in sentences.

PRESENT PARTICIPLES	PAST PARTICIPLES
A *whining* sound came from the man's horse.	The *ground* corn was used to make tortillas.
Competing, each tribe tried to show off its riches.	*Disgusted,* Len walked away without saying goodbye.

Exercise 7 **Identifying Participles** Underline the participle in each sentence. Then, label each as *present* or *past.*

EXAMPLE: The Pueblo tribe was a dignified tribe. (past)

1. The Pueblo Native Americans lived simplified lives.
2. Attaining wealth and high social status was not prized.
3. The good of the community and personal integrity were the most respected values.
4. Their chosen ideal was to live a good, pious life.
5. Everyone helped to teach values to the growing youth.

Spelling Tip

Not all past participles end in *-ed.* Verbals that do not follow the pattern include *frozen, broken, chosen, sought, caught,* and others.

More Practice

On-line Exercise Bank
- Section 21.1

Grammar Exercise Workbook
- pp. 44–45

Verb or Participle?

Because verbs often have endings such as *-ing* and *-ed*, you must be careful not to confuse them with participles acting as adjectives.

KEY CONCEPTS A **verb** shows an action, a condition, or the fact that something exists. A **participle** acting as an adjective modifies a noun or pronoun. ■

The same word can be used as a verb and as a participle.

VERBS	PARTICIPLES
The train was *chugging* down the track.	The *chugging* train puffed down the track.
The directions *confused* her.	*Confused*, she could not follow the directions.

Exercise 8 **Distinguishing Between Verbs and Participles**
Identify each underlined word as a *verb* or *participle*. If the word is used as a participle, also write the word it modifies.

EXAMPLE: The Shoshone people valued the land and its usefulness.

ANSWER: verb

1. To the north of the Pueblo tribes lived scattered bands of people.
2. They were known as the Shoshone, and they inhabited the deserts of the West.
3. They hunted small game such as rabbits or lizards for food.
4. For clothes, they used scraps of skins from the hunted rabbits.
5. Using the resources they had, the Shoshone in this area made their homes of dried brush and desert plants.
6. They used sharpened sticks to dig out edible roots and insects for food.
7. Large gatherings were uncommon as the amount of food in one area sustained very few people.
8. Occasionally, tribes gathered for meetings or ceremonies, which were always simple in style.
9. Dreamed visions were often sung during these ceremonies.
10. Sometimes, the whole community danced to ask for protection for one or more of its members.

Participial Phrases

Because participles are forms of verbs, they can be expanded with modifiers and complements.

KEY CONCEPT A **participial phrase** is a participle modified by an adverb or adverb phrase or accompanied by a complement. The entire phrase acts as an adjective. ■

In the following chart, note how the participial phrases are constructed and which words they modify:

PARTICIPIAL PHRASES
Studying carefully, she learned much about Native American people.
Frightened by its sudden appearance, I yelled, "Snake!"
Her sister, *using a calm voice,* told us to stand still.

Placement A participial phrase can usually be placed either before or after the word it modifies.

EXAMPLES: *Gleaming in the sun,* Aztec temples and towers were awesome.

Aztec temples and towers, *gleaming in the sun,* were awesome.

Punctuation The participial phrases you have seen so far have been set off by commas or dashes. However, when a participial phrase distinguishes one person, place, or thing from another, it is not set off by commas. In the following example, *wearing the war bonnet* is essential to the meaning of the sentence.

EXAMPLE: The man *wearing the war bonnet* was a chief of the Sioux people.

Exercise 9 **Recognizing Participial Phrases** Write the participial phrase in each sentence. Then, write the word or words it modifies.

EXAMPLE: Being a resourceful people, the Nootka used their surroundings to make many things.

ANSWER: Being a resourceful people (the Nootka)

1. Living in the Northwest, the Nootka and other tribes built their lives around fish and wood.
2. Hollowed-out trees were turned into boats.
3. Fishing from these boats, the tribes brought in abundant amounts of salmon and halibut.
4. Some boats measuring 60 feet were even strong enough to bring in a whale.
5. Hunting whales with great skill, the Nootka tribe of Vancouver Island became well known for its catches.
6. Men, wearing armor carved from wood, had protection when fighting during their battles.
7. They made masks in the hope that their enemies, frightened by the horrible faces, would run away.
8. Fashioned to the form of the body, even everyday clothes were often made of bark.
9. Houses, built of wooden planks, often contained several families living together.
10. Door poles, fantastically carved and painted, held family symbols and emblems prized by the Nootka.

More Practice

On-line Exercise Bank
- Section 21.1

Grammar Exercise Workbook
- pp. 71–74

▼ Critical Viewing
Include one of these words—*reaching* or *caught*—as a participle in a participial phrase in a sentence about this picture. **[Speculate]**

21.1

Gerunds and Gerund Phrases

Many of the nouns you use are actually forms of verbs called *gerunds.*

KEY CONCEPT A **gerund** is a form of a verb that acts as a noun. ■

Gerunds always end in *-ing* and function as nouns—subject, indirect object, direct object, predicate nominative, object of a preposition, or appositive. The following chart shows how a gerund may be used.

GERUNDS	
Subject:	*Writing* by the Aztecs was often recorded on paper made of cactus.
Direct Object:	On their vacation, the Rezendes discovered *canoeing.*
Indirect Object:	His performance gives *acting* a bad reputation.
Predicate Nominative:	One relaxing exercise is *swimming.*
Object of a Preposition:	The Aztecs obtained much of their food by *fishing.*
Appositive:	I have a new hobby, *cooking.*

Exercise 10 **Identifying Gerunds** Write the gerund in each sentence, and identify its function in the sentence.

EXAMPLE: Displaying one's social status was important to some Native American tribes.

ANSWER: Displaying (subject)

1. For some tribes, prospering was easy on the west coast.
2. Fishing and hunting for berries there took little time.
3. This meant time spent working was reduced.
4. There was more free time for entertaining.
5. Dancing was less important than the wealth of a person or tribe.

More Practice

On-line Exercise Bank
- Section 21.1

Grammar Exercise Workbook
- pp. 46–47

GRAMMAR IN LITERATURE

from There Is a Longing . . .

Chief Dan George

In the following excerpt, the gerunds are highlighted in blue italics.

. . . There is a *longing* among
the young of my nation to secure for
themselves
and their people the skills that will
provide them with a sense of worth and
purpose. They will be our new warriors.
Their *training* will be much longer and
more demanding than it was in olden days. . . .

Verb, Participle, or Gerund?

Sometimes distinguishing between verbs, participles, and gerunds can be difficult.

The following examples of a verb, a participle, and a gerund demonstrate their differences.

VERB: Small Dove is weaving cloth.

PARTICIPLE: Small Dove, weaving cloth, uses the Incan method.

GERUND: Weaving is a Native American art.

Exercise 11 Distinguishing Between Verbs, Participles, and Gerunds Identify each underlined word as a *verb*, *participle*, or *gerund*.

1. People of the Crow tribe once made a living by farming.
2. When horses were introduced, the tribe changed to hunting for a living.
3. Making tepees from the skins of the animals they hunted, the Crow were more comfortable in freezing winter temperatures than they had been.
4. The tribe was growing in size and staying in one place longer.
5. Since the advantages of hunting far outweighed the advantages of farming, the Crow became mostly a hunting tribe.

Gerund Phrases

A gerund, like a participle, may be part of a phrase.

KEY CONCEPT A **gerund phrase** is a gerund with modifiers or a complement, all acting together as a noun. ■

GERUND PHRASES

Carving in stone was how the Aztecs made their calendars.
The Aztecs were skilled at *building in dense forests.*
Denise's greatest accomplishment was *weaving a blanket.*
They ran into the tepee without *removing muddy moccasins.*
Vicky's morning routine includes *showering leisurely.*
The loud, irregular snoring annoyed him.

In the first sentence, the gerund *carving* is modified by an adjective phrase. In the next sentence, the gerund is modified by a prepositional phrase. In the third and fourth sentences, the gerund is modified by direct objects. In the fifth, *showering* is modified by the adverb *leisurely.* And in the last sentence, *snoring* is modified by the adjectives *loud* and *irregular.*

Note About *Gerunds* and *Possessive Pronouns*: Always use the possessive form of a personal pronoun before a gerund.

INCORRECT: Mr. Avery disliked *him smirking.*
CORRECT: Mr. Avery disliked *his smirking.*

▼ **Critical Viewing** Notice the geometric designs the Caddo used to decorate these artifacts. Write two sentences telling what the designs make you think of. Use gerunds or gerund phrases in each sentence. **[Analyze]**

Exercise 12 **Identifying Gerund Phrases** Write the gerund phrases in each sentence, and identify their functions.

EXAMPLE: By invading Native American territory, the Europeans caused great hardship.
ANSWER: invading Native American territory (object of a preposition)

1. Pilgrims learned about planting crops from the Wampanoags.
2. Advanced weapons made fighting the Sioux a successful effort for the Chippewa.
3. The Sioux became a tribe that lived by hunting buffalo.
4. Beads brought by the Europeans were used in decorating clothing and other costumes.
5. Trading with Native Americans allowed Europeans to survive.

Infinitives and Infinitive Phrases

A third kind of verbal, in addition to the participle and the gerund, is the *infinitive.*

KEY CONCEPT An **infinitive** is a form of a verb that generally appears with the word *to* and acts as a noun, adjective, or adverb. ■

The following chart shows the different functions that an infinitive can have in a sentence.

INFINITIVES	
Subject:	*To decorate* requires gold, tropical feathers, and rare furs.
Direct Object:	Alone and frightened, she wanted *to survive.*
Predicate Nominative:	The purpose of pictures was *to record* an idea.
Object of a Preposition:	He had no choice except *to relent.*
Appositive:	His goal, *to travel,* was never realized.
Adjective:	The director of the camp is the person *to notify.*
Adverbs:	Cortés plotted *to take over* the Aztec Empire. Afraid *to speak,* he looked at his shoes.

Exercise 13 **Identifying Infinitives** Write the infinitive in each sentence. Then, tell how each functions in the sentence.

1. Native Americans had a variety of ways to travel.
2. To walk on top of the snow is the purpose of snowshoes.
3. If a woman wanted to carry many objects at a time, she may have used a carrying basket.
4. It was made especially to fit on her shoulders and head.
5. Those who planned to travel by water used boats made of wood, bark, or animal skins.

More Practice

On-line Exercise Bank
- Section 21.1

Grammar Exercise Workbook
- pp. 48–49

Prepositional Phrase or Infinitive?

You should take care not to confuse a prepositional phrase beginning with *to* with an infinitive.

KEY CONCEPT A **prepositional phrase** always ends with a noun or pronoun. An infinitive always ends with a verb. ■

Notice the difference in the following examples.

PREPOSITIONAL PHRASE	INFINITIVE
We went *to the movies* last week.	I didn't want the movie *to end.*

Exercise 14 Distinguishing Between Prepositional Phrases and Infinitives Write each phrase beginning with *to* in the sentences below. Then, label each *prepositional phrase* or *infinitive.*

1. Clothing of different tribes varied from area to area.
2. Plains tribes used tubes of bone to make a hair-pipe breastplate.
3. Breechcloths, cloths hung around the waist to cover the lower body, were used by several different tribes.
4. Women in the California area wore grass skirts to their knees.
5. Chiefs of the Southwest wore robes of feathers to important ceremonies.
6. Many Native Americans living in colder climates made their clothing out of fur to keep themselves warm.
7. Many tribes went to the forest for materials.
8. Those that lived in the Northwest often used bark and reed to make their clothing.
9. Moccasins were worn to protect feet.
10. To the Native Americans living in warmer climates, clothing was not always an important part of survival.

◀ **Critical Viewing** Compare the way these Native Americans dance with the way you and your friends dance. Use at least three infinitives. **[Compare and Contrast]**

Infinitive Phrases

Like other verbals, infinitives can be used to form phrases.

KEY CONCEPT An **infinitive phrase** is an infinitive with modifiers, complements, or a subject all acting together as a noun, adjective, or adverb. ■

NOUN: Professional dancers need *to practice daily.*

ADJECTIVE: Aztecs had a complex system *to irrigate the land.*

ADVERB: The Aztecs used these floating islands *to grow crops.*

Sometimes infinitives do not include the word *to.* After the verbs *dare, hear, help, let, make, please, see,* and *watch, to* will usually be understood.

EXAMPLE: Slave labor helped *build* many Aztec buildings.

Exercise 15 Identifying Infinitive Phrases Write the infinitive phrases in the following passage. Then, identify their function.

To dance in a powwow was to participate in a formal ceremony. Starting in the 1920's, ceremonial tribal boundaries loosened and tribes came together to participate. Dancing styles became competitive, and groups practiced many hours to show their very best. Today, people come more to celebrate dancing than to observe a formal ceremony. Powwow dancers like to use brighter colors, more motions, and new styles of dance. Their observance has spread across the United States where tribespeople prepare to dance. The desire of participants and visitors is to take part in a modern-day powwow. Before visiting a powwow, one might take a course to study the culture or etiquette. Of course, the dancers and singers have certain behaviors to perform. However, powwow etiquette makes visitors behave in a certain way, too.

More Practice

On-line Exercise Bank

- Section 21.1

Grammar Exercise Workbook

- pp. 75–82

Exercise 16 Writing Sentences With Infinitives Write a sentence for each infinitive phrase, using the infinitive phrase as the part of speech indicated

1. to succeed in school (subject)
2. to call home (direct object)
3. to leave on vacation (adverb modifying adjective *happy*)
4. to travel to another state (predicate noun)
5. to go to the ceremony (appositive)

21.1

Hands-on Grammar

"Where to?" Wheel

There are two kinds of phrases that begin with the word *to.* Infinitives and infinitive phrases begin with the word *to* and are followed by a verb. Some prepositional phrases also begin with the word *to* followed by a noun or pronoun. The phrase wheel illustrated below will help you to determine which is an infinitive and which is a prepositional phrase.

Cut out a wheel, and put a variety of phrases beginning with *to* around the wheel. Make a window frame with two windows, as shown. Make sure that the words on your wheel will show through the windows. One side of the frame tests for prepositional phrases by completing the sentence *They drove.* The other side of the frame tests for infinitives by completing the phrase *He wanted.* You will have to turn the frame upside down to read the infinitive side.

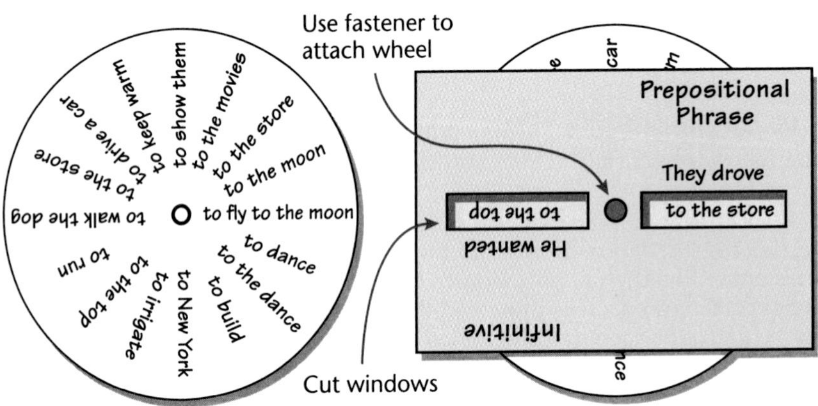

Find It in Your Reading In a short story or a textbook, find examples of phrases beginning with the word *to.* Make a second wheel to test to see whether the phrases are infinitives or prepositional phrases. (You can use the same window frames; just replace the wheel.)

Find It in Your Writing Look through a piece of your writing to find examples of prepositional phrases and infinitive phrases. Find at least three examples of each. If you cannot find any, challenge yourself to add details to your writing by adding three of each.

Section 21.1 Section Review

GRAMMAR EXERCISES 17–22

Exercise 17 **Identifying Adjective and Adverb Phrases** Write the phrase(s) from each sentence. Label prepositional phrases either *adjective* or *adverb*. Indicate the word each modifies. For appositive phrases, indicate the word that is renamed.

1. Tribes from the Northeast were called the Woodland tribes.
2. One of these, the Powhatan tribe, lived in the Virginia area.
3. They seemed unfriendly, but when the English settlers came to the American continent, the Powhatans saved them more than once.
4. The Native Americans taught the settlers to survive on American foods—corn, succotash, and baked beans.
5. Another tribe, the Delaware, was a group of extremely peaceful people.

Exercise 18 **Identifying Verbals** Write the verbal phrases in the following sentences. Label them *participial*, *infinitive*, or *gerund*. Identify the word or words the verbals modify or the way each is used in the sentence.

1. Five tribes came together to form the Iroquois nation.
2. This united league was known as "The Tree of Peace."
3. In Iroquoian culture, to live peacefully under one roof was expected.
4. The Tree of Peace, based on the same idea, showed that many people could live under one sky in peace.
5. Governing the nation was the job of fifty men from each of the five tribes.

Exercise 19 **Combining Sentence Phrases** Combine the following pairs of sentences into one sentence using an appositive or an appositive phrase.

1. The Iroquois were divided into the Mohawk, Seneca, Onondaga, Oneida, and Cayuga nations. Each Iroquois nation had its own council.
2. The Council of Fifty made important decisions. The council was made up of fifty men from the five tribes.
3. Mothers of the clan chose the council members. The council members were the decision makers of the tribe.
4. The council was formed to prevent fighting among the nations. It was called the League of the Iroquois.
5. The most powerful people in the Eastern Woodlands were the Iroquois. The Iroquois lived in what is now New York State.

Exercise 20 **Find It In Your Reading** Read the excerpt from "The Man to Send Rain Clouds." Identify each underlined phrase, and tell how it is used.

> The priest approached the grave slowly, <u>wondering how</u> they had managed <u>to dig into the frozen ground</u>; and then he remembered that this was New Mexico, and saw the pile of cold loose sand <u>beside the hole</u>.

Exercise 21 **Find It in Your Writing** Look through your writing portfolio. Find examples of sentences with prepositional phrases, participial phrases, or infinitive phrases. Underline the phrases, and tell how they are used.

Exercise 22 **Writing Application** Write an article on Native American crafts for your school paper. Make sure that prepositional, appositive, and verbal phrases are used correctly.

Section 21.2

Clauses

Clauses, like phrases, are groups of related words, but unlike phrases, they have a subject and a verb.

KEY CONCEPT A **clause** is a group of words with its own subject and verb. ■

Independent and Subordinate Clauses

There are two basic kinds of clauses: *independent clauses* and *subordinate clauses.*

KEY CONCEPT An **independent clause** can stand by itself as a complete sentence. ■

All complete sentences must contain at least one independent clause. *My aunt visited Africa for two weeks* is an independent clause. *Flora went to South Africa, and her sister went to Egypt* is one independent clause added to another.

KEY CONCEPT A **subordinate clause** cannot stand by itself as a complete sentence; it can only be part of a sentence. ■

Note how each subordinate clause works with an independent clause to form a complete idea in the following examples:

EXAMPLES: We visited Kenya, *which is a country in Africa,* for two weeks.
Because he woke up late, he missed the flight.
They have decided *that you should study more.*

There are three different kinds of subordinate clauses: *adjective, adverb,* and *noun.*

Exercise 23 **Identifying Independent and Subordinate Clauses** Identify each clause as *independent* if the clause can stand alone or *subordinate* if the clause cannot stand alone.

1. weavers of this tribe make beautiful cloth
2. each one has a different pattern
3. because one is mostly yellow
4. it is called "Gold Dust"
5. when Ghana elected its first president

Theme: Africa

In this section, you will learn about clauses and how to classify sentences by structure. The examples and exercises in this section are about the continent of Africa.

Cross-Curricular Connection: Social Studies

Adjective Clauses

Adjective clauses modify nouns or pronouns in ways often not possible with one-word adjectives or adjective phrases.

KEY CONCEPT An **adjective clause** is a subordinate clause that modifies a noun or pronoun by telling *what kind* or *which one.* ■

Adjective clauses usually begin with a relative pronoun, such as *that, which, who, whom,* or *whose.* Sometimes, they may begin with a relative adverb, such as *before, since, when, where,* or *why.*

ADJECTIVE CLAUSES
Ghana, *which means "land of gold,"* lies just north of the equator in Africa.
It was called "Gold Coast" by European traders *who found gold in abundance in this area.*
In the year *since I last saw you,* I have been to Africa twice.
The sun never shines on days *when I can enjoy it.*

Adjective clauses are set off by commas only when they are not essential to the meaning of a sentence.

Exercise 24 **Identifying Adjective Clauses** Write the adjective clause in each sentence. Then, circle the relative pronoun or relative adverb in each.

EXAMPLE: The ports where major trading occurs are the biggest cities of Ghana.
(where) major trading occurs

1. Algeria, which is a country in Africa, is a diverse combination of land, people, and culture.
2. Early invaders settled in Tell, which is north of the Atlas mountain range.
3. The high plateaus that run south of the Atlas Mountains are used for cattle grazing.
4. Members of the Ouled Nail tribe, who are known for their distinctive silver jewelry, live in this area.
5. Men of the Tuareg tribe, whose history is full of caravan raids, wear veils.

More Practice

On-line Exercise Bank
- Section 21.2

Grammar Exercise Workbook
- pp. 83–84

Modifying Nouns and Pronouns Adjective clauses, like single-word adjectives or adjective phrases, may modify any noun or pronoun in a sentence. The following examples suggest only a few of the many possibilities:

MODIFYING A SUBJECT: The city *where I would like to live* is Nairobi.

MODIFYING A DIRECT OBJECT: We ate cookies *that were made from rice.*

An adjective clause must closely follow the word it modifies. If it does not, the meaning of the sentence may be unclear.

INCORRECT: The person on the boat *who went* is my cousin.

CORRECT: The person *who went on the boat* is my cousin.

Combining Sentences Adjective clauses often allow you to combine information from two sentences into one sentence. They not only add detail to sentences but also indicate the relationship between ideas.

TWO SENTENCES: Ghana has a varied landscape. It is most densely populated along the coast.

COMBINED: Ghana, *whose landscape is varied,* is most densely populated along the coast.

▼ Critical Viewing Use adjective phrases in sentences to describe these women from Ghana carrying grain on their heads. **[Infer]**

Exercise 25 Combining Sentences With Adjective Clauses

Combine each pair of sentences by making one an adjective clause.

1. South of the Atlas Mountains lies the Sahara. It comprises 85 percent of Algeria.
2. The people are mostly Muslim and still speak their traditional dialect. They are approximately 80 percent Arab.
3. The majority of the other 20 percent also speak their own language. This group is given the name Berber.
4. They both speak different languages. This does not stop them from having similar lifestyles.
5. Both races work to produce coffee. Coffee is the major crop of their area.

Exercise 26 Writing Sentences With Adjective Clauses
Use each of the adjective clauses below to write a complete sentence on a separate sheet of paper.

1. who explored the river
2. which is where I want to live
3. when I am older
4. since he was last in Morocco
5. whose handwriting this is
6. whom I wanted to see
7. when they need someone to row
8. that lies in the valley below
9. that you can find in Nigeria
10. before you were born

More Practice
On-line Exercise Bank
• Section 21.2
Grammar Exercise Workbook
• pp. 53–54

Relative Pronouns A relative pronoun has two functions in a sentence with an adjective clause. First, it connects the adjective clause to the word the clause modifies. Second, it acts within the clause as a subject, direct object, object of a preposition, or adjective.

RELATIVE PRONOUNS				
who	*whom*	*whose*	*which*	*that*

◀ Critical Viewing In this village in Ghana, residents spread grain out to dry in the sun. Compare the clothing of the people in the picture using relative pronouns in your sentences. **[Compare and Contrast]**

KEY CONCEPT **Relative pronouns** connect adjective clauses to the words they modify and act as subjects, direct objects, objects of prepositions, or adjectives in the clauses. ■

You can tell how a relative pronoun is being used within a clause by separating the clause from the rest of the sentence and then finding the subject and verb in the clause.

USED AS A SUBJECT IN A CLAUSE:	The city *(that) is the largest* is Accra.
USED AS A DIRECT OBJECT IN A CLAUSE:	The movie *(that) you recommended* is no longer playing.
USED AS AN OBJECT OF A PREPOSITION IN A CLAUSE:	The person *of (whom) you spoke* is my friend.

Note About *Understood Words*: Sometimes a relative pronoun is left out of an adjective clause. The missing word, nevertheless, is understood and still functions in the sentence.

EXAMPLES: The flowers [*that*] *she bought* made him sneeze.
The relatives [*whom*] *they visited* were cousins.

Exercise 27 Recognizing the Uses of Relative Pronouns

Write the adjective clause in each sentence, and circle the relative pronoun. Then, label the use of the relative pronoun within the clause as *subject, direct object, object of a preposition*, or *adjective*.

EXAMPLE: Ghana's western frontier, which borders the Ivory Coast, is a stretch of warm, tropical forests.
ANSWER: (which) borders the Ivory Coast (subject)

Ghana, whose people make their living mostly by farming, produces the most cocoa in the world. This product, which makes up thirty-five percent of Ghana's exports, provides more jobs for Ghana's people than any other. However, many people, whom the big factories have attracted, have been migrating to the cities. Tema is a major port that has also attracted many people. Fortunately, the people of big cities, for whom disease was a problem, have been improving sanitation. Disease is no longer as widespread.

▼ **Critical Viewing** Use the relative pronouns *that, which,* and *who* to describe this African forest. **[Analyze]**

Relative Adverbs Like a relative pronoun, a *relative adverb* connects clauses while playing a role within the adjective clause.

KEY CONCEPT **Relative adverbs**—*where* and *when*—connect adjective clauses to the words they modify and act as adverbs in the clauses. ■

Unlike the relative pronoun, the relative adverb has only one use within the clause. It acts only as an adverb.

EXAMPLE: The settlers cleared a plot of land *where they could build.*

Exercise 28 Recognizing the Use of Relative Adverbs

Write the adjective clause in each sentence, and circle the relative adverb. Then, tell what word the clause modifies.

EXAMPLE: The land where Ghana's forests lie is full of valuable resources.

ANSWER: where Ghana's forests lie (land)

1. Many Yoruba people choose to live along the banks of the Niger River, where the soil is fertile.
2. Do you remember the time when we went to the museum?
3. The rooms in the museum where they keep the artifacts are very carefully guarded.
4. I was thinking about the visit when we saw the African masks.
5. The exhibit hall where you can see dioramas is my favorite.

Exercise 29 Writing Sentences With Adjective Clauses

Use each of the adjective clauses to modify a noun in a complete sentence. Write your sentences on a separate sheet of paper.

1. that is the most annoying
2. of which I am a part
3. when we arrived
4. who makes me laugh
5. that he wanted

More Practice

On-line Exercise Bank
- Section 21.2

Grammar Exercise Workbook
- pp. 85–86

21.2

Adverb Clauses

In addition to acting as adjectives, subordinate clauses can act as adverbs.

KEY CONCEPT An **adverb clause** is a subordinate clause that modifies a verb, an adjective, an adverb, or a verbal by telling *where, when, in what way, to what extent, under what condition,* or *why.* ■

KEY CONCEPT All adverb clauses begin with subordinating conjunctions. ■

The chart lists some of the most commonly used subordinating conjunctions. (See Section 19.2 for a more complete list and a review of subordinating conjunctions.)

SUBORDINATING CONJUNCTIONS		
after	even though	unless
although	if	until
as	in order that	when
as if	since	whenever
as long as	so that	where
because	than	wherever
before	though	while

▼ Critical Viewing Compare this scene in the African grasslands to what you see out the window of your house or apartment. Use two subordinate clauses in your response. **[Compare and Contrast]**

ADVERB CLAUSES

Wherever they need to go, Vai people carry their possessions on their heads.

I will help you with your history *whenever you ask.*

He ran *as if he had twisted an ankle.*

She ran more rapidly *than I did.*

If you visit the Uge people, they may give you kola nuts as a sign of welcome.

Jeanette wanted to stay *because the band was good.*

Adverb clauses answer the same questions adverbs answer. The first clause above tells *where*, the second tells *when*, and so on. The last two clauses are special in that they answer questions that simple adverbs cannot: *Under what condition*? and *Why*?

Exercise 30 **Identifying Adverb Clauses** Write the adverb clause in each sentence. Then, circle the subordinating conjunction in each.

EXAMPLE: Because Africa has both coast regions and deserts, its animal life is widely varied.

ANSWER: (Because) Africa has both coast regions and deserts

1. Because Africa's grasslands provide a wide grazing range, many large plant-eating animals are able to survive there.
2. Meat-eaters, such as lions, jackals, and hyenas, live in the grasslands because they hunt the plant-eaters.
3. Elephants, giraffes, zebras, hippopotamuses, and antelopes stay in one area until they have eaten most of the vegetation.
4. They then graze wherever they find more plants.
5. Elephants gather in a herd when they are threatened.
6. Lions won't attack a herd unless they are very hungry.
7. Jackals can hunt, although they usually eat what other animals have caught.
8. A jackal eats well as long as it can scavenge from other animals.
9. They eat after the other animal is finished.
10. Jackals check the area before they approach another animal's catch.

More Practice

On-line Exercise Bank
• Section 21.2
Grammar Exercise Workbook
• p. 55

GRAMMAR IN LITERATURE

from Talk

an Ashanti folk tale retold by Harold Courlander and George Herzog

The highlighted adverb clause adds information to the sentence. The clause modifies the verb became *and answers the question* Why?

The man became angry, *because his dog had never talked before,* and he didn't like his tone besides.

Modification of Different Words An adverb clause can modify a verb, an adjective, or an adverb.

MODIFYING A VERB: They will be caught *unless they can run faster.*

MODIFYING AN ADJECTIVE: The cheetah is swift *because his legs are built for speed.*

MODIFYING AN ADVERB: The storm struck sooner *than the forecasters expected.*

◀ **Critical Viewing** Compare the landscape in this picture with the landscape in the part of the country where you live. Use at least two adverb clauses in your comparison. **[Compare and Contrast]**

Placement in Sentences Adverb clauses can be placed at the beginning, in the middle, or at the end of a sentence. When the clause is at the beginning or in the middle of a sentence, it is set off by commas.

EXAMPLES: *When it rains*, the river often floods.

The river, *when it rains*, often floods.

The river often floods *when it rains*.

Sometimes the position of an adverb clause can affect the meaning of the sentence. To be safe, you should generally place the clause as close as possible to the word it modifies. Notice in the following examples how the placement of the adverb clause changes the word that the clause modifies.

EXAMPLES: *After the meeting ended*, they decided to stay.

They decided to stay *after the meeting ended*.

Exercise 31 **Revising Sentences With Adverb Clauses** Supply an adverb clause to complete each sentence below. Introduce the adverb clause with the subordinating conjunction shown in parentheses. You can put your adverb clause at the beginning or at the end of the sentence, whichever is more appropriate.

1. The Ashanti folk tale teaches a lesson. (while)
2. I laughed. (after)
3. We read it. (when)
4. I will probably read more folk tales. (since)
5. Reading the tale was fun. (because)
6. We did not go to the lake. (because)
7. Mark looks gloomy. (whenever)
8. Susan planned to stay. (until)
9. We wanted to stop. (so that)
10. You will enjoy the story. (if)

More Practice

Language Lab CD-ROM

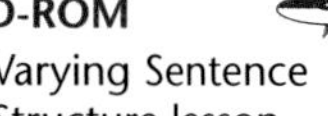

- Varying Sentence Structure lesson

On-line Exercise Bank

- Section 21.2

Grammar Exercise Workbook

- pp. 87–88

Adverb Clauses Used to Combine Sentences Like adjective clauses, adverb clauses often can be used to combine information from two sentences into one sentence.

TWO SENTENCES: We were outside. The cat broke the vase.
COMBINED: *While we were outside*, the cat broke the vase.

Exercise 32 Combining Sentences Using Adverb Clauses Combine each pair of sentences by changing one into an adverb clause.

EXAMPLE: Africa enjoys varied weather patterns. Its coastline and many inland areas receive an abundance of rain.
ANSWER: Because Africa enjoys varied weather patterns, its coastline and inland areas receive an abundance of rain.

1. Africa does have dry regions. It also has enormous rain forests.
2. The rain forests offer rich vegetation. Monkeys, bats, and flying squirrels find the forests hospitable.
3. Gorillas live in the deep jungle. They roam without fear of any predators but humans.
4. These giants can grow as tall as humans. They weigh much more.
5. Gorillas will sleep on the ground or in trees. Gorillas make new sleeping nests each night.

▼ **Critical Viewing** Come up with several adverb clauses used in sentences to explain why the gorilla is making that face. **[Infer]**

Elliptical Adverb Clauses When adverb clauses beginning with *as* or *than* are used to express comparisons, words are sometimes left out. Such adverb clauses are called *elliptical clauses.*

KEY CONCEPT An **elliptical clause** is a clause in which the verb or the subject and verb are understood but not actually stated. ■

The missing words in an elliptical clause still function in the sentence. In the following examples, the missing words have been added in brackets.

VERB UNDERSTOOD: I respect him more *than she* [*does*].

SUBJECT AND VERB UNDERSTOOD: I respect him more *than* [*I respect*] *her.*

When writing elliptical clauses, you should mentally add the missing words to ensure that the sentence retains its meaning.

Exercise 33 **Recognizing Elliptical Adverb Clauses** Write each sentence, adding the missing words in any elliptical clause. Then, underline the complete adverb clause in each sentence, and circle any words you have added.

EXAMPLE: Currently, Africa has more native languages spoken than the United States.
Currently, Africa has more native languages spoken than the United States *does*.

1. More than 700 different languages were developed in Africa by tribes of people who lived more apart than together.
2. Although similar, these languages have significant differences.
3. Strong boundaries were created by climate as much as by geographical features.
4. Their languages were as varied as their cultures.
5. When studying a group, anthropologists consider geographic features as well as cultural ones.

More Practice

Language Lab CD-ROM
- Varying Sentence Structure lesson

On-line Exercise Bank
- Section 21.2

Grammar Exercise Workbook
- p. 87–88

21.2

Noun Clauses

In addition to acting as adjectives and adverbs, subordinate clauses can also act as nouns.

KEY CONCEPT A **noun clause** is a subordinate clause that acts as a noun. ■

The following chart shows noun clauses functioning as several different parts of sentences.

NOUN CLAUSES	
Subject:	*Whomever you bring* will be welcome.
Direct Object:	The nomads can find *whatever water is in the desert.*
Indirect Object:	The teacher gave *whoever presented an oral report* extra credit.
Predicate Nominative:	The big question is *whether he will be allowed to play on the team.*
Object of a Preposition:	They store their food in plastic or in *whatever containers they have.*

◀ **Critical Viewing** What do you think of this Ghanian woman's abilities? Use a noun clause beginning with *who-ever* to respond. **[Speculate]**

Exercise 34 **Identifying Noun Clauses** Write the noun clause in each sentence. Then, label the clause *subject, direct object, predicate nominative,* or *object of a preposition.*

EXAMPLE: We know that some organisms cause health problems.

ANSWER: that some organisms cause health problems (direct object)

1. Our biology book says that many parasites breed in tropical regions.
2. Whatever animal is infested with a hookworm will also become severely anemic.
3. A hookworm causes severe problems for whatever animal it infects.
4. Mosquitoes may transmit malaria to whomever they bite.
5. Locusts fly in large swarms and devour whatever crops lie in their way.
6. Whatever area contains tsetse flies is dangerous for cattle.
7. Tsetse flies carry sleeping sickness and can quickly take the lives of whatever herd they infest.
8. Scientists say that they will soon breed disease-resistant cattle.
9. One organization gives a research grant to whoever works on this project.
10. This work is what will save the cattle of Africa.

▲ **Critical Viewing** Use a noun clause in a sentence to explain the importance of this fishing boat to the Ghanian people who are repairing it. **[Draw Conclusions]**

Exercise 35 **Writing Sentences With Noun Clauses** Use each clause below in a complete sentence. Identify whether the noun clause functions as a *subject,* a *direct object,* an *indirect object,* a *predicate nominative,* or the *object of a preposition.*

1. what they discovered
2. whoever travels farthest
3. what the name of the country is
4. that I could travel in the boat
5. whoever arrives last
6. that traveling by boat is best
7. what is in the boat
8. how long it will take
9. who is interested
10. how people get from here to there

More Practice

On-line Exercise Bank
- Section 21.2

Grammar Exercise Workbook
- pp. 89–90

21.2

Sentences Classified by Structure

All sentences can be classified in two ways. First, they can be classified by structure—that is, by the number and types of clauses they contain. Second, they can be classified by function—that is, by whether they state ideas, ask questions, give orders, or express surprise.

The Four Structures of Sentences

There are two kinds of clauses: *independent* and *subordinate*. These can be used to form four basic sentence structures: *simple*, *compound*, *complex*, and *compound-complex*.

KEY CONCEPT A **simple sentence** consists of a single independent clause. ■

Although a *simple sentence* is just one independent clause with one subject and one verb, the subject, verb, or both may be compound. A simple sentence may also have modifying phrases and complements. However, it cannot have a subordinate clause.

In the following simple sentences, the subjects are underlined once and the verbs twice.

ONE SUBJECT AND VERB: The snow melted.

COMPOUND SUBJECT: Diamonds and manganese are mined in Ghana.

COMPOUND VERB: The tree rotted and died.

COMPOUND SUBJECT AND VERB: Neither the driver nor the skier heard or saw the other boat.

WITH PHRASES AND COMPLEMENT: Loading everything on a boat, the Lozi move from flooding land to higher ground every year.

KEY CONCEPT A **compound sentence** consists of two or more independent clauses. ■

The clauses in a compound sentence can be joined by a comma and a coordinating conjunction (*and, but, for, nor, or, so, yet*) or by a semicolon (;). Like a simple sentence, a compound sentence contains no subordinate clauses.

EXAMPLES: A Sotho bride carries a beaded doll at her wedding, and she keeps the same doll for a year.
Stan read the book Friday; he wrote his essay today.

KEY CONCEPT A **complex sentence** consists of one independent clause and one or more subordinate clauses. ■

The independent clause in a complex sentence is often called the *main clause* to distinguish it from the subordinate clause or clauses. The subject and verb in the independent clause are called the *subject of the sentence* and the *main verb*. The second example shows that a subordinate clause may fall between the parts of a main clause.

EXAMPLES:

MAIN CLAUSE / SUBORD CLAUSE
No one answered the phone when she called us.

MAIN / SUBORD CLAUSE / CLAUSE
The doll that the bride carries doesn't have arms.

KEY CONCEPT In complex sentences with noun clauses, the subject of the main clause may sometimes be the subordinate clause itself. ■

EXAMPLE:

SUBORD CLAUSE / MAIN CLAUSE
That I wanted to go bothered them.

KEY CONCEPT A **compound-complex sentence** consists of two or more independent clauses and one or more subordinate clauses. ■

EXAMPLES:

IND CLAUSE
After a year, the first child is born, and the
IND CLAUSE
baby receives the same name
SUBORD. CLAUSE
that the doll was given
SUBORD. CLAUSE
when the bride was married.

SUBORD. CLAUSE / IND CLAUSE
When the lights went out, we felt extremely
IND CLAUSE
uneasy, but we always knew
SUBORD. CLAUSE
that morning would eventually come.

Exercise 36 Identifying the Structure of Sentences

Identify each sentence as *simple, compound, complex,* or *compound-complex.*

1. South Africa is the southernmost country of Africa.
2. It is the most powerful and the wealthiest country of the region.
3. Gold and diamonds are mined in both South Africa and Namibia, yet it was South Africa where the biggest diamond in the world was found.
4. Although it is not as wealthy as South Africa, Mozambique is the site of the second biggest port in all of Africa.
5. Its capital, Maputo, is the city where the port is located; it is linked by rail with South Africa, Swaziland, and Zimbabwe.
6. Even though most people think of Africa as a desert, Zimbabwe has a hot, tropical climate, so mangoes, passion fruit, pineapples, and avocados grow well.
7. In fact, only a small percentage of southern Africa is desert.
8. However, because soil quality is poor, farms thrive only in places that receive more than 20 inches of rain annually.
9. One of the many surprising facts about west Africa is that the Sahara was not always a desert.
10. Rock paintings show that as recently as several thousand years ago, people hunted hippopotamuses in the region's rivers and chased buffalo on its wide, grassy plains.

More Practice

On-line Exercise Bank
- Section 21.2

Grammar Exercise Workbook
- pp. 91–92

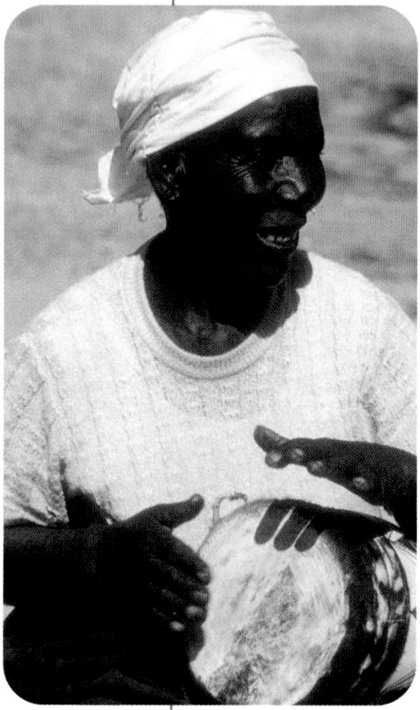

▲ **Critical Viewing** In a complex sentence, describe this picture. Begin with the simple sentence "The musician smiles." **[Apply]**

Exercise 37 Writing Sentences With Different Structures

Use the following instructions to write five sentences of your own.

1. Write a simple sentence with a compound subject and verb.
2. Write a compound sentence with two independent clauses joined by *and.*
3. Write a complex sentence with one independent and one subordinate clause.
4. Write a complex sentence with one independent clause and two subordinate clauses.
5. Write a compound-complex sentence.

Section 21.2 Section Review

GRAMMAR EXERCISES 38–43

Exercise 38 **Recognizing Adjective, Adverb, and Noun Clauses** Write the adjective, adverb, or noun clause from each sentence. Label each correctly.

1. The Zaire River, which is also known as the Congo, runs almost the whole length of the country.
2. Because it has many tributaries, it is an important source of transportation.
3. The river drains a vast area of rain forests so its levels are always high.
4. The climate of the Democratic Republic of the Congo is hot and humid because it lies on the equator.
5. Besides whatever cooking and cleaning African women do, they also work in the fields and sell crops in the market.

Exercise 39 **Identifying Sentence Structure** Label each sentence in the following paragraph *simple, complex, compound,* or *compound-complex.*

(1) The Sahel is a region defined by location, climate, and vegetation. (2) The Sahel, which extends across Africa, separates the Sahara to the north from the tropical rain forests to the south. (3) For centuries, the region was a busy crossroads and a meeting place for different cultures. (4) Today, the area contains more than a dozen independent countries; each one has its own vision of the past, present, and future.

Exercise 40 **Combining Sentences With Clauses** Combine each of the following sentence pairs by making the second sentence into an adjective, an adverb, or a noun clause.

1. The book is no longer in print. You wanted a book on the Democratic Republic of the Congo.
2. We left on vacation. First we took the dogs to the kennel.
3. Chinua Achebe is a Nigerian writer. I read his book *Arrow of God.*
4. This museum was built in 1896. This is the museum in our travel guide.
5. The plane trip to Zimbabwe was long. It took 20 hours.

Exercise 41 **Find It in Your Reading** Read the following lines from "Talk," an Ashanti folk tale. Identify the two sentence structures that are used.

Once, not far from the city of Accra on the Gulf of Guinea, a country man went out to his garden to dig up some yams to take to market. While he was digging, one of the yams [spoke] to him.

Exercise 42 **Find It in Your Writing** In a piece of your own writing, find an example of each type of sentence structure. If you cannot find an example of complex or compound-complex sentences, challenge yourself to use adjective and adverb clauses to combine sentences.

Exercise 43 **Writing Application** Write a brief description of a dry climate. Use at least three of the following clauses, and identify the type of each clause you use. Then, identify each of the sentence structures you have made.

that is hot and dry
where there isn't much rain
whatever rain falls
since the last rainfall
when the temperature rises
where the temperature rises
who can farm the land

Chapter 22 Effective Sentences

▲ **Critical Viewing** Write sentences about this tiger in which you make a statement, ask a question, give an order, or express an exclamation. **[Respond]**

Both domestic and wild cats have various forms of communication. The position and movement of the tail indicates mood. Roars, purrs, and squeals help cats share information about their surroundings.

Humans, on the other hand, use sentences to communicate in writing and in speaking. We use sentences every day—to ask questions, make statements, express emotion, or share information. In writing, putting words together to form effective sentences is the first step in clear communication.

Diagnostic Test

Directions: Write all answers on a separate sheet of paper.

Skill Check A. Label each sentence *declarative, interrogative, imperative*, or *exclamatory*.

1. Have you ever seen a Bengal cat?
2. The word *Bengal* brings to mind tigers.
3. Think about a wildcat as a pet.
4. Do you know that house cats are domesticated wildcats?
5. What an incredible temperament that cat has!

Skill Check B. Combine the following sentences using the method indicated in parentheses.

6. Bengal cats were bred to help increase the number of endangered wildcats. Many wildcats were sold in pet shops. (join with subordinating conjunction)
7. The female is an Asian leopard. The male is a domestic cat. (join with a comma and coordinating conjunction)
8. The Bengal cat growls. The traditional domestic cat hisses. (join with subordinating conjunction)
9. The Bengal cat plays fetch. It walks in a harness. It retrieves objects. (use a compound verb)
10. Bengal cats have friendly, inquisitive, and affectionate personalities. This is true if they are treated kindly and with respect. (turn one sentence into a phrase)

Skill Check C. Rewrite the following sentences to be more direct or to vary their beginnings as shown in parentheses.

11. Bengal cats may be spotted like a leopard, with black or brown spots accenting a light coat of the color tan, orange, rust, or gold.
12. The coat of the Bengal cat is different from that of tabbies since it has chocolate-brown or brick-red spots. (participial phrase)
13. If the Bengal cat has a gray coat with black spots, it could be referred to as a charcoal-spotted cat.
14. A beautiful Bengal, the seal lynx point snow, is a cat that is white as snow and has bright blue eyes like a Siamese cat.
15. The seal sepia snow cat is unusual, with yellow eyes and a dark brown coat. (prepositional phrase)

Skill Check D. Label each of the following items *fragment, run-on*, or *misplaced modifier*. Then, rewrite the item so that it is correct.

16. Talking about the coloring of the coat, the beautiful patterns were described by her.
17. The spotted variety.
18. A rosetted Bengal is spotted, what makes the spots different is that they have two colors.
19. Like the spots on a jaguar.
20. I saw the most beautiful cat the other day at Joe's house with golden glitter in its fur.

Section 22.1

The Four Functions of a Sentence

Sentences can be classified according to what they do—that is, whether they state ideas, ask questions, give orders, or express strong emotions. The four types of sentences in English are *declarative, interrogative, imperative,* and *exclamatory.*

Declarative sentences are the most common type. They are used to "declare," or state, facts.

KEY CONCEPT A **declarative sentence** states an idea and ends with a period. ■

DECLARATIVE: In many Asian countries, wildcats are common. The leopard has a beautiful pattern of brown spots edged in black.

To *interrogate* means "to ask." An *interrogative sentence* is a question.

KEY CONCEPT An **interrogative sentence** asks a question and ends with a question mark. ■

INTERROGATIVE: Whose Bengal cat is this?
In what country do tigers live?

The word *imperative* is related to the word *emperor,* a person who gives commands. *Imperative* sentences are like emperors: They give commands.

KEY CONCEPT An **imperative sentence** gives an order or a direction and ends with either a period or an exclamation mark. ■

Most imperative sentences start with a verb. In this type of imperative sentence, the subject is understood to be *you.*

IMPERATIVE: Follow the directions carefully.
Watch out for lions while on the safari!

Notice the punctuation in the examples on the next page. In the first sentence, the period suggests that a mild command is being given in an ordinary tone of voice. The exclamation mark at the end of the second sentence suggests a strong command, one given in a loud voice.

To *exclaim* means to "shout out." *Exclamatory sentences* are used to "shout out" emotions, such as happiness, fear, or anger.

Theme: Wild and Domestic Cats

In this section, you will learn to classify sentences according to their function. The examples and exercises are about different types of wild and domestic cats.

Cross-Curricular Connection: Science

▼ Critical Viewing
Write an exclamatory sentence and an imperative sentence you might use in talking with someone about an endangered animal, such as this lynx. **[Connect]**

GRAMMAR IN LITERATURE

from The Most Dangerous Game

Richard Connell

The following passage illustrates three of the four types of sentences.

"Don't talk rot, Whitney," said Rainsford. "You're a big-game hunter, not a philosopher. Who cares how a jaguar feels?"

"Perhaps the jaguar does," observed Whitney.

KEY CONCEPT An **exclamatory sentence** conveys strong emotion and ends with an exclamation mark. ■

EXCLAMATORY: She's not telling the truth!
This is an outrage!

Exercise 1 **Identifying the Four Types of Sentences** Read each of the following sentences carefully, and identify it as *declarative, interrogative, imperative,* or *exclamatory.* Then, write the appropriate punctuation mark for each sentence.

EXAMPLE: Have you ever seen a lynx
ANSWER: interrogative (?)

1. The lynx is a wildcat that measures up to three feet in length
2. What color is the lynx
3. It has a brownish-gray coat with a black, bobbed tail and black ear tufts
4. It is so adorable
5. Look for the lynx in dense forests
6. What is the purpose of camouflage
7. Lynxes are successful hunters because their prey cannot differentiate between them and the dense forest
8. Have you ever wondered why the lynx is endangered
9. What a sad thing that is
10. Read this article if you want to learn more

More Practice

Language Lab CD-ROM
- Effective Sentences lesson

On-line Exercise Bank
- Section 22.1

Grammar Exercise Workbook
- pp. 93–94

Section 22.1 **Section Review**

GRAMMAR EXERCISES 2–7

Exercise 2 Identify the Four Types of Sentences Read each sentence carefully, and label it *declarative*, *interrogative*, *imperative*, or *exclamatory*.

1. Saber-toothed tigers get their name from their large, sharp teeth.
2. Study the saber-toothed tiger if you are interested in extinct cats.
3. Evidence of these animals has appeared in two different eras.
4. Do you know why they had such big teeth?
5. Researchers have proposed that they used them to attack prey.
6. Watch out for the saber-toothed tiger!
7. Could they break their teeth by using them that way?
8. Look for a broken tooth in the fossil record.
9. I can't find one!
10. Saber-toothed tigers also used their teeth to tear the flesh off their prey.

Exercise 3 Revising to Vary Sentence Type Rewrite the following sentences to fit the type indicated in italics.

EXAMPLE: Saber-toothed tigers once lived in California. *interrogative*

ANSWER: Did saber-toothed tigers once live in California?

1. Have you ever gone to the La Brea tar pits? *imperative*
2. You found another fossil! *interrogative*
3. Does the short tail of the saber-toothed tiger indicate that it did not chase its prey? *declarative*
4. How dangerous was the saber-toothed tiger? *exclamatory*
5. Go to Berkeley to see representations of these ferocious animals. *declarative*

Exercise 4 Punctuating the Four Types of Sentences Copy the following sentences onto your paper. Add the appropriate punctuation mark for each sentence, and identify its type.

1. Do you know what a saber is
2. A saber is a large sword with a blade that is slightly curved
3. Don't call that animal a tiger
4. Why is it not a tiger
5. These ice age animals were unlike any wildcats that live today
6. Their weight allowed them to attack mastodons and mammoths
7. What a powerful animal it was
8. How could the cats eat their prey without sharp teeth
9. Look at those strong muscles in its head, neck, and shoulders
10. We're so lucky they aren't alive today

Exercise 5 Find It in Your Reading The excerpt from "The Most Dangerous Game" on page 493 contains three of the four sentence types. Add an example of the fourth kind of sentence to continue the conversation.

Exercise 6 Find It in Your Writing Look through your portfolio for examples of each of the four types of sentences. If you can't find all four kinds, challenge yourself to add the missing types to a piece of your writing.

Exercise 7 Writing Application Write a short essay comparing wildcats and domestic cats. Discuss their similarities and their differences. Include all four types of sentences.

Section 22.2 Sentence Combining

If you use too many short sentences, your writing may seem choppy and disconnected. One way to avoid the excessive use of short sentences and to achieve sentence variety is to combine sentences—to express two or more related ideas or pieces of information in a single sentence.

EXAMPLE:	We went to the zoo. We saw tigers.
COMBINED SENTENCES:	We went to the zoo and saw tigers. We saw tigers at the zoo. We saw tigers when we went to the zoo.

KEY CONCEPT Sentences can be combined by using a compound subject, a compound verb, or a compound object. ■

TWO SENTENCES:	Moira enjoyed watching the lions. Jon enjoyed watching the lions.
COMPOUND SUBJECT:	Moira and Jon enjoyed watching the lions.
TWO SENTENCES:	Lisa played the game. Lisa won a prize.
COMPOUND VERB:	Lisa played the game and won a prize.
TWO SENTENCES:	Scott saw the cheetah. Scott saw the hyena.
COMPOUND OBJECT:	Scott saw the cheetah and the hyena.

Exercise 8 **Combining Sentences Using Compound Subjects, Verbs, and Objects** Combine each pair of sentences in the way that makes the most sense. Identify what you have done to combine them.

EXAMPLE:	Lions eat gazelles. Lions eat warthogs.
ANSWER:	Lions eat gazelles and warthogs. (compound object)

1. Thomas heard the roar of the lion. Micah heard the roar of the lion.
2. Lions are social animals. Lions live in groups called prides.
3. As many as twelve females live in a pride. Their cubs live in a pride.
4. The lionesses stalk prey. The lionesses hunt for food.
5. Cubs get milk from their mother. Cubs get milk from other female lions.

Theme: Wild and Domestic Cats

In this section, you will learn to combine sentences. The examples and exercises tell more about wild and domestic cats.

Cross-Curricular Connection: Science

▲ Critical Viewing In a single sentence describing this tiger, mention at least two of its features. **[Analyze]**

KEY CONCEPT Sentences can be combined by joining two independent clauses to create a compound sentence. ■

Use a compound sentence when combining ideas that are related but independent. Compound sentences are created by joining two independent clauses with a comma and a coordinating conjunction (such as *and, but, or, yet,* or *so*) or with a semicolon.

EXAMPLE:	The antelope was on the lookout for enemies. It did not notice the lion hiding in the high grass nearby.
COMPOUND SENTENCE:	The antelope was on the lookout for enemies, but it did not notice the lion hiding in the high grass nearby.
EXAMPLE:	The lion waited patiently. Its prey kept moving closer.
COMPOUND SENTENCE:	The lion waited patiently; its prey kept moving closer.

Exercise 9 **Creating Compound Sentences** Combine each pair of sentences according to the method indicated in parentheses.

EXAMPLE:	The tiger is a cat. It is not likely that anyone would want one as a pet. (comma and conjunction)
ANSWER:	The tiger is a cat, but it is not likely that anyone would want one as a pet.

1. The tiger is the largest species in the cat family. It can weigh up to 675 pounds. (semicolon)
2. The eye of the tiger is specialized to help the tiger see in dim light. It is able to hunt at night. (comma and conjunction)
3. Tigers live in areas that are thick with grasses and trees. This natural cover allows them to hide and ambush their prey. (semicolon)
4. Tigers are solitary animals. They will keep their young with them until the young reach the age of two or three. (comma and conjunction)
5. At this age, young tigers can find their own food. They are able to find and mark their own territory. (comma and conjunction)

More Practice

Language Lab CD-ROM
- Effective Sentences lesson

On-line Exercise Bank
- Section 22.2

Grammar Exercise Workbook
- pp. 95–96

KEY CONCEPT Sentences can be combined by changing one into a subordinate clause to create a complex sentence. ■

Use a complex sentence when you are combining sentences to show the relationship between ideas in which one depends on the other. The subordinating conjunction will help readers understand the relationship.

EXAMPLE:	We were frightened. We thought the lion we saw on safari was hungry.
COMBINED WITH A SUBORDINATE CLAUSE:	We were frightened because we thought the lion we saw on safari was hungry.

Exercise 10 **Combining Sentences Using Subordinate Clauses** Combine each pair of sentences using the subordinating conjunction that is given in parentheses.

EXAMPLE:	The tiger is an endangered species. It has been overexploited as a resource. (because)
ANSWER:	The tiger is an endangered species because it has been overexploited as a resource.

1. There are eight species of tigers. Three of them are extinct. (although)
2. People see pictures of these magnificent creatures. They don't realize they are endangered. (when)
3. The resources required to sustain the life of the tigers are diminishing. Tigers have few places to live and little food to eat. (so that)
4. Poachers diminish the tiger population. They can get high prices for tiger parts. (since)
5. Forty years ago there were four thousand South China tigers living in the wild. Today there are fewer than thirty. (while)
6. The government mistakenly declared the South China tiger a pest in the 1950's. Thousands of the animals were slaughtered. (after)
7. The Chinese government has become actively involved in efforts to preserve the South China tiger. The government wants to prevent the animal's extinction. (because)
8. The South China tiger is the most critically endangered tiger. Other subspecies are also threatened. (although)
9. Efforts were made to halt the hunting of Siberian tigers. There were fewer than fifty of these huge beasts surviving in the wild. (until)
10. Strong pressure has been brought to protect tigers. More people have learned of their peril. (as)

KEY CONCEPT Sentences can be combined by changing one of them into a phrase. ■

EXAMPLE:	My team plays tomorrow. We play the Cougars.
COMBINED WITH PREPOSITIONAL PHRASE:	My team plays *against the Cougars* tomorrow.
EXAMPLE:	My team will play against the Cougars. They are the only undefeated team in the league.
COMBINED WITH: APPOSITIVE PHRASE:	My team will play against the Cougars, *the only undefeated team in the league.*
EXAMPLE:	The Cougars scored quickly. The Cougars jumped out to a two-goal lead.
COMBINED WITH PARTICIPIAL PHRASE:	*Scoring quickly,* the Cougars jumped out to a two-goal lead.

Learn More

To review information about different types of phrases, see Chapter 21.

Exercise 11 **Combining Sentences Using Phrases**
Combine each pair of sentences by turning one sentence into a phrase that adds detail to the other.

EXAMPLE:	The cheetah has a tawny-colored coat. It has round, black spots.
ANSWER:	The cheetah has a tawny-colored coat with round, black spots.

1. The cheetah moves stealthily. It moves through the tall grass.
2. It watches its prey. Its prey is a gazelle.
3. The cheetah runs quickly. It runs after the gazelle.
4. The cheetah tires quickly. It is unable to chase the gazelle very far.
5. The gazelle is relieved to have escaped. The gazelle stops running and catches its breath.

More Practice

Grammar Exercise Workbook
- pp. 93–94

◀ **Critical Viewing** Think of a sentence that combines several details about the way this cheetah moves. **[Analyze]**

Section 22.2 **Section Review**

GRAMMAR EXERCISES 12–17

Exercise 12 **Combining Sentence Parts** Combine each pair of sentences by creating a compound subject, verb, or object.

1. Lions are majestic animals. Tigers are majestic animals.
2. The male lion is a strong fighter. The male lion is called King of the Jungle.
3. Lions hunt zebras. Lions hunt antelopes.
4. Lions inhabit grassland. Lions inhabit thinly forested areas.
5. Lion cubs are born with spots. Lion cubs lose the spots by their third month.

Exercise 13 **Combining Clauses and Phrases** Combine each pair of sentences by creating a compound sentence, forming a complex sentence, or changing one sentence into a phrase.

1. I have often visited the zoo. The zoo is in San Diego.
2. I visit the zoo. My first stop is the tiger habitat.
3. Tigers are cats. They do not purr.
4. Instead, tigers have a variety of roars. They communicate with these roars.
5. A tiger's tail serves two purposes. The tail is long and flexible.
6. The tail aids balance during running. It also expresses emotion.
7. A tiger with its tail upright and moving slowly is friendly. A tiger with its tail lowered and twitching is angry.
8. The natural habitat of the Bengal tiger and Indochinese tiger has declined. It has declined because of overhunting.
9. The Sumatran tiger is similar to the Bengal tiger. It is smaller and its stripes are closer together.
10. I plan to study tigers in college. I hope to work at the San Diego Zoo someday.

Exercise 14 **Revising a Paragraph by Combining Sentences** Revise the paragraph below by combining some of the short sentences to form longer ones.

(1) Cheetahs live on the grassy plains and in the dense bush. (2) The plains and bush are in Africa. (3) Cheetahs once lived in southern and central Asia. (4) Their habitat has shrunk. (5) Many of their former lands have been taken over by farms. (6) Their wooded homelands have been replaced by manufacturing plants. (7) Cheetahs are known for their beauty. (8) Cheetahs are known for their speed. (9) Cheetahs can run up to 60 miles per hour. (10) They can capture even the fastest prey.

Exercise 15 **Find It in Your Reading** Several ideas have been combined in this sentence from "The Most Dangerous Game." Write the ideas that have been combined as separate sentences.

He struggled up to the surface and tried to cry out, but the wash from the speeding yacht slapped him in the face and the salt water in his open mouth made him gag and strangle.

Exercise 16 **Find It in Your Writing** Look in your portfolio for examples of short, choppy sentences. Combine some of these to form longer sentences.

Exercise 17 **Writing Application** Write a short essay telling why endangered animals should or should not be protected. Combine clauses and phrases to form longer, more interesting sentences.

Section 22.3

Varying Sentences

Varying the length and form of your sentences can make them more interesting. It can help to create a rhythm, to achieve an effect, or to emphasize the connections between ideas. There are several ways you can create variety in your sentences:

Vary Sentence Length

You have already learned that you can combine several short, choppy sentences to create a longer, more fluid and stylistically mature sentence. However, too many long sentences one after another can be as uninteresting as too many short sentences. When you want to emphasize a point or surprise a reader, insert a short, direct sentence to interrupt the flow of several long sentences. You can also break some longer sentences that contain two or more ideas into shorter sentences to achieve variety.

Some sentences contain only one idea and can't be broken up. It may be possible, however, to state the idea in a shorter sentence. Other sentences contain two or more ideas and might be shortened by breaking up the ideas.

ONE LONG SENTENCE: Although bicycles have evolved into several forms from the original three-wheeled transportation machine, the originators could not have fathomed the daredevil stunts that people would attempt on mountain bikes, and even much of the population is not aware of the adventure, the adrenaline rush, and the extreme athleticism that are all part of a trip through the mountains.

TWO SENTENCES: Although bicycles have evolved into several forms from the original three-wheeled transportation machine, the originators could not have fathomed the daredevil stunts that people would attempt on mountain bikes. Even much of the population is not aware of the adventure, the adrenaline rush, and the extreme athleticism that are all a part of a trip through the mountains.

Theme: Bicycles and Cyclists

In this section, you will learn ways to vary sentence length and beginnings to make your writing more interesting. The examples and exercises are about bicycles and cyclists.

Cross-Curricular Connection: Physical Education

▼ Critical Viewing Think of three or four ideas that this picture brings to mind. Which ideas should go in separate sentences? Which should be combined in one sentence? **[Make a Judgment]**

Exercise 18 **Making Simpler Sentences** Rewrite the following sentences. Break each one into two sentences or rewrite the sentence in a simpler, more direct way.

EXAMPLE: The casual observer may think of the unicycle as a circus toy, but it is a complex machine that requires great coordination and skill, as you will learn if you ever try one.

ANSWER: The unicycle looks like a simple circus toy. However, if you ever try one, you will see that it requires great coordination and skill.

1. The height of the frame of the giraffe unicycle, also known as the tall unicycle, gives it its name, and it ranges in height from five to eight feet.
2. The biverticycle has two wheels stacked vertically to improve the balance and momentum in turning the wheels and to propel the cycle forward, but it can be considered a unicycle because only one of its wheels touches the ground when the trained professional rides the cycle.
3. In order to learn to ride the biverticycle, it is necessary to train new muscle and nerve reactions because the movement is a backward pedaling motion, which is not the same as the movements required on a normal unicycle.
4. The triverticycle has three wheels, as the name implies, and is easier to ride than the biverticycle because you pedal in a forward direction.
5. Although it may not seem practical, unicycles having up to four or five vertically stacked wheels have been built for entertainment and sport, although the potential hazards of these cycles have not made these cycles popular.

More Practice

Language Lab CD-ROM

- Effective Sentences lesson

On-line Exercise Bank

- Section 22.3

Grammar Exercise Workbook

- pp. 97–98

Vary Sentence Beginnings

Another way to create sentence variety is to avoid starting each sentence in the same way. You can start sentences with different parts of speech.

START WITH A NOUN:	Bicycles are difficult to make.
START WITH AN ADVERB:	Naturally, bicycles are difficult to make.
START WITH A PARTICIPLE:	Having tried to make several bicycles, I know they are very difficult to make.
START WITH A PREPOSITIONAL PHRASE:	For the average person, bicycles are very difficult to make.
START WITH AN INFINITIVE PHRASE:	To win the race is his goal.

Spelling Tip

If you are having difficulty spelling a word, try to think of another form of the word that might indicate the correct spelling. For example, if you are trying to spell *bicycle,* you may want to spell it like it sounds, *bicicle.* However, by thinking of the word *cycle,* the correct spelling, *bicycle,* becomes clear.

Exercise 19 **Varying Sentence Beginnings** Rewrite the following sentences so that they begin with the part of speech indicated in parentheses.

1. The initials *BMX* stand for "Bicycle Motocross" to cycling enthusiasts. (prepositional phrase)
2. This sport is different from MMX, Motorcycle Motocross, because BMX depends on the power of a rider's legs instead of the power of an engine. (adverb)
3. BMX has grown from a simple beginning into a sport with many components. (prepositional phrase)
4. Vert riding is an exciting sport done on ramps known as half-pipes or quarter-pipes, similar to those used in skateboarding. (participial phrase)
5. In their sport, BMX riders use ramps, ledges, and rails. (noun)
6. Flatland is the sport of doing stunts while on a normal, flat surface. (gerund phrase)
7. Dirt jumping is one of the preferred aspects of BMX. (adverb)
8. Dirt jumping consists of riding over dirt trails and jumps. (adverb)
9. Jon knows this sport is the most similar to MMX. (prepositional phrase)
10. Much strength and skill are required to succeed in this sport. (infinitive phrase)

More Practice

Language Lab CD-ROM
- Effective Sentences lesson

On-Line Exercise Bank
- Section 22.3

Grammar Exercise Workbook
- pp. 99-100

Invert Subject-Verb Order

You can also vary sentence beginnings by reversing the traditional subject-verb order.

SUBJECT-VERB ORDER:	The bus is here. The ship sailed into the bay.
INVERTED ORDER:	Here is the bus. Into the bay sailed the ship.

Exercise 20 **Inverting Sentences** Invert the following sentences by reversing the order of the subject and verb. Rearrange other words as needed.

1. The recumbent bicycle is driven by human power.
2. A recumbent bicycle races at a top speed of 65 miles per hour.
3. A picture of the bicycle is here.
4. Recumbent bicycles sit close to the ground.
5. A rider's abdomen is toned and strengthened by recumbent riding.

GRAMMAR EXERCISES 21–26

Exercise 21 **Revising to Simplify Long Sentences** Rewrite each sentence, either breaking it into two sentences that each contain one idea or forming a simpler, more direct sentence.

1. Discipline, professionalism, and commitment have been the key elements in helping Steve Larsen, who excelled in mountain biking after fifteen years of road racing, to achieve a success that is uncommon for the ordinary man.
2. Steve wore the Stars-and-Stripes jersey as a member of the World Championship Team and as a U.S. National Champion, raising his ranking and establishing himself as a hero in mountain-biking history.
3. Although mechanical problems prevented Steve from finishing first in many races, his success through determination and willpower is encouraging for others who wish to follow that same course.
4. Unless you are an avid mountain biker who knows much about bikes, the various components of a bike, such as ergonomic shift levers, brake levers with quick index-barrel adjusters, and chain rings, will be foreign to you.
5. Perhaps the most important equipment that a person can wear while mountain biking is a helmet that is lightweight, provides superior protection, and allows good visibility.

Exercise 22 **Revising Sentences by Varying Beginnings and Inverting Subject-Verb Order** Rewrite the sentences following the direction in parentheses.

1. In the 1996 Olympics in Atlanta, Georgia, the gold medalist was an Italian woman, Paola Pezzo. (start with a noun)
2. She was victorious in the championship race by a significant margin. (invert)
3. She was later honored by her country with a victory parade. (invert)
4. She maintained her dominance with a win in the European mountain bike championship. (start with preposition)
5. As part of her training, Paola typically takes a four-hour bike ride early each morning. (start with adverb)

Exercise 23 **Revising Sentences in Several Ways** Revise the paragraph below by varying sentence beginnings and word order.

(1) A tandem bicycle is there in the store window. (2) Two riders sit one behind the other on a tandem bike. (3) The riders must keep pace with each other for best performance. (4) It is not easy to stay perfectly synchronized. (5) Riders sometimes lose their balance.

Exercise 24 **Find It in Your Reading** Look through a book by one of your favorite authors. How does the author vary his or her sentences?

Exercise 25 **Find It in Your Writing** Look through your portfolio for examples of long sentences. Rewrite them by using shorter, more direct sentences. Also, try to vary the sentence beginnings.

Exercise 26 **Writing Application** Write a short narrative describing the first time that you rode a bicycle. Include short and long sentences, and invert some sentences to provide more interest.

Section 22.4

Avoiding Sentence Errors

Fragments, run-on sentences, and misplaced modifiers can all confuse your readers. Being aware of these common writing problems can help you avoid them.

Theme: Musical Instruments

In this section, you will learn to recognize and correct certain types of sentence errors. The examples and exercises are about different types of musical instruments.

Cross-Curricular Connection: Music

Recognizing Fragments

Some groups of words, even though they have a capital letter at the beginning and a period at the end, are not complete sentences. They are *fragments.*

KEY CONCEPT A **fragment** is a group of words that does not express a complete thought but is punctuated as if it were a sentence. ■

FRAGMENTS
In the early evening. Felt happy and relaxed. The sign in the rehearsal hall. The violinist performing the concerto. When she first touched the drums.

Reading the words aloud can often help you tell if a group of words expresses a complete thought. In the following chart, words have been added to the preceding fragments to make complete sentences. Read each italicized fragment; then, read the complete sentence. Can you hear the difference?

COMPLETED SENTENCES
The opera began *in the early evening.* I *felt happy and relaxed.* *The sign in the rehearsal hall* indicated the audition results. *The violinist* was *performing the concerto.* *When she first touched the drums,* her family wondered why they had consented to let her play.

Each of the preceding examples needed one or more new parts. The first needed both a subject and a verb. The second needed only a subject. The third became complete when a verb and complement were added. The fourth became complete when a helping verb was added. The final example needed an independent clause to go with the subordinate clause.

Exercise 27 **Recognizing Sentence Fragments** Write *F* if an item below is a fragment and *S* if it is a complete sentence.

EXAMPLE: Musicians sounding their instruments.
ANSWER: F

1. An array of finely tuned instruments.
2. Will play any instrument in the band.
3. In the concert hall on the stage.
4. Stringed, woodwind, brass, and percussion instruments.
5. That's loud.
6. Wanting to play the harp.
7. To play the violin takes many years of practice.
8. Performers playing electronic instruments such as synthesizers or electric guitars.
9. Achieved popularity in the 1970's and 1980's.
10. After you finish reading, I will practice the cello.

More Practice

Language Lab CD-ROM
- Effective Sentences lesson

On-line Exercise Bank
- Section 22.4

Grammar Exercise Workbook
- pp. 101–102

Correcting Phrase Fragments

A phrase by itself is a fragment. It cannot stand alone because it does not have a subject and verb.

KEY CONCEPT A phrase should not be capitalized or punctuated as if it were a sentence. ■

Three types of phrases—prepositional, participial, and infinitive—are often mistaken for sentences. A *phrase fragment* can be changed into a sentence in either of two ways. The first way is to try adding the fragment to a nearby sentence.

FRAGMENT:	The orchestra began rehearsing. *At 8:00 in the morning.*
ADDED TO NEARBY SENTENCE:	The orchestra began rehearsing *at 8:00 in the morning.*

In the next example, the participial phrase fragment can easily be corrected by attaching it to the beginning of the sentence that follows it.

FRAGMENT:	*Arriving at the airport.* The members of the choir were exhausted from the long flight.
ADDED TO NEARBY SENTENCE:	Arriving at the airport, the members of the choir were exhausted from the long flight.

Sometimes, however, you may not be able to correct a phrase fragment by adding it to a nearby sentence. In this case, you will need to correct the fragment by adding to the phrase whatever is needed to make it a complete sentence. Often, this method requires adding a subject and a verb.

CHANGING PHRASE FRAGMENTS INTO SENTENCES	
Phrase Fragments	Complete Sentence
Near the historic park.	The band played a tribute *near the historic park.*
Touching his hand.	*Touching his hand,* she asked for her father's advice.
To play well.	Sam learned *to play well.*

Exercise 28 Changing Phrase Fragments Into Sentences
Turn each phrase fragment into a sentence. You may use the phrase at the beginning, at the end, or in any other position in a sentence. Check to be sure that each of your sentences contains a subject and verb.

EXAMPLE: In the morning after breakfast.
ANSWER: Sheri practices in the morning after breakfast.

1. In the woodwind section of the band.
2. Playing the ocarina.
3. After hearing the harmonica.
4. Pressing the keys of the clarinet.
5. To break the reed.
6. Before buying a flute.
7. Trying to learn how to play the oboe.
8. Being more difficult to play than the bassoon.
9. Plays the saxophone in the jazz band.
10. To include the bagpipes.

More Practice

Language Lab CD-ROM
- Effective Sentences lesson

On-line Exercise Bank
- Section 22.4

Grammar Exercise Workbook
- pp. 103–104

Exercise 29 Revising to Correct Phrase Fragments
Rewrite the following paragraph, connecting phrase fragments to nearby sentences or adding needed sentence parts.

After practicing in my garage for nearly four months. Our band was ready to make its public debut. Entered a "battle of the bands" competition at the high school. We were the third band to perform. Following two well-known groups. From our place backstage. We listened to the loud applause the first two groups received. Just added to our nervousness. Walking on stage, I tripped over one of our amps and caused the electricity to short out. Didn't win but did make a lasting impression on the audience.

Correcting Clause Fragments

All clauses have subjects and verbs, but some cannot stand alone as sentences.

KEY CONCEPT A subordinate clause should not be capitalized and punctuated as if it were a sentence. ■

Subordinate clauses do not express complete thoughts. Although a subordinate adjective or adverb clause has a subject and a verb, it cannot stand by itself as a sentence. (See Sections 19.2 and 21.2 for more information about subordinate clauses and the words they begin with.)

Like phrase fragments, *clause fragments* can usually be corrected in one of two ways: by attaching the fragment to a nearby sentence or by adding whatever words are needed to make the fragment into a sentence.

Notice how the following clause fragments are corrected by using the first method.

FRAGMENT: The class enjoyed the lyrics. *That I recited to them as part of my oral report.*

ADDED TO NEARBY SENTENCE: The class enjoyed the lyrics *that I recited to them as part of my oral report.*

FRAGMENT: I'll play the piano. *As long as you play, too.*

ADDED TO NEARBY SENTENCE: I'll play the piano *as long as you play, too.*

To change a clause fragment into a sentence by the second method, you must add an independent clause to the fragment.

CHANGING CLAUSE FRAGMENTS INTO SENTENCES

Clause Fragments	Complete Sentence
That you described.	I found the zither *that you described.* The zither *that you described* has been found.
When he knocked.	I opened the door *when he knocked.* *When he knocked,* I opened the door.

▲ Critical Viewing
Add three different independent clauses to the clause fragment "When I heard the drums beating" to create complete sentences. **[Connect]**

Exercise 30 Changing Clause Fragments Into Sentences

Turn each of the clause fragments into a sentence. Make sure that each sentence contains an independent clause.

EXAMPLE: That she wanted to use.
ANSWER: I lent her the drum set that she wanted to use.

1. Before you go to the Caribbean.
2. Since steel-drum bands are popular there.
3. That they use to strike the instruments.
4. If you can play the tambourine.
5. Although the beat is steady.
6. Since he knows how to play the conga.
7. When the musician plays her solo.
8. Because he had never heard of the guiro.
9. Since another drum was needed.
10. After I heard the beat.
11. Whenever I think of the Caribbean.
12. While the band was playing.
13. Until we returned from the concert.
14. As much as she does.
15. Provided that tickets are available.

▼ **Critical Viewing** Imagine that this band played song after song, without taking a break. In what ways would that be similar to a run-on sentence? **[Compare]**

Run-on Sentences

A fragment is an incomplete sentence. A *run-on* is two or more sentences that are punctuated as one.

KEY CONCEPT A **run-on** is two or more complete sentences that are not properly joined or separated. ■

Run-ons are usually the result of haste. Learn to check your sentences carefully to see where one sentence ends and the next one begins.

Two Kinds of Run-ons

There are two kinds of run-ons. One kind is made up of two or more sentences run together without any punctuation between them. This type of run-on is called a *fused sentence.* The other type of run-on consists of two or more sentences separated only by a comma (instead of a comma and a conjunction or a semicolon). This is called a *comma splice.*

RUN-ONS	
With No Punctuation	With Only a Comma
I use our library often the reference section is my favorite part.	The keyboard makes sound when the keys are depressed, the harpsichord, piano, and organ are keyboard instruments.

Exercise 31 **Recognizing Run-ons** On your paper, write *S* if an item is a sentence and *RO* if it is a run-on. Indicate whether each run-on is a *fused sentence* or a *comma splice.*

1. Percussion instruments produce sound when struck or shaken, some examples are drums, rattles, and bells.
2. The marimba is a percussion instrument with wooden bars arranged like the keys on a piano, mallets are used to strike the bars and produce sound.
3. If you are near a beach, you can collect driftwood to make your own marimba.
4. Gather several pieces of driftwood test each one for sound quality by striking it in the center.
5. To make the marimba, place the driftwood pieces in order by tone, then attach the pieces side by side over two long support pieces.

More Practice

Language Lab CD-ROM
- Effective Sentences lesson

On-line Exercise Bank
- Section 22.4

Grammar Exercise Workbook
- pp. 105–106

Three Ways to Correct Run-on Sentences

There are three easy ways to correct a run-on:

Using End Marks End marks are periods, question marks, and exclamation marks.

KEY CONCEPT Use an end mark to separate a run-on into two sentences. ■

Properly used, an end mark splits a run-on into two shorter but complete sentences. Be sure to use an end mark that is appropriate to the function of the first sentence.

RUN-ON:	Though he began losing his hearing early in his career the composer Ludwig van Beethoven continued to write music he completed some of his most famous works after he was totally deaf.
CORRECTED SENTENCES:	Though he began losing his hearing early in his career, the composer Ludwig van Beethoven continued to write music. He completed some of his most famous works after he was totally deaf.
RUN-ON:	Have you heard of the kettledrum, I thought kettles were for the kitchen.
CORRECTED SENTENCES:	Have you heard of the kettledrum? I thought kettles were for the kitchen.

▼ **Critical Viewing** How are rests and pauses in a musical composition like end marks that separate complete thoughts in writing? **[Compare]**

Using Commas and Coordinating Conjunctions

Sometimes, the two parts of a run-on are related and should stay in the same sentence. In that case, the run-on can be changed into a compound sentence.

KEY CONCEPT Use a comma and a coordinating conjunction to combine two independent clauses into a compound sentence. ■

The five coordinating conjunctions used most often are *and, but, or, for,* and *nor.* To separate the two clauses properly, it is necessary to use both a comma and a coordinating conjunction. A comma by itself is not enough.

RUN-ON:	My mother and father practice the viola with the Cleveland Orchestra on Saturday, I stay home to practice the violin.
CORRECTED SENTENCE:	My mother and father practice the viola with the Cleveland Orchestra on Saturday, and I stay home to practice the violin.
RUN-ON:	I want to go to the symphony, I haven't any money.
CORRECTED SENTENCE:	I want to go to the symphony, but I haven't any money.

Using Semicolons You can sometimes use a semicolon to punctuate the two parts of a run-on.

KEY CONCEPT Use a semicolon to connect two closely related ideas. ■

Do not overuse the semicolon. Remember, semicolons should be used only when the ideas in both parts of the sentence are closely related.

RUN-ON:	The first performance begins at 6:30, the second show doesn't start until 9:15.
CORRECTED SENTENCE:	The first performance begins at 6:30; the second show doesn't start until 9:15.
RUN-ON:	The oboist sounded an A, the rest of the orchestra tuned their instruments to that note.
CORRECTED SENTENCE:	The oboist sounded an A; the rest of the orchestra tuned their instruments to that note.

GRAMMAR IN LITERATURE

from Rules of the Game

Amy Tan

In the following excerpt, the author has used a semicolon to join two clauses; without the semicolon, the sentence would be a run-on.

. . . My brother Winston chose wisely as well. His present turned out to be a box of intricate plastic parts**;** the instructions on the box proclaimed that when they were properly assembled he would have an authentic miniature replica of a World War II submarine.

Exercise 32 **Revising to Eliminate Run-on Sentences** On a separate sheet of paper, revise the sentences below to eliminate run-on sentences. Use any of the methods described in this section. Use each method at least two times in the exercise.

EXAMPLE: Play the maracas, they are easier than most instruments.

ANSWER: Play the maracas. They are easier than most instruments.

1. Maracas are rattles with a round or oval shape, centuries ago they were made from hollow gourds filled with seeds.
2. Ana spends hours playing the maracas in a band her wrists get tired from shaking the instruments.
3. The maracas are a common instrument in Latin American bands, they are used to add Caribbean flavor to the music.
4. Ruben could hardly wait to play percussion in the *Jeremiah Symphony* the maracas would be used as drumsticks.
5. Would you know which ancient instrument was found in Peru, would you be able to play it?
6. If you know how to play the recorder, you could probably play the kena they have similar mouthpieces and fingering they are both woodwind instruments.
7. Although the kena is now made of cane, in ancient times it was made from human or animal bones, clay, or hollowed-out gourds, some were even made of silver or gold.
8. Don't try to use the barimbau as a bow to play the violin, it is intended to be played as an instrument on its own.
9. A stick that taps the string produces the sound, a small wicker basket rattle, known as a caxixi, keeps the rhythm.
10. This instrument from Brazil has a hollowed-out gourd at the base of the bow it alters the pitch of the sound.

Misplaced Modifiers

A phrase or clause that acts as an adjective or adverb should be placed close to the word it modifies. Otherwise, the meaning of the sentence may be unclear.

KEY CONCEPT A modifier should be placed as close as possible to the word it modifies in order to avoid confusion. ■

▲ **Critical Viewing** What happens if you misplace your fingers while playing a recorder? What happens when you misplace a modifier in a sentence you have written? **[Speculate]**

Recognize Misplaced Modifiers

A modifier placed too far away from the word it modifies is called a *misplaced modifier.* Because they are misplaced, such phrases and clauses seem to modify the wrong word in a sentence.

MISPLACED MODIFIER: We rented a recorder from the music store *with an instruction booklet.*

The misplaced modifier is the phrase *with an instruction booklet.* In the sentence, it sounds as though this music store is the only one that has an instruction booklet. The sentence needs to be reworded slightly to place the modifier closer to *recorder.*

CORRECTED SENTENCE: At the music store, we rented a recorder *with an instruction booklet.*

Below is a somewhat different type of misplaced modifier.

MISPLACED MODIFIER: *Walking toward the house,* the tree on the lawn looked beautiful to Elizabeth.

In this sentence, *walking toward the house* should modify a person. Instead, it incorrectly modifies *tree.* The sentence needs to be rewritten to indicate who is actually doing the walking.

CORRECTED SENTENCE: *Walking toward the house,* Elizabeth admired the beautiful tree on the lawn.

Exercise 33 **Recognizing Misplaced Modifiers** Read each sentence carefully, and check the placement of the modifiers. If the sentence is correct, write *C* on your paper. If the sentence contains a misplaced modifier, write *MM.*

EXAMPLE: Vivaldi taught the violin after he discovered that he had a breathing disorder at a music seminary for young orphan girls.

ANSWER: MM

1. The violin is held between the shoulder and the chin, a small four-stringed instrument.
2. In its primitive form, pig bladders, tortoise shells, and wooden boxes were used to enhance the resonance of the violin.
3. Carved to imitate a tortoise shell, ancient forms of the violin include the lyre.
4. The zither, with a polygonal shaped drum, is another ancient form of the violin.
5. Playing the note, the instrument was held against a person's left shoulder.

▲ **Critical Viewing** In a sentence that begins *Holding the bow gently,* should the next words be *the boy* or *the violin* in order to avoid a misplaced modifier? **[Connect]**

Revise Sentences With Misplaced Modifiers

Among the most common misplaced modifiers are prepositional phrases, participial phrases, and adjective clauses. All are corrected in the same way—by placing the modifier as close as possible to the word it modifies.

First, consider a misplaced prepositional phrase. This error usually occurs in a sentence with two or more prepositional phrases in a row.

MISPLACED: Lydia played the trombone in the band *with great enthusiasm.*

The misplaced modifier should be moved to make it clear that it modifies *played.*

CORRECTED: *With great enthusiasm,* Lydia played the trombone in the band.

A participial phrase is sometimes used at the beginning of a sentence. When such a phrase is used this way, it must be followed immediately by a word that it can logically modify.

KEY CONCEPT When a participial phrase introduces a sentence, place the word it modifies directly after the introductory phrase. ■

MISPLACED: *Flying over the mountains*, the electrical storm endangered our plane.

It seems as if the storm is flying over the mountains. Rewrite the sentence to put the word *plane* next to the modifier.

CORRECTED: *Flying over the mountains*, our plane was endangered by an electrical storm.

An adjective clause should also go near the word it modifies. The clause below seems to modify *practicing*, not *piccolo*.

MISPLACED: I played the piccolo after several months of practicing *that my grandfather gave me.*

CORRECTED: After several months of practicing, I played the piccolo *that my grandfather gave me.*

Exercise 34 Revising Sentences to Eliminate Misplaced Modifiers On your paper, revise the following sentences. Eliminate the misplaced modifiers. In each rewritten sentence, underline the modifier that had been misplaced and draw an arrow from the modifier to the word it modifies.

1. The harp had already been purchased by someone else that Chelsea wanted.
2. Reaching the concert hall, Chelsea's harp was already on the stage.
3. Anyone could buy a harp at the auction without pedals.
4. Told to keep playing, the fingers and shoulders of the harpist ached.
5. He played the harp in the orchestra with great enthusiasm.
6. The angular harp was prevalent in Egypt, having a separate top that is attached to a resonator.
7. The five-foot-high harp is a part of the orchestra with a range of six-and-a-half octaves.
8. Wagner and Tchaikovsky used the pedal harp to add color to their orchestral pieces, who are renowned composers.
9. Hae Jin received a new harp from her dad with a pillar that gives better structure and a higher pitch.
10. Stretching from top to bottom, the harp has a strong frame within which there are strings.

More Practice

Language Lab CD-ROM
- Effective Sentences lesson

On-line Exercise Bank
- Section 22.4

Grammar Exercise Workbook
- pp. 109–112

22.4

Hands-on Grammar

Movable Modifiers

Phrases used as modifiers can create confusion if they are misplaced in a sentence. To avoid confusion, place the phrase as close as possible to the word it modifies. To practice putting misplaced modifiers in their proper place in sentences, do the following activity.

Take several paper clips and pairs of self-sticking removable notes. You will also need several long, thin strips of paper on which to write sentences. Put each paper clip inside two notes, so that its clip side remains free (see the diagram below). Stick the notes together around the paper clip.

On one of the notes, write a phrase such as *filled with water and ice*. On one of the strips of paper, write a sentence such as: *A glass sat on the windowsill.* Attach the clipped phrase to the sentence strip. Slide the clip along the sentence until you have placed the phrase in its proper location. In this case, the phrase should go between the words *glass* and *sat*, so that the complete sentence reads: *A glass filled with water and ice sat on the windowsill.* What confusion might result if you placed the phrase after the word *windowsill*, instead?

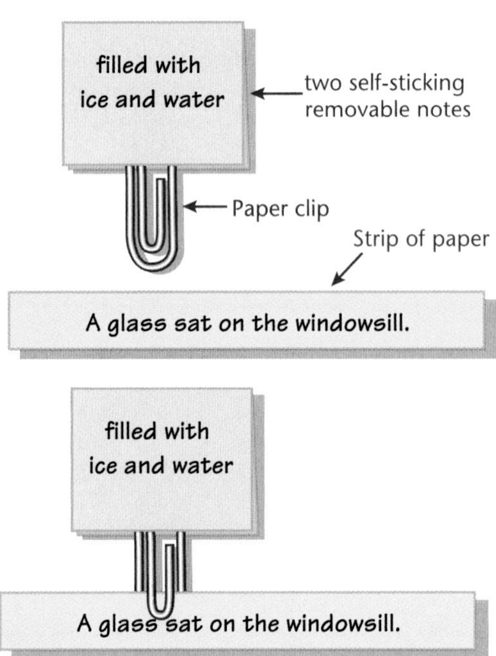

Write several more sentences and phrases of your own on the remaining strips of paper and pairs of removable notes, and test your friends. You can also use this activity to help correct the sentences in Exercise 34 on page 365.

Find It in Your Reading Select a paragraph from a story in your literature book that contains sentences with phrase modifiers. Discuss with a partner why the modifiers are correctly placed.

Find It in Your Writing Look for misplaced modifiers in your own compositions. Then, use this activity to determine the correct location for each modifier.

Section 22.4

Section Review

GRAMMAR EXERCISES 35–40

Exercise 35 **Revising Fragments to Form Sentences** Change each of the following fragments into a sentence. Check to see that each of your sentences contains an independent clause.

1. Playing the piano.
2. To understand why there are three pedals.
3. Since it takes much practice.
4. Of ivory and ebony.
5. Called a pianoforte.

Exercise 36 **Revising to Eliminate Run-on Sentences** On your paper, revise each of the following sentences to eliminate run-ons.

1. Before the appearance of the lute, there was an instrument called an *oud*, it was brought to Spain by the Moors around 711.
2. Europeans changed the oud by adding more strings and frets, the oud evolved into the lute.
3. The lute was probably the most popular instrument during the Renaissance there is more music for the lute than for any other instrument.
4. The lute reached its golden age in the 1500's, lute composers and performers were popular and well paid.
5. By the 1800's, the lute was replaced by the guitar it is believed to have been invented by the people of Malaga.

Exercise 37 **Revising a Paragraph to Eliminate Sentence Errors** Revise the following paragraph, correcting any fragments, run-ons, or misplaced modifiers.

To make every piece of music distinct. Composers use the qualities of emotional expression, rhythm, harmony, and form, the combination of these qualities gives music its style. Through the nineteenth century, musical styles adopted the names of the era from which they came, these eras include Medieval, Renaissance, Baroque, Classical, Romantic, and Impressionist. Much of the music was cultivated by the Roman Catholic Church during the Middle Ages. To use in its worship services. Plain song was promoted by church leaders, which was also known as Gregorian Chant. The Renaissance period in music produced fuller and richer sounds, which lasted from about 1450 to 1600. Composers of the Romantic Era believed music should be imaginative, developing their own personal style.

Exercise 38 **Find It in Your Reading** In this sentence from "Rules of the Game," identify how the writer has avoided creating a run-on sentence.

> I learned about opening moves and why it's important to control the center early on; the shortest distance between two points is straight down the middle.

Exercise 39 **Find It in Your Writing** Review the compositions in your writing portfolio to see if they contain fragments, run-ons, or misplaced modifiers. Rewrite the sentences, correcting, the errors.

Exercise 40 **Writing Application** Write a description of music or instruments you have seen or heard. Avoid fragments, run-ons, and misplaced modifiers in your description.

Chapter

23 Verb Usage

▲ **Critical Viewing** Think of the present and past tense forms of three different verbs that describe actions that occur on Thanksgiving Day. How do the two tenses vary in form? **[Connect, Contrast]**

Using verbs correctly is one of the most important language skills to acquire. Most native speakers of English usually choose the right verb when they speak, but some verbs cause trouble. For example, someone might say, "A new season begun" instead of "A new season began" or "A new season has begun."

Just as seasons change, verbs also change their forms and tenses to suit different meanings. Because there are many chances to misuse verbs, you should take special care to learn the various forms of verbs. This chapter explains how verbs are formed, how they are used to indicate time, and how they are used to show who is performing an action.

Diagnostic Test

Directions: Write all answers on a separate sheet of paper.

Skill Check A. Identify the tense of each verb. Then, tell whether the form is *basic* or *progressive.*

1. Thanksgiving Day is a holiday that we celebrate in the fall.
2. As usual, it will fall on the fourth Thursday in November in the United States.
3. Canadians have been celebrating Thanksgiving Day on the second Monday in October.
4. Most people will be gathering with family and friends.
5. A holiday feast has become a tradition.
6. Thanksgiving Day has been celebrated in New England every year since the Pilgrims and Native Americans began the tradition in the 1600's.
7. The Pilgrims were giving thanks for the survival of their colony.
8. However, the idea had originated with the harvest festivals of ancient times.
9. Children in Pilgrim costumes often march in Thanksgiving Day parades.
10. Such costumes have included bonnets or hats, dark clothes, and shoes with large buckles.

Skill Check B. Choose the correct form of the verb in parentheses.

11. Two years after the feast of the Pilgrims and Native Americans, a drought (striked, struck).
12. The people might have (lose, lost) their crops.
13. Instead, the rains (came, come) during their prayers.
14. From these events, the custom of setting a special day of Thanksgiving annually after the harvest (arose, arisen).
15. Many Thanksgiving celebrations have (began, begun) with a horn-shaped basket overflowing with fruits and vegetables.
16. You may have (call, called) this basket a *cornucopia.*
17. For centuries, many European communities have (choose, chosen) to decorate with cornucopias.
18. The tradition of a Thanksgiving feast has (took, taken) hold in the United States.
19. Turkey, stuffing, cranberry sauce, squash, mashed potatoes, sweet potatoes, and pumpkin pie have (become, became) traditional Thanksgiving Day foods.
20. Most of these foods are (grew, grown) in North America today.

Skill Check C. Identify each verb as *active* or *passive.*

21. Teams in the National Football League established traditions of playing football games on Thanksgiving Day afternoon.
22. The televised games are watched by millions of fans.
23. Retailers sponsor large parades.
24. The annual Thanksgiving Day parade in New York has been enjoyed by all.
25. Floats in the parade are accompanied by gigantic balloons.

Section 23.1

Verb Tenses

In speaking and writing, you often need to indicate when something happens—now, yesterday, or tomorrow. In English, the different tenses of verbs are used to show when something occurs.

KEY CONCEPT A **tense** is a form of a verb that shows the time of an action or a condition. ■

Recognizing the Six Tenses of Verbs

Verbs have six tenses that indicate whether something is happening now, was happening at some time in the past, or will be happening at some time in the future. Each of these tenses can be expressed in two different forms:

KEY CONCEPT Each tense has a basic and a progressive form. ■

The following chart gives examples of the six tenses in their basic forms:

BASIC FORMS OF THE SIX TENSES	
Present	She *skis* for a hobby.
Past	She *skied* every day last year.
Future	She *will ski* again this year.
Present Perfect	She *has skied* at many different resorts.
Past Perfect	She *had skied* when she was only three years old.
Future Perfect	She *will have skied* ten times this season by Valentine's Day.

The basic forms are identified simply by their tense names. The progressive forms, however, are identified by their tense names plus the word *progressive.*

The next chart gives examples of the six tenses in their *progressive form.* Note that all these forms end in *-ing.*

Theme: Seasons

In this section, you will learn to recognize and use the six tenses of verbs. The examples and exercises are about the seasons of the year and seasonal activities.

Cross-Curricular Connection: Social Studies

Spelling Tip

When you are spelling words that end in *-ing* and the vowel in the root has a short sound, add a double letter before the *-ing.* For example, *swimming* has a double *m* before the *-ing.*

PROGRESSIVE FORMS OF THE SIX TENSES	
Present Progressive	She *is skiing* down a mountain now.
Past Progressive	She *was skiing* yesterday morning.
Future Progressive	She *will be skiing* again very soon.
Present Perfect Progressive	She *has been skiing* for years.
Past Perfect Progressive	She *had been skiing* when she broke her leg.
Future Perfect Progressive	She *will have been skiing* for a decade by the end of this year.

As you can see, the forms of a verb change in order to show present, past, and future time.

GRAMMAR IN LITERATURE

from On Summer

Lorraine Hansberry

Several past *tense verbs in the following excerpt are shown in blue italics, and* past perfect *tense verbs are shown in red italics.*

It also *seemed* to me, esthetically speaking, that nature *had got* inexcusably carried away on the summer question and *let* the whole thing get to be rather much. By duration alone, for instance, a summer's day *seemed* maddeningly excessive; an utter overstatement. Except for those few hours at either end of it, objects always *appeared* in too sharp a relief against backgrounds; shadows too pronounced and light too blinding. It always gave me the feeling of walking around in a motion picture which had been too artsily-craftsily exposed.

▼ **Critical Viewing** Use tenses of the same verb in three sentences about making a sand castle—yesterday, today, and tomorrow. How does the verb change from sentence to sentence? **[Connect, Contrast]**

Exercise 1 **Recognizing Tenses and Forms of Verbs** Write the verb or verb phrase in each sentence. Then, identify the tense and form of each verb. Be careful to avoid choosing words that look like verbs but are acting as other parts of speech. In the first sentence, for example, *skiing* is a gerund that acts like a noun.

EXAMPLE: He has been skiing in Colorado.
ANSWER: has been skiing (present perfect progressive)

1. Skiing has become a very popular winter sport.
2. By the twenty-first century, people had skied for thousands of years.
3. Millions of people worldwide are skiing for recreation.
4. This article describes the two types of recreational skiing, alpine and nordic.
5. Alpine, or downhill, skiing developed in the late 1800's as a way of moving down snow-covered slopes.
6. In alpine skiing, people have been using lifts as transportation to the top of a slope.
7. Before alpine skiing, some skiers will have tried nordic, or cross-country, skiing.
8. Most nordic skiers will ski on flat trails prepared for their convenience.
9. Many people have taken lessons from professionals.
10. By the end of the day, many people will have been skiing for hours.

More Practice

Language Lab CD-ROM
- Verb Usage lesson

On-line Exercise Bank
- Section 23.1

Grammar Exercise Workbook
- pp. 113–114

▶ **Critical Viewing** Think of two sentences—one with a basic form verb and one with a progressive form verb—to describe actions of the person in this picture. **[Analyze]**

The Four Principal Parts of Verbs

Tenses are formed from *principal parts* and helping verbs.

KEY CONCEPT A verb has four **principal parts**: the *present*, the *present participle*, the *past*, and the *past participle*. ■

The chart below lists the principal parts of two verbs:

FOUR PRINCIPAL PARTS			
Present	Present Participle	Past	Past Participle
walk run	walking running	walked ran	(have) walked (have) run

The first principal part is used to form the present and future tenses. To form the present, an *-s* or *-es* is added whenever the subject is *he, she, it*, or a singular noun (*she walks, Paul runs*). To form the future tense, the helping verb *will* is added (*she will walk, Paul will run*).

The second principal part is used with various helping verbs to produce all six of the progressive forms (*she is walking, Paul was walking*, and so on).

The third principal part is used to form the past tense (*she walked, Paul ran*).

The fourth principal part is used with helping verbs for the three perfect tenses (*she has walked, Paul had run, we will have run*).

Exercise 2 **Recognizing Principal Parts** Identify the principal part used to form each verb in Exercise 1 on page 528. The example sentence from Exercise 1 is provided as a model below.

EXAMPLE: He has been skiing in Colorado.
ANSWER: present participle (skiing)

Exercise 3 **Writing Sentences With Principal Parts of Verbs** For each numbered item, write a sentence using the subject and the principal part of the verb indicated. Then, identify the tense of the verb in the sentence you have written.

1. We, past participle of talk
2. Mike, present participle of wait
3. People, present of laugh
4. I, past of stop
5. You, present participle of help

23.1

Forming Regular and Irregular Verbs

The way the past and the past participle of a verb are formed determines whether the verb is *regular* or *irregular.*

Regular Verbs Most of the verbs in the English language, such as the verb *walk*, are regular.

KEY CONCEPT The past and past participle of a **regular verb** are formed by adding *-ed* or *-d* to the present form. ■

The past and past participle of regular verbs have the same form. In the following chart, *has* is in parentheses in front of the past participle to remind you that this verb form is a past participle only if it is used with a helping verb.

Notice that the final consonant is sometimes doubled to form the present participle (*skipping*) as well as the past and the past participle (*skipped*). Notice also that the final *e* may be dropped in forming the present participle (*typing*).

PRINCIPAL PARTS OF REGULAR VERBS

Present	Present Participle	Past	Past Participle
play	(is) playing	played	(has) played
skip	(is) skipping	skipped	(has) skipped
type	(is) typing	typed	(has) typed

▲ **Critical Viewing** Think of a sentence with a basic form verb to describe the catcher's actions in this picture. Think of a sentence with a progressive form verb to describe the batter's actions. **[Analyze]**

Irregular Verbs Although most verbs are regular, a number of very common verbs, such as *run*, are irregular.

KEY CONCEPT The past and past participle of an **irregular verb** are not formed by adding *-ed* or *-d* to the present form. ■

The past and past participle of irregular verbs are formed in various ways. Some common irregular verbs are shown in the charts that follow. Just as with regular verbs, the final consonant is sometimes doubled to form the present participle (for example, *sitting*).

Whenever you are in doubt about the principal parts of an irregular verb, use a dictionary to check.

IRREGULAR VERBS WITH THE SAME PAST AND PAST PARTICIPLE			
Present	**Present Participle**	**Past**	**Past Participle**
bind	binding	bound	(have) bound
bring	bringing	brought	(have) brought
build	building	built	(have) built
buy	buying	bought	(have) bought
catch	catching	caught	(have) caught
fight	fighting	fought	(have) fought
find	finding	found	(have) found
get	getting	got	(have) got or (have) gotten
hold	holding	held	(have) held
keep	keeping	kept	(have) kept
lay	laying	laid	(have) laid
lead	leading	led	(have) led
leave	leaving	left	(have) left
lose	losing	lost	(have) lost
pay	paying	paid	(have) paid
say	saying	said	(have) said
send	sending	sent	(have) sent
sit	sitting	sat	(have) sat
sleep	sleeping	slept	(have) slept
spend	spending	spent	(have) spent
spin	spinning	spun	(have) spun
stand	standing	stood	(have) stood
stick	sticking	stuck	(have) stuck
swing	swinging	swung	(have) swung
teach	teaching	taught	(have) taught
win	winning	won	(have) won
wind	winding	wound	(have) wound

IRREGULAR VERBS THAT CHANGE IN OTHER WAYS			
Present	Present Participle	Past	Past Participle
begin	beginning	began	(have) begun
break	breaking	broke	(have) broken
choose	choosing	chose	(have) chosen
come	coming	came	(have) come
do	doing	did	(have) done
draw	drawing	drew	(have) drawn
drive	driving	drove	(have) driven
eat	eating	ate	(have) eaten
fall	falling	fell	(have) fallen
freeze	freezing	froze	(have) frozen
go	going	went	(have) gone
grow	growing	grew	(have) grown
know	knowing	knew	(have) known
lie	lying	lay	(have) lain
ring	ringing	rang	(have) rung
rise	rising	rose	(have) risen
run	running	ran	(have) run
see	seeing	saw	(have) seen
shake	shaking	shook	(have) shaken
sing	singing	sang	(have) sung
sink	sinking	sank	(have) sunk
speak	speaking	spoke	(have) spoken
steal	stealing	stole	(have) stolen
swim	swimming	swam	(have) swum
take	taking	took	(have) taken
write	writing	wrote	(have) written

Exercise 4 **Using the Correct Forms of Irregular Verbs**
Choose the correct form of the verb in parentheses.

EXAMPLE: Baseball has (became, become) my best sport.
ANSWER: become

1. No one knows for sure when baseball (began, begun), but legend claims it was around 1839.
2. Baseball (growed, grew) in popularity, and many people saw the sport as a source of financial profit.
3. Until 1869, the National Association of Baseball Players had not (gave, given) players any form of payment for playing.
4. In 1869, the Cincinnati Red Stockings (become, became) the first professional baseball team. They (winned, won) 60 games without a loss in their first year.
5. Soon, major cities across the United States (seeked, sought) to form their own baseball teams.

More Practice

Language Lab CD-ROM
- Verb Usage lesson

On-line Exercise Bank
- Section 23.1

Grammar Exercise Workbook
- pp. 115–116

Conjugating the Tenses

With the principal parts of verbs and helping verbs, you can form all of the tenses. One way to become familiar with the variety of verb forms is through *conjugation.*

KEY CONCEPT A **conjugation** is a complete list of the singular and plural forms of a verb in a particular tense. ■

For each tense, singular and plural forms correspond to the first-, second-, and third-person forms of personal pronouns.

The following charts conjugate the verb *see.* To conjugate the six tenses in their basic form, you need only three of the principal parts: the present (*see*), the past (*saw*), and the past participle (*seen*). To conjugate the six tenses in their progressive form, you need the present participle and a form of the verb *be.*

CONJUGATION OF THE BASIC FORMS OF *SEE*		
Person	**Singular**	**Plural**
Present		
First person Second person Third person	I see you see he, she, it sees	we see you see they see
Past		
First person Second person Third person	I saw you saw he, she, it saw	we saw you saw they saw
Future		
First person Second person Third person	I will see you will see he, she, it will see	we will see you will see they will see
Present Perfect		
First person Second person Third person	I have seen you have seen he, she, it has seen	we have seen you have seen they have seen
Past Perfect		
First person Second person Third person	I had seen you had seen he, she, it had seen	we had seen you had seen they had seen
Future Perfect		
First person Second person Third person	I will have seen you will have seen he, she it will have seen	we will have seen you will have seen they will have seen

23.1

CONJUGATION OF THE PROGRESSIVE FORMS OF *SEE*

Person	Singular	Plural
Present Progressive		
First person Second person Third person	I am seeing you are seeing he, she, it is seeing	we are seeing you are seeing they are seeing
Past Progressive		
First person Second person Third person	I was seeing you were seeing he, she, it was seeing	we were seeing you were seeing they were seeing
Future Progressive		
First person Second person Third person	I will be seeing you will be seeing he, she, it will be seeing	we will be seeing you will be seeing they will be seeing
Present Perfect Progressive		
First person Second person Third person	I have been seeing you have been seeing he, she, it has been seeing	we have been seeing you have been seeing they have been seeing
Past Perfect Progressive		
First person Second person Third person	I had been seeing you had been seeing he, she, it had been seeing	we had been seeing you had been seeing they had been seeing
Future Perfect Progressive		
First person Second person Third person	I will have been seeing you will have been seeing he, she, it will have been seeing	we will have been seeing you will have been seeing they will have been seeing

More Practice

Language Lab CD-ROM
- Verb Usage lesson

On-line Exercise Bank
- Section 23.1

Grammar Exercise Workbook
- pp. 117–118

Note About *Be:* The verb *be* is highly irregular. The following conjugation of the first two tenses lists some of its forms.

PRESENT:	I am you are he, she, it is	we are you are they are
PAST:	I was you were he, she, it was	we were you were they were

Exercise 5 **Conjugating Basic Forms of Verbs** Conjugate the basic forms of the five verbs below as shown in the example.

EXAMPLE: spend (conjugated with *we*)

Present: we spend	Present perfect: we have spent
Past: we spent	Past perfect: we had spent
Future: we will spend	Future perfect: we will have spent

1. move (conjugated with *I*)
2. see (conjugated with *you*)
3. teach (conjugated with *he*)
4. start (conjugated with *they*)
5. go (conjugated with *we*)

Exercise 6 **Conjugating Progressive Forms of Verbs** Conjugate the progressive forms of the five verbs below as shown in the example.

EXAMPLE: spend (conjugated with *we*)

Present progressive: we are spending
Past progressive: we were spending
Future progressive: we will be spending
Present perfect progressive: we have been spending
Past perfect progressive: we had been spending
Future perfect progressive: we will have been spending

1. play (conjugated with *I*)
2. watch (conjugated with *you*)
3. hit (conjugated with *he*)
4. leave (conjugated with *they*)
5. grow (conjugated with *we*)

Exercise 7 **Supplying the Correct Tense** Write the indicated form for each verb in parentheses.

1. Present perfect progressive—We (swim) by moving our hands and feet in or on the water.
2. Past—Human beings (develop) a variety of body movements to move them through water.
3. Future progressive—Many people (go) to their local swimming pool this summer to swim.
4. Past perfect—Before today, currents (make) swimming in the inlet hazardous.
5. Present progressive—Wherever you (travel) this summer, you will find a place to swim.

▼ **Critical Viewing** Describe the action in this picture using sentences with present progressive verbs. **[Describe]**

Expressing Time With Verb Tenses

You know that the tense of a verb indicates the time of the action or the state of being expressed by the verb. The chart below shows the different uses of the various verb tenses:

TENSES AND THEIR USES		
Tenses	**Uses**	**Examples**
Present	Present action or condition	It is below freezing.
	Continuing action or condition	He is enjoying winter.
Past	Completed action or condition	We tried ice fishing.
	Continuous completed action or condition	The weather was being agreeable.
Present Perfect	Completed action or condition	She has been on skates before.
	Action or condition continuing to present	They have fished for hours.
	Action continuing to present	We have been waiting for them.
Past Perfect	Past action or condition completed before another	I had been there before Thanksgiving.
	Continuing past action interrupted by another	We had been eating when you called.
Future	Future action or condition	You will catch something soon.
	Continuing future action or condition	He will be wearing a parka.
Future Perfect	Future action or condition completed before another	By noon, he will have caught some fish.
	Continuing future action completed before another	By then, we will have been fishing for four hours.

Exercise 8 **Revise to Create Consistent Verb Tense** Revise this paragraph so that it is written in a consistent tense.

(1) My brother took me fishing last weekend. (2) We rent a small motorboat and buy some bait. (3) By the time we will reach our favorite fishing spot, I feel very excited. (4) Almost as soon as I cast my line over the side of the boat, I hook a fish. (5) As I brought the fish into the boat, my brother is cheering at my good luck.

Exercise 9 **Identifying the Uses of Tense** Identify the tense as well as the use of each underlined verb in the following sentences.

EXAMPLE: He has gone sailing every summer.
ANSWER: present perfect (action continuing to present)

1. Sailing attracts people to lakes and rivers all over the world.
2. Many have enjoyed the excitement and the challenge of the sport.
3. That boat was sailing directly into the wind.
4. The crew had checked the sails before leaving the dock.
5. They have always maintained the boats well.
6. Sailboat races often will cover a triangular course.
7. To maneuver the boat, the crew will be changing the position of the rudder and the sails.
8. You will have learned about trimming and tacking by the end of the day.
9. Windsurfing, another water sport, is also gaining in popularity.
10. In this sport, a sail has been attached to a surfboard.

More Practice

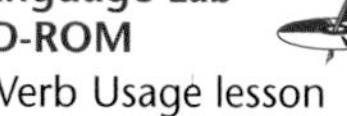

Language Lab CD-ROM
- Verb Usage lesson

On-line Exercise Bank
- Section 23.1

Grammar Exercise Workbook
- pp. 119–126

◀ **Critical Viewing** Based on the picture, describe an action that began before and is continuing to the present. What verb did you use? What is its tense? **[Connect]**

Section 23.1 **Section Review**

GRAMMAR EXERCISES 10–19

Exercise 10 Recognizing Tenses and Forms of Verbs Identify the tense and form of the verb or verbs in each sentence.

1. We were studying the reasons for the change of season.
2. The position of the Earth in orbit around the sun determines the season.
3. The sun had been shining for more hours per day during the summer season.
4. The seasons will change because of the tilt of the Earth's axis.
5. This tilt will have caused the North Pole to be closer to the sun for half of the year.
6. The hemisphere toward the sun is receiving the sun's rays more directly.
7. In summer, the Northern Hemisphere will be tilting toward the sun.
8. In winter, the Northern Hemisphere has tilted away from the sun.
9. Mars has been orbiting the sun in a similar way.
10. Knowing this, we have been assuming for many years that Mars' seasons are similar to Earth's.

Exercise 11 Recognizing Principal Parts Identify the principal part used to form each verb in Exercise 10.

Exercise 12 Using the Correct Forms of Irregular Verbs Choose the correct form of the verb in parentheses.

1. Baseball fans are happy when spring training has (began, begun).
2. The mayor (throwed, threw) out the first ball to start the game.
3. That player has (stole, stolen) more bases than any other player.
4. The pitcher has also (broke, broken) the record for scoreless innings.
5. He just (striked, struck) out another batter.
6. Finally, a batter (drove, driven) a ball into the outfield.
7. We have always (ate, eaten) peanuts at baseball games.
8. The playoff game has (drew, drawn) a large crowd.
9. Have you (chose, chosen) your favorite team?
10. We already (did, done) that.

Exercise 13 Conjugating the Basic Forms of Verbs Use the person indicated to conjugate the basic forms of the verbs in each of the six tenses.

1. open (conjugated with *I*)
2. move (conjugated with *you*)
3. know (conjugated with *he*)
4. begin (conjugated with *we*)
5. fall (conjugated with *they*)

Exercise 14 Conjugating the Progressive Forms of Verbs Use the person indicated to conjugate the progressive forms of the verbs in each of the six tenses.

1. go (conjugated with *I*)
2. teach (conjugated with *you*)
3. spin (conjugated with *he*)
4. shake (conjugated with *we*)
5. swim (conjugated with *they*)

Exercise 15 Identifying Uses of Tenses Identify the tense of each underlined verb, and explain how it indicates time.

1. An equinox <u>occurs</u> when both hemispheres are the same distance from the sun.
2. This <u>will happen</u> about March 21 and

September 23 each year.

3. In March, spring will have started in the Northern Hemisphere when the vernal equinox occurs.
4. When the autumnal equinox occurs in September, autumn has begun in the Northern Hemisphere.
5. The sun appeared directly over the Earth's equator during the equinox.
6. When this has happened, the lengths of day and night are equal over almost all the Earth, except at the poles.
7. A solstice has occurred when the distance from either pole to the sun is at its greatest.
8. On about June 21, the sun is standing at its northernmost position; this is the summer solstice in the Northern Hemisphere.
9. The Southern Hemisphere's winter solstice will have occurred at the same time.
10. Whichever hemisphere tilts toward the sun on the solstice will have the longest day and the shortest night.

Exercise 16 **Revising Sentences by Changing the Verb Tense** Rewrite each sentence, changing the tense of the underlined verb as indicated in parentheses. You do not need to change the tense of other verbs in the sentence.

1. The change in the length of daylight accompanying the seasons differed at different latitudes. (present)
2. In this article, you discover that summer near the poles is six months of daylight and winter is six months of darkness. (future)
3. Those who live at the equator will experience the hottest climate. (future progressive)
4. Some people have thought that the days near the summer solstice are the hottest days of the year; however, they are not. (past progressive)
5. Scientists are discovering that temperature depends not only on the amount of heat the atmosphere receives but also the amount it loses. (past)
6. The atmosphere loses heat through absorption into the ground or through reflection. (future perfect)
7. The ocean's temperature changed much more slowly than the atmosphere's temperature. (present perfect)
8. The atmosphere warmed up quickly in the spring and summer but was still losing much heat to the oceans. (past perfect)
9. The oceans had absorbed enough heat to reach equilibrium with the temperature of the atmosphere. (present perfect progressive)
10. Some people were using temperature to determine the season instead of looking at the calendar! (past perfect progressive)

Exercise 17 **Find It in Your Reading** In the excerpt from "On Summer" on page 527, identify the tense of each of the verbs in the last sentence and tell whether the verb is regular or irregular.

Exercise 18 **Find It in Your Writing** Choose a paragraph from a piece of your own writing. Identify the tenses of the verbs, and tell whether they are basic or progressive.

Exercise 19 **Writing Application** Write a short essay about your favorite season and some activities you particularly enjoy doing at that time. Underline the verbs you use, and identify the tense and form of each verb.

Section 23.2

Active and Passive Voice

In addition to indicating time, most verbs can indicate whether the subject is performing an action or having an action performed upon it. Two different voices of verbs are used to show how an action is performed.

KEY CONCEPT **Voice** is the form of a verb that shows whether the subject performs or receives the action. ■

Linking verbs do not show voice. Only action verbs show voice. The voice may be either *active* or *passive*.

Recognizing Active and Passive Voice

Any action verb, with or without a direct object, can be in the *active* voice.

KEY CONCEPT A verb is **active** if its subject performs the action. ■

In the two examples below, the subjects are the performers.

ACTIVE VOICE: Laura *found* a dinosaur bone.
The archaeologist *called* yesterday.

Most action verbs can also be used in the *passive* voice.

KEY CONCEPTS A verb is **passive** if its action is performed upon the subject. ■

A passive verb is made from a form of *be* plus the past participle of a transitive verb. ■

In a sentence with a passive verb, the performer of the action may or may not be named. In the first example below, Laura is still the performer. The word *Laura*, however, is no longer the subject but the object of the preposition *by*. In the second example, the person who will be calling tomorrow is not identified.

PASSIVE VOICE: A dinosaur bone *was found* by Laura.
The archaeologist *will be called* tomorrow.

Theme: Anthropology

In this section, you will learn to recognize and use verbs in active and passive voice. The examples and exercises are about anthropology and archaeology.

Cross-Curricular Connection: Social Studies

Grammar and Style Tip

To make your writing more interesting, use a balance of active and passive voice.

Exercise 20 **Distinguishing Between the Active and Passive Voice** Write the verb phrase in each sentence. Then, label each verb as *active* or *passive*.

1. The study of all aspects of human life and culture is called anthropology.
2. Anthropologists examine such things as people's lives and their interactions with their environments.
3. Human diversity has been explored by anthropologists.
4. They investigate the common interests of people.
5. Some common questions about humans are asked by anthropologists.
6. Have people developed differently in different environments?
7. Societies from the ancient past to the present have been studied by anthropologists.
8. The work of anthropologists has uncovered clues to our past.
9. As a result, we will learn much about the present-day needs of people.
10. Better ways of life for the future may also be found.

More Practice

Language Lab CD-ROM
- Verb Usage lesson

On-line Exercise Bank
- Section 23.2

Grammar Exercise Workbook
- pp. 127–128

Using Voice Correctly

To write well, you need to know when to use the active voice and when to use the passive voice. There are no firm rules, but here are some suggestions:

KEY CONCEPT Use the active voice whenever possible. ■

Good writing is crisp and direct. Sentences with active verbs are less wordy and more direct than those with passive verbs.

ACTIVE VOICE: The scientist *opened* the package.
PASSIVE VOICE: The package *was opened* by the scientist.

◀ **Critical Viewing** Use the verbs *found* and *were found* in two sentences about the Egyptian hieroglyphics in this photograph. Which sentence is in the active voice and which is in the passive voice? **[Connect]**

23.2

GRAMMAR IN LITERATURE

from Caucasian Mummies Mystify Chinese

Keay Davidson

A passive voice verb phrase in this passage is in blue italics. An active voice verb phrase is in red italics.

A former Stanford scientist is analyzing the mummies' DNA in hopes of answering haunting questions: Who are they? Where did they come from? And what on earth were these European-looking men, women and children doing in China's parched out-back 2,000 years before Jesus, when Europe was largely a dark forest? Sixteen years after the first mummies *were found*, the Chinese government *has granted* Western researchers their first close look at these faces from prehistory: a baby in colorful swaddling clothes; a 20-year-old girl with braided hair, found buried in a curled-up position with her hands by her chest, as if dozing; a man with a pigtail, scarlet-colored clothes and red, blue, and amber leg wrappings. . . .

KEY CONCEPT Use the passive voice when you want to emphasize the receiver of an action rather than the performer of an action. ■

EXAMPLE: My best friend was awarded a medal by the archaeological society.

KEY CONCEPT Use the passive voice to point out the receiver of an action whenever the performer is not important or not easily identified. ■

EXAMPLE: The mysterious find was made at midnight.
At noon, the doors to the tomb were unlocked, and the archaeologists entered it.

Spelling Tip

Many words have letters that are not pronounced. *Archaeology,* for instance, has a silent *a.* Be sure to include it when you write the word!

Exercise 21 **Using the Passive Voice** Explain why the passive voice is appropriate in each of the following sentences.

EXAMPLE: Anthropologist Dr. Black was taught by my uncle.
ANSWER: emphasizing receiver of action

1. The work of anthropologists has been divided into different specialties.
2. Cultural anthropology, linguistic anthropology, archaeology, and physical anthropology were made areas of specialization in the United States.
3. Special training is required of all anthropologists.
4. Different research techniques are used by many scientists.
5. In the United States, courses are taught covering all of the subfields.

More Practice

Language Lab CD-ROM
- Verb Usage lesson

On-line Exercise Bank
- Section 23.2

Grammar Exercise Workbook
- pp. 129–130

Exercise 22 **Revising a Paragraph to Eliminate Unnecessary Use of the Passive Voice** Rewrite the following paragraph, changing at least five uses of the passive voice to the active voice. Explain why you chose to revise or leave each use of passive voice.

EXAMPLE: Anthropology *is being studied* by many students.
ANSWER: Many students are studying anthropology. (shorter and more direct)

(1) Archaeology is also studied by anthropologists. (2) The study of past human societies and culture is focused on by archaeologists. (3) Various artifacts have been studied by archaeologists. (4) The remains of items made by past humans—such as tools, pottery, and buildings—are referred to as artifacts. (5) Fossils, or hardened remains of plant and animal life, have also been looked at by archaeologists. (6) Past environments are also examined by archaeologists to understand how natural forces shaped the development of human culture. (7) Such factors as climate and the amount of food available at that time are referred to as past environments. (8) Cultures existing before the development of writing have been studied by some archaeologists. (9) This period is known as prehistory. (10) The study of the periods prior to the first development of agriculture is called paleoanthropology. (11) This period took place thousands of years ago. (12) More recent cultures have been studied in historical archaeology. (13) The material remains of the past as well as written documents have been examined by archaeologists. (14) Archaeology is only one of the fields of interest to anthropologists. (15) All of their findings are used in understanding human life today.

▲ Critical Viewing Use the active voice to describe what the animals in the cave painting are doing. Use the passive voice to describe the artwork itself. **[Analyze, Connect]**

Hands-on Grammar

Active Arrows and Passive Points

You should write most sentences in the active voice unless you want to emphasize the receiver of an action or you are not indicating the performer of an action. To practice revising sentences by changing them from passive to active voice, do the following activity:

Cut out several arrows, similar to the ones shown below. On the side of an arrow pointing to the right, write a past tense form of a verb. Examples: *addressed, bought, drew, knew, saw.*

Flip the arrow over so that it points to the left. Write the same verb in the passive voice. (Remember that a passive voice verb includes a form of *be* and a past participle.) Examples: *has been addressed, was bought, are drawn, was known, has been seen.* Fold the flat end of the arrow, and write the word *by* on it, to be hidden or revealed as needed.

Next, take two equal piles of index cards. On each card in one pile, write a performer of an action—*a boy, an anthropologist, a scientist, my brother.* On each card in the other pile, write a noun that can receive the action—*a house, a pyramid, a fossil, the portrait.*

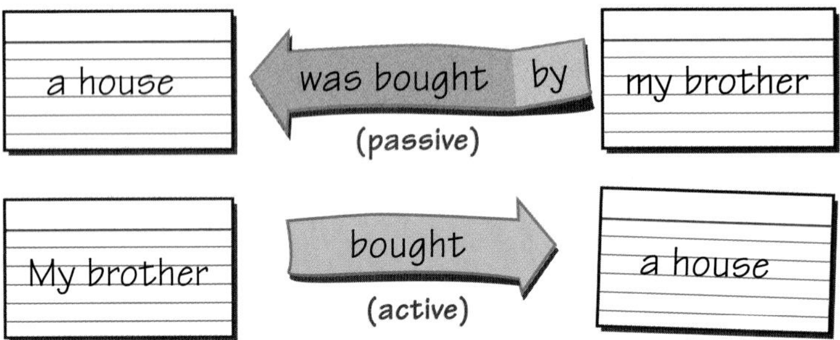

Working alone or with a partner, place a receiver and a performer card words up, with a space between them. Choose an arrow to fill the space. Point the arrow toward the receiver of the action. Read this passive voice sentence. Then, flip the arrow over, and shift the two index cards to create a new active voice sentence. Your second sentence should be shorter and more direct. Experiment by creating some sentences in your fold under the word *by* and do *not* state the performer of the action. Note that these sentences must stay in the passive voice.

Find It in Your Reading Select a paragraph from a story in your literature book that contains sentences with both active and passive voice verbs. Discuss with a partner why the writer chose each voice.

Find It in Your Writing Use this activity to evaluate the voice of several sentences in your own writing. If you discover some passive voice sentences, consider whether you should revise them to be in the active voice.

Section 23.2 Section Review

GRAMMAR EXERCISES 23–28

Exercise 23 **Distinguishing Between the Active and Passive Voice** Write the verbs or verb phrase in each sentence. Then, identify each verb as *active* or *passive.*

1. Archaeologists have uncovered artifacts from a great span of time.
2. They have identified different time periods and different cultures.
3. They specialize in these different areas and also in particular study methods.
4. The ancient civilizations of the Middle East or Europe are studied by some.
5. Later historical time periods are also explored by archaeologists.
6. Many other fields important to archaeological study have been examined by archaeology students.
7. Physical anthropology, geology, ecology, and climatology are all included in the archaeologist's study.
8. Archaeologists have studied with three goals in mind: chronology, reconstruction, and explanation.
9. Explanations of scientific theories have been proposed by archaeologists.
10. These theories explain what the people who lived in the past thought and did.

Exercise 24 **Using the Passive Voice** Explain why the passive voice is appropriate in each of the following sentences.

1. Chronological data relating to the spread of ideas have been studied by archaeologists.
2. Ideas were spread from one region to another over time.
3. This information about past cultures has been analyzed by archaeologists.
4. Information from various archaeological sites has been used.
5. Assembling a sequence or pattern has been made easier.

Exercise 25 **Revising to Eliminate Unnecessary Use of the Passive Voice** Revise the following paragraph, changing at least three uses of the passive voice to the active. Explain why you chose to revise or leave each use of passive voice.

(1) The appearance of people and life in the past has been reconstructed by archaeologists. (2) How well the material remains have been documented by archaeologists will determine the accuracy of the reconstruction. (3) Environmental remains have been found as well. (4) Animal body parts have been included in the environmental remains that archaeologists have found. (5) Environmental remains also include parts of plants, which would also be found by the archaeologist.

Exercise 26 **Find It in Your Reading** In the excerpt from "Caucasian Mummies Mystify Chinese" on page 542, identify the voice of all the verbs that are not highlighted.

Exercise 27 **Find It in Your Writing** Look through your writing portfolio. Find at least three examples of passive verbs. Could any of the sentences be improved by changing the verbs to the active voice?

Exercise 28 **Writing Application** Write a description of a job that you find interesting. Be sure to identify the actions people perform in that job. Label each verb *active* or *passive.*

Chapter 24

Pronoun Usage

▲ **Critical Viewing** What details in this photograph show pride of possession? Answer using the personal pronouns *he, his, him, it.* **[Analyze]**

Cars come in many shapes and forms. Some cars are built for speed; others are built to travel over rough roads. The form of a car usually indicates its function, or purpose. This chapter will explain the different forms of pronouns and their functions in sentences.

At one time in the history of the English language, the form of nouns and pronouns was changed to indicate how they were being used in a sentence. Today, the form of nouns changes only to show possession. In modern English, however, the form of pronouns still changes to show how they are being used in a sentence.

Diagnostic Test

Directions: Write all answers on a separate sheet of paper.

Skill Check A. Identify the underlined pronoun in each sentence as *nominative, objective,* or *possessive.*

1. You and I have consumer protection rights because of the efforts of government organizations, individuals, and businesses.
2. Consumers should know the laws protecting their rights.
3. Some consumers are unaware of the laws that protect them.
4. Mrs. Larson bought a shirt that she later wanted to return.
5. The salesperson helped her to choose another one.

Skill Check B. Choose the correct case of the pronoun to complete each sentence.

6. The saleswoman helped my brother Paul and (I, me).
7. We seemed like good customers to (she, her).
8. Other customers thought (they, them) might buy the same car.
9. Paul and (I, me) did purchase the car.
10. To drive the car legally, it is necessary for (we, us) to buy insurance.

Skill Check C. Supply a pronoun to complete each sentence.

11. Insurance agent Jane spoke to Paul about __?__ new car.
12. "I want to know if this is __?__," Jane asked.
13. Paul told her that it was also __?__.
14. "If it is __?__ also," Jane said, "the cost of insurance will go up."
15. Paul told the agent that the car was __?__.

Skill Check D. Write *who, whom, whose,* or *who's* to complete each of the following sentences.

16. From __?__ did you get that product?
17. I want to meet the salesperson __?__ sold this to you.
18. __?__ name should I give when I call the company?
19. __?__ the best person to call for a refund?
20. It is she __?__ you should contact.

Skill Check E. Choose the correct pronoun in the elliptical clause. Then, write any words or phrases that are understood to come before or after the noun.

21. I worked longer last night than (he, him) __?__.
22. He feels that he is as skilled as (I, me) __?__.
23. Helen has a more flexible schedule than (us, we) __?__.
24. However, we work longer hours than (she, her) __?__.
25. The supervisor knows me better than (she, her) __?__.

Section 24.1

Identifying Case

The case of a pronoun reflects its function.

KEY CONCEPT **Case** is the form of a noun or a pronoun that indicates its use in a sentence. ■

In this section, you will learn how to recognize the three cases of pronouns and when to use them in sentences.

The Three Cases

Both nouns and pronouns have three cases. The chart below shows the uses of each of these three cases.

KEY CONCEPT The three cases are the *nominative,* the *objective,* and the *possessive.* ■

Case	Use in Sentence
Nominative	Subject or predicate nominative
Objective	Direct object, indirect object, object of a preposition, or object of a verbal
Possessive	To show ownership

Using the correct case of nouns is seldom a problem because the form changes only in the possessive case.

Personal pronouns, on the other hand, often require a change in form for all three cases. The chart below shows the various forms of the personal pronouns in the three cases.

Nominative	Objective	Possessive
I	me	my, mine
you	you	your, yours
he, she, it	him, her, it	his, her, hers, its
we	us	our, ours
they	them	their, theirs

Theme: Employment

In this section, you will learn about the nominative, objective, and possessive cases of pronouns. The examples and exercises in this section are about working in a store.

Cross-Curricular Connection: Social Studies

Learn More

To review what you have already learned about pronouns, turn to Chapter 16.

Exercise 1 **Identifying Case** Write the case of each underlined pronoun.

EXAMPLE: The manager gave me the good news about the job.

ANSWER: me (objective)

1. After waiting ten minutes, we finally spoke to the manager.
2. My friend gave him our résumés.
3. He asked us to fill out applications.
4. Later in the week, he called me for an interview.
5. The other associates said that they would help me learn the job.
6. There are a variety of duties involved in my job.
7. The trainer and I worked all day on Friday.
8. She taught me how to interact with customers.
9. I must always be ready to answer their questions.
10. They ask for a certain item, and I give it to them.

More Practice

Language Lab CD-ROM
- Pronoun Case lesson

On-line Exercise Bank
- Section 24.1

Grammar Exercise Workbook
- pp. 131–132

Using the Nominative Case

There are two major uses of pronouns in the nominative case:

KEY CONCEPT Use the nominative case for the subject of a verb. ■

EXAMPLES: *I* do most of the advertising.
You know we are friends.

Informal usage is appropriate for casual conversations, but you should use the nominative case after linking verbs in formal writing.

If the pronoun is part of a compound subject, remove the other subject to check that you have used the nominative case.

COMPOUND SUBJECT: Janie and I do most of the advertising. (*I* do most of the advertising.)

KEY CONCEPT Use the nominative case for a predicate nominative. ■

A predicate nominative is the noun or pronoun that appears after a linking verb and identifies or renames the subject.

EXAMPLE: Who's there? It is *I*.

Exercise 2 **Identifying Pronouns in the Nominative Case** Choose the pronoun in the nominative case. Then, write the use of the pronoun.

EXAMPLE: Greg and (me, I) will start our new job.
ANSWER: I (subject)

1. The manager for two years has been (he, him).
2. The new members of the store's staff are Greg and (she, her).
3. Mary and (I, me) will work the morning shift tomorrow.
4. The manager and (he, him) will work the evening shift.
5. It is (them, they) who will clean up at closing.

▲ Critical Viewing What does this woman do as part of her market job? Answer using a nominative case pronoun. **[Infer]**

Exercise 3 **Supplying Pronouns in the Nominative Case** Write a nominative case pronoun to complete each sentence. Then, write the use of the pronoun.

EXAMPLE: Alma and __?__ will do the shopping.
ANSWER: I (subject)

1. __?__ are hoping to close the store quickly tonight.
2. It is __?__ who must restock the shelves right away.
3. __?__ is the associate I enjoy working with the most.
4. You know that __?__ am a fast worker.
5. The fastest worker, however, is __?__.

Exercise 4 **Writing Sentences Using the Nominative Case Pronouns** Write sentences about a shopping trip, using nominative case pronouns according to the instructions below.

1. Use a person's name and *I* as a compound subject.
2. Use *we* as a predicate pronoun.
3. Use *he and they* as a compound subject.
4. Use *he* (or *she*) *and I* as a compound predicate pronoun.
5. Use *you and they* as a compound subject.

More Practice

Language Lab CD-ROM
- Pronoun Case lesson

On-line Exercise Bank
- Section 24.1

Grammar Exercise Workbook
- pp. 133–134

Using the Objective Case

The *objective case* is used when a pronoun functions as the object of a verb, the object of a preposition, or the object in a verbal phrase.

KEY CONCEPT Use the objective case for the object of a verb or preposition and as the object in most verbal phrases. ■

The chart below provides examples of objective pronouns used as direct objects, indirect objects, objects of prepositions, and objects of participles, gerunds, and infinitives.

OBJECTIVE PRONOUNS	
Use	**Examples**
Direct Object	I sold *them* yesterday. Our manager praised *her.*
Indirect Object	Give *him* the new product. Alice gave *us* the paychecks.
Object of Preposition	Between *us*, there are no unserved customers. Stock the shelves beside *them.*
Object of Participle	Racing *her,* I stock the shelves in minutes. The girl chasing *them* was her employer.
Object of Gerund	The manager likes helping *me* with difficult customers. Warning *them* was my primary concern.
Object of Infinitive	To tell *her* clearly, he had to shout. He wants to ask *me* about the warranty.

Identifying Objective Pronouns in Compounds If an objective pronoun is part of a compound, make sure that you have selected the correct form by removing the other part of the compound.

EXAMPLES: Mr. Rodriguez promoted Carlos and *her.*
Mr. Rodriguez promoted *her.* (*Her* is a direct object.)

Tom gave my sister and *me* five dollars.
Tom gave *me* five dollars. (*Me* is an indirect object.)

This matter is between you and *me.*
(*Me* is the object of the preposition *between.*)

Speaking and Listening Tip

When using compound pronouns as objects, people often make the mistake of using the nominative case, as in these incorrect examples: *It's between you and I. Beth told Tom and she.* To accustom yourself to using compound objective pronouns correctly, pair up with a classmate and practice reading aloud the examples on this page and in Exercise 5 on page 396.

Exercise 5 **Identifying Pronouns in the Objective Case** Choose the pronoun in the objective case. Then, write the use of the pronoun.

EXAMPLE: The manager asked only (us, we) workers for a conference.

ANSWER: us (direct object)

1. This secret is just between you and (I, me).
2. The manager gave both Greg and (I, me) a raise.
3. Between the other associates and (we, us), there is a big difference.
4. The man training (they, them) is the manager.
5. We are training (them, they) to be more effective in customer service.

Exercise 6 **Using Pronouns in the Objective Case** Write an objective pronoun to complete each sentence. Then, write the use of the pronoun.

EXAMPLE: My parents gave __?__ a watch for my birthday.

ANSWER: me (indirect object)

1. We gave __?__ advice on how to handle customer-service problems.
2. Ask for the manager or __?__ if you cannot handle a customer.
3. Training __?__ did not take long.
4. The associates gave __?__ a good example to follow.
5. I congratulated __?__ for their improved job performance.

▶ **Critical Viewing** What is the role of the young man, and what might his purpose be in showing the jacket? Include two objective pronouns in your response. **[Speculate]**

Using the Possessive Case

The *possessive case* of personal pronouns shows possession before nouns and gerunds. It can also be used alone.

KEY CONCEPT Use the possessive case before nouns to show ownership. ■

EXAMPLES: *My* shoes do not fit properly.
The store owner visited *our* class.
Their purchase came as a surprise.

KEY CONCEPT Use the possessive case before gerunds. ■

EXAMPLES: *Your* complaining bothers all of us.
We did not like *his* chattering during work.

KEY CONCEPT Use certain possessive pronouns by themselves to indicate possession. ■

EXAMPLES: That book is *hers*, not *his*.
Is this money *yours* or *theirs?*

Sometimes, possessive pronouns cause problems because they are incorrectly spelled with an apostrophe. Spellings such as *your's*, *our's*, *their's*, and *her's* are incorrect. In addition, do not confuse a possessive pronoun with a contraction.

POSSESSIVE PRONOUN: The monkey wanted to get out of *its* cage.

CONTRACTION: The store is closed today, but *it's* open tomorrow.

Spelling Tip

The pronoun *their* is spelled differently from the adverb *there. Their* is a possessive pronoun, and *there* indicates a location or acts as a sentence opener. Remember also that *theirs* is a pronoun and *there's* is the contraction of *there is.*

Exercise 7 **Using Pronouns in the Possessive Case** Supply a possessive pronoun to complete each sentence.

EXAMPLE: Doing a job well is often __?__ own reward.
ANSWER: its

1. I spoke to Ralph about __?__ offering me a job.
2. I asked him if the job was __?__.
3. Marty works with Shelly on __?__ shared register.
4. Everybody comes in to __?__ store at once.
5. The store is at __?__ fullest near lunchtime.
6. The staff members do most of __?__ work in the afternoon.
7. Together, __?__ line serves the most customers.
8. __?__ paying attention to each customer is important.
9. __?__ brother wants to work with us.
10. I asked Ralph if __?__ store had another opening.

More Practice

Language Lab CD-ROM
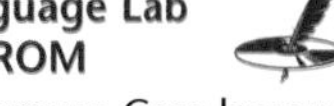
• Pronoun Case lesson

On-line Exercise Bank
• Section 24.1

Grammar Exercise Workbook
• pp. 133–136

Section 24.1 **Section Review**

GRAMMAR EXERCISES 8–13

Exercise 8 **Choosing Pronouns in the Correct Case** Choose the pronoun that is in the correct case to complete each sentence. Identify the case of the pronoun you choose.

1. School fund-raisers taught (we, us) how to sell products to the public.
2. When promoting a product to customers, a salesperson should provide an incentive for (they, them) to buy.
3. (Them, Their) buying often depends on how they react to the seller.
4. This year, my teammates and (I, me) are selling team-spirit banners.
5. The treasurer is (she, her).
6. We will deliver Mr. Barouski's purchase to (he, him).
7. (Our, Us) delivering saves him from having to pick up his order.
8. This fund-raiser is important to my teammates and (I, me).
9. (Me, My) learning to interact with the public is an important part of the experience.
10. Customers know that the sale helps (we, us) earn money for the team.

Exercise 9 **Supplying Pronouns** Supply a pronoun to fill in each blank.

The business of selling things has been practiced for thousands of years. Prehistoric people traded for the things that ___(1)___ needed. If one man was a good hunter, he might have traded some of ___(2)___ catch for clothing or tools. The bargaining skills that ___(3)___ would use would involve some techniques used in selling. Many historical documents that reveal how people lived are actually sales orders. ___(4)___ looking at what people bought and sold helps us to learn what was important or necessary to ___(5)___.

Exercise 10 **Revision Practice: Pronouns** Revise the following passage by replacing some nouns with pronouns in the appropriate case.

The theater manager hired Verna and Max to work in the movie theater. Several of Verna and Max's classmates work at the theater. Karen sells movie tickets. Customers often ask Karen if the movie has already begun. Kenny works at the concession stand. Kenny enjoys selling snacks and beverages.

Exercise 11 **Find It in Your Reading** Identify the case of each pronoun in the following excerpt from Edgar Allan Poe's "The Cask of Amontillado."

"Come," I said, with decision, "we will go back; your health is precious. You are rich, respected, admired, beloved; you are happy, as once I was. You are a man to be missed. For me it is no matter."

Exercise 12 **Find It in Your Writing** Using the chart on page 552, find at least one example in your own writing of each pronoun in each case. On a separate sheet of paper, write the sentences in which you have used the pronouns.

Exercise 13 **Writing Application** Write a brief dialogue between a salesperson and a customer. In your dialogue, use a possessive pronoun with a gerund, a nominative case pronoun as a predicate nominative, and an objective case pronoun in a verbal phrase.

Section 24.2 Special Problems With Pronouns

In this section, you will study the proper uses of *who*, *whom*, and *whose* and the related forms *whoever* and *whomever*. You will also study the use of pronouns in clauses in which some words are omitted but understood.

Theme: William Shakespeare

In this section, you will learn correct uses of *who*, *whom*, and *whose* and of pronouns in elliptical clauses. The examples and exercises in this section are about William Shakespeare.

Cross-Curricular Connection: Literature

Using *Who*, *Whom*, and *Whose* Correctly

KEY CONCEPT *Who* and *whoever* are nominative. *Whom* and *whomever* are objective. *Whose* and *whosever* are possessive. ■

Case	Pronoun	Use in Sentence
Nominative	who, whoever	Subject or predicate nominative
Objective	whom, whomever	Direct object, object of a verbal, or object of a preposition
Possessive	whose, whosever	To show ownership

Note About *Whose*: Do not confuse the contraction *who's*, which means *who is*, with the possessive pronoun *whose*.

POSSESSIVE PRONOUN: Whose short story won the contest?
CONTRACTION: Who's our first singer tonight?

GRAMMAR IN LITERATURE

from The Tragedy of Romeo and Juliet

William Shakespeare

In the following excerpt, the prince questions a young nobleman about the start of a street fight. The nominative case is highlighted in blue italics. The objective case is highlighted in red italics.

PRINCE. Benvolio, *who* began this bloody fray?
BENVOLIO. Tybalt, here slain, *whom* Romeo's hand did slay.

Using the Nominative Case: *Who*

The nominative case is used for subjects and for predicate nominatives.

KEY CONCEPT Use *who* for the subject. ■

EXAMPLES: *Who* is the main character in *Romeo and Juliet*? (*Who* is the subject of the sentence.)
I know *who* is the main character in the play. (*Who* is the subject of the subordinate clause.)

KEY CONCEPT Use *who* for a predicate nominative. ■

EXAMPLE: The villain is *who*? (*Who* is a predicate nominative because it renames *villain.*)

Using the Objective Case: *Whom*

The objective case of personal pronouns is used for direct objects of verbs, the objects of verbals, and objects of prepositions.

KEY CONCEPT Use *whom* and *whomever* for the direct object of a verb or the object of a verbal. ■

In the following example, *whom* is the object of the verb *ask*. *She* is the subject performing the action and *whom* is the one receiving the action; therefore, *whom* is an object.

EXAMPLE: *Whom* did she ask to the dance?

Pronouns in the objective case also occur in the subordinate clauses of complex sentences.

EXAMPLES: She did not know *whom* he chose.
You can select *whomever* you wish.

▼ **Critical Viewing** What details can you learn from the cover of this play script? Use *who* and *whom* in your response. **[Analyze]**

THE
MOST EX-
cellent and lamentable
Tragedie, of Romeo
and *Iuliet.*

Newly corrected, augmented, and amended:

As it hath bene sundry times publiquely acted, by the right Honourable the Lord Chamberlaine his Seruants.

LONDON
Printed by Thomas Creede, for Cuthbert Burby, and are to be sold at his shop neare the Exchange.
1599.

Note About *Checking for the Correct Use of* Who *or* Whom To see if the correct pronouns have been used, first isolate the subordinate clause (*whom he chose*). Next, put the clauses in normal word order: *he chose whom.* It now becomes clear that the subject is *he* and that the direct object is *whom.*

KEY CONCEPT Use *whom* for the object of a preposition. ■

A common error is to use the nominative case in sentences in which the pronoun is separated from the preposition for which it is the object. It is best to rewrite or restate such sentences so that the pronoun immediately follows the preposition.

INCORRECT: *Who* did Romeo receive the message from?
I spoke to the actor *who* we had lunch with.

BETTER: *Whom* did Romeo receive the message from?
I spoke to the actor *whom* we had lunch with.

BEST: From *whom* did Romeo receive the message?
I spoke to the actor *with whom we had lunch.*

PRONOUN IMMEDIATELY FOLLOWS THE PREPOSITION: From *whom* did Romeo receive the message?

Exercise 14 **Using *Who* and *Whom* Correctly** Choose the correct pronoun from each pair in parentheses.

EXAMPLE: With (who, whom) are you going to the play?
ANSWER: whom

1. (Who, Whom) knows the characters of Shakespeare's play *Romeo and Juliet*?
2. From (who, whom) did you hear about the play *Romeo and Juliet*?
3. (Who, Whom) is Romeo's love for most of the play?
4. At (whose, who's) party did the star-crossed lovers meet?
5. The Capulets expected Juliet to marry (who, whom)?
6. (Whose, Who's) Juliet's choice?
7. In (who, whom) did the lovers confide?
8. (Who, Whom) will Tybalt insist on fighting?
9. (Who, Whom) spoke to the Montagues and Capulets about their feud?
10. Escalus, the prince of Verona, punished (who, whom) for the death of Tybalt?

More Practice

Language Lab CD-ROM
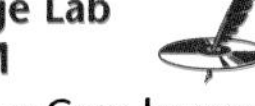
- Pronoun Case lesson

On-line Exercise Bank
- Section 24.2

Grammar Exercise Workbook
- pp. 137–138

Exercise 15 **Proofreading for the Correct Usage of *Who* and *Whom*** Copy the following passage onto a separate sheet of paper. Change any incorrect uses of *who* and *whom.* Leave correct uses as is.

In 1594, William Shakespeare belonged to a company of actors whom presented a variety of plays. These actors, who were called the Lord Chamberlain's Men, were very popular. Not everyone who Shakespeare worked with admired him. Some critics who wrote for the newspapers of the time wrote poor reviews of his work. As time passed, people began to wonder whether a common actor could be the one by who the plays were written. Today, few scholars doubt that Shakespeare is the one to whom the plays should be credited.

More Practice

Language Lab CD-ROM
- Pronoun Case lesson

On-line Exercise Bank
- Section 24.2

Grammar Exercise Workbook
- pp. 137–138

Using Pronouns Correctly in Elliptical Clauses

In an *elliptical clause,* some words are omitted because they are understood. Sentences with elliptical clauses are often used to draw comparisons. *Fran is smarter than he,* or *Tom is as happy as I.* In selecting the case of the pronoun, you must know what the unstated words are.

KEY CONCEPT In elliptical clauses beginning with *than* or *as,* use the form of the pronoun that you would use if the clause were fully stated. ■

The case of the pronoun depends upon whether the omitted words belong before or after the pronoun.

WORDS LEFT OUT AFTER PRONOUN:	Jo is as talented as *he.* Jo is as talented as he [is].
WORDS LEFT OUT BEFORE PRONOUN:	We gave Scott the same choices as *her.* We gave Scott the same choices as [we gave] her.

If the words left out come *after* the pronoun, use a nominative pronoun. If the words left out come *before* the pronoun, use an objective pronoun because the pronoun will be an object.

Often, the entire meaning of the sentence depends on the case of the pronoun, as in the following examples.

WITH A NOMINATIVE PRONOUN:	We liked him better than *she.* We liked him better than she [did].
WITH AN OBJECTIVE PRONOUN:	We liked him better than *her.* We liked him better than [we liked] her.

Internet Tip

To find a wealth of information and links about Shakespeare, visit the Shakespeare Resources page of the Internet School Library Media Center at:

http://falcon.jmu.edu/~ramseyil/shakes.htm

Exercise 16 **Identifying the Correct Pronoun in Elliptical Clauses** Rewrite each sentence, choosing one of the pronouns in parentheses and correctly completing the elliptical clause.

EXAMPLE: We studied Shakespeare more than (he, him).
ANSWER: We studied Shakespeare more than *he* did.

1. Beth has more experience with Shakespeare than (I, me).
2. She feels that I know as much as (she, her).
3. The director gave her the part of Juliet because she fit the role better than (I, me).
4. The actor who plays Romeo is as talented as (she, her).
5. They gave more advice to her than to (me, I).

More Practice
Grammar Exercise Workbook
• pp. 137–138

Exercise 17 **Supplying Pronouns in Elliptical Clauses** Rewrite each sentence, supplying an appropriate pronoun and completing the elliptical clause.

EXAMPLE: Joanne reads plays more often than __?__.
ANSWER: Joanne reads plays more often than I do.

1. My teacher knows much more about Shakespeare than __?__.
2. When we were taught his plays, our teacher was as excited as __?__.
3. His enthusiasm led us to enjoy the plays as much as __?__.
4. We have also read works by Christopher Marlowe, but I like Shakespeare better than __?__.
5. Although I thought I was the biggest Shakespeare fan in the class, Sarah enjoyed reading *Hamlet* more than __?__.
6. Luisa, who learned to play madrigals on her guitar, was an even greater Shakespeare fan than __?__.
7. The teacher said that Luisa knew more about Elizabethan music than __?__.
8. Elizabeth I favored the songs of the madrigalists, and members of her court liked them as much as __?__.
9. Playing the lute and singing these cheerful part-songs gave as much pleasure to the queen as __?__.
10. Luisa has heard more songs performed in Shakespearean plays than __?__.

▼ **Critical Viewing** Using at least one elliptical clause, compare two kinds of guitars or guitar music. **[Compare and Contrast]**

24.2

Hands-on Grammar

Who/Whom Pickup

To learn when to use the nominative *who* or the objective *whom*, get together with three or four classmates and play *Who/Whom* Pickup. To begin, cut out sixteen 2" x 2" squares from one piece of heavy paper and sixteen 2" x 3" rectangles from another piece, preferably of a different color. On eight of the square cards, print *WHO*, and on the other eight, print *WHOM*. Then, mix them up and stack them neatly upside down on a desk or table. Next, write a short statement on each rectangular card; for example: *Joe drove Michelle to the game. We talked to Mara and Al. Lucy wrote about Shakespeare. Mr. Ames visited Dr. Frye.* Make sure that the subjects and objects are people. When you have sixteen sentences, mix them up and stack them neatly upside down next to the WHO/WHOM pile. (See illustrations.)

To play, the first person picks up a card from each stack. He or she must then turn the statement into a question using either *who* or *whom*, depending on the word drawn. If *who* is drawn, it must substitute for the subject of the sentence. If *whom* is drawn, it must substitute for an object. Write down your questions as you go along.

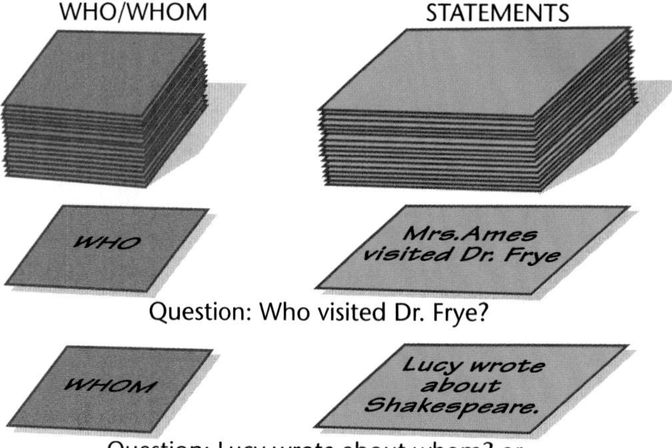

Take turns until all the cards have been drawn. Then, trade sentence cards with another group, and play another round. Pay close attention to when you use the nominative *who* and the objective *whom*.

Find It in Your Reading Read a passage of biographical writing in a book or a magazine, and look for uses of *who* and *whom*. See if you can determine if each one is used correctly or if the author used *who* informally when he or she should have used *whom*.

Find It in Your Writing Look through one or more pieces of writing in your portfolio to see if you have used *who* and *whom* correctly. Revise any that are in the wrong case.

Section 24.2 Section Review

GRAMMAR EXERCISES 18–23

Exercise 18 **Supplying *Who* and *Whom*** Supply *who* or *whom* to complete each sentence.

1. Can you tell us __?__ Shakespeare's most popular characters are?
2. We listen to opinions from all __?__ will give them.
3. The character of Hamlet, __?__ you like, is a favorite of mine.
4. It is he to __?__ Shakespeare gave the most lines of any role in all his plays.
5. Hamlet's father is the ghost __?__ haunts the castle.

Exercise 19 **Proofreading Practice: *Who* and *Whom*** Copy the following passage onto a separate sheet of paper. With different-colored pens, correct any errors in the usage of *who* and *whom.*

I know whom the villain is in *Othello.* He is an officer who, we see, will scheme to destroy Othello's marriage and career. Desdemona is the woman to whom Othello is married. Whomever meets her is charmed by her love for her husband. Roderigo, who's jealous of Othello, schemes with Iago. Because of their trickery, Othello becomes insanely jealous of whoever goes near Desdemona. In the end, Cassio knows whose schemes brought ruin to the characters of the play. In Shakespeare's tragedies, only one character is left alive to whom everyone can go for the whole story.

Exercise 20 **Completing Elliptical Clauses** Write the pronoun and the understood words to complete the elliptical clause in each of the following sentences.

1. In the play *Henry IV,* Falstaff, comparing himself with others in the play, believes that he is more witty than __?__.
2. However, Prince Hal, who will become King Henry V, is just as clever as __?__.
3. Falstaff talks bravely to everyone but runs away from danger faster than __?__.
4. Falstaff plays dead on the battlefield while his friends fight because his own life is more important to him than __?__.
5. Nonetheless, we didn't like the other characters as much as __?__.

Exercise 21 **Find It in Your Reading** Identify the cases of *who* as used in the following excerpt from *The Tragedy of Romeo and Juliet.*

Of Tybalt deaf to peace, but that he tilts / With piercing steel at bold Mercutio's breast; / Who, all as hot, turns deadly point to point, / And, with a martial scorn, with one hand beats / Cold death aside and with the other sends / It back to Tybalt, whose dexterity / Retorts it. . . .

Exercise 22 **Find It in Your Writing** Find three examples in your own writing of *who* and *whom.* Copy the sentences onto a separate sheet of paper. If you cannot find examples, compose sentences that include these pronouns.

Exercise 23 **Writing Application** Write a scene between two characters in a play. Include at least one elliptical clause, one *who,* one *whom,* and the possessive pronoun *whose.*

Chapter 25

Agreement

▲ **Critical Viewing** Which parts of this picture would you name with plural nouns? Which parts would you name with singular nouns? **[Analyze]**

When you speak, you automatically use words that agree with other words. You might say, for example, "She *speaks* faster than they *speak.*" You know you must add an *-s* to *speak* when the subject is *she* to make the verb agree with the subject.

Agreement is the match—the "fit"—between words or grammatical forms. Because grammatical agreement is not always obvious, you need to study some sentences more closely than others. In this chapter, you will learn to make a verb agree with its subject and to make a pronoun agree with its antecedent.

Diagnostic Test

Directions: Write all answers on a separate sheet of paper.

Skill Check A. Choose the verb in parentheses that agrees with the subject in each of the following sentences.

1. In most democracies, the people (enjoys, enjoy) basic rights.
2. Freedom of speech, along with other ideals, (is, are) treasured.
3. Neither dictatorships nor most monarchies (grants, grant) broad freedoms to their people.
4. In some countries, either secret police or the military (enforces, enforce) the law.
5. The people and their government (needs, need) to work together for the common good.
6. Dear to the hearts of many (is, are) the concept of liberty.
7. Today in the world, there (is, are) many changes taking place.
8. Among the changes (is, are) a struggle for a free society.
9. Collapsing communist governments (is, are) one reason for the changes.
10. A group of Russians (wants, want) to return to communism.
11. Politics (is, are) difficult in many former communist countries.
12. Each of the countries (deals, deal) with different conditions.
13. Roger Manser's *Failed Transitions* (describes, describe) problems in the Eastern European economy after the fall of communism.
14. Fifty years (was, were) a long time to wait for freedom.
15. More than half the world's population (is, are) still waiting.

Skill Check B. Choose the pronoun in parentheses that agrees with the antecedent in each of the following sentences.

16. Many say our culture takes (its, their) freedom for granted.
17. The development of democracy has changed the way in which people around the world conduct (his or her, their) lives.
18. Neither Thomas Jefferson nor Benjamin Franklin could have judged the impact (his, their) work would someday have.
19. Every person enjoying democracy today may owe some of (his or her, their) opportunities to America's founders.
20. Each of us should be grateful for (his or her, our) freedom.

Skill Check C. Revise the following sentences to correct problems in pronoun reference.

21. Even in a corrupt democracy, the government may prevent your progress.
22. Officials may demand bribes from ordinary citizens in exchange for basic services. This practice makes them rich.
23. When opposing forces unseat a corrupt leader, most citizens are relieved. Then, they have a big job ahead.
24. In the newspaper article, it said that a free election was held.
25. You hear about these changes in the news every day.

Subject and Verb Agreement

For a subject and verb to agree, both must be singular or both must be plural. In this section, you will learn how to distinguish between singular and plural subjects, how to make verbs agree with compound subjects, and how to deal with special agreement problems caused by confusing subjects.

Theme: Governments

In this section, you will learn about subject and verb agreement. The examples and exercises in this section are about governments.

Cross-Curricular Connection: Social Studies

Singular and Plural Subjects

When making a verb agree with its subject, you identify the subject and determine whether it is singular or plural.

KEY CONCEPT A singular subject must have a singular verb. A plural subject must have a plural verb. ■

SINGULAR SUBJECT AND VERB:	Hungary *is* a small European country.
PLURAL SUBJECT AND VERB:	Hungarians *vote* in free elections.

Exercise 1 **Making Verbs Agree With Their Subjects**
Choose the verb in parentheses that agrees with the subject of each sentence.

1. Before 1940, most Hungarians (was, were) farmers.
2. Today, many people (works, work) in industry.
3. When thinking of the past, my uncle (remembers, remember) the restrictions of Communist party rule.
4. Since the fall of the communist government, a great change (has, have) occurred.
5. Today, the citizens (elects, elect) their leaders.

More Practice

Language Lab CD-ROM
- Special Problems in Agreement lesson

On-line Exercise Bank
- Section 25.1

Grammar Exercise Workbook
- pp. 139–140

KEY CONCEPT A phrase or clause that interrupts a subject and its verb does not affect subject-verb agreement. ■

EXAMPLES: Citizens of the country *vote.*
The legislature, which has 386 members, *is called* the National Assembly.

In the first example, the plural subject *citizens* takes the plural verb *vote.* Even though the singular noun *country* is closer to the verb, it is the object of a preposition and does not affect the agreement of the subject and the verb. In the second example, the singular subject *legislature* takes the singular verb *is.* The clause that interrupts the subject and verb does not affect the agreement.

▲ Critical Viewing
Describe three features of this building. Write the subject and verb you use in each sentence. Label each *singular* or *plural*. **[Describe]**

Exercise 2 **Making Separated Subjects and Verbs Agree**
Choose the verb in parentheses that agrees with the subject of each sentence.

1. In Hungary, a system of multiple parties (guarantees, guarantee) electoral choice.
2. The legislative body, representing local and national interests, (holds, hold) office for four years.
3. Hungary's Supreme Court, the final court of appeals, (comprises, comprise) two citizens and one judge.
4. Members of the Socialist Workers' party no longer (attracts, attract) much popular appeal.
5. Citizens, exercising their right to vote, currently (seems, seem) to prefer the more conservative political party.

Exercise 3 **Correcting Subject and Verb Agreement**
Revise the following paragraph, correcting all errors in subject and verb agreement.

(1) Hungary's capital city, Budapest, are really three separate cities combined to form one. (2) Obuda and Buda sits on the west bank of the Danube River. (3) The city of Pest stands majestically on the east bank. (4) The three cities was merged into one in the late nineteenth century. (5) Budapest, now one of Europe's busiest capitals, have become an industrial and commercial center.

25.1

Compound Subjects

A compound subject consists of two or more subjects, usually connected by *or* or *and,* that have the same verb. A number of different rules apply to compound subjects.

Subjects Joined by *and* Only one rule applies to compound subjects connected by *and:* Whether the parts of the compound subject are all singular, all plural, or mixed, the verb is usually plural.

KEY CONCEPT A compound subject joined by *and* is generally plural and must have a plural verb. ■

TWO SINGULAR SUBJECTS:	The chancellor and his cabinet *are going* to meet.
TWO PLURAL SUBJECTS:	The ministers and their assistants *discuss* a new bill.
A SINGULAR AND A PLURAL SUBJECT:	The chancellor and the cabinet members *go* over the agenda.

There are two exceptions to the preceding rule. If the parts of the compound subject are the same thing or are thought of as one item, then a singular verb is needed. A singular verb is also needed if the word *every* or the word *each* precedes a compound subject.

EXAMPLES: Germany's capital and largest city *is* Berlin.

Give and take *is* a rule of negotiations.

Each issue and proposal *is discussed.*

Singular Subjects Joined by *or* or *nor* When both parts of a compound subject connected by *or* or *nor* are singular, a singular verb is required.

KEY CONCEPT Two or more singular subjects joined by *or* or *nor* must have a singular verb. ■

EXAMPLE: Schroeder or Kohl *was going* to win.

In the preceding example, the conjunction *or* connects two singular subjects that act as a singular compound subject. Either Schroeder or Kohl would be the winner, not both.

▼ Critical Viewing
In 1989, Berliners destroyed the wall that had divided their city for twenty-eight years. Identify three other verbs besides *tear* that agree in number with *Berliners.* **[Connect]**

Plural Subjects Joined by *or* or *nor* When both parts of a compound subject connected by *or* or *nor* are plural, a plural verb is required.

KEY CONCEPT Two or more plural subjects joined by *or* or *nor* must have a plural verb. ■

EXAMPLE: The liberals or the conservatives *are going* to win.

Subjects of Mixed Number Joined by *or* or *nor* If one part of a compound subject is singular and the other is plural, the verb agrees with the subject that is closer to it.

KEY CONCEPT If a singular subject is joined to a plural subject by *or* or *nor*, the subject closer to the verb determines whether the verb is singular or plural. ■

EXAMPLES: Either Schroeder or the ministers *are going* to speak.
Either the ministers or Schroeder *is going* to speak.

Exercise 4 Making Verbs Agree With Compound Subjects
Choose the verb in parentheses that agrees with the subject in each sentence.

EXAMPLE: Neither East Germany nor West Germany (was, were) interested in remaining divided.
ANSWER: was

1. East Germany and West Germany (is, are) now reunited under a federal republic.
2. Neither the Berlin Wall nor many other aspects of division (exists, exist) any longer.
3. East Germany and West Germany (is, are) united.
4. In the current German government, the president and the chancellor (works, work) as partners.
5. Neither the president nor the Parliament (selects, select) ministers for the chancellor's cabinet.
6. In the Parliament, either the upper house or the lower house (passes, pass) laws.
7. Either one political party or a coalition (governs, govern) the country.
8. The six parties and each candidate (participates, participate) actively in the political process.
9. Often, labor issues or the environment (forms, form) the basis for some political platforms.
10. Each state and major city (has, have) some Social Democrats and some Christian Democrats.

Technology Tip

When writing with a word-processing program, use the "Search" feature to locate places in a document where you have used *and, or,* or *nor.* If you have used these conjunctions to join the parts of a compound subject, check these sentences carefully for subject-verb agreement.

More Practice

Language Lab CD-ROM
- Special Problems in Agreement lesson

On-line Exercise Bank
- Section 25.1

Grammar Exercise Workbook
- pp. 141–142

25.1

Confusing Subjects

Some subjects create special agreement problems:

Inverted Sentences Foremost among the confusing subjects are hard-to-find subjects that come after their verbs. A sentence in which the subject comes after the verb is said to be inverted. Subject and verb order is usually inverted in questions.

KEY CONCEPT A verb that comes before its subject must still agree with the subject in number. ■

EXAMPLES: On the wall *are* slogans. (Slogans *are* on the wall.)
Is the message clear? (The message *is* clear.)

In the first example, the plural verb *are* agrees with the plural subject *slogans.* In the second example, a question, the singular verb *is* agrees with the singular subject *message.* Check the verb by mentally rewording the sentence so that the subject comes at the beginning.

The words *there* and *here* at the beginning of a sentence often signal an inverted sentence. The words *there* and *here* never function as the subjects of sentences.

EXAMPLES: There *is* only one government in Germany.
There *are* several parties in the government.

The subject in the first of the preceding examples is *government.* It is singular and takes the singular verb *is.* The plural subject *parties* in the second sentence takes the plural verb *are.*

Note About *There's* and *Here's*: The contractions *there's* (*there is*) and *here's* (*here is*) contain singular verbs. They should not be used with plural subjects.

CORRECT: Here*'s* the minister now.
Here *are* the ministers now.

Exercise 5 Making Subjects and Verbs Agree in Inverted Sentences For each sentence, choose the verb in parentheses that agrees with the subject.

1. Making up Germany's Parliament (is, are) two houses.
2. There (is, are) an election held every four years to select members of the Bundestag.
3. Chosen as chancellor (is, are) the leader of the strongest party.
4. In the Bundestag (is, are) 662 deputies.
5. (Does, do) the chancellor vote?

More Practice

Language Lab CD-ROM
- Special Problems in Agreement lesson

On-line Exercise Bank
- Section 25.1

Grammar Exercise Workbook
- pp. 82–84

Subjects of Linking Verbs Subjects with linking verbs may also cause agreement problems. Do not be misled by a predicate nominative.

KEY CONCEPT A linking verb must agree with its subject, regardless of the number of the predicate nominative. ■

EXAMPLES: Economic conditions *are* one cause for concern.
One cause for concern *is* economic conditions.

In the first example, the verb *are* agrees with the plural subject *conditions* even though the predicate nominative *cause* is singular. In the second example, the subject is now *cause*, which requires the singular verb *is*, and *conditions* becomes the predicate nominative.

Collective Nouns Collective nouns—such as *assembly, audience, class, club,* and *committee*—name groups of people or things. A collective noun is considered singular if it refers to the group acting as a unit. The noun is considered plural if it refers to the members of the group acting as individuals.

KEY CONCEPT A collective noun takes a singular verb when the group it names acts as a single unit. A collective noun takes a plural verb when the group it names act as individuals with different points of view. ■

EXAMPLES: Singular: The committee *votes* on the issue.
Plural: The committee *have split* their votes.

Plural-Looking Nouns Some nouns that end in *-s* appear to be plural but are actually singular in meaning. Some of these nouns name branches of knowledge, such as *civics, economics, physics, mathematics,* and *social studies.* Others are singular because, like collective nouns, they name single units: *molasses* (one kind of syrup), *mumps* (one disease), *news* (one body of information), and so on.

KEY CONCEPT Nouns that are plural in form but singular in meaning take singular verbs. ■

EXAMPLES: Social studies *has become* my favorite subject.
Measles *is* a dangerous disease for unborn babies.

Grammar and Style Tip

Use inverted sentences to vary the sentence patterns in your writing. When used after several sentences in subject-verb order, an inverted sentence creates a mental pause for emphasis or thought.

25.1

GRAMMAR IN LITERATURE

from Glory and Hope

Nelson Mandela

In the following passage, the indefinite pronoun all *refers to the plural pronoun* us. *Therefore, it takes the plural verb* do.

Your majesties, your royal highnesses, distinguished guests, comrades and friends: Today, *all* of us *do*, by our presence here, and by our celebrations in other parts of our country and the world, confer glory and hope to newborn liberty.

Our daily deeds as ordinary South Africans must produce an actual South African reality that will reinforce humanity's belief in justice, strengthen its confidence in the nobility of the human soul and sustain all our hopes for a glorious life for all.

Indefinite Pronouns Some indefinite pronouns are always singular, some are always plural, and some may be either singular or plural.

ALWAYS SINGULAR:	anybody, anyone, anything, each, either, every, everybody, everyone, everything, neither, nobody, no one, nothing, somebody, someone, something
ALWAYS PLURAL:	both, few, many, others, several
SINGULAR OR PLURAL:	all, any, more, most, none, some

KEY CONCEPT Singular indefinite pronouns take singular verbs. Plural indefinite pronouns take plural verbs. ■

Do not be misled by a prepositional phrase that interrupts the subject and verb. The interrupting phrase does not affect subject-verb agreement.

SINGULAR: Either of your plans *is* acceptable to me.

PLURAL: Few of the representatives *are* here.

Spelling Tip

To remember that *neither* is an exception to the *i before e* rule, recognize the word *either* in *neither*. You are not likely to begin *either* with an *i*, and remembering the connection between the words will help you spell *neither* correctly.

KEY CONCEPT The pronouns *all, any, more, most, none,* and *some* take a singular verb if they refer to singular words and a plural verb if they refer to plural words. ■

SINGULAR: Most of South Africa *was* proud.
PLURAL: Most of the South Africans *were* proud.

Exercise 6 **Making Verbs Agree With Indefinite Pronouns** Choose the verb in parentheses that agrees with the indefinite pronoun in each sentence.

1. Everyone in Kenya (learns, learn) about the country's history.
2. Few (recalls, recall) when the British took over their country.
3. Most of Kenya's best land (was, were) controlled by British settlers during the late 1890's.
4. Many (was, were) unhappy with British rule of their country.
5. Some still (remembers, remember) the day Kenya gained its independence.

More Practice

Language Lab CD-ROM
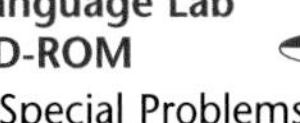

- Special Problems in Agreement lesson

On-line Exercise Bank

- Section 25.1

Grammar Exercise Workbook

- pp. 145–150

Titles of Creative Works and Names of Organizations Plural words in the title of a creative work or in the name of an organization do not affect subject-verb agreement when the title or name is the subject of a verb.

KEY CONCEPT A title or the name of an organization is singular and must have a singular verb. ■

EXAMPLES: *Hard Times* *is* a novel by Charles Dickens.
Sunflowers *is* Van Gogh's most famous painting.
DiCuffa Brothers *makes* the best pizza.

Learn More

For more about capitalization of titles of creative works or names of organizations, see Chapter 28.

Amounts and Measurements Most amounts and measurements, although they appear to be plural, actually express single units or ideas.

KEY CONCEPT A noun expressing an amount or a measurement is usually singular and requires a singular verb. ■

EXAMPLES: Fifty cents *is* more than enough.
Twenty feet *was* the length of the voting line.
Usually, only one third of the country *votes*.
Half the votes *were* counted.

In the first three examples, the subjects take singular verbs. *Fifty cents* equals one sum of money; *twenty feet* is one measurement; and *one third* is one part of a total country. In the last example, however, the subject *half* refers to many individual items and is therefore plural.

Exercise 7 **Making Verbs Agree With Confusing Subjects** Choose the item in parentheses that agrees with the subject of each sentence.

1. Only after years of protest and sanctions (was, were) apartheid abolished in South Africa.
2. Almost every country, including the United States, (was, were) critical of South Africa's racial policies.
3. A television audience of millions (was, were) thrilled to watch Nelson Mandela's inauguration.
4. There (is, are) now reasons for hope throughout the country.
5. More than three fourths of the population (consists, consist) of blacks; the remaining quarter (comprises, comprise) whites, Asians, and people of mixed race.
6. Human rights for all South Africans (is, are) the focus of the new government.
7. (Isn't, Aren't) economics also a great concern?
8. Anybody from one of the poorer areas (hopes, hope) conditions will improve.
9. Watching South Africa's progress (is, are) leaders of many other nations.
10. Catherine Bradley's *Causes and Consequences* (discusses, discuss) problems in the new South Africa.

More Practice

Language Lab CD-ROM
- Special Problems in Agreement lesson

On-line Exercise Bank
- Section 25.1

Grammar Exercise Workbook
- pp. 82–84

▼ Critical Viewing Describe the flags. What verb did you use with *flags*? With *stripes*? **[Describe]**

Hands-on Grammar

Subject-Verb Agreement Color Match

Cut two strips of paper of equal length. Draw a blue line across the center of one. Draw a red line across the center of the other. Fold the strip into thirds, as shown in the illustration. Then, write a sentence with a singular subject, a singular verb form, and a phrase across the blue line. Write the subject in the first fold, the verb in the second, and the remaining words in the third fold. Write the same sentence on the strip with the red line but use a plural subject and plural verb form. Next, cut each strip on the folds. Finally, try to line up the parts of the sentence. You will find that you can't create a color match between a singular subject and a plural verb form.

The Minister	attends	every session

The Ministers	attend	every session

The Ministers	attends	every session

Find It in Your Reading Do this activity with a sentence from the Grammar in Literature passage from "Glory and Hope," on page 414. If the sentence has too many phrases, just use the subject and verb.

Find It in Your Writing Review a recent piece of writing in your portfolio. Use this activity with several sentences from the piece.

Section 25.1 Section Review

GRAMMAR EXERCISES 8–17

Exercise 8 **Choosing Verbs That Agree** Choose the verb in parentheses that agrees with the subject of each sentence.

1. Democracy (exists, exist) when the people direct the nation's activities.
2. Free systems of government (is, are) common in Western nations.
3. Concepts of democracy (includes, include) the election of representatives.
4. An individual in a free system (possesses, possess) many basic rights.
5. Freedom of speech and freedom of the press (is, are) protected.
6. There (is, are) no letup in the ads.
7. When (is, are) the voting and the counting of ballots?
8. In November (comes, come) the vote.
9. There (is, are) predictions of the winner immediately after the polls close.
10. However, only after several hours (is, are) there an official count.

Exercise 9 **Revising Sentences for Subject-Verb Agreement** Read each sentence. If it is correct, write *correct*. If the verb does not agree with the subject, rewrite the sentence correctly.

1. Toward the end of a political convention comes the nominations.
2. Then begin the campaign.
3. During the fall, is each candidate's campaign in full swing?
4. Yes, there is numerous personal appearances by the candidates.
5. Is there many ads on television?
6. Unreasonable search and seizure is forbidden under the law.
7. Neither Congress nor the President have absolute authority.
8. The President and each elected member of Congress swear to uphold the Constitution.
9. Either the citizens or the press monitor the government.
10. Neither police nor soldiers rules.

Exercise 10 **Choosing the Correct Linking Verb** Choose the verb in parentheses that agrees with the subject of each sentence.

1. Our courts (is, are) a large system.
2. Criminal and civil cases (is, are) the responsibility of the district courts.
3. The responsibility of the Supreme Court (is, are) appeals from the district courts.
4. The Court (has, have) nine justices.
5. The courts (is, are) now the domain of female as well as male justices.

Exercise 11 **Revising Sentences With Difficult Subjects** Revise the paragraph, correcting errors in subject-verb agreement.

Not everybody know how laws are established. However, each of us realize the importance of laws. A committee votes on whether to send the bill further. In the House or Senate, many debates aspects of the bill. Politics always play a role.

Exercise 12 **Choosing Verbs That Agree With Titles, Names, and Amounts and Measurements** Choose the verb in parentheses that agrees with the subject of each sentence.

1. Since 1790, the United States (has, have) taken a census of the population.

2. Ten years (is, are) the interval between censuses.
3. For the first census, $45,000 (was, were) paid by the government.
4. About 2.5 percent of the population (was, were) undercounted in 1970.
5. Deirdre Gaquin's *Places, Towns, and Townships* (provides, provide) census data for businesses.

Exercise 13 **Revising Sentences for Subject-Verb Agreement** Rewrite each sentence, revising it according to the instructions given in brackets. Change the verb form as needed. Not all verbs will change.

1. Local government is important in the daily lives of Americans. [Change *government* to *governments*.]
2. The importance of the township differs from state to state. [Change *the township* to *townships*.]
3. Waste removal is regulated. [Add *and water supply* after *Waste removal*.]
4. There is usually a zoning law. [Change *a zoning law* to *zoning laws*.]
5. The town council votes on the laws. (Begin the sentence with *Members of*.]
6. Neither the council nor the mayor acts alone. [Add *members* after *council*.]
7. About 40 percent of the budget goes to schools. [Change *budget* to *budgets*.]
8. Policies interest most citizens. [Change *policies* to *politics*.]
9. Each of the states has county governments. [Change *Each* to *All but one*.]
10. *The Future of Us All* examines local politics. [Change *The Future of Us All* to *City Trenches*.]

Exercise 14 **Revising a Paragraph for Subject Verb Agreement** Copy the paragraph on a separate sheet of paper. Revise to correct all errors in subject-verb agreement. Not all verbs will change.

(1) Are lower taxes an important issue to you? (2) This question and others like it are often asked by pollsters. (3) Does any of your friends think about big issues? (4) Have your mother or father ever been polled? (5) There's many issues in which a large percentage of the population take an interest. (6) The public's views on an issue forms public opinion. (7) Every pollster and politician try to keep abreast of public opinion. (8) The results of a poll, along with the margin for error, are often reported in the press. (9) Here's one of many books on polls: Susan Herbst's *Numbered Voices*. (10) It tells how politics have been shaped by opinion polls.

Exercise 15 **Find It in Your Reading** Read the following lines from Nelson Mandela's "Glory and Hope." Then, on your paper, write each subject and its verb, and identify whether each is singular or plural.

> Each time one of us touches the soil of this land, we feel a sense of personal renewal. The national mood changes as the seasons change.
>
> We are moved by a sense of joy and exhilaration when the grass turns green and the flowers bloom.

Exercise 16 **Find It in Your Writing** Review a draft from your portfolio written in the present tense. Underline each subject once and its verb twice. Make sure your subjects and verb forms agree.

Exercise 17 **Writing Application** Summarize the plot of a novel or a movie that you enjoyed. Describe the events in the present tense. Then, carefully check the agreement of your subjects and verbs.

Section 25.2

Pronoun and Antecedent Agreement

Antecedents are the nouns (or the words that take the place of nouns) to which pronouns refer. The word *antecedent* comes from a Latin word meaning "to go before." In English, an antecedent usually precedes its pronoun. This section will explain how pronouns agree with their antecedents.

Theme: Technology and Communications

In this section, you will learn about pronoun and antecedent agreement. The examples and exercises are about communications and technology.

Cross-Curricular Connection: Science

Agreement Between Personal Pronouns and Antecedents

The following rule of pronoun and antecedent agreement is the basis for almost all the other rules:

KEY CONCEPTS A personal pronoun must agree with its antecedent in number and gender. ■

The grammatical number of a noun or pronoun indicates whether it is singular or plural.

Some pronouns and nouns also indicate one of three genders: masculine, feminine, or neuter. Nouns referring to males, such as *uncle* and *boy*, are masculine. Nouns referring to females, such as *actress* and *mother*, are feminine. Nouns that do not refer to either males or females, such as *stone* and *freedom*, are neuter. Only pronouns in the third-person singular indicate gender.

GENDER OF THIRD-PERSON SINGULAR PRONOUNS

Masculine	Feminine	Neuter
he, him, his, himself	she, her, hers, herself	it, its, itself

In the following example, the pronoun and antecedent agree completely. Both the antecedent *Charlene* and the pronoun *her* are singular and feminine.

EXAMPLE: *Charlene* accessed *her* friend's Home Page.

Agreement in Number Making personal pronouns agree with their antecedents in number is usually a problem only when the antecedent is a compound.

KEY CONCEPT Use a singular personal pronoun to refer to two or more singular antecedents joined by *or* or *nor*. ■

EXAMPLE: Neither *Keith nor Rob* remembers *his* password.

KEY CONCEPT Use a plural personal pronoun to refer to two or more antecedents joined by *and*. ■

EXAMPLE: *Gene and Rita* have checked *their* e-mail.

Agreement in Person Errors in agreement between personal pronouns and their antecedents often involve a shift in person.

KEY CONCEPT When dealing with pronoun-antecedent agreement, take care not to shift person. ■

SHIFT IN PERSON: Becca is studying programming, a course you need for a degree in computer science.

CORRECT: Becca is studying programming, a course she needs for a degree in computer science.

Note About Generic Masculine Pronouns: Historically, a masculine pronoun (*he, his, him, himself*) has been used to refer to a singular antecedent whose gender is not specified. Such use of the masculine pronoun is said to be generic, meaning it covers both the masculine and feminine genders. Today, however, many writers prefer to use both the masculine and feminine pronouns (*he or she, him or her, his or her, himself or herself*) instead of the generic masculine form. When using both forms becomes awkward, it is best to rewrite the sentence.

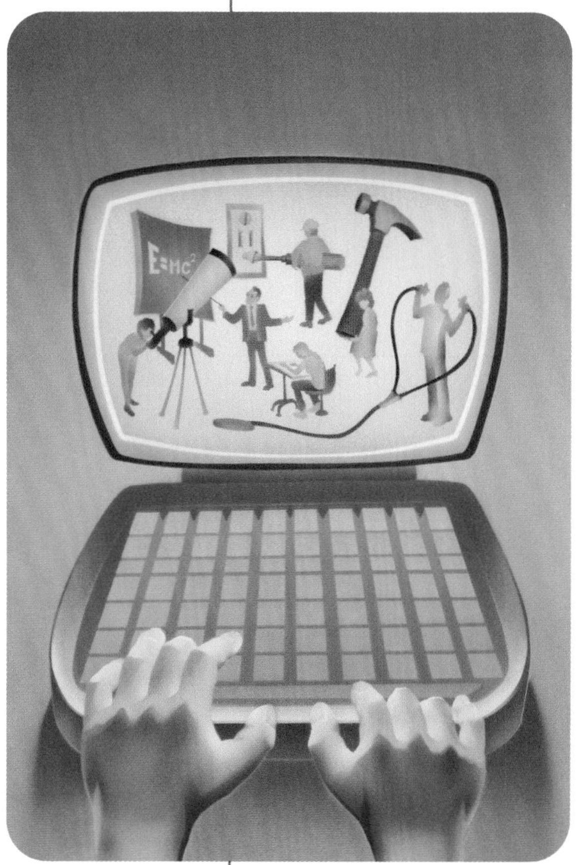

▲ Critical Viewing
In what ways has technology changed the way people communicate? **[Analyze]**

KEY CONCEPT When gender is not specified, use the masculine and feminine pronouns or rewrite the sentence. ■

EXAMPLES: A *student* should keep *his or her* password a secret.
Students should keep *their* passwords a secret.

Exercise 18 **Making Personal Pronouns Agree With Their Antecedents** Write an appropriate personal pronoun to complete each sentence.

EXAMPLE: Personal computers are in the process of expanding __?__ capabilities.

ANSWER: their

1. One computer pioneer is Alan Kay. __?__ is noted for __?__ role in the development of the laptop computer.
2. Before Kay introduced graphics and animation, __?__ had not been seen before on PCs.
3. The PCs of today have much more memory than __?__ predecessors.
4. In the 1970's, the average person did not have a computer in __?__ home.
5. However, once the microprocessor was invented, __?__ hastened the development of the PC.
6. When the fully assembled PC went on the market, __?__ became a sales phenomenon.
7. At first, neither computer developers nor manufacturers realized what __?__ had.
8. These days, a PC usually comes with several programs as part of __?__ initial package.
9. Diana Adams, who sees __?__ as a modern woman, takes a laptop computer with __?__ wherever __?__ goes.
10. However, you and I don't even have to leave home. __?__ can access the world through __?__ PCs.

More Practice

Language Lab CD-ROM

- Pronoun Antecedent Agreement lesson

On-line Exercise Bank

- Section 25.2

Grammar Exercise Workbook

- pp. 145–148

Using Reflexive Pronouns

A reflexive pronoun ends in *-self* or *-selves* and points back to a noun or pronoun near the beginning of the sentence, as in "*David* taught *himself* to use the Internet."

KEY CONCEPT A reflexive pronoun must have an antecedent in the sentence in which it appears. ■

POOR USE: Todd helped Jen and *myself* to search the Internet.

CORRECT: Todd helped Jen and *me* to search the Internet.

CORRECT: Jen searched the Internet *herself*.

Exercise 19 **Correcting Misuse of Reflexive Pronouns** Correct the sentences that misuse a reflexive pronoun. If a sentence is correct, write *C*.

1. The assignment directed Sean and myself to find information on a space shuttle.
2. Sean said that himself and I should try the Internet.
3. The results of our Internet searches were a surprise to both the teacher and ourselves.
4. I came up with 102,700 sites myself.
5. Won't it be an effort for yourself to check all those sites?

Exercise 20 **Supplying Reflexive Pronouns** Supply a reflexive pronoun to complete each sentence.

1. I can do that __?__.
2. Sean said he would search the Internet __?__.
3. We were proud of __?__.
4. They created a Web site __?__.
5. Do you want to check the sites __?__?

▼ **Critical Viewing** *Antennae* is the plural form of *antenna*. Write a sentence with the word *antenna*. Then, use the same verb in a sentence with *antennae*. How does the verb change? **[Analyze]**

Agreement With Indefinite Pronouns

When you write a sentence with a personal pronoun that has an indefinite pronoun as its antecedent, you must always make sure that the two pronouns agree.

KEY CONCEPTS Use a singular pronoun to refer to a singular indefinite pronoun. Use a plural pronoun to refer to a plural indefinite pronoun. ■

SINGULAR: *One* of the boys will print *his* document.
PLURAL: *All* of the boys will print *their* documents.

If no gender is specified, you can use *his* or *his or her*, or you can reword the sentence, as in the following examples:

EXAMPLES: *Everyone* saved *his or her* document.
All the students saved *their* documents.

With an indefinite pronoun that can be either singular or plural, agreement depends on the word to which the indefinite pronoun refers. In the first example below, *some* refers to part of the *document*, a singular noun. In the second example, *some* refers to part of the *students*, a plural noun.

EXAMPLES: *Some* of the document lost *its* formatting.
Some of the students printed *their* documents.

Exercise 21 **Making Personal Pronouns Agree With Indefinite Pronouns** On your paper, write a pronoun or pronouns to complete each sentence correctly.

EXAMPLE: Each of the students must have __?__ own password.

ANSWER: his or her

1. Software companies have profited greatly from __?__ word-processing programs.
2. Each of the editing features is valued for __?__ ability to help people save time.
3. For example, some text in a document can be cut; then, __?__ can be moved or copied as needed.
4. Few who do word processing make full use of the technology available to __?__.
5. Many are comfortable with basic computer tools, but __?__ don't want to figure out how to create tables.
6. Anyone who practices for a short time will find __?__ job easier.
7. Others improve __?__ computer skills by taking classes.
8. Practice and classes—both are helpful in __?__ own way.
9. Once somebody masters word processing, __?__ may want to go on to learn about charts and graphs.
10. Shouldn't every one of us explore __?__ computer programs thoroughly?

▲ Critical Viewing Use an indefinite pronoun in a sentence that describes the picture. What verb did you use? Why? **[Relate]**

Three Special Problems in Pronoun Agreement

When you use personal pronouns, make sure that they have antecedents that are clearly defined. Problems can occur when the antecedent is unstated or unclear or when the personal pronoun refers to the wrong antecedent.

KEY CONCEPT A personal pronoun requires an antecedent that is either stated or clearly understood. ■

POOR: The *program* was easy, but *they* didn't explain it clearly.

CORRECT: The *program* was easy, but *it* wasn't explained clearly.

More Practice

Language Lab CD-ROM
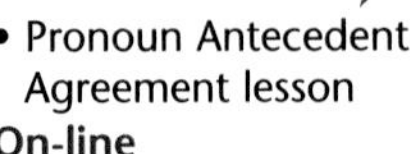
- Pronoun Antecedent Agreement lesson

On-line Exercise Bank
- Section 25.2

Grammar Exercise Workbook
- pp. 149–150

GRAMMAR IN LITERATURE

from The Road Ahead

Bill Gates

Bill Gates uses both the masculine and feminine pronouns (his or her) *to refer to the indefinite antecedent* anybody.

Before the invention of writing 5,000 years ago, the only form of communication was the spoken word and the listener had to be in the presence of the speaker or miss his message. Once the message could be written, it could be stored and read later by *anybody,* at *his* or *her* convenience. I'm writing these words at home on a summer evening, but I have no idea where or when you'll read them. One of the benefits the communications revolution will bring to all of us is more control over our schedules.

In the example on page 588, there is no antecedent for the pronoun *they*. The sentence can be corrected by replacing *they* with a noun or a personal pronoun that agrees with the antecedent *program.*

KEY CONCEPT A personal pronoun should always refer to a single, obvious antecedent. ■

If a pronoun can refer to more than one antecedent, the sentence should be rewritten.

POOR: I saw the *procedure* in the *manual,* but now I can't find *it.*

CORRECT: I saw the *procedure* in the *manual,* but now I can't find the *procedure.*
I can't find the *procedure* I saw in the *manual.*

POOR: When the *technician* adjusted the sound, the *musician* was pleased. Even so, *he* wasn't satisfied.

CORRECT: When the *technician* adjusted the sound, the *musician* was pleased. Even so, the *technician* wasn't satisfied.
When the *technician* adjusted the sound, *he* wasn't satisfied. Even so, the *musician* was pleased.

▲ Critical Viewing In what ways has communication changed during the last fifty years? **[Analyze]**

KEY CONCEPT Use the personal pronoun *you* only when the reference is truly to the reader or the listener. ■

POOR:	In a sound studio, *you* see high-tech equipment.
CORRECT:	In a sound studio, *one* sees high-tech equipment.
	In a sound studio, *there is* high-tech equipment.

Exercise 22 Recognizing Proper Pronoun Usage Identify the sentence that better follows the conventions of English usage of pronouns. Explain your choices.

1. (A) The concert was being held in the park, and we finally found it. (B) We finally found the park where the concert was being held.
2. (A) The sound was good, but they didn't play long enough. (B) The sound was good, but the musicians didn't play long enough.
3. (A) Everyone brought their own chair. (B) Everyone brought his or her own chair.
4. (A) The crowd was huge, but you could hear the music. (B) The crowd was huge, but everyone could hear the music.
5. (A) Next year, you should go to the concert. (B) Next year, he or she should go to the concert.

Exercise 23 Correcting Special Problems in Pronoun Agreement Revise the following paragraph, correcting all errors in pronoun and antecedent agreement.

(1) In sound recording, they convert acoustic energy into sound. (2) It can then be either stored or reproduced for later use. (3) Thomas Edison made improvements in recording in the late 1800's, when they invented a reproduction of audible sound. (4) Record players, which were the next great innovation, used an amplifier to magnify it. (5) In current recordings, you have the sound waves go into a microphone. (6) The microphone converts them into a signal that is recorded on tape. (7) If the engineer needs to, he or she can edit it. (8) You use laser technology to create compact discs. (9) Sound is written and read digitally without physical contact with them. (10) Motion picture recordings are called *optical* because they use a beam of light to create them.

More Practice

Language Lab CD-ROM
- Special Problems in Agreement lesson

On-line Exercise Bank
- Section 25.2

Grammar Exercise Workbook
- pp. 85–87

Section 25.2 **Section Review**

GRAMMAR EXERCISES 24–29

Exercise 24 **Correcting Errors in Pronoun-Antecedent Agreement** In the following sentences, most of the pronouns do not agree with their antecedents. Identify pronouns that do not agree. Then, write the correct form. If the sentence is correct, write *C*.

1. Anyone who has e-mail probably corresponds with their friends often.
2. Both Marissa and Tashina check their mailboxes every day.
3. Neither likes to open their mailbox to find that no one has written to them.
4. However, each of the girls always has messages waiting for them.
5. One feature of an e-mail program is their ability to store messages.

Exercise 25 **Correcting Special Problems in Pronoun-Antecedent Agreement** Rewrite the following paragraph, correcting the errors in pronoun and antecedent agreement. Not all sentences have errors.

(1) There is a little gray thing attached to every computer. (2) It is a device that is needed to operate it. (3) They call it a mouse. (4) A mouse is a small, gray object that you roll along a hard, flat surface. (5) The connecting wire looks like its tail. (6) You use a mouse to control the movement of the pointer on the screen. (7) As it moves, the pointer on the screen moves in the same direction. (8) Mice have at least one button and sometimes three. (9) They have different uses, depending on which program is running. (10) Some newer ones include a scroll wheel for scrolling through long documents quickly and easily.

Exercise 26 **Revision Practice: Pronoun Antecedent Agreement** Revise the following paragraph, correcting errors in pronoun and antecedent agreement.

(1) There are homes in America in which they don't watch much TV. (2) Instead, each family member spends their time on other activities. (3) This is much better for you. (4) One health expert reports that when someone stares at TV, they don't use their imagination. (5) National TV-Turnoff Week is sponsored by TV-Free America, and millions of Americans participate in it.

Exercise 27 **Find It in Your Reading** Reread the excerpt from Bill Gates's *The Road Ahead* on page 589. Find at least three personal pronouns, and write them down along with their antecedents.

Exercise 28 **Find It in Your Writing** Select a writing sample from your portfolio. On your draft, draw a circle around each pronoun and underline its antecedent. Finally, check to be sure that the pronouns and the antecedents agree.

Exercise 29 **Writing Application** Write an e-mail message in which you describe an event you attended with a friend. Make sure that each pronoun has a clear antecedent and that the pronouns and antecedents agree.

Chapter 26 Using Modifiers

▲ **Critical Viewing** Describe this Alaskan scenery using adjectives in comparative forms. **[Describe]**

On a hike through the forest, you may have to climb over some rocks. Some rocks are large, some are larger, and one is the largest rock you've ever seen. When comparing the size of rocks, we use modifying words to make our meaning more explicit. *Large, larger,* and *largest* help the reader understand these different sizes.

As you have learned, adjectives and adverbs modify other words. They are also used to make comparisons. You might say, for instance, that summer nights in a forest are *cool;* autumn nights, *cooler;* and winter nights, *coolest.* Notice that in using the word *cool,* you change the form depending on whether two or more things are being compared.

In this chapter, you will learn how to use adjectives and adverbs correctly in comparisons.

Diagnostic Test

Directions: Write all answers on a separate sheet of paper.

Skill Check A. In each line, one form of the adjective or adverb is missing. Write the missing word on your paper.

	Positive	Comparative	Superlative
1.	green	greener	
2.	dense		densest
3.		shadier	shadiest
4.	wet	wetter	
5.	good		best
6.		more rapidly	most rapidly
7.	leafy		leafiest
8.	many	more	
9.		warmer	warmest
10.	complex		most complex

Skill Check B. Select the correct form of the adjective or adverb in parentheses, and write it on your paper.

11. A forest is a (large, larger, largest) area of land where the main plants are trees.
12. Evergreen forests of cone-bearing trees are located in the regions (far, farther, farthest) north in North America.
13. In southern Canada and the eastern United States, where the weather is (warm, warmer, warmest), broadleaf forests are common.
14. In the fall, broadleaf trees—such as maples, beeches, oaks, and hickories—are (colorful, more colorful, most colorful) than cone-bearing trees, which stay green.
15. The (moist, moister, moistest) air of the west coast of North America provides an ideal climate for temperate rain forests.

Skill Check C. Write the appropriate comparative or superlative form of the modifier in parentheses.

16. The redwood is the (tall) tree in the forest.
17. It grows (fast) in wet climates than in dry climates.
18. Which of the two trees grows (good)?
19. The trees in Costa Rica are (far) from the United States than are the trees in Guatemala.
20. Central America has the (strange) trees in the world.

Skill Check D. Rewrite each sentence, correcting the unbalanced or illogical comparison.

21. Central America's rain forests are more numerous than North America.
22. The eye of a lizard is larger than a frog.
23. Southern Mexico's forests are more lush than any I've visited.
24. The expedition leader had traveled more miles than anyone I know.
25. This mountain is steepest than any in the area.

Section 26.1 Degrees of Comparison

Often, instead of simply describing something, you may want to compare it with something else. There are three *degrees*, or forms, of adjectives and adverbs that are used to modify and make comparisons.

KEY CONCEPT Most adjectives and adverbs have different forms to show degrees of comparison. ■

Recognizing Degrees of Comparison

In order to make comparisons, you need to know the three degrees of comparison.

KEY CONCEPT The three degrees of comparison are the *positive*, the *comparative*, and the *superlative*. ■

EXAMPLES: cold colder coldest
possible more possible most possible

The following chart lists the three degrees of some common adjectives and adverbs. As you can see, the *comparative* and *superlative* degrees of modifiers are formed in various ways. With the adjective *high*, for example, an *-er* is added for the comparative degree and an *-est* is added for the superlative, while *more* and *most* are used with the adjective *eager*.

ADJECTIVES		
Positive	**Comparative**	**Superlative**
high	higher	highest
eager	more eager	most eager
ADVERBS		
Positive	**Comparative**	**Superlative**
early	earlier	earliest
eagerly	more eagerly	most eagerly
well	better	best

Theme: Nature

In this section, you will learn how to form the comparative and superlative degrees of modifiers. The examples and exercises in this section are about the beauty of nature.

Cross-Curricular Connection: Science

Spelling Tip

When adding *-er* or *-est* to words ending in *y*, change the *y* to an *i*. For example, *dry* becomes *drier* and *driest*, and *sunny* becomes *sunnier* and *sunniest*.

Exercise 1 **Recognizing Positive, Comparative, and Superlative Degrees** Identify the degree of each underlined modifier.

EXAMPLE: That tree is the <u>tallest</u> tree in my yard.
ANSWER: superlative

1. Thousands of years ago, the only nonforested areas of the Earth were those where the land was the <u>driest</u>.
2. In areas where the environment was <u>more favorable</u>, forests extended from the equator to the far north.
3. Forests expanded by moving into formerly <u>icy</u> regions.
4. However, forests are <u>rapidly</u> declining, as clearing by humans and fire outpace the natural expansion of forest regions.
5. About 30 percent of the world is forested today, the <u>lowest</u> percentage ever.

▲ **Critical Viewing** Describe the colors in this photograph using at least three superlatives. **[Describe]**

Regular Forms

Modifiers are either regular or irregular. The comparative and superlative degrees of most regular adjectives and adverbs are formed using one of two rules. The first rule applies to modifiers with one or two syllables.

KEY CONCEPT Use *-er* or *more* to form the comparative degree and *-est* or *most* to form the superlative degree of most one- and two-syllable modifiers. ■

The more common method for forming the comparative and superlative degrees of one- and two-syllable modifiers is to add *-er* and *-est* to the modifier rather than to use *more* and *most.*

EXAMPLES:	green	greener	greenest
	dark	darker	darkest

More and *most* are used with one- and two-syllable modifiers when adding *-er* or *-est* would sound awkward. Notice that the words below would sound awkward with *-er* or *-est.*

EXAMPLES:	crisp	more crisp	most crisp
	humid	more humid	most humid

To form the comparative and superlative degrees of adverbs that end with the suffix *-ly*, use *more* and *most.*

EXAMPLES:	quickly	more quickly	most quickly
	smoothly	more smoothly	most smoothly

KEY CONCEPT Use *more* and *most* to form the comparative and superlative degrees of all modifiers with three or more syllables. ■

EXAMPLES: popular | more popular | most popular

Note About *Comparisons With Less and Least:* *Less* and *least,* the opposite of *more* and *most,* can be used to form the comparative and superlative degrees of most modifiers.

EXAMPLES:

favorable	less favorable	least favorable
quickly	less quickly	least quickly

Exercise 2 **Forming Regular Comparative and Superlative Degrees** Write the comparative and the superlative forms of each modifier.

1. tall 2. ancient 3. difficult 4. new 5. strong
6. beautiful 7. noisy 8. slowly 9. shiny 10. odd

More Practice
On-line Exercise Bank
• Section 26.1
Grammar Exercise Workbook
• pp. 151–154

Irregular Forms

KEY CONCEPT Memorize the irregular comparative and superlative forms of certain adjectives and adverbs. ■

The most commonly used irregular modifiers are listed in the following chart. Notice that some modifiers differ only in the positive degree. For instance, the modifiers *bad, badly,* and *ill* all have the same comparative and superlative forms (*worse, worst*).

IRREGULAR MODIFIERS

Positive	Comparative	Superlative
bad	worse	worst
badly	worse	worst
far (distance)	farther	farthest
far (extent)	further	furthest
good	better	best
ill	worse	worst
late	later	last or latest
little (amount)	less	least
many	more	most
much	more	most
well	better	best

GRAMMAR IN LITERATURE

from Children in the Woods

Barry Lopez

The writer has used comparative and superlative modifiers. Most moving *is superlative,* heavily *and* wet *are positive,* older *is comparative.*

The most moving look I ever saw from a child in the woods was on a mud bar by the footprints of a heron. We were on our knees, making handprints beside the footprints. You could feel the creek vibrating in the silt and sand. The sun beat down heavily on our hair. Our shoes were soaking wet. The look said: I did not know until now that I needed someone much older to confirm this, the feeling I have of life here. I can now grow older, knowing it need never be lost.

Grammar and Style Tip

You can make comparisons to help your readers understand your exact meaning. The right forms of adjectives and adverbs will help you add color and depth to your writing.

Exercise 3 **Forming Irregular Comparative and Superlative Degrees** Write the comparative and the superlative degree of each modifier.

EXAMPLE: little
ANSWER: less, least

1. bad
2. good
3. far
4. much
5. well

▶ **Critical Viewing** Use the superlative degree of adjectives in sentences to compare the trees in this photograph of Alaskan scenery. **[Compare and Contrast]**

Exercise 4 Using Comparative and Superlative Degrees Correctly Rewrite each sentence, replacing the modifier in italics with the comparative or superlative degree indicated in brackets. You may need to add *the* before some superlatives.

EXAMPLE: This year had *little* rainfall. [superlative]
ANSWER: This year had the least rainfall.

1. A woodland differs from a forest in that it consists of *small*, more widely separated trees. [comparative]
2. Woodlands form a transition between *moist* conifer forests and *dry* grasslands or deserts. [comparative]
3. Western forests and woodlands also cover a *wide* variety of terrains, which enhances their beauty: mountains, canyons and mesas, and cliffs and headlands. [superlative]
4. The forests in the western United States boast *large*, *tall*, and *old* trees. [superlative]
5. Fire can have a *devastating* effect on a forest, but it is not always considered a tragedy. [superlative]
6. Native Americans periodically set ground fires to clear out the underbrush to provide *good* forage conditions for big game. [comparative, irregular]
7. Forests that have developed over *long* periods without catastrophic disturbance of either natural or human origin are known as old-growth forests. [superlative]
8. Old-growth forests are *complex* and *beautiful* than many young forests. [comparative]
9. Old-growth forests are important because they provide some of the *good* wildlife habitats, recreation areas, and commercial timber. [superlative, irregular]
10. Because of their great commercial value, *many* old-growth forests have been eliminated, except for those in national parks and wilderness areas. [superlative, irregular]

More Practice

On-line Exercise Bank
• Section 26.1
Grammar Exercise Workbook
• pp. 151–154

Critical Viewing Compare this Alaskan forest with your own backyard or neighborhood. **[Compare and Contrast]**

Section **26.1** Section Review

GRAMMAR EXERCISES 5–10

Exercise 5 Identifying Positive, Comparative, and Superlative Degrees
Identify the degree of each underlined modifier.

1. Temperatures within the forest are often <u>cooler</u> than in nearby open areas.
2. The canopy blocks the sunlight, resulting in <u>lower</u> temperatures on the forest floor.
3. At night, however, the forest remains <u>warmer</u> than in open areas.
4. Plants in the forest are <u>less</u> subject to frost damage than those in the open.
5. Mature forest conifers often shed their <u>lowest</u> limbs.
6. The <u>warmest</u> rain forests produce their own rain beneath the forest canopy.
7. Mosses are everywhere in <u>damper</u> forests, forming plush carpets.
8. Each plant in the forest functions to its <u>best</u> ecological capabilities.
9. Some plant species have so <u>completely</u> adapted to life in the forest that they never occur outside it.
10. Mammals of the forest tend to be <u>darkly</u> pigmented.

Exercise 6 Forming Regular Comparative and Superlative Degrees
Write sentences using the comparative and the superlative form of each modifier.

1. shady
2. mossy
3. late
4. chilly
5. humid
6. rare
7. far
8. remote
9. dense
10. spectacular

Exercise 7 Supplying Comparative and Superlative Degrees Rewrite each sentence, replacing the modifier in italics with the degree indicated. You may need to add *the* before some superlatives.

1. All visitors to the forest should take precautions to ensure the *safe* visit possible. (superlative)
2. The *good* times for viewing birds and mammals are near dawn and dusk. (superlative)
3. The best place to see birds is in an area that is *much* open. (comparative)
4. One is *likely* to see animals by sitting quietly in one place for a time than by walking around. (comparative)
5. *Many* experts say not to feed or tease animals in the forest. (superlative)
6. It is *safe* not to approach baby animals. (comparative)
7. Cleaning up after meals is *effective* in discouraging bears. (superlative)
8. Insects can be *troublesome* pests in the forest. (superlative)
9. Learn to recognize the *unpleasant* plants and avoid them. (comparative)
10. When traveling in a forest, it is *good* to have a map and a compass. (comparative)

Exercise 8 Find It in Your Reading
Read a description in a travel magazine. Find five examples of modifiers used in the comparative and superlative degrees.

Exercise 9 Find It in Your Writing
Review your portfolio, and find examples of comparative and superlative modifiers. Make sure you have used them correctly.

Exercise 10 Writing Application
Write five sentences comparing places you have visited. In each sentence, include at least one modifying adjective or adverb. Underline the modifier, and identify it as positive, comparative, or superlative.

Section 26.2 Making Clear Comparisons

The problems you are likely to have with comparisons generally involve using the wrong degree, comparing unrelated things, or comparing something with itself.

In this section, you will learn how to make clear and balanced comparisons. The examples and exercises in this section are about theater, dance, and opera.

Cross-Curricular Connection: Performing Arts

Using Comparative and Superlative Degrees

There are two simple rules to keep in mind in order to use the correct degree of comparison:

KEY CONCEPTS Use the comparative degree to compare two people, places, or things. Use the superlative degree to compare three or more people, places, or things. ■

Notice in the following examples that it is not necessary to mention specific numbers when making a comparison.

COMPARATIVE: Steve is *more creative* than Michael.
The stage is *closer* to us than the exit.
My costume is *more colorful* than hers.

SUPERLATIVE: Sue is the *most creative* pupil in our class.
That door is the *closest* exit to our seats.
Of the costumes in the play, Teresa's is the *most colorful.*

Note About *Double Comparisons:* A double comparison is an error caused by using both *-er* and *more* to form the comparative degree or both *-est* and *most* to form the superlative. It can also be caused by adding any of these endings or words to an irregular modifier.

INCORRECT: Amy is *more smarter* than I.
Jim's acting is *worser* than Jon's.

CORRECT: Amy is *smarter* than I.
Jim's acting is *worse* than Jon's.

▶ Critical Viewing Compare and contrast the positions of the actors on the stage. **[Compare and Contrast]**

Exercise 11 **Using the Comparative and Superlative Degrees Correctly** Choose the correct comparative or superlative form in parentheses to complete each sentence.

EXAMPLE: Acting is (more, most) complicated than it may appear on stage.

ANSWER: more

1. The history of the performing arts begins with one of the (more, most) ancient sources of Western civilization, the culture of ancient Greece.
2. Some of the (earlier, earliest) plays still performed were written by the Greeks more than 2,500 years ago.
3. Of the two types of plays written and performed by the Greeks, tragedies were (more, most) serious than comedies.
4. The (more, most) common subjects of Greek tragedy were the myths, which emphasized moral issues.
5. Present-day historians believe that (more, most) of a play was chanted, or sung.

More Practice

On-line Exercise Bank
- Section 26.2

Grammar Exercise Workbook
- pp. 155–158

Exercise 12 **Supplying the Comparative and Superlative Degrees** Write the appropriate comparative or superlative degree of the modifier in parentheses.

EXAMPLE: Of the two types of plays, tragedy is (intense).

ANSWER: more intense

1. While tragedy produced the (wide) variety of responses, comedy always invoked laughter.
2. The masks of Greek comedy were (ugly) and (silly) than those of tragedies.
3. Greek comedy employed a (great) amount of speech than tragedy, but the chorus was often sung.
4. Comedy deals with (humorous) subjects than tragedy, such as the quirks of daily living and trivial problems.
5. The Greek dramas that flourished in the 500's and 400's B.C. have had the (great) influence on Western drama.
6. When the Romans conquered Greece, they adapted Greek texts to depict even (glorious) tales of Rome.
7. During the Middle Ages, the (common) subjects of plays were saints and characters from the Bible.
8. The (great) and (influential) playwright was William Shakespeare, who wrote in the late 1500's and early 1600's.
9. Even though music and singing had been incorporated into plays in (early) times, people began writing plays in which the characters only sang.
10. In a (late) time period, the French planned stage productions using dancers who did not speak at all.

Balanced Comparisons

Whenever you write a comparison, you must check the sentence to make sure that the things being compared are properly balanced. Otherwise, you may compare two or more items that cannot logically be compared.

KEY CONCEPT Make sure that your sentences compare only items of a similar kind. ■

The following examples show unbalanced sentences. These sentences are illogical because they unintentionally compare dissimilar things. An audition cannot be compared to a person, and the blade of a sword cannot be compared to an entire sword.

UNBALANCED: *Joe's audition* was more dramatic than *Ken.*
CORRECT: *Joe's audition* was more dramatic than *Ken's.*

UNBALANCED: The *blade of a sword* is longer than a *dagger.*
CORRECT: The *blade of a sword* is longer than a *dagger's.*

Exercise 13 Revising to Eliminate Errors in Comparisons

Rewrite each sentence, correcting the unbalanced comparison.

EXAMPLE: Dancing's effect on an audience is just as significant as music.

ANSWER: Dancing's effect on an audience is just as significant as *music's.*

1. Dance's origins go back even farther than theater.
2. When a dance is performed more for the audience's pleasure than for the dancer, it is considered theatrical dance.
3. Around 1400, the reigning princes of the Italian states used theatrical dance as a way to proclaim that their courts' brilliance and taste exceeded their neighbor.
4. The first ballet that combined movement, music, décor, and special effects only vaguely resembled today.
5. Even though the steps differed little, the earliest ballet steps were more polished and studied than ballroom steps.
6. Early ballet's format varied slightly from opera.
7. Later, ballet moved from the ballroom to the theater, and the professional's role replaced the court member.
8. Dancing was considered an art of the gentleman, but women's importance as choreographers rivaled men.
9. The choreographer's role may be more significant than the dancer.
10. Women's roles in court ballets were minimal compared to men until 1681.

Spelling Tip

Many words in the English language have more than one acceptable spelling. *Theater* and *theatre* is an example. It is best to use the same spelling of a word consistently throughout any one piece of writing. The preferred spelling of a word is listed first in the dictionary entry. *Theater* is the preferred spelling.

Other and *Else* in Comparisons

Another common error in making a comparison is to compare something with itself.

KEY CONCEPT When comparing one of a group with the rest of the group, make sure that your sentence contains the word *other* or the word *else.* ■

Adding *other* or *else* in these situations will prevent comparing something with itself. For example, because Shakespeare was one English playwright, he cannot logically be compared to all English playwrights. He must be compared to all *other* English playwrights.

ILLOGICAL: Shakespeare was *greater than any* English playwright.
CORRECT: Shakespeare was *greater than any other* English playwright.

ILLOGICAL: I had more *lines than anyone* in the play.
CORRECT: I had more *lines than anyone else* in the play.

Exercise 14 **Using *Other* and *Else* in Comparisons** Rewrite each sentence, correcting the illogical comparison.

EXAMPLE: Beth is a better dancer than anyone in class.
ANSWER: Beth is a better dancer than anyone *else* in class.

1. Opera is different from any art form.
2. From the earliest times, civilized humans have conveyed drama through music as much as any art form.
3. My knowledge of Greek drama is greater than any knowledge I have.
4. As opera evolved, Greek tragedy demonstrated a greater influence on opera than on any art form.
5. During the Middle Ages, theater became less musical because it cost more to train a singer than any performer.
6. King Louis XIV loved to participate in the court entertainment of dance and music more than anyone.
7. The "pre-operatic" theater was entertainment that was available to royal courts more than to anyone.
8. During the Renaissance, Italy, more than any country, claimed to be home to all the arts.
9. In the early operas, music was secondary to any characteristic of the play.
10. The opera *Euridice,* more than any opera, is considered to be the earliest that has survived intact.

More Practice

On-line Exercise Bank
- Section 26.2

Grammar Exercise Workbook
- pp. 155–158

26.2

Hands-on Grammar

Comparison-Star Standout

A common error in making a comparison is to compare something with itself. With this exercise, you will illustrate how one stands out from the group in a comparison.

1. Cut a 3" circle. Put slots in it as shown in the illustration. On the circle above the slots, write *all the other.*
2. Cut a long strip of paper to feed through the slots in the circle. On it, write names of groups you will be comparing, such as *actors, writers, dancers, teachers, boys, girls,* and *students.* Space out the words so that they will show through the window.
3. Cut out seven stars. On each of the stars, write the person you want to compare with all the others.
4. Cut out seven strips of paper, each approximately 3" long and 1/2" wide. On each strip of paper, write the comparison. For example, *is more graceful than, is smarter than,* or *is nicer than.*
5. Fold each strip of paper up like an accordion. Attach one end to the star and the other end to the circle with pieces of tape.
6. Now, slide your strip of paper through the slots to make a balanced and logical comparison. For example, *George is more graceful than all the other dancers.*
7. Illustrate the following sentences:

   Mrs. Dardis is nicer than all the other teachers.
   Sam is smarter than all the other students.

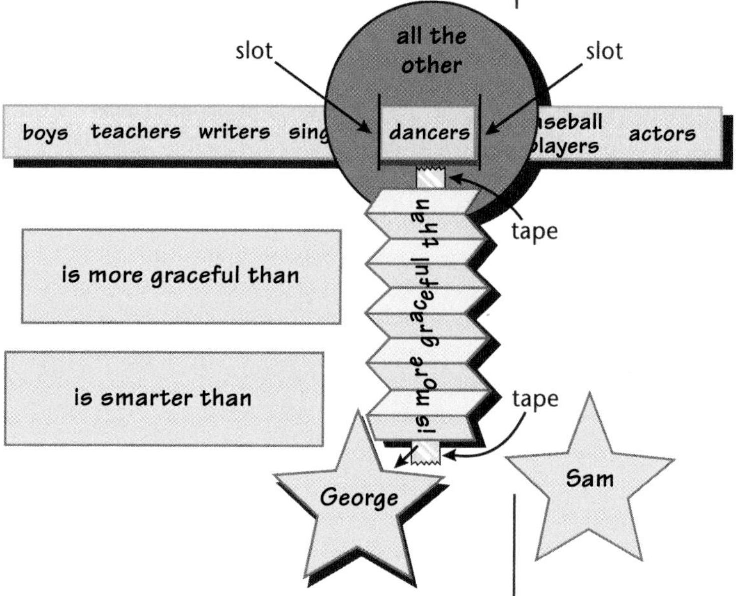

Find It in Your Reading Find some comparisons in your reading that compare one person with a group. Illustrate your comparisons.

Find It in Your Writing Review a piece of your writing that has comparatives in it. Make sure that you have used balanced and logical comparisons and that you have not compared something with itself.

Section 26.2 **Section Review**

GRAMMAR EXERCISES 15–20

Exercise 15 **Using Degrees of Modifiers Correctly** Choose the correct comparative or superlative form in parentheses to complete each sentence.

1. Many experts agree that Shakespeare wrote with (great, greater, greatest) wisdom than any other writer.
2. Shakespeare found the (more interesting, most interesting) stories for his plays in history books.
3. In *Macbeth*, a Scottish noble, whose (deep, deeper, deepest) desire is to be king, kills the ruling king.
4. Critics regard *The Tragedy of King Lear* as Shakespeare's (greater, greatest) work.
5. *Hamlet* kills his stepfather, who had (earlier, earliest) murdered Hamlet's father and taken his throne.

Exercise 16 **Supplying the Comparative and Superlative Degrees** Write the appropriate comparative or superlative degree of the modifier in parentheses.

1. Although Shakespeare died nearly 400 years ago, his plays are among those (often) read and performed.
2. Even the (bad) actor will learn to recognize at least one Shakespearean character.
3. Shakespeare's popularity as a playwright is unequaled by even the (good) modern-day writer.
4. His plays still command some of the (large) number of ticket sales.
5. The movie *West Side Story* is one of the (successful) modern versions of Shakespeare's *Romeo and Juliet.*

Exercise 17 **Revising to Eliminate Errors in Comparisons** Rewrite each sentence, correcting the unbalanced or illogical comparison.

1. In most of Shakespeare's tragedies, the hero's role is more significant than the heroine.
2. However, Juliet's role is equally as important as Romeo.
3. *Twelfth Night* is more musical than any Shakespeare play.
4. Lady Macbeth's character is colder and more cruel than Macbeth.
5. It is said that Shakespeare's comedies are more difficult to act than any of his plays.

Exercise 18 **Find It in Your Reading** Read the following from Romeo and Juliet. Explain why this is a logical comparison.

. . . That which we call a rose
By any other name would smell as sweet.

Exercise 19 **Find It in Your Writing** Look through your portfolio. Find examples of comparisons. Make sure that your comparisons are logical and balanced.

Exercise 20 **Writing Application** Write a logical and balanced comparison for each item below.

1. you and your father
2. a dog and a cat
3. an apple and an orange
4. two basketball teams
5. two flowers

Chapter 27 Miscellaneous Problems in Usage

▲ **Critical Viewing** Use negative sentences to explain how this crab is different from a mammal such as a dog. **[Distinguish]**

In addition to the usage problems you have already studied, certain other words and expressions can sometimes cause problems for writers.

Consider this sentence: *There ain't no creatures who are more beautiful and fascinating then those living under the sea.* The sentence contains common usage errors. Written correctly, it could say: *There aren't any creatures that are more beautiful and fascinating than those living under the sea.*

This chapter discusses usage problems that have not been presented earlier. You will learn how to form negative sentences correctly, and you will examine a list of troublesome words and expressions.

Diagnostic Test

Directions: Write all answers on a separate sheet of paper.

Skill Check A. Choose the word in parentheses that best completes each sentence.

1. Many people won't eat (no, any) fish, even if it is fresh.
2. Sardines don't eat (nothing, anything) except zooplankton.
3. The fish don't have (no, any) spines on their heads.
4. Unless it is between noon and sunset, sardines won't eat (nothing, anything).
5. Sardines do not eat their own eggs because they don't lay (no, any) eggs in the deep, cold water where they feed.
6. Although crabs are closely related to lobsters, they don't walk (nothing, anything) like the way lobsters do.
7. Crabs don't do (none, any) of their walking forward or backward; they walk sideways.
8. Don't go (nowhere, anywhere) near the pincers of an angry crab.
9. A crab doesn't have (no, any) skeleton inside its body.
10. A hermit crab doesn't have (no, any) shell.

Skill Check B. Choose the correct word to complete each sentence.

11. Hermit crabs (adopt, adapt) abandoned snail shells.
12. Hermit crabs use (they're, their, there) enlarged right claw to defend themselves.
13. Crabs have (too, to, two) sensory antennae.
14. Crabs can burrow (anywheres, anywhere) in the sandy bottom.
15. (Being as, Because) the lobster has an external skeleton like the crab, it must shed its shell to grow.
16. The lobster (don't, doesn't) eat during the day; it eats at night.
17. The (farther, further) from shore, the fewer lobsters you'll find.
18. If you look (in, into) the stomach of a lobster, you can find small invertebrates or algae.
19. (That there, That) lobster is tasty.
20. I have a friend in Australia (who, which) calls lobsters "crayfish."

Skill Check C. Rewrite each sentence, correcting any usage problems that you find. If the sentence is correct as is, write *correct.*

21. Buried in the mud or sand is where you can find ghost shrimp.
22. She never seen a ghost shrimp.
23. Ghost shrimp have a positive effect on the marine ecosystem.
24. Due to burrowing by the ghost shrimp, the amount of oxygen in the sediment increases.
25. Beside being an important resource under the sea, the ghost shrimp is used as bait by those who fish.
26. There are similarities between shrimp, lobsters, and crabs.
27. We set down at a seafood restaurant for a meal of shrimp.
28. We tasted the shrimp and decided they were cooked bad.
29. The reason the shrimp tasted funny was because of the sauce.
30. Since we had all ready paid for them, we ate the shrimp.

Section 27.1

Negative Sentences

Negative words, such as *not* or *never,* are used to deny or to refuse something. Only one negative word is necessary in a sentence to make the sentence negative.

Recognize Double Negatives

A *double negative* is the use of two negative words in a sentence when one is sufficient.

KEY CONCEPT Do not use double negatives in sentences. ■

The chart below provides examples of double negatives and the two ways that each might be corrected.

CORRECTING DOUBLE NEGATIVES	
Double Negatives	**Corrections**
Starfish *don't* bother *no one.*	Starfish *don't* bother *anyone.* Starfish bother *no one.*
I *haven't* seen *no* whales.	I *haven't* seen *any* whales. I have seen *no* whales.
Tom *never* said *nothing.*	Tom *never* said *anything.* Tom said *nothing.*

Exercise 1 **Avoiding Double Negatives** Choose the word in parentheses that best completes each sentence.

EXAMPLE: There aren't (no, any) biomes that occupy more of the Earth's surface than aquatic biomes.

ANSWER: any

1. Scientists can't classify (no, any) protists as exclusively animals or exclusively plants because protists have characteristics of both groups.
2. Brown algae are not found (nowhere, anywhere) on land; they are found in cold ocean waters.
3. Green algae won't live (nowhere, anywhere) that has a dry climate because they depend on water for survival.
4. There isn't (no, any) ice cream that does not contain red algae.
5. We could not see (none, any) of the single-celled golden algae, or diatoms, without a microscope.

Theme: Marine Life

In this section, you will learn to form negative sentences correctly. The examples and exercises in this section are about marine life, including algae, coral, and sharks.

Cross-Curricular Connection: Science

More Practice

Language Lab CD-ROM
- Problems With Modifiers

On-line Exercise Bank
- Section 27.1

Grammar Exercise Workbook
- pp. 159–160

Form Negative Sentences Correctly

There are three common ways to form negative sentences:

Using One Negative Word The most common way to make a statement negative is to use one negative word, such as *never, no, nobody, none, not, nothing,* or *nowhere.*

▲ **Critical Viewing** Write three sentences that discuss the variety of life in a coral reef using the words *barely, hardly,* and *scarcely.* **[Analyze]**

KEY CONCEPT Do not use two negative words in the same clause. ■

Using two negative words in the same clause will result in a double negative.

DOUBLE NEGATIVE: We *don't* want *no* help from you.
CORRECT: We *don't* want any help from you.
We want *no* help from you.

Using *But* in a Negative Sense When *but* means "only," it generally acts as a negative. Do not use it with another negative word.

DOUBLE NEGATIVE: There *wasn't but* one whale at the park.
CORRECT: There was *but* one whale at the park.

Using *Barely, Hardly,* and *Scarcely* All three of these words are negative.

KEY CONCEPT Do not use *barely, hardly,* or *scarcely* with another negative. ■

DOUBLE NEGATIVE: The dull-gray coral *wasn't barely* visible in the dim light.
CORRECT: The dull-gray coral was *barely* visible in the dim light.

DOUBLE NEGATIVE: We *didn't scarcely* recognize the bright fluorescent coral in the ultraviolet light.
CORRECT: We *scarcely* recognized the bright fluorescent coral in the ultraviolet light.

DOUBLE NEGATIVE: I *couldn't hardly* believe the beauty of the coral when it was illuminated with ultraviolet light.
CORRECT: I could *hardly* believe the beauty of the coral when it was illuminated with ultraviolet light.

Exercise 2 **Avoiding Problems With Negatives** Fill in the blank to make each sentence negative without forming a double negative.

EXAMPLE: Jon __?__ hardly believe he had caught such an odd-looking fish.

ANSWER: could

1. The anglerfish, camouflaged to look like the algae, could not be found __?__ by the photographer.
2. The anglerfish lives on the ocean floor where there __?__ barely any light.
3. When a frogfish enters a bed of algae, other fishes cannot see __?__ trace of it.
4. The anglerfish __?__ hardly be able to hunt for food without its dorsal fin, which glows in the dark.
5. The anglerfish __?__ scarcely eat for days after consuming such a large meal.

Exercise 3 **Revising to Eliminate Double Negatives** On a separate sheet of paper, rewrite each sentence, correcting the double negative.

EXAMPLE: Sharks don't have no bones.

ANSWER: Sharks don't have any bones.

1. Unless they are disturbed, sharks will not attack nobody.
2. The whale shark, the largest fish, does not eat nothing but plankton and small fish.
3. The great white shark doesn't usually attack no person unless it confuses the person for a sea lion or seal.
4. The skeptic would not believe nobody who told him that the great white shark can grow up to 25 feet long and weigh 7,300 pounds.
5. The bull shark will attack with hardly no provocation.
6. These animals often live in shallow inlets and rivers where they can't hardly be seen because of the murky water.
7. Reports about the blue shark indicate that a swimmer couldn't hardly count on being safe around these creatures.
8. Blue sharks cannot scarcely be seen from above or below because their skin is blue on top and white underneath.
9. There isn't nothing that you couldn't find in the stomach of a tiger shark; household objects have even been found.
10. Swimmers were not given no chance to survive the attack of the fierce-looking sand tiger sharks.

More Practice

Language Lab CD-ROM
- Problems With Modifiers

On-line Exercise Bank
- Section 27.1

Grammar Exercise Workbook
- pp. 159–160

▼ Critical Viewing Imagine seeing this blue shark in the wild. Use negative sentences in a description of your encounter. **[Speculate]**

Section 27.1 Section Review

GRAMMAR EXERCISES 4–9

Exercise 4 Avoiding Double Negatives Choose the word in parentheses that best completes each sentence.

1. The horseshoe crab is (nothing, anything) like a typical crab.
2. This marine animal hasn't (no, any) living relatives.
3. While it has positive medical uses, no one says (nothing, anything) positive about eating horseshoe-crab meat.
4. They may look frightening, but there isn't (nothing, anything) dangerous about horseshoe crabs.
5. They are not used (nowhere, anywhere) for fertilizer anymore.

Exercise 5 Revising Sentences to Correct Double Negatives Rewrite each sentence, correcting the double negative. If there is no double negative, write *correct.*

1. Without no shell, the octopus must rely on other resources for protection.
2. Prey can't scarcely tell the difference between an octopus's arm and a worm.
3. If not for large, complex eyes, the octopus wouldn't be able to locate nothing.
4. There is not hardly any other animal in the sea that has a nervous system as complex as that of the octopus.
5. They squeeze between rocks so that they are not easy targets for predators.
6. Because of their camouflage, a hidden octopus cannot barely be seen.
7. If an octopus is firmly attached to a rock, there isn't no way to pull it off.
8. An octopus will not never have fewer than eight legs because new legs grow in to replace lost ones.
9. Most octopuses cannot live no longer than about three years.
10. Many young octopuses cannot protect themselves and are eaten by fish.

Exercise 6 Revising a Paragraph to Avoid Problems With Negatives Revise the following, correcting any errors in double negatives.

The giant red mysid, a shrimplike animal, cannot be seen by nothing underwater. Although it appears as bright red to humans, it is not perceived that way by no underwater life. There isn't no mysid bigger than the giant red mysid. Where red mysids live, there aren't but low levels of oxygen. The animal defends itself by releasing a bioluminescent fluid. Attackers can't hardly see through the fluid and are unable to find their prey.

Exercise 7 Find It in Your Reading Review newspaper and magazine articles to find examples of correct usage of negatives. Write down five examples in your notebook.

Exercise 8 Find It in Your Writing Review several pieces of writing from your portfolio, checking for double negatives. If necessary, revise them to correct any problems with double negatives.

Exercise 9 Writing Application Write a paragraph describing two people scuba-diving in a warm tropical sea. Use at least five of the following words. Be sure to avoid double negatives.

nothing	didn't	never
shouldn't	hardly	hadn't
not	couldn't	scarcely

Section 27.2

Common Usage Problems

This section provides a list of forty-one usage problems arranged in alphabetical order.

KEY CONCEPT Study the items in this glossary, paying particular attention to similar meanings and spellings. ■

(1) accept, except *Accept* is a verb meaning "to receive." *Except* is a preposition meaning "other than."

VERB: I *accept* your gift gratefully.

PREPOSITION: Everyone *except* Craig was at the dance.

(2) adapt, adopt *Adapt* means "to change." *Adopt* means "to take as one's own."

EXAMPLES: The frogfish *adapts* its appearance to blend into its environment.
The young man *adopted* his hero's style of dress.

(3) affect, effect *Affect* is almost always a verb meaning "to influence." *Effect*, usually a noun, means "result." Occasionally, *effect* is a verb meaning "to bring about" or "to cause."

VERB: The President's speech deeply *affected* me.

NOUN: Scientists study the *effects* of nuclear radiation.

VERB: The Student Council *effected* many changes.

(4) ain't *Ain't* was originally a contraction of *am not.* It is not considered standard English.

NONSTANDARD: Anglerfish *ain't* easy to find or identify.

CORRECT: Anglerfish *aren't* easy to find or identify.

(5) all ready, already The two words *all ready* are used as an adjective meaning "ready." *Already* is an adverb meaning "by or before this time" or "even now."

ADJECTIVE: I am *all ready* to go scuba-diving.

ADVERB: I have *already* checked my gear.

(6) all right, alright *Alright*, though it is seen more and more frequently in print, is not considered a correct spelling.

NONSTANDARD: That new album is *alright.*

CORRECT: He is feeling *all right* today.

(7) all together, altogether These two adverbs have different meanings. *All together* means "together as a group." *Altogether* means "completely" or "in all."

Theme: Marine Animals

In this section, you will learn about forty-one common usage problems. The examples and exercises in this section are about marine animals such as octopuses, dolphins, and rays.

Cross-Curricular Connection: Science

Spelling Tip

When you refer to many fish of the same species, use the word *fish*. If you want to refer to many fish of different species, use the word *fishes*.

EXAMPLES: Fish in a school travel *all together.*
The old television set finally broke *altogether.*

(8) among, between *Among* and *between* are both prepositions. *Among* always implies three or more. *Between* is generally used only with two.

EXAMPLES: The fish swam *among* the coral.
The surfers passed *between* two sharks.

(9) anywhere, everywhere, nowhere, somewhere None of these adverbs should ever end with an *-s.*

NONSTANDARD: The child lost the money *somewheres.*
CORRECT: The child lost the money *somewhere.*

(10) at Do not use *at* after *where.* Simply eliminate it.

NONSTANDARD: Can you tell me *where* to catch crabs *at?*
CORRECT: Can you tell me *where* to catch crabs?

(11) awhile, a while *Awhile* is used as an adverb and is never preceded by a preposition. *A while* is the word *while* used as a noun, and it is usually preceded by a preposition like *after, for,* or *in.*

ADVERB: Lie down *awhile* and rest.
NOUN: For *a while* he lay still without moving.

(12) bad, badly *Bad* is an adjective meaning "defective," "hurtful," or "ill." It cannot be used after an action verb. *Badly* cannot be used as an adjective, but it can be used as an adverb after an action verb.

ADJECTIVE: Fishing without a license is a *bad* idea.
We felt *bad* after a long day in the cold.
ADVERB: Despite much practice, she played *badly.*

▲ **Critical Viewing** Using the words *among* and *between,* write three sentences about the fish in this picture. **[Analyze]**

(13) because Do not use *because* after *the reason.* Say "The reason . . . is that" or reword the sentence altogether.

NONSTANDARD: *The reason* the fish were eaten is *because* they did not swim fast enough.
CORRECT: *The reason* the fish were eaten is *that* they did not swim fast enough.
The fish were eaten *because* they did not swim fast enough.

(14) being as, being that Avoid using both expressions. Use *because* or *since* instead.

NONSTANDARD: *Being as* it was so late, we went home.
CORRECT: *Because* it was so late, we went home.

(15) beside, besides These two prepositions are different. *Beside* means "at the side of." *Besides* means "in addition to."

EXAMPLES: Mary saw a clownfish *beside* the anemone.
Other animals live in the coral reef *besides* coral.

(16) bring, take *Bring* means "to carry from a distant place to a nearer one." *Take* means "to carry from a near place to a more distant place."

EXAMPLES: *Bring* me the lobster platter, please.
They *take* their daily catches to the restaurants.

(17) different from, different than *Different from* is preferred.

LESS ACCEPTABLE: The frogfish is *different than* any other species of fish.

PREFERRED: The frogfish is *different from* any other species of fish.

(18) doesn't, don't Use *doesn't* instead of *don't* with all third-person singular pronouns and nouns.

NONSTANDARD: The machine *don't* work.

CORRECT: The machine *doesn't* work.

(19) done *Done* is the past participle of *do*. It should always follow a helping verb.

NONSTANDARD: He *done* his homework.

CORRECT: He *has done* his homework.

(20) due to *Due to* means "caused by" and should be used only when the words *caused by* can logically be substituted.

NONSTANDARD: *Due to* hunting and pollution, the monk seal has become endangered.

CORRECT: The near extinction of the monk seal is *due to* humans' hunting it and polluting its waters.

(21) farther, further *Farther* refers to distance. *Further* means "additional" or "to a greater degree or extent."

EXAMPLES: The *farther* from the surface of the ocean, the colder the water becomes.
I looked *further* into the sport of scuba diving.

(22) fewer, less Use *fewer* for things that can be counted. Use *less* for quantities that cannot be counted.

EXAMPLES: *fewer* calories, *fewer* dollars, *fewer* assignments
less sugar, *less* money, *less* homework

(23) gone, went *Gone* is the past participle of *go*. It should be used as a verb only with a helping verb. *Went* is the past tense of *go* and is never used with a helping verb.

NONSTANDARD: Craig and Louise *gone* to the movies.
You really *should have went* to the party.

CORRECT: Craig and Louise *went* to the movies.
You really *should have gone* to the party.

(24) in, into *In* refers to position. *Into* suggests motion.

EXAMPLES: The vampire squid lives *in* the deep sea.
The octopus can crawl *into* tiny spaces.

(25) just When you use *just* as an adverb meaning "no more than," place it right before the word it logically modifies.

LESS ACCEPTABLE: She *just* wants one piece of candy.
PREFERRED: She wants *just* one piece of candy.

(26) kind of, sort of Do not use in place of *rather* or *somewhat*.

NONSTANDARD: Siphonophores are *sort of* like jellyfish.
CORRECT: Siphonophores are *rather* like jellyfish.

(27) lay, lie *Lay* means "to put or set (something) down." Its principal parts—*lay, laying, laid,* and *laid*—are usually followed by a direct object. *Lie* means "to recline." Its principal parts—*lie, lying, lay,* and *lain*—are never followed by a direct object.

LAY: Please *lay* the basket on the counter.
Those turtles *are laying* their eggs on the beach.
Before she left, she *laid* the books on the table.
The masons have *laid* three rows of bricks.

LIE: If you are sick, you should *lie* down.
They are *lying* in the sunshine.
Last week, he *lay* in the hammock every evening.
The children have *lain* in bed long enough.

(28) learn, teach *Learn* means "to receive knowledge." *Teach* means "to give knowledge."

EXAMPLES: Dolphins can *learn* to follow commands.
The trainer *taught* the killer whale a new trick.

(29) leave, let *Leave* means "to allow to remain." *Let* means "to permit." Do not use one in place of the other.

NONSTANDARD: People should *let* animal habitats alone.
CORRECT: People should *leave* animal habitats alone.

NONSTANDARD: *Leave* me go!
CORRECT: *Let* me go!

▼ **Critical Viewing** Write down your impressions of the octopus in the photograph below. Use the words *gone, went, in, into, lay,* and *lie.* **[Interpret]**

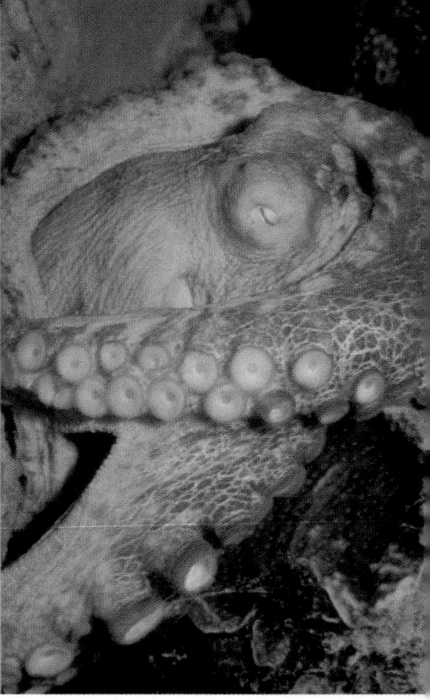

▲ **Critical Viewing** These and other fish living around coral reefs are extremely colorful. How does their color affect the way they relate to their environment? **[Analyze]**

(30) like, as *Like* is a preposition meaning "similar to" or "such as." It should not be used in place of the conjunction *as.*

NONSTANDARD: She writes *like* she speaks—graciously.
CORRECT: She writes *as* she speaks—graciously.

(31) of, have Do not use the preposition *of* in place of the verb *have.*

NONSTANDARD: The octopus could *of* squirted its pursuer.
CORRECT: The octopus could *have* squirted its pursuer.

(32) only Because the position of *only* can affect the entire meaning of a sentence, be sure to place it before the word that should be modified.

EXAMPLES: *Only* Rita wanted to go bowling. (No one else wanted to go bowling.)
Rita *only* wanted to go bowling. (Rita did not want to do anything else.)

(33) set, sit *Set* means "to put (something) in a certain place." Its principal parts—*set, setting, set,* and *set*—are usually followed by a direct object. *Sit* means "to be seated." Its principal parts—*sit, sitting, sat,* and *sat*—are never followed by a direct object.

SET: *Set* the peaches on the table.
He should be *setting* the table now.
They *set* the television on the corner table.
We have *set* all the clocks to go off at seven.

SIT: I will *sit* in his place tonight.
You must have been *sitting* there for hours.
She *sat* in her office and thought.
We have *sat* in the front row for three weeks now.

(34) seen *Seen* is a past participle and can be used as a verb only with a helping verb.

NONSTANDARD: We *seen* the bright colors in the coral reef.
CORRECT: We *have seen* the bright colors in the coral reef.

(35) so *So* is a coordinating conjunction. It should not be used alone when you mean "so that."

LESS ACCEPTABLE: Sponges use filters *so* they can eat food.
PREFERRED: Sponges use filters *so that* they can eat food.

(36) than, then *Than* is used in comparisons. Do not confuse it with the adverb *then*, which usually refers to time.

EXAMPLES: Some sharks are more aggressive *than* others.
We finished shopping and *then* ate lunch.

(37) that, which, who Use these relative pronouns correctly. *That* and *which* refer to things (*which* is set off by commas). *Who* refers only to people.

EXAMPLES: I saw the fish *that* you told me about.
Conch, which is a kind of shellfish, was served for dinner.
We thanked the waiter *who* helped us.

(38) that there, this here Avoid these nonstandard expressions. Simply leave out *here* and *there*.

NONSTANDARD: *That there* nudibranch is a beautiful creature.
This here sea slug is a nudibranch.

CORRECT: *That* nudibranch is a beautiful creature.
This sea slug is a nudibranch.

(39) their, there, they're *Their*, a possessive pronoun, always modifies a noun. *There* can be used either as an expletive at the beginning of a sentence or as an adverb. *They're* is a contraction for *they are*.

PRONOUN: Nag fish tie *their* bodies into knots.

EXPLETIVE: *There* are some reasons for doing this.

ADVERB: They can find food *there*.

CONTRACTION: *They're* trying to escape predators.

(40) to, too, two *To*, a preposition, begins a prepositional phrase or an infinitive. *Too*, an adverb, modifies adjectives and other adverbs; it can be used to mean "also" as well. *Two* is a number.

PREPOSITION: *to* the ocean floor

INFINITIVE: *to* swim

ADVERB: *too* tall, *too* quickly

NUMBER: *two* eggs, *two* fins

(41) when, where Do not use *when* or *where* directly after a linking verb, and do not use *where* in place of *that*.

NONSTANDARD: At night is *when* you can watch the fish feed.
Under the sea is *where* you find fish.
We read *where* taxes are rising.

CORRECT: At night is the time to watch fish feed.
Under the sea is the place for you to find fish.
We read that taxes are rising.

Exercise 10 **Avoiding Usage Problems** Choose the correct word to complete each sentence.

EXAMPLE: The (affects, effects) of predators on all undersea life are amazing.

ANSWER: effects

1. (Being that, Because) there are many undersea animals that are attacked by predators, many defense techniques have been developed.
2. In order to propel itself quickly to escape from predators, the octopus (brings, takes) water into its mantle cavity and quickly shoots a jet of water through a separate opening.
3. Another defense for the octopus is to squirt an inky fluid (that, which) causes the water to become cloudy and makes it very difficult for an attacker to see.
4. Lacking bones or a hard shell, the octopus can move (in, into) tight spaces between rocks to hide from its enemies.
5. The octopus can change its color to that of its surroundings (so, so that) it can hide from predators.
6. Rays use camouflage, (to, too, two), as a method of defense.
7. (Besides, Beside) being a color that blends into the ocean floor, a ray has poisonous spines on its tail.
8. A puffer fish can scare its enemies by inflating its body for (a while, awhile).
9. The porcupine fish, which is (different from, different than) the puffer, has sharp spines all over its body to discourage predators.
10. The reason the lionfish has venomous spines sticking out of its fins is (because, that) they help it to defend itself from enemies.

More Practice

On-line Exercise Bank
- Section 27.2

Grammar Exercise Workbook
- pp. 161–162

▼ **Critical Viewing** Why do you think this fish is called a lionfish? Using three problem words correctly, discuss how the lionfish got its name. **[Speculate]**

Exercise 11 **Revising Sentences to Eliminate Usage Problems** Rewrite each sentence, correcting any usage problems that you find. If the sentence is correct as is, write *correct.*

1. Dolphins ain't fish; they are mammals.
2. If he had wanted, he could of gone diving with the dolphins.
3. The dolphin brain is kind of the same size as the human brain.
4. A dolphin does not breathe through its nose, but through a hole in the top of its head.
5. Scientists seen dolphins surface in order to breathe.
6. That there beak on the dolphin is called a *rostrum.*
7. Dolphins have grown thick layers of blubber under their skin due to the cold water in which they live.
8. Dolphins navigate by producing sounds and by listening to the echoes that come from their surroundings.
9. Dolphins have a language of there own.
10. Dolphins have an amazing ability to communicate their emotions by the sounds that they make.

More Practice

On-line Exercise Bank

- Section 27.2

Grammar Exercise Workbook

- pp. 161–162

Exercise 12 **Revising a Paragraph to Eliminate Usage Problems** Revise the following paragraph. Correct any usage problems that you find.

Their are animals living on coral reefs that have unique relationships with other species. They live this way in order to enhance there own lives or to help them to avoid the risks of undersea life. The clownfish, or anemone fish, and the sea anemone live together in a relationship called *obligate symbiosis.* This term means that the clownfish benefits from living between the poisonous tentacles of the anemone. However, the anemone doesn't gain nothing from the relationship. In order too survive among the stinging tentacles of the anemone, the body of the clownfish is coated with a protective mucus layer. Scientists believe that these fish have adapted this coating in order to survive better under the sea. This feature has a few benefits for the clownfish. First of all, the clownfish can lie its eggs between the many tentacles of the anemone. By doing this, it protects the eggs from any predators who would die from the sting of the anemone's tentacles. Second, the anemone provides a refuge and hiding place for clownfish that are escaping predator fish. Although the clownfish reaps many benefits from this relationship, the anemone is uneffected by the relationship.

Hands-on Grammar

Working on Usage Problems With Pictographs

Work on common usage problems by forming pictographs—pictures that represent ideas or words. In the examples below, *further* and *farther* are illustrated with arrows showing that *farther* refers to distance and *further* means "to a greater extent." *Among* and *between* are illustrated with balls showing that *among* implies three or more, while *between* is generally used with two.

Farther
Further

Each of the ten word pairs below represents a common usage problem. Using the Common Usage Problems glossary on pages 620–625, form pictographs for each word. Your pictures do not need to be elaborate, as long as they clearly illustrate what you have learned is the main difference between the proper usage of the two words. Use one index card for each word pair, and use the same side of the index card to illustrate both words.

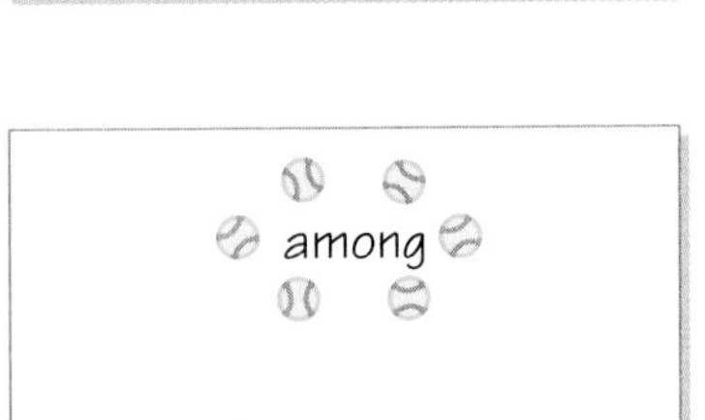

After you have completed your pictographs, work with a partner to practice the correct usage of each word. Select your partner's cards at random, studying the pictographs and then coming up with sentences that use each word correctly. Refer to the Common Usage Problems glossary to check your answers.

1. all together, altogether
2. beside, besides
3. bring, take
4. learn, teach
5. than, then
6. in, into
7. lay, lie
8. fewer, less
9. set, sit
10. that, who

Find It in Your Reading In your literature or other textbooks, find examples of the words above used correctly in sentences. Write the example sentences on the backs of the appropriate index cards.

Find It in Your Writing Look through pieces of writing in your writing portfolio for examples of the words above used correctly in sentences. Write the example sentences on the back of the appropriate index cards. If you cannot find examples of any of the words, challenge yourself to write new sentences on the backs of the cards using the words correctly

Section 27.2 Section Review

GRAMMAR EXERCISES 13–17

Exercise 13 **Avoiding Usage Problems** Choose the correct word to complete each sentence.

1. (Being that, Being as, Because) ocean life varies according to depth, the ocean is divided into zones.
2. There is less oxygen and light (farther, further) down in the ocean.
3. The mesopelagic zone is lower (than, then) the surface layer of the ocean.
4. In the mesopelagic zone, there are (fewer, less) streamlined fish.
5. The fish in the mesopelagic zone go (into, in) the upper zone to feed at night because (farther, further) down (fewer, less) food is available.
6. The teeth of the mid-zone fish are often long and sharp, and (their, there, they're) jaws and stomachs are enlarged to accommodate larger fishes.
7. The bigscale fish is an example of a fish (who, that) lives in this zone.
8. The large scales and plates that cover its body make the bigscale fish (different from, different than) fishes (that, which) live in the most shallow zone.
9. A bigscale fish (don't, doesn't) chase its prey (so, so that) it can save energy.
10. The ctenophore is (kind of, somewhat) like the jellyfish.

Exercise 14 **Revising to Eliminate Usage Problems** Rewrite each sentence, correcting any usage problems. If the sentence is correct as is, write *correct.*

1. The firefly squid is more advanced then the ctenophore because it has three organs who generate light.
2. Photophores are organs that produce light.
3. The firefly squid doesn't just glow for any reason.
4. They probably have this feature so predators will let them alone.
5. After studying the squid closely, scientists learned us that the firefly squid glows in order to attract other firefly squid.
6. Like humans use speech to communicate, firefly squid may use light to communicate.
7. The squid seen their prey because their glowing organs light up the darkness of the ocean.
8. In the darkness of the deep ocean is where photophores are useful.
9. Another animal that has photophores is the hatchet fish.
10. There are fish who have glowing organs on the undersides of their bodies and under there eyes.

Exercise 15 **Find It in Your Reading** Read an article about fish in a science magazine. Identify five areas where problems in usage could have occurred, and explain how the writers avoided those problems.

Exercise 16 **Find It in Your Writing** Choose one piece of writing in your portfolio. Check it carefully for the usage problems discussed in this chapter. If you find any usage problems, revise your writing to correct them.

Exercise 17 **Writing Application** Write an original sentence for one of the words in each set listed below. Underline the word in your sentence, and check to be sure you have used it correctly.

awhile, a while	bring, take	their, there
farther, further	to, too, two	so, so that
sit, set	lie, lay	then, than

Chapter 28

Capitalization

Central Park

▲ **Critical Viewing** Name some of the people, places, or things in this photo that you would start with a capital letter. **[Identify]**

Capital letters are important signals in your writing. They show when a new sentence begins. They also indicate names of specific people, places, or things and show which words are most significant in a title.

If you visit New York City, many famous and exciting places will stand out in your mind—such as Central Park, the Empire State Building, the Statue of Liberty, and Yankee Stadium. They should also stand out in your writing by beginning with capital letters.

You have probably already mastered the major rules of capitalization. This chapter will help you review the rules you already know and give you a chance to master some new rules to help you communicate even more clearly.

Diagnostic Test

Directions: Write all answers on a separate sheet of paper.

Skill Check A. Copy the following sentences, adding the missing capitals.

1. there are many beautiful and exciting places to see in New York state!
2. Adirondack park is located in the northern corner of the state.
3. Whiteface mountain is the highest skiing peak in the east, and it is the only high peak in the adirondacks reachable by car.
4. in 1935, president Franklin D. Roosevelt opened the new state highway to the mountaintop.
5. The 1932 and 1980 winter olympic games were held at lake placid, located just south of whiteface mountain.

Skill Check B. Copy the following sentences, correcting any capitalization errors.

6. The Niagara river and niagara falls are located in Western New York.
7. More than 10 million visitors a year come to see the great Falls, which Native americans called the "Thunder of the waters."
8. There are five homes designed by the american Architect Frank Lloyd wright in the Western new York city of Buffalo.
9. To cross over to Central New York, you can rent a Houseboat and cruise the historic Erie canal.
10. The New York State capitol building is in Albany.

Skill Check C. Rewrite the following sentences, correcting all errors in capitalization.

11. For Bob smith, his first day at Washington high school had not begun well.
12. Bob had not wanted to move to New York and leave his old school in centerville, Indiana.
13. However, his Father had accepted a job at Saint John's university, and his mother had been offered a job as a reporter for *the new york times*, so they moved in august.
14. The bus this morning had been delayed in traffic on maple Street.
15. Bob's first class was history with mr. Harris.
16. finally, He found room 302 and took a seat.
17. mr. Harris was telling the class about the field trips they would be taking throughout the semester.
18. When Mr. Harris finished his lecture, the girl sitting next to bob smiled and extended her hand.
19. "I am Sarah carter," she said, "And this is my first day here."
20. perhaps tuesday, September 2, was going to be a good day after all.

Capitalizing Words in Sentences

One of the most important uses of capitals is to signal the beginning of each new sentence.

KEY CONCEPT Capitalize the first word in declarative, interrogative, imperative, and exclamatory sentences. ■

DECLARATIVE: The taxi stopped when I waved.
INTERROGATIVE: Do you know where we are going?
IMPERATIVE: Bring the travel brochures home tomorrow.
EXCLAMATORY: I would love to take a trip to New York City!

KEY CONCEPT Capitalize the first word in a quotation if the quotation is a complete sentence. ■

Each quotation below is a complete sentence. In the last example, note that the full quotation consists of two complete sentences. Each of the sentences begins with a capital letter.

EXAMPLES: She said, "The art museum is closed."
"The art museum is closed," she said.
"The art museum is closed," she said. "We will come back in the morning."

When a quotation consists of one complete sentence separated into two parts, only one capital letter is required.

EXAMPLE: "The art museum is closed," she said, "because they are setting up a new exhibit that opens tomorrow."

A fragment of a quotation contained within a larger sentence should not be capitalized.

EXAMPLE: June told us that the art exhibit was "better than the one last year."

Here is one more capitalization rule to keep in mind when writing sentences:

KEY CONCEPT Capitalize the first word after a colon only if the word begins a complete sentence. ■

EXAMPLES: We all had the same thought: How are we going to decide which attractions to visit?
We all agreed that the city has many worthwhile attractions: museums, theaters, parks, and zoos.

Theme: New York City Attractions

In this chapter, you will learn when to capitalize words in sentences, names, and titles. The examples and exercises are about tourist attractions in New York City.

Cross-Curricular Connection: Social Studies

Exercise 1 **Using Capitalization Correctly in Sentences and Quotations** Copy the following sentences on your paper, adding the missing capitals.

1. we have decided to take a family vacation in New York City this year.
2. our travel agent said, "it's one of the most exciting places in the world."
3. "you need to plan ahead," she said, "because there are many fascinating attractions to choose from."
4. there is one thing every visitor should know: the city is divided into five regions, and each has many educational and cultural attractions.
5. we spent all week reading about the many attractions we could visit while in the city: museums, art galleries, theaters, parks, historic landmarks, and many others.

More Practice

Language Lab CD-ROM

- Problems With Capitalization lesson

On-line Exercise Bank

- Chapter 28

Grammar Exercise Workbook

- pp. 163–164

GRAMMAR IN LITERATURE

from One Ordinary Day, With Peanuts

Shirley Jackson

The first word of each quote in this passage is capitalized. The first word of each sentence or fragment inside the quote is also capitalized to show where each new thought begins.

. . . They sat on the steps cracking peanuts in a comradely fashion, and Mr. Johnson said, "So you're moving?"

"Yep," said the boy.

"Where you going?"

"Vermont."

"Nice place. Plenty of snow there. Maple sugar, too; you like maple sugar?"

"Sure."

"Plenty of maple sugar in Vermont. You going to live on a farm?"

"Going to live with Grandpa."

Capitalizing Proper Nouns

As you may recall, a proper noun names a specific person, place, or thing. All proper nouns are capitalized.

KEY CONCEPT Capitalize each part of a person's full name. ■

EXAMPLES: Diana T. Cheng B. L. Baker

KEY CONCEPT Capitalize geographical names. ■

GEOGRAPHICAL NAMES	
Streets Towns and Cities Counties	Madison Avenue, Aborn Road Evansdale, New York City, London Macon County, Bergen County
States and Provinces Nations Continents	Vermont, Saskatchewan United States of America, Japan North America, Europe, Asia
Valleys and Deserts Mountains Sections of a Country Islands Scenic Spots	Hudson Valley, the Sahara Sierra Nevadas, Adirondacks the Great Plains, the Northeast the Canary Islands, Maui the Grand Canyon, Yellowstone National Park
Rivers and Falls	the Amazon River, the Tigris, Niagara Falls
Lakes and Bays Seas and Oceans	Lake Huron, Chesapeake Bay South China Sea, Atlantic Ocean

When a compass point names a specific area of a country, it is capitalized. It is not capitalized when it simply refers to a physical direction.

EXAMPLES: My family lives in the Northeast.
The wind came from the west.

KEY CONCEPT Capitalize the names of other special places. ■

EXAMPLES: the Statue of Liberty, John F. Kennedy Memorial, the Theater of Fine Arts, the Empire State Building, Room 114, the Madison Room, Conference Room B, the Milky Way, Earth, Venus, the Big Dipper

KEY CONCEPT Capitalize the names of specific events and periods of time. ■

SPECIFIC EVENTS AND TIMES	
Historic Periods Historic Events Documents	the Renaissance, the Middle Ages, the Age of Enlightenment the Revolutionary War, World War II the Declaration of Independence, the Magna Carta
Days Months	Tuesday, Saturday April, November
Holidays Religious Days	Fourth of July, Groundhog Day, Labor Day Christmas, Easter, Passover, Ramadan
Special Events	Ashland Shakespeare Festival, Parade of Roses, New York City Marathon

Although they stand for specific times of the year, seasons are not capitalized.

EXAMPLES: We visited Manhattan last winter.
The spring is my favorite time of year.

▼ **Critical Viewing**
If you were writing a sentence about someone you know who was skating at this rink on a certain day, what words would you capitalize? **[Connect]**

The skating rink at Rockefeller Center is a famous tourist attraction.

KEY CONCEPT Capitalize the names of various organizations, government bodies, political parties, races, nationalities, and languages. ■

SPECIFIC GROUPS AND LANGUAGES	
Clubs, Organizations, Institutions, and Businesses	Kiwanis Club, Weld Chess Club, Red Cross, Fund for Animals, University of Washington
Government Bodies Political Parties	the Congress of the United States, the Department of Transportation the Republican party, the Democratic party, the Conservative party
Nationalities and Languages	Chinese, British English, Dutch, Swahili, Russian

KEY CONCEPT Capitalize references to religions, deities, and religious scriptures. ■

RELIGIOUS REFERENCES	
Christianity	God, the Lord, the Father, the Son, the Holy Spirit, the Bible, books of the Bible (that is, Genesis, Revelations, and so on)
Judaism	God, the Lord, the Father, the Prophets, the Torah, the Talmud, the Midrash
Islam	Allah, the Prophet, the Koran
Hinduism	Brahma, the Bhagavad Gita, the Vedas
Buddhism	the Buddha, Mahayana, Hinayana

The only exception to the rule for capitalizing religious terms occurs when you refer to a god or goddess of ancient mythology. In these cases, the word *god* is not capitalized.

EXAMPLES: the *god* Zeus, the *goddess* Hera

A number of other proper nouns not mentioned as yet also need capitalization. The following rule covers these.

More Practice

Language Lab CD-ROM
- Problems With Capitalization lesson

On-line Exercise Bank
- Chapter 28

Grammar Exercise Workbook
- pp. 165–166

KEY CONCEPT Capitalize the names of other special proper nouns. ■

OTHER SPECIAL PROPER NOUNS	
Awards	the Nobel Peace Prize, the John Newbery Medal
Air, Sea, Space, and Land Craft	the *Concorde*, the *Nautilus*, *Apollo I*, the Model T
Trademarks	Instaflash Film, Melody Records

When you use a trademark, all the words should be capitalized. If you are using only part of the trademark (the brand name), capitalize only the word that comes from the trademark.

TRADEMARK: Snapzit Instaphoto
BRAND NAME ALONE: Snapzit camera

Exercise 2 **Capitalizing Proper Nouns** Copy the following sentences, adding the missing capitals.

1. Jazz musicians in the 1920's nicknamed new york city the big apple.
2. The city is divided into five boroughs: manhattan, brooklyn, the bronx, queens, and staten island.
3. Each year, millions of tourists travel to this beautiful city in the northeast to visit its wide variety of attractions.
4. In the middle of manhattan is central park, the best known of the city's more than one hundred parks.
5. The brooklyn bridge has been linking brooklyn with manhattan since 1883.
6. Although the empire state building is no longer the world's tallest building, it is still one of the most famous.
7. On liberty island in new york harbor is the world-famous statue of liberty.
8. Manhattan is the home of a floating sea, air, and space museum that is on board the *intrepid*, a world war II aircraft carrier.
9. The oldest church building in new york, saint paul's chapel, stands on broadway across from city hall park.
10. A golden statue of the ancient greek god prometheus looks over the lower plaza at rockefeller center.

▼ **Critical Viewing** Write a sentence describing this bridge and the two places it connects. What words should you capitalize? **[Connect]**

The Brooklyn Bridge has a unique appearance.

Hands-on Grammar

Rule Reminder Reference Cards

This chapter includes dozens of important rules about capitalization that you will need to remember. Try this activity to devise your own "rule reminder reference."

Take stacks of index cards in two different colors. On each card of one color write a rule category, such as *Sentence Starters, Quotations, Proper Nouns, Proper Adjectives, Titles, or Abbreviations.* On the front of each card of the second color, write a rule from this chapter or that your teacher gives in class. The headings in the different charts in the chapter can help you select rules. On the back of each rule card, write sentences or lists to illustrate the rule.

Take a category card, and arrange under it any rule cards that fit that category. This will help you find the rule you want.

Now, punch a hole into the upper left corner of each card. Place a single loose-leaf ring through the holes to hold the stacks of cards together, or tie them with a piece of heavy string. You can now flip through your reference cards to find the category and rule you need. If you learn new rules, you can open the ring or string and insert a new rule card into its appropriate category. Then, refasten your stack of cards.

Store your rule reminder reference cards in your notebook.

Find It in Your Reading In your reading, find sentences with capitalized proper nouns, proper adjectives, and titles. You might write these sentences as examples on the back of your rule cards.

Find It in Your Writing Look through samples of your own writing to find sentences in which you have used both proper and common nouns to see if you have capitalized them properly. Also, look at any examples of quotations that you have used to see if they are capitalized correctly.

Capitalizing Proper Adjectives

A proper adjective is a proper noun used as an adjective or an adjective formed from a proper noun.

KEY CONCEPT Capitalize most proper adjectives. ■

EXAMPLES: New York cabdriver
a Korean restaurant

Some proper adjectives, however, have been used so often that they have lost their capitals, such as *french fries* and *teddy bear.*

Here are a few exceptions that you should know concerning proper adjectives.

KEY CONCEPT Do not capitalize prefixes with proper adjectives unless the prefix refers to a nationality. ■

EXAMPLES: all-American
pre-Renaissance
pro-Mexican
Sino-Russian
Anglo-American

KEY CONCEPT In a hyphenated adjective, capitalize only the proper adjective. ■

EXAMPLE: French-speaking Canadians

Exercise 3 Capitalizing Proper Adjectives Copy the following sentences on your paper, adding needed capitals.

EXAMPLE: I am taking a chinese history course at NYU.
ANSWER: I am taking a Chinese history course at NYU.

1. Tourists love New York City's ethnic diversity. They can find everything from an egyptian mummy exhibit at the Metropolitan Museum of Art to an authentic mongolian, greek, or ethiopian meal at an ethnic restaurant.
2. During the 1650's, only about 1,000 people lived in the dutch colony of New Amsterdam on Manhattan Island.
3. During the 1800's and early 1900's, millions of european immigrants came to the city seeking a better life.
4. Since the mid-1900's, many african Americans from the southern states have moved to New York City.
5. Many spanish-speaking americans from caribbean and south american countries have also looked to New York City as a place to find a better life.

▲ **Critical Viewing** What proper adjectives would you capitalize in a sentence describing immigrants from different countries viewing the Statue of Liberty? **[Describe]**

Capitalizing Titles

KEY CONCEPT Capitalize titles of people and titles of works of art, literature, and music. ■

Titles of People Several rules apply to the titles of people. The first applies to titles used before names and in direct address.

KEY CONCEPT Capitalize a person's title when it is followed by the person's name or is used in direct address. ■

SOCIAL:	Sir, Madam or Madame, Lord, Lady
BUSINESS:	Professor, Doctor, Superintendent
RELIGIOUS:	Reverend, Bishop, Father, Pope, Sister, Rabbi
MILITARY:	Sergeant, Major, Lieutenant, Admiral, General
GOVERNMENT:	Mayor, Governor, President, Ambassador, Secretary of Defense

KEY CONCEPT Capitalize the titles of certain high government officials when the titles are not followed by a proper name or used in direct address. ■

The titles of some high government officials are almost always capitalized. These include the titles of the incumbent President and Chief Justice of the Supreme Court and the Queen of England. Notice in the following examples that these titles are often capitalized even when they do not refer to a particular person holding the office.

EXAMPLES: The visiting diplomats were presented to the Queen at a reception.
The Chief Justice is one of nine justices on the Supreme Court.
The President was vacationing at Camp David.

KEY CONCEPT Capitalize all important words in compound titles, but do not capitalize prefixes and suffixes. ■

EXAMPLES: Vice President
Commander in Chief

If a prefix or suffix is part of the title, it is not capitalized.

EXAMPLES: ex-Senator Smith
President-elect Jefferson

More Practice

Language Lab CD-ROM
- Problems With Capitalization lesson

On-line Exercise Bank
- Chapter 28

Grammar Exercise Workbook
- pp. 167–168

KEY CONCEPT Capitalize titles showing family relationships when they refer by themselves to a specific person or when they are used in direct address. ■

EXAMPLES: Long ago, Grandfather Pleski took me to the Bronx Zoo.
I need a new jacket, Mother.
Did Father buy the tickets for the play?
Stan's grandmother once played the violin.

Titles of Things Titles are given not only to people but also to things such as written works and other works of art.

KEY CONCEPT Capitalize the first word and all other key words in the titles of books, periodicals, poems, stories, plays, paintings, and other works of art. ■

All words in a title should be capitalized except articles (*a, an, the*) and prepositions and conjunctions with fewer than four letters. These words are capitalized only when they are the first and last word in a title.

EXAMPLES: *The Grapes of Wrath*
"There Is a Longing"
A Tour Through America's Museums

When capitalizing a subtitle, use the same rule that you use for titles. Notice in the following example that *A* is capitalized because it is the first word in the subtitle.

EXAMPLE: *Art History: A Look at Great Masterpieces*

◀ **Critical Viewing** Write a title that includes a subtitle for a new book about the Bronx Zoo. What words should be capitalized in your title? **[Connect]**

KEY CONCEPT Capitalize titles of courses when the courses are language courses or when the courses are followed by a number. ■

EXAMPLES: French Chemistry 1A Economics 313

The capital letters are dropped when school subjects are discussed in a general way and no specific course is named. Languages, however, always receive capitals.

EXAMPLES: Last year, I studied chemistry and French.
After English class, I have to rush to biology.

Exercise 4 **Capitalizing Titles of People** Copy the following sentences, adding the missing capitals.

1. Could you direct me, sir, to Times Square?
2. We invited general Sadler to the play.
3. Last week, the president of the United States had a meeting at the United Nations headquarters in New York City.
4. While visiting in New York City, reverend Casey was sure to stop at Saint Patrick's Cathedral.
5. Last summer, we visited grandmother Johnson and several aunts in Idaho.

Exercise 5 **Capitalizing Titles of Things** Copy the titles that need capitalization in the following sentences, adding the missing capitals. Underline any titles that appear in italics.

EXAMPLE: Have you read the novel *the red pony* by Steinbeck?

ANSWER: <u>The Red Pony</u>

1. I went to Lincoln Center to see *the nutcracker* performed by the New York City Ballet.
2. *the wall street journal* is a respected newspaper that presents the news from the point of view of business people.
3. The New York City composer George Gershwin wrote the famous folk opera *porgy and bess.*
4. Langston Hughes, a famous poet of the Harlem Renaissance of the 1920's, also wrote the children's books *the sweet and sour animal book* and *the dream keeper.*
5. We saw a revival of Neil Simon's play *the sunshine boys* at a theater on Broadway.

The Federal Building (in front) is the spot where George Washington was inaugurated as President.

▲ **Critical Viewing** When would you capitalize the word *building* in a caption about this photo? When would you not need a capital letter? **[Analyze]**

Section 28

Chapter Review

GRAMMAR EXERCISES 6–8

Exercise 6 Capitalizing Sentences and Proper Nouns Correctly Copy the following sentences onto your paper, adding the missing capitals.

1. movies have made central park perhaps one of the best-known city parks in the world.
2. this park, designed by frederick law olmsted and calvert vaux, occupies 5 percent of the land area of manhattan.
3. central park was developed between 1856 and 1875, and it has many interesting features: the great lawn, the sheep meadow, belvedere castle, bethesda fountain, and wollman rink.
4. "let's skate at wollman rink in Central park," my brother suggested, "to try out our new skates."
5. "sure," I replied. "can we take the subway directly to the park?"

Exercise 7 Capitalizing Titles Correctly Copy the titles below onto your paper, and add capitals where necessary. Underline titles that are printed in italics.

1. book: *the empire state building: the making of a landmark*
2. play: *lost in yonkers*
3. magazine: *the new yorker*
4. song: "east side, west side"
5. movie: *manhattan murder mystery*
6. elected official: mayor edward koch
7. newspaper: the *new york daily news*
8. poem: "spring and all"
9. military title: lieutenant commander
10. clergy: reverend william d. morrison

Exercise 8 Capitalizing Proper Nouns, Proper Adjectives, and Titles Correctly Copy the following sentences onto your paper, adding the missing capitals. Underline any titles that appear in italics.

1. New York City served as the first american capital, and president george washington was inaugurated there.
2. Throughout history, many influential new yorkers have entertained and educated us and helped us create a better american way of life.
3. Have you read the short story "*rip van winkle,*" written by Washington Irving, who was born in New York city?
4. One of the most celebrated american poets, Walt Whitman, spent most of his life in brooklyn.
5. james baldwin—author of many essays, plays, and novels, including *go tell it on the mountain*—was born and raised in new york city.
6. The director Woody Allen has used the city for the setting of many of his films, such as *manhattan, broadway danny rose,* and *annie hall.*
7. Eleanor Roosevelt, the wife of president Franklin d. Roosevelt, helped improve conditions for minorities and the poor.
8. Colin Powell, the son of caribbean immigrants, grew up in the south bronx.
9. general Powell became the first african American chairman of the joint chiefs of staff in 1989.
10. The retired general wrote a book about his life, *my american journey*, in 1995.

Chapter

29 Punctuation

▲ **Critical Viewing** Why are pauses and stops important to a rock climber? **[Connect]**

Hiking is a sport steeped in variety. Some hikes are short, while others are long; some wind through shady forests, while others trek through dry deserts. Certain tools, like a compass, help hikers navigate an overland course.

Writing sentences, like hiking, takes readers on a course through your ideas. Certain tools, like the punctuation marks you add, will help guide your readers.

When used accurately and effectively, punctuation marks help your readers follow your ideas. In this chapter, you will learn about the most important punctuation marks: commas, semicolons, colons, quotation marks, dashes, parentheses, apostrophes, and end marks.

Diagnostic Test

Directions: Write all answers on a separate sheet of paper.

Skill Check A. Rewrite the following sentences, adding the appropriate commas and end marks.

1. Mountain climbing which is also called alpinism or mountaineering can be a life-threatening sport
2. Which steep dangerous mountains are considered the most important
3. The Himalayas attract the very best mountaineers who face high altitudes extreme cold and severe weather
4. Someone may ask you which peak is the highest in the Himalayas Surprise It is Mt Everest
5. Mt. Everest the highest peak in all the Himalayas and in all the world was first climbed by Sir Edmund Hillary and Tenzing Norgay

Skill Check B. Rewrite the following sentences, adding the appropriate semicolons and colons.

6. Mountaineers climbing on ice slopes must bring the appropriate tools climbing ropes, ice axes, and metal spikes or crampons.
7. They use the ropes in a rope harness that fits around the climbers' waists this protects them if they fall.
8. The job of a belayer is to stand at the bottom of a cliff, to keep tight the ropes connecting climbers, and to pull in the slack yet, surely, the most important role is to prevent the climbers from falling.
9. The *World Book Encyclopedia* explains "While advancing, the lead climber inserts pieces of gear into the snow, ice, or cracks in the rock, securing the rope to them with a snap link."
10. The lead climber belays the second climber the second climber reaches the top of the cliff the lead climber belays the third climber.

Skill Check C. Rewrite the following sentences, adding commas, quotation marks, underlining, dashes, hyphens, or parentheses. Divide any underlined words as if they were at the end of a line.

11. While hiking or mountain climbing, you might ask Are there any tips that I should keep in mind?
12. Yes answered George and I would suggest you read The Rock Climber's Handbook.
13. While I was hiking Brenda continued I saw a sign that read Please keep it cleaner than when you arrived.
14. Alpine style climbing you have to be half crazy to be a true fan of this! is said to be the purest and most dangerous way to climb a mountain.
15. Those who participate in mountaineering no matter how young or how old are usually serious climbers looking for new routes and new adventures.

Section 29.1 End Marks

Just as every sentence must begin with a capital letter, so every sentence must end with an end mark. The three end marks are the period (.), the question mark (?), and the exclamation mark (!). These marks clearly indicate to a reader that you have arrived at the end of a thought. End marks also indicate the emotion or tone of a sentence so that the reader knows with what kind of expression it should be read. End marks can serve other important functions, as well. In this section, you will have the opportunity to review the more common uses of end marks and to study some of their other functions.

Theme: Mountain Climbing

In this section, you will learn about the end marks used to punctuate different types of sentences. The examples and exercises are about mountain climbing.

Cross-Curricular Connection: Physical Education

Basic Uses of End Marks

The period, the most common end mark, has three basic uses:

KEY CONCEPT Use a period (.) to end a declarative sentence, a mild imperative, and an indirect question. ■

Declarative sentences include statements of fact and statements of opinion. Both types of statements require a period.

STATEMENT OF FACT: Some hikes can last for weeks.
STATEMENT OF OPINION: Hiking is the most exciting sport.

You should also place a period at the end of a mildly worded command called a *mild imperative*. You can recognize these sentences easily because they often begin with a verb and have an "understood you" as their subject.

MILD IMPERATIVE: Change your shoes quickly.

Indirect questions also require a period. An indirect question needs no answer; instead, it is a statement that refers to a question that might be or has been asked.

DIRECT QUESTION: Are the pants on sale?
INDIRECT QUESTION: I asked whether the pants were on sale.

A sentence that asks a direct question, one to which an answer might be made, is an interrogative sentence. The end mark used for interrogative sentences is the question mark.

▼ **Critical Viewing** What questions might these climbers ask someone coming down the path that they are climbing? **[Speculate]**

KEY CONCEPT Use a question mark (?) to end a direct question, an incomplete question, or a statement intended as a question. ■

A direct question demands an answer; it stands as a direct request. All direct questions must end with a question mark.

DIRECT QUESTIONS: Did you dress appropriately for the hike**?**
Which mountain are you planning to scale**?**

In some cases, only a portion of the question is written out and the rest is simply understood.

INCOMPLETE QUESTIONS: Where**?** What color**?** How much**?**

Sometimes, a question is phrased as if it were a declarative sentence. Use a question mark to show that the sentence is a question.

STATEMENTS INTENDED AS QUESTIONS: You called me**?**
They have four dogs**?**

An exclamatory sentence shows strong emphasis or emotion. It expresses more feeling than other sentences do. An exclamation mark is used at the end of an exclamatory sentence to indicate the emphasis or emotion it expresses.

KEY CONCEPT Use an exclamation mark (!) to end an exclamatory sentence, a forceful imperative sentence, or an interjection expressing strong emotion. ■

EXCLAMATORY SENTENCE: The view from the top of the mountain is stunning**!**

A strongly worded imperative that demonstrates forcefulness or strong emotion will also take an exclamation mark.

STRONG IMPERATIVE: Get away from the cliff before you fall**!**

Occasionally (especially in conversations), one or two words are delivered emphatically. These strong interjections should also be followed by an exclamation mark.

STRONG INTERJECTIONS: Breathtaking**!** Ouch**!** Oh**!**

Sometimes, a strong interjection may appear before a short exclamatory sentence. If this occurs, you may use either a comma or an exclamation mark after the interjection.

WITH A COMMA: Goodness, that thunder was loud**!**

WITH AN EXCLAMATION MARK: Goodness**!** That thunder was loud**!**

▲ Critical Viewing Write three sentences about this picture. Use a different end mark for each sentence. [Apply]

Exercise 1 **Using the Period, Question Mark, and Exclamation Mark** Write the appropriate period, question mark, or exclamation mark with the word preceding it.

EXAMPLE: In mountain climbing, the objective is to reach the peak of a mountain by climbing its slopes

ANSWER: slopes.

1. Mountain climbing started in Europe, where people climbed peaks simply for the fun of it
2. Have all of the major mountain peaks been climbed
3. Yes With the exception of a few peaks in remote areas of the world, most major peaks have been climbed
4. Mount McKinley, the tallest peak in North America, was first climbed in 1913
5. In 1953, Sir Edmund Hillary of New Zealand and Tenzing Norgay of Nepal were the first to reach the summit of Mt. Everest in Asia
6. Can you believe that they were able to climb the tallest mountain in the world Amazing
7. Even today, mountaineers want to be the first to conquer the challenge of a new peak
8. However, the biggest attraction of competitive mountain climbing is finding new routes up challenging mountains
9. Where
10. I have never climbed anywhere more exhilarating and challenging than the Himalayas

More Practice

On-line Exercise Bank
- Section 29.1

Grammar Exercise Workbook
- pp. 169–170

Section 29.1 Section Review

GRAMMAR EXERCISES 2–6

Exercise 2 Punctuating the Ends of Sentences Write the end mark required in each of the following sentences.

1. Backpacking is a popular type of hiking
2. Items that are packed must be as lightweight as possible
3. For crying out loud, you can't expect a backpacker to walk for 50 miles with 200 pounds of equipment.
4. By carrying clothes, food, and plenty of water, a backpacker can spend many days in remote areas where these supplies would normally be unavailable
5. Where Anyplace you want

Exercise 3 Identifying Uses of End Marks Write the correct end mark for each of the following sentences. Then, label each sentence *statement of fact, opinion, mild imperative, direct question, indirect question, incomplete question, statement intended as a question, exclamatory sentence, strong imperative,* or *strong interjection.*

1. Besides backpacking, the sport of hiking has several other variations
2. You, as a competitor in orienteering, will compete in a course in the wilderness
3. Don't you dare go anywhere near the edges of cliffs
4. When you find all the checkpoints before the other teams, you win
5. Snowshoeing, another type of hiking, takes place in the snow
6. How can we learn more about the sport
7. If I tell you that the hiker wears large strung frames on her feet, does that bring an image to your mind
8. These frames distribute body weight over a larger area, so the hiker is better able to walk on top of the snow
9. Who is credited with the invention of this sport
10. Long before Europeans arrived, Native Americans enjoyed walking on the snow.

Exercise 4 Find It in Your Reading Read this excerpt from "Uphill" by Christina Rosetti. Explain the pattern formed by the end marks. Then, restate each line that ends with a period as a complete sentence.

Does the road wind uphill all the way?
  Yes, to the very end.
Will the day's journey take the whole
      long day?
  From morn to night, my friend.

But is there for the night a resting
      place?
  A roof for when the slow dark hours
      begin.
May not the darkness hide it from my
      face?
  You cannot miss that inn.

Exercise 5 Find It in Your Writing Select a piece of writing from your portfolio. Identify two sentences that express strong emotion and that state an opinion.

Exercise 6 Writing Application Write three original sentences to fit each situation below. Write each sentence according to the directions for each situation.

1. You missed your bus.
   a. statement of fact
   b. direct question
   c. explanation for being late
2. The cat walked through flour.
   a. humorous exclamation
   b. mild imperative
   c. statement of opinion

Section 29.2

Commas

A comma represents a short pause. It tells the reader to hesitate before continuing the sentence. Commas also help set up relationships among parts of a sentence and make long sentences easier to read.

The comma is used more than any other internal punctuation mark. As a result, many errors are made in its use. Keep in mind two basic uses of the comma: (1) Commas can be used *to separate* similar items, and (2) one or more commas can be used *to set off* a single item at the beginning, middle, or end of a sentence. Do not use a comma unless there is a comma rule for it.

This section presents rules to help you use the comma correctly to separate basic elements and to set off added elements in sentences.

Theme: Stores

In this section, you will learn about the various uses of commas. The examples and exercises are about different kinds of stores.

Cross-Curricular Connection: Social Studies

Commas With Compound Sentences

A compound sentence is two or more independent clauses joined by a coordinating conjunction (*and, but, for, nor, or, so,* and *yet*).

KEY CONCEPT Use a comma before the conjunction to separate two independent clauses in a compound sentence. ■

EXAMPLES: Many families in developing countries produce their own food, but most families in the United States rely on the food industry for their food.

The food industry takes food from the place where it is grown, and it distributes the food where it is needed.

Always check to make sure that you have written two complete sentences joined by a coordinating conjunction before you insert a comma.

Sometimes, conjunctions merely join two words, phrases, or subordinate clauses. When they are used in one of these ways, no comma is required.

COMPOUND SUBJECT: Diana and Jill met for lunch at the mall.

COMPOUND VERB: The old friends chatted and laughed as they ate lunch.

TWO PREPOSITIONAL PHRASES: They ate lunch in the restaurant and then walked around the mall.

TWO SUBORDINATE CLAUSES: My brothers enjoy shopping trips only if they are relatively short and only if they are productive.

Exercise 7 **Using Commas in Compound Sentences** Write each sentence, adding the necessary commas. If no comma is needed, write *correct.*

EXAMPLE: I try to save money but I still overspend.
ANSWER: I try to save money, but I still overspend.

1. The food industry includes the production and distribution of food as well as the people involved in this most important business.
2. About 3 million Americans work in farming or other related fields to produce basic foods for the food market.
3. Livestock farmers raise animals for beef yet not all our meat comes from this type of farming.
4. Private fishermen and large commercial fleets gather huge quantities of fish and shellfish.
5. Food is shipped to processing plants and it is then prepared and packaged for the market.
6. Fruits and vegetables are washed and sorted before they are sent to market.
7. Much food is put through a process called irradiation so that most of the bacteria on the food is killed by radiation.
8. Neither light nor moisture is good for food preservation so most food products are packaged immediately after they are processed.
9. Shipping companies transport the food from producers to consumers in refrigerated trucks for fresh food spoils quickly.
10. The finished food product can be sold in a variety of locations but in the United States the most common place is a supermarket or grocery store.

More Practice

Language Lab CD-ROM

- Commas lesson

On-line Exercise Bank
- Section 29.2

Grammar Exercise Workbook
- pp. 171–172

◀ **Critical Viewing** How would you express the contrast between the trees and the boxes? Would you need a comma to separate clauses? **[Describe]**

29.2

Commas Between Items in a Series

Items in a series must be separated by commas. A series consists of three or more similar items. These items may be words, phrases, or clauses.

KEY CONCEPT Use commas to separate three or more words, phrases, or clauses in a series. ■

The number of commas that should be used in a series is one fewer than the number of items in the series. For example, if you have a series of three items, you should use two commas; if you have a series of four items, you should use three commas; and so on.

SERIES OF WORDS:	Some farmers sell grain, dairy, and fruits directly to the processor.
SERIES OF PREPOSITIONAL PHRASES:	Other farmers belong to a marketing cooperative, to a terminal market, or to an auction market.
SERIES OF CLAUSES:	The bank filled quickly with people who transferred their accounts, who cashed checks, and who opened their safe-deposit boxes.

In the preceding examples, each series consists of three items; therefore, two commas are used in each of the series.

Some writers omit the last comma in a series except when it is needed to prevent confusion. In your own work, you will find that the full use of commas generally works better.

CONFUSING:	Endless streams of people, honking geese and police officers were all leaving the fair.
ALWAYS CLEAR:	Endless streams of people, honking geese, and police officers were all leaving the fair.

Two Exceptions

When each of the items in a series is joined to the next item by a conjunction, no commas are necessary.

EXAMPLE: Supermarkets and grocery stores and restaurants all sell a variety of foods to consumers.

Commas are not necessary between pairs of items that are thought of as a single item.

EXAMPLE: I asked for ham and eggs, coffee and cream, and bread and butter.

Exercise 8 **Proofreading for Commas With Items in a Series** Copy each sentence that needs commas, adding the necessary commas. For sentences that need no commas, write *correct.*

EXAMPLE: I bought oregano parsley and garlic for the spaghetti sauce.

ANSWER: I bought oregano, parsley, and garlic for the spaghetti sauce.

1. In many developing countries, foods are sold to the general public in an open-market setting without being processed.
2. Markets are made up of individual merchants who set up shop under a tent on a blanket or behind a stand.
3. In the market, you can find shoes furniture dishes or fruits and vegetables.
4. In the Dominican Republic, food is also sold in street carts in supermarkets or in *colmados.*
5. *Colmados* are shops built onto a house or small business and run by one person.
6. There are usually two or three to a street, and they sell basic items, such as eggs soap salt and pepper and fresh meat.
7. Items are sold in bulk, such as flour butter sugar and bananas sold by the pound.
8. Food is not bought and stored in cupboards on shelves or in the refrigerator in the house. It is bought only when it is needed.
9. For this reason, the ability to buy in small amounts to be able to shop often and to serve the food quickly is very important.
10. Those who sell fruits and vegetables who clean shoes or who run errands may call out their services as they walk up and down the street.

More Practice

Language Lab CD-ROM
- Commas lesson

On-line Exercise Bank
- Section 29.2

Grammar Exercise Workbook
- pp. 171–172

▼ **Critical Viewing** In a sentence, list the foods that you like in this picture. Where would you use commas in your sentence? **[Apply]**

Adjectives

Use commas to divide adjectives of equal rank. Such adjectives are called *coordinate adjectives.*

KEY CONCEPT Use commas to separate adjectives of equal rank. ■

Two or more adjectives are considered equal in rank if the word *and* can be placed between the adjectives without changing the meaning of the sentence. Another test is to change the order of the adjectives. If the sentence still sounds correct, then the adjectives are of equal rank and a comma should be placed between them.

EXAMPLE: The dog's matted, filthy coat needed washing.

KEY CONCEPT Do not use commas to separate adjectives that must stay in a specific order. ■

EXAMPLE: The tightly restricted food market is regulated by the government.

These adjectives must stay in the order in which they are written. Therefore, no comma is used to separate them.

Note About *Commas With Adjectives:* Do not use a comma to separate the last adjective in a series from the noun it modifies.

INCORRECT: The food-delivery truck followed a long, twisting, scenic, road.

CORRECT: The food-delivery truck followed a long, twisting, scenic road.

Exercise 9 **Using Commas Between Adjectives** Write the following phrases, and add any necessary commas. If no commas are needed, write *correct.*

EXAMPLE: a vivid beautiful scene

ANSWER: a vivid, beautiful scene

1. rented selling space
2. attractive colorful packaging
3. busy powerful market
4. many new marketplaces
5. cooperative grocery merchants

More Practice

Language Lab CD-ROM
- Commas lesson

On-line Exercise Bank
- Section 29.2

Grammar Exercise Workbook
- pp. 171–172

Commas After Introductory Material

Commas are usually needed to set off introductory material from the rest of the sentence.

KEY CONCEPT Use a comma after an introductory word, phrase, or clause. ■

Following are examples of commas with introductory material.

KINDS OF INTRODUCTORY MATERIAL		
Words	Introductory Words	No, I will not order the magazine you want.
	Nouns of Direct Address	Cindy, could you search appliances on the Internet?
	Common Expressions	Of course, we can get that printed for you.
	Introductory Adverbs	Obviously, the student had tried. Hurriedly, she hid the present she had wrapped.
Phrases	Prepositional Phrases (of four or more words)	In the catalog next to the sink, you can find the shoes you are looking for.
	Participial Phrases	Jumping over the fence, the horse caught its back hoof.
	Infinitive Phrases	To buy things on the Internet, a credit card is often required.
Clauses	Adverb Clauses	When World War II ended, shopping centers became popular.

GRAMMAR IN LITERATURE

from Checkouts

Cynthia Rylant

The introductory words and clauses are highlighted in blue italics. Each introductory element is followed by a comma.

Incredibly, it was another four weeks before they saw each other again. *As fate would have it,* her visits to the supermarket never coincided with his schedule to bag. *Each time she went to the store,* her eyes scanned the checkouts at once, her heart in her mouth. *And each hour he worked,* the bag boy kept one eye on the door, watching for the red-haired girl with the big orange bow.

Exercise 10 Using Commas After Introductory Material For each of the following sentences, write the introductory material and the comma.

EXAMPLE: My friend do you know how malls are run?
ANSWER: My friend,

1. No shopping centers have not always been centers of American shopping.
2. In fact before 1945 very few shopping centers existed.
3. When retailers began to think of combining businesses they focused on the automotive industry.
4. With automobiles in mind the first modern shopping center was designed in Baltimore in 1896.
5. For more than fifty years the idea grew slowly.
6. After World War II ended America became obsessed with the shopping center.
7. Suddenly new shopping centers were springing up everywhere.
8. To keep up with the growing trend of convenience shopping centers were built with enclosed areas.
9. By the end of the 1980's there were about 35,000 shopping centers in the United States.
10. Attracting businesses of all kinds the shopping center industry is very profitable.

More Practice

Language Lab CD-ROM

- Commas lesson

On-line Exercise Bank
- Section 29.2

Grammar Exercise Workbook
- pp. 173–174

Commas With Parenthetical and Nonessential Expressions

Commas are often used within a sentence to set off parenthetical and nonessential expressions.

▲ Critical Viewing Describe this mall, comparing it parenthetically to a mall or shopping center near you. **[Compare and Contrast]**

Parenthetical Expressions

A parenthetical expression is a word or a phrase that is unrelated to the rest of the sentence and interrupts the general flow of the sentence. Study the following list of common parenthetical expressions.

NAMES OF PEOPLE BEING ADDRESSED:	Don, Judge Burke, my son,
CONJUNCTIVE ADVERBS:	also, besides, furthermore, however, indeed, instead, moreover, nevertheless, otherwise, therefore, thus
COMMON EXPRESSIONS:	by the way, I feel, in my opinion, in the first place, of course, on the other hand, you know
CONTRASTING EXPRESSIONS:	not that one, not there, not mine

For any parenthetical expressions, use the following rule:

KEY CONCEPT Use commas to set off parenthetical expressions. ■

Two commas are used to enclose the entire parenthetical expression when the expression is located in the middle of the sentence.

NAMES OF PEOPLE BEING ADDRESSED:	We will go, Marge, as soon as your father arrives.
CONJUNCTIVE ADVERB:	The boys, therefore, decided to call a tow truck.
COMMON EXPRESSION:	The Internet, in my opinion, has made shopping easier than ever.
CONTRASTING EXPRESSION:	It was here, not there, that we found the camera we were looking for.

If one of these expressions is used at the end of a sentence, however, only one comma is necessary.

EXAMPLE:	We will go as soon as your father arrives, Marge.

Exercise 11 **Setting Off Parenthetical Expressions** Copy each of the following sentences, inserting any commas necessary to set off parenthetical expressions. If no comma is needed, write *correct.*

EXAMPLE: The mall is so big in fact that there are three restaurants and a theater.

ANSWER: The mall is so big, in fact, that there are three restaurants and a theater.

1. Most shopping centers are owned by one company and rented out to retail businesses.
2. Each business pays rent plus a percentage of its profit of course to keep its location in the shopping center.
3. This extra percentage called overage makes up most of the profit of owning a shopping center.
4. The company in charge therefore hopes that each of the businesses will succeed.
5. The location of a shopping center is chosen with great care.
6. It must be a place that is easily reached by shoppers.
7. The property furthermore must provide ample parking.
8. The owner rents the available spaces to stores that as a group will attract a large consumer pool.
9. After the center opens, it is the owner not the individual businesses that takes care of security and fire protection.
10. Sanitation and grounds care moreover are also provided by the shopping center firm.

More Practice

Language Lab CD-ROM
- Commas lesson

On-line Exercise Bank
- Section 29.2

Grammar Exercise Workbook
- pp. 173–174

▼ Critical Viewing What features make the location pictured a good location for a shopping center? Use the details you select to complete the following sentence: "This street, ______, is a good location for a shopping center." **[Draw Conclusions]**

Nonessential Expressions

Because commas are used only with nonessential expressions, writers must learn to distinguish between essential and nonessential material. (The terms *restrictive* and *nonrestrictive* are sometimes used to refer to the same type of expressions.)

An *essential expression* is a word, phrase, or clause that provides information that cannot be removed without changing the meaning of the sentence. It is restrictive.

Nonessential expressions provide additional, nonrestrictive, information in a sentence. You can remove nonessential material from a sentence, and the remaining sentence will still contain all the necessary information required by the reader.

Once you have decided whether or not an expression is essential, you can apply this rule.

KEY CONCEPT Use commas to set off nonessential expressions. ■

An appositive, a participial phrase, or an adjective clause can be either essential or nonessential. In the following chart, note that essential material is not set off with commas. Nonessential items, however, are set off with two commas if they are in the middle of a sentence and with one comma if they are at the end.

ESSENTIAL AND NONESSENTIAL EXPRESSIONS		
Appositive	Essential	My sister Joanne went to the Nicollet Mall in Minnesota.
	Nonessential	Joanne, my sister, went to the Nicollet Mall in Minnesota.
Participial Phrase	Essential	The teacher wearing a blue dress took the students to the mall.
	Nonessential	Mrs. Goff, wearing a blue dress, took the students to the mall.
Adjective Clause	Essential	The mall that we enjoyed the most had three levels and a swimming pool.
	Nonessential	The Pine-Woods Center, which was our favorite, had three levels and a swimming pool.

The examples in the chart show only expressions that are located in the middle of the sentence; each nonessential expression is set off with two commas. If the expression shifts to the beginning or the end of the sentence, use only one comma.

EXAMPLE: That evening, he met Joanne**,** my sister.

Exercise 12 **Distinguishing Between Essential and Nonessential Expressions** If one of the following sentences contains an essential expression needing no additional commas, write *essential*. If the sentence contains a nonessential expression, copy the sentence, adding the necessary commas.

EXAMPLE: Shopping in the United States has changed since the 1800's.
ANSWER: essential

1. In small towns of the 1800's, the variety of clothing stores as well as food stores was limited.
2. Foods such as fruits and vegetables were grown on family farms.
3. Ice was sold by the iceman who traveled around in an ice wagon.
4. Small items such as household goods, tools, or fabrics were sold in the town's general store.
5. Specialists such as the blacksmith, the baker, and the tailor offered goods or services of other kinds.
6. Oftentimes, any special purchase like clothes or toys had to be ordered by catalog, and the consumer waited months for it to arrive.
7. Auctions which were held periodically would attract buyers for miles around.
8. Eventually, general stores grew into larger mercantile establishments department stores.
9. They started to carry items in the store that were available only by catalog before.
10. Specialty foods bakery and butcher products became available in one place called the supermarket.

More Practice

Language Lab CD-ROM
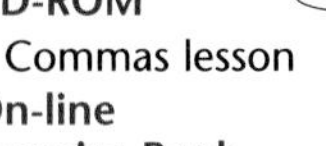
- Commas lesson

On-line Exercise Bank
- Section 29.2

Grammar Exercise Workbook
- pp. 175–176

▼ **Critical Viewing** If you described the place pictured as a store, would the fact that it sells pumpkins and flowers be essential or nonessential to the description? What if you described the place as a farmer's market? **[Apply]**

Commas With Places, Dates, and Titles

The names of places are often made up of several parts. The name of a town may be followed by the name of a county, which in turn may be followed by the name of a state.

KEY CONCEPT When a geographical name is made up of two or more parts, use a comma after each item. ■

EXAMPLE: I traveled from Taos**,** New Mexico**,** to Oklahoma City**,** Oklahoma.

Dates are also often made up of several parts, such as months, days, and years. Commas can help avoid confusion.

KEY CONCEPT When a date is made up of two or more parts, use a comma after each item except in the case of a month followed by a day. ■

EXAMPLES: On Friday**,** April 17**,** we will have a special meeting.
The city's new subway system ran its first train on June 11**,** 1890.

You may omit the commas if the date contains only the month and the year.

EXAMPLE: February 1980 was one of the wettest months on record.

If the parts of a date have already been joined by prepositions, no comma is needed.

EXAMPLE: The city's new subway system ran its first train in June of 1890.

KEY CONCEPT When a name is followed by one or more titles, use a comma after the name and after each title. ■

EXAMPLE: I noticed that Jeremy McGuire**,** Sr.**,** works here.

A similar rule applies with some business abbreviations.

EXAMPLE: Bookwright**,** Inc.**,** published a book about food technology.

Other Uses of the Comma

▲ **Critical Viewing** For what kinds of work-related writing might this store owner use commas? **[Speculate]**

KEY CONCEPT Use a comma after each item in an address of two or more parts. ■

EXAMPLE: My new address is Katie Wedel, 243 Park Street, St. Louis, Missouri 63131.

When an address is written on an envelope, most of the commas are omitted. Notice in both cases that extra space, instead of a comma, is left between the state and the ZIP Code.

EXAMPLE: Katie Wedel
243 Park Street
St. Louis, Missouri 63131

KEY CONCEPT Use a comma after the salutation in a personal letter and after the closing in all letters. ■

SALUTATIONS: Dear Rupert, Dear Aunt Dolly,
CLOSINGS: Sincerely, In appreciation,

KEY CONCEPT With numbers of more than three digits, use a comma after every third digit starting from the right. ■

EXAMPLE: The company has sold 498,362,719 jelly beans.

Note About *Commas in Numbers:* Do not use commas in ZIP Codes, phone numbers, page numbers, serial numbers, years, or house numbers.

EXAMPLES: ZIP Code: 26413 Page number: 1047
Telephone number: (201) 236-7000

KEY CONCEPT Use a comma to indicate the words left out of an elliptical sentence. ■

In the following example, the omitted word is clearly understood. The comma serves as a visual clue to the reader that an omission exists.

EXAMPLE: Developed countries buy food from the grocery store; undeveloped countries, the market.

Commas are also used to help show where direct quotations begin and end.

KEY CONCEPT Use commas to set off a direct quotation from the rest of the sentence. ■

Notice in the next examples that the placement of the commas depends on the location of the nonspoken words in the sentence.

EXAMPLES: The guest asked, "Do you know of any nearby supermarkets that are open all night?"
"If you don't mind a little drive," the host said, "you will find one about three miles down the road."
"Oh, that will be perfect," the guest replied.

Commas help readers by giving visual clues to avoid misreading.

KEY CONCEPT Use a comma to prevent a sentence from being misunderstood. ■

UNCLEAR: Near the highway developers were building a shopping mall.

CLEAR: Near the highway, developers were building a shopping mall.

Exercise 13 **Using Commas in Other Situations** Copy the following sentences, adding the necessary commas. If no comma is needed, write *correct.*

EXAMPLE: Number (702) 555-4818 was billed for $2352.
ANSWER: Number (702) 555-4818 was billed for $2,352.

1. Thursday October 17 Bearnson and Sons Inc. delivered twenty boxes of soap.
2. On Friday of the same week, a check was sent for $1309.46 to Bearnson and Sons Inc. 1298 Ether Road Butler Idaho 83440.
3. She charged the amount to her credit card number 3565 3334 25 3676 on Monday October 21 2001.
4. The store next door was cited for the safety violation on page 1096 of the handbook; our store nothing.
5. John of Mayberry Street in Indianapolis is a friend of mine.

Learn More

To learn more about punctuating direct quotations, see 29.4, Quotation Marks With Direct Quotations

More Practice

Language Lab CD-ROM
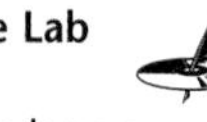
- Commas lesson

On-line Exercise Bank
- Section 29.2

Grammar Exercise Workbook
- pp. 177–178

29.2

Hands-on Grammar

Punctuation Spots

To analyze how commas and end marks can affect meaning, do the following activity with a group of three other people. Photocopy a passage from your literature textbook. Keep one copy complete with punctuation. Then, use correction fluid or correction tape to eliminate the commas and end marks. Make three photocopies of the passage without commas or end marks, and distribute them to the group. Other group members should choose their own passages and eliminate the commas and end marks. Each member in the group should end up with three passages.

Use self-sticking dots from a stationery store to color-code the photocopies where you think commas and end marks should go. As a group, agree to use one color for periods, a second color for question marks, a third color for exclamation marks, and a fourth color for commas. Independently, mark the photocopies with the self-sticking dots. Then, compare your results with other group members, and discuss your choices. Finally, compare your color-coded versions to the originals.

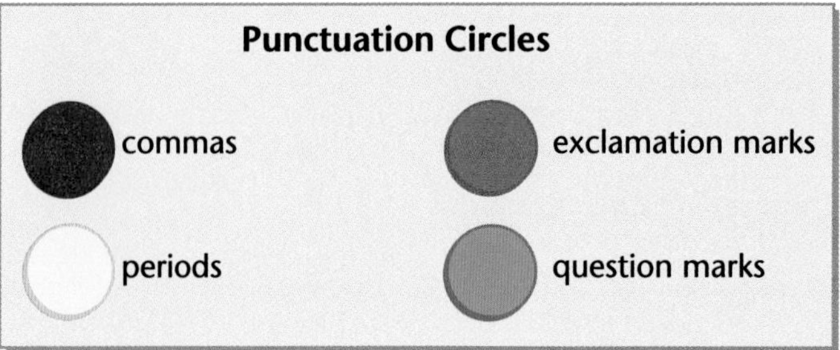

Find It in Your Reading In a literature selection, find examples of commas used to separate items in a series, commas used to set off introductory material, and commas used to set off parenthetical expressions.

Find It in Your Writing Choose one piece of writing from your portfolio. Proofread it for the correct use of commas. If the writing sample you chose does not have any sentences that contain introductory phrases or clauses, challenge yourself to add at least two introductory elements, and punctuate them correctly.

Section 29.2 Section Review

GRAMMAR EXERCISES 14–19

Exercise 14 Using Commas Correctly Rewrite each sentence, inserting commas where necessary. If the sentence is written correctly, write *correct.*

1. The modern shopping mall was made possible by the automobile the growth of the suburbs and television advertising.
2. Some consist of one long or angled building usually of one story divided into several stores.
3. To get from store to store in an open mall a customer must go outdoors.
4. The enclosed mall is covered by a roof which can be eight stories tall.
5. This type of mall is large completely protected from the weather and temperature-controlled.
6. The Mall of America located in Bloomington Minnesota was the largest shopping mall in the United States when it was built in the 1990's.
7. Its nearest rival at the time the Del Amo Fashion Center in Torrance California was half its size.
8. Malls have become all-purpose entertainment centers where a person may shop or eat or go to the movies.
9. Shopping in cities presents problems lack of parking space for example that suburban malls do not have.
10. The mall has the best solution to the problem of scarce parking spaces: huge lots for all-day free parking.

Exercise 15 Proofreading for Commas On a separate sheet of paper, copy the following paragraph. Add or delete commas as needed.

Shopping in older cities like Bombay India is a bustling activity. Buildings are crowded into small, spaces and people seem to be everywhere.

Traders often specializing in one line of business sell their items, in small shops, that have fronts open to the streets. Going from shop, to shop you may ride in a rickshaw a hand-pulled cart. You will have to compete for space with people animals, automobiles other rickshaws and bicycles.

Exercise 16 Using Commas in Special Situations Rewrite the phrase, number, or situation for which a comma is needed. If no comma is needed, write *correct.*

1. Food production began around 8000 B.C.
2. "Shopping" explained the teacher "has existed since man started to trade."
3. The book was published by World Book Inc. 525 W. Monroe Chicago, IL 60661.
4. Look on page 2006 for the answer.
5. Last year 2,067,981 socks were sold.

Exercise 17 Find It in Your Reading Reread the excerpt from "Checkouts" by Cynthia Rylant on page 664. Identify the purpose of each comma.

Exercise 18 Find It in Your Writing Select a piece of writing from your portfolio. Find two examples of the use of commas to set off introductory material.

Exercise 19 Writing Application Follow each set of directions to form new sentences. Use commas correctly.

- Use the conjunction *but* to join two sentences.
- Write a sentence with a series of phrases.
- Write a sentence with an introductory phrase or clause.

Section 29.3

Semicolons and Colons

The semicolon (;) is a punctuation mark that serves as the happy medium between the comma and the period. It signals to the reader to pause longer than for a comma but to pause without the finality of a period. The colon (:) is used primarily to point ahead to additional information. It directs the reader to look further.

Theme: Space Travel

In this section, you will learn how to use semicolons and colons. The examples and exercises are about space travel.

Cross-Curricular Connection: Science

The Semicolon

The semicolon is used to separate independent clauses that have a close relationship to each other. A semicolon is also used to separate independent clauses or items in a series that already contain a number of commas.

Use the Semicolon With Independent Clauses

KEY CONCEPT Use a semicolon to join independent clauses that are not already joined by the conjunction *and, but, for, nor, or, so,* or *yet.* ■

EXAMPLE: The astronaut trainee sat in the spinning, swinging chair**;** she soon grew dizzy going in circles.

Do not use a semicolon to join unrelated independent clauses.

INCORRECT: Astronauts train for their missions; tomorrow, rain is expected.

CORRECT: The word *astronaut* is of Greek origin; it means "sailor among the stars."

Sometimes, the independent clauses will share a similar structure as well as a similar meaning. Occasionally, independent clauses may set up a contrast between each other.

EXAMPLES: With enthusiasm, he cast his line out into the lake; with pleasure, he later cooked his fish.

My sister excels at art; I can barely draw a straight line.

Semicolons can be used to join more than two independent clauses.

EXAMPLE: Alexei A. Leonov was the first human being to float freely in space; Edward H. White II was the first American to spacewalk; Valentina Tereshkova was the first woman in space.

KEY CONCEPT Use a semicolon to join independent clauses separated by either a conjunctive adverb or a transitional expression. ■

The following list contains common conjunctive adverbs and transitional phrases.

CONJUNCTIVE ADVERBS:	also, besides, consequently, furthermore, however, indeed, instead, moreover, nevertheless, otherwise, therefore, thus
TRANSITIONAL EXPRESSIONS:	as a result, at this time, first, for instance, in fact, on the other hand, second, that is

Notice in the following examples that the semicolon is placed before the conjunctive adverb or the transitional expression. A comma follows the conjunctive adverb or the transitional expression because it serves as an introductory expression in the second independent clause.

CONJUNCTIVE ADVERB:	In 1967, the United States *Apollo* was scheduled to fly as the first manned *Apollo* spacecraft; however, the command module caught fire during a ground test, and the flight was cancelled.
TRANSITIONAL EXPRESSION:	We needed to get to the spare tire in the trunk; as a result, we had to unload the trunk.

Because words used as conjunctive adverbs and transitions can also interrupt one continuous sentence, use a semicolon only when there is an independent clause on each side of the conjunctive adverb or transitional expression.

INCORRECT:	The flight was; consequently, cancelled.
CORRECT:	The flight was, consequently, cancelled.

In these examples, *consequently* interrupts one continuous sentence; therefore, a semicolon would be incorrect.

▼ **Critical Viewing** In what way does this picture illustrate the importance of the correct connection? **[Relate]**

29.3

Use the Semicolon to Avoid Confusion

The semicolon can also be used to avoid confusion in sentences that contain other internal punctuation.

KEY CONCEPT Consider the use of semicolons to avoid confusion when independent clauses already contain commas. ■

When a sentence consists of two independent clauses joined by a coordinating conjunction, the tendency is to place a comma before the conjunction. However, when one or both of the sentences also contain commas, a semicolon may be used before the conjunction to prevent confusion.

EXAMPLE: The astronauts who were aboard the first manned spaceflight to the moon in 1968 were William Anders, Frank Borman, and James Lovell; but they did not land on the moon.

KEY CONCEPT Use a semicolon between items in a series if the items themselves contain commas. ■

EXAMPLE: Some of the women that the space program has trained include the Russian, Valentina Tereshkova, who orbited Earth in 1963; Sally K. Ride, the first American woman in space; and Christa McAuliffe, who was killed in a tragic accident seconds after liftoff in the shuttle *Challenger.*

You will use the semicolon in a series most commonly when the items contain either nonessential appositives, participial phrases, or adjective clauses.

APPOSITIVES: I sent notes to Mr. Nielson, my science teacher; Mrs. Jensen, my history instructor; and Mrs. Seltz, the librarian.

PARTICIPIAL PHRASES: I developed a fascination with space travel from television, watching live rocket launches; from school, learning about the science; and from movies, watching science-fiction adventures.

ADJECTIVE CLAUSES: The toy rocket that I bought has spare tires, which are brand new; a siren, which has just been installed; and a great engine, which has been newly tuned up.

Notice that commas are used to separate the nonessential material from the word or words they refer to or modify; the semicolons separate the complete items in the series.

More Practice

Language Lab CD-ROM
- Quotation Marks, Colons, and Semicolons lesson

On-line Exercise Bank
- Section 29.3

Grammar Exercise Workbook
- pp. 179–180

Exercise 20 **Using the Semicolon With Independent Clauses** Decide where a semicolon is needed in each of the following sentences. Write the word that goes before the semicolon, write the semicolon, and write the word that goes after it.

EXAMPLE: Not all astronauts fly in space those who work on the Earth's surface for NASA are also considered astronauts.

ANSWER: space; those

1. Knowledge about space has not come easily since 1959 about 250 astronauts have flown in space.
2. For the first Mercury program, seven test pilots were chosen the group consisted of Air Force officers.
3. In 1962, nine more pilots were selected fourteen were chosen in 1963.
4. These pilots flew on two-person *Gemini* missions and *Apollo* flights to the moon this was the last time only Air Force officers were chosen as pilots.
5. The year 1965 marked the beginning of scientist astronauts a group of six men and five civilians was chosen.
6. All had received master's or doctor's degrees, and only two were jet pilots consequently, the rest received one year of military flight training.
7. In 1978, NASA changed the organization of the astronauts twenty mission specialists and fifteen new pilot astronauts were chosen.
8. This group included the first six women astronauts from the United States indeed, Russia had already sent a woman into space in 1963.
9. Many of the astronauts selected since the late 1970's have held advanced degrees this education was useful for mission specialists.
10. In 1983, Sally K. Ride, the first American woman to travel in space, orbited Earth on the space shuttle *Challenger* in 1990 NASA selected the first woman to become a pilot astronaut, a pilot who commands or controls a spacecraft.

▼ **Critical Viewing** Which sentence in the exercise at left gives you a clue to the identity of this astronaut? **[Connect]**

▲ Critical Viewing What qualities do you think these cosmonauts need to function well in a setting such as the one shown here? **[Deduce]**

Exercise 21 **Using Semicolons With Internal Punctuation** Copy each sentence, adding semicolons where they are needed to avoid confusion. Hint: Some commas may need to be replaced with a semicolon.

EXAMPLE: Cosmonauts work in space, handling equipment for space stations, satellites for communication, and experiments for scientific research.

ANSWER: Cosmonauts work in space, handling equipment for space stations; satellites for communication; and experiments for scientific research.

1. One who works in the space field may be called an astronaut, a space worker from the United States or a cosmonaut, a space worker from the Commonwealth of Independent States.
2. Cosmonauts work and train at the Gagarin Center, also called *Star Town* and the Baykonur Cosmodrome, where crews lift off into space.
3. Since 1961, more than one hundred cosmonauts, which means "sailors of the universe," have traveled into space four of them were killed during flight.
4. One cosmonaut, Vladimir Komarov, was killed when his parachute did not open three others, members of the *Soyez II* crew, died when air leaked out of their capsule and asphyxiated them.
5. The former cosmonaut program consisted of two years of athletic activity, parachute jumping, and the use of chambers to push the physical limits of its trainees, but the modern-day program focuses on mental preparation and lasts 8–10 years.

More Practice

Language Lab CD-ROM
- Quotation Marks, Colons, and Semicolons lesson

On-line Exercise Bank
- Section 29.3

Grammar Exercise Workbook
- pp. 179–180

The Colon

The colon acts mainly as an introductory device. It is also used in several special situations.

Colons as Introductory Devices

KEY CONCEPT Use a colon before a list of items following an independent clause. ■

EXAMPLE: Astronaut trainees go through the following five phases of training: classroom work, flight training, survival training, mission training, and special training.

As shown in this example, the independent clause before a list often ends in a phrase such as *the following* or *the following items*. You should familiarize yourself with these phrases because they often indicate the need for a colon. Of course, you should not depend on these phrases alone to signal the need for a colon. The most important point to consider is whether or not an independent clause precedes the list. If it does, use a colon.

EXAMPLE: He had the right qualities to be an astronaut: fitness, courage, and commitment.

KEY CONCEPT Use a colon to introduce a quotation that is formal or lengthy or a quotation that does not contain a "he said/she said" expression. ■

Often, a formal quotation requiring a colon will consist of more than one sentence. However, your best guideline for inserting a colon should be the formality of the quotation. The more formal the quotation, the more likely you will need a colon.

Do not use a colon to introduce a casual quoted remark or dialogue, even if more than one sentence is used.

EXAMPLE: The speaker began with these words: "I have never been so honored in all my life."

KEY CONCEPT Use a colon to introduce a sentence that summarizes or explains the sentence before it. ■

Capitalize the first word after a colon if the word begins a complete sentence.

EXAMPLE: The technician provided her with one piece of advice: Check the water level often.

In this example, the colon points to the explanation contained in the next sentence.

Use a colon, instead of a comma, to introduce an appositive that follows an independent clause to give additional emphasis to the appositive.

KEY CONCEPT Use a colon to introduce a formal appositive that follows an independent clause. ■

EXAMPLE: The Russian 1971 flight ended in an accident: a sudden loss of air in the cabin.

When you are using colons in sentences, always check to be sure that an independent clause comes before the colon.

INCORRECT: We decided to: see an old movie.

CORRECT: We decided to see an old movie: *The Right Stuff.*

INCORRECT: The lunar trips helped: collect lunar dust, bring back lunar rock, and set up scientific stations on the moon.

CORRECT: The lunar trips had three side-missions: to collect lunar dust, to bring back lunar rock, and to set up scientific stations on the moon.

Although an independent clause must precede a colon, it is not necessary that the words following the colon be an independent clause.

EXAMPLE: From the window, I looked out at the expanse of space and saw a familiar sight: Earth.

As you can see, the word *Earth* is an appositive for the words *familiar sight.* You could argue successfully that a comma would also be appropriate where the colon is inserted. However, the colon provides a slightly more dramatic, profound effect than that which would be achieved by the comma. As a writer, you will have the responsibility of deciding whether the comma or the colon more precisely fits the tone you are trying to establish in your writing.

Learn More

For more information about capitalizing with colons, see Chapter 28.

Special Uses of the Colon The colon has several specialized functions that you will probably encounter in your reading and writing.

Many special situations require the use of a colon. Among them are references to time, volume and page numbers, chapters and verses in the Bible, book subtitles, business letter salutations, and labels that are used to introduce important ideas. Study the examples that are given in the following chart; it shows how the colon is used in each of these special situations.

▲ **Critical Viewing** In a sentence using a colon, list words that describe the texture of the lunar surface pictured here. **[Apply]**

SPECIAL SITUATIONS REQUIRING COLONS	
Numerals Giving the Time	5:22 A.M. 7:49 P.M.
References to Periodicals (Volume Number: Page Number)	*Forbes* 4:8
Biblical References (Chapter Number: Verse Number)	Genesis 1:5
Subtitles for Books and Magazines	*Fixing Hamburger: One Hundred Ways to Prepare Delicious Meals*
Salutations in Business Letters	Dear Mr. Biggs: Ladies: Dear Sir:
Labels Used to Signal Important Ideas	WARNING: Cigarette smoking can be hazardous to your health. Note: This letter must be postmarked no later than the tenth of this month.

Exercise 22 **Using Colons as Introductory Devices** Decide where a colon is appropriate. On your paper, write the word that comes before the colon, write the colon, and write the word that comes after the colon with the correct capitalization.

EXAMPLE: NASA teaches classes that their trainees will need as astronauts aerodynamics, physics, physiology, and spacecraft-tracking techniques.

ANSWER: astronauts: aerodynamics

1. After one year at the Johnson Space Center, astronauts experience the first phase of specialized training classroom work.
2. In the early years of the space program, astronauts began the study of important space technology rocket engines, flight mechanics, and computer theory.
3. *Apollo* astronauts took additional classes astronomy, Earth geology, life sciences, and geology of the moon.
4. NASA also discusses what makes spaceflight possible qualified people, equipment, and funds.
5. NASA hires well-qualified instructors experienced astronauts, pilots, doctors, and university professors.

More Practice

Language Lab CD-ROM
- Quotation Marks, Colons, and Semicolons lesson

On-line Exercise Bank
- Section 29.3

Grammar Exercise Workbook
- pp. 181–182

Exercise 23 **Using Colons for Special Writing Situations** Copy each of the following items, adding the necessary colons. If an item requires no colons, write *correct.*

EXAMPLE: For more information on astronauts, read *Liftoff The Story of America's Adventure in Space.*
For more information on astronauts, read *Liftoff: The Story of America's Adventure in Space.*

1. October 13, 20--
   6 35 P.M.
2. Dear Sirs
   I am writing to tell you what I know about some moon trips.
3. On one trip to the moon, the astronauts read from Genesis 1 1–10 over national television.
4. Upon landing in the Sea of Tranquillity, these famous words came from the spacecraft "Tranquillity Base here . . . the Eagle has landed." Note The prior landing destination proved unsuitable.
5. Sincerely yours,
   George Tuckett

Section 29.3 **Section Review**

GRAMMAR EXERCISES 24–29

Exercise 24 **Using Semicolons Correctly** Decide where a semicolon is needed in each of the following sentences. Write the word before the semicolon, write the semicolon, and write the word after the semicolon.

1. Astronaut trainees work hard to fill the requirements as a result, they are physically and mentally ready for the arduous tasks that lay before them.
2. Applicants are physically tested and interviewed for a period of one week trainees are selected from those who score the highest.
3. Those applying as pilot astronauts must also complete 1,000 hours in a top-level flight post, such as a command pilot in a high-performance jet aircraft following that, they must pass a spaceflight physical.
4. Pilot astronauts must be between 5'4" tall and 6'4" tall mission-specialist astronauts must be between 5' tall and 6'4" tall payload specialists have no height requirement.
5. To fit the requirements, an astronaut applicant must have the appropriate education, physical health and stature, and experience but, in most cases, an applicant may be of any age.

Exercise 25 **Using Colons Correctly** Rewrite each item, adding colons where appropriate. Some items may require more than one colon. Write *correct* if an item needs no additional punctuation.

1. August 1, 1998
2. To whom it may concern
3. Meeting Friday, September 8, for Junior Space Camp
4. Place American Hills High School
5. Time 7 00 P.M.

Exercise 26 **Proofreading for Semicolons, Colons, and Capitalization** On a separate sheet of paper, write the following paragraph. Add any needed semicolons or colons. Correct any capitalization errors.

It is important for pilot astronauts to experience the next phase of training flight training. Flight training, done in a T-38 jet aircraft, is not as extensive as it once was astronauts used to have one year of military flight training before they could fly in space. Candidates practice maneuvering, reaching altitudes of above 5,000 feet, and they are taught to use the ejection seat. They also study other systems the aircraft's electrical system, life support, and ejection seat. Note mission specialists are also given flight training, but they do not pilot the jets during takeoffs or landings.

Exercise 27 **Find It in Your Reading** On a notice on your school bulletin board, identify how colons and semicolons are used to transmit information.

Exercise 28 **Find It in Your Writing** Select a piece of writing from your portfolio. Find examples of the use of colons and semicolons. If you are unable to locate such examples, challenge yourself to write two sentences using colons and semicolons.

Exercise 29 **Writing Application** Write a brief letter to a local or national politician asking about the future of America's space exploration. Use at least two semicolons in your letter.

Quotation Marks With Direct Quotations

Writers try to provide concrete support for their ideas and arguments. Quoting an expert directly can provide support for your statements while making your writing more colorful.

Theme: Trains

In this section, you will learn how to use quotation marks to set off direct quotations. The examples and exercises are about trains.

Cross-Curricular Connection: Social Studies

Punctuating Direct Quotations

This section will take a close look at direct quotations to help clarify any uncertainties you may have regarding their punctuation.

KEY CONCEPT A **direct quotation** represents a person's exact speech or thoughts and is enclosed in quotation marks (" "). ■

DIRECT QUOTATION: "I can make a steam carriage that will run 15 miles an hour on good, level railways."
—Oliver Evans

Sometimes, you will insert only a quoted phrase into a sentence. You must set this fragment off with quotation marks also. Notice in the following examples that the first word of a phrase or fragment is capitalized only when it falls at the beginning of a sentence or when it would be capitalized regardless of its position in a sentence.

EXAMPLES: In the early years of the locomotive, people often called it "the iron horse."
"The iron horse" is what people often called the locomotive in its early years.

KEY CONCEPT An **indirect quotation** reports only the general meaning of what a person said or thought and does not require quotation marks. ■

INDIRECT QUOTATION: Oliver Evans, who had built a steam-powered scow with wheels in 1804, said that he could build a locomotive that could run 15 miles an hour on level track.

KEY CONCEPT Use a comma or colon after an introductory expression. ■

INTRODUCTORY EXPRESSION: A representative of the Smithsonian Institution wrote, "Railroad is one of the most important means of transportation."

If you do not use a "he said/she said" expression in your introduction to a quotation or if the introductory phrase takes a more formal tone, use a colon instead of a comma before the quotation.

EXAMPLES: Walter Larson, mayor of Washington, Missouri, spoke with the reporter: "We are looking forward to the renovated station spurring additional visitors to our community."

Solemnly, she stated: "I will resign as treasurer of this corporation."

▲ Critical Viewing With a partner, role-play a conversation that might occur between two travelers on this platform. Write a few sentences of the dialogue you exchange, correctly punctuating with commas and quotation marks. **[Apply]**

KEY CONCEPT Use a comma, a question mark, or an exclamation mark after a quotation followed by a concluding expression. ■

CONCLUDING EXPRESSION: "Railroad is one of the most important means of transportation," wrote a representative of the Smithsonian Institution.

KEY CONCEPT Use a comma after part of a quoted sentence followed by an interrupting expression. Use another comma after the expression. ■

INTERRUPTING EXPRESSION: "Railroad," wrote a representative of the Smithsonian Institution, "is one of the most important means of transportation."

KEY CONCEPT Use a comma, a question mark, or an exclamation mark after a quoted sentence that comes before an interrupting expression. Use a period after the expression. ■

EXAMPLE: "Should we expect the train any time soon?" he asked. "It was an hour late yesterday."

Grammar and Style Tip

When using a direct or an indirect quotation, give the speaker's name whenever possible to add credibility to your writing and to avoid plagiarizing others' works.

Exercise 30 **Indicating and Capitalizing Quotations** Copy the following sentences, making the necessary corrections in punctuation and capitalization. Quoted phrases are italicized.

EXAMPLE: in 1812 Colonel Stevens announced to the Legislature of New York *I could build a railroad at much less the cost of the proposed Erie Canal.*

ANSWER: In 1812, Colonel Stevens announced to the Legislature of New York, "I could build a railroad at much less the cost of the proposed Erie Canal."

1. colonel Stevens stated: *the transportation by means of cars drawn by steam locomotives could be carried on at a considerably cheaper rate.*
2. *I had read of your very ingenious proposition as to the railway communication* wrote his friend *I fear, however, that they will be liable to serious objection.*
3. *they would ultimately prove more expensive than a canal* the chancellor continued.
4. He spoke of the great strength that the rails would need to have to *sustain so heavy a weight.*
5. *the wall on which they are placed* he explained *must be at least four feet below the surface, to avoid frost.*

More Practice

Language Lab CD-ROM
- Quotation Marks, Colons, and Semicolons lesson

On-line Exercise Bank
- Section 29.4

Grammar Exercise Workbook
- pp. 183–184

▼ Critical Viewing

Find a quotation about progress that you would use as a caption for this picture. On a separate sheet of paper, write and punctuate the quotation, including the words that indicate the speaker. **[Connect]**

Other Punctuation Marks With Quotation Marks

Whether to place punctuation inside or outside the quotation marks presents a problem for some writers. Four basic rules, once learned, will help you avoid most of the confusion.

KEY CONCEPT Always place a comma or a period inside the final quotation mark. ■

EXAMPLES: "You exhibited greater skill in today's lesson," the driving instructor announced.

"August 1829," the President of the Delaware and Hudson Canal Company wrote, "marked the first locomotive run upon this continent."

Note in the second example that the quotation is split but that this makes no difference in the placement of the comma. It still goes inside the quotation marks.

KEY CONCEPT Always place a semicolon or colon outside the final quotation mark. ■

EXAMPLE: His history book reports, "John Stevens built the first steam locomotive in the United States"; however, it had many flaws.

KEY CONCEPT Place a question mark or exclamation mark inside the final quotation mark if the end mark is part of the quotation. ■

EXAMPLE: Horatio Allen asked in a letter, "When was the exact date of the first locomotive trip in the United States?"

KEY CONCEPT Place a question mark or exclamation mark outside the final quotation mark if the end mark is not part of the quotation. ■

EXAMPLE: Did you hear that speaker say, "We must reduce energy consumption"?

With question marks and exclamation marks, only one mark is needed. In the following, the quotation is a question and the sentence is a statement. No period, however, is needed.

EXAMPLE: My mother asked, "Did you feed the animals?"

Grammar and Style Tip

Use dialogue to improve characterization in short stories. The exact words a character speaks sometimes reveal more about a character than a description can.

Exercise 31 **Using Quotation Marks With Other Punctuation Marks** Copy the following sentences, adding quotation marks and any needed commas, colons, semicolons, or end marks. *Note:* Italics included in some of the sentences are a clue to which text should be in quotations.

EXAMPLE: Marion de Lorme wrote a letter in 1641 to the Marquis about a *poor creature named Solomon de Cause;* Solomon had been locked up in Paris by the king for his *crazy* ideas about steam power.

ANSWER: Marion de Lorme wrote a letter in 1641 to the Marquis about a "poor creature named Solomon de Cause"; Solomon had been locked up in Paris by the king for his "crazy" ideas about steam power.

1. Solomon was sent away without being admitted to the king, but he was so persistent that the king *had him shut up as a madman!*
2. Nineteenth-century locomotives powered by steam were created by expanding on these basic ideas. *Air expands as it heats. Steam has a lot of power.*
3. Was it really the Marquis of Worcester who first discovered the power of steam from observing *the motion of the lid of a teakettle of boiling water?*
4. Perhaps, but the author of <u>The First Locomotives</u> writes *it does seem far more likely that Solomon . . . would be the one to observe the effects of the steam upon the lid of a teakettle.*

More Practice

Language Lab CD-ROM
- Quotation Marks, Colons, and Semicolons lesson

On-line Exercise Bank
- Section 29.4

Grammar Exercise Workbook
- pp. 185–186

▼ Critical Viewing Why might it be difficult to hear a speaker's exact words when traveling on this train? **[Speculate]**

Quotation Marks in Special Situations

Several special situations may occur when you write direct quotations. These include dialogues, quotations of more than one paragraph, and quotations within other quoted material.

First, consider the use of quotation marks when writing dialogue—a direct conversation between two or more people. Use quotation marks to enclose the directly quoted conversation, and begin a new paragraph for each change of speaker.

KEY CONCEPT When writing dialogue, begin a new paragraph with each change of speaker. ■

EXAMPLE: The station attendant shouted from behind the hood, "You're a quart low on oil, Mrs. Lowell. Would you like me to put some in for you?"

"Yes, thank you," she replied.

"What kind of oil do you use in the car?"

She hesitated and then replied, "I believe the car takes multigrade."

KEY CONCEPT For quotations longer than a paragraph, put quotation marks at the beginning of each paragraph and at the end of the final paragraph. ■

EXAMPLE: "In July of 1831, the West Point Foundry Works of New York first put a steam vehicle on the road. They called it the De Witt Clinton, and to many it seemed like a steam locomotive without tracks.

"This De Witt Clinton was not a lightweight vehicle. It weighed about six tons, and its wheels were about five feet across.

"Two names associated with this project were John B. Jervis, the man who contracted for the vehicle to be built, and another man, known as Sir Matthew, who served as chief engineer of the project."

KEY CONCEPT Use single quotation marks for a quotation within a quotation. ■

EXAMPLE: The fund-raiser concluded, saying, "As we try to raise money for this worthy cause, let us not forget that old English proverb that says, 'Where there's a will there's a way.'"

▲ **Critical Viewing** Find an article about the "bullet train." Choose a fact or detail from the article and write it out as a direct quotation. Include in your sentence the author's name. **[Apply]**

Exercise 32 **Punctuating and Capitalizing in Longer Selections** The following dialogue has no paragraphing, quotation marks, capitalization, or punctuation. Each number indicates a new speaker. Copy the dialogue, indicating paragraphs and adding the necessary quotation marks, capitalization, and punctuation.

1. what is an electric railroad asked peter
2. it is replied raajita an electrically powered railway system
3. oh, would that include subways and streetcars
4. raajita looked at him and explained yes, they are a lot quieter than other trains, and they don't produce any smoke or exhaust
5. peter was doubtful maybe, but how do they run
6. well, the encyclopedia says the world's fastest is france's tgv train and that it can reach up to 160 mph
7. there are magnetic-levitation electrical trains interrupted desmond being designed by engineers right now
8. how do the two of you know so much about electric trains inquired Peter
9. desmond turned to him with a smile
10. we have been to europe, he explained electric trains are common in europe, but in the united states, less than 1 percent of inter-city track is electrified.

More Practice

Language Lab CD-ROM
- Quotation Marks, Colons, and Semicolons lesson

On-line Exercise Bank
- Section 29.4

Grammar Exercise Workbook
- pp. 185–186

Underlining and Other Uses of Quotation Marks

In printed material, italics and quotation marks are used to set some titles, names, and words apart from the rest of the text. In handwritten or typed material, italics are not available, so underlining is used instead. Quotation marks, on the other hand, are used in both printed and handwritten materials.

Technology Tip

Use the formatting tools of a word-processing program to italicize the titles of full-length works.

Underlining

KEY CONCEPT Underline the titles of long written works and the titles of publications that are published as a single work. ■

Following are examples of titles you should underline.

TITLES OF WRITTEN WORKS THAT ARE UNDERLINED	
Titles of Books	Jane Eyre by Charlotte Brontë
Titles of Plays	A Raisin in the Sun by Lorraine Hansberry The Man Who Came to Dinner by Moss Hart
Titles of Periodicals (magazines, journals, pamphlets)	Eastern Railroad News Time Journal of American History TRAINS Magazine
Titles of Newspapers	The New York Times the Palm Beach Post the Chicago Sun-Times
Titles of Long Poems	Idylls of the King by Alfred, Lord Tennyson Beowulf

Note About *Newspaper Titles:* The portion of the title that should be underlined will vary from newspaper to newspaper. *The New York Times* should always be fully capitalized and underlined. Other papers, however, can usually be treated in one of two ways: *The Los Angeles Times* or the Los Angeles *Times.* Unless you know the true name of a paper, choose one of these two forms and use it consistently.

KEY CONCEPT Underline the titles of movies, television and radio series, lengthy works of music, paintings, and sculpture. ■

OTHER ARTISTIC WORKS THAT ARE UNDERLINED	
Titles of Movies	The Caine Mutiny
Titles of Radio and Television Series	The Shadow Happy Days
Titles of Long Musical Compositions and Record Albums (any musical work made up of several parts, such as operas, musical comedies, symphonies, and ballets)	Bach's Christmas Oratorio The Beatles' Abbey Road Puccini's Tosca Haydn's Surprise Symphony Tchaikovsky's Swan Lake
Titles of Paintings and Sculpture	Dancers at the Bar (Degas) Indian on Horseback (Mestrovic)

KEY CONCEPT Underline the names of individual air, sea, space, and land craft. ■

the Spirit of St. Louis — the S.S. Seagallant
the De Witt Clinton

KEY CONCEPT Underline foreign words not yet accepted into English. ■

EXAMPLE: It is verboten to board the train without a ticket. (German: forbidden)

Since the process of accepting words and phrases into the English language is a continuous one, you cannot be certain whether a phrase is still considered foreign.

KEY CONCEPT Underline numbers, symbols, letters, and words used to name themselves. ■

NUMBERS: When I say the number three, you start running.
SYMBOLS: Is that an ! at the end of that sentence?
LETTERS: Is that first letter a G or an S?
WORDS: She wrote the word fluid, but she meant fluent.

KEY CONCEPT Underline words that you wish to stress. ■

EXAMPLE: We will need a minimum of six dollars for the trip.

Exercise 33 **Underlining Titles, Names, and Words** Write and underline titles, names, or words that require underlining. If a sentence needs no correction, write *correct.*

EXAMPLE: She graduated magna cum laude.
ANSWER: magna cum laude

1. He read the book Murder on the Orient Express.
2. The words all aboard signal the last boarding of the train.
3. They had to get some dinero before they could buy the TV.
4. Flimsies West and Hot Off the Rails Newsletter are both magazines about railroads.
5. In the former Soviet Union, President Mikhail Gorbachev introduced glasnost, beginning a major reform period.
6. You may read about a change in railroad legislation in The New York Times.
7. We won't get on this car but the next one.
8. The cast of Our Town took the subway to Times Square.
9. Although locomotives were built and tested up to the year 1829, the first locomotive to run for public use was the De Witt Clinton in the year 1831.
10. The advances in technology from steam engines to the launching of Apollo 12 happened amazingly fast.

More Practice
On-line Exercise Bank
• Section 29.4
Grammar Exercise Workbook
• pp. 187–188

▼ Critical Viewing
Name three stories, novels, movies, or songs that this picture calls to mind. Which ones would be underlined or italicized in writing? **[Connect]**

Other Uses of Quotation Marks

Earlier in Section 29.4, the use of quotation marks (" ") with spoken words was discussed. Quotation marks also set off certain titles.

KEY CONCEPT Use quotation marks around the titles of short written works. ■

Short works include short stories, chapters from books, short poems, essays, and articles.

SHORT STORY:	"The Jockey" by Carson McCullers
CHAPTER FROM A BOOK:	"Railroads in America"
SHORT POEM:	"Boy Breaking Glass" by Gwendolyn Brooks
ESSAY TITLES:	"Self-Reliance" by Ralph Waldo Emerson
ARTICLE TITLE:	"The Benefits of Train Travel"

KEY CONCEPT Use quotation marks around the titles of episodes in a series, songs, and parts of long musical compositions. ■

EPISODE:	"The Iran File" from 60 Minutes
SONG TITLE:	"I've Been Working on the Railroad"
PART OF A LONG MUSICAL COMPOSITION:	"Spring" from The Four Seasons

Occasionally, you may refer to the title of one long work contained in a larger work. Singly, each title would require underlining; when used together, another rule applies.

Use quotation marks around the title of a work that is mentioned as part of a collection.

EXAMPLE: "Plato" from Great Books of the Western World

▶ **Critical Viewing** Explain how this picture illustrates the importance of understanding and following visual clues and signals. **[Analyze]**

Exercise 34 **Using Quotation Marks With Titles** From each of the following sentences, copy the unpunctuated title and enclose it in quotation marks.

EXAMPLE: The story The Necklace has an interesting theme.
ANSWER: "The Necklace"

1. Streetcars Tie the City Together is an article about the importance of streetcars in the city.
2. Edgar Allan Poe wrote the famous story The Tell-Tale Heart.
3. A popular song about a train is The Chattanooga Express.
4. An important chapter to read from that book is Letters From Officials.
5. Robert Frost, one of my favorite poets, wrote Nothing Gold Can Stay.
6. The newspaper clipping was entitled Local Officials Celebrate New Train Station in Washington.
7. The story The Lottery speaks against blindly following the crowd.
8. Read The Inspector-General in *Prentice Hall Literature: Timeless Voices, Timeless Themes,* Gold.
9. Be sure to cover the chapter entitled The Industrial Revolution in your history books tonight.
10. They decided to sing Good Night, Ladies as the train left the station.

More Practice

Language Lab CD-ROM

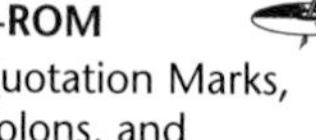

- Quotation Marks, Colons, and Semicolons lesson

On-line Exercise Bank

- Section 29.4

Grammar Exercise Workbook

- pp. 187–188

Titles Without Underlining or Quotation Marks

Some titles require neither underlining nor quotation marks. The first such classification consists of various religious works.

KEY CONCEPT Do not underline or place in quotation marks the name of the Bible, its books, divisions, or versions or the names of other holy scriptures, such as the Koran. ■

EXAMPLE: He found a Bible in his hotel room.

Similarly, you should not underline or enclose in quotation marks certain government documents.

KEY CONCEPT Do not underline or place in quotation marks the titles of government charters, alliances, treaties, acts, statutes, or reports. ■

EXAMPLES: the Declaration of Independence
the Civil Rights Act

Exercise 35 **Punctuating Different Types of Titles** Copy the titles, and enclose them in quotation marks or underline them. If neither quotation marks nor underlining is needed, write *correct.*

EXAMPLE: The Bill of Rights protects the rights of individuals.

ANSWER: correct

1. The Constitution was a collection of compromises.
2. The astronaut read from the first chapter of Genesis when he saw the Earth from space.
3. The family studied the Koran as they rode the train.
4. The Americans With Disabilities Act provides accommodations to those with disabilities.
5. They read Electric Railroad from the World Book Encyclopedia.
6. The Railroads: Opening the West would have several chapters about the history of railroads.
7. The English locomotive John Bull had four driving wheels of four feet in diameter.
8. There was a Bible in our hotel room.
9. The San Diego Times is a newspaper published in California.
10. All the leaders signed the Treaty of Versailles.

▲ Critical Viewing
Based on details from this picture, why might some people prefer traveling by train to traveling by plane? **[Infer]**

More Practice

Language Lab CD-ROM
- Quotation Marks, Colons, and Semicolons lesson

On-line Exercise Bank
- Section 29.4

Grammar Exercise Workbook
- pp. 187–188

Section 29.4

Section Review

GRAMMAR EXERCISES 36–41

Exercise 36 **Punctuating Direct Quotations** Rewrite the following sentences, punctuating correctly.

1. John Edgar, a reporter, writes of a new program: this program offers train customers car-rental services at select stations throughout the country.
2. He is speaking of a new program many train stations have adopted with the facilities housing rental desks.
3. We have come together explains Executive Vice President Barbara J. Wylie to deliver a more seamless journey for our customers.
4. She continues it is the very kind of service that today's travelers expect.
5. You can read the paper to find out how this service works Upon arrival at participating stations, travelers may simply walk across the street to the car-rental location.

Exercise 37 **Using Punctuation in Direct Quotations** Rewrite the following dialogue, punctuating correctly. Each number indicates a new speaker.

1. Was it the Robert Fulton that was the first locomotive-engine that came from England and was afterward put on the road?
2. It certainly was he said and when it came, great preparations were made for a large crowd of passengers
3. I read what happened on the day of the excursion Something [went] wrong with the Robert Fulton and the DeWitt Clinton took its place at the head of the train.
4. Of course, the rest of the train Tom pointed out was too heavy for so small a machine
5. Some of the cars were pulled by the DeWitt, and the other popular mode of transportation pulled the rest of the amusing-looking cavalcade: horses.

Exercise 38 **Using Quotation Marks and Underlining** Rewrite the title(s) from each sentence. Add underlining or quotation marks where appropriate.

1. In 1832, the Baltimore and Ohio Railroad Company introduced a steam locomotive called the York.
2. For those who own passenger cars, the American Association of Private Railroad Car Owners is a good society to join.
3. We listened to Summer from The Four Seasons during the trip.
4. We pulled the information from Chapter 38: Additional Letters.
5. An informative paper designed for rail-road fans is the Eastern Railroad News.

Exercise 39 **Find It in Your Reading** Explain the purpose of the quotation marks and underlining in the following passage.

"Space travel is humanity's greatest adventure," says Eugene F. Kranz, who describes the history and development of the space program in an article in the World Book Encyclopedia.

Exercise 40 **Find It in Your Writing** Choose a piece of writing from your portfolio. Find examples of direct quotations and indirect quotations.

Exercise 41 **Writing Application** Write a conversation between two or more people who are discussing travel plans. Use quotation marks correctly.

Dashes, Parentheses, and Hyphens

Dashes

The dash, a long horizontal mark made above the writing line (—), functions to set off material in three basic ways:

KEY CONCEPT Use dashes to indicate an abrupt change of thought, a dramatic interrupting idea, or a summary statement. ■

USES OF THE DASH	
To indicate an abrupt change of thought	I cannot believe what the barber did to my beautiful hair—oh, I don't even want to think about it!
To set off interrupting ideas dramatically	Oatmeal—which tastes delicious with honey and raisins—makes a nutritious breakfast when served with milk. The ruby-throated hummingbird—wow, what a beautiful bird—gets its name from the male's red throat.
To set off a summary statement	Vanilla, rocky road, strawberry, blackberry, and butter pecan—deciding which of these flavors to get took me a full five minutes. To eat twice its body weight in a day—this is the feeding goal of the hummingbird.

It may help you to know that words such as *all, these, this,* and *that* frequently begin a summary sentence preceded by a dash.

In certain circumstances, nonessential appositives and modifiers are also set off with dashes.

KEY CONCEPT Use dashes to set off a nonessential appositive or modifier when it is long, when it is already punctuated, or when you want to be dramatic. ■

Only those appositives or modifiers that follow the rule need a dash. Notice how the examples in the following charts each meet at least one of the three criteria in the rule.

Theme: Birds

In this section, you will learn about the various uses of dashes, parentheses, and hyphens. The examples and exercises are about birds.

Cross-Curricular Connection: Science

USING DASHES WITH NONESSENTIAL APPOSITIVES	
Reasons for Use	**Examples**
Length	The ruby-throated hummingbird—a bird that lives in woods, orchards, and gardens but moves to the forests in the winter—eats nectar and small insects.
Internal Punctuation	Some of the stores in the mall—for example, The Bathing Beauties Bath Shop—never have any customers.
Strong Emphasis	The movies—three box-office blockbusters—were not among our favorites.

Nonessential modifiers are generally set off only when they have internal punctuation or when strong emphasis is desired.

USING DASHES WITH NONESSENTIAL MODIFIERS	
Internal Punctuation	The ruby-throated hummingbird—which migrates to Central America for the winter—must build up a layer of body fat equal to half its body weight before migrating.
Strong Emphasis	Our new dog's hopeful expression—which he has mastered so well that even Lassie could take lessons from him—is so appealing that he is slowly winning me over.

Consider a final kind of sentence interrupter—a parenthetical expression. You may recall that a parenthetical expression consists of words or phrases that are inserted into a sentence but have no essential grammatical relationship to it. Parenthetical expressions are often enclosed by dashes.

Grammar and Style Tip

Do not overuse dashes; they will lose their impact if they appear too frequently in your writing.

KEY CONCEPT Use dashes to set off a parenthetical expression when it is long, already punctuated, or especially dramatic. ■

Of course, not every parenthetical expression will take a dash. Short expressions hardly need dashes.

EXAMPLES: I will, I think, go.
Give it to me, Susan.

However, as with nonessential appositives, if the parenthetical expression is long or contains its own punctuation, you will often want to set it off with dashes.

EXAMPLE: This continual downpour—we had two inches Monday, one inch yesterday, and an inch already today—will certainly help the birds.

The use of dashes is especially likely if the parenthetical expression is a question or an exclamation.

EXAMPLE: After Mr. Mathers was caught stealing the exotic bird—did you have any idea?—he was taken to the police station and booked.

You can also enclose a parenthetical expression in dashes if you want the expression to stand out dramatically from the rest of the sentence.

EXAMPLE: Hummingbirds time their migration—a trip of over 1,850 miles, crossing 600 miles of the Gulf of Mexico—to arrive back at their North American homes just when their favorite nectar flowers bloom.

Although the dash has many uses, be careful not to overuse it. Using an occasional dash adds sentence variety and interest; putting dashes in too often will make your thoughts seem confused and disjointed. Therefore, always follow one of the rules when you use dashes. In all other situations, insert commas or, in some cases, parentheses for maximum effectiveness.

▼ **Critical Viewing** Write a sentence about the hummingbird pictured here. Include the phrase "tiny and fast" as a parenthetical expression set off by dashes. **[Describe]**

Exercise 42 **Using the Dash** Copy the following sentences, adding one or two dashes in each.

EXAMPLE: Hummingbirds feed on the nectar from red flowers that is, most of the time.

ANSWER: Hummingbirds feed on the nectar from red flowers—that is, most of the time.

1. There are actually some flowers at least thirty-one varieties of blossoms that attract the ruby-throated hummingbird.
2. The fantastic agility of the hummingbird a hummingbird beats its wings ninety times per second lets it skip from flower to flower in the same movements an insect uses.
3. Flying from flower to flower, gathering nectar with its long beak it can hover for long periods of time it pollinates the flowers from which it feeds.
4. Honeysuckle, petunias, nasturtiums, and lilacs all these flowers attract a hummingbird.
5. The hummingbird's main source of food nectar is supplemented with small insects and spiders.

More Practice

Language Lab CD-ROM
- Section 29.5

Grammar Exercise Workbook
- pp. 189–190

Parentheses

Parentheses set off supplementary material not essential to the understanding of the sentence. Though not as dramatic as the dash, parentheses are the strongest separator you can use.

KEY CONCEPT Use parentheses when the material is not essential or when it consists of one or more sentences. ■

Note that you can take out all the material in parentheses in the following example without altering the meaning.

EXAMPLE: The diet (seeds, nuts, berries, fruits, flowers, corn, and some insects) of the sulphur-crested cockatoo is especially varied for a bird.

Supplementary numbers may also be enclosed in parentheses.

KEY CONCEPT Use parentheses to set off numerical explanations—such as dates of a person's birth and death—and around numbers and letters marking a series. ■

EXAMPLE: We established a memorial fund for Mary Tsai (1965–1981), which will be used to buy books.

Capitalizing and Punctuating With Parentheses

Several guidelines will help you punctuate and capitalize the material in parentheses.

KEY CONCEPT When a phrase or declarative sentence interrupts another sentence, do not use an initial capital or end mark inside the parentheses. ■

EXAMPLE: Cockatoos (my sister just bought one) look like parrots.

If the sentence is exclamatory or interrogative, however, the rule changes.

KEY CONCEPT When a question or exclamation interrupts another sentence, use both an initial capital and an end mark inside the parentheses. ■

EXAMPLE: Cocky (That bird lived 82 years compared to the normal 50 in captivity!) lived in the London Zoo.

KEY CONCEPT With any sentence that falls between two complete sentences, use both an initial capital and an end mark inside the parentheses. ■

EXAMPLE: We drove to the Ashland bird sanctuary. (It took more than fifteen hours.) The quality of the facility surpassed even our high expectations.

Be aware of punctuation that falls after a parenthetical phrase.

KEY CONCEPT In a sentence that includes parentheses, place any punctuation belonging to the main sentence after the parenthesis. ■

Apply this rule for commas, semicolons, colons, and end marks.

EXAMPLES: The ocean water felt icy cold (about 45°)!

Nesting in a cliff or high niche (a dead eucalyptus tree with a hole in it is ideal), both the male and female cockatoos take care of the young.

More Practice

Language Lab CD-ROM
- Section 29.5

Grammar Exercise Workbook
- pp. 191–192

Exercise 43 **Using Parentheses** Copy the following sentences, adding the necessary parentheses.

EXAMPLE: The sulphur-crested cockatoo Have you ever seen one up close? is one of the most popular birds to keep as a pet.

ANSWER: The sulphur-crested cockatoo (Have you ever seen one up close?) is one of the most popular birds to keep as a pet.

1. The sulphur-crested cockatoo has been kept as a pet I have one since the nineteenth century.
2. Its shrill voice heard mostly early in the morning or when it becomes alarmed can be trained to mimic the human voice.
3. Cockatoos that make the best pets are those that are bred in captivity. They are calmer and easier to train. Buying only birds that are captivity-bred also helps protect the birds of the wild.
4. A cockatoo will use the crest of feathers on its head to show strong emotion fear or aggression.
5. When buying a cockatoo, be sure to buy a large cage; cockatoos will grow to be over a foot 18–20 inches long.

▶ **Critical Viewing** Include a parenthetical comment in a statement about the bird in this picture. **[Apply]**

Exercise 44 **Using Capitals and Punctuation With Parentheses** Copy each sentence that needs capitalization or punctuation, making the necessary changes. If no corrections are needed, write *correct.*

EXAMPLE: When I finished the assignment (what a tough one it was) I took a nap.

ANSWER: When I finished the assignment (What a tough one it was!), I took a nap.

1. Cockatoos are common in the wild throughout parts of Australia the eastern area and some islands close to the mainland.
2. In the North, these birds travel in small (at least two birds) groups.
3. In the South, they travel in huge flocks (Looking like a blanket of snow flying around) that can contain hundreds of birds.
4. Cockatoos spend the morning and evening looking for food. (Afternoons are spent entertaining themselves by pulling bark and leaves off trees.) They then return to their roosting grounds at nightfall.
5. Because they eat all the seeds until they are gone of course that is their natural diet they are sometimes a nuisance to farmers.

More Practice

Language Lab CD-ROM
- Section 29.5

Grammar Exercise Workbook
- pp. 193–194

▼ Critical Viewing Identify several words of two or more syllables that describe this picture. Write each word, inserting hyphens between syllables. **[Analyze]**

Hyphens

As a writer, you should appreciate the versatility of the hyphen, for this punctuation mark makes it possible not only to join but also to divide certain words. Unfortunately, the hyphen is often mistaken for its cousin, the dash, because the two share a similar appearance. However, you should note that the hyphen is distinctly shorter than the dash; in fact, typing the hyphen takes one mark (-), while the dash takes two (--). In books and other printed material, the hyphen is less than half as long as the dash.

The primary uses of the hyphen are to divide certain numbers and parts of words, to join some compound words, and to divide words at the ends of lines. This section will focus on the rules governing the appropriate use of the hyphen in these cases.

With Numbers

When you write out numbers in words, some of them require hyphens.

KEY CONCEPT Use a hyphen when writing out two-word numbers from *twenty-one* through *ninety-nine.* ■

EXAMPLE: The average cockatoo is about thirty-two centimeters long.

Some fractions also require a hyphen.

KEY CONCEPT Use a hyphen with fractions used as adjectives. ■

EXAMPLE: The typical cockatoo diet is one-half seeds and nuts and one-half fruit.

In the preceding example, the fractions function as adjectives. If they were used as nouns, the hyphen would then be omitted.

EXAMPLE: Only *one third* of the birds in the parrot family are called parrots.

With Word Parts

Some word parts require the use of a hyphen.

KEY CONCEPT Use a hyphen after a prefix that is followed by a proper noun or adjective. ■

EXAMPLE: Eclectus parrots live on islands in the *east-Pacific* islands.

Certain prefixes and suffixes require the use of hyphens even when no proper noun or adjective is involved.

KEY CONCEPT Use a hyphen in words with the prefixes *all-*, *ex-*, and *self-* and in words with the suffix *-elect.* ■

EXAMPLES: all-powerful, ex-teacher, self-addressed, senator-elect

With Compound Words You must also use hyphens with some compound words.

KEY CONCEPT Use a hyphen to connect two or more words that are used as one word unless the dictionary gives a contrary spelling. ■

EXAMPLES: merry-go-round crow's-feet sit-in

KEY CONCEPT Use a hyphen to connect a compound modifier that comes before a noun. ■

EXAMPLE: Eclectus parrots were kept as pets by *forest-dwelling* natives.

If a compound modifier comes after the noun, however, the hyphen is dropped.

BEFORE: We got the bird food from an *all-night* pet store.
AFTER: A pet store open *all night* sold us the food.

If the compound modifier is hyphenated, the word remains hyphenated regardless of its position in the sentence.

EXAMPLES: We rode in a *jet-propelled* boat.
Our ski boat was *jet-propelled.*

KEY CONCEPT Do not use hyphens with compound modifiers that include words ending in *-ly* or with compound proper adjectives or compound proper nouns acting as adjectives. ■

INCORRECT: The *badly-damaged* wing healed slowly.
CORRECT: The *badly damaged* wing healed slowly.

For Clarity

KEY CONCEPT Use a hyphen within a word when a combination of letters might otherwise be confusing. ■

EXAMPLES: *co-op* versus *coop*
re-create versus *recreate*

KEY CONCEPT Use a hyphen between words to keep the reader from combining them erroneously. ■

EXAMPLES: *thirty-dollar tickets* versus *thirty dollar tickets*

◀ Critical Viewing Why do you think people like to teach parrots to mimic speech? **[Speculate]**

Exercise 45 **Using Hyphens in Numbers, Word Parts, and Words** Rewrite the words that need hyphens, adding the necessary hyphens. Use a dictionary when in doubt. If no hyphen is needed, write *correct.*

EXAMPLE: The male eclectus parrot is a bright yellow green color.

ANSWER: yellow-green

1. The female, in contrast, is a bright red and bluish purple color.
2. Because they are so different in color, at one time it was thought that they were two completely different species.
3. The male is considered to be a medium sized bird, and the female is slightly smaller.
4. When she is ready to lay eggs, a female parrot lays chewed up wood at the bottom of a hole in a tree for her nest.
5. The ever caring mother then stays with the eggs until they hatch.
6. For the twenty six days of incubation, the male makes frequent visits to the nest to feed the female.
7. The male's brightly colored feathers help him to hide in the treetops as he searches for food.
8. After hatching, fledglings spend 85 days in the nest, approximately one eleventh of the time required to reach adulthood.
9. The six week old female chicks are almost as multicolored as they will be as adults.
10. The male, in contrast, has a color that is still blue gray.

More Practice

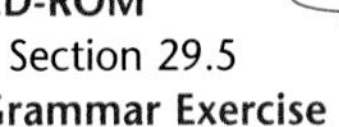

Language Lab CD-ROM
- Section 29.5

Grammar Exercise Workbook
- pp. 193–194

Exercise 46 **Using Hyphens to Avoid Ambiguity** Copy the sentences, adding hyphens to make each sentence clear. If no hyphens are required, write *correct as is.*

EXAMPLE: We had to relay the bricks in the garden wall.
ANSWER: We had to re-lay the bricks in the garden wall.

1. New Zealand, an island close to Australia, has short winged birds.
2. They are strange looking animals with stubby, coarse feathers that cannot be used to fly.
3. This bird, a night walking bird, is called the brown kiwi.
4. The male is a light brown kiwi that weighs around five pounds, while the female weighs about 20 percent more.
5. Kiwis have three clawed feet that they use for finding food or for self defense.
6. They have long bills decorated with small bill hairs whose sensitivity helps the kiwi find food.
7. At the base of its bill, the kiwi has long, threadlike feathers that help it find its way in the dark.
8. Full fledged biologists know that the kiwi comes in four species.
9. A five pound kiwi lays an egg that weighs over one pound.
10. The kiwi is the national symbol of New Zealand; "kiwis" is the worldwide symbol for New Zealanders.

More Practice

Language Lab CD-ROM
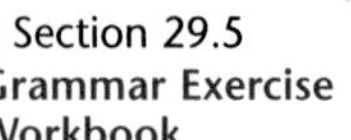
- Section 29.5

Grammar Exercise Workbook
- pp. 193–194

▼ Critical Viewing
Choose three compound modifiers to describe three different nouns in this picture. Which modifiers require hyphens? **[Describe]**

Using Hyphens at the Ends of Lines

KEY CONCEPT If a word must be divided, always divide it between syllables. ■

EXAMPLE: The egg takes approximately twenty-six days to hatch.

Always place the hyphen at the end of the first line—never at the start of the next line.

INCORRECT: The cuckoo bird inhab
-its Africa.

CORRECT: The cuckoo bird inhabits Africa.

KEY CONCEPT If a word contains word parts, it can almost always be divided between the prefix and the root or the root and the suffix. ■

PREFIX:	ex-tend	out-side	mis-fortune
SUFFIX:	hope-less	incuba-tion	fif-teen

If the suffix is composed of only two letters, however, do not divide the word between the root and suffix.

INCORRECT: walk-ed

CORRECT: walked

Be on the lookout for one-syllable words that sound like two-syllable words or look as if they are long enough to be two syllables. Do not divide them.

INCORRECT:	lod-ge	clo-thes	thro-ugh
CORRECT:	lodge	clothes	through

KEY CONCEPT Do not divide a word so that a single letter stands alone. ■

INCORRECT:	stead-y	a-ble	e-vict
CORRECT:	steady	able	evict

KEY CONCEPT It is preferable not to divide proper nouns and proper adjectives. ■

The following divisions have traditionally been considered undesirable or even incorrect.

INCORRECT: We recently hired Sylvia Rodriguez.

I just finished eating a South American banana.

KEY CONCEPT Divide a hyphenated word only after the hyphen. ■

If you use the word *apple-pie* as an adjective, you would hyphenate it. When dividing the word at the end of a line, divide it only at the hyphen.

INCORRECT: Everything appeared to be in apple-pie order.

CORRECT: Everything appeared to be in apple-
pie order.

KEY CONCEPT Do not divide a word so that part of the word is on one page and the remainder is on the next page. ■

Exercise 47 **Using Hyphens to Divide Words** If a word has been divided correctly, write *correct*. If not, divide the word correctly or write it as one word if it cannot be divided.

EXAMPLE: Have you ever thought why a peacock calls so loudly?

ANSWER: Have you ever thought
why a peacock calls so loudly?

1. The peafowl is numerous in India, and many native Indians believe that their call is a sign of rain.
2. Blue peafowl live in hill-
y forest areas and tend to stay in groups.
3. During the day, they may sit in a thick-
et, but as the sun starts to set, they climb trees to roost.
4. As it climbs higher, the pea-
cock will screech loudly.
5. The peacock, the male of the peafowl species, re-
enacts the same routine every day.

Section Review

GRAMMAR EXERCISES 48–53

Exercise 48 **Using Dashes Correctly** Rewrite the following sentences, adding dashes where appropriate.

1. Blue and yellow macaws which belong to the parrot family but are not actually called "parrots" live in South America.
2. Nuts, fruits, seeds, and berries these are the staple foods of the macaw diet.
3. Bonding between the pair is reinforced as the birds preen, they groom each other's feathers.
4. When eggs are laid usually only two at a time the female incubates them.
5. Baby macaws always hatched in pairs are blind and featherless at hatching.

Exercise 49 **Using Hyphens Properly in Words and to Clarify Sentences** Rewrite the words that require hyphens. If no hyphen is needed, write *correct.*

1. The all powerful beak of a macaw is hinged to crush tough nuts that other birds are not able to eat.
2. From the top of the body to the tip of the tail, macaws can reach up to thirty six inches.
3. Nearly two thirds the length is accounted for in the tail.
4. Cuckoo birds create a coop with other species when raising their young.
5. A female cuckoo looks for an insect eating host species like the one she was raised in.

Exercise 50 **Revising With Dashes, Parentheses, and Hyphens** Rewrite the following paragraph, adding dashes, parentheses, and hyphens where necessary.

The Princess Parrot an endangered bird so rarely found that it is strictly protected by law lives mostly in central Australia. These birds live in a fair sized group twenty and stay in areas with eucalyptus trees or dry scrubland. Frequently moving, these birds are nomadic following the blossoming of the acacia plant. Princess parrots in flight communicate with a long, chattering note. These birds so surprisingly tame in the wild that you can approach them frequently without startling them fly high, fast, and seemingly without much effort.

Exercise 51 **Find It in Your Reading** Read the following excerpt from "The Scarlet Ibis" by James Hurst. On your paper, indicate why the parentheses and hyphen are used.

> . . . But sometimes (like right now), as I sit in the cool, green-draped parlor, the grindstone begins to turn, and time with all its changes is ground away—and I remember Doodle.

Exercise 52 **Find It in Your Writing** Review a piece of writing from your portfolio. Challenge yourself to write two sentences using both a dash and parentheses.

Exercise 53 **Writing Application** Write a brief observation of a bird or other animal with which you are familiar. Include dashes to set off a nonessential phrase in the middle of a sentence; parentheses around an explanation within a sentence; and a hyphen in a word at the end of a line of writing.

Section 29.6

Apostrophes

Apostrophes With Possessive Nouns

An apostrophe must be used with nouns to indicate ownership or relationship.

With Singular Nouns

First, consider possessives formed from singular nouns.

KEY CONCEPT Add an apostrophe and *s* to show the possessive case of most singular nouns. ■

EXAMPLES: The government of *India* becomes *India's* government.
The sleeve of the *dress* becomes the *dress's* sleeve.

When a singular noun ends in *s*, as in the last example, you can still follow this style in most cases. However, if the apostrophe and *s* make the word difficult to pronounce, the apostrophe may be used alone.

EXAMPLES: Burns's poetry is not well known in India.
Burns' poetry is not well known in India.

With Plural Nouns

Showing possession with plural nouns ending in *s* or *es* calls for a different rule.

KEY CONCEPT Add an apostrophe to show the possessive case of plural nouns ending in *s* or *es*. ■

EXAMPLE: The decision of the *representatives* becomes the *representatives'* decision.

KEY CONCEPT Add an apostrophe and *s* to show the possessive case of plural nouns that do not end in *s* or *es*. ■

EXAMPLE: The books of the *men* becomes the *men's* books.

Theme: India

In this section, you will learn about the various uses of apostrophes. The examples and exercises are about India.

Cross-Curricular Connection: Social Studies

With Compound Nouns

KEY CONCEPT Add an apostrophe and *s* (or just an apostrophe if the word is a plural ending in *s*) to the last word of a compound noun to form the possessive. ■

APOSTROPHES WITH COMPOUND NOUNS	
Businesses and Organizations	The House of the People's building the Lions Club's motto
Names With Titles	the Prime Minister's visit Edward VIII's abdication
Hyphenated Compound Nouns Used to Describe People	my father-in-law's glasses the secretary-treasurer's pen

With Expressions Involving Time and Amounts

If you use possessive expressions involving time amounts, you will need to use an apostrophe.

KEY CONCEPT To form possessives involving time, amounts, or the word *sake*, use an apostrophe and *s* or just an apostrophe if the possessive is plural. ■

TIME:	a day's journey	six years' time
AMOUNT:	one quarter's worth	fifty cents' worth

To Show Joint and Individual Ownership

KEY CONCEPT To show joint ownership, make the final noun possessive. ■

EXAMPLE: The president and the prime minister's term (They share one term.)

KEY CONCEPT To show individual ownership, make each noun possessive. ■

EXAMPLE: The president's and the prime minister's term (Each has a different term.)

CHECKING THE USE OF APOSTROPHES		
Incorrect	**Explanation**	**Correction**
Jame's car	The owner is not *Jame*, but *James*.	James's
one boys' book	The owner is not *boys*, but *boy*.	boy's
two girl's lunches	The owner is not *girl*, but *girls*.	girls'

If you place the apostrophe correctly, the letters to the left of the apostrophe should spell out the owner's complete name.

Exercise 54 **Using Apostrophes With Single-Word Possessive Nouns** Copy the underlined nouns, putting them into the possessive form.

EXAMPLE: A person extended family is important in Indian society.
ANSWER: person's

1. In India, one personal life tends to be arranged around traditional extended families.
2. When a woman marries, she moves in with her husband family.
3. Parents usually arrange the marriages, but the couple may reject their parents decision.
4. According to society expectations, the couple will have a child within the first few years of a marriage.
5. Especially within small villages and farming communities, the parents preference is to have a male child.

Learn More

To review possessive and compound nouns, see Chapter 16.

Exercise 55 **Using Apostrophes With Compound Nouns** Write the underlined noun in the possessive form, as required by the sentence.

EXAMPLE: The prime minister power is significant.
ANSWER: prime minister's

1. It is the head of state job to appoint the prime minister.
2. All heads of state responsibilities include working with other government leaders to make laws.
3. The Council of Ministers appointment is made by the president on the advice of the prime minister.
4. The two houses of India's government are usually controlled by the prime minister political party.
5. Lok Sabha, Rajya Sabha, the president, and the prime minister terms all last five years.

Exercise 56 **Using Apostrophes to Show Joint and Individual Ownership** Write the underlined words, changing them to show joint or individual ownership, as the instructions indicate.

EXAMPLE: Dravidians and Indo-Aryans ancestry lies in India. (individual)
ANSWER: Dravidians' and Indo-Aryans'

1. Western India and Pakistan mountains are the places where Dravidians established their ancient but advanced civilization. (joint)
2. Jammu and Kashmir people emigrated from central Asia. (individual)
3. In India, the forests and hills inhabitants are fewer than the cities' inhabitants. (individual)
4. Because of the people and cultures differences, languages in India number over 1,000. (individual)
5. For this reason, elementary schools and secondary schools requirements include studies in Hindi and English. (individual)
6. The national language of India is Hindi; this language or its dialect use is known by more than two fifths of the population. (joint)
7. Bureaucrats and businesspersons language is most often English. (joint)
8. English is widespread in the media as well as in colleges and universities courses. (individual)
9. Because non-Hindu speakers and politicians needs have varied, the government created many state boundaries based on language use. (individual)
10. Today, Bengal and Tamil Nadu official languages are different from that of the country of India. (individual)

More Practice

Language Lab CD-ROM 
- Types of Nouns lesson

On-line Exercise Bank
- Section 29.6

Grammar Exercise Workbook
- pp. 197–198

◄ **Critical Viewing** What might these women own jointly? **[Connect]**

29.6

Apostrophes With Pronouns

Some pronouns showing ownership require an apostrophe.

KEY CONCEPT Use an apostrophe and *s* with indefinite pronouns to show possession. ■

EXAMPLES:	another's	nobody's	one's
	anyone's	someone's	everybody's

If you form a two-word indefinite pronoun, add the apostrophe and *s* to the last word only.

EXAMPLE: nobody else's one another's

Possessive personal pronouns do not need an apostrophe.

KEY CONCEPT Do not use an apostrophe with the possessive forms of personal pronouns. ■

With the words *yours, his, hers, theirs, its, ours,* and *whose,* no apostrophe is necessary. These already show ownership.

EXAMPLE: *Its* sacred writing makes the Vedas a guide to moral conduct for Hindus.

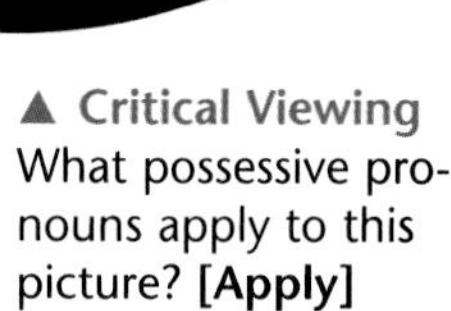

▲ Critical Viewing What possessive pronouns apply to this picture? **[Apply]**

Pay special attention to the possessive forms *whose* and *its* since they are easily confused with the contractions *who's* and *it's*. Just remember, *whose* and *its* show possession.

PRONOUNS: *Whose* temple is this?
Its chimes rang out clearly.

Who's and *it's,* on the other hand, are contractions of the words *who is* and *it is*. They both require apostrophes to indicate the missing letters.

CONTRACTIONS: *Who's* taking notes for the meeting?
It's the main religion in India.

Exercise 57 **Proofreading for Apostrophes With Pronouns** Rewrite any sentences in which pronouns are used incorrectly, making the necessary changes. If a sentence is already correct, write *correct.*

EXAMPLE: I think this book about yoga is your's.
ANSWER: I think this book about yoga is yours.

1. Hindus believe in one spiritual force, Brahman, who's presence takes many forms.
2. The many gods and goddesses of Hindu beliefs are representations of his forms.
3. Several different cultures accept the basic beliefs of Hinduism as their's.
4. In India, almost everybody's life was once influenced by the caste system.
5. Ones' occupation and opportunities were affected by the caste system.
6. Although the caste system is now weakening, it was once a factor in everyones' existence.
7. Its power to separate people is not as great as it once was.
8. Although they are rooted in Hinduism, yoga and meditation are used by many whose beliefs are not Hindu.
9. Another belief, *ahimsa,* refers to nonviolence in everyone's life.
10. This is achieved largely through a popular practice of their's: yoga.

More Practice

Language Lab CD-ROM

- Types of Nouns lesson

On-line Exercise Bank
- Section 29.6

Grammar Exercise Workbook
- pp. 197–198

▼ **Critical Viewing** Write a sentence describing this scene. Include a pronoun showing ownership. **[Describe]**

Apostrophes With Contractions

The meaning of a contraction is implied by its name. It is a word contracted in size by the removal of some letter or letters and the insertion of an apostrophe to indicate the missing letters. Use the following basic rule for contractions:

KEY CONCEPT Use an apostrophe in a contraction to indicate the position of the missing letter or letters. ■

Contractions With Verbs

Verbs often come in contracted form. Look at the chart, taking a moment to notice how often these verb contractions are used in common speech patterns.

COMMON CONTRACTIONS WITH VERBS		
Verbs with *not*	are not = aren't do not = don't	was not = wasn't were not = weren't
Pronouns with *will*	I will = I'll you will = you'll	she will = she'll they will = they'll
Pronouns and nouns with the verb *be*	I am = I'm you are = you're	who is = who's Mark is = Mark's
Pronouns with *would*	I would = I'd he would = he'd	we would = we'd they would = they'd

One special contraction changes letters as well as drops them: *Will not* becomes *won't* in contracted form.

Contractions With Years

In writing about years, insert an apostrophe in places where a number is left out.

EXAMPLE: Decathlon Champion of '05

Contractions With *o'*, *d'*, and *l'*

These letters followed by the apostrophe make up the abbreviated form of the words *of the* or *the*, as spelled in several different languages.

EXAMPLES: o'clock d'Carlo
O'Sullivan l'Abbé

As you can see, these letters and apostrophes are combined most often with surnames.

Spelling Tip

Do not confuse the uses of *their*, *they're*, and *there*. When in doubt, ask yourself, "Would substituting *they are* be correct?" If so, you may use the contraction *they're*.

Contractions With Dialogue

When writing dialogue, you will usually want to keep the flavor of the speaker's individual speaking style. Therefore, you should use any contractions the speaker might use. You may also want to include a regional dialect or a foreign accent. Because this often includes pronunciations with omitted letters, insert apostrophes to show those changes.

EXAMPLES: C'mon—aren't you comin' fishin'?
'Tis a fine spring morn we're havin'.
That li'l horse is afeelin' his oats!

As with most punctuation, overuse reduces the effectiveness and impact, so watch the overuse of the apostrophe with contractions—even in dialogue.

Exercise 58 **Using Apostrophes With Contractions** If a contraction is underlined in the following sentences, write the complete word or words from which the contraction is formed. If two words are underlined, write the contraction they would form.

EXAMPLE: Most Indian women wear a long piece of material that's draped around the body like a dress.

ANSWER: that is

1. From 6 o'clock until dark, Indian women wear a wide variety of clothing.
2. Sometimes, they are influenced by their region, religion, or ethnic backgrounds.
3. However, most Indian women wear light, loose clothing that doesn't trap in the heat of the hot climate.
4. Women who are unmarried often wear *shalwar,* long flowing pants.
5. They're worn with a long blouse that is called a *kameez.*
6. I've seen many tribal women who'll wear long skirts.

More Practice

On-line Exercise Bank
- Section 29.6

Grammar Exercise Workbook
- pp. 199–200

◀ Critical Viewing What features of the clothing worn by the women in this picture make the clothing suitable for a hot climate? **[Analyze]**

29.6

Special Uses of the Apostrophe

One final method for employing the apostrophe exists—using it to show the plural of numbers, symbols, letters, and words used to name themselves.

KEY CONCEPT Use an apostrophe and *-s* to write the plurals of numbers, symbols, letters, and words used to name themselves. ■

EXAMPLES: There are two *8*'s in that number.
You need two more *?*'s.
Her *b*'s and *d*'s all look the same.
A's and *an*'s cause confusion.

Exercise 59 **Using the Apostrophe in Special Cases** Copy the following sentences, adding an apostrophe and an *-s* to numbers, symbols, letters, and words whenever necessary. Underline all items in italics. If no apostrophe or *-s* is needed, write *correct.*

EXAMPLE: Many Indian Jews moved to Israel in *1950* and *1960*.

ANSWER: Many Indian Jews moved to Israel in the 1950's and 1960's.

1. They had been living in India since A.D. *100*.
2. While writing that down, please be sure to include two *0* in the date.
3. Make sure that your capital *I* and lowercase *l* do not all look the same.
4. A large group of Zoroastrians fled to India about 1,000 years ago.
5. They are called Parsis (that has two *s* in the word) in India.
6. They fled to India when Iran was converted to Islam.
7. Maybe you feel some sentences deserve a few *?*?.
8. Christianity came to India in the *1500*.
9. The religion came with the Europeans and spread from its small communities to larger *ones*.
10. Christians in India live mostly in the southern states of Kerala and Tamil Nadu.

More Practice

On-line Exercise Bank
- Section 29.6

Grammar Exercise Workbook
- pp. 199–200

Section 29.6 **Section Review**

GRAMMAR EXERCISES 60–65

Exercise 60 Using Apostrophes With Possessive Nouns Write the correct possessive for each underlined noun.

1. Also, the Buddhist temples walls are frequently covered in wall paintings.
2. They depict scenes from some Buddhist men stories.
3. Literature has a strong background in India; the Nobel Prize Committee selection in 1913 was Rabindranath Tagore.
4. Many of the famous folk tales beginnings came from India.
5. Music is also important in India; recently film music popularity has grown.

Exercise 61 Using Apostrophes in Special Situations Use apostrophes to form plurals where appropriate. If no corrections are needed in a sentence, write *correct.*

1. *India* is spelled with two *i.*
2. Since the 1950, the government has worked hard to increase the literacy rate.
3. The new Constitution of 50 provided education for children ages 6 to 14.
4. All Indian children receive the same education, learning to write their *ABC* and more.
5. However, by the time they reach 10, only half of the children continue with their education.

Exercise 62 Proofreading for Apostrophes Rewrite the following passage, adding, deleting, or moving apostrophes as necessary.

Most villagers possession's are few in number. (Household items they can claim as their's include pots theyll use for cooking and carrying water.) The peoples' cooking takes place in a clay oven that burns coal. Even in the 90s people were still sleeping on string cots. The village and huts electric power frequently fails.

Exercise 63 Find It in Your Reading Copy the following paragraph on your paper, and explain why each apostrophe is used.

India was a British colony from the late 1700's until it became independent in 1947. Since then, the Indian government has been trying to develop the country's resources and improve people's standard of living.

Exercise 64 Find It in Your Writing Select a sample of dialogue from your writing portfolio. Identify where you have used contractions. If you have not used any contractions, challenge yourself to add at least two. Check that you have correctly placed the apostrophe in each contraction.

Exercise 65 Writing Application Write a paragraph describing your neighborhood to someone who lives in a faraway country, such as India. Use apostrophes in your paragraph to form plurals and to show ownership. Use at least three of these words and phrases in your paragraph:

1. friends' and neighbors'
2. 2's and 3's
3. teacher and students'
4. morning's
5. they're

PART

3

Academic and Workplace Skills

Books II, 1993, Polly Kraft, Private Collection, Courtesy Fischbach Gallery, New York

Chapter 30

Speaking, Listening, Viewing, and Representing

Communication travels between people in many forms. You convey information through speaking or through visual representations. You receive information by listening to others or by viewing visual representations. The more developed these four skills are—your speaking, listening, viewing, and representing skills—the more you will be able to communicate your ideas, as well as to comprehend the ideas of others. This chapter will help you increase your ability in these four areas of communication.

▲ **Critical Viewing** Identify several different means of communication that you see in this photograph. **[Analyze]**

Section 30.1

Speaking and Listening Skills

If you develop good speaking skills, you will be better prepared to contribute effectively in group discussions, to give formal presentations with more confidence, and to communicate your feelings and ideas to others more easily. If you improve your listening skills, it will become easier to focus your attention on classroom discussions and to identify important information more accurately.

Speaking in a Group Discussion

In a group discussion, you openly discuss ideas and topics in an informal setting. The group discussions in which you participate will involve, for the most part, your classmates and focus on the subjects you are studying. To get the most out of a group discussion, you need to participate in it.

KEY CONCEPT Use group discussions to express and to listen to ideas in an informal setting. ■

Communicate Effectively The points you want to make, the order in which you want to make them, the words you will use to express them, and the examples that will support these points should all be thought of carefully before you speak. By thinking through your thoughts, your message will be clear.

Ask Questions Asking questions can help you in two ways. First, asking questions can help you improve your comprehension of another speaker's ideas. Second, asking questions may call attention to possible errors in another speaker's points.

Make Relevant Contributions Stay focused on the topic being discussed. Relate comments to your own experience and knowledge. When you contribute information or ideas, make clear how your contributions are connected to the topic.

Exercise 1 **Holding a Group Discussion** With three to five other students, hold a fifteen-minute group discussion about a topic you are studying in class. Review some related material from your textbooks to generate ideas and supporting information for your statements.

Technology Tip

Search the Internet for more information on a topic you are studying. Use key words that are related to the topic. If you do not have good results with your first key word, try using other words related to it.

More Practice

Academic and Workplace Skills Activity Book
- p. 1

Giving a Speech

Giving a presentation or speech before an audience is generally recognized as *public speaking.* To become an effective speaker and to deliver a good speech, you must become familiar with the different kinds of speeches, be well prepared, and deliver your speech smoothly and with confidence.

Recognizing Different Kinds of Speeches There are four main kinds of speeches: *informative speeches, persuasive speeches, entertaining speeches,* and *extemporaneous speeches.*

KEY CONCEPT Consider the purpose of your speech and your audience before deciding what kind of speech you will give. ■

- Give an **informative** speech to explain an idea, a process, an object, or an event. In an informative speech, you may include technical language or terms to more accurately describe your topic.
- Give a **persuasive** speech to try to get your listeners to agree with your position or to take some action. In a persuasive speech,the language is usually formal English.
- Give an **entertaining** speech to offer your listeners something to enjoy or to amuse them. An entertaining speech may vary between informal and formal language.
- An **extemporaneous** speech is given to suit the occasion. It is an informal impromptu speech, because you do not rely on a prepared manuscript.

Exercise 2 **Listing Kinds of Speeches** Give two topic examples for each kind of speech above. Then, speculate about who your audience might be for each kind of speech.

▶ Critical Viewing What kind of a speech do you think this student is making? What makes you think that? **[Infer]**

Learn More

To learn more about persuasive writing, read Chapters 7 and 8. To learn more about expository writing, read Chapters 9–11.

Preparing and Presenting a Speech If you are asked to deliver a speech, begin by thinking carefully about your topic. Choose a topic that you like or know well. Once you have completed this first step, you will need to prepare your speech so that you can present it to your audience.

KEY CONCEPT To prepare your speech, research your topic, make an outline, and use numbered note cards. ■

Gather Information Use the library and other resources to gather reliable information and to find examples to support your ideas.

Make an Outline Organize your information in an outline of main ideas and major details. Use Roman numerals to list main ideas and capital letters for supporting details.

Outline

I. Main Idea

A. Supporting detail

B. Supporting detail

C. Supporting detail

Use Numbered Note Cards Write the main ideas and major details on note cards that you can use when you deliver your speech. Include quotations and facts you want to remember. Use underlining and capital letters to make important information stand out.

KEY CONCEPT When presenting your speech, use rhetorical forms of language and verbal and nonverbal strategies. ■

Use Rhetorical Language Repeat key words and phrases to identify your most important points. Use active verbs and colorful adjectives to keep your speech lively and interesting. Use parallel phrases or series of words to insert a sense of rhythm in your speech.

Use Verbal Strategies Vary the pitch and tone of your voice, as well as the rate at which you speak. Speak loudly enough, so the entire audience can hear your voice. Pronounce key words or phrases slower or louder for emphasis.

Use Nonverbal Strategies Maintain eye contact with members of the audience. Use gestures, facial expressions, and other movements to emphasize key points in your message.

Research Tip

For more tips on how to deliver a speech effectively, use the card catalog in your library to find books on the subject. Start your search with the key words *Public Speaking.*

Exercise 3 **Preparing and Presenting a Speech** Prepare an informative or persuasive speech on a topic in which you are interested. Use the steps in this section to prepare your speech and to present it to your classmates.

More Practice

Academic and Workplace Skills Activity Book

• p. 2

Evaluating a Speech Evaluating a speech gives you the chance to judge another speaker's skills. It also gives you the opportunity to review and improve your own methods for preparing and presenting a speech.

KEY CONCEPT When you evaluate a speech, you help the speaker and yourself. ■

The checklist below offers some criteria, or guidelines, for evaluating another person's speech as well as your own speeches.

CHECKLIST FOR EVALUATING A SPEECH

- ☐ Did the speaker introduce the topic clearly, develop it well, and conclude it effectively?
- ☐ Did the speaker support each main idea with appropriate details?
- ☐ Did the speaker approach the platform confidently and establish eye contact with the audience?
- ☐ Did the speaker's facial expressions, gestures, and movements appropriately reinforce the words spoken?
- ☐ Did the speaker vary the pitch of his or her voice and the rate of his or her speaking?
- ☐ Did the speaker enunciate all words clearly?

Exercise 4 **Evaluating a Speech** Use the checklist above to help you make an evaluation of a speech given in class. List what you feel to be the areas at which the speaker excelled and those where he or she could have been more prepared. Give your evaluation to the speaker.

Using Critical Listening

Did you know that there is a difference between hearing and listening? Hearing happens naturally as sounds reach your ears. Listening, or critical listening, requires that you understand and interpret these sounds.

KEY CONCEPT Critical listening requires preparation, active involvement, and self-evaluation from the listener. ■

Learning the Listening Process Like all forms of communication, listening is interactive; the more you involve yourself in the listening process, the more you will understand.

Focus Your Attention Focus your attention on the speaker and his or her words. Block out all distractions—people, noises, and objects—that may redirect your attention. Before attending a formal speech or presentation, find out more about the subject that will be discussed.

Interpret the Information To interpret a speaker's message successfully, you need to identify and understand important information. Use the following suggestions to guide you:

- Listen for words and phrases that are emphasized or repeated.
- Pause momentarily from listening to silently repeat and to memorize important statements.
- Write down important statements, and summarize ideas.
- Watch for nonverbal signals—a change in the tone or pitch of the voice, gestures, and facial expressions—that may signal important information.
- Link the information currently being given into a meaningful pattern by combining it with the information you already have.

Respond to the Speaker's Message Respond to the information you have heard by identifying the kind of speech, its overall message, its most interesting and useful points, and whether you agree or disagree with the speaker. If possible, ask questions to clarify your understanding.

Exercise 5 Using the Listening Process Apply the strategies described on this page to a lecture, speech, or classroom discussion. In writing, summarize the speaker's main points and respond to the message. Share your response with your classmates.

More Practice

Academic and Workplace Skills Activity Book
- p. 3

Using Different Types of Listening You use different listening skills when you listen to a friend from those you use when you listen to a teacher or to a speech by one of your classmates. Different situations call for different types of listening. Learn more about the four main types of listening—*critical, empathic, appreciative,* and *reflective*—in the chart below.

Types of Listening

Type	How to Listen	Situations
Critical	Listen for facts and supporting details to understand and evaluate the speaker's message.	Informative or persuasive speeches, class discussions, announcements
Empathic	Imagine yourself in the other person's position, and try to understand what he or she is thinking.	Conversations with friends or family
Appreciative	Identify and analyze aesthetic or artistic elements, such as character development, rhyme, imagery, and descriptive language.	Oral presentations of a poem, dramatic performances
Reflective	Ask questions to get information, and use the speaker's responses to form new questions.	Class or group discussions

Using Different Types of Questions A speaker's ideas may not always be clear to you. The best way to clarify your understanding is by asking questions. You can ask a variety of questions, each with a different purpose. If you understand the different types of questions, you will be able to get the information you need.

- An **open-ended** question does not lead to a specific response. Use this question to open up a discussion: "What did you think of the piano recital?"
- A **closed** question leads to a specific response and must be answered with a yes or no: "Did you play a piece by Chopin at your recital?"
- A **factual** question is aimed at getting a particular piece of information and must be answered with facts: "How many years have you been playing the piano?"

Exercise 6 **Using Different Types of Listening and Questions** Identify at least one example of each type of listening and each type of question. Use examples from life, from television, from movies, or from descriptions in stories.

More Practice

Academic and Workplace Skills Activity Book
- p. 3

Evaluating Your Listening

A good way to improve your listening is to evaluate it: to find out which listening skills work for you and which skills you need to improve. Use the following strategies to evaluate your listening skills.

Rephrase and Repeat Statements Test your understanding of a speaker's statements by rephrasing and then repeating them to the speaker. If the speaker agrees with your paraphrase, you know that you have understood him or her. If, however, the speaker disagrees with your paraphrase, ask the speaker for correction or clarification.

Compare and Contrast Interpretations Write your interpretation of a speaker's message, and then compare and contrast it with another student's interpretation. Use a Venn diagram to list the points with which you agree and disagree. Resolve these points of disagreement through discussion and, if necessary, by appealing to the speaker.

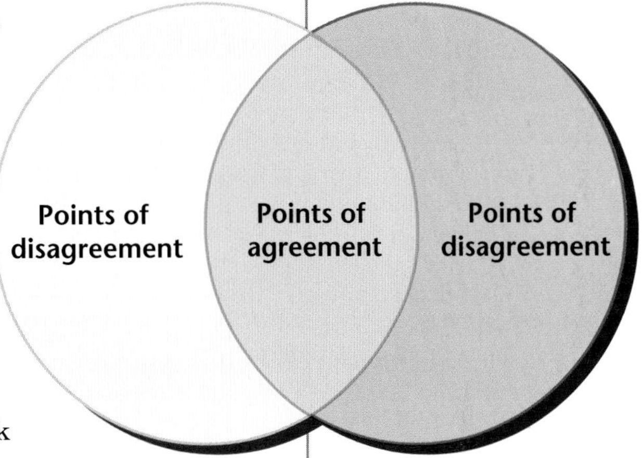

Research Points of Interest or Contention Use the library or other reference tools to acquire more information about the speaker's topic or to check questionable facts in the presentation.

Exercise 7 **Evaluating Your Listening Skills** Working with two other classmates, have one classmate read a speech or paper that he or she has recently written.

1. Tell the speaker to pause after every paragraph or after every few sentences, and take turns with your other classmate to rephrase and repeat the speaker's statements.
2. Have the speaker read the entire speech or paper while you and your classmate take notes. Then, compare and contrast your interpretations.
3. Write an evaluation of your listening skills. Identify areas of strength and areas in which you need to improve.

Viewing Skills

Visual representation, or the use of images, is an important method of communicating. You see examples of this in television programs, magazines, billboards, textbooks, and works of art. In this section, you will learn how to use visual representations as sources of information.

Interpreting Maps and Graphs

Maps and graphs are useful tools to help readers clarify difficult, complicated information. Because these tools help you to understand information visually, they are sometimes called *visual aids*. To interpret these visual aids, you need to know the special features of each.

KEY CONCEPT Interpret maps and graphs in order to obtain information visually. ■

Maps

A map can present much more information than simply the locations of cities and geographical formations. For example, maps can identify areas of population clusters, clarify battle activities in war, or report weather forecasts. To interpret a map, **(1)** determine the type and purpose of the map; **(2)** examine the symbols, distance, scale, and other data on the map; and **(3)** relate the information on the map to any written information accompanying it.

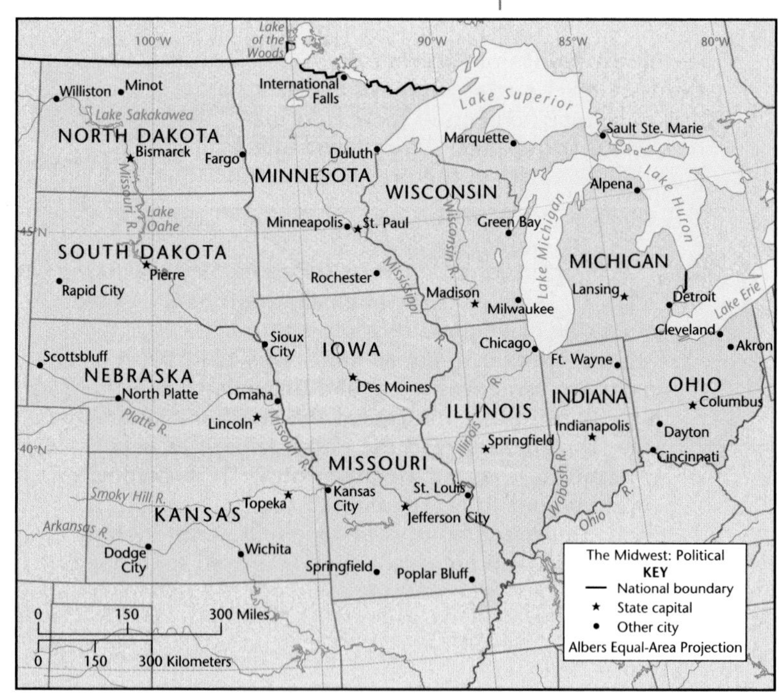

Research Tip

To get a better idea of the kinds of information maps can show, go to the reference section of your library and browse through a few atlases.

Graphs

Graphs provide a visual way to compare several pieces of related information. Study the following three types of commonly used graphs.

Line Graph A **line graph** shows changes over a certain period of time. It features a line that connects points. The points, which may appear as dots on the graph, represent numbers or amounts of something. To interpret a line graph, **(1)** read the title of the graph and its labels to find out what type of information is represented and the time interval over which the data is being reported; **(2)** read each axis of the graph: the main vertical line and main horizontal line that make up the graph; **(3)** compare and contrast the data.

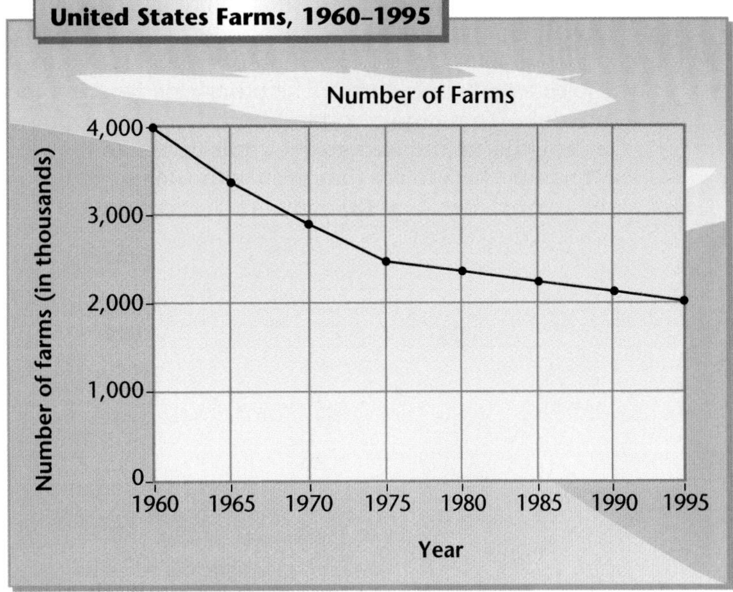

Pie Graph A **pie graph** shows the relationship of parts to each other and to a whole. To interpret a pie graph, **(1)** look at the numbers that go with the individual parts; **(2)** match the parts with the key; and **(3)** use the numbers and parts to make comparisons.

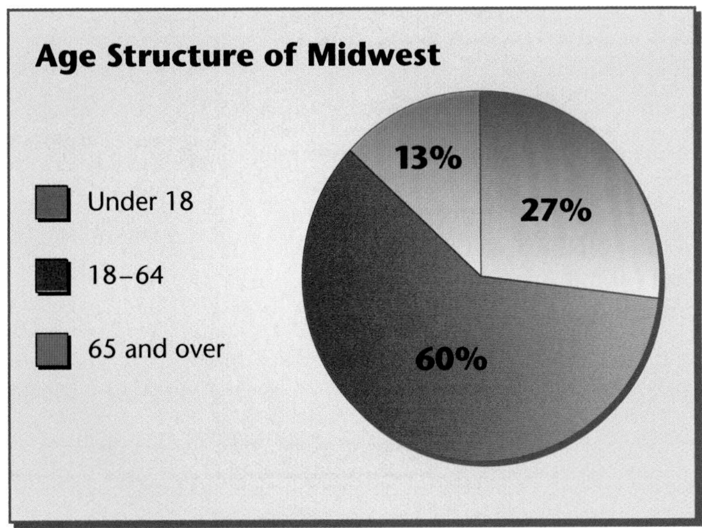

Bar Graph A **bar graph** shows changes over a period of time or compares and contrasts information. A bar graph has a vertical axis and a horizontal axis. One axis shows the subjects being measured. The other axis lists numbers or amounts. To interpret a bar graph, **(1)** look at the "heights" or "lengths" of the bars to see what numbers they represent; **(2)** match the subject that goes with the bar to the number the bar reaches; and **(3)** compare and contrast the "heights" or "lengths" of bars.

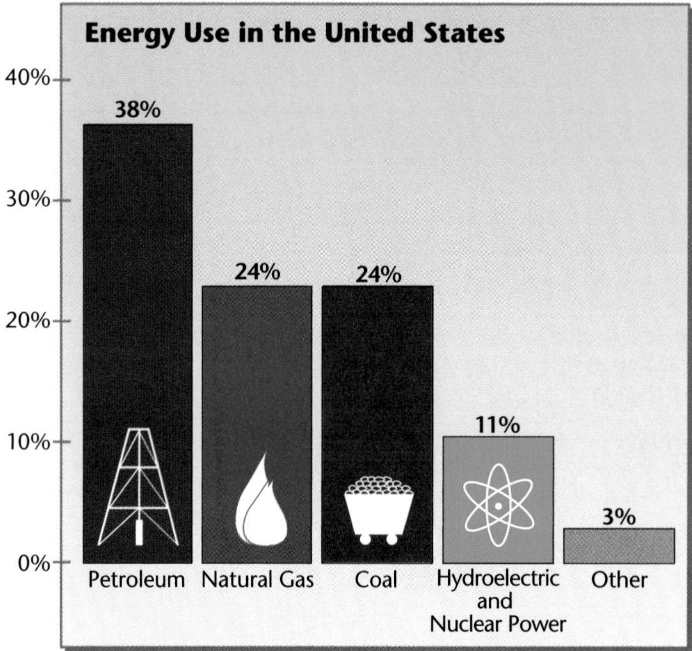

Exercise 8 **Reading Information Visually** Find an example from your textbooks or other sources of each type of visual aid (a map and a line, pie, and bar graph). Use the general guidelines and steps for interpretation to help you describe the visual aid and tell what kinds of information you can learn from each. Report your findings to your classmates.

More Practice

Academic and Workplace Skills Activity Book

- pp. 4–5

Viewing Information Media Critically

When you view information media critically, you think carefully about what you see and hear. Because the media distributes large amounts of information, it is important to learn the differences between various kinds of media as well as to evaluate the information being presented.

KEY CONCEPT Learn to identify and evaluate the various kinds of information and images found in nonprint media. ■

Recognizing the Kinds of Information Media

Television, documentary films, and other media provide news and other information. The quality and importance of the information you get depends on the kind of program or film you are watching.

The following chart describes several forms of nonprint information media.

NONPRINT INFORMATION MEDIA

Form of Medium	Topic(s)	Coverage and Content	Point of View
Television News Program	Current events or news	Brief summaries illustrated by video footage	Gives objective information
Documentary	One topic of social interest	Story shown through narration and video footage	Expresses controversial opinions
Interview	Topics of social interest	Conversations of questions and answers	Presents opinions of those involved
Editorial	Current or controversial topics	Commentary by a single person supported by statistics or facts	Presents the opinions of a single individual
Commercial	Products, people, and ideas	Short message of images and slogans	Presents information to sell something

Learn More

Advertisements often use loaded language and images. To learn more about the techniques used in advertisements, read Chapter 8.

Evaluating Persuasive Techniques When you are reading or watching any form of media, you should be aware of persuasive techniques that are being used so that your understanding of the information is not distorted.

KEY CONCEPT Be aware of persuasive techniques in media that may distort your understanding of actual events. ■

- **Facts and opinions** are two primary means of persuasion. A *fact* is a statement that can be proved to be true. An *opinion* is a viewpoint that cannot be proved to be true.
- **"Loaded" language and images** are words and visuals that appeal to your emotions in order to persuade you to think a certain way.
- **Bias** is a tendency to think from a particular point of view. As you view, consider whether the information is being presented objectively or with an intended viewpoint.

Evaluating Information From the Media Once you understand the different forms of media and their persuasive techniques, you are ready to evaluate the programs themselves.

KEY CONCEPT Use critical viewing strategies to help you evaluate the media more effectively. ■

- As you watch a program, be aware of its form, its purpose, and its limitations.
- Separate facts from opinions. Be on the lookout for loaded language or sensational images that might cause you to react in a certain way. Listen for bias, and note any points of view that might be ignored.
- Check surprising or questionable information in other sources.
- View the complete program, and develop your own views about the issues, people, and information.

Exercise 9 **Analyzing Information Media** Watch a television program that provides information, such as a news program, a documentary, or an interview. Notice the commercials as well. Then, write an essay in which you identify the type of program and describe the topics covered. In addition, comment on what the commercials were selling. Finally, evaluate the information on each topic in the program and in the commercials using the strategies listed above.

Viewing Fine Art Critically

When you view fine art—such as a painting, drawing, photograph, or a sculpture—you use different standards for evaluation from those you use when viewing a program from the media—even if the work has a political or social message. The critical emphasis on bias, loaded words, and opinions gives way to an examination of line, shape, color, and motion.

KEY CONCEPT To enrich your understanding and enjoyment of fine art, interpret the various elements of which the artwork is composed. ■

Interpreting Elements of Fine Art Consider the following questions as you observe a work of art:

Starry Night, Vincent van Gogh, Museum of Modern Art, New York

- What kind of work are you viewing: a painting, drawing, photograph, engraving, or collage?
- What are the subject and central focus of the piece of art?
- What technique does the artist use—color *versus* black and white, bold lines *versus* impressionistic ones (lines of short strokes), vivid *versus* muted colors?
- What mood, theme, or message does the work convey?
- Is your overall response to the work more positive or more negative? Why?

Exercise 10 **Interpreting Fine Art** Interpret the painting *Starry Night* by Vincent van Gogh by asking and answering the questions listed above. Write your answers to these questions in your notebook. Add any other observations.

More Practice

Academic and Workplace Skills Activity Book

• p. 7

Section 30.3

Representing Skills

Visual representation, or the use of images, is an important method of communicating. You can design your own visual representations by using graphic organizers, multimedia presentations, and performances.

Creating Visual Representations

When you are reading, researching, studying, or presenting complicated ideas, you can use graphic organizers and other visual aids to give structure to the material. This makes the information easier to comprehend.

KEY CONCEPT Large amounts of information or technical data can be absorbed more easily if you put them into visual form. ■

Use these strategies to help you present information visually:

Use Text Descriptions In some types of writing, you will notice headings and subheadings that indicate various sections. A good way to organize this information visually is to design a graphic organizer, which is a tool that helps you organize information visually. For text with detailed descriptions, a drawing would help clarify the parts and details.

Look at Text Structure As you read, notice how the text is organized. Is it comparison-and-contrast, cause-and-effect, main idea and details, or chronological order? If it is a comparison and contrast, you can use a Venn diagram or a comparison chart to show similarities and differences. If the text shows cause-and-effect relationships, you can use a flowchart to show the information visually. If the text uses many details to support a main idea, you can use an outline to organize the material. A good way to visualize chronological order is a timeline.

Chronology

Harold meets Margaret. ▶ They go out to dinner. ▶ The diamonds disappear. ▶ Margaret leaves town.

Identify Your Purpose Think about what parts of the material you want to represent visually. Then, decide which type of graphic organizer will work best for your purposes. For example, you might want to show what two political systems have in common and how they differ, or you may want to chart three possible outcomes of an election. You might want to compare and contrast the percentages of people who have dogs, cats, or birds as pets.

Learn More

To learn more about graphic organizers, read "Using Graphic Organizers" in Chapter 32, "Reading."

Charts, Graphs, and Tables For columns of numbers, survey statistics, and other complex information, you can prepare a chart, graph, or table. A chart can be any shape or color, and it can display any type of information, such as the heights of tall mountains. A graph, such as a bar or line graph, is a good way to show changes that take place over time, such as the daily outdoor temperature. Tables enable you to present scientific and numerical information in a clear and logical way.

Diagrams and Illustrations Diagrams and illustrations are line drawings that indicate the features of something. If you were describing the solar system, for example, you might make a diagram like the one below:

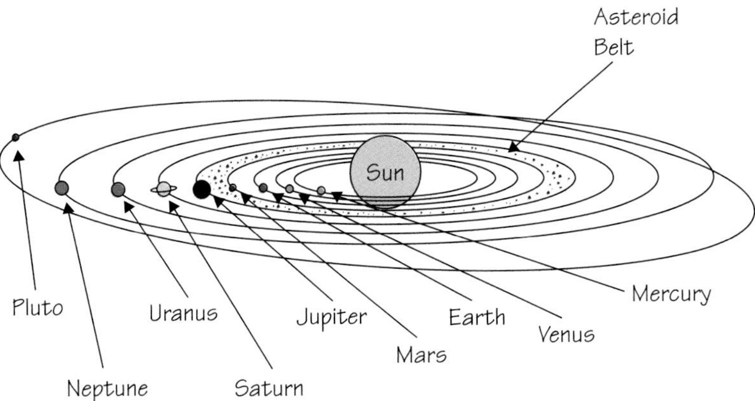

Maps If you want to know how to get somewhere or if you are studying the geography of several regions, a map can be quite useful. Maps can show almost any type of geographical information.

Exercise 11 **Creating Visual Representations** Use your knowledge of visual representations to complete one of the following activities:

1. Examine a chapter from one of your textbooks and prepare a chart, graph, or table to illustrate a portion of its information. Present your visual representation to the class, and explain why you chose to present the information in this way.
2. Make a map or diagram of your school or of an area of your town or city.

Technology Tip

You can get maps from the Internet by using the key word *Maps*. You can also get directions from any one location to another, as long as you have the two addresses. Print out some directions from a map Web site, and study the maps that accompany the directions.

More Practice

Academic and Workplace Skills Activity Book
- p. 8

Using Formatting

You can enhance any written text by using the basic formatting features in your word-processing program. Formatting features include boldface, italics, capital letters, font sizes, and bullets, to name a few. Notice how this flyer uses formatting features to get its message across.

Here are some tips for using these features:

Capitals Use capital letters in heads to draw attention to important ideas and topics.

Boldface Use boldface type to emphasize key concepts or ideas on a page.

Italics Use italics to give special emphasis to a written line or word.

Numbered Lists Use a numbered list when you have steps that need to be followed in sequence.

Bulleted Lists For items that can be presented in any order, use a bulleted list.

Graphics Use graphics to attract a viewer's attention and to give an idea of what kind of information can be expected.

Go Now and Save With International Quality Tours!

If your vacation time and funds are limited, then you should check us out! Unlike lesser quality charter tours, we've got added value built into our prices.

We've Got It ... Do They?

- transfers to and from airports
- complimentary breakfasts
- a dazzling array of side trips
- gratuities included in price

Here's a sample day's itinerary:

1. Visit the historic district, famous for its period architecture.
2. Break for lunch at the renowned Foods Around the World Hall, where you can sample international cuisine.
3. Head to the outlet center, where name brands meet unrivaled discount prices.
4. Dine at a fine local restaurant.

Our tour packages have been rated as outstanding by our clients. Because we offer great packages at great prices, you can enjoy a quality vacation without depleting your budget.

Exercise 12 Using Formatting to Summarize a Textbook Page Read a page from your textbook. Then, use the tips on formatting listed above to design a flyer that summarizes the textbook information. Give reasons for your formatting choices.

Working With Multimedia

An oral report becomes a multimedia presentation when the speaker illustrates the main points with media selections. If this type of presentation is well planned and executed, it can be effective and memorable.

KEY CONCEPT Multimedia presentations make use of a variety of media in order to explain information. Among the media used are text, slides, videos, music from audiotapes and CDs, maps, charts, and art. ■

Preparing a Multimedia Presentation First, prepare an outline of your report. Then, decide which parts of your report could best be illustrated through the use of media.

- Choose an appropriate form of media for your topic. For example, if you were discussing the music of Beethoven, a picture of the composer, video clips from movies based on his life, and music that he wrote would help enhance your presentation.
- As you deliver your report, incorporate the media at appropriate points. Do not show all the media at once.
- Check to be sure that the media you plan to present will be able to be seen and/or heard by everyone. A small photograph, for example, might not be clear to people in the back. It would be better to project the image using an overhead projector.
- Before the day of your presentation, rehearse with the equipment. Make sure that the use of visuals does not distract from your presentation. You should not be fumbling around with equipment during your presentation.
- Before your presentation, make sure that all your equipment (slide projectors, overhead projectors, microphones, cassette players, CD players) are in working condition.
- Always have an alternate plan in case something goes wrong with the equipment.

Exercise 13 **Preparing a Multimedia Presentation** Look through the writings in your portfolio. Find one piece to use as a multimedia presentation. Prepare an outline of your presentation, including the media you'd use and the order in which you would use it. Practice a few times, and then present it to your class.

Learn More

You will have to do research as you prepare your presentation. The steps you would follow to prepare the presentation are basically the same as the steps you would follow to prepare a research paper. To learn more about research methods, read Chapter 12.

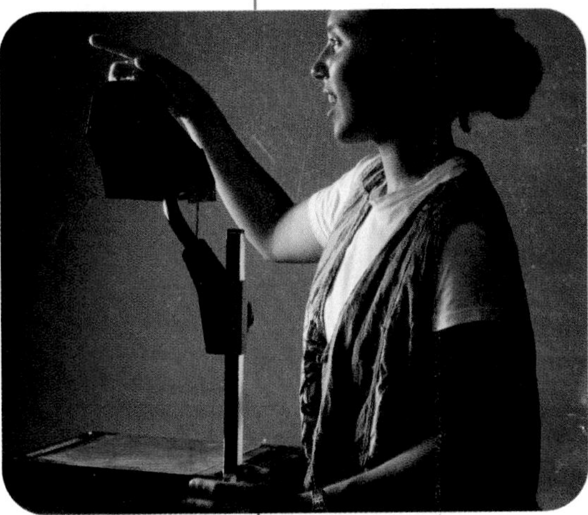

▲ **Critical Viewing** How can this student use this form of media to enhance her report? **[Deduce]**

More Practice

Academic and Workplace Skills Activity Book
- p. 10

Preparing a Flip Chart

Flip charts are effective visual aids that help your audience remember the key points of your speech.

KEY CONCEPT Prepare a flip chart to help your audience follow the sequence of events in your story, the main points of your argument, or the steps to be followed in your directions. ■

Follow these steps to prepare and use a flip chart:

1. Determine the most important points in your presentation.
2. Obtain enough sheets of posterboard to allow one sheet per point.
3. Write each point on a separate sheet of posterboard. Be sure that the writing is large enough to be seen by all audience members. Keep it short—you can elaborate in your presentation. You can use charts, diagrams, and other visuals, but they must be clear.
4. Arrange the sheets in the order in which the points appear in your presentation.
5. Punch two or three holes in the top of each sheet of posterboard. Use shower curtain hooks or similar devices to attach the sheets and make them easy to flip.
6. Set the flip chart on an easel. If you are right-handed, stand on the left side of the chart. If you are left-handed, stand on the right side of the chart. This will make it easy for you to flip the pages and point out the important information on the chart.
7. Do not turn your back to your audience as you flip the pages. Face the audience at all times.

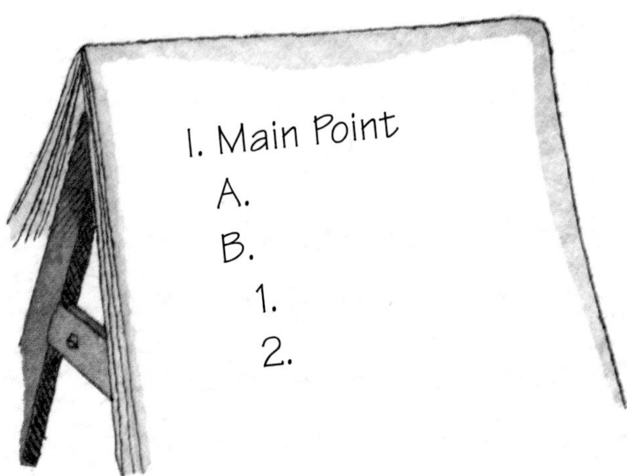

Exercise 14 **Preparing a Flip Chart** Prepare a flip chart of at least three pages. Follow the steps in the list above to make your chart. Be sure that each page of your flip chart is clear and concise. Remember that the purpose of a flip chart is to accompany and clarify your more elaborate presentation.

Performing or Interpreting

A live performance is one of the oldest and most effective forms of communication.

KEY CONCEPT You can use a wide variety of techniques to convey the meaning of a text or song. ■

Preparing to Perform Whether you plan a performance of someone else's work or of an original piece of your own, keep the following tips in mind.

1. Write the text in a notebook or photocopy it. Then, highlight its most important words and ideas.
2. Read the text aloud several times, experimenting with the tone and pitch of your voice and with the emphasis you give to certain words and phrases.
3. Practice using different kinds of body language—such as hand gestures, posture, and facial expressions—to convey meaning.
4. Costumes, props, background setting, and music are all important elements that can contribute to the mood.
5. Rehearse until you feel comfortable enough to perform.

Exercise 15 **Giving an Oral Interpretation** Choose a poem or a story you'd like to interpret for an audience. Copy it and highlight its key ideas and words. Then, write a list of performance notes, planning the effect you'd like to create, the mood you'd like to set, and other details related to the performance.

Technology Tip

You might want to use the computer to make a copy of your text. If you do, you can highlight the most important words and ideas in various ways:

- You can use large type.
- You can use boldface type.
- You can use different colors for the type or for the background.

More Practice

Academic and Workplace Skills Activity Book
- p. 12

Reflecting on Your Speaking, Listening, Viewing, and Representing

Review the various concepts discussed in this chapter. Write a one-page reflection on these experiences. Begin your observations by responding to these questions:

- How has my understanding of being a good speaker and listener changed? In what ways can I improve each of these skills?
- What strategies have most improved my ability to view information critically?
- Which representing experiences did I find the most enjoyable?
- What have I learned about viewing and representing?

Share your insights with your classmates.

Chapter 31

Vocabulary and Spelling

▲ **Critical Viewing** Describe the tools for writing that you see in this picture. How do our tools differ? **[Compare]**

The words you use and the way you present them can combine to create a powerful message. Your vocabulary includes all the words available to you in your speaking, reading, and writing. By increasing your vocabulary, you will understand more and communicate your ideas more precisely. Correct spelling is another key to clear communication.

This chapter will show you ways to learn and remember new words. It will also offer some practical suggestions and specific spelling rules to help you improve your spelling.

Section 31.1

Developing Your Vocabulary

Words are the building blocks of communication. The more words you have at your command, the more elaborate and complete your communication can be.

To increase your vocabulary, you must have a desire to expand your knowledge of word meanings, as well as a commitment to learning new words. There are many methods and helpful techniques for building vocabulary.

Listening, Discussing, and Reading

Most of our everyday words and expressions we learned when we were small children. We learned by listening and by practicing.

KEY CONCEPT The most common ways to increase your vocabulary are listening, reading, and taking part in conversations. ■

Listen for and Use New Words Try to imagine what it must have been like when you were a baby. You had no language to communicate your wants and needs. You made a lot of noise, but everyone had to guess what you wanted. You quickly began to learn language. Before you could speak one word, you understood many. People spoke to you, and you listened very carefully to their words. Soon, you began to speak, and before long you were stringing words into sentences and following grammar rules that you didn't even know existed.

Now, as then, listening is an excellent way to expand your vocabulary. When you talk to other people, listen and take notes in class, watch television, listen to the radio, or listen to literature on audiocassettes, notice the unfamiliar words. Jot the words down, and find out their meanings by using a dictionary or by asking someone. Whenever possible, try to use new words in conversation.

Wide Reading You will probably run into more unfamiliar words when you read than when you listen and discuss. People's written vocabulary is usually larger than their spoken vocabulary. You will encounter familiar words used in new ways, as well as brand-new words.

The more variety you have in your reading, the more variety you will have in your vocabulary. Try to expand your vocabulary by reading as widely as possible. Read textbooks, newspapers, magazines, novels, and articles on the Internet.

31.1

Recognizing Context Clues

By examining the meaning of a sentence, you can often find clues to the meaning of any unfamiliar words in it.

KEY CONCEPT A word's **context** is the sentence, the surrounding words, or the situation in which the word is used. ■

There are many types of context clues, including *description, example, restatement, comparison* or *contrast*, and *synonyms* or *antonyms*. Look at the following example:

EXAMPLE: The winning record of our team *intimidated* the other team so much that they didn't want to play against us.

CLUES: In this sentence, the *description* "winning record" suggests strength and skill. The words "didn't want to play against us" suggest the *contrast* between the ability of the two teams.

POSSIBLE MEANING: *Intimidate* must mean "frighten."

The steps in the following chart explain how to use the context of a word to find clues to its meaning.

USING CONTEXT CLUES
1. Read the sentence, leaving out the unfamiliar word. 2. Find clues in the sentence that suggest the word's meaning. 3. Read the sentence again, substituting your possible meaning for the unfamiliar word. 4. Check your possible meaning by looking up the unfamiliar word in the dictionary. Write the word and its definition in your vocabulary notebook.

Exercise 1 **Recognizing Context Clues** Use context clues to determine the meaning of the underlined word in each sentence below. Check your answers in a dictionary.

1. After examining the evidence, Sherlock Holmes surmised that the criminal had escaped through the back door.
2. Because of his hesitation, I was skeptical that he really wanted to join our group.
3. My father remained intransigent and would not change his mind about buying me a new computer.
4. The store salesman showed us battery-operated staplers, labelmakers, and other such gadgets.
5. His mendacity was so well known in the town that no one believed him when he said he would never tell a lie again.

Research Tip

Find a science book in the library. Locate three sentences in the book that provide context clues to help determine the meaning of a word. Add the new words to your notebook.

Using Possible Sentences You can have fun with unfamiliar words by using the Possible Sentences strategy outlined in the illustration below.

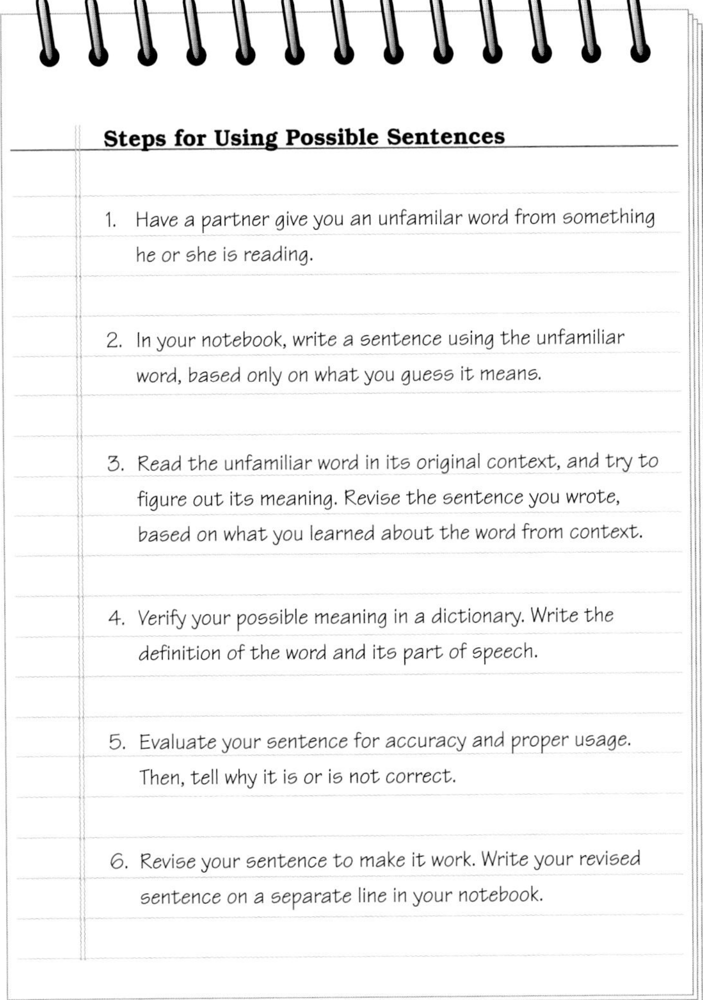

Exercise 2 **Using Possible Sentences** Using the steps mentioned above, apply the Possible Sentences strategy to increase your understanding of seven vocabulary words from your next reading assignment.

31.1

Denotation and Connotation

Context can help you determine a word's exact meaning. Knowing the denotations and connotations of a word can help you discriminate among different shades of meaning.

KEY CONCEPT The **denotation** of a word is its literal definition. Its **connotations** include the ideas, images, and feelings that are associated with the word. ■

The denotation of the word *doctor* is "physician" or "surgeon"—a person licensed to practice any of the healing arts. The connotations of the word suggest prestige, success, and hard work. As you increase your vocabulary, be aware of both positive and negative connotations of words you use.

Exercise 3 **Revising Sentences to Change Connotations** Read each sentence below. Then, revise each sentence by replacing the underlined word with a word that has a similar denotation but a different connotation.

1. The cashier was <u>forgetful</u>, often adding the sales tax twice.
2. The doctor's positive report <u>consoled</u> us.
3. The radio on the windowsill <u>played</u> endlessly.
4. Robert had trouble making friends because he was <u>shy</u>.
5. He made a <u>clumsy</u> attempt to apologize.

Recognizing Related Words

Three kinds of related words are *synonyms*, *antonyms*, and *homophones*. Examining the relationships between words will strengthen your understanding of their meanings and will help you remember new words.

KEY CONCEPTS **Synonyms** are words that are similar in meaning. **Antonyms** are words that are opposite in meaning. **Homophones** are words that sound alike but have different meanings and spellings. ■

Exercise 4 **Recognizing Synonyms, Antonyms, and Homophones** Identify each pair of words below as synonyms, antonyms, or homophones.

1. negative/positive
2. there/their
3. oppose/defend
4. careful/negligent
5. our/hour

Using Related Words in Analogies

Working with analogies, or word relationships, strengthens your vocabulary by increasing your understanding of connections between word meanings. It will also benefit you to practice analogies because they are typical items found in aptitude and achievement tests.

Learn More

Analogies can be used to explain the relationship between objects or ideas. They are also useful in setting up dynamic description. For more about descriptive writing, see Chapter 6.

KEY CONCEPT **Analogies** present word pairs that have some relationship to each other. ■

Look at the following analogy, and see whether you can find the relationship between the given word pairs:

EXAMPLE: SMALL : MINUTE :: large : tremendous

The relationship between the word pairs appears to be that they are *synonyms*, but a closer look reveals the finer relationship of *degree*. Just as the word *minute* means very small, *tremendous* means very large. Other common analogy relationships include *part to whole*, *defining characteristic*, *instrument*, and *kind*.

Exercise 5 **Working With Analogies** First, identify the analogy relationship expressed in the capitalized pair. Then, choose the lettered pair that best expresses this relationship.

1. POODLE : DOG ::
   a. ram : bull
   b. Arabian : horse
   c. fox : wolf
2. PETAL : FLOWER ::
   a. bale : hay
   b. wood : axe
   c. branch : tree
3. HILL : MOUNTAIN ::
   a. tree : forest
   b. climber : rock
   c. pony : horse
4. BRUSH : ARTIST ::
   a. painting : color
   b. pen : author
   c. model : person
5. FIRE : HEAT ::
   a. ice : cold
   b. sun : moon
   c. volcano : eruption

▼ Critical Viewing These students appear to be studying together. How does studying with a partner help you to learn? **[Infer]**

Section 31.2

Studying Words Systematically

Using a Dictionary and a Thesaurus

A dictionary and a thesaurus can help you increase your vocabulary. Every time you come across an unfamiliar word, consult a dictionary to learn its meaning. Use a thesaurus to find new words that will better express your meaning.

KEY CONCEPT A **dictionary** gives the meaning, spelling, and proper pronunciation of words. ■

- Look up the base form of the word, the form without endings showing tense or number.
- Study the pronunciation of the word you look up. It is usually given in parentheses right after the word.
- Notice the different meanings that a single word can have.
- Notice the abbreviations that are used in the definitions to indicate the part of speech of the word.

KEY CONCEPT A **thesaurus** provides lists of words that are similar in meaning. ■

- Do not choose a word just because it sounds interesting. Choose the word that expresses the meaning you intend.
- To avoid errors, look up the word in a dictionary to check its precise meaning and to make sure it is properly used.

Exercise 6 **Using a Dictionary** Look up each word in a dictionary. Write the definition for the part of speech indicated in parentheses.

1. tattle (verb)
2. avail (noun)
3. fray (verb)
4. sallow (noun)
5. knell (verb)

Exercise 7 **Using a Thesaurus** Use a thesaurus to find a more precise word for the underlined word in each sentence.

1. The boy was happy when he won the raffle.
2. After the ten-mile hike, we were tired.
3. The speech that brought a standing ovation was good.
4. She felt afraid to walk home alone through the dark woods.
5. Because it was his first day on the job, he was a beginner.

Research Tip

Choose five words, and use a thesaurus to find a synonym for each of them. Then, use a dictionary to see whether there are any subtle differences in meaning between each word and its synonym.

Remembering New Vocabulary

Even if you use a dictionary and thesaurus regularly, there still may be some word meanings that are harder for you to remember than others. Use these suggestions to reinforce your memory of new words once you have determined their meanings.

KEY CONCEPT Study and review new words a few times a week, using a variety of methods. ■

Using a Vocabulary Notebook Keep track of your new vocabulary in a separate section in your notebook. Use the following illustration to set up a notebook page for vocabulary words:

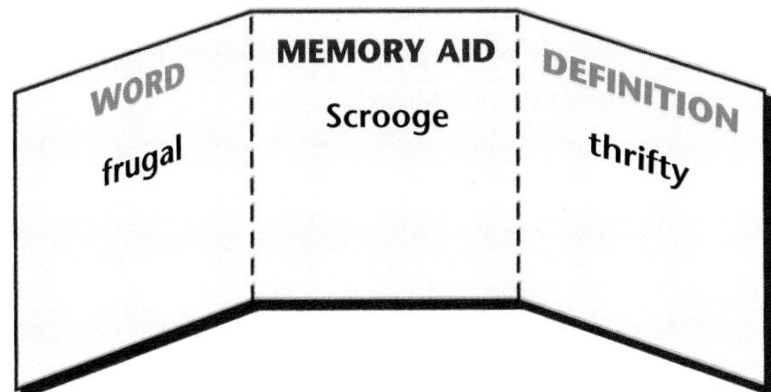

When studying, you can either cover the third column with another piece of paper or fold the paper back to hide the word's definition.

Using a Tape Recorder When reviewing your new words at home, you may find that a tape recorder is helpful. Saying, repeating, and hearing your new words can often make it easier to learn them.

Follow these steps when you study with a tape recorder:

1. Record a word on the tape.
2. Leave five seconds of space on the tape, and then give a definition followed by a sentence using the word. Leave another five-second pause before reading the next word.
3. Continue with the remainder of the words.
4. Study the words by replaying the entire tape and saying each definition aloud in the pause before the recorded definition plays and then again during the second pause.
5. Rerun the tape until you can give all the definitions.

Listening to your tape several times a week will help you make new words a permanent part of your vocabulary.

Using Flashcards Flashcards can also help you learn new words. On the front of an index card, write the word you want to learn. If it is difficult to pronounce, copy the phonetic spelling of the word from the dictionary, as shown below. On the lower right corner of the card, write in pencil a bridge word—a word or image that you associate with the meaning of the vocabulary word. When you no longer need this hint to remember the definition of the word, you can erase it. On the back of the card, write the definition of the word.

Front
Frugal
(fro͞o′gəl)
Scrooge

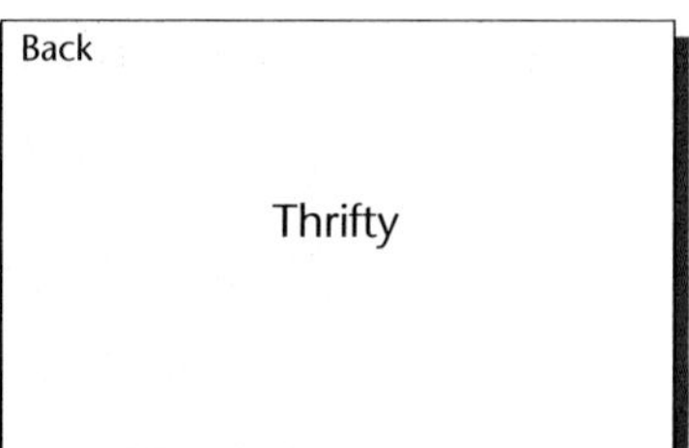

Use the following steps to drill yourself:

1. Flip through the cards, looking at both sides of each card, and try to associate each word with its definition.
2. Then, look at just the front side of each card, defining each word and using it in a sentence.
3. Place cards with words you cannot define in a review pile.
4. Repeat the first three steps with the cards in the review pile until you are able to define all the words.

Working With a Partner Reviewing vocabulary with a partner provides a chance for reinforcement as well as encouragement. In the first round, read the words from your partner's vocabulary notebook or flashcards and have your partner define them. If your partner is slow to respond, you should provide the bridge word if it is given. Repeat the words until your partner can correctly define all of them. During the second round, exchange roles with your partner, and have your partner read you the words from your vocabulary notebook or flashcards.

Exercise 8 **Using Different Study Methods** After reviewing vocabulary words using at least three of the methods explained here, decide which method works best for you. Then, choose a second method to add variety to your study. Explain the reasons for both choices.

Section 31.3

Studying Word Parts and Origins

When you analyze the parts of an unfamiliar word, you can find clues to its meaning. Many words have a *prefix*, a *root*, and a *suffix*.

Using Prefixes

One of the best ways to build your vocabulary is to learn how prefixes change the meanings of words.

KEY CONCEPT A **prefix** is one or more syllables placed before the root. ■

You may want to memorize these prefixes and their meanings.

TEN COMMON PREFIXES		
Prefixes	Meanings	Examples
de-	away from, off	*de*face, or take away from the "face" or appearance of
dis-	away, apart	*dis*arm, or take the arms *away*
ex-	from, out	*ex*change, or change *from*
in-	not	*in*human, or *not* human
in-	in, into	*in*dent, or "bite" *into*
inter-	between	*inter*national, or *between* nations
mis-	wrong	*mis*understand, or understand *incorrectly*
re-	back, again	*re*new, or make new *again*
sub-	beneath, under	*sub*marine, or *beneath* the sea
un-	not	*un*happy, or *not* happy

Exercise 9 **Working With Prefixes** Using your knowledge of prefixes, figure out the meaning of each word below. Then, check your answers by looking up each word in a dictionary.

1. *re*kindle
2. *mis*interpret
3. *in*flame
4. *inter*continental
5. *ex*clude

Exercise 10 **Defining Prefixes and Prefix Origins** Using a dictionary, write the definition of each prefix and its origin. Then, provide an example for each prefix.

1. ad-
2. circum-
3. post-
4. trans-
5. com-

Recognizing Roots

The root carries the basic meaning of a word. The same root can be used to form many different words.

KEY CONCEPT A **root** is the base of the word. ■

This chart lists ten common roots used in English words. Alternative spellings are shown in parentheses.

TEN COMMON ROOTS		
Roots	**Meanings**	**Examples**
-duc- (-duct-)	to lead	con*duct*, or *lead* together
-graph-	to write	*graph*ic, or of *writing*
-mit- (-mis-)	to send	trans*mit*, or *send* across
-pon- (-pos-)	to put or place	com*pon*ent, or something *put* with something else
-puls- (-pel-)	to drive	re*pulse*, or *drive* back
-scrib- (-script-)	to write	in*scribe*, or *write* into
-spec- (-spect-)	to see	in*spect*, or *see* into
-ten- (-tain-)	to hold	con*tain*, or *hold* together
-ven- (-vent-)	to come	in*vent*, or *come* into
-vert- (-vers-)	to turn	re*verse*, or *turn* back

Exercise 11 **Using Roots to Define Words** In your notebook, write each word, paying close attention to the word's root, shown in italics. Then, next to each word, write the letter of its meaning.

1. sub*script*
2. re*vert*
3. re*ten*tive
4. con*ven*tion
5. im*pose*

a. to place a burden on
b. able to hold on to
c. a group meeting
d. a character written below another
e. to turn back to

Exercise 12 **Finding Common Roots** Look up each pair of words in a dictionary, paying close attention to each word's root, shown in italics. Then, write the basic meaning shared by each pair of words.

1. in*capa*citate, *capt*ive
2. contra*dict*ion, *dict*ation
3. *fact*itious, *fac*ilitate
4. *mot*ion, *mov*ing
5. en*vis*ion, *vid*eo

Using Suffixes

Some suffixes—word endings—form plurals of nouns, such as the *-s* in *dogs*. Others show the tenses of verbs, such as the *-ed* in *wanted* or the *-ing* in *wanting*. The suffixes in this section form new words.

Ten common suffixes used to form new words are listed in the next chart.

KEY CONCEPT A **suffix** is one or more syllables added at the end of a root, which can be used to form new words. ■

TEN COMMON SUFFIXES

Suffixes	Meanings	Examples
-able (-ible)	capable of being	sustain*able*, or *capable of being* sustained
-ance (-ence)	the act of	clear*ance*, or *the act of* being cleared
-ate	make or apply	activ*ate*, or *make* active
-ful	full of	scorn*ful*, or *full of* scorn
-ity	the state of being	intens*ity*, or *the state of being* intense
-less	without	hope*less*, or *without* hope
-ly	in a certain way	careless*ly*, or done *in a* careless *way*
-ment	the result of being	improve*ment*, or *the result of being* improved
-ness	the state of being	hopeless*ness*, or *the state of being* hopeless
-tion (-ion, -sion)	the act or state of being	admis*sion*, or *the act of being* admitted

Suffixes can indicate the word's part of speech. The following list shows the parts of speech indicated by the suffixes. Notice that *-ful* and *-ly* can each form two parts of speech.

NOUNS:	-ance -ful -ity -ment -ness -tion	ADJECTIVES:	-able -ful -less -ly
VERB:	-ate	ADVERB:	-ly

Learn More

To learn more about parts of speech, see Chapter 16, "Nouns and Pronouns," and Chapter 17, "Verbs."

Exercise 13 **Determining Parts of Speech and Meaning From Suffixes** Using your knowledge of suffixes, write the part of speech and meaning of each word below. Then, check and correct your answer by looking up each word in a dictionary.

1. contain*ment*
2. divis*ible*
3. bounti*ful*
4. biolog*ist*
5. motiv*ate*
6. good*ness*
7. commun*ity*
8. wit*less*
9. adapta*tion*
10. norther*ly*

Exercise 14 **Defining Suffixes and Suffix Origins** Using a dictionary, write the definition of each suffix and its origin. Then, provide an example of a word using each suffix.

1. -ic
2. -ward
3. -logy
4. -ist
5. -ous

▲ Critical Viewing What adjectives would you use to describe the attitudes of the girls in this picture? Which words have suffixes? What are the suffixes? **[Analyze]**

Exploring Etymologies (Word Origins)

The **etymology** of a word is its origin and history.

KEY CONCEPT Knowing the etymology of a word can help you understand its meaning. ■

Listed below are several ways in which words evolve:

- Words are borrowed from other languages.
- Words change meaning over time and through usage.
- Words are invented, or coined, to serve new purposes.
- Words are combined or shortened.
- Words are formed from acronyms, or the use of initials.

Exercise 15 **Using a Dictionary to Learn About Etymologies** Find the word origins of each word below. Write the word origin, and then write a sentence using the word.

1. mosquito
2. geometry
3. scuba
4. dollar
5. southpaw
6. chowder
7. magazine
8. quark
9. plaid
10. pretzel

Keeping a Spelling Notebook

Make it a practice to keep a list of all the words that you regularly have trouble spelling. These words can be grouped into two categories. The first category contains the words that present special difficulty and have repeatedly caused you trouble. It is often best to memorize these spelling words.

The second category contains the words that you misspell because of error patterns, which will be further discussed in this section.

KEY CONCEPT Make a personal spelling list of words that repeatedly cause you problems and the error patterns in your misspellings. ■

Identify Your Error Patterns Learn to identify the error patterns in your misspellings. The chart below lists common error patterns:

COMMON ERROR PATTERNS	
Error	**Example**
Doubling consonants	coming *not* comming
Adding syllables	athletic *not* atheletic
Deleting syllables	mathematics *not* mathmatics
Using apostrophes for plurals	ten boys *not* ten boy's
Dropping final *e*	management *not* managment
Retaining final *e*	debatable *not* debateable
Retaining final *y*	merriment *not* merryment
Blending sounds	length *not* lenth
Omitting silent letters	wealthy *not* welthy
Transposing letters	relevant *not* revelant
Separating combined words	classroom *not* class room
Confusing homophones	to/too/two
Confusing contractions and possessive pronouns	it's/its

Exercise 16 **Identifying Error Patterns** Each sentence below contains one or more incorrect spellings. Identify the error pattern of the misspelled word, and write the correct spelling. Then, look over the writing you have done in the past two weeks. Proofread your work for misspelled words, and identify your error patterns.

1. A completely empty space is called a vacum.
2. Accept for Rob, we all went out to lunch.
3. The group did not condem the person who was late.
4. There were three girl's sitting on the porch that morning.
5. Some one was in the car, but no one knew who it was.

Using Memory Aids

Most words can be easily learned through well-organized strategies and the use of rules, such as those listed in the following section. For some words, however, you may find that spelling success can best be achieved through the development and use of special memory aids or hints.

KEY CONCEPT Use memory aids to remember the spelling of words that you find especially difficult to spell. ■

Some problem words lend themselves to the development of memory aids. With some words, for example, you can find a short, easy-to-spell word hidden within the more difficult word.

EXAMPLES:	believe	Never believe a lie.
	necessary	The word *necessary* causes problems.
	calendar	A calendar shows the days of the week.
	prairie	The air smells fresh on the prairie.

Exercise 17 **Developing Memory Aids** Perhaps the best memory aids are the ones you develop yourself. Create a memory aid for each word below. Then, choose five words in your spelling notebook, and find some memory aid for each. Enter the hints in your spelling notebook.

1. tomorrow
2. handkerchief
3. extraordinary
4. capital
5. lawyer

Following Spelling Rules

Although some words present spelling problems, the vast majority of English words follow some regular pattern. For example, you can learn rules for writing plurals, writing words with prefixes and suffixes, and choosing between *ie* and *ei*.

Plurals

The plural form of a noun is the form that means "more than one." The plural forms can be either *regular* or *irregular*.

KEY CONCEPT The regular plural form of most nouns is formed by adding -*s* or-*es* to the singular. ■

Regular Plurals As a general rule, you can just add -*s* to form a regular plural. With certain regular plurals, however, you may have to choose whether to add -*s* or -*es*. Occasionally, you may also have to change a letter or two in the word.

1. To form the plurals of words ending in *s*, *ss*, *x*, *z*, *sh*, or *ch*, add -*es* to the base word:

circus + -es = circuses	dress + -es = dresses
box + -es = boxes	waltz + -es = waltzes
dish + -es = dishes	church + -es = churches

2. To form the plurals of words ending in *y* or *o* preceded by a vowel, add -*s* to the base word:

journey + -s = journeys	holiday + -s = holidays
rodeo + -s = rodeos	patio + -s = patios

3. To form the plurals of words ending in *y* preceded by a consonant, change the *y* to *i* and add -*es*. For most words ending in *o* preceded by a consonant, add -*es*. For musical terms ending in *o*, simply add -*s*:

city + -ies = cities	enemy + -ies = enemies
echo + -es = echoes	tomato + -es = tomatoes
piano + -s = pianos	solo + -s = solos

4. To form the plurals of some words ending in *f* or *fe*, you might just add -*s* or you might have to change the *f* or *fe* to *v* and add -*es*. For words ending in *ff*, add -*s*:

leaf + -es = leaves	loaf + -es = loaves
wife + -es = wives	life + -es = lives
chief + -s = chiefs	proof + -s = proofs
staff + -s = staffs	cliff + -s = cliffs
staff + -es = staves (in music)	

▼ **Critical Viewing** What steps should this student take to make sure that she has no spelling errors in her writing? **[Analyze]**

Irregular Plurals Irregular plurals are not formed according to the rules on the previous page. You can, however, find them in some dictionaries, listed right after the pronunciation of the word.

KEY CONCEPT Consult a dictionary for irregular plurals. ■

The following chart lists some irregular plurals.

IRREGULAR PLURALS		
Singular Forms	**Ways of Forming Plurals**	**Plural Forms**
ox	add *-en*	oxen
child	add *-ren*	children
tooth, mouse, woman	change one or more letters	teeth, mice, women
radius, focus, alumnus	change *-us* to *-i*	radii, foci, alumni
alumna	change *-a* to *-ae*	alumnae
crisis, emphasis	change *-is* to *-es*	crises, emphases
medium, datum, curriculum	change *-um* to *-a*	media, data, curricula
phenomenon, criterion	change *-on* to *-a*	phenomena, criteria
deer, sheep	plural form same as singular	deer, sheep
	plural form only	scissors, slacks

Note About *Plurals of Compound Words*: Compound words written as single words follow the general rules for forming plurals (*cookbooks*, *footballs*, and *Englishmen*). To form the plurals of compound words written with hyphens or as separate words, make the modified word plural (*passers-by*, *all stars*, *suits of armor*, and *field mice*).

Exercise 18 **Spelling Plurals** Write the plural for each word below. Consult a dictionary when necessary.

1. echo
2. bench
3. fox
4. mystery
5. chorus
6. ash
7. loss
8. veto
9. daughter-in-law
10. turkey
11. proof
12. alley
13. bush
14. potato
15. soprano
16. sheep
17. peach
18. scarf
19. alto
20. calf
21. goose
22. runner-up
23. tragedy
24. mosquito
25. knife

Prefixes and Suffixes

A **prefix** is one or more syllables added at the beginning of a word to form a new word. A **suffix** is one or more syllables added to the end of a word.

KEY CONCEPT Adding a prefix to a word does not affect the spelling of the original word. Adding a suffix often involves a spelling change in the word. ■

Prefixes When a prefix is added to the word, the spelling of the root remains the same.

EXAMPLES: dis- + appear = disappear
in- + sincere = insincere
mis- + inform = misinform

Exercise 19 **Spelling Words With Prefixes** Add one of the five prefixes below to each of the following words. Then, check each word in a dictionary.

in- *mis-* *un-* *dis-* *com-*

1. spell
2. satisfied
3. understand
4. possess
5. ability
6. mend
7. necessary
8. form
9. pose
10. dependent
11. take
12. organic
13. guide
14. charge
15. lodge
16. fort
17. mission
18. known
19. cast
20. like

Suffixes When adding suffixes to some words, a spelling change is required. The three charts that follow summarize the major kinds of spelling changes that can take place when a suffix is added.

SPELLING CHANGES IN WORDS ENDING IN *y*			
Word Endings	Suffixes Added	Rules	Exceptions
consonant + *y* (defy, happy)	most suffixes (*-ance, -ness*)	change *y* to *i* (defiance, happiness)	most suffixes beginning with *i: defy* becomes *defying*
vowel + *y* (employ, enjoy)	most suffixes (*-er, -ment*)	make no change (employer, enjoyment)	a few short words: *day* becomes *daily*

SPELLING CHANGES IN WORDS ENDING IN *e*			
Word Endings	Suffixes Added	Rules	Exceptions
any word ending in *e* (believe, recognize)	suffix beginning with a vowel (*-able*)	drop the final *e* (believable, recognizable)	1. words ending in *ce* or *ge* with suffixes beginning in *a* or *o*: *trace* becomes *traceable; outrage* becomes *outrageous* 2. words ending in *ee: agree* becomes *agreeable*
any word ending in *e* (price, nice)	suffix beginning with a consonant (*-less, -ly*)	make no change (priceless, nicely)	a few special words: *true* becomes *truly; argue* becomes *argument; judge* becomes *judgment*

DOUBLING THE FINAL CONSONANT BEFORE SUFFIXES			
Word Endings	Suffixes Added	Rules	Exceptions
consonant + vowel + consonant in one-syllable words or in a stressed syllable (rob´, admit´)	suffix beginning with a vowel (*-er, -ed*)	double the final consonant (rob´ber, admit´ted)	1. words ending in *x* or *w: bow* becomes *bowing; wax* becomes *waxing* 2. words in which the stress changes after the suffix is added: *prefer´* becomes *pref´erence*
consonant + vowel + consonant in an unstressed syllable (an´gel, fi´nal)	suffix beginning with a vowel (*-ic, -ize*)	make no change (angel´ic, fi´nalize)	no major exceptions

Exercise 20 **Spelling Words With Suffixes** Write the new word formed by combining each of the words and suffixes below. Check the spellings in a dictionary, and add the difficult words to your list.

1. accidental + -ly
2. occur + -ence
3. favor + -able
4. imply + -ing
5. survey + -or
6. silly + -ness
7. encourage + -ment
8. amplify + -er
9. rebel + -ion
10. continue + -ous

Exercise 21 **Using Words With Suffixes in Sentences** Make a new word to complete each sentence below by combining the words and suffixes in parentheses. Write each new word on your paper, spelled correctly. Check the spelling in a dictionary, and add the difficult words to your list.

1. The (shop + -er) had too many packages to carry.
2. I think a letter has been (omit + -ed) from this word.
3. Standing in a grocery store line with a (cry + -ing) child is frustrating for parents.
4. This is a (beauty + -ful) butterfly specimen.
5. We learned a (value + -able) lesson while watching them swim.
6. The (amuse + -ment) park was very crowded because it was spring break.
7. To get the most benefit, one must exercise (day + -ly).
8. It is rash to make a (judge + -ment) too quickly.
9. When wet, ceramic tile can be very (slip + -ery).
10. Let's get together on Friday to (final + -ize) plans for the (confer + -ence).

▶ Critical Viewing How can an interest in a subject like butterflies encourage you to learn the spelling of specialized vocabulary? **[Relate]**

31.4

Understanding Rules and Exceptions

Because English contains many words **borrowed from other languages**, most spelling rules have exceptions—words that do not follow the pattern and therefore must be memorized.

KEY CONCEPT For most words containing *ie* or *ei*, you can use the traditional rule: "Place *i* before *e* except after *c* or when sounded like *a*, as in *neighbor* or *weigh*." For its exceptions as well as the words ending in *-cede*, *-ceed*, and *-sede*, it is often best to memorize the correct spellings.

Spelling *ie* and *ei* Words

The *ie* and *ei* rule applies for many of these words, but like most rules, it has exceptions.

Exceptions for *ie* Words: counterfeit, either, foreign, forfeit, heifer, height, leisure, neither, seismology, seize, seizure, sheik, sleight, sovereign, weird

Exercise 22 **Spelling *ie* and *ei* Words** Use *ie* or *ei* to complete the word in each sentence below.

1. Her ach _ _ vements in the modern art world are great.
2. He was warned to stay out of misch _ _ f.
3. She felt a moment of anx _ _ ty as she entered the room.
4. We were not sure we had suffic _ _ nt money.
5. They bel _ _ ve in freedom of action.

Words Ending in *-cede*, *-ceed*, and *-sede*

The best way to handle words that end with these suffixes is to memorize the correct spelling.

Words ending in *-cede*: accede, concede, intercede, precede, recede, secede

Words ending in *-ceed*: exceed, proceed, succeed

Word ending in *-sede*: supersede

Exercise 23 **Spelling Words Ending in *-cede*, *-ceed*, and *-sede*** Write the incomplete word for each sentence, filling in the blanks with *-cede*, *-ceed*, or *-sede*.

1. Despite the setback, we must pro _ _ _ _ according to plan.
2. It is unlikely that he will suc _ _ _ _ in his efforts.
3. The country might se _ _ _ _ from the organization.
4. Clare will super _ _ _ _ Chuck as vice president.
5. I will gladly con _ _ _ _ that I was wrong.

Technology Tip

You can use the spell checker on your word processor to alert you when words are misspelled. Remember that if you have used a word incorrectly, a spell checker will not pick it up.

▼ **Critical Viewing** How does this picture illustrate one strategy for memorizing exceptions? **[Connect]**

Proofreading Carefully

One good strategy to use to improve your spelling skills is to proofread everything you write. By looking closely at the way you have spelled each word, you will become more conscious of the way words are supposed to look on the page.

KEY CONCEPT Proofread everything you write. ■

Following are some common proofreading strategies and tips:

- Proofread by reading your work slowly.
- Proofread only one line at a time. Use a ruler or other device to focus on the line you are proofreading and to cover up the lines you are not proofreading.
- Read backward, from the last word to the first. This forces you to focus only on the words themselves.
- Consult a dictionary when you come across a word that you suspect is spelled incorrectly.
- Use peer proofreading. Exchange papers with a classmate, and check each other's work for spelling errors.
- Always proofread more than once.

Exercise 24 **Proofreading Carefully** Each sentence below contains one incorrectly spelled word. Write the correct spelling of each misspelled word, using a dictionary when necessary.

1. We had a very pleasent picnic in the park.
2. The doctor advised her to get more exersise.
3. The prisonor denied that he had taken part in the crime.
4. The actor's performence was applauded by the critics.
5. The nurse said that he would accept the responsability.

Reflecting on Your Spelling and Vocabulary

Review your personal spelling list, the spelling rules in your notebook, and the methods you use to increase your vocabulary. See whether the spelling lists contain a pattern of the types of words with which you have difficulty. In a journal entry, ask yourself:

- Which words are easiest for me, and which words are hardest?
- What kinds of spelling errors do I typically make?
- Which method helped me to learn the greatest number of words?

Chapter 32 Reading Skills

▲ **Critical Viewing** What special sections of the textbook might these students be using to help them in their work? **[Analyze]**

Your teachers in earlier years stressed learning to read; now, the stress is on reading to learn. Being a good reader of both fiction and nonfiction involves knowing how to approach the material and using the critical thinking skills of evaluating and judging. In this chapter, you will learn ways to improve your skills in reading books related both to your schoolwork and personal reading.

Section 32.1

Reading Methods and Tools

To understand more fully the contents of a book, you have to be able to construct your own meaning of the material.

Using Sections in Textbooks

A good way to start improving your textbook reading skills is to become familiar with the parts of your textbook. The front and back of most textbooks include a number of sections.

KEY CONCEPT Use the special sections of the textbook to familiarize yourself with its contents. ■

Table of Contents In the front of the textbook, the table of contents shows the book's organization by listing the units and chapters and indicating the pages where they are located.

Preface or Introduction This information is located just after or just before the table of contents. The preface states the author's purpose in writing the book. The introduction gives an overview of the book's ideas.

Index The index, found in the back of the textbook, lists alphabetically the specific topics and terms covered in the textbook, along with the pages on which they can be found.

Glossary The glossary is a list of terms with definitions, located in the back of many textbooks. Generally, it includes specialized words taken directly from the textbook.

Appendix Located in the back of the textbook, the appendix contains a variety of information that the author considers useful in understanding the material in the book.

Bibliography The bibliography includes publication information about books and articles referred to by the author, as well as other related materials you might want to read.

Exercise 1 **Examining Your Textbooks** Examine two of your textbooks to become acquainted with their various sections. Answer the following questions for each book:

1. According to the table of contents, how many units and chapters does the textbook have?
2. What do the preface and the introduction each contain?
3. What are two pieces of information located in the index?
4. Does the textbook have a glossary? What are two pieces of information you can learn from it?
5. Does the textbook have an appendix or a bibliography? What kind of information does each contain?

More Practice

Academic and Workplace Skills Activity Book
• p. 28

32.1

Using Different Reading Styles

You can also improve your reading skills through knowledge of different reading styles. The three types of reading styles are *skimming*, *scanning*, and *close reading*. Each style of reading has a different purpose. Before you begin reading any material, consider your purpose, and then decide which reading style is the most suitable.

KEY CONCEPT Choose the style of reading suitable for your purpose and material. ■

Skimming When you **skim** a text, you look it over quickly to get a general idea of its contents. Look for highlighted or bold type, headings, and topic sentences. Use skimming to preview, review, and locate information.

Scanning When you **scan** a text, you look it over to find specific information. Look for words related to your topic or purpose for reading. Use scanning to research, review, and find information.

Close Reading When you **closely read** a text, you read it carefully to understand and remember its ideas, to find relationships between ideas, and to draw conclusions about what you read. Use close reading to organize, study, and remember information.

As you become familiar with the three styles of reading, you will learn to adjust your mind and eyes to the appropriate style for the material you are reading.

Exercise 2 **Determining Which Style of Reading to Use** Decide which style or styles of reading you would use for each of the following purposes.

EXAMPLE: Finding an article in a magazine *(scanning)*

1. Seeing if a book will be suitable for pleasure reading
2. Surveying the questions at the end of a chapter
3. Finding a word in the glossary of a textbook
4. Locating a particular place on a map
5. Reading and taking notes for a chapter test
6. Checking the contents of a book by using the index
7. Locating the time a bus should arrive using a bus schedule
8. Previewing a chapter
9. Reading a short story for an assignment in English class
10. Finding statistics about the population in a book of facts

More Practice

Academic and Workplace Skills Activity Book
• p. 29

Using the SQ4R Method

You can also use the organization of a textbook to study individual assignments by mastering the following skills: Survey, Question, Read, Record, Recite, and Review. The SQ4R method will guide you as you read, and it will later help you recall information.

KEY CONCEPT Use the SQ4R method to gain a better understanding of textbook material. ■

The SQ4R method can help you to study textbook material more efficiently and increase your comprehension skills.

SQ4R: STEPS IN READING TEXTBOOKS	
Preparing for reading:	*Survey* for an overview of the material
Focusing your reading:	*Question* before you read each section *Read* to answer the questions *Record* by taking notes on the main ideas and major details
Remembering what you read:	*Recite* by reading your notes aloud *Review* on a regular basis

Surveying allows you to become acquainted with the material you will be reading. When you survey textbook material, look for these features: titles, headings, and subheadings; words in italics or bold print; introductions and summaries; pictures and captions; and questions at the end of a section or chapter. The survey should take no more than a few minutes.

Questioning is a good way to force yourself to think about the material before you read it. As you come to each heading and subheading, ask yourself what might be covered under each. Your ability to ask yourself questions can help you focus on the main ideas and major details as you read.

Reading is the time for comprehension and for finding the answers to the questions you posed in the previous step. In addition, you should determine the main ideas and major details of the material.

Recording involves taking notes on the main ideas and major details. Recording information is one of the best ways to remember what you have read. By organizing the ideas in your mind as you read and then writing them in outline form, you improve your chances of remembering the material.

Reciting reinforces what you have already learned, by requiring you to listen to the material from the textbook and from your notes. There are a number of ways to carry out this step:

- Recite aloud the information you want to master.
- Mentally recite the information you want to remember.
- Read the summaries, outlines, or other notes into a tape recorder. Then, play back the tape several times.
- Pair up with a classmate for a question-and-answer session.

Reviewing will help ensure that you have retained what you have been studying. When you review, you should repeat some of the previous steps. For example, you might want to reread your notes and look again at the headings and subheadings of your textbook. *When* you review is almost as important as *how* you review. You should never allow so much time to elapse that the material seems unfamiliar to you. In order to master material, you will need to review it a number of times before taking a test on it.

▲ Critical Viewing
Which step of the SQ4R method does this student appear to be using? **[Infer]**

Exercise 3 **Surveying and Questioning** Choose a chapter from one of your textbooks. Survey all the chapter headings and subheadings. Then, go back and turn each heading and subheading into a question.

More Practice
Academic and Workplace Skills Activity Book
- pp. 30–31

Exercise 4 **Reading and Recording** Using the same textbook chapter you used for Exercise 3, Surveying and Questioning, read and take notes on the chapter. Write the main ideas and major details in an outline form.

Exercise 5 **Reciting and Reviewing** Using the outline you made for the textbook chapter in Reading and Recording, work with another student to ask and answer questions about the outlined material. Then, review the material by asking yourself and answering questions about the chapter headings and subheadings.

Using Outlines

Making an outline for the material you read will help you to better understand the information. When you make an **outline**, you list the main ideas and supporting details of a topic.

KEY CONCEPT Use an outline to arrange important information and ideas. ■

The examples below illustrate the organization of a topic outline and a sentence outline on the same topic:

TOPIC OUTLINE:

I. Habitat of wild boar ← Main Idea
 A. North Africa
 B. Southwest Asia } Major details explaining I
 C. Central Asia
II. Physical appearance ← Main Idea
 A. Three feet high
 B. Four hundred pounds } Major details explaining II
 C. Grayish black hide
  1. Short hair } Minor details explaining C
  2. Bristly hide

SENTENCE OUTLINE:

I. The wild boar inhabits several continents.
 A. The wild boar lives in North Africa.
 B. It can also be found in Southwest Asia.
 C. It also lives in Central Asia.

Exercise 6 **Making Outlines** Using a section from your textbook, make a formal topic outline and a sentence outline of the material.

▼ **Critical Viewing** Think of a topic for this photograph of wild boars in India. Add some details that you observe in the photograph. **[Analyze]**

Using Graphic Organizers

A graphic organizer is a good tool to use to summarize and review information, as well as to show relationships among ideas. Because the information is organized visually, the graphic organizer provides you with a quick overview of the subject. Before you make a graphic organizer, consider how the various parts of the subject are related. The format you choose depends on those relationships.

KEY CONCEPT Use graphic organizers to help you understand relationships among ideas in the text. ■

Following is a summary of some of the graphic organizers you can use to increase your understanding of the text.

Venn Diagram Use this graphic organizer to compare and contrast two subjects. To make a Venn diagram, draw two overlapping circles. In the overlapping section of the circles, write the characteristics that the two subjects share. In the other sections of the circles, write their differences.

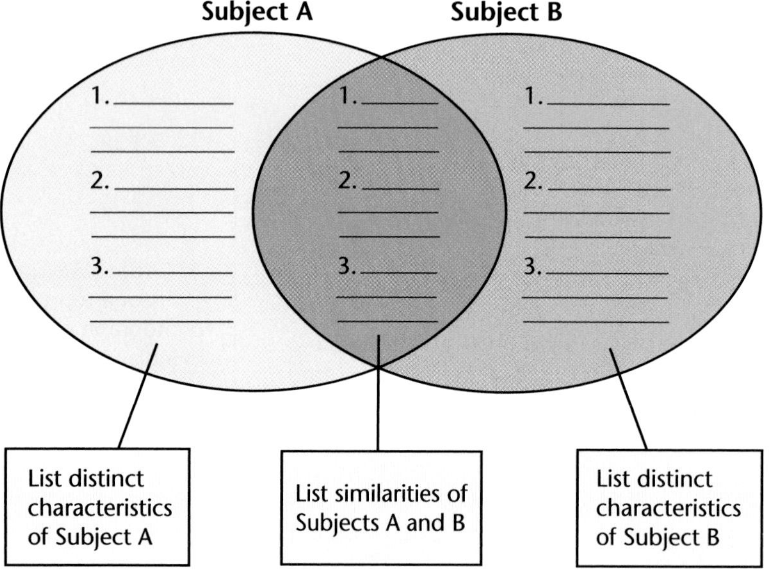

Web Diagram This graphic aid, sometimes called a cluster diagram in a slightly different format, is a useful tool for developing and organizing related ideas and supporting details. Begin your web diagram by writing your topic in the center of a sheet of paper. Circle that topic. Then, write any related ideas, and link them to the main topic with a line. Finally, write details that support each related idea.

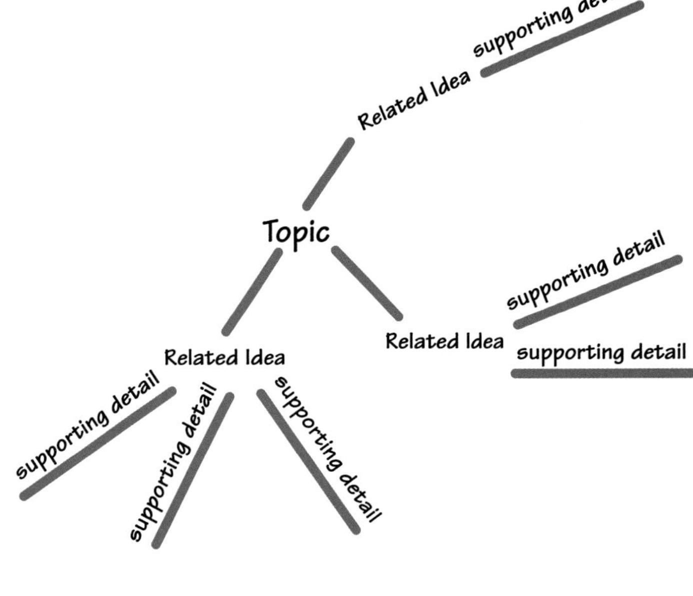

Sequence Chart This graphic organizer, often used to review nonfiction, clarifies the sequence of a series of events from beginning to end. To make a sequence chart, write the initial event in sequence on a sheet of paper. Put a circle or square around it. Then, write each additional event in a square or circle, and use arrows to indicate how one event leads to the next.

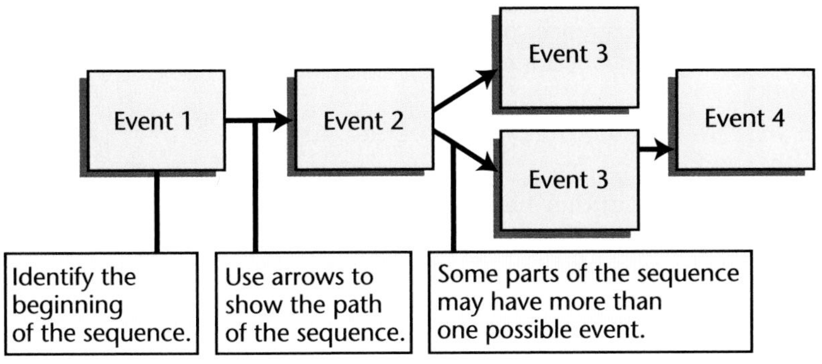

Exercise 7 **Using Graphic Organizers** Read a chapter from one of your textbooks or a work of fiction. Then, use a Venn diagram, a web diagram, or a sequence chart to present this information.

More Practice

Academic and Workplace Skills Activity Book
- pp. 32–33

Section 32.2

Reading Nonfiction Critically

When you read critically, you examine and question the writer's ideas, especially in light of his or her purpose. You also evaluate the information the writer includes as support, and you form a judgment about the content of the work.

Comprehending Nonfiction

When you read, your primary goal is to comprehend, or understand, the main ideas of the material.

KEY CONCEPT Use general reading strategies to learn more about the author's ideas in the text. ■

To help increase your ability to comprehend nonfiction, use these general strategies:

- **Establish a Purpose for Reading** Before you begin to read, decide why you are reading the material. Once you have established your purpose, look for information and other details in your reading that support this purpose.
- **Identify Main Points and Details** The main points are the most important ideas in the work. Details are the facts and examples used to support each main point.
- **Identify Relationships** As you read, determine the relationships between the ideas and events in the text. Some common relationships include sequence, part to whole, order of importance, cause and effect, comparison and contrast, and spatial order.
- **Interpret** State in your own words what you have read, to better understand the work.
- **Respond** Think about what the author has said and how you personally feel about the topic. Also, consider how you may apply this knowledge to your life.

Exercise 8 **Using General Strategies for Reading Nonfiction** Read a section from one of your textbooks, and use the strategies mentioned above to increase your understanding of the text. Then, answer the following questions:

1. What was your purpose for reading?
2. What main points and supporting details did you identify?
3. How was the material organized?
4. What is the importance of the information you read?
5. How might this information be applied to your own life?

More Practice

Academic and Workplace Skills Activity Book
• p. 34

Evaluating What You Read

Once you have a general understanding of the work, the next step is to evaluate the material, especially in light of the author's purpose and the reliability of the information given.

KEY CONCEPT Be an attentive reader so you can determine the purpose and reliability of the material you read. ■

Author's Purpose Part of being a critical reader is being able to determine why the author is writing. The chart below lists common purposes and clues to identifying them.

IDENTIFYING AUTHOR'S PURPOSE IN WRITING	
Purpose	**Informational Clues**
To inform	Series of factual statements that are verified by experimentation, records, or personal observation
To instruct	Sequential development of an idea or a process
To offer an opinion	Presentation of an issue with predominant point of view backed up by valid authority
To sell	Persuasive techniques, including facts and propaganda, designed to sell an idea or a product
To entertain	Narration of an event in a humorous manner; often used to lighten a serious topic

Inferences Sometimes, an author states his or her purpose in writing directly. More often, however, the purpose is implied. As you read, you must make inferences about the author's purpose from clues you find in the reading.

Exercise 9 Determining the Author's Purpose by Making Inferences Read the following sentences. Then, make an inference about the author's purpose. Explain your answer.

1. Today's session will guide you through the steps of how to build an oak cabinet with brass handles.
2. The temperature is 60 degrees Fahrenheit, and there is a light rain falling over the city.
3. Have you ever wondered why computers are so slow? Well, I have. Here are my solutions to solve this problem.
4. The political turmoil in the world reminds me of a funny joke my friend used to tell.
5. The X1-Viper snowboard has a rugged look and is designed from the latest technology that snowboarding has to offer.

Fact and Opinion In order to decide whether the material you read is reliable, you have to be able to distinguish between fact and opinion statements. A *statement of fact* is one that can be verified, or proved true by written authority, personal observation, or experimentation. A *statement of opinion* cannot be proved true, but the opinion can be considered valid if it is supported by related facts.

FACT STATEMENT: The United States government has three branches. (True)

FACT STATEMENT: "The Raven" was written by the author Shirley Jackson. (False)

The first fact statement is *true* because it can be verified by written authority, an encyclopedia, almanac, or social studies textbook. On the other hand, the second statement is *false* because a literary or biographical dictionary tells us that Edgar Allan Poe—not Shirley Jackson—is the author of "The Raven."

OPINION STATEMENT: Scientists at the university feel that life was less stressful in past centuries since fewer people died of heart attacks, which are stress related. (Valid)

OPINION STATEMENT: Life was easier a century ago because people did not have cars. (Invalid)

The first opinion statement is valid because it gives supporting facts by an authority. The second opinion statement, however, is invalid because its reasoning is explained using a relationship that cannot be verified.

More Practice

Academic and Workplace Skills Activity Book
• pp. 36–37

▼ **Critical Viewing** Identify a fact about William Shakespeare that can be validated. Then, give an opinion based on the picture. **[Connect]**

Exercise 10 **Analyzing Fact and Opinion Statements** Identify each statement as a *fact* or an *opinion*. Then, analyze whether each fact statement is *true* or *false* and whether each opinion statement is *valid* or *invalid*.

1. *The Wizard of Oz* is the best movie ever made.
2. Jan is a great swimmer; she has won six swim meets.
3. William Shakespeare wrote *A Midsummer Night's Dream*.
4. The World Trade Center is the tallest building in the world.
5. Hank Aaron broke Babe Ruth's record for total career home runs.

Evaluating Forms of Reasoning

One way to improve your critical reading skills is by evaluating ideas to see if they are reasonable. Following is a list of three common forms of reasoning:

KEY CONCEPT *Generalization, analogy,* and *cause and effect* are common forms of reasoning that can be used by an author to convey valid or invalid information. ■

A **generalization** is a statement made on the basis of a number of particular facts or cases.

VALID: There are seventy-four girls and sixty-six boys in Sue's ninth-grade class. Therefore, the majority of the students in Sue's ninth-grade class are girls.

HASTY: Sue's ninth-grade class has more girls than boys. Therefore, all ninth grades have more girls than boys.

The first example is a valid generalization because it is clearly supported by evidence. The second example, however, is a hasty generalization, because the author's statement is made about a whole group based on only one example.

RECOGNIZING VALID/HASTY GENERALIZATIONS

1. What facts or cases are being presented as evidence to support the general statement?
2. Are there any exceptions to the statement?
3. Are enough cases or examples being presented?

An **analogy** is a comparison between two things that are similar in some ways but are essentially unlike. An author will often use an analogy to convey an idea about one thing by showing its similarity to something more familiar.

COMPLETE: Like the human brain, a computer stores and processes information.

INCOMPLETE: A computer is like the human brain.

The first analogy is complete because it explains the functions of a computer by comparing them to the more familiar functions of the human brain. The second analogy is incomplete because a computer and the human brain are essentially dissimilar in structure and origin.

IDENTIFYING COMPLETE/INCOMPLETE ANALOGIES

1. How are the two things being compared essentially different?
2. How are the two things alike? Is the comparison logical?
3. What is the truth that the comparison tries to show?

A **cause-and-effect** sequence may be used by an author to conclude that one event has caused a second event because the first event happened immediately before the second. An author uses a *valid* cause-and-effect sequence when something is caused by one or more events that occurred before it. An author uses an *invalid* cause-and-effect sequence when the first event did not cause the second event.

VALID: Thunder occurs after each lightning flash because the lightning causes the air to heat and expand, forming a compression wave heard as thunder.

INVALID: The lights went out because the lightning flashed.

DETERMINING CAUSE/EFFECT SEQUENCES

1. What evidence is there that the first event or situation could have caused the second?
2. What other events may have caused the second event?
3. Could the second event have occurred without the first?

Exercise 11 **Analyzing Forms of Reasoning** Identify the form of reasoning *(generalization, analogy, cause and effect)* found in each statement below. Then, identify whether each conclusion is *valid* or *invalid,* and explain your answer.

1. The cost of raising cattle has risen sharply; therefore, meat prices will go up this year.
2. The new highway that is being built will solve all of the city's traffic problems.
3. Sarah placed second in the tennis tournament, so she will place second in all tennis tournaments.
4. Wearing this shirt to the exam will help me get an *A.*
5. Students who spend all of their free time watching television instead of studying usually receive poor grades.

▶ Critical Viewing Make a valid generalization about this picture. **[Analyze]**

Examining the Author's Language

Authors can use different kinds of language to make you think or feel a certain way about the ideas presented.

KEY CONCEPT *Denotative* and *connotative* words and *jargon* are some of the ways authors use language to change the meaning of a fact or an event. ■

A **denotative word** refers to a word's literal or exact meaning and has a neutral tone. A **connotative word** suggests or implies meaning in a positive or negative tone. In the following example, words with strong connotations are italicized. Words that are not italicized do not carry strong connotations.

CONNOTATIVE: The *ill-planned* highway project has *dragged on* for six years at an *ever-escalating* annual expense of more than one million dollars.

DENOTATIVE: The *extensive* highway project has *continued* for six years at an annually *increasing* expense of more than one million dollars.

Jargon is the specialized words and phrases unique to a specific field. While it is frequently useful, jargon can sometimes appear to be scientific or technical but instead be vague and meaningless. An author might use jargon to confuse or deceive the reader about the real meaning behind the words.

JARGON: Due to *business reversals*, the company is forced to *eliminate your position*.

DIRECT LANGUAGE: Because the company has *lost money*, you will *lose your job*.

Exercise 12 **Analyzing the Author's Language** Read the following passage, and identify the following uses of language: *denotative words*, *negative* and *positive connotative words*, and *jargon*.

1. The decline in students' educational performance is the result of disturbing inadequacies in the way the educational process itself is constructed.
2. It is not our new school buildings or fancy enrichment programs that will restore the good old values of hard work and the three "R's" to our halls of learning.
3. "Back to Basics" must be the watchword of every school's educational policy.
4. If we pursue our goal with single-minded purpose, we can dispel the mists that cloud our vision like a wet blanket and concentrate on graduating students with a sound knowledge of basic educational skills.

More Practice

Academic and Workplace Skills Activity Book
- p. 38

Section 32.3

Reading Literary Writings

Literature is an imaginative form of writing that encompasses works by fiction writers, playwrights, and poets.

Reading Actively

Reading literary works involves using your judgment and imagination and responding to the work on a personal level.

KEY CONCEPT Use a variety of reading strategies to increase your understanding of literary works. ■

To increase your comprehension and add to your appreciation of prose, plays, and poetry, use these general strategies:

Establish a Purpose for Reading Before you begin to read, decide why you're reading the piece. Establishing a purpose for reading focuses your thoughts.

Ask Questions As you read, question what is happening in the text. Then, search the text for answers as you read further.

Reread or Read Ahead Reread a sentence, paragraph, or stanza to find the connections among the words or to connect the ideas in several sentences. Read ahead to find more information about difficult words or ideas.

Make Personal Connections Use your own experiences to help you get a better understanding of what you are reading. As you read, look for connections between people and events in your own life and those in the text.

Be Aware of the Historical Context When does the action occur? What are the manners, customs, and morals of the times? What mood does the historical context suggest?

Respond As you read, determine how you feel about the characters or speakers and the situations in which they are described. When you have finished reading, think about what the work means to you.

Exercise 13 Using Strategies to Comprehend Literature Read a short story, an act or scene from a play, a chapter of a novel, or a poem, and use the strategies mentioned above to increase your comprehension of the material. Then, write a summary describing what you learned.

More Practice

Academic and Workplace Skills Activity Book
• pp. 39–40

Reading Fiction

Short stories and novels are literature of the imagination in which the characters and events are made up by the author.

KEY CONCEPT Short stories and novels usually focus on a central conflict that a character must face. ■

Determine the Point of View The **point of view** is the perspective from which the narrator tells a story. In *omniscient third-person point of view*, the narrator has complete knowledge of all the characters and tells what they feel and think. In *limited third-person point of view*, the narrator has knowledge of the thoughts and feelings of only one character, and the world that the author creates is viewed from this character's perspective. In the *first-person point of view*, the narrator assumes the role of one character in the story and refers to himself or herself with the first-person pronoun *I*.

Identify the Stages of Plot The **plot** is the sequence of events that make up the story. The *exposition* provides background information and sets the scene for the conflict. The *conflict* is a struggle between opposing people or forces that drives the action of the story. The introduction of the conflict marks the beginning of the *rising action*, in which the conflict intensifies until it reaches the high point, or *climax*, of the story. After the climax, the action falls to a *resolution*, which shows how the story turns out.

Describe the Characters A **character** is someone or something that takes part in the story. There are *major characters*, who play a significant role in the action, and *minor characters*, who play a less important role. In addition, a character can be *dynamic*, or experience change as the work progresses. If a character does not change, the character is said to be *static*.

Identify the Conflict **Conflict** is the struggle between opposing forces. There are two kinds of conflict: external and internal. An external conflict is a physical struggle between the character and an outside force. An internal conflict is a mental or emotional struggle that takes place within the character.

Exercise 14 **Reading Short Stories and Novels** Read a short story from your textbook, or choose one from your own collection. As you read, answer the following questions: What is the point of view in the story? What kind of characters are in the story? Do they experience an internal or external conflict? The next time you read a novel, ask these same questions.

32.3

Reading Drama

The story in a play is told mostly through dialogue and action. The stage directions indicate when and how the actors move and sometimes suggest sound and lighting effects.

KEY CONCEPT When you read a drama, it is important to remember that it was written to be performed. ■

Read the Cast of Characters Before the first act or first scene of a play, you will see a list—often with descriptions of the characters that take part in the play. Reading this list can tell you the various relationships among the characters, as well as offer you some insight into their personalities.

Use Stage Directions to Envision the Play As you read the drama, use your imagination to mentally re-create the play. Use characters' descriptions of places and other characters, as well as the playwright's stage directions.

Summarize the Events After Acts or Scenes Dramas are often broken into acts or scenes. These natural breaks give you an opportunity to review the action that has taken place.

Exercise 15 **Reading Drama** Read the first act or first few scenes of a play. As you read, do the following: List three details describing the play's historical context. Name five stage directions that you feel contribute most to the play's action. Describe the main characters and the conflicts they face.

More Practice

Academic and Workplace Skills Activity Book
- pp. 41–43

Reading Poetry

Poetry is a unique form that expresses meaning in few words. Poets achieve this concentration by selecting details and by using imaginative and sensory language.

KEY CONCEPT A poem is a combination of images and details that work to create a total impression. ■

Identify and Understand the Speaker To identify and understand the speaker of the poem, ask yourself these questions: Who is the speaker? What does the speaker look like? In what situation or setting is the speaker placed? To whom is he or she speaking? What is the speaker's outlook on life?

Follow Punctuation The words of a poem are often put together and punctuated as sentences. As you read through a poem, be sure to follow the punctuation.

Speaking and Listening Tip

One of the best ways to truly understand and appreciate a poem is to read it aloud. Listen to the sounds of the words and the rhythms of the lines. How does the poet use sound to enhance the poem's meaning?

Examine the Imagery Imagery is the descriptive language that writers use to create word pictures. These pictures, or images, are created through the details that appeal to the senses: sight, sound, smell, taste, and touch.

Paraphrase the Poem Paraphrasing, restating the speaker's experiences and feelings in your own words, is a helpful way to check your understanding of what you read. Before you paraphrase a poem, make sure you understand what is happening, who is speaking, and what ideas and images are being expressed.

Exercise 16 **Reading Poetry** Choose a poem from your textbook or from your personal reading. Read the poem accurately by paying close attention to the punctuation. As you read, identify the speaker, list three specific images, and paraphrase each stanza or every few lines in the poem.

Reading Myths and Folk Tales

Many folk songs, ballads, folk tales, legends, and myths originated in the oral tradition. A *myth* is a fictional tale that explains the actions of gods or the causes of natural phenomena. Myths have little historical truth and involve supernatural elements. Every culture has its collection of myths. *Folk tales* are entertaining stories about heroes or adventures.

Identify the Cultural Context Understanding the culture from which a myth or folk tale comes will help you to understand the ideas presented in it. Read any notes that accompany a story to find out more about the culture. While you read the story, look for details that tell you about the culture.

Predict Look for clues to help you make guesses about what will happen next. Revise your predictions as new details unfold, and check to see whether your predictions come true.

Recognize the Storyteller's Purpose Knowing why a myth or folk tale was told will help you understand why the characters in it behave in certain ways. It will also help you learn more about the culture that created the story.

▲ Critical Viewing Does this look like a good setting for reading a piece of literary writing? Why or why not? **[Evaluate]**

Exercise 17 **Reading Myths and Folk Tales** Read a myth or folk tale from your literature textbook, and answer the following questions.

1. List details of the story, and explain what they suggest about the culture presented in the piece.
2. What predictions did you make about events in the piece? Were you correct? Why or why not?
3. What is the purpose of this piece? What does the purpose suggest about the culture's values or beliefs?

Section 32.4

Reading From Varied Sources

Information is made available to you in a wide variety of formats, including books, magazines, Web pages, advertisements, newspapers, letters, and speeches. By familiarizing yourself with different types of sources, you will widen the range and type of information you can learn and use.

Read Diaries, Letters, and Journals

Diaries, letters, and journals are firsthand accounts of events or circumstances. They are often published after the writer's death with the permission of his or her family. Some may be written by people whose achievements make them interesting subjects. Others are written by people who lived in interesting times. Keep in mind when you read these primary sources that not all the information in them will be strictly factual. Much of it will reflect the writer's personal opinions.

Read Newspapers

Newspapers are a good source of information on current events and issues in your community, in the United States, and around the world. When you read a newspaper, notice whether the coverage is local, national, or global. Different sections of newspapers have different purposes. Editorial pages offer opinions of the topics they cover. Other sections give an unbiased account of the topics they cover. Read newspapers critically. Keep an eye out for bias or faulty logic.

Read Transcripts of Speeches and Interviews

A transcript is a written record of what was spoken. You can obtain transcripts of most famous speeches in library resources. Books and other references contain the printed record of what a speaker said. Interview transcripts are usually available through the media that produced the interview. Speeches and interviews offer one person's perspective on an issue, a situation, or a condition. These thoughts, unlike those set down in diaries or letters, are usually intended for publication. Like diaries and letters, speeches and interviews reflect the person's opinions.

Read Forms and Applications

One of the most practical purposes for reading is to fill out forms and applications. Read these documents carefully. Understanding what information is being requested will help you fill out forms accurately. Filling out forms accurately leads to quicker results than if the form must be resubmitted again with new information.

Read Electronic Texts

Web pages, electronic advertising, and e-mail present text through an electronic medium. Whether you read text on screen or on a page, read critically. When you read a Web page, consider the source when you evaluate the reliability of the information. Look for evidence that the writer of the page has background in the subject area. Determine whether the page is sponsored by a company that wants to promote a particular point of view. The Internet can be a fine resource, but you must use it with a critical awareness.

Exercise 18 **Reading Varied Sources** Choose an event or a time period from American history, such as the Civil War or the Depression. Find an account of the event or the period in at least three different sources discussed in this chapter. Write a summary of the information you find in each. Then, in a brief evaluation, compare and contrast the information you found in each and explain the unique perspective you gained from reading each source.

Reflecting on Your Reading

After a week of practicing your reading skills, write a paragraph about the areas in which you found success and those in which you need to improve. Use the following questions as a starting point:

- Which sections of my textbooks did I find most useful?
- Which steps of the SQ4R method did I find most useful?
- Which graphic organizers have I recently used to organize ideas or explain a story's development?
- How have critical reading skills helped me to analyze and evaluate nonfiction material?
- Which strategies for reading fiction did I find the most useful? Which strategies did I find the most difficult to use?

Chapter 33

Study, Reference, and Test-Taking Skills

▲ **Critical Viewing** What subject do you think this student is studying? Why do you think so? **[Deduce]**

Studying, researching, taking tests—all are vital skills to develop as you progress through school. Most of these skills will also come in handy later in life as you train on the job or pursue your personal interests. In this chapter, you will learn how to make the most of your study time. You will also learn more about researching information in printed and electronic sources. Finally, you will receive valuable tips that can help improve your test scores.

Section 33.1 Basic Study Skills

Good study habits require time, organization, and practice. You need to schedule your study time in a suitable study area, keep track of assignments, and keep an organized notebook in which you take useful notes.

Developing a Study Plan

To study effectively, you need a space where there are no distractions, a space that you associate only with studying. It is also important to schedule set times in which to study. Plan your days so that you have enough time for studying, extra-curricular activities, chores, and relaxation.

KEY CONCEPT Establish a workable study area and regular periods for studying. ■

Plan a schedule that fits your personal needs. Vary the amount of time spent on each subject, depending on upcoming tests and long-term projects. Allow extra review time for those subjects that are challenging for you.

Study Schedule

	7–8:00	8:00–9:00
Mon	Daily assignments	Study for math test tomorrow
Tues	Daily assignments	Work on research project / Review for Friday's science test
Wed	Review for Friday's science test / Daily assignments	More review for Friday's science test

Exercise 1 **Planning Your Study Schedule** Develop your own study schedule, using the sample as a model. Follow your schedule for a week. Then, evaluate it and make any needed changes. Keep a copy in your notebook.

More Practice

Academic and Workplace Skills Activity Book
• p. 44

Keeping an Assignment Book Instead of trusting your memory to recall homework and long-term projects, write them down in an assignment book that shows the due dates clearly.

▲ **Critical Viewing** What subject do you think this student is working on? Give reasons for your answer. **[Speculate]**

KEY CONCEPT Use an assignment book to record homework, long-range projects, and their due dates. ■

One simple way to set up your assignment book is to make four columns on each page. Use one column for subjects, one for detailed descriptions of assignments, one for dates the assignments are due, and one for checks when the assignments are completed. The sample below from an assignment book lists two short-term homework assignments and a long-term science project. Notice how the long-term project is divided into a series of steps.

Assignments - October 13

Subject	Description	Date Due	Completed
Math	Exercise 4, p. 32	10/14	✓
English	Read Act 1, Romeo & Juliet	10/15	✓
Science	Science Fair Satellite Model	1/20	
	1. Do library research	11/2	✓
	2. Draw up plan with Jo	11/9	✓
	3. Submit plan to Mrs. S	11/9	✓
	4. Meet with Mrs. S	11/16	

Exercise 2 **Setting Up an Assignment Book** In a special section of your notebook or a separate notebook, set up an assignment book. Date each page and record assignments, using the sample above as a model.

Taking Notes

To understand and remember what you learn, it is important to take notes. Organize your notebook by school subject. Then, in the appropriate sections, take notes on what you learn in class as well as what you read in textbooks.

KEY CONCEPT Use a modified outline to take notes while listening or reading. ■

One of the best ways to take notes quickly is to use a *modified outline form,* in which you list main ideas along the margin, indent to show major details, and indent further to show more supporting details.

MODIFIED OUTLINE

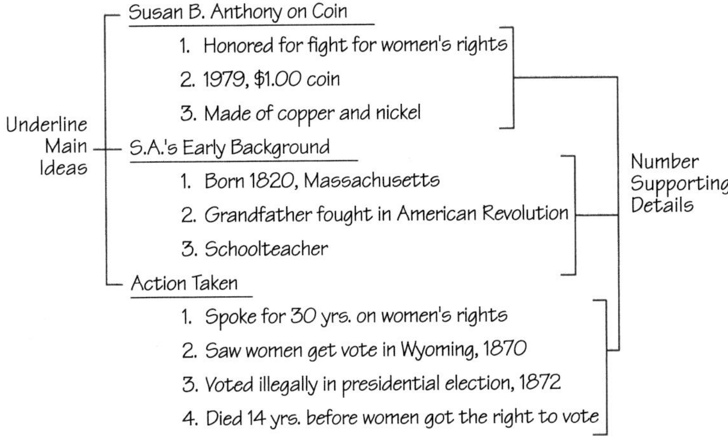

KEY CONCEPT Write summaries of chapters or lectures to review what you have learned. ■

After reading a chapter or attending a class, summarize by identifying the main points and explaining how they are connected. Write your summary in your notebook, and use it to review at a later time.

Exercise 3 **Taking Notes in Outline Form** Choose a section in your mathematics textbook, and take notes on the important information. Use a modified outline form.

Exercise 4 **Making a Summary** Write a summary of a chapter or section of your social studies book.

More Practice

Academic and Workplace Skills Activity Book
- p. 45

Section 33.2

Reference Skills

You are living in what has been called the Information Age. To access the wealth of information available, you need to develop your reference skills. Just about every major form of printed reference now has its electronic equivalent on either CD-ROM, the Internet, or both. Many of the works, in both printed and electronic form, are available at school or public libraries.

Technology Tip

Many libraries have Web sites and offer services on-line. You may be able to access the library card catalog. There may be links to county or state resources. Check with your librarian.

Using the Library: An Overview

Most school and public libraries contain at least some of these resources: fiction and nonfiction books, audiocassettes and videocassettes, periodicals (newspapers, magazines, and scholarly journals), microfilm, vertical files of pamphlets and other small printed material, reference works in printed and electronic form, and computer access to the Internet.

KEY CONCEPT Use the library catalog to find valuable information about the resources that a library contains. ■

The library catalog will be in one of these three forms:

Card Catalog This system lists books on index cards, with a separate *author card* and *title card* for each book. If the book is nonfiction, it also has at least one *subject card*. Cards are filed alphabetically in small drawers, with author cards alphabetized by last names and title cards alphabetized by the first words of the titles, excluding *A*, *An*, and *The*.

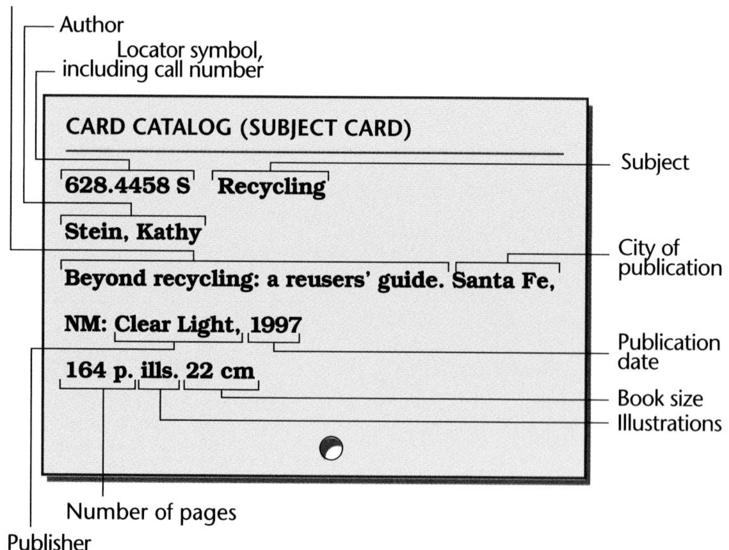

Printed Catalog This catalog lists books in printed booklets, with each book listed alphabetically by author, by title, and—if nonfiction—by subject. Often, there are separate booklets for author, title, and subject listings.

▼ **Critical Viewing** What key words could this student type in to access the book listed in the printed catalog art at left? **[Apply]**

Electronic Catalog An electronic catalog lists books in a CD-ROM or on-line database that you access from special computer terminals in the library. Usually, you can access an entry by typing in a title, key words in the title, an author's name, or, for nonfiction, an appropriate subject.

Exercise 5 **Using the Library Catalog** Visit your school or local library and answer these questions.

1. What kind of catalog does the library use: card, printed, or electronic? Where is it located?
2. Who wrote *Little Women*? Is it fiction or nonfiction?
3. What are the titles, subjects, and call numbers of two books that your library carries by author Bill Bryson?
4. What are the titles, authors, and call numbers of three books about Mexico published since 1985?
5. What are the titles, authors, and call numbers of two nonfiction books about birds that are more than 100 pages long?

More Practice

Academic and Workplace Skills Activity Book
• p. 46

Finding Books on Library Shelves The library distinguishes between two kinds of books: *fiction* (made-up stories) and *nonfiction* (factual material). Nonfiction also includes two smaller groups that are often shelved separately: *biographies* and *reference books.*

KEY CONCEPT Fiction and nonfiction books are shelved separately in the library, and each follows a special method of organization. ■

Most school and public libraries use the **Dewey Decimal System** to classify books. The Dewey Decimal System divides all knowledge into ten main classes, numbered from 000 to 999. The first digit on the left tells you the general subject.

This chart shows the number spans for the content areas.

MAIN CLASSES OF THE DEWEY DECIMAL SYSTEM

Number	Subject
000–099	General Works (encyclopedias, periodicals, etc.)
100–199	Philosophy
200–299	Religion
300–399	Social Sciences
400–499	Language
500–599	Science
600–699	Technology (applied science)
700–799	Arts and Leisure
800–899	Literature
900–999	History and Geography

Fiction Books In most libraries, fiction books (literature) are shelved in a special section and are alphabetized by authors' last names. In the library catalog and on the book's spine, a work of fiction may be labeled *F* or *FIC*, followed by one or more letters of the author's last name.

Nonfiction Books Nonfiction books are assigned different numbers and letters. These number-letter codes, called *call numbers*, are placed on the spine of each book, and the books are arranged in number-letter order on the shelves; for example, 619.1, 619.2, 619.31A, 619.31D, 619.32A. To find a nonfiction book, you look it up in the library catalog, find its call number, and then follow number-letter order to locate the book on the shelves.

Biographies Life stories of real people are technically 921 in the Dewey Decimal System. Sometimes, however, biographies are not assigned call numbers but instead are shelved in a special section alphabetized by the last names of their subjects (the people they are about). In the library catalog and on

Technology Tip

In electronic database searches, be sure to type carefully and spell everything correctly. One wrong letter often means inaccurate results.

the book's spine, a biography may be labeled *B* or *BIO*, followed by one or more letters of the subject's last name; for example, *BIO Lin* may appear on a biography of Abraham Lincoln.

Reference Books These types of books may also be shelved in their own special section of a library. Frequently, the sources in the library's reference section are labeled *R* or *REF.* Because the book is nonfiction, a call number follows the abbreviation. Thus, if a book you look up in the card catalog has *REF* before its call number, go first to the library's reference section and then use the call number to locate the book on the shelves in that section.

Many college and research libraries use the **Library of Congress System.**

LIBRARY OF CONGRESS SYSTEM			
A	General Works	L	Education
B	Philosophy, Psychology, Religion	M	Music
		N	Fine Arts
C	History	P	Language and Literature
D	General History	Q	Science
E–F	American History	R	Medicine
G	Geography, Anthropology, Recreation	S	Agriculture
		T	Technology
H	Social Sciences	U	Military Science
J	Political Science	V	Naval Science
K	Law	Z	Bibliography and Library Science

Exercise 6 Finding Books on Library Shelves

1. To find fiction by Louise Erdrich, would you look before or after fiction by Elizabeth Enright?
2. To find a nonfiction book with the call number 910.72M, would you look before or after a book with the call number 911.30B?
3. For a book with the call number R523.4R, would you look in the reference, biography, or children's section?
4. Arrange these works of fiction in the order in which you would find them on the library shelves: *Child of the Owl* by Laurence Yep, *White Fang* by Jack London, *The Left Hand of Darkness* by Ursula K. Le Guin, *Pedro Paramo* by Juan Rulfo, *Zeely* by Virginia Hamilton.
5. Arrange these call numbers in the order in which you would find them on the library shelves: 598.2P, 598.3A, 598.1L, 597.6Z, 599.1S. What would be the general subject matter of these books?

More Practice

Academic and Workplace Skills Activity Book
• p. 47

33.2

Using Periodicals, Periodical Indexes, and the Vertical File

Periodicals are printed materials, such as newspapers and magazines, that are published on a regular basis. To find all the articles on a particular subject in periodicals, you need to consult a *periodical index*. You can find the information contained in booklets or pamphlets in the *vertical file*.

KEY CONCEPT Use periodicals to find current information, use periodical indexes to find articles in periodicals, and use the vertical file to find small printed materials. ■

Periodical Indexes When you want to find articles on a particular subject, you need to consult a periodical index. Periodical indexes, issued in printed or electronic form, are published or updated regularly. They cite articles that appeared during a specified period of time. Some periodical indexes cover articles from many periodicals; others cover articles from only one newspaper or magazine.

Citations in periodical indexes provide the information you need to find an article; namely, the title and date of the publication in which the article appears.

In *printed indexes*, citations are listed alphabetically by subject or author. The citations in printed indexes also may contain *abstracts*, or brief summaries, of the articles. In *electronic indexes*, citations appear in a database that you can search by subject, the author's name, or a key word or phrase. Some electronic indexes also provide the *full text*, or complete article, for some or all of the articles cited.

Below is a sample citation from a recent print edition of the *Readers' Guide to Periodical Literature:*

SAMPLE *READERS' GUIDE* ENTRY

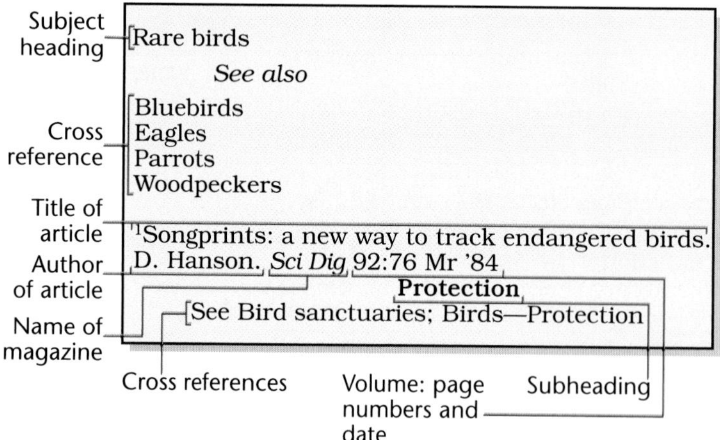
Rare birds

See also

Bluebirds
Eagles
Parrots
Woodpeckers

Songprints: a new way to track endangered birds. D. Hanson. *Sci Dig* 92:76 Mr '84

Protection

See Bird sanctuaries; Birds—Protection

Technology Tip

Many leading newspapers and magazines have free Internet sites where you can read current editions of the material.

The Vertical File The vertical file is a special filing cabinet used to house small printed materials of various kinds, such as pamphlets, booklets, folded maps, newspaper and magazine clippings, and photographs. The materials are placed in files that are labeled and arranged alphabetically by subject.

Exercise 7 **Using Periodicals and Periodical Indexes** Visit your school or local library to answer these questions on periodicals and periodical indexes.

1. What newspapers does the library carry?
2. Give the titles of three newsmagazines the library carries. Find out how far back each goes and in what format(s) they are archived.
3. Use a periodical index to find citations for articles on a subject you are studying in science or social studies. Then, find at least one of the articles in your library.

More Practice

Academic and Workplace Skills Activity Book

- p. 48

Exercise 8 **Exploring the Vertical File** Find out whether your school or library has a vertical file. If it does, survey and summarize the main kinds of materials that it contains.

Using Dictionaries

A dictionary tells you how words are pronounced, how they are used in context, and, often, their history.

KEY CONCEPT Dictionaries contain a wealth of information about words. ■

Distinguishing Types of Dictionaries All dictionaries are not the same. Some dictionaries are for scholars; others are for general readers; still others are intended for people studying a special field.

THREE TYPES OF DICTIONARIES	
Unabridged	Exhaustive study of the English language containing more than 250,000 words
Abridged	Compact edition containing listings of 55,000 to 160,000 words
Specialized	Edition limited to words of a particular field, such as foreign languages or mathematics

Finding Words in Dictionaries A word listed in a dictionary, along with all the information about it, is called an *entry*.

In *printed dictionaries*, all the items are listed in strict *alphabetical order*. To speed your search for a word, use these features:

- **Thumb Index** This series of right-hand notches makes it easier to thumb alphabetically through the dictionary. Each notch, labeled *A*, *B*, and so on, shows the section of entries for words that start with that particular letter.
- **Guide Words** At the top of a dictionary page appear the first and last words covered on the page. All other entries on the page are for words that fall alphabetically between the two guide words. For instance, if the guide words are *need* and *neglect*, *needle* and *negative* will also be on the page; *necessary* will not be on that page.

In *electronic dictionaries*, you usually find a word's entry simply by typing the word and having the computer search the dictionary database.

Understanding Dictionary Entries In a dictionary, a word and all the information about it are called a *main entry*. The word itself is called an *entry word*.

1. Entry Word This may may be a single word, a compound word (two or more words acting as a single word), an abbreviation, a prefix or suffix, or the name of a person or place. Dots, spaces, or slashes in an entry word indicate the syllables. When you break a word at the end of a line, remember that you cannot leave a syllable of just one letter on a line by itself. Words with one syllable are never divided.

SAMPLE DICTIONARY ENTRY

① **liv·ery** ② (liv´ər ē) ③ *n.*, ④ pl. **-er·ies** ⑤ [ME, allowance of food, gift of clothes to a servant, thing delivered <OFr *livree*, pp. of *livrer*, to deliver < L *liberare*, to LIBERATE] ⑥ **1** an identifying uniform such as was formerly worn by feudal retainers or is now worn by servants or those in some particular group, trade, etc. **2** the people wearing such uniforms **3** characteristic dress or appearance **4** a) the keeping and feeding of horses for a fixed charge b) the keeping of horses, vehicles, or both, for hire ☆c) LIVERY STABLE ☆**5** a place where boats can be rented ⑦ **6** [Historical] *Eng. Law* the legal delivery of property, esp. landed property, into the hands of the new owner

Learn More

For information on how dictionaries can help improve your vocabulary, see Chapter 32.

2. Pronunciation Appearing right after the entry word, the pronunciation uses symbols to show how to say the word. The syllable that gets the most emphasis has a *primary stress,* usually shown by a heavy mark after the syllable (´). Words of more than one syllable may also have a *secondary stress,* usually shown by a shorter, lighter mark (´).

3. Part-of-Speech Label A dictionary also tells you how a word can be used in a sentence—whether it functions as a noun, verb, or some other part of speech. This information is given in abbreviated form, usually after the pronunciation.

4. Plurals and Inflected Forms After the part-of-speech label, a dictionary may also show the plural forms of nouns and inflected forms of verbs—past tense and participle forms—if there is anything irregular about their spelling.

5. Etymology The origin and history of a word is called its *etymology.* The etymology usually appears in brackets, parentheses, or slashes near the start or end of the entry. Abbreviations (explained in the dictionary's key to abbreviations) are often used for languages.

6. Definition A definition is the meaning of a word. Definitions are numbered if there are more than one. Often, they include an example illustrating the use of the particular meaning in a phrase or sentence.

7. Usage Labels Such labels note how the word is generally used. Words labeled *Archaic (Arch.), Obsolete (Obs.), Poetic,* or *Rare* are not widely used today. Those labeled *Informal (Inf.), Colloquial (Colloq.),* or *Slang* are not considered part of formal English. Those labeled *Brit.* are used mainly in Britain, not in the United States.

8. Field Labels These labels indicate whether a word is used in a special way by people in a certain occupation or activity, such as *History (Hist.), Mathematics (Math.),* or *Chemistry (Chem.)*

9. Idioms and Derived Words The end of an entry may list and define idioms or expressions that contain the entry word. It may also list derived words, words formed from the entry word, and their parts of speech.

Exercise 9 **Working With a Dictionary** Use a dictionary to answer the following questions.

1. In what order would these entry words appear?
   dolphin—knife—hand—length—mushroom
2. Which of these entry words would appear on a page with the guide words *contempt* and *continuation*?
   contact—contemptuous—contest—continue—continuity
3. What two guide words appear on the page with *neutron*?
4. Which word is not spelled correctly?
   lollipop—gasoline—kindergarden—judgment—license
5. Which word is spelled correctly?
   inflamable—psychology—truely—nesessary—tomorow

Technology Tip

Abridged electronic dictionaries are now available in a format similar to pocket calculators. Foreign-language dictionaries in this format may be especially useful to travelers.

More Practice

Academic and Workplace Skills Activity Book
• p. 48

33.2

Using Other Reference Works

Periodical indexes and dictionaries are two examples of *reference works*, resources to which you refer for information instead of reading in their entirety. Most reference works—available in both printed and electronic form—are usually found in the reference section of the library.

KEY CONCEPT Use articles in encyclopedias to get an overview of a variety of subjects. ■

Encyclopedias When you are investigating an unfamiliar subject, one of the best places to start is a general encyclopedia. A *general encyclopedia* is a collection of articles that provide basic information on a great many subjects. If you want to find more comprehensive and detailed articles in a particular subject area, use a *specialized encyclopedia.*

Printed encyclopedias list articles alphabetically by subject or, when the subject is a person, by last name. Encyclopedias usually span several volumes, with letters or words on each spine to show you which subjects that volume contains. In *electronic encyclopedias*, you can usually find articles by typing the subject or a key term and then having the computer search the encyclopedia database. You may also be able to browse an alphabetical list of subjects.

Biographical References These books provide brief histories of all kinds of famous people. Biographical references may offer short entries similar to those in dictionaries or longer articles more like those in encyclopedias.

Almanacs Annually issued handbooks, almanacs provide various lists and statistics on a host of subjects, including government, history, geography, weather, science, technology, industry, sports, and entertainment. To find a subject in a *printed almanac*, refer to the index, which may be at the front or back of the book. In an *electronic almanac*, you can usually find information by typing a subject or key word.

Atlases, Gazetteers, and Electronic Map Collections *Atlases* and *electronic map collections* contain maps and geographical information based on them, such as cities, bodies of water, mountains, and landmarks. Some also supply statistics about population, climate, agricultural and industrial production, natural resources, and so on.

In *printed atlases*, use the index to learn on which map to look for a particular place. A *gazetteer* is a dictionary or index of place names. Often, it gives populations and sizes. You may find a gazetteer at the back of an atlas or a textbook. In *electronic atlases*, or map collections, you usually type the place name and have the computer search the database for the appropriate map.

Technology Tip

Electronic maps often have zoom and other features in which you simply click the mouse to enlarge or change the area shown.

◀ **Critical Viewing** How do you think these students found the books they are reading? What methods may have been available to them? **[Speculate]**

Thesauruses A specialized dictionary, a thesaurus gives extensive lists of *synonyms*, or words with similar meanings. It may also list *antonyms*, or words with opposite meanings.

Many *printed thesauruses* arrange words alphabetically. Some arrange them thematically. For these thesauruses, you must look up the word in the index and then turn to the appropriate section to find its synonyms. In *electronic thesauruses*, you usually type in the word and have the computer search the database.

Exercise 10 **Using Other Reference Works** Use printed or electronic reference works to find answers to these questions. Indicate the type of reference you used.

1. Who was the first American woman to walk in space?
2. What did Europe's national borders look like in 1945?
3. List the title, editor, publisher, and publication date of an anthology that contains Sara Teasdale's poem "Barter."
4. Find a quotation about love from any work by William Shakespeare. Include the name of the work.
5. What are five synonyms for the verb *offer*?

More Practice

Academic and Workplace Skills Activity Book

- pp. 49–50

Exercise 11 **Using All Types of Reference Works** Give at least two specific examples of something you would research in each of the following types of references.

1. atlas
2. almanac
3. thesaurus
4. dictionary
5. periodical index

33.2

Using the Internet

The *Internet* is a worldwide network, or Web, of computers connected over phone and cable lines. When you go *on-line*, or hook up with the Internet, you have access to an almost unlimited number of Web sites where an amazing amount of information can be found. Each Web site has its own address, or *URL* (Universal Resource Locator). The site usually consists of several Web pages of text and graphics, and sometimes audio or video displays, which you can download and save on your computer.

Learn More

For more information on how to use the Internet, see the Internet Research Handbook section on pp. 855–859.

KEY CONCEPT You can use the Internet for all kinds of information, but evaluate Web sites for reliability. ■

Here are some guidelines for finding reliable information on the Internet:

- If you know a reliable Web site and its address (URL), simply type the address into your Web browser. Often, television programs, commercials, magazines, newspapers, and radio stations provide Web site addresses where you can find more information about a show, product, company, and so on.
- Consult Internet coverage in library journals (like *Booklist* and *Library Journal*) to learn addresses of Web sites that provide useful and reliable information.
- If you don't know a specific Web site, you can do a general search for a key term on a search engine. Then, evaluate any sites you access by considering the credentials of whoever constructed and whoever now maintains the site.
- Remember to bookmark or add to Favorites interesting and reliable sites you find searching the Web.

Exercise 12 **Using the Internet** On a library, school, or home computer, use the Internet to do this research.

1. Learn the ZIP Code for 1 Fifth Avenue, New York, NY.
2. Find the director and cast members of the movie *Casablanca*.
3. Choose a topic for a history paper. List names and URLs (addresses) of four Web sites that you think can help you.
4. Locate lyrics for a version of the ballad "Barbara Allen." Be sure to record the name and URL (address) of your source.
5. From a reliable source, find out about household problems posed by Indian meal moths. Record source information.

More Practice

Academic and Workplace Skills Activity Book
- p. 51

Section 33.3 Test-Taking Skills

This section provides strategies that will improve your performance on tests and help you answer the different kinds of questions they may contain.

Answering Objective Questions

If you are familiar with the different kinds of objective questions that are frequently asked on tests, you may improve your performance on the tests.

KEY CONCEPT Know the different kinds of objective questions and the strategies for answering them. ■

Multiple-Choice Questions This kind of question asks you to choose from four or five possible responses.

EXAMPLE: The opposite of energetic is ___.

a. frantic c. busy
b. lethargic d. certain

In the preceding example, the answer is *b*. Follow these strategies to answer multiple-choice questions:

- Try answering the question before looking at the choices. If your answer is one of the choices, select that choice.
- Eliminate the obviously incorrect answers, crossing them out if you are allowed to write on the test paper.
- Read all the choices before answering. For multiple-choice questions, there are often two possible answers but only one best answer.

Matching Questions Matching questions require that you match items in one group with items in another.

EXAMPLE:

___ 1. functional a. aware
___ 2. remote b. explanation
___ 3. interpretation c. hold back
___ 4. refrain d. working
___ 5. cognizant e. distant

In the preceding example, the answers are *d, e, b, c,* and *a*. Follow these strategies to answer matching questions:

- Count each group to see if items will be left over. Check the directions to see if items can be used more than once.
- Read all the items before you start matching.
- Match the items you know first.
- Then, match items about which you are less certain.

True-or-False Questions True-or-false questions require you to identify whether or not a statement is accurate.

▲ **Critical Viewing** What kind of test questions do you think this student is answering? What advice could you offer him for test taking? **[Connect]**

EXAMPLE: ___ All citizens vote on Election Day.
___ High-school students always take three math courses.
___ Some schools have a foreign-language requirement.

In the preceding example, the answers are *F, F,* and *T.* Follow these strategies to answer true-or-false questions:

- If a statement seems true, be sure all of it is true.
- Pay special attention to the word *not,* which often changes the whole meaning of a statement.
- Look carefully at the words *all, always, never, no, none,* and *only.* They often make a statement false.
- Notice the words *generally, much, many, most, often, some,* and *usually.* They often make a statement true.

Fill-in Questions A fill-in question asks you to supply an answer in your own words. The answer may complete a statement or it may simply answer a question.

EXAMPLE: An __?__ is a word that is the opposite of another word.

In the preceding example, the answer is *antonym.* Follow these strategies to answer fill-in questions:

- Read the question or incomplete statement carefully.
- If you are answering a question, change it into a statement by inserting your answer and see if that makes sense.

Exercise 13 **Answering Objective Questions** Using a subject you are studying in a class, prepare a short objective test on the material. Write five multiple-choice questions, five matching questions, five true-or-false questions, and five fill-in questions. Exchange tests with another student, and take the other student's test. Then, exchange again and grade the test.

Analogies An analogy asks you to match pairs of words that express a similar relationship.

EXAMPLE: ELM : TREE ::

a. whale : mammal c. cart : horse
b. painting : artist d. cloud : rain

In the preceding example, the answer is *a*. The relationship between the pairs of words is *kind*. An elm is a *kind* of tree, and a whale is a *kind* of mammal.

COMMON ANALOGY RELATIONSHIPS	
Relationship	**Example**
Synonym	joy : elation
Antonym	despair : hope
Quality	library : quiet
Degree (greater or lesser)	shout : speak
Part to whole	page : book
Kind	milk : beverage
Sequence	engagement : marriage
Proximity	shore : water
Device	telescope : astronomer

Exercise 14 **Answering Analogies** Choose the pair of words that has the same relationship as the first pair.

1. joy : elation ::
   A happiness : sadness C wonder : amazement
   B curiosity : fear D unrest : ease
2. page : book ::
   A sleeve : shirt C page : paper
   B library : quiet D hat : head
3. sob : cry ::
   A whisper : talk C run : dash
   B shout : anger D run : walk
4. despair : hope ::
   A hunger : eating C love : hate
   B danger : peril D shovel : gardener
5. molar : tooth ::
   A cow : horse C orange : peel
   B carrot : vegetable D vegetable : fruit

More Practice

Academic and Workplace Skills Activity Book

• pp. 51–52

33.3

Answering Short-Answer and Essay Questions

Some test questions require you to supply an answer, rather than just identifying a correct answer. Identify these questions when you preview the test. Allow time to write complete, accurate answers.

KEY CONCEPT Allow time and space to respond to short-answer and essay questions. ■

Identify Key Words Whether you are responding to a short-answer question or an essay prompt, identify the key words in the test item. Look for words like *discuss, explain, identify,* and any numbers or restrictions. If the question asks for three causes, make sure you supply three.

Check Your Space On some tests, you will be given a certain number of lines on which to write your answer. Make sure you understand whether you are limited to that space or whether you can ask for more paper. If you are limited to a certain amount of space, use it for the most significant and relevant information.

Stick to the Point Do not put down everything you know about a topic. If the question asks you to identify three steps Jefferson took to limit government power, you will not get extra credit for including information about Jefferson's childhood. In fact, including unrelated information may cause you to lose points.

For more extensive instruction on responding to essay questions, see Chapter 14, "Writing for Assessment."

Exercise 15 **Answering Essays** Evaluate an essay answer that you wrote based on what you have learned. In your evaluation, honestly answer these questions:

1. What was the key issue of the question? Did you respond directly to it?
2. Was there any irrelevant information that you included in your response?
3. What might you do to improve the essay that you are evaluating?

More Practice

Academic and Workplace Skills Activity Book
• p. 53

Types of Standardized Tests

Besides the tests in your subject areas, you will be taking standardized tests. These may include state tests, high-school exit exams, and college board tests such as the SAT and the ACT. Following are descriptions of some of these tests:

PSAT The PSAT, the Preliminary Scholastic Aptitude Test, is given nationwide and provides students with the opportunity to practice for the SAT. The PSAT has the same format as the SAT with the following exceptions: (1) The PSAT contains fewer sections than the SAT. (2) The PSAT contains items that test your knowledge of usage and mechanics; the SAT does not.

SAT The SAT, the Scholastic Aptitude Test, is used by many colleges as one factor in admissions decisions. It is given nationwide once a month from October through June, except in February. If you are dissatisfied with your SAT scores, you may repeat the test; however, all previous scores will be reported to schools as well as the most recent score. SATs have a math portion and a verbal portion. The verbal portion contains the following sections:

1. **Sentence-completion questions** test your knowledge of vocabulary by asking you to fill in a blank within a sentence or passage with an appropriate word.
2. **Analogy questions** are like those on page 623.
3. **Critical-reading questions** are multiple-choice questions asked in response to a pair of related reading passages.
4. **Writing sections** ask you to respond to a prompt.

ACT The ACT, the American College Test, is another test used by colleges as one factor in admissions decisions. The questions—all multiple choice—focus on English, math, reading, and science reasoning. The English portion asks you to identify errors in grammar, usage, mechanics, logic, and organization. The reading portion presents four passages from different content areas, followed by questions that test your reading and reasoning skills.

Learn More

The Standardized Test Preparation Workshops that appear at the ends of every chapter throughout this book provide instruction and practice in all of the types of items covered on these tests.

Reflecting on Your Study, Reference, and Test-Taking Skills

Answer the following questions that will help you think about what you have learned concerning your study, reference, and test-taking habits and skills.

- Which strategies seemed new or unusual? How can using these strategies help me improve my academic performance?
- Which strategies do I already use? Why do I find these most comfortable or useful?

Chapter 34

Workplace Skills and Competencies

▲ **Critical Viewing** How can effective writing, speaking, and listening skills improve a training session, such as the one shown here? **[Support]**

Many of the skills that contribute to school success also contribute to success in the workplace. Whether you interact with the public, pursue a field that involves the research and development of new products, or work in a labor-oriented job, your abilities to speak clearly, listen closely, read carefully, and interact effectively with people are keys to a productive career.

This chapter will help you to build new skills or to improve existing ones in a number of critical areas, such as communicating with others, setting and achieving goals, and solving problems efficiently. It will also offer suggestions on how to manage your time and money as well as how to apply math and computer skills in the workplace.

Working With People

In school, you learn to work together with classmates and teachers. In the workplace, you will be expected to interact effectively with supervisors, co-workers, and clients. This section offers some practical suggestions to refine your communication skills in one-on-one and group situations.

Learn to Communicate One on One

On a formal interview or when interacting with peers, you will need to use communication skills.

Interviewing When you apply to a college, compete for a job, or show interest in a school committee, knowing how to interview can greatly increase your chances of success.

TIPS FOR A SUCCESSFUL INTERVIEW

1. Find out when, where, and with whom the interview is.
2. Prepare references and a copy of your résumé.
3. Learn about the company, group, or person with whom you have the interview.
4. Select a neat, appropriate outfit for the interview.

1. Smile and maintain eye contact.
2. Ask and answer questions politely and concisely.
3. Thank the interviewer, and ask when a decision will be made.

1. In a follow-up letter, restate your interest in the internship, job, or college, and extend your thanks.
2. When the deadline for a decision arrives, call to check the status.

Speaking and Listening Tip

During an interview, work to maintain a positive impression. Be polite and confident, speak courteously, and listen carefully to the person conducting the interview.

Interacting Successfully In school or at work, communication requires respectful interaction with people who have different priorities or opinions than you do. In fact, the people you encounter may have different personalities and working styles, too. In order to work successfully, strike a balance between communicating your own ideas and listening to those expressed by others. When you work on a project with a partner, speak to a teacher or supervisor, or deal with customers, the ability to compromise can often make everyone's job easier and more pleasant.

KEY CONCEPT Effective interaction requires respect for and sensitivity to others. ■

Follow these guidelines for successful interaction:

- **Consider the other person's point of view.** Ask yourself how you would feel if you were in another's situation.
- **Listen without interrupting.**
- **Clarify by asking questions.**
- **Respect differences.** Recognize and accept that others may have different backgrounds, abilities, and opinions.
- **Express disagreement in nonconfrontational terms.** For example, rather than saying, "You're wrong," try saying, "I don't see it that way."
- **Be polite and professional.** A temper tantrum may be dramatic, but it is not an accepted behavior in the workplace. Whenever possible, avoid raising your voice. You can be more persuasive when you are in control of your emotions.

Exercise 1 **Interviewing for a Job on the School Newspaper** With another classmate, role-play an interview for a job as a reporter for the school newspaper. The interviewer should ask questions that will prompt the interviewee to describe the reasons for wanting the job. Present your role-play to a group, and discuss what others can learn from the experience.

More Practice

Academic and Workplace Skills Activity Book

- pp. 54–55

Exercise 2 **Interacting in a Variety of Situations** Working with another student, role-play the following situations:

1. Two classmates are collaborating on a project. They each participate in different activities, so coordinating their schedules is difficult. Role-play a conversation in which they arrive at two mutually agreeable times to work.
2. A bank teller must interact with an angry customer who has a problem with a bank statement. Role-play a conversation in which they try to solve the problem.

Learning Teamwork

To succeed in any team effort, such as organizing a fund-raiser, studying for a test, or preparing a job-related presentation, group members must work together to achieve a common goal. Although personalities and opinions may differ, the shared goal should direct each member's focus.

Participating in Group Discussions The benefit of a group discussion is that it allows each person to access and consider a pool of ideas. For example, when embarking on a major project, businesses often ask members of different departments to share their knowledge and expertise to make the planning effective. This benefit is realized only if each member of the group participates,

KEY CONCEPT Effective participation involves both contributing and allowing others to contribute. ■

▲ Critical Viewing What problems might arise when people work in groups, as shown here? **[Hypothesize]**

Taking on Group Roles Group discussions held at meetings can be improved by a systematic sharing of responsibilities. In a group that meets regularly, these roles and responsibilities should rotate among the members.

KEY CONCEPT Members of a group assume distinct, yet important, roles to realize a common goal. ■

These roles and responsibilities make meetings run smoothly:

Facilitator: Guides the discussion and makes sure that everyone has a chance to be heard

Note-taker: Records the discussion and prepares the notes for distribution

Timekeeper: Watches the time and keeps the discussion on schedule

Participants: Contribute ideas, help problem-solve, and participate in the discussion

Tips for Effective Participation Whether you are involved in a regularly scheduled meeting or are participating in a single-session group discussion, consider these tips:

- Bring relevant documents or ideas to the meeting.
- Use an agenda, a prepared list of subjects to address.
- Share your perspective, and encourage others to provide their points of view.
- Focus your attention on the topic.
- Follow up on any decisions or plans the group makes.

Exercise 3 **Conducting an Informal Group Discussion** Working with a group of four or five students, hold an informal discussion to identify three objects you'd want to save in a scrapbook. Then, evaluate how successfully the group encouraged participation and interaction from all members.

Exercise 4 **Using Group Roles** With a group of four or five students, hold a meeting using the following suggested agenda. Before beginning, set a time limit for each part of the discussion, and assign group roles. After the discussion, explain how the group roles affected the interaction.

TOPIC: Raising money for a class trip
Part 1: Brainstorm for ideas
Part 2: Narrow the number of ideas down to three or four
Part 3: Analyze ideas by listing pros and cons
Part 4: Reach agreement on a single idea

Learn More

For instructions on writing minutes or notes of a meeting, see pages 210–211 in the "Workplace Writing" chapter.

Moving Toward Your Goals

Goals—attainable, measurable outcomes—may take a short or a long time to fulfill. They may focus on improving your grades or your tennis serve, on becoming class president or a clerk at a local convenience store. As you set goals for various parts of your life, they may conflict with one another, leaving you to decide which one is most important to you.

▲ **Critical Viewing** Identify an attainable goal for an athlete beginning to learn tennis. **[Apply]**

Personal and Professional Goals

Personal goals focus on your lifestyle and how you want to develop as a person. For example, you decide to learn more about a favorite hobby or to be kinder to others. *Professional goals* focus on your career; for example, you may want to learn a new computer program or complete an important project within a set budget. While personal and professional goals are different, they often affect each other. Therefore, you may need to identify the ones you consider most important.

Setting and Achieving Goals To set a goal, clearly define the outcome so that you know what you are working toward. This first step is followed by the equally important step of achieving the goal, which requires a plan with a set time limit.

KEY CONCEPT Goals should be specific and should include a set time limit for completion. ■

By following the steps on the timeline below, you can develop an action plan that will help you realize your goals.

TIMELINE FOR MEETING GOALS

Write down the goal in detail.

Break the goal down into specific steps.

Set a reasonable time frame to complete each step.

Adjust your progress on a regular basis.

Adjust the steps as needed.

GOAL

Exercise 5 **Developing an Action Plan** Using the steps above, develop an action plan for achieving a school-related goal. Outline the steps you will need to take to achieve your goal, and set a daily or weekly time limit for each one. Discuss your plan with your teacher, a family member, or a classmate. Then, follow your action plan. At the end of each interval, evaluate your progress, and adjust your plan as needed.

More Practice

Academic and Workplace Skills Activity Book
• p. 56

Solving Problems and Thinking Creatively

Whether you are working to achieve personal or professional goals, be prepared for the problems that will undoubtedly arise. Many successful people view these bumps in the road as opportunities because problems challenge people to see a situation in a new light. Keep in mind that not every problem can be solved in exactly the way you would like. Sometimes, solving the problem means accepting a compromise, or finding a solution you hadn't originally considered.

Problem Solving Effectively Use a graphic organizer like the one below to help you analyze a problem. These tips also offer useful advice:

- Keep a positive attitude.
- Identify the reason or reasons that the problem exists. If you can identify several elements that caused the problem, address one element at a time.
- Evaluate the pros and cons of a variety of solutions.
- Be willing to accept a less-than-perfect solution.

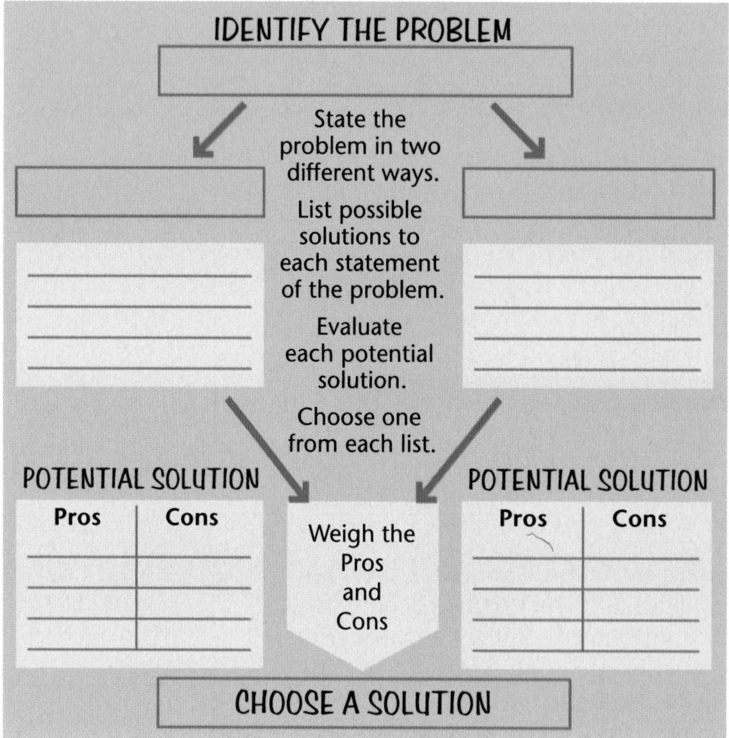

Learn More

For more instruction about problem-and-solution writing, see Chapter 11.

Thinking Creatively Sometimes, solving problems means thinking creatively—looking beyond the ordinary. When you are problem solving, think creatively by looking at the problem from several angles. The illustration below shows one method for approaching a problem from more than one angle. You may discover other techniques that help you come up with creative solutions.

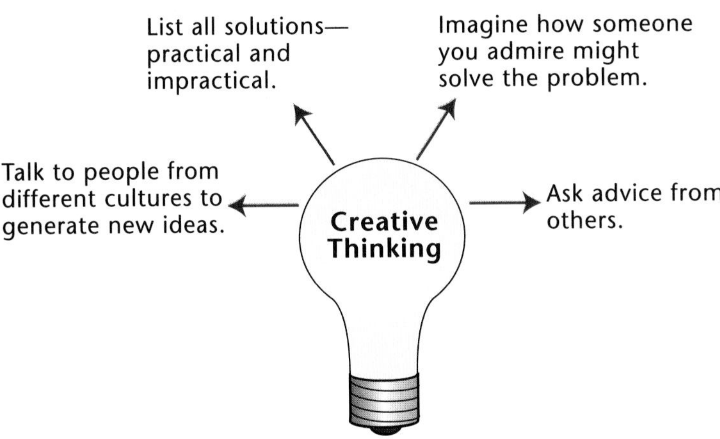

Exercise 6 **Applying Problem-Solving Skills** Use problem-solving skills to arrive at a potential solution for each of the following problems. In each case, write a brief explanation of how you arrived at the solution.

1. You spend at least fifteen minutes each morning looking for your house keys. Often, by the time you find them, you are late leaving the house.
2. You are nervous about speaking in front of a group, and you have a class presentation coming up in two weeks.

▶ **Critical Viewing** What are some of the benefits of problem-solving with a group? **[Analyze]**

Managing Time

In whatever career you choose, you will likely face a task that must be completed in a set amount of time. Between answering e-mails, phone calls, and dealing with unexpected problems, knowing how to use your time efficiently can mean the difference between success and failure.

Keeping Weekly and Daily Schedules Proper time management takes planning and the ability to decide which of your goals and activities is most important.

KEY CONCEPT To manage your time, keep a schedule of activities and plan for upcoming events. ■

The following strategies will help you accomplish what you must with minimal scrambling.

- Write down activities and goals for the week. Decide which projects are most important, and devote more time to them.
- Break big tasks into manageable steps.
- Make a daily to-do list.

Internet Tip

Some Web sites offer on-line opportunities for managing your time. Locate such resources on-line, and use them to keep an electronic calendar.

WEEKLY SCHEDULE

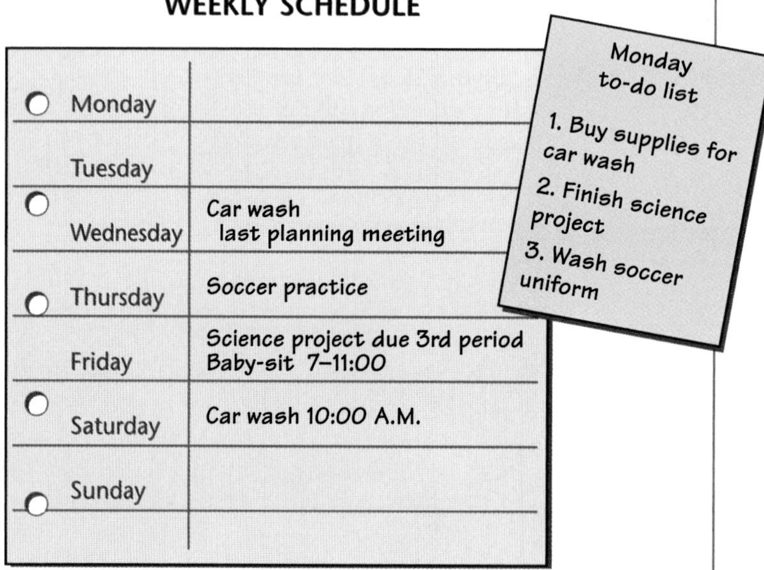

Exercise 7 **Managing Your Time** In your notebook or in a weekly planner, record your schedule for a week. Include a daily to-do list. Break large projects or tasks into smaller activities or steps. After a week, identify one positive aspect of such a system.

Managing Money

In order to keep spending in line, a budget, or a spending plan, can be effective. From the chief financial officer in charge of a company's budget to the office manager who orders supplies, many employees are expected to record and manage expenses. This may present difficult choices about cutting spending or increasing income.

KEY CONCEPT To manage money, keep track of spending, set financial goals, and save money to meet them. ■

More Practice
Academic and Workplace Skills Activity Book
• pp. 57–58

Developing a Budget In order for a budget to be successful, the money coming in should exceed the money going out. To outline a budget, show credits or money earned in black. Show debts or outgoing money in red. In the example below, income can cover the expenses identified.

Freshman Dance Budget

	Regular Income	Regular Expenses	Projected Expenses
Total Ticket Sales	1,000.00		
From Sponsors	250.00		
Raffle Prize			150.00
Disc Jockey		200.00	
Lights/Balloons		115.00	
Total	$1,250.00	$315.00	$150.00

Exercise 8 **Managing a Budget** Plan one month's budget for a hiking club with thirty members who each pay $1.00 a week in dues. Once a month, the club holds a bake sale. The supplies for the sale cost $20.00, and the sale brings in $130.00. Each month, the club sponsors a bus for $75.00 to take the members to a hiking site. Insurance for the trip costs $25.00. The club is saving to purchase a $100.00 tree for the school in June. Use your budget to answer these questions:

1. How many months will it take to save money for the tree?
2. Make two suggestions: one for reducing expenses and one for increasing income.

Applying Math Skills

When it comes to applying the skills you have learned in class to the workplace, you will discover that math has many common applications and that a working knowledge of computers can give you an edge in your chosen career.

Internet Tip

Some Web sites offer math support on-line. Search for a Web site that can help you with budgeting and calculations.

KEY CONCEPT Math skills help you shop wisely, plan for a profit, and determine the value of your time. ■

Determining the Best Buy Math skills can help you calculate the best price for a product or service. For example, some "buy one, get one free" sales actually work out to cost more than if you bought the two items at their regular price at another store. By calculating the difference, you can make an educated decision and save money.

Planning for Profit Any job or project that requires materials, space, or people's time usually involves costs that must be balanced by the income generated by sales. To figure out the cost of each finished item or each service performed, determine your investment and divide that number by the quantity of items you are making. In order to make a profit, you must sell the item or service at a higher rate than it costs you.

Setting the Value of Your Time When you are looking for a job, the wage you are quoted (if a flat rate) may be misleading. To effectively evaluate an offer that doesn't include an hourly wage, divide the offer by the number of hours the job will take. Then, decide whether the offer presented seems fair to you.

Exercise 9 **Using Math Skills to Evaluate Two Job Offers**

A neighbor has offered you $40 to baby-sit his child on the weekends (Saturday and Sunday), five hours each day. Another neighbor has offered you $40 to feed and walk her dog five times a week, which takes approximately one hour each day.

1. Identify the amount of time you would need to invest in each job.
2. What other factors might influence your decision?
3. Which job would you accept? Explain your answer.

▼ **Critical Viewing** How can calculators help workers increase efficiency? **[Analyze]**

Applying Computer Skills

▲ Critical Viewing What are two benefits of learning strong computer skills? [Analyze]

The more you learn about your computer, the more useful it can be. You should begin by learning to keyboard quickly and accurately. Then, study your computer's special formatting features. You may even want to learn specialized spreadsheet programs or graphics applications.

KEY CONCEPT A working knowledge of your computer can enhance your work. ■

Practice your typing skills. Being an accurate and quick typist gives you more time to focus on other tasks. A good typing speed is 45 words per minute, but remember that accuracy is more important than speed.

Use the thesaurus and spell-check tools. With the click of a mouse, you can find just the right word or catch errors that you may have missed while proofreading.

Learn how to format. Use fonts, bullets, and other features to organize and emphasize information.

Exercise 10 **Examining Computer Skills** Using a computer at home or in school, do the following activities:

1. Working with a partner who will time you, type a page from a textbook as quickly and accurately as you can for one minute. Then, count how many words you typed and review your work for accuracy.
2. Review the classified section of a newspaper to identify the computer skills and programs that are most frequently requested in job openings. Choose one application or skill that interests you, and learn more about it. Share your findings with classmates.

More Practice

Academic and Workplace Skills Activity Book
• pp. 59–60

Reflecting on Your Workplace Skills and Competencies

Consider your own readiness for the workplace. In your journal or notebook, begin by answering the following questions:

- Consider the job you want to pursue. Which skills will it require?
- What are your strengths? What are your weaknesses?

Citing Sources and Preparing Manuscript

The presentation of your written work is important. Your work should be neat, clean, and easy to read. Follow your teacher's directions for placing your name and class, along with the title and date of your work, on the paper.

For handwritten work:

- Use cursive handwriting or manuscript printing, according to the style your teacher prefers. The penmanship reference below shows the accepted formation of letters in cursive writing.
- Write or print neatly.
- Write on one side of lined $8\,^{1}/_{2}$" x 11" paper with a clean edge. (Do not use pages torn from a spiral notebook.)
- Indent the first line of each paragraph.
- Leave a margin, as indicated by the guidelines on the lined paper. Write in a size appropriate for the lines provided. Do not write so large that the letters from one line bump into the ones above and below. Do not write so small that the writing is difficult to read.
- Write in blue or black ink.
- Number the pages in the upper right corner.
- You should not cross out words on your final draft. Recopy instead. If your paper is long, your teacher may allow you to make one or two small changes by neatly crossing out the text to be deleted and using a caret [^] to indicate replacement text. Alternatively, you might make one or two corrections neatly with correction fluid. If you find yourself making more than three corrections, consider recopying the work.

PENMANSHIP REFERENCE

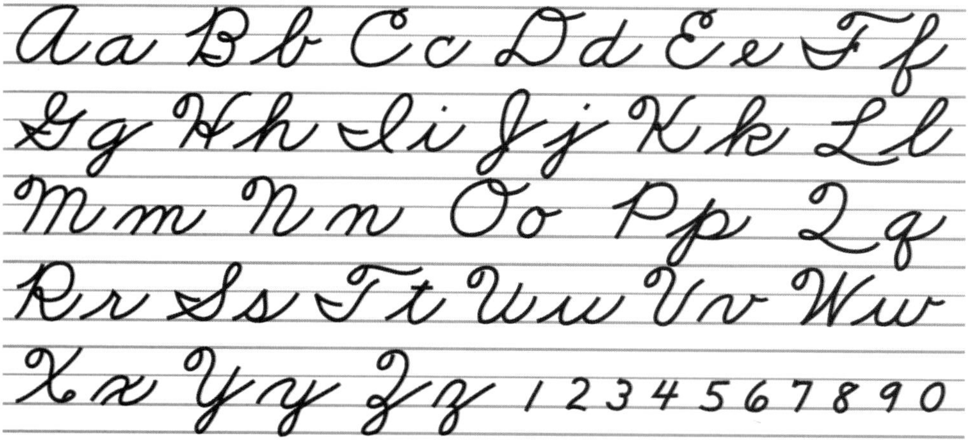

Aa Bb Cc Dd Ee Ff
Gg Hh Ii Jj Kk Ll
Mm Nn Oo Pp Qq
Rr Ss Tt Uu Vv Ww
Xx Yy Zz 1 2 3 4 5 6 7 8 9 0

For word-processed or typed documents:

- Choose a standard, easy-to-read font.
- Type or print on one side of unlined $8\,^1/_2$" x 11" paper.
- Set the margins for the side, top, and bottom of your paper at approximately one inch. Most word-processing programs have a default setting that is appropriate.
- Double-space the document.
- Indent the first line of each paragraph.
- Number the pages in the upper right corner. Many word-processing programs have a header feature that will do this for you automatically.
- If you discover one or two errors after you have typed or printed, use correction fluid if your teacher allows such corrections. If you have more than three errors in an electronic file, consider making the corrections to the file and reprinting the document. If you have typed a long document, your teacher may allow you to make a few corrections by hand. If you have several errors, however, consider retyping the document.

For research papers:

Follow your teacher's directions for formatting formal research papers. Most papers will have the following features:

- Title page
- Table of Contents or Outline
- Works-Cited List

Incorporating Ideas From Research

Below are three common methods of incorporating the ideas of other writers into your work. Choose the most appropriate style by analyzing your needs in each case. In all cases, you must credit your source.

- **Direct Quotation:** Use quotation marks to indicate the exact words.
- **Paraphrase:** To share ideas without a direct quotation, state the ideas in your own words. While you haven't copied word-for-word, you still need to credit your source.
- **Summary:** To provide information about a large body of work—such as a speech, an editorial, or a chapter of a book—identify the writer's main idea.

Avoiding Plagiarism

Whether you are presenting a formal research paper or an opinion paper on a current event, you must be careful to give credit for any ideas or opinions that are not your own. Presenting someone else's ideas, research, or opinion as your own—even if you have rephrased it in different words—is *plagiarism*, the equivalent of academic stealing, or fraud.

You can avoid plagiarism by synthesizing what you learn: Read from several sources and let the ideas of experts help you draw your own conclusions and form your own opinions. Ultimately, however, note your own reactions to the ideas presented.

When you choose to use someone else's ideas or work to support your view, credit the source of the material. Give bibliographic information to cite your sources of the following information:

- Statistics
- Direct quotations
- Indirectly quoted statements of opinions
- Conclusions presented by an expert
- Facts available in only one or two sources

Crediting Sources

When you credit a source, you acknowledge where you found your information and you give your readers the details necessary for locating the source themselves. Within the body of the paper, you provide a short citation, a footnote number linked to a footnote, or an endnote number linked to an endnote reference. These brief references show the page numbers on which you found the information. To make your paper more formal, prepare a reference list at the end of the paper to provide full bibliographic information on your sources. These are two common types of reference lists:

- A **bibliography** provides a listing of all the resources you consulted during your research.
- A **works-cited list** indicates the works you have referenced in your paper.

Choosing a Format for Documentation

The type of information you provide and the format in which you provide it depend on what your teacher prefers. These are the most commonly used styles:

- **Modern Language Association (MLA) Style** This is the style used for most papers at the middle-school and high-school level and for most language arts papers.
- **American Psychological Association (APA) Style** This is used for most papers in the social sciences and for most college-level papers.
- ***Chicago Manual of Style* (CMS) Style** This is preferred by some teachers.

On the following pages, you'll find sample citation formats for the most commonly cited materials. Each format calls for standard bibliographic information. The difference is in the order of the material presented in each entry and the punctuation required.

MLA Style for Listing Sources

Book with one author	Pyles, Thomas. *The Origins and Development of the English Language.* 2nd ed. New York: Harcourt Brace Jovanovich, Inc., 1971.
Book with two or three authors	McCrum, Robert, William Cran, and Robert MacNeil. *The Story of English.* New York: Penguin Books, 1987.
Book with an editor	Truth, Sojourner. *Narrative of Sojourner Truth.* Ed. Margaret Washington. New York: Vintage Books, 1993.
Book with more than three authors or editors	Donald, Robert B., et al. *Writing Clear Essays.* Upper Saddle River, NJ: Prentice-Hall, Inc., 1996.
A single work from an anthology	Hawthorne, Nathaniel. "Young Goodman Brown." *Literature: An Introduction to Reading and Writing.* Ed. Edgar V. Roberts and Henry E. Jacobs. Upper Saddle River, NJ: Prentice-Hall, Inc., 1998. 376–385. [Indicate pages for the entire selection.]
Introduction in a published edition	Washington, Margaret. Introduction. *Narrative of Sojourner Truth.* By Sojourner Truth. Ed. Washington. New York: Vintage Books, 1993. v–xi.
Signed article in a weekly magazine	Wallace, Charles. "A Vodacious Deal." *Time* 14 Feb. 2000: 63.
Signed article in a monthly magazine	Gustaitis, Joseph. "The Sticky History of Chewing Gum." *American History* Oct. 1998: 30–38.
Unsigned editorial or story	"Selective Silence." Editorial. *Wall Street Journal* 11 Feb. 2000: A14. [If the editorial or story is signed, begin with the author's name.]
Signed pamphlet	[Treat the pamphlet as though it were a book.]
Pamphlet with no author, publisher, or date	*Are You at Risk of Heart Attack?* n.p. n.d. [n.p. n.d. indicates that there is no known publisher or date]
Filmstrips, slide programs, videocassettes, DVDs, and other audiovisual media	*The Diary of Anne Frank.* Dir. George Stevens. Perf. Millie Perkins, Shelley Winters, Joseph Schildkraut, Lou Jacobi, and Richard Beymer. 1959. DVD. Twentieth Century Fox, 2004.
Radio or television program transcript	"Washington's Crossing of the Delaware." Host Liane Hansen. Guest David Hackett Fischer. *Weekend Edition Sunday.* Natl. Public Radio. WNYC, New York City. 23 Dec. 2003. Transcript.
Internet	"Fun Facts About Gum." NACGM site. National Association of Chewing Gum Manufacturers. 19 Dec. 1999. <http://www.nacgm.org/consumer/funfacts.html>. [Indicate the date of last update if known and the date you accessed the information. Content and addresses at Web sites change frequently.]
Newspaper	Thurow, Roger. "South Africans Who Fought for Sanctions Now Scrap for Investors." *Wall Street Journal* 11 Feb. 2000: A1+ [For a multipage article that does not appear on consecutive pages, write only the first page number on which it appears, followed by a plus sign.]
Personal interview	Smith, Jane. Personal interview. 10 Feb. 2000.
CD (with multiple publishers)	Simms, James, ed. *Romeo and Juliet.* By William Shakespeare. CD-ROM. Oxford: Attica Cybernetics Ltd.; London: BBC Education; London: HarperCollins Publishers, 1995.
Article from an encyclopedia	Askeland, Donald R. "Welding." *World Book Encyclopedia.* 1991 ed.

APA Style for Listing Sources

The list of citations for APA is referred to as a Reference List and not a bibliography.

Book with one author	Pyles, T. (1971). *The Origins and Development of the English Language* (2nd ed.). New York: Harcourt Brace Jovanovich, Inc.
Book with two or three authors	McCrum, R., Cran, W., & MacNeil, R. (1987). *The Story of English.* New York: Penguin Books.
Book with an editor	Truth, S. (1993). *Narrative of Sojourner Truth* (M. Washington, Ed.). New York: Vintage Books.
Book with more than three authors or editors	Donald, R. B., Morrow, B. R., Wargetz, L. G., & Werner, K. (1996). *Writing Clear Essays.* Upper Saddle River, New Jersey: Prentice-Hall, Inc. [With six or more authors, abbreviate second and following authors as "et al."]
A single work from an anthology	Hawthorne, N. (1998) Young Goodman Brown. In E. V. Roberts, & H. E. Jacobs (Eds.), *Literature: An Introduction to Reading and Writing* (pp. 376–385). Upper Saddle River, New Jersey: Prentice-Hall, Inc.
Introduction to a work included in a published edition	[No style is offered under this heading.]
Signed article in a weekly magazine	Wallace, C. (2000, February 14). A vodacious deal. *Time, 155,* 63. [The volume number appears in italics before the page number.]
Signed article in a monthly magazine	Gustaitis, J. (1998, October). The sticky history of chewing gum. *American History, 33,* 30–38.
Unsigned editorial or story	Selective Silence. (2000, February 11). *Wall Street Journal,* p. A14.
Signed pamphlet	Pearson Education. (2000). *LifeCare* (2nd ed.) [Pamphlet]. Smith, John: Author.
Pamphlet with no author, publisher, or date	[No style is offered under this heading.]
Filmstrips, slide programs, and videotape	Stevens, G. (Producer & Director). (1959). *The Diary of Anne Frank.* [Videotape]. (Available from Twentieth Century Fox) [If the producer and the director are two different people, list the producer first and then the director, with an ampersand (&) between them.]
Radio or television program transcript	Broderick, D. (1999, May 23). The First Immortal Generation. (R. Williams, Radio Host). *Ockham's Razor.* New York: National Public Radio.
Internet	National Association of Chewing Gum Manufacturers. Available: http://www.nacgm.org/consumer/funfacts.html [References to Websites should begin with the author's last name, if available. Indicate the site name and the available path or URL address.]
Newspaper	Thurow, R. (2000, February 11). South Africans who fought for sanctions now scrap for investors. *Wall Street Journal,* pp. A1, A4.
Personal interview	[APA states that, since interviews (and other personal communications) do not provide "recoverable data," they should only be cited in text.]
CD (with multiple publishers)	[No style is offered under this heading.]
Article from an encyclopedia	Askeland, D. R. (1991). Welding. In *World Book Encyclopedia.* (Vol. 21 pp. 190–191). Chicago: World Book, Inc.

CMS Style for Listing Sources

The following chart shows the CMS author-date method of documentation.

Book with one author	Pyles, Thomas. *The Origins and Development of the English Language,* 2nd ed. New York: Harcourt Brace Jovanovich, Inc., 1971.
Book with two or three authors	McCrum, Robert, William Cran, and Robert MacNeil. *The Story of English.* New York: Penguin Books, 1987.
Book with an editor	Truth, Sojourner. *Narrative of Sojourner Truth.* Edited by Margaret Washington. New York: Vintage Books, 1993.
Book with more than three authors or editors	Donald, Robert B., et al. *Writing Clear Essays.* Upper Saddle River, New Jersey: Prentice-Hall, Inc., 1996.
A single work from an anthology	Hawthorne, Nathaniel. "Young Goodman Brown." In *Literature: An Introduction to Reading and Writing.* Ed. Edgar V. Roberts and Henry E. Jacobs. 376–385. Upper Saddle River, New Jersey: Prentice-Hall, Inc., 1998.
Introduction to a work included in a published edition	Washington, Margaret. Introduction to *Narrative of Sojourner Truth,* by Sojourner Truth. New York: Vintage Books, 1993. [According to CMS style, you should avoid this type of entry unless the introduction is of special importance to the work.]
Signed article in a weekly magazine	Wallace, Charles. "A Vodacious Deal." *Time,* 14 February 2000, 63.
Signed article in a monthly magazine	Gustaitis, Joseph. "The Sticky History of Chewing Gum." *American History,* October 1998, 30–38.
Unsigned editorial or story	*Wall Street Journal,* 11 February 2000. [CMS states that items from newspapers are seldom listed in a bibliography. Instead, the name of the paper and the relevant dates are listed.]
Signed pamphlet	[No style is offered under this heading.]
Pamphlet with no author, publisher, or date	[No style is offered under this heading.]
Filmstrips, slide programs, and videotape	Stevens, George. (director). *The Diary of Anne Frank.* 170 min. Beverly Hills, California: Twentieth Century Fox, 1994.
Radio or television program transcript	[No style is offered under this heading.]
Internet	[No style is offered under this heading.]
Newspaper	*Wall Street Journal,* 11 February 2000. [CMS states that items from newspapers are seldom listed in a bibliography. Instead, the name of the paper and the relevant dates are listed.]
Personal interview	[CMS states that, since personal conversations are not available to the public, there is no reason to place them in the bibliography. However, the following format should be followed if they are listed.] Jane Smith. Conversation with author. Wooster, Ohio, 10 February 2000.
CD (with multiple publishers)	Shakespeare, William. *Romeo and Juliet.* Oxford: Attica Cybernetics Ltd.; London: BBC Education; London: HarperCollins Publishers, 1995. CD-ROM.
Article from an encyclopedia	[According to CMS style, encyclopedias are not listed in bibliographies.]

Sample Works-Cited List (MLA)

Carwardine, Mark, Erich Hoyt, R. Ewan Fordyce, and Peter Gill. *The Nature Company Guides: Whales, Dolphins, and Porpoises*. New York: Time-Life Books, 1998.

Ellis, Richard. *Men and Whales*. New York: Knopf, 1991.

Whales in Danger. "Discovering Whales." 18 Oct. 1999. <http://whales.magna.com.au/DISCOVER>

Sample Internal Citations (MLA)

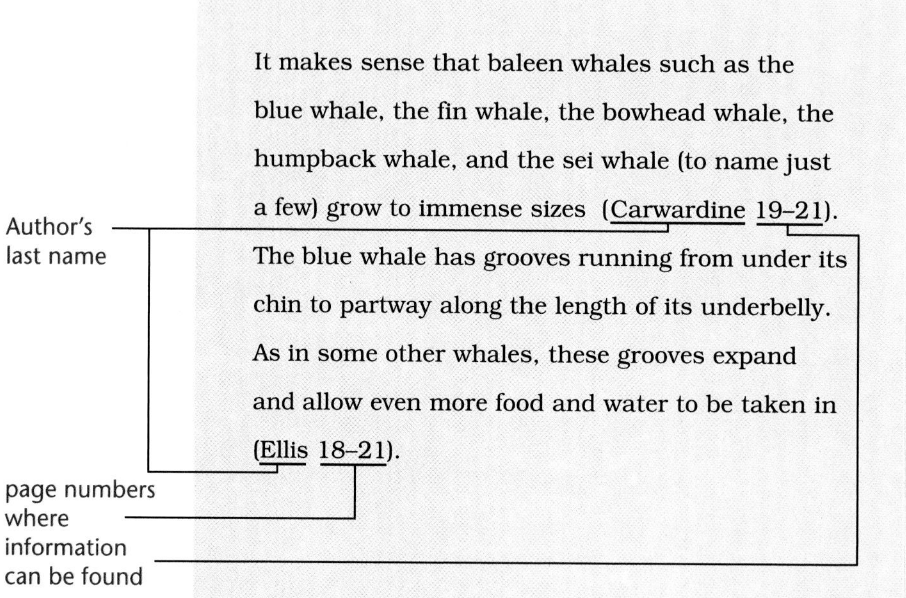
It makes sense that baleen whales such as the blue whale, the fin whale, the bowhead whale, the humpback whale, and the sei whale (to name just a few) grow to immense sizes (Carwardine 19–21). The blue whale has grooves running from under its chin to partway along the length of its underbelly. As in some other whales, these grooves expand and allow even more food and water to be taken in (Ellis 18–21).

Introduction to the Internet

The Internet is a series of networks that are interconnected all over the world. The Internet allows users to have almost unlimited access to information stored on the networks. Dr. Berners-Lee, a physicist, created the Internet in the 1980's by writing a small computer program that allowed pages to be linked together using key words. The Internet was mostly text-based until 1992, when a computer program called the NCSA Mosaic (National Center for Supercomputing Applications at the University of Illinois) was created. This program was the first Web browser. The development of Web browsers greatly eased the ability of the user to navigate through all the pages stored on the Web. Very soon, the appearance of the Web was altered as well. More appealing visuals were added, and sound was also implemented. This change made the Web more user-friendly and more appealing to the general public.

Using the Internet for Research

Key Word Search

Before you begin a search, you should identify your specific topic. To make searching easier, narrow your subject to a key word or a group of key words. These are your search terms, and they should be as specific as possible. For example, if you are looking for the latest concert dates for your favorite musical group, you might use the band's name as a key word. However, if you were to enter the name of the group in the query box of the search engine, you might be presented with thousands of links to information about the group that is unrelated to your needs. You might locate such information as band member biographies, the group's history, fan reviews of concerts, and hundreds of sites with related names containing information that is irrelevant to your search. Because you used such a broad key word, you might need to navigate through all that information before you find a link or subheading for concert dates. In contrast, if you were to type in "Duplex Arena and [band name]" you would have a better chance of locating pages that contain this information.

How to Narrow Your Search

If you have a large group of key words and still don't know which ones to use, write out a list of all the words you are considering. Once you have completed the list, scrutinize it. Then, delete the words that are least important to your search, and highlight those that are most important.

These **key search connectors** can help you fine-tune your search:

- AND: narrows a search by retrieving documents that include both terms. For example: *baseball AND playoffs*
- OR: broadens a search by retrieving documents including any of the terms. For example: *playoffs OR championships*
- NOT: narrows a search by excluding documents containing certain words. For example: *baseball NOT history of*

Tips for an Effective Search

1. Keep in mind that search engines can be case-sensitive. If your first attempt at searching fails, check your search terms for misspellings and try again.
2. If you are entering a group of key words, present them in order, from the most important to the least important key word.
3. Avoid opening the link to every single page in your results list. Search engines present pages in descending order of relevancy. The most useful pages will be located at the top of the list. However, read the description of each link before you open the page.
4. When you use some search engines, you can find helpful tips for specializing your search. Take the opportunity to learn more about effective searching.

Other Ways to Search

Using On-line Reference Sites *How* you search should be tailored to *what* you are hoping to find. If you are looking for data and facts, use reference sites before you jump onto a simple search engine. For example, you can find reference sites to provide definitions of words, statistics about almost any subject, biographies, maps, and concise information on many topics. Some useful on-line reference sites:

On-line libraries
On-line periodicals
Almanacs
Encyclopedias

You can find these sources using subject searches.

Conducting Subject Searches As you prepare to go on-line, consider your subject and the best way to find information to suit your needs. If you are looking for general information on a topic and you want your search results to be extensive, consider the subject search indexes on most search engines. These indexes, in the form of category and subject lists, often appear on the first page of a search engine. When you click on a specific highlighted word, you will be presented with a new screen containing subcategories of the topic you chose. In the screen shots below, the category *Sports & Recreation* provided a second index for users to focus a search even further.

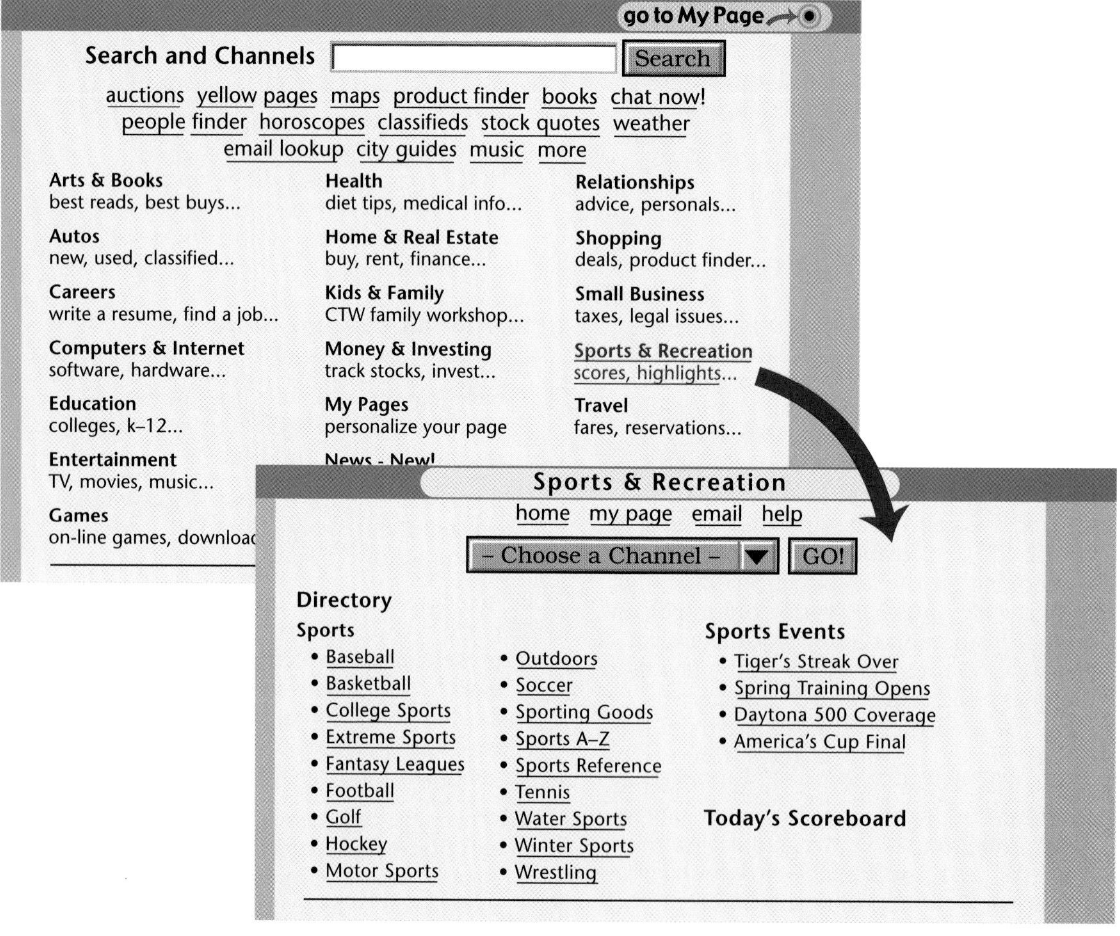

Evaluating the Reliability of Internet Resources Just as you would evaluate the quality, bias, and validity of any other research material you locate, check the source of information you find on-line. Compare these two sites containing information on the poet and writer Langston Hughes:

Site A is a personal Web site constructed by a college student. It contains no bibliographic information or links to sites that he used. Included on the site are several poems by Langston Hughes and a student essay about the poet's use of symbolism. It has not been updated in more than six months.

Site B is a Web site constructed and maintained by the English Department of a major university. Information on Hughes is presented in a scholarly format, with a bibliography and credits for the writer. The site includes links to other sites and indicates new features that are added weekly.

For your own research, consider the information you find on Site B to be more reliable and accurate than that on Site A. Because it is maintained by experts in their field who are held accountable for their work, the university site will be a better research tool than the student-generated one.

Tips for Evaluating Internet Sources

1. Consider who constructed and who now maintains the Web page. Determine whether this author is a reputable source. Often, the URL endings indicate a source.
   - Sites ending in *.edu* are maintained by educational institutions.
   - Sites ending in *.gov* are maintained by government agencies (federal, state, or local).
   - Sites ending in *.org* are normally maintained by nonprofit organizations and agencies.
   - Sites with a *.com* ending are commercially or personally maintained.
2. Skim the official and trademarked Web pages first. It is safe to assume that the information you draw from Web pages of reputable institutions, on-line encyclopedias, on-line versions of major daily newspapers, or government-owned sites produce information as reliable as the material you would find in print. In contrast, unbranded sites or those generated by individuals tend to borrow information from other sources without providing documentation. As information travels from one source to another, the information has likely been muddled, misinterpreted, edited, or revised.
3. You can still find valuable information in the less "official" sites. Check for the writer's credentials and then consider these factors:
   - Don't let official-looking graphics or presentations fool you.
   - Make sure the information is updated enough to suit your needs. Many Web pages will indicate how recently they have been updated.
   - If the information is borrowed, see whether you can trace it back to its original source.

Respecting Copyrighted Material

Because the Internet is a relatively new and quickly growing medium, issues of copyright and ownership arise almost daily. As laws begin to govern the use and reuse of material posted on-line, they may change the way that people can access or reprint material.

Text, photographs, music, and fine art printed on-line may not be reproduced without acknowledged permission of the copyright owner.

Commonly Overused Words

When you write, use the most precise word for your meaning, not the word that comes to mind first. Consult this thesaurus to find alternatives for some commonly overused words. Consult a full-length thesaurus to find alternatives to words that do not appear here. Keep in mind that the choices offered in a thesaurus do not all mean exactly the same thing. Review all the options, and choose the one that best expresses your meaning.

about approximately, nearly, almost, approaching, close to

absolutely unconditionally, perfectly, completely, ideally, purely

activity action, movement, operation, labor, exertion, enterprise, project, pursuit, endeavor, job, assignment, pastime, scheme, task

add attach, affix, join, unite, append, increase, amplify

affect adjust, influence, transform, moderate, incline, motivate, prompt

amazing overwhelming, astonishing, startling, unexpected, stunning, dazzling, remarkable

awesome impressive, stupendous, fabulous, astonishing, outstanding

bad defective, inadequate, poor, unsatisfactory, disagreeable, offensive, repulsive, corrupt, wicked, naughty, harmful, injurious, unfavorable

basic essential, necessary, indispensable, vital, fundamental, elementary

beautiful attractive, appealing, alluring, exquisite, gorgeous, handsome, stunning

begin commence, found, initiate, introduce, launch, originate

better preferable, superior, worthier

big enormous, extensive, huge, immense, massive

boring commonplace, monotonous, tedious, tiresome

bring accompany, cause, convey, create, conduct, deliver, produce

cause origin, stimulus, inspiration, motive

certain unquestionable, incontrovertible, unmistakable, indubitable, assured, confident

change alter, transform, vary, replace, diversify

choose select, elect, nominate, prefer, identify

decent respectable, adequate, fair, suitable

definitely unquestionably, clearly, precisely, positively, inescapably

easy effortless, natural, comfortable, undemanding, pleasant, relaxed

effective powerful, successful

emphasize underscore, feature, accentuate

end limit, boundary, finish, conclusion, finale, resolution

energy vitality, vigor, force, dynamism

enjoy savor, relish, revel, benefit

entire complete, inclusive, unbroken, integral

excellent superior, remarkable, splendid, unsurpassed, superb, magnificent

exciting thrilling, stirring, rousing, dramatic

far distant, remote

fast swift, quick, fleet, hasty, instant, accelerated

fill occupy, suffuse, pervade, saturate, inflate, stock

finish complete, conclude, cease, achieve, exhaust, deplete, consume

funny comical, ludicrous, amusing, droll, entertaining, bizarre, unusual, uncommon

get obtain, receive, acquire, procure, achieve

give bestow, donate, supply, deliver, distribute, impart

go proceed, progress, advance, move

good satisfactory, serviceable, functional, competent, virtuous, striking

great tremendous, superior, remarkable, eminent, proficient, expert

happy pleased, joyous, elated, jubilant, cheerful, delighted

hard arduous, formidable, complex, complicated, rigorous, harsh

help assist, aid, support, sustain, serve

hurt injure, harm, damage, wound, impair

important significant, substantial, weighty, meaningful, critical, vital, notable

interesting absorbing, appealing, entertaining, fascinating, thought-provoking

job task, work, business, undertaking, occupation, vocation, chore, duty, assignment

keep retain, control, possess

kind type, variety, sort, form

know comprehend, understand, realize, perceive, discern

like (adj) similar, equivalent, parallel

like (verb) enjoy, relish, appreciate

main primary, foremost, dominant

make build, construct, produce, assemble, fashion, manufacture

mean plan, intend, suggest, propose, indicate

more supplementary, additional, replenishment

new recent, modern, current, novel

next subsequently, thereafter, successively

nice pleasant, satisfying, gracious, charming

old aged, mature, experienced, used, worn, former, previous

open unobstructed, accessible

part section, portion, segment, detail, element, component

perfect flawless, faultless, ideal, consummate

plan scheme, design, system, plot

pleasant agreeable, gratifying, refreshing, welcome

prove demonstrate, confirm, validate, verify, corroborate

quick brisk, prompt, responsive, rapid, nimble, hasty

really truly, genuinely, extremely, undeniably

regular standard, routine, customary, habitual

see regard, behold, witness, gaze, realize, notice

small diminutive, miniature, minor, insignificant, slight, trivial

sometimes occasionally, intermittently, sporadically, periodically

take grasp, capture, choose, select, tolerate, endure

terrific extraordinary, magnificent, marvelous

think conceive, imagine, ponder, reflect, contemplate

try attempt, endeavor, venture, test

use employ, operate, utilize

very unusually, extremely, deeply, exceedingly, profoundly

want desire, crave, yearn, long

Commonly Misspelled Words

The list on these pages presents words that cause problems for many people. Some of these words are spelled according to set rules, but others follow no specific rules. As you review this list, check to see how many of the words give you trouble in your own writing. Then, read the instruction in the "Vocabulary and Spelling" chapter in the book for strategies and suggestions for improving your own spelling habits.

abbreviate
absence
absolutely
abundance
accelerate
accidentally
accumulate
accurate
ache
achievement
acquaintance
adequate
admittance
advertisement
aerial
affect
aggravate
aggressive
agreeable
aisle
all right
allowance
aluminum
amateur
analysis
analyze
ancient
anecdote
anniversary
anonymous
answer
anticipate
anxiety
apologize
appall
appearance
appreciate
appropriate
architecture
argument
associate

athletic
attendance
auxiliary
awkward
bandage
banquet
bargain
barrel
battery
beautiful
beggar
beginning
behavior
believe
benefit
bicycle
biscuit
bookkeeper
bought
boulevard
brief
brilliant
bruise
bulletin
buoyant
bureau
bury
buses
business
cafeteria
calendar
campaign
canceled
candidate
capacity
capital
capitol
captain
career
carriage
cashier

catastrophe
category
ceiling
cemetery
census
certain
changeable
characteristic
chauffeur
chief
clothes
coincidence
colonel
column
commercial
commission
commitment
committee
competitor
concede
condemn
congratulate
connoisseur
conscience
conscientious
conscious
contemporary
continuous
controversy
convenience
coolly
cooperate
cordially
correspondence
counterfeit
courageous
courteous
courtesy
criticism
criticize
curiosity

curious
cylinder
deceive
decision
deductible
defendant
deficient
definitely
delinquent
dependent
descendant
description
desert
desirable
dessert
deteriorate
dining
disappointed
disastrous
discipline
dissatisfied
distinguish
effect
eighth
eligible
embarrass
enthusiastic
entrepreneur
envelope
environment
equipped
equivalent
especially
exaggerate
exceed
excellent
exercise
exhibition
existence
experience
explanation

extension
extraordinary
familiar
fascinating
February
fiery
financial
fluorescent
foreign
forfeit
fourth
fragile
gauge
generally
genius
genuine
government
grammar
grievance
guarantee
guard
guidance
handkerchief
harass
height
humorous
hygiene
ignorant
illegible
immediately
immigrant
independence
independent
indispensable
individual
inflammable
intelligence
interfere
irrelevant
irritable
jewelry
judgment
knowledge
laboratory
lawyer
legible
legislature
leisure
liable
library
license
lieutenant
lightning
likable
liquefy
literature
loneliness
magnificent
maintenance
marriage
mathematics
maximum
meanness
mediocre
mileage
millionaire
minimum
minuscule
miscellaneous
mischievous
misspell
mortgage
naturally
necessary
negotiate
neighbor
neutral
nickel
niece
ninety
noticeable
nuclear
nuisance
obstacle
occasion
occasionally
occur
occurred
occurrence
omitted
opinion
opportunity
optimistic
outrageous
pamphlet
parallel
paralyze
parentheses
particularly
patience
permanent
permissible
perseverance
persistent
personally
perspiration
persuade
phenomenal
phenomenon
physician
pleasant
pneumonia
possess
possession
possibility
prairie
precede
preferable
prejudice
preparation
prerogative
previous
primitive
privilege
probably
procedure
proceed
prominent
pronunciation
psychology
publicly
pursue
questionnaire
realize
really
recede
receipt
receive
recognize
recommend
reference
referred
rehearse
relevant
reminiscence
renowned
repetition
restaurant
rhythm
ridiculous
sandwich
satellite
schedule
scissors
secretary
siege
solely
sponsor
subtle
subtlety
superintendent
supersede
surveillance
susceptible
tariff
temperamental
theater
threshold
truly
unmanageable
unwieldy
usage
usually
valuable
various
vegetable
voluntary
weight
weird
whale
wield
yield

Abbreviations Guide

Abbreviations, shortened versions of words or phrases, can be valuable tools in writing if you know when and how to use them. They can be very helpful in informal writing situations, such as taking notes or writing lists. However, only a few abbreviations can be used in formal writing. They are: *Mr., Mrs., Miss, Ms., Dr., A.M., P.M., A.D., B.C., M.A, B.A., Ph.D.,* and *M.D.*

The following pages provide the conventional abbreviations for a variety of words.

Abbreviations of Common Titles

Ambassador	Amb.	Lieutenant	Lt.
Attorney	Atty.	Major	Maj.
Brigadier-General	Brig. Gen.	President	Pres.
Brother	Br.	Professor	Prof.
Captain	Capt.	Representative	Rep.
Colonel	Col.	Reverend	Rev.
Commander	Cmdr.	Secretary	Sec.
Commissioner	Com.	Senator	Sen.
Corporal	Cpl.	Sergeant	Sgt.
Doctor	Dr.	Sister	Sr.
Father	Fr.	Superintendent	Supt.
Governor	Gov.	Treasurer	Treas.
Honorable	Hon.	Vice Admiral	Vice Adm.

Abbreviations of Academic Degrees

Bachelor of Arts	B.A. (or A.B.)	Esquire (lawyer)	Esq.
Bachelor of Science	B.S. (or S.B.)	Master of Arts	M.A. (or A.M.)
Doctor of Dental Surgery	D.D.S.	Master of Business Administration	M.B.A.
Doctor of Divinity	D.D.		
Doctor of Education	Ed.D.	Master of Fine Arts	M.F.A.
Doctor of Laws	LL.D.	Master of Science	M.S. (or S.M.)
Doctor of Medicine	M.D.	Registered Nurse	R.N.
Doctor of Philosophy	Ph.D.		

Abbreviations of States

State	Traditional	Postal Service	State	Traditional	Postal Service
Alabama	Ala.	AL	Montana	Mont.	MT
Alaska	Alaska	AK	Nebraska	Nebr.	NE
Arizona	Ariz.	AZ	Nevada	Nev.	NV
Arkansas	Ark.	AR	New Hampshire	N.H.	NH
California	Calif.	CA	New Jersey	N.J.	NJ
Colorado	Colo.	CO	New Mexico	N.M.	NM
Connecticut	Conn.	CT	New York	N.Y.	NY
Delaware	Del.	DE	North Carolina	N.C.	NC
Florida	Fla.	FL	North Dakota	N.Dak.	ND
Georgia	Ga.	GA	Ohio	O.	OH
Hawaii	Hawaii	HI	Oklahoma	Okla.	OK
Idaho	Ida.	ID	Oregon	Ore.	OR
Illinois	Ill.	IL	Pennsylvania	Pa.	PA
Indiana	Ind.	IN	Rhode Island	R.I.	RI
Iowa	Iowa	IA	South Carolina	S.C.	SC
Kansas	Kans.	KS	South Dakota	S.Dak.	SD
Kentucky	Ky.	KY	Tennessee	Tenn.	TN
Louisiana	La.	LA	Texas	Tex.	TX
Maine	Me.	ME	Utah	Utah	UT
Maryland	Md.	MD	Vermont	Vt.	VT
Massachusetts	Mass.	MA	Virginia	Va.	VA
Michigan	Mich.	MI	Washington	Wash.	WA
Minnesota	Minn.	MN	West Virginia	W. Va	WV
Mississippi	Miss.	MS	Wisconsin	Wis.	WI
Missouri	Mo.	MO	Wyoming	Wyo.	WY

Common Geographical Abbreviations

Apartment	Apt.	National	Natl.
Avenue	Ave.	Park, Peak	Pk.
Block	Blk.	Peninsula	Pen.
Boulevard	Blvd.	Point	Pt.
Building	Bldg.	Province	Prov.
County	Co.	Road	Rd.
District	Dist.	Route	Rte.
Drive	Dr.	Square	Sq.
Fort	Ft.	Street	St.
Island	Is.	Territory	Terr.
Mountain	Mt.		

Abbreviations of Traditional Measurements

inch(es)	in.	ounce(s)	oz.
foot, feet	ft.	pound(s)	lb.
yard(s)	yd.	pint(s)	pt.
mile(s)	mi.	quart(s)	qt.
teaspoon(s)	tsp.	gallon(s)	gal.
tablespoon(s)	tbsp.	Fahrenheit	F.

Abbreviations of Metric Measurements

millimeter(s)	mm	liter(s)	L
centimeter(s)	cm	kiloliter(s)	kL
meter(s)	m	milligram(s)	mg
kilometer(s)	km	centigram(s)	cg
milliliter(s)	mL	gram(s)	g
centiliter(s)	cL	Celsius	C

Other Commonly Used Abbreviations

about (used with dates)	c., ca., circ.	manager	mgr.
and others	et al.	manufacturing	mfg.
anonymous	anon.	market	mkt.
approximately	approx.	measure	meas.
associate, association	assoc., assn.	merchandise	mdse.
auxiliary	aux., auxil.	miles per hour	mph
bibliography	bibliog.	miscellaneous	misc.
boxes	bx(s).	money order	M.O.
bucket	bkt.	note well; take notice	N.B.
bulletin	bull.	number	no.
bushel	bu.	package	pkg.
capital letter	cap.	page	p., pg.
cash on delivery	C.O.D.	pages	pp.
department	dept.	pair(s)	pr(s).
discount	disc.	parenthesis	paren.
dozen(s)	doz.	Patent Office	pat. off.
each	ea.	piece(s)	pc(s).
edition, editor	ed.	poetical, poetry	poet.
equivalent	equiv.	private	pvt.
established	est.	proprietor	prop.
fiction	fict.	pseudonym	pseud.
for example	e.g.	published, publisher	pub.
free of charge	grat., gratis	received	recd.
General Post Office	G.P.O.	reference, referee	ref.
government	gov., govt.	revolutions per minute	rpm
graduate, graduated	grad.	rhetorical, rhetoric	rhet.
Greek, Grecian	Gr.	right	R.
headquarters	hdqrs.	scene	sc.
height	ht.	special, specific	spec.
hospital	hosp.	spelling, species	sp.
illustrated	ill., illus.	that is	i.e.
including, inclusive	incl.	treasury, treasurer	treas.
introduction, introductory	intro.	volume	vol.
italics	ital.	weekly	wkly
karat, carat	k., kt.	weight	wt.
left	L.		

Proofreading Symbols Reference

Proofreading symbols make it easier to show where changes are needed in a paper. When proofreading your own or a classmate's work, use these standard proofreading symbols.

insert	I proofred. (a inserted)
delete	Ip proofread.
close up space	I proof read.
delete and close up space	I proofreade.
begin new paragraph	¶I proofread.
spell out	I proofread (10) papers. (sp)
lowercase	I Proofread. (lc)
capitalize	i proofread. (cap)
transpose letters	I proofraed. (tr)
transpose words	I only proofread her paper. (tr)
period	I will proofread
comma	I will proofread and she will help.
colon	We will proofread for the following errors
semicolon	I will proofread she will help.
single quotation marks	She said, "I enjoyed the story The Invalid."
double quotation marks	She said, I enjoyed the story.
apostrophe	Did you borrow Sylvias book?
question mark	Did you borrow Sylvia's book ?/
exclamation point	You're kidding !/
hyphen	online /=/
parentheses	William Shakespeare 1564–1616

Student Publications

To share your writing with a wider audience, consider submitting it to a local, state, or national publication for student writing. Following are several magazines and Web sites that accept and publish student work.

Periodicals

Creative Kids P.O. Box 8813, Waco, TX 76714

Merlyn's Pen: The National Magazine of Student Writing P.O. Box 1058, East Greenwich, RI 02818

Skipping Stones P.O. Box 3939, Eugene, OR 97403

The McGuffey Writer McGuffey Foundation School, 5128 Westgate Drive, Oxford, OH 45056

Writing! General Learning Corporation, 900 Skokie Boulevard, Northbrook, IL 60062

On-line Publications

Stone Soup http://www.stonesoup.com/

MidLink Magazine http://www.cs.ucf.edu:80/~MidLink/

Wild Guess Magazine http://members.tripod.com/~WildGuess/

Contests

Annual Poetry Contest National Federation of State Poetry Societies, 3520 State Route 56, Mechanicsburg, OH 43044

National Written & Illustrated By . . . Awards Contest for Students Landmark Editions, Inc., 1402 Kansas Avenue, Kansas City, MO 64127

Paul A. Witty Outstanding Literature Award International Reading Association, Special Interest Group for Reading for Gifted and Creative Students, c/o Texas Christian University, P.O. Box 32925, Fort Worth, TX 76129

***Seventeen* Magazine Fiction Contest** *Seventeen* Magazine, 850 Third Avenue, New York, NY 10022

The Young Playwrights Festival National Playwriting Competition 321 East 44th Street, Suite 906, New York, NY 10036

Sentence Diagraming Workshop

Diagraming is a visual means of helping you understand how all the different parts of a sentence relate to one another. Diagraming allows you to see a sentence not as a string of separate words, but as several groups of words arranged in a logical pattern.

Subjects, Verbs, and Modifiers

In a diagram, the subject and verb are placed on a horizontal line with the subject on the left and the verb on the right. A vertical line separates the subject from the predicate. The following examples show how to diagram a subject and verb.

S V

EXAMPLE: Jonathan sneezed.

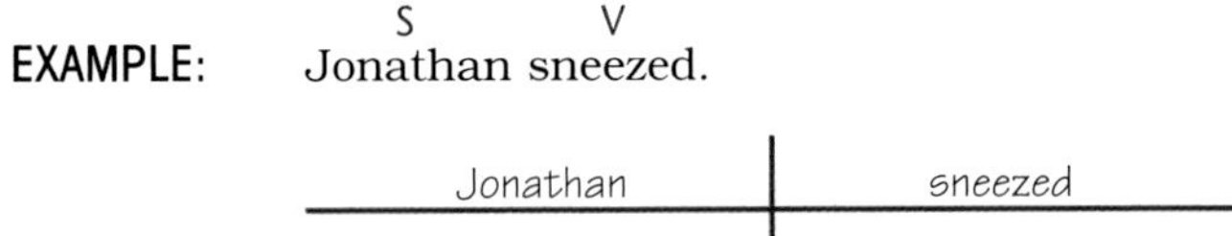

Adjectives and adverbs are placed on slanted lines directly below the words they modify.

ADJ ADJ ADV ADV

EXAMPLE: The weary hikers were walking very slowly.

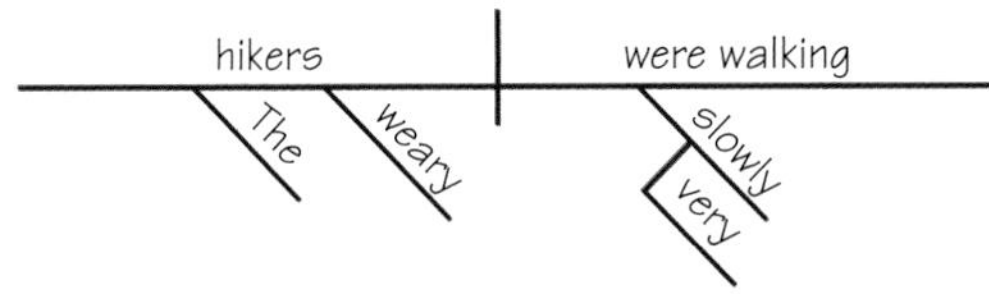

A sentence whose subject is understood to be *you* is diagramed in the usual way. Often, however, the word *there* is used just to get the sentence started. When that is the case, the word *there* is an expletive. Interjections are also expletives. The following examples show how to diagram expletives.

EXAMPLES: There was an accident. (There = EXP) Hooray, we won! (Hooray = INT)

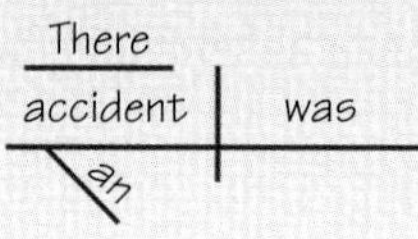

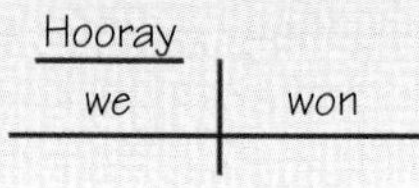

Exercise 1 **Diagraming Subjects, Verbs, and Modifiers**

Correctly diagram each sentence.

1. Sit down.
2. The weary runner suddenly sprinted ahead.
3. Your exceptionally studious friend thinks very quickly.
4. There was no test given today.
5. Goodness, Sandy sings very poorly.

Adding Conjunctions

Conjunctions that connect words are written on dotted lines drawn between the words that they connect. The following example shows where to place conjunctions that connect adjectives and adverbs.

EXAMPLE: The black and tan dog barked loudly and constantly. (and = CONJ; and = CONJ)

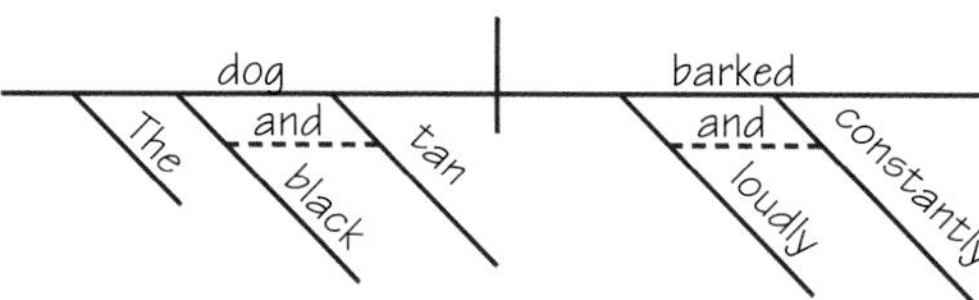

Conjunctions that connect compound subjects or compound verbs are also placed on dotted lines drawn between the words that they connect. Notice how the horizontal line must be split when a sentence has a compound subject or a compound verb.

EXAMPLE: Jean and I neither dance nor sing. (and = CONJ; neither = CONJ; nor = CONJ)

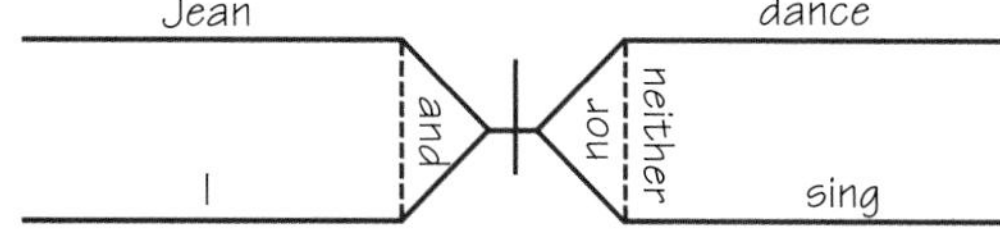

In sentences with compound subjects or verbs, a modifier is placed under the part of the sentence it modifies. If a word modifies both parts of a compound subject or verb, it is placed under the main line of the diagram.

EXAMPLE: My (ADJ) older (ADJ) sister and younger (ADJ) brother left early (ADV) but arrived late (ADV).

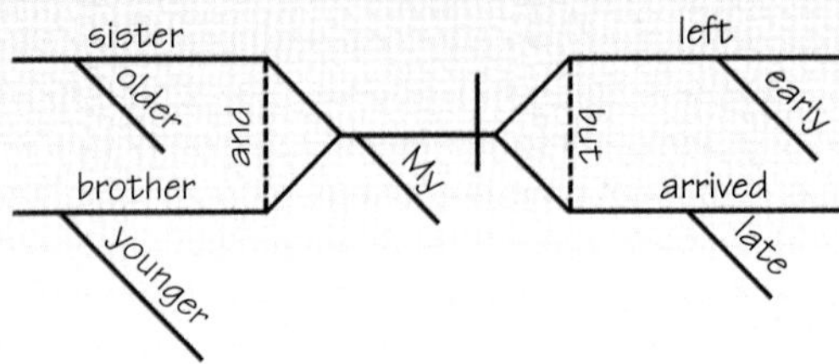

If each part of a compound verb has its own helping verb, each helping verb is placed on the line with its verb. If compound verbs share a helping verb, however, the helping verb is placed on the main line of the diagram.

EXAMPLE: Tomorrow I will (HV) either swim or fish.

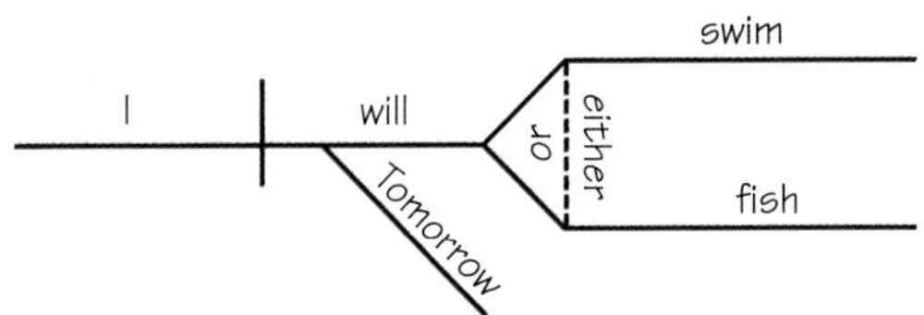

Exercise 2 **Diagraming Sentences With Conjunctions**

Correctly diagram each sentence.

1. Ferns and palms were everywhere.
2. He can stay but should go.
3. Kim and Lan were leaving now but returning later.
4. The eighteen boys and girls waited quietly.
5. Very agile and highly skilled acrobats tumbled about.

Complements

The following diagrams show how to add direct objects and indirect objects to sentence diagrams.

EXAMPLE: Bill plays chess. (chess = DO) I told Joan a story. (Joan = IO, story = DO)

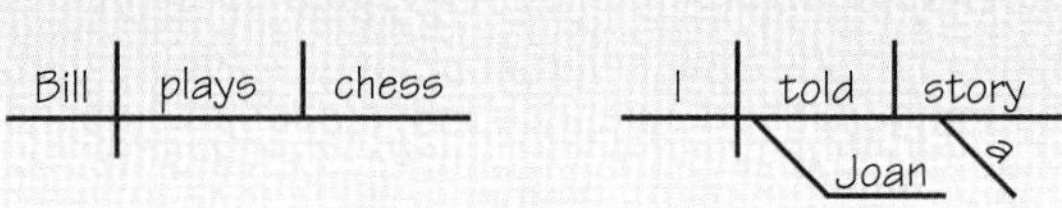

The next diagram shows where to place an objective complement.

EXAMPLE: Our class elected Beth Green treasurer. (Beth Green = DO, treasurer = OC)

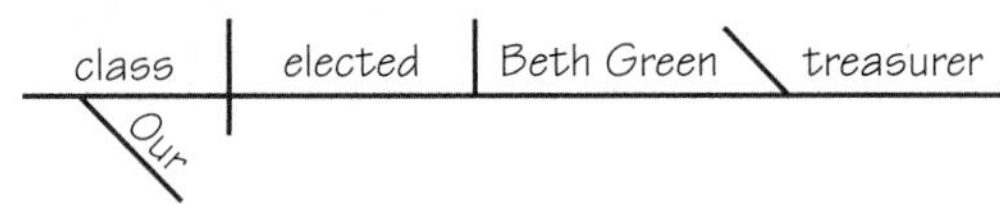

Predicate nominatives and predicate adjectives are diagramed in a similar way

EXAMPLE: Sean is an actor. (actor = PN) He is talented. (talented = PA)

Compound complements are diagramed by splitting the lines on which they are placed and adding on dotted lines any conjunctions that connect them.

EXAMPLE: We gave Ann and Ed some crackers and cheese. (Ann = IO, Ed = IO, crackers = DO, cheese = DO)

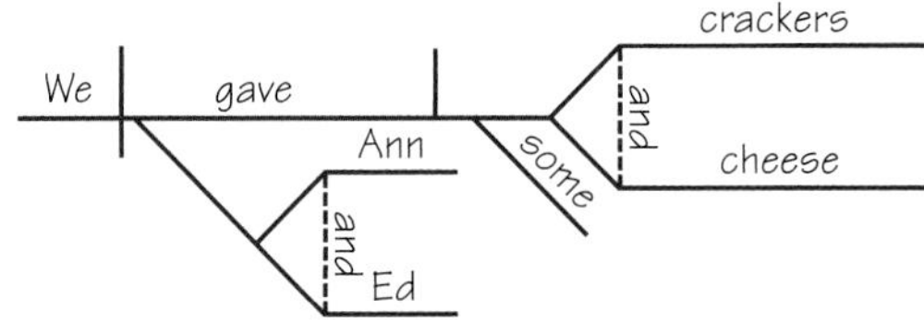

Exercise 3 **Diagraming Complements** Correctly diagram each sentence.

1. Several urgent callers distracted the doctor.
2. Cathy wrote her name and her new address.
3. I bought my mother and my sister beautiful designer scarves.
4. The dance committee selected Alan Stavinsky chairperson.
5. The happy parents named one twin Christopher and the other twin Christine.
6. That is it!
7. The fog grew deeper and more mysterious.
8. The Chinese cooking tasted strange but delicious.
9. The largest airplane was silver and blue.
10. The coin was very old but still shiny.

Prepositional Phrases

A prepositional phrase can act as either an adjective or an adverb in a sentence. In a diagram, an adjective phrase is placed directly below the noun or pronoun it modifies. An adverb phrase is placed directly below the verb, adjective, or adverb it modifies. The preposition is placed on a slanted line with its object on a horizontal line below the slanted line. Any adjectives that modify the object of the preposition are placed on slanted lines below the horizontal line.

EXAMPLE: The woman with the large hat went into the store.
(PREP PHRASE: with the large hat; PREP PHRASE: into the store)

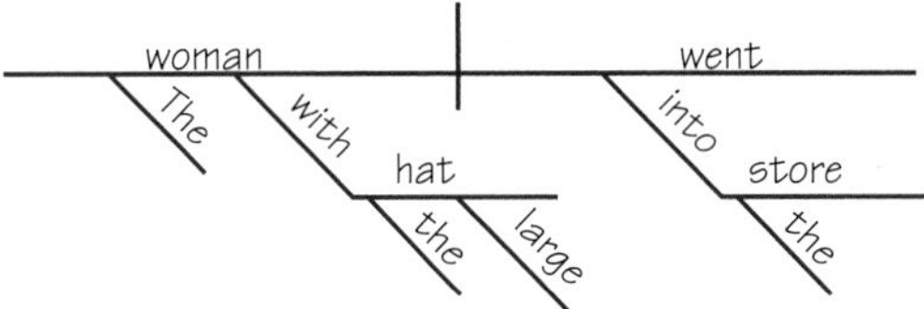

The first example on the next page shows how to diagram a prepositional phrase that modifies the object of another prepositional phrase. The other example shows how to diagram a prepositional phrase that modifies an adjective or an adverb.

PREP PHRASE

EXAMPLE: I ate pizza with mushrooms on it.

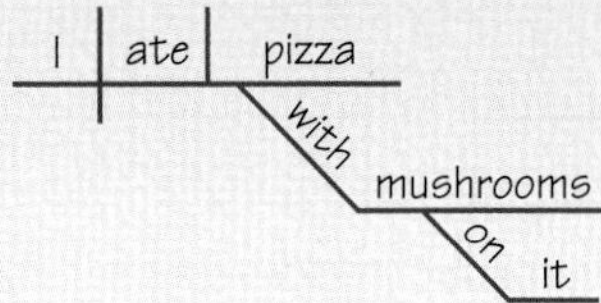

PREP PHRASE

The rain started yesterday after lunch.

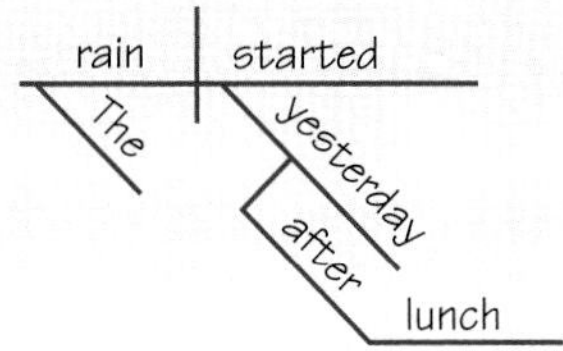

A prepositional phrase with a compound object is diagramed in the same way other compound sentence parts are diagramed. The diagram below is an example of a sentence containing a prepositional phrase with a compound object.

PREP PHRASE

EXAMPLE: I eat whole-wheat bread with breakfast and lunch.

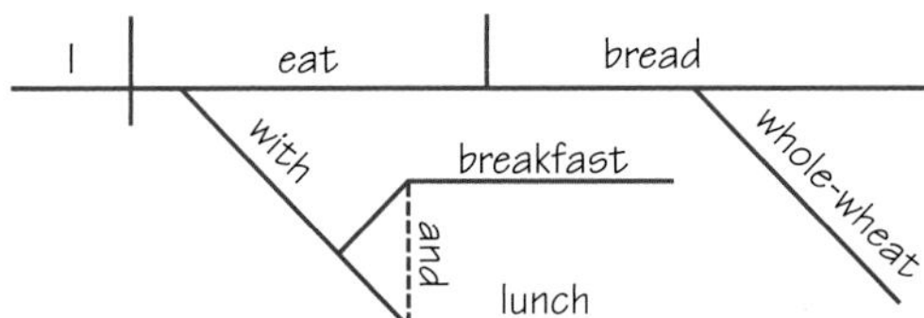

Exercise 4 **Diagraming Prepositional Phrases** Correctly diagram each sentence.

1. Mark is working at the radio station.
2. You may take the television to your room.
3. The boy on the bench played in the first half.
4. She runs for exercise.
5. The roof of the old house on the corner collapsed.

Appositives and Appositive Phrases

To diagram an appositive, place it in parentheses beside the noun or pronoun it identifies, renames, or explains. Any adjectives or adjective phrases included in an appositive phrase are placed directly beneath the appositive.

EXAMPLE: Blue whales, the largest animals in the world, are rare. (APPOSITIVE PHRASE: the largest animals in the world)

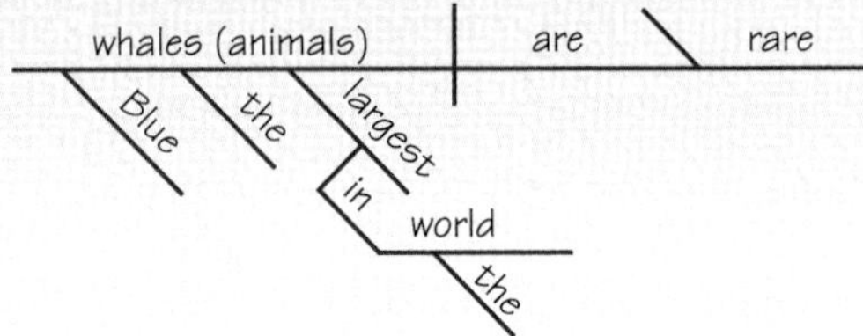

Exercise 5 Diagraming Appositives and Appositive Phrases Correctly diagram each sentence.

1. The governor announced the appointee, his wife!
2. Give to Colonel Gray, the commandant, this message.
3. That is our representative, Miss Hoyt.
4. The results of the exam, the Scholastic Aptitude Test, have arrived.
5. My uncle, a bachelor for fifty years, finally married.

Participles and Participial Phrases

Participles function as adjectives. Thus, in a diagram, they are placed directly beneath the nouns or pronouns they modify. Participles are placed partly on a slanted line and partly on a horizontal line extending from the slanted line. Any adverbs or adverb phrases included in a participial phrase are placed on slanted lines beneath the horizontal line. When a participle has a complement, it is placed on the horizontal line with the participle and separated from it by a short vertical line.

EXAMPLE: Carefully following the instructions, Karen assembled the model airplane. (PARTICIPIAL PHRASE: Carefully following the instructions)

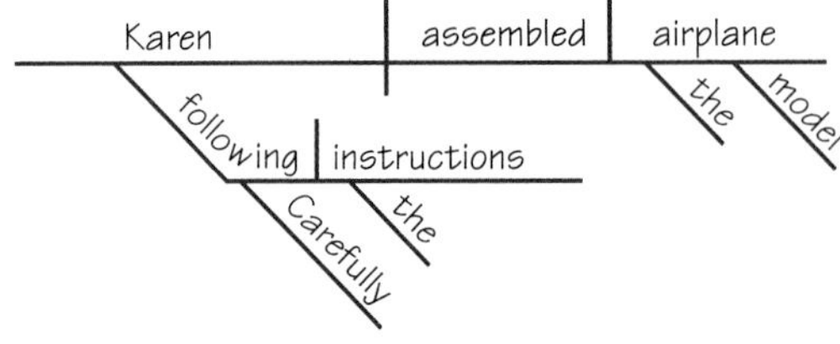

Exercise 6 **Diagraming Participles and Participial Phrases**

1. Laughing, she turned toward me.
2. Carefully detailed reports will be available.
3. Exhausted, we finally reached our destination.
4. My grandmother, speaking in low tones, continued the bedtime story.
5. Closing the door, I heard the kettle whistling on the stove.

Gerunds and Gerund Phrases

Because gerunds act as nouns, they can be subjects, complements, objects of prepositions, or appositives. When a gerund acts as a subject, direct object, or predicate nominative, it is placed on a pedestal above the main horizontal line of the diagram. Notice in the following diagram the stepped line on which all gerunds are written. Notice also that any modifiers and complements that are part of a gerund phrase are added to the diagram in the usual way.

EXAMPLE: We will not allow your reading comics in class. (GERUND PHRASE: your reading comics in class)

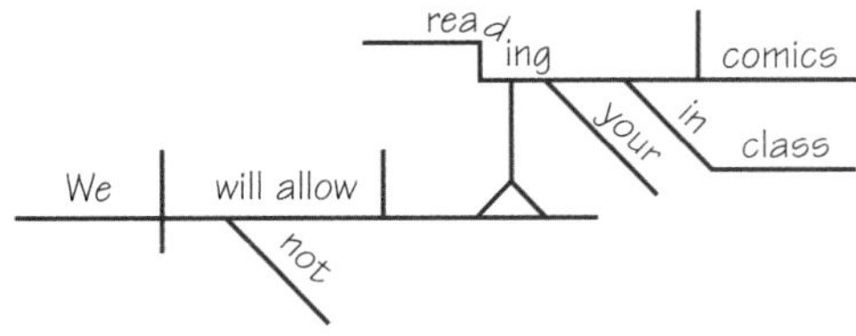

When a gerund acts as indirect object or an object of a preposition, it is placed on a line slanting down from the main horizontal line.

EXAMPLE: His performance gives acting a bad name. (GERUND: acting)

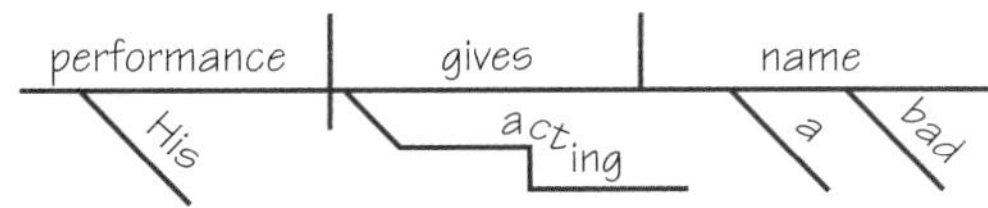

Exercise 7 **Diagraming Gerunds and Gerund Phrases**

Correctly diagram each sentence.

1. Exercising can be a form of relaxation.
2. By exercising, you can improve your physical fitness.
3. Exercise is a way of dealing with some diseases.
4. Being in good physical condition contributes to good emotional health.
5. Exercise is performing activities for your health.

Infinitives and Infinitive Phrases

Infinitives can act as nouns, adjectives, or adverbs. An infinitive acting as a noun is generally diagramed on a pedestal like a gerund, but the line on which the infinitive is written is simpler. Modifiers included in an infinitive phrase are added to a diagram in the usual way. Complements are also added in the usual way.

INFINITIVE PHRASE

EXAMPLE: To leave early was his goal.

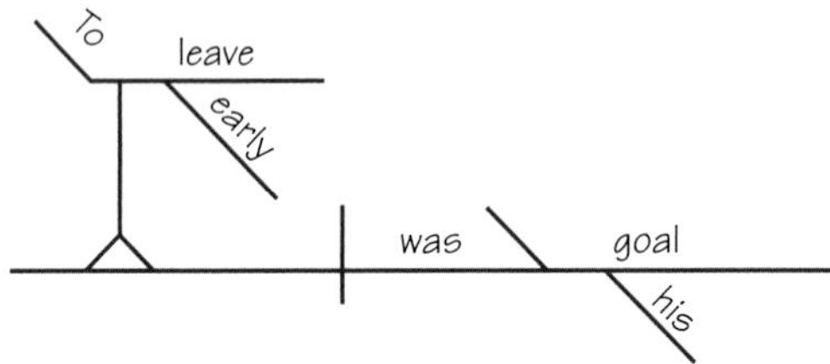

When an infinitive phrase has a subject, it is added to the left on a horizontal line.

INFINITIVE PHRASE

EXAMPLE: I want you to pay me the ten dollars.

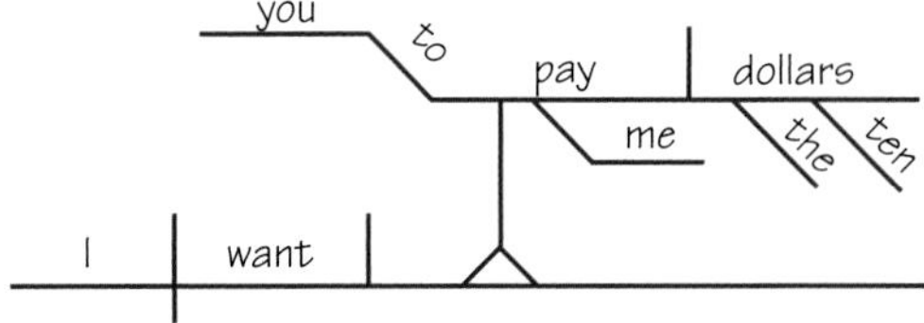

An infinitive used as an adjective or adverb is diagramed in much the same way as a prepositional phrase.

EXAMPLE: He will be happy to drive. (INFINITIVE: to drive)

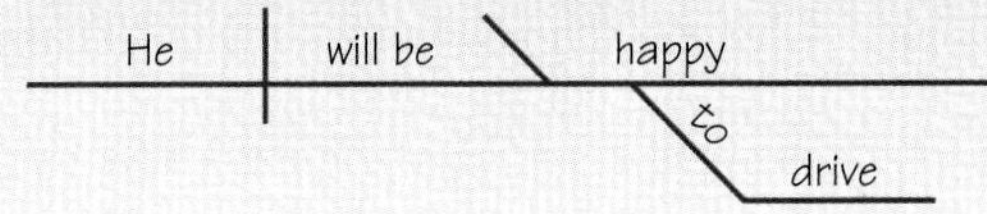

If an infinitive does not include the word *to,* add the word to the sentence diagram but place it in parentheses.

EXAMPLE: They watched the ship sail into the harbor. (INFINITIVE PHRASE: ship sail into the harbor)

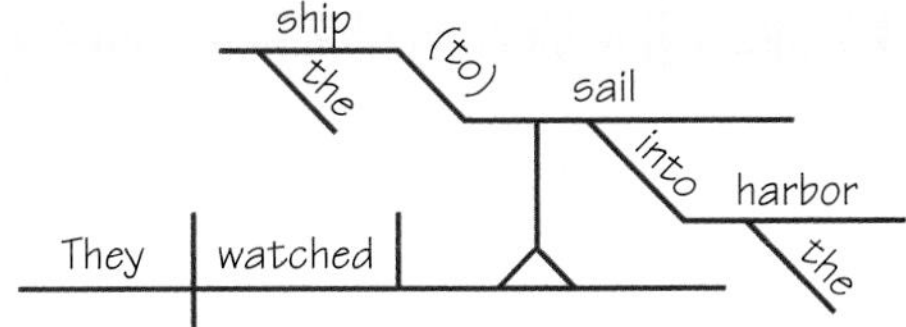

Exercise 8 **Diagraming Infinitives and Infinitive Phrases**

Correctly diagram each sentence.

1. This is the road to take.
2. Our goal is to drive across the continent.
3. To pack the car is our next job.
4. My father wants me to study German.
5. We saw Bernstein conduct three symphonies.

Compound Sentences

To diagram a compound sentence, simply diagram each of the independent clauses separately, join the verbs with a dotted line, and write the conjunction or semicolon on the dotted line.

INDEPENDENT CLAUSE

EXAMPLE: I found his books, and I returned them to him.

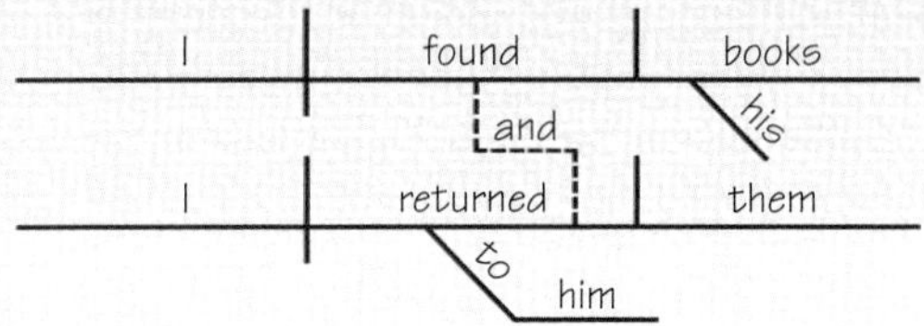

Exercise 9 **Diagraming Compound Sentences** Correctly diagram each sentence.

1. We installed insulation, and our fuel bills are much lower.
2. We can go to the beach today, or we can wait for better weather.
3. School ends soon, and Pauline has not started her paper.
4. Money can be enjoyable, but happiness is more important.
5. The chimpanzee shook the doll, and then he cuddled it in his arms.

Complex Sentences

Complex sentences contain an independent clause and one or more subordinate clauses. The subordinate clauses can be adjective clauses, adverb clauses, noun clauses, or any combination of these.

Adjective Clauses The line on which an adjective clause is placed goes beneath the main line, to which it is connected by a dotted line. The dotted line extends from the noun or pronoun being modified by the clause to the relative pronoun or relative adverb in the adjective clause. The position of the relative pronoun varies depending on its function in the adjective clause. In the following diagram, the relative pronoun is the direct object in the subordinate clause.

ADJECTIVE CLAUSE

EXAMPLE: The table lamps that you ordered have just arrived.

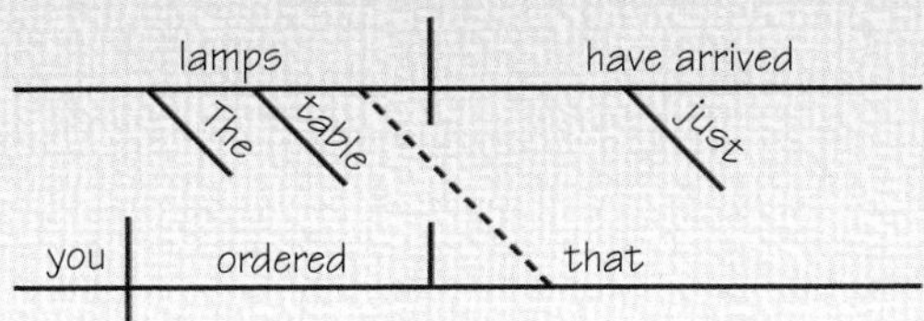

Sometimes, an adjective clause may be introduced by a relative pronoun acting as either an object of a preposition or as an adjective. The dotted line must be bent to connect the clauses properly. This is also true when the adjective clause is introduced by a relative adverb, as the following example illustrates.

ADJECTIVE CLAUSE

EXAMPLE: We visited a laboratory where testing was done.

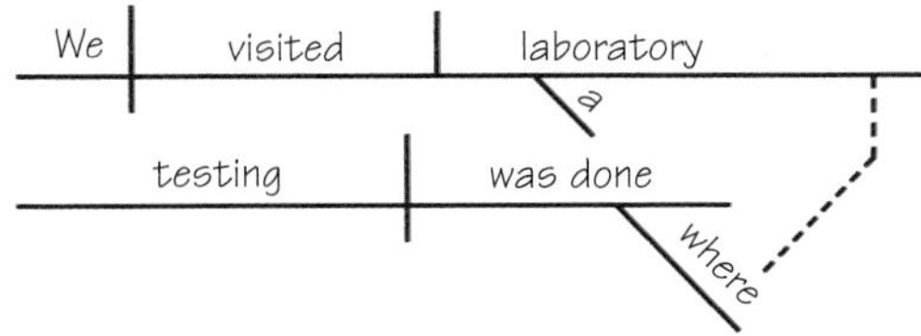

Adverb Clauses An adverb clause is diagramed in the same way as an adjective clause, except that the subordinate conjunction is written along the dotted line. This line extends from the verb, adjective, adverb, or verbal being modified by the clause to the verb in the adverb clause.

ADVERB CLAUSE

EXAMPLE: Gas will be rationed whenever a shortage occurs.

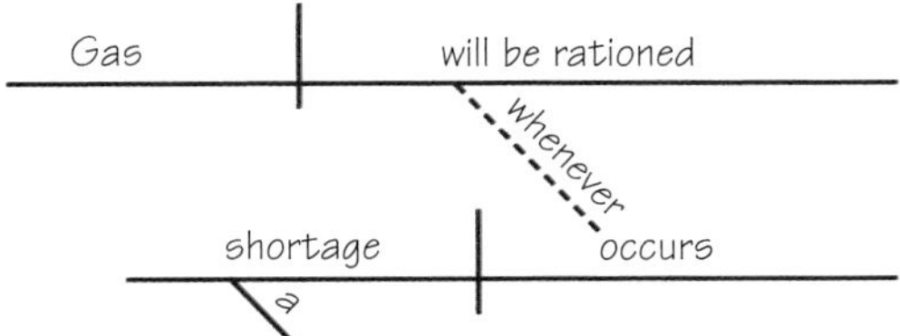

If the adverb clause is elliptical, the understood but unstated words are placed in the diagram in parentheses.

EXAMPLE: The tree in our yard is taller than the tree in yours. (ADVERB CLAUSE)

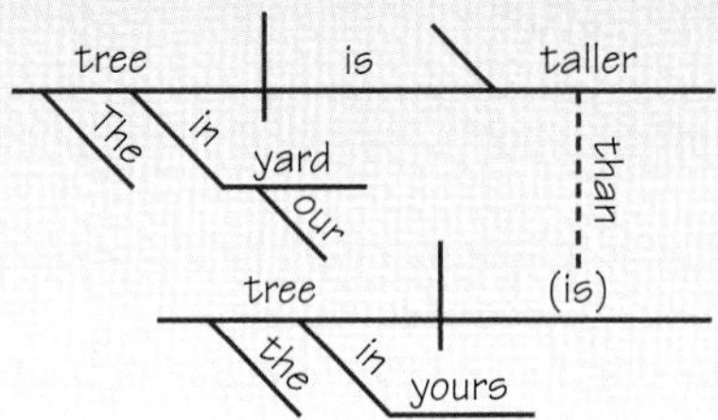

Noun Clauses To diagram a sentence containing a noun clause, first diagram the independent clause. Then, place the noun clause on a pedestal extending upward from the position the clause fills in the sentence. The noun clause in the following is acting as the subject of the sentence.

EXAMPLE: Whoever is responsible will pay for the damage. (NOUN CLAUSE)

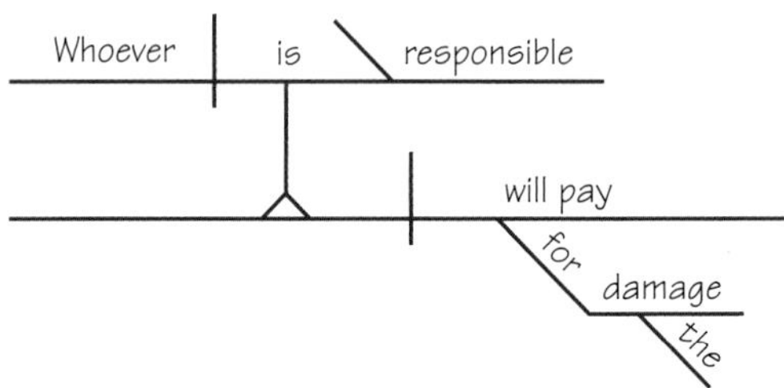

When the introductory word in a noun clause has no function in the clause, it is written alongside the pedestal.

EXAMPLE: I wonder whether we should wait for them. (NOUN CLAUSE)

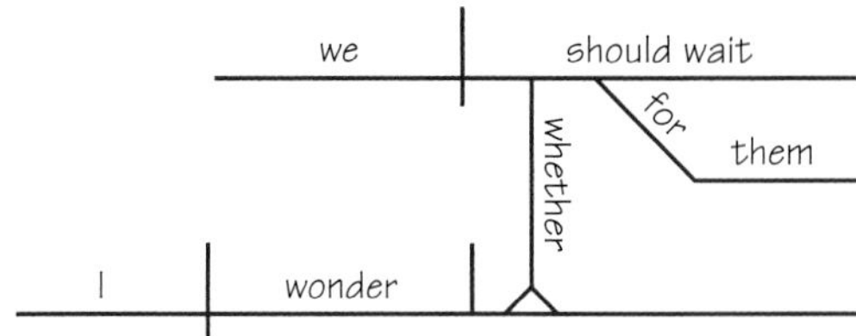

Exercise 10 **Diagraming Complex Sentences** Correctly diagram each sentence.

1. The restaurant that we chose is famous for its pastry.
2. When we were in New York City, we toured the New York Stock Exchange.
3. Whatever boat we rent must accommodate six people.
4. The director was furious because the star quit the picture.
5. This chair adjusts to whatever position you desire.

Compound-Complex Sentences

When diagraming a compound-complex sentence, begin by diagraming each of the independent clauses. Then, diagram each subordinate clause.

EXAMPLE: Before the play began, the audience was restless and the actors were nervous.
(ADVERB CLAUSE: Before the play began; INDEPENDENT CLAUSE: the audience was restless; INDEPENDENT CLAUSE: and the actors were nervous.)

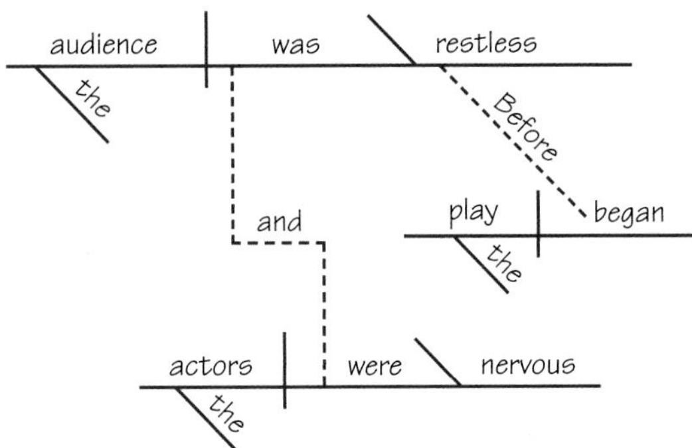

Exercise 11 **Diagraming Compound-Complex Sentences** Correctly diagram each sentence

1. When their father returned, Jill set the table and Peter poured milk.
2. The letter that he received was short, but he read it very slowly.
3. We hoped that it would be sunny, but it was not.
4. After they reached the city, they bought a newspaper and Judy looked for a good restaurant.
5. The children gasped at their luck when they found the wallet, for they had been very worried.

Note: **Bold numbers** show pages on which basic definitions and rules appear.

A

B

C

E

F

G

H

I

J

K

L

P

Q

T

U

Acknowledgments

Staff Credits
The people who made up the *Prentice Hall Writing and Grammar: Communication in Action* team—representing design services, editorial, editorial services, electronic publishing technology, manufacturing & inventory planning, marketing, marketing services, market research, on-line services & multimedia development, product planning, production services, project office, and publishing processes—are listed below. Bold type denotes the core team members.

Ellen Backstrom, Betsy Bostwick, Evonne Burgess, **Louise B. Capuano, Sarah Carroll, Megan Chill,** Katherine Clarke, Rhett Conklin, Martha Conway, Harold Crudup, **Harold Delmonte,** Laura Dershewitz, Donna DiCuffa, Amy Fleming, Libby Forsyth, Ellen Goldblatt, Elaine Goldman, Jonathan Goldson, **Rebecca Graziano,** Rick Hickox, Kristan Hoskins, Jim Jeglikowski, Carol Lavis, **George Lychock,** Gregory Lynch, William McAllister, **Frances Medico,** Perrin Moriarty, Loretta Moser, Margaret Plotkin, Maureen Raymond, Shannon Rider, **Steve Sacco,** Gerry Schrenk, **Melissa Shustyk,** Annette Simmons, Robin Sullivan, **Elizabeth Torjussen, Doug Utigard**

Additional Credits
Ernie Albanese, Diane Alimena, Susan Andariese, Michele Angelucci, Penny Baker, Susan Barnes, Louise Casella, Lorena Cerisano, Cynthia Clampitt, Jaime Cohen, Elizabeth Crawford, Ken Dougherty, Vince Esterly, Kathy Gavilanes, Beth Geschwind, Michael Goodman, Diana Hahn, Jennifer Harper, Evan Holstrom, Alex Ivchenko, Leanne Korszoloski, Sue Langan, Rebecca Lauth, Dave Liston, Maria Keogh, Christine Mann, Vicki Menanteaux, Gail Meyer, Artur Mkrtchyan, LaShonda Morris, Karyl Murray, Omni-Photo Communications, Kim Ortell, Patty Rodriguez, Brenda Sanabria, Carolyn Sapontzis, Ken Silver, Slip Jig Image Research Services, Sunnyside, NY, Ron Spezial, Barbara Stufflebeem, Gene Vaughan, Karen Vignola, Linda Westerhoff

Photo Credits

Cover: Corel Professional Photos CD-ROM™; Stamp Design ©United States Postal Service, All Rights Reserved.; **vi:** (top) Michael P. Gadomski/Photo Researchers, Inc.; (bottom) Corel Professional Photos CD-ROM™; **vii:** (top) Corel Professional Photos CD-ROM™; (bottom) ©1996, Bob Gage/FPG International Corp.; **ix;** ©The Stock Market/Mark Gamba; **x:** Nik Wheeler/CORBIS; **xi:** Nick Gunderson/Tony Stone Images; **xii:** Photofest; **xiii:** Al Campanie/ The Image Works; **xiv:** Pierre Berger/Photo Researchers, Inc.; **xv:** Courtesy Rebecca Graziano; **xvi:** *Gust of wind at Ejiri, in the province of Suruga.* From the series The Thirty-six Views of Fuji, The Metropolitan Museum of Art, Rogers Fund, 1936. (JP 2553) © 1984/87 by The Metropolitan Museum of Art; **xvii:** ©StockFood America/Beery; **xviii:** Marshian Boy, Christian Pierre, Private Collection/SuperStock ; **xix:** (top) David Young-Wolff/Tony Stone Images; (bottom) ©1996, Rob Gage/FPG International Corp.; **xx:** (top) ©1993 Jack Vartoogian; (bottom) Corel Professional Photos CD-ROM™; **xxi:** (top) Corel Professional Photos CD-ROM™; (bottom) NASA; **xxii:** (top & bottom) Corel Professional Photos CD-ROM™; **xxiii:** (top & bottom) Corel Professional Photos CD-ROM™; **xxiv:** Corel Professional Photos CD-ROM™; **xxv:** (top, middle, bottom) Corel Professional Photos CD-ROM™; **xxvi:** Andy Sacks/Tony Stone Images; **xxvii:** (top) ©The Stock Market/Mug Shots; (bottom) Corel Professional Photos CD-ROM™; **1:** *Benjamin Comfort* (detail), Percy Ives, Detroit Historical Museum; **2:** ©1991 Arthur Tilley/FPG International Corp.; **4:** David Young-Wolff/PhotoEdit; **5:** ©The Stock Market/Jose L. Pelaez; **6:** ©Jeff Greenberg/PhotoEdit/PictureQuest; **20:** ©StockFood America/Grand; **23:** Ken Kerbs/Monkmeyer; **25:** Corel Professional Photos CD-ROM™; **31:** Fotopic/Omni-Photo Communications, Inc.; **32:** ©The Stock Market/Mark Gamba; **35:** *Travelling Carnival,* John Sloan, National Museum of American Art/Art Resource, NY; **36:** ©1999, Telegraph Colour Library/FPG International Corp.; **47:** Esbin-Anderson/The Image Works; **48:** Nik Wheeler/CORBIS; **51:** *Basketball Superstars* by LeRoy Neiman. Copyright © LeRoy Neiman, Inc. All Rights Reserved.; **57:** Laura Dwight/CORBIS; **60:** ©The Stock Market/John Henley; **63:** CORBIS; **65:** Amos Zezmer/ Omni-Photo Communications, Inc.; **66:** Nick Gunderson/Tony Stone Images; **69:** Vincent van Gogh, "The Bedroom of Van Gogh at Arles," 1889. Oil on canvas. 57.5 x 74 cm. Musée d'Orsay, Paris, France. Erich Lessing/Art Resource, NY; **70:** (left) ©1993, S. Malmone/ FPG International Corp.; (right) ©1991, Ron Thomas/FPG International Corp.; **73:** ©1999 Terry Qing/FPG International Corp.; **74:** Rudi Von Briel/ PhotoEdit; **82:** *Trial by Jury,* 1964, Thomas Hart Benton, oil on canvas; 30" x 40" (76.0 x 1010.7cm), The Nelson-Atkins Museum of Art, Kansas City, Missouri, bequest of the artist. ©T.H. Benton and R.P. Benton Testamentary Trusts/Licensed by VAGA, New York, NY; **85:** *The Pond,* 1985, Adele Alsop, Courtesy of Schmidt Bingham Gallery, NYC; **89:** CORBIS/Bettmann; **95:** Ken Karp Photography; **98:** Artwork copyright 2000 by Phil Yeh www.ideaship. com; **100:** Michigan Opera Theatre; **105:** Al Campanie/The Image Works; **111:** Courtesy Megan Chill; **112:** Pierre Berger/Photo Researchers, Inc.; **115:** *Love In Ice,* Veronica Ruiz de Velasco, Courtesy of the artist; **119:** (top) Janecek/Monkmeyer; (bottom) Leslye Borden/ PhotoEdit; **121:** David W. Hamilton/The Image Bank; **124:** Bob Daemmrich/The Image Works; **127 & 129:** Michael Newman/PhotoEdit; **130:** NASA; **133:** *Two Lane Road Cut,* Woody Gwyn, Courtesy of the artist; **139:** Michael Newman/PhotoEdit; **145–146:** David Young-Wolff/PhotoEdit; **147:** Courtesy Rebecca Graziano; **148:** R. Crandall/The Image Works; **151:** *Gust of wind at Ejiri, in the province of Suruga.* From the series The Thirty-six Views of Fuji, The Metropolitan Museum of Art, Rogers Fund, 1936. (JP 2553) © 1984/87 by The Metropolitan Museum of Art; **161:** image ©Copyright 1998 PhotoDisc, Inc.; **162:** *Icebergs,* Frederic Edwin Church, Art Resource, NY; **165:** *Three Studies of a Dancer in Fourth Position,* Charcoal and pastel with stumping, with touches of brush and black wash on greyish-tan laid paper with blue fibers (discolored from pinkish-blue). c. 1879/80, 48 x 61.5 cm. Bequest of Adele R. Levy, 1962.703. Photograph © 1999, The Art Institute of Chicago. All rights reserved.; **172:** Tony Freeman/ PhotoEdit; **175:** ©The Stock Market/John Henley; **179:** Tony Freeman/PhotoEdit; **180:** *Marshian Boy,* Christian Pierre, Private Collection/SuperStock; **183:** *Mexican Market* (detail), Jane Scott, Schalkwijk/Art Resource, NY; **187:** image©Copyright 1998 PhotoDisc, Inc.; **193:** Jeff Greenberg/The Picture Cube; **196:** ©1996, Rob Gage/FPG International Corp.; **203:** Tony Freeman/PhotoEdit; **206:** Corel Professional Photos CD-ROM™; **214:** *In Celebration,* 1987, Sam Gilliam, National Museum of American Art, Washington, DC/Art Resource, NY; **235:** Corel Professional Photos CD-ROM™; **243:** NASA; **246–260:** Corel Professional Photos CD-ROM™; **266:** Pearson Education/PH

College; **269–275:** Corel Professional Photos CD-ROM™; **276:** NASA; **278:** Corel Professional Photos CD-ROM™; **281:** Mark D. Longwood/Pearson Education/PH College; **282:** Ken Karp/PH photo; **287–306:** Corel Professional Photos CD-ROM™; **308:** Silver Burdett Ginn; **309 & 313:** Corel Professional Photos CD-ROM™; **316:** Silver Burdett Ginn; **318:** Corel Professional Photos CD-ROM™; **324–360:** Corel Professional Photos CD-ROM™; **363:** Frank Siteman/Omni-Photo Communications, Inc.; **364–387:** Corel Professional Photos CD-ROM™; **390:** Pearson Education/PH College; **394:** image©Copyright 1998 PhotoDisc, Inc.; **396:** Michael Littlejohn/Pearson Education/PH College; **400:** Courtesy of the Library of Congress; **403:** M. Lopez/Pearson Education/PH School; **420–427:** Corel Professional Photos CD-ROM™; **431:** PH College; **431–433:** Corel Professional Photos CD-ROM™; **434:** PH College; **434–488:** Corel Professional Photos CD-ROM™; **495–501:** NASA; **505:** Corel Professional Photos CD-ROM™; **506:** Courtesy of the Library of Congress; **508–539:** Corel Professional Photos CD-ROM™; **542:** *Books II,* 1993, Polly Kraft, Private Collection, Courtesy Fischbach Gallery, New York; **544:** Elizabeth Crews/The Image Works; **546:** Richard Hutchings/ PhotoEdit; **557:** *Starry Night,* Vincent van Gogh, 1889, Oil on Canvas, 29 x 36 1/4 in. The Museum of Modern Art, New York. Acquired through the Lillie P. Bliss Bequest; **561:** Ken Karp/ PH Photo; **562:** Lane Yerkes; **564:** Corel Professional Photos CD-ROM™; **579:** ©The Stock Market/ Michal Heron; **583:** Corel Professional Photos CD-ROM™; **584:** ©1996, Bob Gage/FPG International Corp.; **586:** Will Faller; **590:** Ken Karp/PH Photo; **591:** Grace Davies/Omni-Photo Communications, Inc.; **596:** Courtesy of the Library of Congress; **598:** ©The Stock Market; **603:** Myrleen Ferguson/ PhotoEdit; **606:** ©The Stock Market/Mug Shots; **608:** Will Hart; **611:** David Young-Wolff/PhotoEdit; **619:** Will Faller; **622:** Will Faller; **626:** David Aronson/Stock, Boston/ PictureQuest; **629:** Tony Freeman/PhotoEdit; **631:** David Young-Wolff/PhotoEdit; **633:** Dennis MacDonald/PhotoEdit/ PictureQuest; **636:** Corel Professional Photos CD-ROM™; **637:** Jeff Greenberg/ PhotoEdit